APPROACHES TO THE

PHILOSOPHY OF RELIGION

A Book of Readings

APPROACHES TO THE
PHILOSOPHY OF RELIGION
A Book of Readings

Edited by

DANIEL JAY BRONSTEIN

and

HAROLD M. SCHULWEIS

Essay Index Reprint Series

 BOOKS FOR LIBRARIES PRESS
FREEPORT, NEW YORK

STANDARD BOOK NUMBER:

8369-1344-2

LIBRARY OF CONGRESS CATALOG CARD NUMBER:

77-93320

PRINTED IN THE UNITED STATES OF AMERICA

PREFACE

We hope this volume will meet the need for a collection of stimulating readings on the basic issues of the philosophy of religion — a need that teachers of the subject have felt for many years.

We gratefully acknowledge the helpful suggestions of friends and colleagues, especially Professor Arthur E. Murphy, general editor of the Prentice-Hall Philosophy Series.

Although this book is a work of collaboration, responsibility for the chapters is as follows:

Chapters 1, 5, 6 — Daniel J. Bronstein
Chapters 2, 3, 4 — Harold M. Schulweis

Following the usual custom, material supplied by the editors has been surrounded by square brackets.

D. J. B.
H. M. S.

CONTENTS

vii

CHAPTER THREE: GOD AND EVIL

CHAPTER FOUR: GOD AND HUMAN FREEDOM

Chapter Five: CHURCH AND STATE

Chapter Six: IMMORTALITY

Bibliography

APPROACHES TO THE

PHILOSOPHY OF RELIGION

A Book of Readings

Chapter One

WHAT IS RELIGION?

INTRODUCTION

Evidence of a growing interest in religion in recent years, after a period of disillusionment, has accumulated from many quarters. Most often cited are the unprecedented popularity of books and films with a religious theme or inspirational message, the figures of church attendance, and the results of surveys of opinion, especially among college students. Three related questions have been asked about these surveys. (1) How can we account for the recent upsurge of religious interest? (2) Are the college students who are "returning to religion" responding to traditional formulations of religion? (3) Are they attracted mainly by theological or by ethical conceptions?

When we try to answer these questions, certain more fundamental questions concerning the meaning of religion inevitably arise. Is religion primarily a question of beliefs, of feelings, or of practices? Does religion necessarily involve belief in a supreme being, an after life, a soul? How does religion differ from theology, from philosophy, from science? Is there an inevitable conflict between

1

religion and science, or can they be reconciled? (Einstein). Is humanism or secularism a religion, or the foe of all religion? (Fromm). Should religious doctrines be judged as true or false, or are truth and falsity irrelevant to religion? (Santayana). Are any religious beliefs verifiably true, or do we accept them only because we have faith? (Brightman). Can religion to-day have the same significance and perform the same functions for man that it did in ancient times? Can one who has lost his faith in the existence of a benevolent God still find enduring values in religious rituals? (Cohen). Is the essential value of religion to be found in its ethical teachings? (Adler). Or is the function of religion to pass beyond the ethical, to go above nature; that is to say, is religion essentially concerned with man's relation to a supernatural God? (Kierkegaard). What is meant by a religion of revelation, and why is it held by some that it alone can satisfy man's deepest needs? (Niebuhr, Maritain). Are we compelled to choose among theism, atheism, and agnosticism, or is it logically possible to reject all these views? (Ayer).

These are some of the questions people are asking today. Answers are given in the selections that follow. But they are not one consistent set of answers. Instead, they constitute a variety of viewpoints. We hope that the reader, seeing the complexity of the religious issues, will feel challenged to do some thinking of his own.

D. J. B.

1. Religion as a Philosophical Problem *

EDGAR S. BRIGHTMAN (1884–1953)

Although it is often supposed that religion by its very nature precludes philosophical investigation, the fact is that almost all great religious thinkers of all branches of Christendom, Judaism, Islam, Brahmanism, and other religions have been far more than

---

* From Edgar S. Brightman, *A Philosophy of Religion*, copyright 1940, Prentice-Hall, Inc., pp. 112–131.

dogmatic expounders of an uncriticized faith; they have also been philosophers who related their tenets to experience as a whole and subjected them to radical criticism. It is a source of distress to the irreligious that many of the philosophers treated in any history of philosophy are also theologians; but, pleasant or unpleasant, it is a fact, and a fact that shows clearly the need of religion for intellectual interpretation. No matter how many may wish to believe or disbelieve in religion without thinking about it, the point of our present remarks is that it is not normal or usual for an intelligent mind to accept religion without thought. Why should this be true? Why not simply "enjoy" religion without critical analysis?

(1) **Coalescence of values.** As was shown in the previous chapter, religious values, like all others, coalesce with other types of value and become meaningless and worthless without such coalescence. But if religious, moral, and intellectual values do coalesce, the question arises as to how this happens. What intellectual values support and sustain religion? Or are the ideas with which religion is fused not values but disvalues, not truths but errors? Again, what moral values interpenetrate with the religious? In the presence of what competing values, if any, does religion wane or perish? In order to cope with such questions, philosophical method is necessary.

(2) **Relations of ideals to existence.** It has already been pointed out that religion is not concerned primarily about abstract ideals, but rather about the production, preservation, and increase of actually existing values. It is not enough for the believer to know that there is an ideal of peace which it would be excellent to attain; but he hears a divine voice say, "Peace *be* unto you"—in short, let the ideal exist in actual, empirical form. As G. E. Moore remarks in his *Principia Ethica*, "Though God may be admitted to be a more perfect object than any actual human being, the love of God may yet be inferior to human love, *if* God does not exist." [1] Religion is not abstract idealism, it is concrete and practical. It asserts that ideals are not only abstractly valid in the Platonic kingdom of Ideas, but also that they are to some extent realizable and realized in the world of actual existence. The belief that ideals are valid but are not potent in actuality is the position of an idealistic pessimist. Such a view, however bravely moral it may be, is not religious, because it denies the basic axiom of the conservation of values. The

---

[1] Moore, *Principia Ethica*, 200.

axiom of the eternal validity of ideals is logical, but not religious; religion requires the conservation of values. Religion, therefore, can be understood only when the philosophical problem of the relation of ideals to existence is thought through.

(3) **Religion, science, and philosophy refer to the same world.** This statement may seem to contradict the views of those who hold that science and philosophy refer to the realm of nature and religion to the realm of grace, or that the former relate to this world and the latter to a superworld. Let it be granted that some religion is predominantly otherworldly. It remains true that such religion implies a judgment on this world. Either this world is a divine creation which has fallen from grace and is under a curse; or this world is an obstacle and temptation to be overcome; or it is the scene of a conflict between the God of light and the God of darkness; or it is a gymnasium or a prison house. In any case, religion means something about the present and visible world; and in this respect its judgments are directed toward the same world that science and philosophy investigate. The relations of these various judgments to each other must be considered, if religion is to be found true or false. Furthermore, if in addition to this world, there is a superworld, it is necessary to consider the evidence in this world for belief in the other, and also to make coherent statements about the relations between the two.

(4) **There are contradictory religious value-claims and beliefs.** This indubitable fact of religious history makes it impossible to believe all religion to be true. A value-claim of one religion is that the merciful are blessed. A value-claim of another religion is that the first-born should be killed as a sacrifice. It is possible that either one of these value-claims may be valid, but not that both are at the same time, unless the aim of religion on the second assumption is to avoid being blessed. Some believe that there are many gods; others, that there is only one. Some hold that the gods have bodily form, others assert that God is a conscious spirit without bodily form, and still others think that the divine is a force, principle, or law with no personal consciousness. Some hold that salvation is by Christ alone; some, by Buddha alone. There is no doubt that systems of belief as different as Judaism, Christian Science, Confucianism, and Roman Catholicism have all produced religious values and noble characters; but it is impossible that all the beliefs of all of them can be

true at the same time. Catholicism affirms the reality of material substance; Christian Science denies it; Judaism and Confucianism do not regard any view on the subject as essential to religion. The facts reveal the presence of conflicting beliefs about religion.

From this conflict the philosophers of ancient Rome inferred, according to Gibbon, that "the various modes of worship were all equally false." [2] But a conflict of opinion about the world or the nearest route to the Indies did not, in the days before Columbus, prove the nonexistence of America or that the world had no shape. Conflicting opinions about the future do not imply that there will be no future, any more than different theories of money show that there is no money. Neither does conflict of opinion prove that all religious opinions are equally valuable, as amiable tolerance often says, when it forgets the claims of logic. All that conflict of opinion proves is that there is need for rational inquiry, unless religion is to degenerate either into the cat-and-dog fight of a war of all against all, or else into a purely subjective emotion that allows itself no rational or social expression.

What Is the Philosophical Problem of Religion?

In view of the claims and counterclaims, the conflicting values and contradicting beliefs entertained by religious men and women, the philosophical problem of religion may be stated very briefly. It is obviously impossible that all religious beliefs can be true or all religious value-claims be true values. The question: Is religion true? would therefore be undiscriminating. The rational problem of philosophy of religion would take the form: Are any religious beliefs true? If so, which ones, and why? Are any religious value-claims truly objective? If so, which ones, and why? The best possible answer to these questions is the best possible philosophy of religion. If no religious beliefs or value-claims are true, then religion is shown to be of no metaphysical importance, and of primary importance only to phenomenologists or psychiatrists.

What Is the Method of Philosophical Interpretation?

If religion is to be investigated philosophically, what we mean by philosophical investigation must be made clear. There are some

---

[2] *Decline and Fall of the Roman Empire,* Chap. II.

whose notion of philosophical method is rather crude. It consists in arriving at a system of philosophical conclusions without regard to the empirical facts of religion, and then accepting or rejecting religious beliefs according to their consistency or inconsistency with that system. Such a method is not an interpretation of religion; it is sheer dogmatism. It is to be condemned regardless of whether the system is piously theistic or impiously atheistic. The philosophical interpreter should apply methods of internal criticism rather than these crudely external ones. Internal criticism starts with the empirical subject matter to be criticized, discovers its meaning and structure, and then relates it to other areas of experience and thought. In the process of interpretation by internal criticism, there are five fairly distinct stages: (1) preliminary synopsis, (2) scientific analyses and syntheses, (3) synoptic hypotheses, (4) verification, and (5) reinterpretation. (See Chapters XV-XVI.) *

(1) **Preliminary synopsis.** Interpretation must begin with something to interpret; yet the first grasp of the material must necessarily be most inadequate. It is a mere orientation (see Chapter I), a sweeping glance with the aim of getting what we call "the hang" or "the feel" of the whole. It is observation on what J. Loewenberg calls the preanalytic stage, and consists of a tentative intuition of the general field of facts to be studied.

(2) **Scientific analyses and syntheses.** The more or less shadowy and foggy whole of the preliminary synopsis acquires firm outlines and definite content only by processes of scientific analysis and synthesis. First of all, the various portions of the field are isolated and broken up into their constituent parts. Ideally, this analysis proceeds until simple elements have been found that can be analyzed no further. Then these elements are seen synthetically in their relations to each other. In Chapter II the results of such analyses and syntheses of religion were summarized. Philosophical interpretation is purely formal and empty of real content unless it rests on the firm ground of the scientific analysis and synthesis of experience.

(3) **Synoptic hypotheses.** The third stage is the most distinctly philosophical one in the process of interpretation. It is that of what Kant called the *Gedankenexperiment* (experiment of thought) or what we may call the synoptic hypothesis. All thought, scientific or philosophical, proceeds by the invention of hypotheses intended

* [Chapter references are to Brightman's book].

to explain the observed data. Without hypotheses, not even analysis can advance; the methods and the goal of analysis would both be blind unless thus guided. Experiment is meaningless unless it either is made for the purpose of testing some hypothesis or else results in a new hypothesis. Facts without hypotheses are mere piles of bricks; facts ordered by hypotheses are buildings fit to dwell in.

Scientific hypotheses, however, differ from philosophical ones. A scientific hypothesis is restricted to the ordering of the limited subject matter under investigation—let us say the radiation of light or the religion of the Algonkins. A philosophical hypothesis, on the other hand, has a far wider scope and is synoptic in a very special sense, for it aims to relate the subject matter under investigation to a view of experience as a whole. The word synopsis, meaning a seeing together, has been used since Plato to denote a comprehensive view of experience, which relates the parts revealed by analysis and the relations established by synthesis to the whole structure of which they are aspects. Synopsis lays stress on the properties of wholes which their parts do not have.[3] This principle is of importance in the field of religion, for any value or ideal may be made to appear petty and worthless if it be analyzed into its simplest elements and attention fixed on those elements. To say that the ideal of worship is nothing but a complex of feelings, sensations, and thoughts, quite disregards the nature of the worship experience as a whole and its function in the ordering and elevation of life. A living whole is always more than the sum of its parts, just as a human body is more than a sum of electrons and protons. Without synoptic hypotheses, the value and function of religion would forever escape us.

An additional word is needed about the nature of a philosophical hypothesis. In being philosophical, an hypothesis relates the particular to the universal, the present to the eternal, the part to the whole. It seems most presumptuous for man, with his fragmentary knowledge, to make any statements, however hypothetical, about the whole which must forever exceed his grasp. Yet it is no more presumptuous to think of the whole than to think of the part, for the part necessarily implies a whole to which it belongs. In fact,

---

[3] Such properties have been discovered and interpreted most frequently by idealists; but many realists, such as G. E. Moore (in his *Principia Ethica*), E. G. Spaulding, and R. W. Sellars, recognize the reality and importance of these properties.

the nature of reason is such that it is impossible to avoid using universals which apply to the whole; we cannot think time without thinking eternity; we cannot think of man's dependence without thinking of something on which he depends. It is futile to try to choke off philosophical thinking by calling it presumptuous. It is more presumptuous to take any attitude without thought than it is after thoughtful consideration. Just as the individual needs integration for his psychological health, so also he needs synoptic hypotheses for his mental health. Yet such hypotheses are not to be tested by their value for health; on the contrary, their value for health is tested by their truth. Religion always includes synoptic hypotheses as its very life; faith is the religious attitude toward them.

(4) **Verification.** The fourth stage of philosophical interpretation is verification. Given a synoptic hypothesis, faith in the goodness of God, for example, some means of testing it must be devised, or else there is no way of knowing whether it points to fact or to fancy.

There is difference of opinion about what constitutes verification. This is at least partly due to the different types of object toward which our hypotheses are directed. There are at least three such types: observable natural processes, mathematical and logical systems, and minds. It is fairly simple to verify an hypothesis about an observable natural process; define your hypothesis exactly, perform an experiment and observe its results exactly, compare the results, and the verification (or falsification) of the hypothesis has taken place. Likewise in logic and mathematics, verification is a simple matter. The consistency or inconsistency of the hypothesis may be shown by repeated deductive operations that can be carried out by any rational mind and will be carried out so that the conclusion will be the same if the premises are the same. But if you ask how the existence of other minds is verified, you find yourself in a muddle. Everyone is sure that there are other minds besides his own and almost everyone thinks he knows how he verifies the hypothesis that they exist. One does it by direct intuition; another, by analogy from behavior; another, by extrasensory perception; another by communication through language.[4] However we do it, it is surely not in the same way that we verify natural processes, for other

---

[4] See the valuable article by H. H. Price on "Our Evidence for the Existence of Other Minds," in *Philosophy*, 13 (1938), 425–456, and H. Dingle's criticism of it in the same journal, 14 (1939), 457–467.

minds are not observable by the senses; nor in the same way that we verify a logical or mathematical result, because other minds are not abstract terms and relations.

What, then, happens to make us so sure that we have verified the presence of another mind which we cannot see physically or prove deductively? Social objects force us to see what is implicit in physical and logical objects, but less patent—namely, that all verification rests on postulates. Unless we presuppose the unity of the verifying self, the presence of data within self-experience, the purpose of verification, the validity of reason, the trustworthiness of memory (when tested by reason), the reality of time, and the reality of an objective world which is there when not observed or verified, no verification can occur. If it is to be shared it also presupposes other minds. None of these presuppositions can be verified either by sense perception or by mathematical proof; yet all of them must be granted if any verification of any kind of hypothesis is to go on. Are these presuppositions merely arbitrary? Or is there some ground for them? Surely they are not wild fancies. They are basic truths. How do we know they are truths? Simply by the fact that they are beliefs which form a system consistent with itself and consistent (as far as we know) with every phase and type of experience.

If the reader inquires what all this has to do with religion, he has a right to an answer. Religion is not an observable physical process; it is not a syllogism or a mathematical formula; it is a conscious experience that includes reference to other minds,[5] human and divine. It is therefore unreasonable to expect a religious belief to be verified or falsified by sense observations or by formal logico-mathematical operations. Religious verification or falsification must take place as all our social knowledge does, and in the light of the presuppositions of verification. A religious belief can be verified only by its relation to the system of our beliefs as a whole which have the marks of consistency with one another and with experience. No verification can hope for more than this in principle. As Dickinson S. Miller has said, the problem can be solved only in "the forum of the individual mind."[6]

(5) **Reinterpretation.** When thought has reached the stage of

---

[5] Mind is here used as synonymous with person.

[6] For a contradictory view of verification, that of logical positivism, see Ayer, *Language, Truth and Logic*, [first published 1936, Oxford University Press, now reissued by Dover Publications; see selection 12, this volume].

verification, is it then at the end of its journey? May it finally rest? No; neither in science nor in religion is there an end. No verification is completely inclusive. There is no test that does not need retesting. Nothing is absolute short of The Absolute—the all-inclusive whole of being. Every stage of insight may lead to deeper insight. Every interpretation requires reinterpretation. The Psalmist's word, "He that sitteth in the heavens shall laugh," must have been written for men who believe that human knowledge can completely compass the infinite. We cannot reach the end; but as long as we live and use sound method, we may grow endlessly.

Reinterpretation does not imply that when it goes on, every belief we now hold will be found to be false. It does not require groundless rejection of any faith. It requires, rather, the recognition of incomplete proof, incomplete understanding, and incomplete information, together with insight into the method of philosophical interpretation which constantly corrects and supplements, but never absolutely completes man's fragmentary but growing grasp of reality.

What Is the Criterion of Religious Truth?

The question about the criterion of religious truth has already been given a preliminary answer, namely, that the consistency of our beliefs with each other and with experience is the test of the truth of religious beliefs.

The suggested criterion is obviously the same criterion that is applied in science and in daily life to detect the presence of error and to measure our approximation to truth. Should a different criterion be applied in religious matters? If a different criterion were proposed, let it be what it will, could it be such as to allow truth to be inconsistent? Could contradictory propositions be true in religion? Or could religious truth be of such a nature as to be irrelevant to experience? Could belief in God be entertained, for example, without regard to its relation to the facts of experience? If a totally different criterion were applied, we should indeed have a "double truth." [7] One kind of truth would be based on a rational interpretation of experience; the other kind would be based on its own cri-

---

[7] Gilson, *Reason and Revelation in the Middle Ages,* gives reasons for maintaining that this view was not held even in the Middle Ages.

terion and would be exempt from any criticism arising in reason or experience (except the privileged experience of its own criterion). To raise such questions is to answer them. All truth accepted by any mind is subject to the jurisdiction of that mind's reason and experience.

But there is implicit in the apparent absurdity of the frequent appeal for a separate criterion for religious truth, one factor of real importance, namely, the justified demand on the part of religion that its claims shall be judged on the basis neither of abstract a priori considerations alone nor of nonreligious experiences alone. In seeking for religious truth, all that a priori logic can offer must be considered; all secular experience must be weighed; but the vital question of the truth and value of religion cannot be said to have been approached until the actual evidence of religious experience is interpreted. Neither physics nor psychology nor philosophy is competent to pass any judgment, favorable or unfavorable, on religion until religious values have been considered; one cannot know whether one is confirming or refuting religion until one knows what religion is.

The patent necessity of considering data before judging them establishes, however, no unique criterion. Yet the human mind has always struggled against the demands of reason, or (to take a more historical view) has come very slowly to a recognition of its universal claims, especially in the field of religion. Not rational interpretation of experience, but *instinct,* or *custom,* or *tradition,* is the criterion appealed to by great masses. The first is often cited by the clergy and is also the support of totalitarian views which found religion on "race and blood"; but the lack of any clear definition of instinct renders the concept useless as a criterion. Conflicting customs and traditions furnish no criterion for choice among them. Others, holding that religion is universal (a questionable proposition in itself), insist that universal agreement (*consensus gentium*) is a test of truth. But there is no universal agreement on any matter of importance; many reject evolution, medicine, and the calculations of astronomy, not to mention God, freedom, and immortality; and even if there were universal agreement on a proposition, the truth of the proposition would not be tested by the agreement (for there was once agreement on animism and a flat earth), but rather by the reasons which led to the agreement. Others have appealed to *feeling* as a test of truth; but the notoriously varying moods of feeling contain no principle for determining which of two equally strong, but conflicting, feelings is true. Hence no religious feeling, either of belief or of doubt, is to be regarded as true because of its intensity.

The five criteria just examined are plainly unacceptable. At least five other criteria have been proposed. *Sense experience,* it is often said, is the one means of access to objective reality. No philosopher would deny that it is a source of real knowledge. But something more than sense experience is needed to test whether a dream, an illusion, an hallucination, or a mirage is a veridical perception; and sense experience is not all of experience. The fundamental problems of philosophy of religion turn about the relation of value experience to sense experience. It is purely arbitrary to elevate sense experience to a preferred position while ignoring the fact that values are as truly present in consciousness as are sense data. To select sense data as being normative without considering the claims of value experience is to be dogmatic. Sense data must be seen in the light of the rest of experience and must be rationally interpreted.

Intuition is a principle often appealed to as criterion. By intuition is meant immediate knowledge, that is, awareness of a content (a quality or a principle) as given in experience and not derived from reasoning. Sense experience, for instance, is one example of intuition; value experience is another; experience of space and time is intuitional. That intuitions lie at the basis of all our knowledge is certain, and that many intuitions are true is at least highly probable. But it is not possible to distinguish a genuine intuition from a disguised appeal to feeling (a rationalization of desire) without consulting some criterion other than intuition itself. Particularly is this true of religious intuitions when they come in the form of belief in revelation. It is characteristic of religions, as we have seen, to make revelation-claims. When God has spoken, it seems irreverent to ask for further evidence, much more so to raise questions. But the fact is that the intuition, "I am now hearing the voice of God," accompanies contradictory beliefs, even within the scriptures of one religion, such as the Judaeo-Christian. Therefore all intuitions, including all religious ones, need to be tested by some criterion that is not merely one more intuition. In common with all of the criteria thus far proposed, intuition, however inadequate as a test of truth, is of the utmost importance as a source of truth. Even instinct, custom, and tradition may suggest some truths to us; what is very widely accepted may be accepted for good reasons, what is strongly felt may also be true; and sense data are certainly sources of truth. Yet in every instance some test must be applied to sift the truth from the error.

In philosophical discussion, *correspondence* often appears as a candidate for criterion in chief. Correspondence is, in fact, the definition of truth; a proposition is true if what it asserts corresponds to the object about which the assertion is made, and we should naturally expect a definition to serve as criterion of the presence or absence of what is defined. Correspondence, however, fails us in this respect; it is not a criterion of truth nor even a source of truth. It is not a criterion of truth for the simple reason that it can never be applied. Propositions are about the past, the present, the future, the timeless, or some combination of them. It is clear that it is now, at this present moment, always impossible to compare a present proposition with a past, a future, or an eternal object; such comparison would require the past, the future, or eternity to be now present for comparison, a plain impossibility. Even propositions about the present are incapable of being tested by correspondence; for the process of comparison would take time and ere it had occurred the present object would have become past. It is equally difficult to doubt that correspondence is what we mean by truth and to believe that it is a usable criterion or a source of truth.[8]

There remain two criteria which are the ones chiefly used at the present time by philosophers. They are *practical results* and *coherence*. Those who regard practical results as being the test of truth are called pragmatists. Pragmatism [9] is one of the few original contributions which American philosophy has made, and it has exerted a wide influence on all fields including philosophy of religion. The empirical method of the present work owes much to both James and Dewey. Pragmatism, however, is a broad phase of the empirical movement rather than a precise system. A pragmatist, as is well

---

[8] See Pratt, *Personal Realism*, New York, The Macmillan Co., 1937, pp. 74–97.

[9] The literature of pragmatism is so extensive that no attempt will be made here to do more than mention four notable works: William James's *Pragmatism*, John Dewey's *Logic*, W. P. Montague's *The Ways of Knowing* (this last contains one of the best criticisms of pragmatism), and Ralph Barton Perry's *The Thought and Character of William James*, a gem of American philosophy.

known, is one who says that an idea is true if it works, or has practical consequences. This makes an immediate appeal to the religious mind, which cares more for the actual religious experience than for the philosophy or theology which interprets or validates it. "By their fruits ye shall know them"; "if any man willeth to do his will, he shall know of the teaching." Jesus seems to be pragmatic, and the religious thinkers of India are even more so.[10] Furthermore, pragmatism brings religion and science close together. Each uses the test of consequences; indeed each speaks of experiment—or at least eighteenth- and nineteenth-century Christians often referred to "experimental Christianity," an empirical testing of religion.

That all practical consequences of ideas are facts which must be considered; that a belief that is not tested in experience is blind and useless; and that pragmatism is a sane, radical challenge to dogmatism cannot well be denied. Yet there is one central difficulty in pragmatism which makes it very difficult to apply. That difficulty is the ambiguity of its fundamental criterion of practical results. What, exactly, is meant by practical? What is meant by saying that an idea works? In one sense, every idea that we can fool ourselves or others with may be said to work to that extent. Belief in transubstantiation works among Catholics; it does not work among Methodists or Quakers; it is utter nonsense to Mohammedans or Shintoists. The belief in the omnipotence of God may work for the purpose of elevating the spirit, yet not work at all for the purpose of explaining concrete evils in the world. Belief in the efficacy of the bones of a saint may work until it is found that his skull is on exhibition at several different shrines.

This ambiguity of terms and of their application is so great that pragmatists have not been able to arrive at any clear agreement on definitions. If "practical" and "work" are not defined exactly, the use of them as criteria only adds to the confusion of thought and belief. But if they are defined exactly and used thoroughly, they turn into a mandate to examine all the evidence, especially all of the consequences of action, in the light of the mind's total experience. In other words, when taken thoroughly, the pragmatist's criterion turns into coherence.

Coherence is essentially the method of verification described earlier

---

[10] For the quotations from Jesus see Mt. 7:16 and Jn. 7:17. See also the sarcastically pragmatic remark of the man born blind: "Why, herein is the marvel, that ye know not whence he is, and yet he opened mine eyes" (Jn. 9:30).

in this chapter. To restate it: according to the criterion of coherence, a proposition is to be treated as true if (1) it is self-consistent, (2) it is consistent with all of the known facts of experience, (3) it is consistent with all other propositions held as true by the mind that is applying this criterion, (4) it establishes explanatory and interpretative relations between various parts of experience, (5) these relations include all known aspects of experience and all known problems about experience in its details and as a whole. It is to be noted that coherence is more than mere consistency; the latter is absence of contradiction, whereas the former requires the presence of the empirical relations mentioned under points (4) and (5); thus consistency is necessary to coherence, but consistency is not sufficient.

Two very important additional points about coherence should be noted. (1) Since coherence requires a reference to the whole of experience, some hypothesis about the nature of the whole is essential to the working of this criterion. (2) Since experience and science are constantly growing, the application of coherence cannot arrive at fixed and static results. It is a principle of constant reorganization, a law of criticism and growth, rather than a closed system. Coherence can never be fully applied until all thinking about all possible experience has been finished; however, in this it is no worse off than pragmatism, which requires all practical results. This does not mean that all our present beliefs are erroneous and that no truth can be known until we know all truth. In fact, it may be a very coherent hypothesis to assume that some truths (such as the validity of coherence and the need of consulting experience) will always be true no matter what else is true. Nevertheless, the criterion of coherence implies that no truth can be completely tested or proved until all truth is known; perhaps just the facts which we do not yet know may be required for the modification or rejection of any known truth. On the other hand, all of the results offered by all other proposed tests, revelations, or insights must come before the tribunal of the whole mind and its grasp on experience as a whole. This, and this only, justifies or "verifies" a scientific hypothesis or a religious faith.

The Problem of Religious Certainty

The author's view of the criterion of coherence just presented has been subjected to criticism on the ground that it fails to afford the certainty that is needed if religion is to be a vital factor in life.

The attack has come both from the right and from the left. The right-winger, Edwin Lewis, speaks of "the right to be certain," and to say to an opposing view "quietly, but finally, even dogmatically, *it is wrong.*" To hold (as the present writer does) that our highest religious affirmations are, from the logical standpoint, at most only probable is said by Lewis to introduce "a fatal and quite unnecessary skepticism into the very heart of existence." [11] On the other hand, the left-winger, Henry Nelson Wieman, opposes the proposed use of the coherence criterion on the ground that it would justify beliefs that have only a speculative probability, whereas we need to build, he thinks, on more certain and stable foundations.[12] Wieman would accordingly restrict religious beliefs to propositions about the structure of nature which have assured scientific certainty. John Dewey, however, in his *The Quest for Certainty* (1929) takes a position differing from that of both Lewis and Wieman. He holds, in substance, that the great error of both philosophy and religion has been to claim or even to seek certainty. In the nature of the case, we cannot get it without deceiving ourselves. What we can get, and all we can get, is an exploration of the possibilities of experience. Dewey's view, which has much to commend it, was in some respects anticipated by F. J. McConnell's little book on *Religious Certainty* (1910).

Additional light on this vexed problem was shed by the German psychologist and philosopher, Karl Groos, in an essay entitled "The Problem of Relativism." [13] He points out (p. 471) that there is no way of securing objective truth except "by the way of subjective conviction." Now, Groos holds that, although "it is one of our beliefs that objective, overindividual validity attaches to many of our subjective intuitions and experiences," it is impossible to prove this strictly. Thus, while theoretically all proof is relative and not absolute, practically it is rational to believe that some propositions are really true. For instance, who can doubt that there are other minds than his own; but who can prove it with absolute certainty? Thus "theoretical relativism is united with practical absolutism." There

---

[11] See Lewis, *God and Ourselves*, New York, The Abingdon Press, 1931.

[12] These views have been expressed in personal correspondence.

[13] This essay appeared in both German and English in the short-lived *Forum Philosophicum*, I (1930–1931), 461–473. The view is developed in a pamphlet, *Die Sicherung der Erkenntnis: theoretischer Relativismus und praktischer Absolutismus* (Tübingen: Osiander, 1927).

seems little objection to this procedure, and much value in it, as long as we follow Groos's demand "that we treat our beliefs, whenever they persist in the face of cool reflection on the situation, as absolute truths, at least 'pending further developments.' " We cannot justify our commonest beliefs about the past or the future without recourse to Groos's postulates; with them, an exploration of the possibilities of religious value experience becomes more rational than on Lewis's assumptions, and more experimental and constructive than on Wieman's.

In this chapter some attempt has been made to show that religion is a philosophical problem, and to indicate by what methods and criteria philosophy may deal with religion.

2. *The Will as a Maker of Truth* *

WILLIAM ERNEST HOCKING *(1873-)*

Whatever value religion has for man will be funded, we now judge, in the religious ideas, especially in the religious world-idea or reality-idea or substance-idea—the idea of God. Judging religion solely by its effectiveness in human affairs we will have no religion without metaphysics, which is but a knowledge of reality. Religion does its work by way of its truth. Creed and theology become again important to us; become the essential treasures of religion: for in them the race preserves from age to age the determining factors of all human worth.

Such is, in fact, my own belief. But there is one formidable question to be met before we can either rest in this conclusion, or wholly understand its meaning. We have been assuming that reality is a finished total which it is our place to recognize and adjust ourselves to, without presuming to alter its general aspect. We have been assuming that if there is a God at all, God is a fixity in the universe; a being whom we must accept and not undertake to change. We

* From *The Meaning of God in Human Experience* (1912), reprinted by permission of the publisher, Yale University Press.

have been assuming that the objects of our religious interest are all made up in advance, and that our own wills have no part to play in determining what *is*; in short that as knowers of reality we must be passive, receptive toward the truth as it is, taking it as we find it, in experience and in idea. But this general asumption of ours, that reality such as religion deals with *is what it is* in independence of our own wills, not to be created or destroyed by anything we may resolve or do about it, — this general assumption is open to doubt.

There are certainly some regions of reality which are *unfinished*. We are endowed with wills only because there are such regions, to which it is our whole occupation to give shape and character. In such regions the will-to-believe is justified, because it is no will-to-make-believe, but a veritable will to create the truth in which we believe. What I believe of my fellow men goes far to determine what my fellow men actually are. Believe men liars—they show themselves such; determine yourself upon their essential goodness, and they do not disappoint your resolve: your belief is not one which can ever be refuted, for the characters of men are not finished parts of reality; they are still being built, and your will is a factor in the building. Where truth is thus waiting to be finished or determined, the will may hold the deciding play.

Every social need, such as the need for friendship, must be a party to its own satisfaction: I cannot passively find my friend as a ready-made friend; a ready-made human being he may be, but his friendship for me I must help to create by my own active resolve. So of the great political reality, the State. This also is nothing which man has found ready-made. The State is a reality which is what it is by dint of the combined resolves of many human wills, through time: we individuals find the State as something apparently finished, standing there as something to be empirically accepted; but at no time does the existence of this object become so independent that it can continue to hold its reality apart from the good-will which from moment to moment recreates it. May it be that the objects in which religion is concerned are in some ways like these, belonging to the unfinished regions of reality?

We find our religion much as we find our State, an inherited possession fixed in its main outlines by no will of our own; yet an expression, perhaps, of the racial good-will of men, depending like the State on the continued good-will of all individuals for its validity,

even for its truth. Religion throws over human life a unity like that
of the State, but vaster: it provides a canopy under which all men
may recognize their brotherhood: in the good-will of religion a
totality of spirit is *brought about* which apart from that good-will
has no independent existence. In holding to this qualification of my
whole-idea — by the idea of a spiritual totality which I must cooperate with other men to make real — I find an immeasurable and
substantial enlargement of my field of vision and so of my whole
level of values. Is not this spiritual unity, though a function of the
will of man, a large part of what I mean by the name of God?
Through religion, too, a still greater totality is accomplished: a world
beyond is brought into conjunction with our present interest, and
our mortal lives are endowed with prospects of immortality. Yet I
strongly doubt whether immortality is any such predetermined
reality that it exists for any person apart from that person's will to
make it real. The future life may well be such an object as my decision can make real or unreal, so far as my own experience is concerned. And in general, when we consider closely the kind of object
which religion presents for our faith we find it such as might well
be plastic to the determinations of the will, more plastic even than
friendship or the State. For these objects are not to be found on
earth like the friend; nor are they to be set up in visible form like
the State: they exist wholly in that region of the spirit, whose coming and going is immediately sensitive to every variation of loyalty
and disloyalty on the part of the souls in which alone it has its life.

Further, the difference between a religious view of the world and
a non-religious view lies chiefly in the quality or *character* which is
attributed to the world as a whole. It does not lie in the circumstance that the religious mind has a whole-idea, while the nonreligious mind has none: every man must have his whole-idea, and
such as it is, it will determine what value existence may have for
him. But the critical difference appears in the judgments *about* the
whole; whether this reality of ours is divine, or infernal, or an indifferent universal gravepit. These differences, we may say, are
differences in *predicates,* rather than in the subject; and it is precisely in the matter of the predicates which can be applied to the
world as a whole that we found the primary difficulty of religious
knowledge to lie. Every one begins with his whole-idea; but it is the
function of religion to *interpret* this whole as divine; in brief, to

make the transition from the whole-idea to the idea of God. These other words of ours, non-committal in regard to quality — "the whole," "substance," "reality" — do they fairly name that with which religion has to do? Is not the problem of religious knowledge a problem of the *attributes* of reality,[1] and are not these attributes indeterminate, apart from the will?

For it is not simply the case that these attributes which religion ascribes to reality (divinity, beneficence, soul-preserving or value-conserving properties) are invisible, spiritual, inaccessible to observation: it is the case that these ideas, so far as reasons go, are in apparent *equilibrium* — neither provable nor disprovable. The world would be consistent without God; it would also be consistent with God: whichever hypothesis a man adopts will fit experience equally well; neither one, so far as accounting for visible facts is concerned, works better than the other. I have often wondered whether in these supermundane matters the universe may not be so nicely adjusted (and withal so justly) that each man finds true the things he believes in and wills for; why should not every man find his religion true, in so far as he has indeed set his heart upon it and made sacrifices for it? However this may be, the religious objects (the predicates given by religion to reality) stand at a pass of intellectual equipoise: it may well seem that some other faculty must enter in to give determination to reason at the point where reason halts, without a deciding voice of its own. The birth of the idea of God in the mind — the judgment "Reality is living, divine, a God exists" — is so subtle, like the faintest breath of the spirit upon the face of the waters, that no look within can tell whether God is here revealing himself to man, or man creating God.

It is because of this position of subtle equilibrium that the religious consciousness is *evanescent;* faith is unstable as empirical knowledge is not. Though at any time I find my world sacred, it only needs a touch of passivity on my part and it will again become secular: I cannot recover nor understand its former worth. My faith in God is subject to fluctuation as my faith in other objects is not, even though these other objects are equally inaccessible (as my

---

[1] The earliest ideas and names for the Deity seem to have been rather adjectives than nouns. Among the Aryans, the divine was expressed as "the shining," "the illustrious"; among Malays and Indians and very generally elsewhere, "the wonderful," "the powerful," "the immense."

faith in China or in the conservation of energy). And noteworthy about this fluctuation is that it passes from extreme to extreme, not pausing in the intermediate stages of probability: the existence of God is to me either wholly certain or wholly absurd. Likewise of immortality: it seems to me at times that man is a fool to believe it, at other times that a man is a fool not to believe it. I have no power of weighing shades of probability in these matters. It must be so, it can't be so: these are the only degrees of which my own religious faith is capable. But alternatives like these belong rather to the will or disposition of the spirit than to the estimating mind. And further, the one thing which is most sure to dispel faith and substitute the secular world-picture is precisely intellectual scrutiny. Faith is not only difficult for reason; it is distinctly diffident toward reason. Its origin, then, and its firmness must be due to some other power, presumably to will.

It would help our thought on this point if we could trace the mental processes in which the idea of God first arises in human consciousness. It is more than doubtful whether any such tracing is possible; and largely because of the circumstances which we have pointed out: the thought of God comes and goes; is often lost and often recovered, both in racial and in individual experience; it appears also in various ways to various minds. No historical nor typical origin of the belief in God can be shown. Nevertheless, taking as a beginning a mood of secularity which often recurs in human experience, there may be some measure of typical psychological truth in such a picture as this which follows:

There is a grim and menacing aspect of reality which remains commonly unemphatic as our lives go but which events may at any time uncover. We are obliged to witness this vast Whole, of which we speak so easily, threatening existence or destroying the things that make our existence valuable. Against such threats our usual methods of protection avail exactly nothing. The merciless processes of nature, of disease and death, of fate generally, are not impressed by entreaty or by effort, are not to be beaten off with clubs nor frightened away by shrieks and gestures of defiance. All these weapons will be tried; and trial best convinces of futility. Fear and hope normally inspire action; fear and hope show themselves alike empty in this situation. That with which one has to do is reality itself; and toward this only some less external attitude can be significant. But in the human creature at bay there are other depths; the recognition of futility is the beginning of human adequacy. For despair ends by calling out a certain touch of *resentment*, — resentment having a tinge of self-assertion in it, even of moral requirement directed against reality. Such a being as I, by virtue of this very power of realizing my situation, by virtue of my whole-idea and my self-consciousness, has some claim to urge upon the reality that surrounds me, threatening; the reality which, after all, has brought me forth. Though by the slightest movement of this deep-lying sense of right, one does, in effect, demand justice of his creator: and thereby, without premeditation, finds himself with the idea of Deity already constituted and possessed. For toward what can moral resentment and demand be addressed but to a living and moral Being? In that deep impulse of self-assertion there was involved, though I knew it not, *the will that my reality should be a living and responsible reality.* And in time I shall find that in imputing this quality to my world, I have already lifted the burden of those anxieties, so helpless upon their own plane. The God-idea thus appears as a postulate of our moral consciousness: an original object of resolve which tends to make itself good in experience.

For the proof of this new-found or new-made relation to reality, expressed in my God-idea, is this: that in meeting my world divinely it shows itself divine. It supports my postulate. And without such act of will, no discovery of divinity could take place. Men cannot *be* worthy of reverence, until I meet them with reverence: for my reverence is the dome under which alone their possible greatness can stand and live. Of the world likewise, — it can have no divinity but only materiality or menacing insensibility, unless I throw over it the category under whose dome its holiness can rise visible and actual. God cannot live, as divine and beneficent, except in the opportunity created by our good-will: but given the good-will, reality is such as will become indeed divine.

In accord with this conjecture as to the position of religious truth, namely that it is determined by the movement of will-to-believe, is an old observation of religious experience. It is written that he who seeks finds: the connection between seeking and finding is infallible. Such infallible connection may be many-wise understood, but it may be thus understood, that the *seeking brings the finding with it.* "Thou wouldst not seek me hadst thou not already found me," said Pascal: and to Sabatier this thought came "like a flash of light . . . the solution of a problem that had long appeared insoluble." [2] The religiousness of man's nature is the whole substance of his revelation. Whatever we *impute* to the world comes back to us as a quality pre-resident there — is not this the whole illusion of reality? Impute then to the world a living beneficence: the world will not reject this imputation, will *be* even as you have willed it.[3] Your belief becomes (as Fichte held) an evidence of your character — not of your learning. He who waits his assent till God is proved to him, will never find Him. But he who seeks finds — has already found.

In all these respects there is the strongest resemblance between the religious idea and human value. The world is consistent without Deity (so it is said); the world is *consistent* also without beauty, or other charm. Before reason, religious assurance is evanescent: so also with any pleasure or other worth when by introspection, or analysis, we determine to seize its secret. The world-body to the eye of Fact is grey, even dead with all its working; if it is to be reanimated with worth, it must be by that miracle which continually repeats itself in our experience — the Spirit breathes upon it from its own resources the breath of life. Thus the birth of value and the birth of God-faith are alike; as indeed we have every reason to believe, if the conclusions of the last chapter are valid: is it not possible that they are the *same thing,* — in both cases the work of an ultimate *good-will* toward our world? If the union which we have proposed between idea and feeling is indeed so intimate and equal that "without feeling the ideas are false; even as without the idea the feelings are meaningless," it is at least possible that some deeper faculty fundamental to both idea and feeling is here *giving laws to reality itself:* deciding what the truth, and therewith the value, of my world shall be.

A new conception of faith appears here: faith is more than passive feeling, more also than the sight which seizes upon the

---

2 *Outlines of a Philosophy of Religion*, p. 32.

3 The Chinese have long had a saying "If you believe in the gods, the gods exist: if you do not believe in them they do not exist." Whence pragmatism as a theory of metaphysics may be said to be of Chinese origin. See A. H. Smith, *Chinese Characteristics*, p. 301.

reality of the world as it is — faith is the loyal determination and resolve which sees the world *as it is capable of becoming,* and commits its fortunes to the effort to make real what it thus sees. The religious creed or world-view becomes a postulate rather than either an empirical discovery or a revelation to be obediently received.

I know not whether this presentation of a voluntaristic foundation for religious truth has been able to provoke any acceptance on the part of the reader: it is a paradoxical doctrine, yet it has in it great power, and especially great relief for the difficult situation of the religious idea. To my mind, I must admit, nothing more illuminating has ever been put forward than just such interpretation of many a religious doctrine; nothing truer to the way in which religious picturing and myth-building does actually take place in the human consciousness.

Taking religious ideas literally and fixedly is, in fact, a modern and Western peculiarity. The Oriental mind realizes that the spiritual atmosphere in which either men or gods may breathe, must be *created;* it knows nothing of empirical truth in matters of religion, truth passively taken; and postulate joins hands with poetry in constituting the medium in which all spirituality may live. (The freedom of the religious poem or myth or parable may be regarded as the will-to-believe at play.) The Oriental mind speaks understandingly of miracles and virgin births, because it sees in them poetic means of lifting what it will pronounce divine above the commonplace of profane event and indolent human character. We also, of the West, have our own style of poetry and imagination; of which we see well enough that it must be understood with imagination and humor also after its kind. But we approach, in religious matters, the poetry of the Orient often with a literal-minded savagery, which must accuse us of some deeper defect than simple lack of humor — a lack, namely, of spirituality itself, which knows that the language of the spirit must be read by the spirit also, and is not to be rudely transferred into empirical text-books of physics and of medicine. I do not doubt that in religion as in human experience generally, each will sets the level of its own life, determines in large measure its own destiny, and helps to create spiritual reality for all other human life. A faith without a large ingredient of will, is no faith at all.

Nevertheless, I must believe that the great heave of the West to get a literal and objective grip upon its major religious objects is an advance, and not a retrogression. We only drive men to make their religion all prose, when we threaten to make it all poetry and postulate. For poetry and postulate are pioneer stages of truth, and live by the ounce of literality and truth-independent that is at their heart. The large scope for our own will and creation is not denied: the world is such as to make this creativity possible. But then our religion attaches itself to the literal truth *that the world is such,* already such, *as to allow these developments* and to respond thus sensitively to our acts of will. This prior element becomes our religious creed; the region of our wills to create becomes the province of art and of morals.

The destiny of religious truth to become universal and imperative must detach it at last from all salient subjectivity; must state and define the *scope* of our creative possibilities *within the frame of that which independently Is.* Literality is an accomplishment of deepening self-consciousness; it marks an achievement of personal equilibrium and stability, which is able to recognize corresponding stability and identity in the world with which it deals, — not as limiting its own freedom, but as upholding it. It has required a Western integrity and self-respect to submit in obedience to the observation of Nature; it is this same integrity which requires in its religious objects that to which it must be obedient, as the basis of whatever creativity and command it will claim.

Early religious objects are like play-objects of children, whose character is partly real, and partly conferred by the player. This, says the child, shall be a soldier, — this a good soldier, and this a bad one — and behold they are such. To hold interest, playthings must become more autonomous as the child grows, more locomotive, more realistic and difficult to manage. In time they are all to be displaced by objects of the same name, — but *real.* As for these real objects, they are more dangerous, more refractory; they have independent inner purposes of their own; our success in dealing with them is uncertain, whereas with the play-objects, whose inner thoughts were such only as we imputed to them, our success was a foregone conclusion. Play is the necessary prologue to life, because, chiefly, it is necessary to meet life with the *habit of success.* Not wholly different may it have been with the maturation of the

religious life in human history. Let the religious instinct have its
full swing and success in its traffic with divinities and world-auspices
which are in large part the work of its own will, if not of its own
hand. Thereby may it be prepared to meet with the temper of
success the ear of a Deity wholly *himself*, wholly identical in his own
counsel. Christianity marks the first great inburst of the Orient
into consciousness of the literal world, with its literal human
problem and world sorrow, the first worship of the literal God of that
world. The work of literalizing our creed is never to be finished;
for imagination and postulate move more rapidly than the leaven of
objectivity can spread; but they move under the protection of the
major literalities. Upon these major literalities religion must hence-
forth and forever be built. For maturity is marked by the preference
to be defeated rather than have a subjective success. We as mature
persons can worship only that which we are compelled to worship.
If we are offered a man-made God and a self-answering prayer, we
will rather have no God and no prayer. There can be no valid
worship except that in which man is involuntarily bent by the
presence of the Most Real, beyond his will.

The problem of loyalty in religion is not different from the problem of loyalty elsewhere. It is true that we cannot be loyal to any
tie that has been imposed upon us without our own consent — this
is the first premise alike of love and of government. On the other
hand, we cannot be loyal to any tie that has been fabricated by a
needless stroke of our own will. Any object which can hold our
allegiance must therefore be at the same time an object of free
choice, and an object of necessary choice. In the expressions of
romantic love it is hard to tell which is uppermost: that this bond
between the lovers is wholly their own, their exclusive knowledge
and will, the highest work of their own freedom; or that this bond
is the work of Fate, such as the stars of heaven from all time have
destined to effect. Unless God is that being for whom the soul is
likewise inescapably destined by the eternal nature of things, the
worship of God will get no sufficient hold on the human heart.
Religion is indeed a manifestation of the generous and creative side
of human nature; but its generosity is not that of creation out of
whole cloth, — it is the generosity of the spirit ready to acknowledge the full otherness of its objects, and to live divinely in a world
which *is* divine.

It is still possible that reality in its whole constitution is a matter of choice, though not of *our* choice. The results of your choice become data to me; your will is my fact: it may be similarly that everything which is fact to our human consciousness is the creative choice of a supreme Will. On such a supposition, voluntaristic views of reality would be true for God, but for no other. It is true that creativity is the essential quality of the will; and in the constitution of reality, man's will is to coöperate with whatever other creative will there may be in the universe. But man has religion because he is not wholly identical with God; and his religion will be founded upon that relation to reality in which he is less creative than dependent, — or more exactly, in which his creatorship is a result of his dependence.[4]

For in truth, our human life is only an apprenticeship in creativity. The small launches of postulation which we make depend on being quickly caught up and floated by a tide of corroboration hailing from beyond ourselves. We leap; but unless we are soon borne up from beyond we make but a sorry flight. And however far my creativity extends, my own creations never become truth for me, until seen through the eye of another than myself they are recognized by him as fact, and so made valid for me also. My best creativity must win the consent of the independent before it can take the status of truth, even in my own eyes. The word truth has in it some reference not to be suppressed to a wholly other than myself, to a will wholly other than mine, as a condition of the reality of anything created. Thus, all finite creativity contemplates this other, which by implication is not a product of its will; it is this radically independent reality which religion seeks to know, and which alone it can worship.

How, then, is religious truth to be known? Are the realities of which religion speaks to be discovered in experience? Or are they matters of hypothesis, or of inference, that is to say, of reason? Our answer has been implied in what has gone before: religious truth

---

[4] There are two uses of the word independent which need to be distinguished. One kind of independence is mutual, a symmetrical relation: A is independent of B, B is independent of A. The other kind is not symmetrical: A is independent of B, B is dependent upon A. It is in this latter sense that we refer to "the independent variable," in mathematical and physical systems. Reality has an element of the latter kind of independence of finite purposes, not of the former.

is founded *upon experience*. In that imaginary picture of ours of the psychological birth of the idea of God — in which it seemed to us as if our resentment, a stroke of moral will, had spontaneously made or recognized our world a living and responsible being — we may discern beside the stroke of will an experience of discovery.[5] If there is any knowledge of God, it must be in some such way a matter of experience. This implies that our experience of reality is not confined to sensation. Sensation itself also brings us into contact with a reality which is independent of our will; sensation is a metaphysical experience. And religious faith must be built upon an experience not wholly different from sensation; but a super-sensible experience, like our experience of our human fellows; an experience which recognizes the reality given in sensation for what, in its true nature, it is.

And whatever is matter of experience must also become, in time, matter of reason; for reason is but the process of finding, by some secure path of connection, a given experience from the standpoint of other experience assumed as better known. The proof of God's existence is (as Hegel put it) but the lifting of the mind to God from out of the affairs of secular business. Such proof, or mental direction, is called for, not because the religious objects are inaccessible to experience, but rather because they *are accessible;* and being found in experience, it is necessary to establish their systematic relations with the rest. It is through reason that the original and evanescent experience of God becomes established as veritable truth.

This, then, is the result to which our labors so far have led. We cannot find a footing for religion in feeling: we must look for valid religious ideas. And these ideas are not to be taken at liberty, nor deduced from the conception of any necessary purpose: we are to seek the truth of religion obediently in experience as something which is established in independence of our finite wills. So far we have done no more than orient our search. The task itself we shall take up in a later part of this book.

In the meantime, while voluntarism cannot define truth for us,

---

[5] Of some such subtle but veritable experience I believe that all "revelation" is built. Revelation is knowledge real and empirical (i.e., received in relative passivity), which is more certain in itself than in its assignable connections with the main body of experience.

religious truth least of all, it remains the most important and valuable of all tests of truth and ballasts of judgment about truth. The question, "What kind of world would best satisfy the requirements of our wills?" can never finally determine what kind of world we, in reality, have. But such questions may go far toward clearing our mind about those requirements themselves; they may give some not-unimportant hints of what we have to expect of reality. To this pragmatic type of inference we shall devote the next few studies.

3. The Will to Believe *

WILLIAM JAMES (1842-1910)

In the recently published Life by Leslie Stephen of his brother, Fitz-James, there is an account of a school to which the latter went when he was a boy. The teacher, a certain Mr. Guest, used to converse with his pupils in this wise: "Gurney, what is the difference between justification and sanctification? — Stephen, prove the omnipotence of God!" etc. In the midst of our Harvard freethinking and indifference we are prone to imagine that here at your good old orthodox College conversation continues to be somewhat upon this order; and to show you that we at Harvard have not lost all interest in these vital subjects, I have brought with me to-night something like a sermon on justification by faith to read to you, — I mean an essay in justification *of* faith, a defence of our right to adopt a believing attitude in religious matters, in spite of the fact that our merely logical intellect may not have been coerced. 'The Will to Believe,' accordingly, is the title of my paper.

I have long defended to my own students the lawfulness of voluntary adopted faith; but as soon as they have got well imbued with the logical spirit, they have as a rule refused to admit my contention to be lawful philosophically, even though in point of fact they were personally all the time chock-full of some faith or other themselves. I am all the while, however, so profoundly

* From *The Will to Believe*. Published in *The New World*, June, 1896.

convinced that my own position is correct, that your invitation has seemed to me a good occasion to make my statements more clear. Perhaps your minds will be more open than those with which I have hitherto had to deal. I will be as little technical as I can, though I must begin by setting up some technical distinctions that will help us in the end.

I

Let us give the name of *hypothesis* to anything that may be proposed to our belief; and just as the electricians speak of live and dead wires, let us speak of any hypothesis as either *live* or *dead*. A live hypothesis is one which appeals as a real possibility to him to whom it is proposed. If I ask you to believe in the Mahdi, the notion makes no electric connection with your nature, — it refuses to scintillate with any credibility at all. As an hypothesis it is completely dead. To an Arab, however (even if he be not one of the Mahdi's followers), the hypothesis is among the mind's possibilities: it is alive. This shows that deadness and liveness in an hypothesis are not intrinsic properties, but relations to the individual thinker. They are measured by his willingness to act. The maximum of liveness in an hypothesis means willingness to act irrevocably. Practically, that means belief; but there is some believing tendency wherever there is willingness to act at all.

Next, let us call the decision between two hypotheses an *option*. Options may be of several kinds. They may be — 1, *living* or *dead;* 2, *forced* or *avoidable;* 3, *momentous* or *trivial;* and for our purposes we may call an option a *genuine* option when it is of the forced, living, and momentous kind.

1. A living option is one in which both hypotheses are live ones. If I say to you: "Be a theosophist or be a Mohammedan," it is probably a dead option, because for you neither hypothesis is likely to be alive. But if I say: "Be an agnostic or be a Christian," it is otherwise: trained as you are, each hypothesis makes some appeal, however small, to your belief.

2. Next, if I say to you: "Choose between going out with your umbrella or without it," I do not offer you a genuine option, for it is not forced. You can easily avoid it by not going out at all. Similarly, if I say, "Either love me or hate me," "Either call my theory true or call it false," your option is avoidable. You may

remain indifferent to me, neither loving nor hating, and you may decline to offer any judgment as to my theory. But if I say "Either accept this truth or go without it," I put on you a forced option, for there is no standing place outside of the alternative. Every dilemma based on a complete logical disjunction, with no possibility of not choosing, is an option of this forced kind.

3. Finally, if I were Dr. Nansen and proposed to you to join my North Pole expedition, your option would be momentous; for this would probably be your only similar opportunity, and your choice now would either exclude you from the North Pole sort of immortality altogether or put at least the chance of it into your hands. He who refuses to embrace a unique opportunity loses the prize as surely as if he tried and failed. *Per contra*, the option is trivial when the opportunity is not unique, when the stake is insignificant, or when the decision is reversible if it later prove unwise. Such trivial optons abound in the scientific life. A chemist finds an hypothesis live enough to spend a year in its verification; he believes in it to that extent. But if his experiments prove inconclusive either way, he is quit for his loss of time, no vital harm being done.

It will facilitate our discussion if we keep all these distinctions well in mind. . . .

In Pascal's *Thoughts* * there is a celebrated passage known in literature as Pascal's wager. In it he tries to force us into Christianity by reasoning as if our concern with truth resembled our concern with the stakes in a game of chance. Translated freely his words are these; You must either believe or not believe that God is — which will you do? Your human reason cannot say. A game is going on between you and the nature of things which at the day of judgment will bring out either heads or tails. Weigh what your gains and your losses would be if you should stake all you have on heads, or God's existence; if you win in such case, you gain eternal beatitude; if you lose, you lose nothing at all. If there were an infinity of chances, and only one for God in this wager, still you ought to stake your all on God; for though you surely risk a finite loss by this procedure, any finite loss is reasonable, even a certain one is reasonable, if there is but the possibility of infinite gain. Go then, and take holy water, and have masses said; belief will come and stupefy your scruples — *Cela vous fera croire et vous*

---

* [See Selection 21, this volume].

abêtira. Why should you not? At bottom, what have you to lose? . . .

The thesis I defend is, briefly stated, this: *Our passional nature not only lawfully may, but must, decide an option between propositions, whenever it is a genuine option that cannot by its nature be decided on intellectual grounds; for to say, under such circumstances, "Do not decide, but leave the question open," is itself a passional decision, — just like deciding yes or no, — and is attended with the same risk of losing the truth.* The thesis thus abstractly expressed will, I trust, soon become quite clear. . . .

VIII

And now, let us go straight at our question. I have said, and now repeat it, that not only as a matter of fact do we find our passional nature influencing us in our opinions, but that there are some options between opinions in which this influence must be regarded both as an inevitable and as a lawful determinant of our choice.

I fear here that some of you my hearers will begin to scent danger, and lend an inhospitable ear. Two first steps of passion you have indeed had to admit as necessary, — we must think so as to avoid dupery, and we must think so as to gain truth; but the surest path to those ideal consummations, you will probably consider, is from now onwards to take no further passional step.

Well, of course, I agree as far as the facts will allow. Wherever the option between losing truth and gaining it is not momentous, we can throw the chance of *gaining truth* away, and at any rate save ourselves from any chance of *believing falsehood*, by not making up our minds at all till objective evidence has come. In scientific questions, this is almost always the case; and even in human affairs in general, the need of acting is seldom so urgent that a false belief to act on is better than no belief at all. Law courts, indeed, have to decide on the best evidence attainable for the moment, because a judge's duty is to make law as well as to ascertain it, and (as a learned judge once said to me) few cases are worth spending much time over: the great thing is to have them decided on *any* acceptable principle, and got out of the way. But in our dealings with objective nature we obviously are recorders, not makers, of the truth; and decisions for the mere sake of deciding promptly and getting on to the next business would be wholly out of place. Throughout the breadth of physical nature facts are what they are quite independently of us, and seldom is there any such hurry about them that the risks of being duped by believing a premature theory need be faced. The questions here are always trivial options, the hypotheses are hardly living (at any rate not living for us spectators), the choice between believing truth or falsehood is seldom forced. The attitude of sceptical balance is therefore the absolutely wise one if we would escape mistakes. What difference, indeed, does it make to most of us whether we have or have not a theory of the Röntgen rays, whether we believe or not in mind-stuff, or have a conviction about the causality of conscious states? It makes no difference. Such options are not forced on us. On every account it is better not to make them, but still keep weighing reasons *pro et contra* with an indifferent hand.

I speak, of course, here of the purely judging mind. For purposes of discovery such indifference is to be less highly recommended, and science would be far less advanced than she is if the passionate desires of individuals to get their own faiths confirmed had been kept out of the game. See for example the sagacity which Spencer and Weismann now display. On the other hand, if you want an absolute duffer in an investigation, you must, after all, take the man who has no interest whatever in its results: he is the warranted incapable, the positive fool. The most useful investigator, because the most sensitive observer, is always he whose eager interest in one side of the question is balanced by an equally keen nervousness lest he become deceived.[1] Science has organized this nervousness into a regular *technique*, her so-called method of verification; and she has fallen so deeply in love with the method that one may even say she she has ceased to care for truth by itself at all. It is only truth as technically verified that interests her. The truth of truths might come in merely affirmative form, and she would decline to touch it. Such truth as that, she might repeat with Clifford,* would be stolen in defiance of her duty to mankind. Human passions, however, are stronger than technical rules. "Le coeur a ses raisons," as Pascal says, "que la raison ne connait pas;" and however indifferent to all

---

[1] Compare Wilfrid Ward's Essay, "The Wish to Believe," in his *Witnesses to the Unseen*, Macmillan & Co., 1893.

* [See Selection 26, this volume].

but the bare rules of the game the umpire, the abstract intellect, may be, the concrete players who furnish him the materials to judge of are usually, each one of them, in love with some pet 'live hypothesis' of his own. Let us agree, however, that wherever there is no forced option, the dispassionately judicial intellect with no pet hypothesis, saving us, as it does, from dupery at any rate, ought to be our ideal.

The question next arises: Are there not somewhere forced options in our speculative questions, and can we (as men who may be interested at least as much in positively gaining truth as in merely escaping dupery) always wait with impunity till the coercive evidence shall have arrived? It seems *a priori* improbable that the truth should be so nicely adjusted to our needs and powers as that. In the great boarding-house of nature, the cakes and the butter and the syrup seldom come out so even and leave the plates so clean. Indeed, we should view them with scientific suspicion if they did.

IX

Moral questions immediately present themselves as questions whose solution cannot wait for sensible proof. A moral question is a question not of what sensibly exists, but of what is good, or would be good if it did exist. Science can tell us what exists; but to compare the *worths*, both of what exists and of what does not exist, we must consult not science, but what Pascal calls our heart. Science herself consults her heart when she lays it down that the infinite ascertainment of fact and correction of false belief are the supreme goods for man. Challenge the statement, and science can only repeat it oracularly, or else prove it by showing that such ascertainment and correction bring man all sorts of other goods which man's heart in turn declares. The question of having moral beliefs at all or not having them is decided by our will. Are our moral preferences true or false, or are they only odd biological phenomena, making things good or bad for *us*, but in themselves indifferent? How can your pure intellect decide? If your heart does not *want* a world of moral reality, your head will assuredly never make you believe in one. Mephistophelian scepticism, indeed, will satisfy the head's play-instincts much better than any rigorous idealism can. Some men (even at the student age) are so naturally cool-hearted that the moralistic hypothesis never has for them any pungent life, and in their supercilious presence the hot young moralist always feels strangely ill at ease. The appearance of knowingness is on their side, of *naïveté* and gullibility on his. Yet, in the inarticulate heart of him, he clings to it that he is not a dupe, and that there is a realm in which (as Emerson says) all their wit and intellectual superiority is no better than the cunning of a fox. Moral scepticism can no more be refuted or proved by logic than intellectual scepticism can. When we stick to it that there *is* truth (be it of either kind), we do so with our whole nature, and resolve to stand or fall by the results. The sceptic with his whole nature adopts the doubting attitude; but which of us is the wiser, Omniscience only knows.

Turn now from these wide questions of good to a certain class of questions of fact, questions concerning personal relations, states of mind between one man and another. *Do you like me or not?* — for example. Whether you do or not depends, in countless instances, on whether I meet you half-way, am willing to assume that you must like me, and show you trust and expectation. The previous faith on my part in your liking's existence is in such cases what makes your liking come. But if I stand aloof, and refuse to budge an inch until I have objective evidence, until you shall have done something apt, as the absolutists say, *ad extorquendum assensum meum*, ten to one your liking never comes. How many women's hearts are vanquished by the mere sanguine insistence of some man that they *must* love him! he will not consent to the hypothesis that they cannot. The desire for a certain kind of truth here brings about that special truth's existence; and so it is in innumerable cases of other sorts. Who gains promotions, boons, appointments, but the man in whose life they are seen to play the part of live hypotheses, who discounts them, sacrifices other things for their sake before they have come, and takes risks for them in advance? His faith acts on the powers above him as a claim, and creates its own verification.

A social organism of any sort whatever, large or small, is what it is because each member proceeds to his own duty with a trust that the other members will simultaneously do theirs. Wherever a desired result is achieved by the co-operation of many independent persons, its existence as a fact is a pure consequence of the precursive faith in one another of those immediately concerned. A government, an army, a commercial system, a ship, a college, an athletic team, all exist on this condition, without which not only is nothing achieved, but nothing is even attempted. A whole train of passengers (individually brave enough) will be looted by a few highwaymen, simply because the latter can count on one another, while each passenger fears that if he makes a movement of resistance, he will be shot before any one else backs him up. If we believed that the whole car-full would rise at once with us, we should each severally rise, and train-robbing would never even be attempted. There are, then, cases where a fact cannot come at all unless a preliminary faith exists in its coming. *And where faith in a fact can help create the fact,* that would be an insane logic which should say that faith running ahead of scientific evidence is the 'lowest kind of immorality' into which a thinking being can fall. Yet such is the logic by which our scientific absolutists pretend to regulate our lives!

X

In truths dependent on our personal action, then, faith based on desire is certainly a lawful and possibly an indispensable thing.

But now, it will be said, these are all childish human cases, and have nothing to do with great cosmical matters, like the question of religious faith. Let us then pass on to that. Religions differ so much in their accidents that in discussing the religious question we must make it very generic and broad. What then do we now mean by the religious hypothesis? Science says things are; morality says some things are better than other things; and religion says essentially two things.

First, she says that the best things are the more eternal things, the overlapping things, the things in the universe that throw the last stone, so to speak, and say the final word. "Perfection is eternal,"— this phrase of Charles Secretan seems a good way of putting this first affirmation of religion, an affirmation which obviously cannot yet be verified scientifically at all.

The second affirmation of religion is that we are better off even now if we believe her first affirmation to be true.

Now, let us consider what the logical elements of this situation

are *in case the religious hypothesis in both its branches be really
true.* (Of course, we must admit that possibility at the outset. If
we are to discuss the question at all, it must involve a living option.
If for any of you religion be a hypothesis that cannot, by any living
possibility be true, than you need go no farther. I speak to the
'saving remnant' alone.) So proceeding, we see, first, that religion
offers itself as a *momentous* option. We are supposed to gain, even
now, by our belief, and to lose by our non-belief, a certain vital good.
Secondly, religion is a *forced* option, so far as that good goes. We
cannot escape the issue by remaining sceptical and waiting for more
light, because, although we do avoid error in that way *if religion be
untrue*, we lose the good, *if it be true*, just as certainly as if we
positively chose to disbelieve. It is as if a man should hesitate indefinitely to ask a certain woman to marry him because he was not
perfectly sure that she would prove an angel after he brought her
home. Would he not cut himself off from that particular angel-
possibility as decisively as if he went and married some one else?
Scepticism, then, is not avoidance of option; it is option of a certain
particular kind of risk. *Better risk loss of truth than chance of
error,* — that is your faith-vetoer's exact position. He is actively
playing his stake as much as the believer is; he is backing the field
against the religious hypothesis, just as the believer is backing the
religious hypothesis against the field. To preach scepticism to us as
a duty until 'sufficient evidence' for religion be found, is tantamount
therefore to telling us, when in presence of the religious hypothesis,
that to yield to our fear of its being error is wiser and better than to
yield to our hope that it may be true. It is not intellect against
all passions, then; it is only intellect with one passion laying down
its law. And by what, forsooth, is the supreme wisdom of this
passion warranted? Dupery for dupery, what proof is there that
dupery through hope is so much worse than dupery through fear?
I, for one, can see no proof; and I simply refuse obedience to the
scientist's command to imitate his kind of option, in a case where
my own stake is important enough to give me the right to choose
my own form of risk. If religion be true and the evidence for it
be still insufficient, I do not wish, by putting your extinguisher upon
my nature (which feels to me as if it had after all some business
in this matter), to forfeit my sole chance in life of getting upon the
winning side, — that chance depending, of course, on my willing-

ness to run the risk of acting as if my passional need of taking the
world religiously might be prophetic and right.

All this is on the supposition that it really may be prophetic
and right, and that, even to us who are discussing the matter,
religion is a live hypothesis which may be true. Now, to most of
us religion comes in a still further way that makes a veto on our
active faith even more illogical. The more perfect and more eternal
aspect of the universe is represented in our religions as having personal form. The universe is no longer a mere *It* to us, but a *Thou*,
if we are religious; and any relation that may be possible from person to person might be possible here. For instance, although in one
sense we are passive portions of the universe, in another we show
a curious autonomy, as if we were small active centres on our own
account. We feel, too, as if the appeal of religion to us were made
to our own active good-will, as if evidence might be forever withheld from us unless we met the hypothesis half-way. To take a trivial illustration: just as a man who in a company of gentlemen made
no advances, asked a warrant for every concession, and believed no
one's word without proof, would cut himself off by such churlishness
from all the social rewards that a more trusting spirit would earn,
— so here, one who should shut himself up in snarling logicality and
try to make the gods extort his recognition willy-nilly, or not get it at
all, might cut himself off forever from his only opportunity of making
the gods' acquaintance. This feeling, forced on us we know not
whence, that by obstinately believing that there are gods (although
not to do so would be so easy both for our logic and our life) we are
doing the universe the deepest service we can, seems part of the
living essence of the religious hypothesis. If the hypothesis *were*
true in all its parts, including this one, then pure intellectualism,
with its veto on our making willing advances, would be an absurdity;
and some participation of our sympathetic nature would be logically
required. I, therefore, for one, cannot see my way to accepting the
agnostic rules for truth-seeking, or wilfully agree to keep my willing
nature out of the game. I cannot do so for this plain reason, that
a rule of thinking which would absolutely prevent me from acknowl-
edging certain kinds of truth if those kinds of truth were really
there, would be an irrational rule. That for me is the long and short
of the formal logic of the situation, no matter what the kinds of
truth might materially be.

I confess I do not see how this logic can be escaped. But sad experience makes me fear that some of you may still shrink from radically saying with me, *in abstracto*, that we have the right to believe at our own risk any hypothesis that is live enough to tempt our will. I suspect, however, that if this is so, it is because you have got away from the abstract logical point of view altogether, and are thinking (perhaps without realizing it) of some particular religious hypothesis which for you is dead. The freedom to 'believe what we will' you apply to the case of some patent superstition; and the faith you think of is the faith defined by the schoolboy when he said, "Faith is when you believe something that you know ain't true." I can only repeat that this is misapprehension. *In concreto*, the freedom to believe can only cover living options which the intellect of the individual cannot by itself resolve; and living options never seem absurdities to him who has them to consider. When I look at the religious question as it really puts itself to concrete men, and when I think of all the possibilities which both practically and theoretically it involves, then this command that we shall put a stopper on our heart, instincts, and courage, and *wait* — acting of course meanwhile more or less as if religion were *not* true [2] — till doomsday, or till such time as our intellect and senses working together may have raked in evidence enough, — this command, I say, seems to me the queerest idol ever manufactured in the philosophic cave. Were we scholastic absolutists, there might be more excuse. If we had an infallible intellect with its objective certitudes, we might feel ourselves disloyal to such a perfect organ of knowledge in not trusting to it exclusively, in not waiting for its releasing word. But if we are empiricists, if we believe that no bell in us tolls to let us know for certain when truth is in our grasp, then it seems a piece of idle fantasticality to preach so solemnly our duty of waiting for the bell. Indeed we *may* wait if we will, — I hope you do not think

---

[2] Since belief is measured by action, he who forbids us to believe religion to be true, necessarily also forbids us to act as we should if we did believe it to be true. The whole defence of religious faith hinges upon action. If the action required or inspired by the religious hypothesis is in no way different from that dictated by the naturalistic hypothesis, then religious faith is a pure superfluity, better pruned away, and controversy about its legitimacy is a piece of idle trifling, unworthy of serious minds. I myself believe, of course, that the religious hypothesis gives to the world an expression which specifically determines our reactions, and makes them in a large part unlike what they might be on a purely naturalistic scheme of belief.

that I am denying that, — but if we do so, we do so at our peril as much as if we believed. In either case we *act,* taking our life in our hands. No one of us ought to issue vetoes to the other, nor should we bandy words of abuse. We ought, on the contrary, delicately and profoundly to respect one another's mental freedom: then only shall we bring about the intellectual republic; then only shall we have that spirit of inner tolerance without which all our outer tolerance is soulless, and which is empiricism's glory; then only shall we live and let live, in speculative as well as in practical things.

I began by a reference to Fitz-James Stephen; let me end by a quotation from him. "What do you think of yourself? What do you think of the world? . . . These are questions with which all must deal as it seems good to them. They are riddles of the Sphinx, and in some way or other we must deal with them. . . . In all important transactions of life we have to take a leap in the dark. . . . If we decide to leave the riddles unanswered, that is a choice; if we waver in our answer, that, too, is a choice: but whatever choice we make, we make it at our peril. If a man chooses to turn his back altogether on God and the future, no one can prevent him; no one can show beyond reasonable doubt that he is mistaken. If a man thinks otherwise and acts as he thinks, I do not see that any one can prove that *he* is mistaken. Each must act as he thinks best; and if he is wrong, so much the worse for him. We stand on a mountain pass in the midst of whirling snow and blinding mist, through which we get glimpses now and then of paths which may be deceptive. If we stand still we shall be frozen to death. If we take the wrong road we shall be dashed to pieces. We do not certainly know whether there is any right one. What must we do? 'Be strong and of a good courage.' Act for the best, hope for the best, and take what comes. . . . If death ends all, we cannot meet death better." [3]

---

[3] Liberty, Equality, Fraternity, p. 353, 2d edition. London, 1874.

4. My Philosophy of Religion *

GEORGE SANTAYANA *(1863–1952)*

This brings me to religion, which is the head and front of everything. Like my parents, I have always set myself down officially as a Catholic: but this is a matter of sympathy and traditional allegiance, not of philosophy. In my adolescence, religion on its doctrinal and emotional side occupied me much more than it does now. I was more unhappy and unsettled; but I have never had any unquestioning faith in any dogma, and have never been what is called a practising Catholic. Indeed, it would hardly have been possible. My mother, like her father before her, was a Deist: she was sure there was a God, for who else could have made the world? But God was too great to take special thought for man: sacrifices, prayers, churches, and tales of immortality were invented by rascally priests in order to dominate the foolish. My father, except for the Deism, was emphatically of the same opinion. Thus, although I learned my prayers and catechism by rote, as was then inevitable in Spain, I knew that my parents regarded all religion as a work of human imagination: and I agreed, and still agree, with them there. But this carried an implication in their minds against which every instinct in me rebelled, namely that the works of human imagination are bad. No, said I to myself even as a boy; they are good, they alone are good; and the rest — the whole real world — is ashes in the mouth. My sympathies were entirely with those other members of my family who were devout believers. I loved the Christian epic, and all those doctrines and observances which bring it down into daily life: I thought how glorious it would have been to be a Dominican friar, preaching that epic eloquently, and solving afresh all the knottiest and sublimest mysteries of theology. I was de-

---

* The first part of this selection (Pages 41 to 42) is from "Brief History of My Opinions," which Santayana wrote for *Contemporary American Philosophy,* Vol. II, edited by Adams and Montague. It is reprinted by permission of the publisher, The Macmillan Company. The rest of the selection is excerpted from *Reason in Religion,* the fourth volume of The Life of Reason, copyright 1905 by Charles Scribner's Sons, 1933 by George Santayana; used by permission of the publishers.

lighted with anything, like Mallock's *Is Life Worth Living?*, which seemed to rebuke the fatuity of that age. For my own part, I was quite sure that life was not worth living; for if religion was false everything was worthless, and almost everything, if religion was true. In this youthful pessimism I was hardly more foolish than so many amateur mediaevalists and religious aesthetes of my generation. I saw the same alternative between Catholicism and complete disillusion: but I was never afraid of disillusion, and I have chosen it.

Since those early years my feelings on this subject have become less strident. Does not modern philosophy teach that our idea of the so-called real world is also a work of imagination? A religion — for there are other religions than the Christian — simply offers a system of faith different from the vulgar one, or extending beyond it. The question is which imaginative system you will trust. My matured conclusion has been that no system is to be trusted, not even that of science in any literal or pictorial sense; but all systems may be used and, up to a certain point, trusted as symbols. Science expresses in human terms our dynamic relation to surrounding reality. Philosophies and religions, where they do not misrepresent these same dynamic relations and do not contradict science, express destiny in moral dimensions, in obviously mythical and poetical images: but how else should these moral truths be expressed at all in a traditional or popular fashion? Religions are the great fairy-tales of the conscience. . . .*

Experience has repeatedly confirmed that well-known maxim of Bacon's, that "a little philosophy inclineth man's mind to atheism, but depth in philosophy bringeth men's minds about to religion." In every age the most comprehensive thinkers have found in the religion of their time and country something they could accept, interpreting and illustrating that religion so as to give it depth and universal application. Even the heretics and atheists, if they have had profundity, turn out after a while to be forerunners of some new orthodoxy. What they rebel against is a religion alien to their nature; they are atheists only by accident, and relatively to a convention which inwardly offends them, but they yearn mightily in their own souls after the religious acceptance of a world interpreted

---

*[The selection from *Contemporary American Philosophy* ends here. The next excerpt is Chapter I of *Reason in Religion*.]

in their own fashion. So it appears in the end that their atheism and loud protestation were in fact the hastier part of their thought, since what emboldened them to deny the poor world's faith was that they were too impatient to understand it. Indeed, the enlightenment common to young wits and worm-eaten satirists, who plume themselves on detecting the scientific ineptitude of religion — something which the blindest half see — is not nearly enlightened enough; it points to notorious facts incompatible with religious tenets literally taken, but it leaves unexplored the habits of thought from which those tenets sprang, their original meaning, and their true function. Such studies would bring the sceptic face to face with the mystery and pathos of mortal existence. They would make him understand why religion is so profoundly moving and in a sense so profoundly just. There must needs be something humane and necessary in an influence that has become the most general sanction of virtue, the chief occasion for art and philosophy, and the source, perhaps, of the best human happiness. If nothing, as Hooker said, is "so malapert as a splenetic religion," a sour irreligion is almost as perverse.

At the same time, when Bacon penned the sage epigram we have quoted he forgot to add that the God to whom depth in philosophy brings back men's minds is far from being the same from whom a little philosophy estranges them. It would be pitiful indeed if mature reflection bred no better conceptions than those which have drifted down the muddy stream of time, where tradition and passion have jumbled everything together. Traditional conceptions, when they are felicitous, may be adopted by the poet, but they must be purified by the moralist and disintegrated by the philosopher. Each religion, so dear to those whose life it sanctifies, and fulfilling so necessary a function in the society that has adopted it, necessarily contradicts every other religion, and probably contradicts itself. What religion a man shall have is a historical accident, quite as much as what language he shall speak. In the rare circumstances where a choice is possible, he may, with some difficulty, make an exchange; but even then he is only adopting a new convention which may be more agreeable to his personal temper but which is essentially as arbitrary as the old.

The attempt to speak without speaking any particular language is not more hopeless than the attempt to have a religion that shall be no religion in particular. A courier's or a dragoman's speech may indeed be often unusual and drawn from disparate sources, not without some mixture of personal originality; but that private jargon will have a meaning only because of its analogy to one or more conventional languages and its obvious derivation from them. So travellers from one religion to another, people who have lost their spiritual nationality, may often retain a neutral and confused residuum of belief, which they may egregiously regard as the essence of all religion, so little may they remember the graciousness and naturalness of that ancestral accent which a perfect religion should have. Yet a moment's probing of the conceptions surviving in such minds will show them to be nothing but vestiges of old beliefs, creases which thought, even if emptied of all dogmatic tenets, has not been able to smooth away at its first unfolding. Later generations, if they have any religion at all, will be found either to revert to ancient authority, or to attach themselves spontaneously to something wholly novel and immensely positive, to some faith promulgated by a fresh genius and passionately embraced by a converted people. Thus every living and healthy religion has a marked idiosyncrasy. Its power consists in its special and surprising message and in the bias which that revelation gives to life. The vistas it opens and the mysteries it propounds are another world to live in; and another world to live in — whether we expect ever to pass wholly into it or no — is what we mean by having a religion.

What relation, then, does this great business of the soul, which we call religion, bear to the Life of Reason? That the relation between the two is close seems clear from several circumstances. The Life of Reason is the seat of all ultimate values. Now the history of mankind will show us that whenever spirits at once lofty and intense have seemed to attain the highest joys, they have envisaged and attained them in religion. Religion would therefore seem to be a vehicle or a factor in rational life, since the ends of rational life are attained by it. Moreover, the Life of Reason is an ideal to which everything in the world should be subordinated; it establishes lines of moral cleavage everywhere and makes right eternally different from wrong. Religion does the same thing. It makes absolute moral decisions. It sanctions, unifies, and transforms ethics. Religion thus exercises a function of the Life of Reason. And a further function which is common to both is that of emancipating man from his personal limitations. In different ways religions promise to transfer the soul to better conditions. A supernaturally favoured kingdom is to be established for posterity upon earth, or for all the faithful in heaven, or the soul is to be freed by repeated purgations from all taint and sorrow, or it is to be lost in the absolute, or it is to become an influence and an object of adoration in the places it once haunted or wherever the activities it once loved may be carried on by future generations of its kindred. Now reason in its way lays before us all these possibilities: it points to common objects, political and intellectual, in which an individual may lose what is mortal and accidental in himself and immortalise what is rational and human; it teaches us how sweet and fortunate death may be to those whose spirit can still live in their country and in their ideas; it reveals the radiating effects of action and the eternal objects of thought.

Yet the difference in tone and language must strike us, so soon as it is philosophy that speaks. That change should remind us that even if the function of religion and that of reason coincide, this function is performed in the two cases by very different organs. Religions are many, reason one. Religion consists of conscious ideas, hopes, enthusiasms, and objects of worship; it operates by grace and flourishes by prayer. Reason, on the other hand, is a mere principle or potential order, on which, indeed, we may come to reflect, but which exists in us ideally only, without variation or stress of any kind. We conform or do not conform to it; it does not urge or chide us, nor call for any emotions on our part other than those naturally aroused by the various objects which it unfolds in their true nature and proportion. Religion brings some order into life by weighting it with new materials. Reason adds to the natural materials only the perfect order which it introduces into them. Rationality is nothing but a form, an ideal constitution which experience may more or less embody. Religion is a part of experience itself, a mass of sentiments and ideas. The one is an inviolate principle, the other a changing and struggling force. And yet this struggling and changing force of religion seems to direct man toward something eternal. It seems to make for an ultimate harmony within the soul and for an ultimate harmony between the soul and all the soul depends upon. So that religion, in its intent, is a more conscious and direct pursuit of the Life of Reason than is society, science, or art. For these approach and fill out the ideal life tentatively and piecemeal, hardly regarding the goal or caring for the ultimate justification of their instinctive aims. Religion also has an instinctive and blind side, and bubbles up in all manner of chance practices and intuitions; soon, however, it feels its way toward the heart of things, and, from whatever quarter it may come, veers in the direction of the ultimate.

Nevertheless, we must confess that this religious pursuit of the Life of Reason has been singularly abortive. Those within the pale of each religion may prevail upon themselves to express satisfaction with its results, thanks to a fond partiality in reading the past and generous draughts of hope for the future; but any one regarding the various religions at once and comparing their achievements with what reason requires, must feel how terrible is the disappointment which they have one and all prepared for mankind. Their chief anxiety has been to offer imaginary remedies for mortal ills, some of which are incurable essentially, while others might have been really cured by well-directed effort. The Greek oracles, for instance, pretended to heal our natural ignorance, which has its appropriate though difficult cure, while the Christian vision of heaven pretended to be an antidote to our natural death, the inevitable correlate of birth and of a changing and conditioned existence. By methods of this sort little can be done for the real betterment of life. To confuse intelligence and dislocate sentiment by gratuitous fictions is a short-sighted way of pursuing happiness. Nature is soon avenged. An unhealthy exaltation and a one-sided morality have to be followed by regrettable reactions. When these come, the real rewards of life may seem vain to a relaxed vitality, and the very name of virtue may irritate young spirits untrained in any natural excellence. Thus religion too often debauches the morality it comes to sanction, and impedes the science it ought to fulfill.

What is the secret of this ineptitude? Why does religion, so near to rationality in its purpose, fall so far short of it in its texture and in its results? The answer is easy: Religion pursues rationality through the imagination. When it explains events or assigns causes, it is an imaginative substitute for science. When it gives precepts, insinuates ideals, or remoulds aspiration, it is an imaginative substitute for wisdom — I mean for the deliberate and impartial pursuit of all good. The conditions and the aims of life are both represented in religion poetically, but this poetry tends to arrogate to itself literal truth and moral authority, neither of which it possesses. Hence the depth and importance of religion become intelligible no less than its contradictions and practical disasters. Its object is the same as that of reason, but its method is to proceed by intuition and by unchecked poetical conceits. These are repeated and vulgarised in proportion to their original fineness and significance, till they pass for reports of objective truth and come to constitute a world of faith, superposed upon the world of experience and regarded as materially enveloping it, if not in space at least in time and in existence. The only truth of religion comes from its interpretation of life, from its symbolic rendering of that moral experience which it springs out of and which it seeks to elucidate. Its falsehood comes from the insidious misunderstanding which clings to it, to the effect that these poetic conceptions are not merely representations of experience as it is or should be, but are rather information about experience or reality elsewhere — an experience and reality which, strangely enough, supply just the defects betrayed by reality and experience here.

Thus religion has the same original relation to life that poetry has; only poetry, which never pretends to literal validity, adds a pure value to existence, the value of a liberal imaginative exercise. The poetic value of religion would initially be greater than that of poetry itself, because religion deals with higher and more practical themes, with sides of life which are in greater need of some imaginative touch and ideal interpretation than are those pleasant or pompous things which ordinary poetry dwells upon. But this initial advantage is neutralised in part by the abuse to which religion is subject, whenever its symbolic rightness is taken for scientific truth. Like poetry, it improves the world only by imagining it improved, but not content with making this addition to the mind's furniture — an addition which might be useful and ennobling — it thinks to confer a more radical benefit by persuading mankind that, in spite of appearances, the world is really such as that rather arbitrary idealisation has painted it. This spurious satisfaction is naturally the prelude to many a disappointment, and the soul has infinite trouble to emerge again from the artificial problems and sentiments into which it is thus plunged. The value of religion becomes equivocal. Religion remains an imaginative achievement, a symbolic representation of moral reality which may have a most important function in vitalising the mind and in transmitting, by way of parables, the lessons of experience. But it becomes at the same time a continuous incidental deception; and this deception, in proportion as it is strenuously denied to be such, can work indefinite harm in the world and in the conscience.

On the whole, however, religion should not be conceived as having taken the place of anything better, but rather as having come to relieve situations which, but for its presence, would have been infinitely worse. In the thick of active life, or in the monotony of practical slavery, there is more need to stimulate fancy than to control it. Natural instinct is not much disturbed in the human brain by what may happen in that thin superstratum of ideas which commonly overlays it. We must not blame religion for preventing the development of a moral and natural science which at any rate would seldom have appeared; we must rather thank it for the sensibility, the reverence, the speculative insight which it has introduced into the world.

We may therefore proceed to analyse the significance and the function which religion has had at its different stages, and, without disguising or in the least condoning its confusion with literal truth, we may allow ourselves to enter as sympathetically as possible into its various conceptions and emotions. They have made up the inner life of many sages, and of all those who without great genius or learning have lived steadfastly in the spirit. The feeling of reverence should itself be treated with reverence, although not at a sacrifice of truth, with which alone, in the end, reverence is compatible. Nor have we any reason to be intolerant of the partialities and contradictions which religions display. Were we dealing with a science, such contradictions would have to be instantly solved and removed; but when we are concerned with the poetic interpretation of experience, contradiction means only variety, and variety means spontaneity, wealth of resource, and a nearer approach to total adequacy.

If we hope to gain any understanding of these matters we must begin by taking them out of that heated and fanatical atmosphere in which the Hebrew tradition has enveloped them. The Jews had no philosophy, and when their national traditions came to be theoretically explicated and justified, they were made to issue in a puerile scholasticism and a rabid intolerance. The question of monotheism, for instance, was a terrible question to the Jews. Idolatry did not consist in worshipping a god who, not being ideal, might be unworthy of worship, but rather in recognising other gods than the one worshipped in Jerusalem. To the Greeks, on the contrary, whose philosophy was enlightened and ingenuous, monotheism and polytheism seemed perfectly innocent and compatible. To say God or the gods was only to use different expressions for the same influence, now viewed in its abstract unity and correlation with all existence, now viewed in its various manifestations in moral life, in nature, or in history. So that what in Plato, Aristotle, and the Stoics meets us at every step — the combination of monotheism with polytheism — is no contradiction, but merely an intelligent variation of phrase to indicate various aspects or functions in physical and moral things. When religion appears to us in this light its contradictions and controversies lose all their bitterness. Each doctrine will simply represent the moral plane on which they live who have devised or adopted it. Religions will thus be better or worse, never true or false. We shall be able to lend ourselves to each in turn, and seek to draw from it the secret of its inspiration. . . .*

Herein lies the chief difference between those in whom religion is spontaneous and primary — a very few — and those in whom it is imitative and secondary. To the former, divine things are inward values, projected by chance into images furnished by poetic tradition or by external nature, while to the latter, divine things are in the first instance objective factors of nature or of social tradition, although they have come, perhaps, to possess some point of contact with the interests of the inner life on account of the supposed physical influence which those super-human entities have over human fortunes. In a word, theology, for those whose religion is secondary, is simply a false physics, a doctrine about eventual experience not founded on the experience of the past. Such a false physics, however, is soon discredited by events; it does not require much experience or much shrewdness to discover that supernatural beings and laws are without the empirical efficacy which was attributed to them. True physics and true history must always tend, in enlightened minds, to supplant those misinterpreted religious traditions. Therefore, those whose reflection or sentiment does not furnish them with a key to the moral symbolism and poetic validity underlying theological ideas, if they apply their intelligence to the subject at all, and care to be sincere, will very soon come to regard religion as a delusion. Where religion is primary, however, all that worldly dread of fraud and illusion becomes irrelevant, as it is

---

* [End of Chapter I, *Reason in Religion*. The next excerpt is from Chapter IX of the same work, pp. 156–158].

irrelevant to an artist's pleasure to be warned that the beauty he expresses has no objective existence, or as it would be irrelevant to a mathematician's reasoning to suspect that Pythagoras was a myth and his supposed philosophy an abracadabra. To the religious men religion is inwardly justified. God has no need of natural or logical witnesses, but speaks Himself within the heart, being indeed that ineffable attraction which dwells in whatever is good and beautiful, and that persuasive visitation of the soul by the eternal and incorruptible by which she feels herself purified, rescued from mortality, and given an inheritance in the truth. This is precisely what Saint Augustine knew and felt with remarkable clearness and persistence, and what he expressed unmistakably by saying that every intellectual perception is knowledge of God or has God's nature for its object.

Proofs of the existence of God are therefore not needed, since his existence is in one sense obvious and in another of no religious interest. It is obvious in the sense that the ideal is a term of moral experience, and that truth, goodness, and beauty are inevitably envisaged by any one whose life has in some measure a rational quality. It is of no religious interest in the sense that perhaps some physical or dynamic absolute might be scientifically discoverable in the dark entrails of nature or of mind. The great difference between religion and metaphysics is that religion looks for God at the top of life and metaphysics at the bottom; a fact which explains why metaphysics has such difficulty in finding God, while religion has never lost Him.

5. *An Ethical Philosophy of Life* *

FELIX ADLER *(1851–1933)*

The predominance of the ethical principle in religion dates from the prophets of Israel. The religious development of the human race

* From: *An Ethical Philosophy of Life* by Felix Adler. Copyright, 1918, D. Appleton & Company. Reprinted by permission of the publishers, Appleton-Century-Crofts, Inc.

took a new turn in their sublime predications, and I for one am certainly conscious of having drawn my first draught of moral inspiration from their writings.[1]

But nevertheless I found myself compelled to separate from the religion of Israel. Now why was it necessary for me to take this step? Why not continue along the path first blazed by the Hebrew prophets — smoothing it perhaps and widening it? Why not separate the dross from the gold, the error from the truth, explicating what is implicit in that truth, and adapting it to the needs and conditions of the modern age? The answer is that the truth contained in the Hebrew, and as I shall presently show, in the Christian religion, is not capable of such adaptation. It claims finality. I have mentioned that there is an element of permanent value in both the Hebrew and the Christian religion, and that it should be restated and fitted into a larger synthesis. But this is impossible unless the Hebrew or Christian setting be broken, unless the element to be preserved is taken out of its context, and treated freshly and with perfect freedom. A religion like the two I am concerned with is a determinate thing. It is a closed circle of thoughts and beliefs. It is capable of a certain degree of change but not of indefinite change. The limits of change are determined by its leading conceptions — the monotheistic idea in the one case, and the centrality of the figure of Christ in the other. Abandon these, and the boundaries by which the religion is circumscribed are passed.

The great religious teachers are men who see the spiritual landscape from a certain point of view, including whatever is visible from their station, excluding whatever is not. The religion which they originate is thus both inclusive and sharply exclusive. What they see with their rapt eyes they describe with a trenchancy and fitness never thereafter to be equalled.[2] But in order to progress in religion it is necessary to advance toward a different station, to reach a different, a higher eminence, and from that to look forth

---

[1] I still go back to that fountain-head for refreshment and inspiration, much as a modern poet may go back to Homer, without attempting to copy him, or as a modern sculptor or architect may go back to the Greek artists without relinquishing his right and his duty to help in producing a different kind of art, which perchance may one day culminate in masterpieces like theirs, though his own performance be but the poor beginning.

[2] Compare the ejaculatory deliverance of Isaiah, the Sermon on the Mount and the Parables of Jesus. Who can attempt in language to express what they saw as they did?

anew upon the spiritual landscape, comprehending the outlook of one's predecessors in a new perspective, seeing what they saw and much besides.

Religious growth may also be compared to the growth of a tree. To expect that development shall continue along the Hebrew or Christian lines is like expecting that a tree will continue to develop along one of its branches. There is a limit beyond which the extension of a branch cannot go. Then growth must show itself in the putting forth of a new branch.

But let me now state with somewhat greater particularity the reasons that compelled me to depart from the faith of Israel, and to leave my early religious home, cherishing pious memories of it, but nevertheless firmly set in my course towards new horizons.[3]

1. The difficulty created by the claim that Israel is an elect people, that it stands in a peculiar relation to the Deity. This claim, at the time when it was put forth, was neither arrogant nor unfounded. It was not arrogant because the mission was understood to be a heavy burden not a privilege: or if a privilege at all, then the tragic privilege of martyrdom, a martyrdom continued through generations. And the claim was not unfounded or preposterous at the time when it was put forth because the Hebrews were in reality the only people who conceived of morality in terms of holiness. It was not absurd for them to assert their mission to be the teachers of mankind in respect to the spiritual interpretation of morality, since there was something, and that something infinitely important, which

---

[3] No seriously religious person will attempt to strike out into a new path unless he be under inward coercion to do so. The advantages of what is commonly called historic continuity (I have just shown wherein real continuity consists, that of growth along the trunk, and not of growth along the branch) are great. There is for one thing the support derived from leaning on an ancient tradition, the proud humility felt in passing on the torch that had been held by mighty predecessors, the self-dedication to that which is larger than self, i.e., to an institution and ideas that existed in the world before one was born, and will exist after one is gone. There is the strength drawn from contact with a large and powerful organization, powerful both in sustaining one's efforts, and in restraining and correcting them when need be. There are, on the other side, the perils of innovation, the errors into which one is led for lack of restraint and correction, the too great dependence on self, the spiritual loneliness and the lack of many gracious and useful aids to the religious life such as a noble ritual, majestic music, the fit emotional expressions of religious feeling, which are not to be had for the asking, the fine embellishments that are precious in their way, and that, like the fruits in the Gardens of the Gods, ripen slowly, and may not be extemporized or anticipated.

they actually had to teach. Moral thinking and moral practices of course had existed from immemorial times everywhere, but the conception of morality as divine in its source, as spiritual in its inmost essence, — this immense idea was the offspring of the Hebrew mind. On the other hand, I asked myself, has not the task of Israel in this respect been accomplished? Have not its Scriptures become the common property of the civilized nations? And does not that teacher mistake his office who attempts to maintain his magisterial authority after his pupils have come to man's estate, and are capable of original contributions? The "nations" are not to be looked upon in the light of mere pupils. The ethical message of Israel so far as it is sane is universalistic. It is founded on the conviction that there is a moral nature in every human being, and that the moral nature is a spiritual nature. And if this be so, then the utterances, the insights, the new visions with which the spiritual nature is pregnant, cannot be supposed to be restricted to members of the Jewish people. If the teaching function is to be maintained it must be exercised by all who have the gift. If there is to be an elect body (a dangerous conception, the meaning of which is to be carefully defined), it must consist of gentiles and Jews, of men of every race and condition in whom the spiritual nature is more awakened than in others, peculiarly vivid, pressing towards utterance.

2. Aside from the spiritual interpretation of morality, the mission of the Jewish people has been said to consist in holding aloft the standard of pure monotheism as against trinitarianism. But pure monotheism is a philosophy rather than a religion. Taken by itself it is too pure, too empty of content to serve the purposes of a living faith. The attributes of omniscience, omnipotence, etc., ascribed to Deity are highly abstract, too abstruse to be even thinkable, save indirectly, and they certainly fail to touch the heart. As a matter of fact it was the image of the Father projected upon the background of these abstractions, that made the object of Jewish piety. Jahweh is the heavenly spouse; Israel is to be his faithful earthly spouse. The Children of Israel are pre-eminently his children. Other nations likewise are his children, — some children of wrath to be cast out and destroyed like the rebellious son in Deuteronomy, others to be eventually gathered into the patriarchal household. But this view comes back to the same general conception of the relations of Israel to other nations which has just been discussed. Moreover, the Father

image, as representing the divine life in the world, even when extended so as to include all mankind on equal terms, is open to a serious objection.[4]

3. If, nevertheless, the Jews have a mission, is it perhaps this: to rehabilitate the prophetic ideal of social justice? Is it not social justice that the world is crying for today? Were not the prophets of Israel the great preachers of righteousness in the sense of social justice? Did they not affirm that religion consists in justice and in its concomitant mercifulness, but above all in justice? Did not Isaiah say: "When ye come to tread my courts, who has demanded this of you? Go wash you, make you clean. Put away the evil that is in your hands. Cease to do evil; learn to do good." And later on, "That ye let the oppressed go free, and that ye break every yoke." These are solemn, marvelous words assuredly! They have been ringing down through the ages, and still find their echo in our hearts. And yet the justice idea of the prophets is inadequate to serve the purpose of social reconstruction today. To go back to it would mean repristination, not renovation. It is sound as far as it goes, but it does not go far enough. It is negative, rather than positive; it is based on the idea of non-violation. What we require today is a positive conception, and this implies a positive definition of that holy thing in man which is to be treated as inviolable. To the mind of the prophets justice meant chiefly resistance to oppression, since oppression is the most palpable exemplification of the forbidden violation. The prophets in their outlook on the external relations of their people stood for the weak, the oppressed, against

---

[4] It gives rise to the belief that men as individuals or collectively are the objects of a special Providence, and that the universe is so arranged as to be adapted to man's needs, not to say his wishes; whereas the facts show that man must adapt himself to the universe, and find his physical safety and his ethical salvation in so doing. The belief in the Father who allows not one hair of our heads to fall unnoticed raises expectations to which actual experience fails to correspond.

As to the issue between monotheism and trinitarianism, it has long since become obsolescent, if not obsolete. The forward-looking men and women of our time are absorbed in far other issues—Is the mechanical theory propounded by science the ultimate account of things? Is the world in which we live a blind machine? Is man a chance product of nature, like the beasts that perish? Not is God one in unity or is He a Triune God, but, is there a God at all? Is there a supersensible reality? Is religion capable of a new lease of life, and of giving a new lease of life to us who now are spiritually dead?

the strong, the oppressor. They stood for their own weak little nation, the Belgium of those days, against the two over-mighty empires, Egypt and Assyria, that bordered it on either side. In the internal affairs of Israel they espoused the cause of the weak against the rich and strong: "Woe unto them that add house to house and field to field, that grind the faces of the poor." Ever and ever again the same note resounds, the same intense, passionately indignant feeling against violation in the form of oppression. But this aspect of justice, as I have said, is the negative aspect, — inestimably important, but insufficient. Where oppression does not occur, have the claims of justice ceased? Is there not something even greater than mere non-infringement, greater than mercifulness or kindness, which in justice we owe to the personality of our fellows, namely, to aid in the development of their personality? Righteousness, yes, by all means, — but does the righteousness of the prophets of Israel exhaust or begin to exhaust the content of that vast idea?

The universalistic ethical idea in the Hebrew religion is bound up with and bound down by racial restrictions. The issue between monotheism and trinitarianism is no longer a vital issue of our day. The father image as the symbol of Deity raises expectations which experience does not confirm. The ideal of social justice as conceived by the prophets of Israel is a valid but incomplete expression of what is implied in social justice. These are weighty considerations that make it difficult to retain the belief in the elect character attributed to the people of Israel. There is one other, of very deep-reaching importance, that must be noticed. An elect people is supposed to be an exemplary people, one that sets a moral example which other nations are expected to copy. But it has become more and more clear to me that the value of example in the moral life has been overestimated and misunderstood. No individual, for instance, can really serve as an example to others so as to be copied by them. The circumstances are always somewhat different, the natures are different, and the obligations, finely examined, are never quite the same. In fact, the best that anyone can do for another by his example is to stimulate him to express with consummate fidelity his different nature in his own different way. I do not of course deny that there are certain uniformities, chiefly negative, in moral conduct, but I have come to think that the ethical quality of moral acts consists in the points in which they differ rather than in those in which they agree. The ideally ethical act, to my mind, is the most completely individualized act.

And what is true of individuals is no less true of peoples. No people can really be exemplary for other peoples, and in this sense elect. Every people possesses a character of its own to which it is to give expression in ways which I shall indicate in the last part of this work. But the way rightly adopted by one nation cannot be a law or a model for its sister nations. If the ideal of the modern Zionists were realized, if the Jews were to return to Palestine, to speak once more the language of the Bible, to cultivate their distinctive gifts, they would not therefore produce a pattern which could be copied in Japan, or among the 400 millions of China, or in the United States, or among the Slavic or Latin peoples.

In concluding these reflections, I may not conceal from myself or from others that the objection to the function of exemplariness, if sustained, affects at the root both the theology and the ethics of the past. If no individual can be in the strict sense an example to others, neither can an individual Deity be an example to be copied by men, neither can Christ be the perfect exemplar to be imitated. There can be no single perfect exemplar.[5] Virtues that bear the same name are not therefore the same virtues. Often it is only the name that is the same, not the substance; and where they are in a broad way the same, yet there remains a difference of accent. The natures of men are unlike. Their moral destiny is to work out the unlikeness of each in harmony with that of the others. The moral equivalence of men, rather than their moral equality, is for me the expression of the fundamental moral relations.

---

[5] Of many ethical types of behavior no examples whatever as yet exist, for instance, of the ethically-minded employer or merchant, ethically-minded in thought and in practice. The standard of ethical behavior which we apply is at present higher and more exacting. The standard itself indeed is in process of being defined, and there are no illustrations of it, or none but very imperfect ones, on which to dwell with satisfaction. But the same is true of other vocations. We are very thankful for any examples that can be found. They seem to prove that that which ought to be can be. But we may not lean on them too hard. They are never quite adequate, even in their limited sphere; and there is ever an Ought-to-be beyond that which has been even partially realized, beyond that which has even as yet been conceived. To make too much of example is to check moral progress. Along with a due appreciation of past moral achievements, there should be encouraged a spirit of brave adventure, a certain intrepidity of soul to venture forth on voyages of discovery into unknown ethical regions, taking the risks but bent upon the prize.

6. My Philosophy of Religion *

MORRIS RAPHAEL COHEN *(1880–1947)*

In the winter of 1890 there had been some question as to whether my mother, my sister and myself should go to join the rest of the family in America, and I wrote a letter to my father expressing my fear of the irreligious surroundings to which I should thus be subject and my hope that he would allow me to continue my pious studies where I was. But my father's efforts to establish a livelihood for himself and his family in the following months in Minsk were doomed to failure. And when my mother, my sister and I traveled to America two years later, my youthful fears of what would happen to my religion in the irreligious atmosphere of America were borne out by events. It was only a few months after we had arrived that my childhood faith was broken on the sharp edge of Mr. Tunick's skepticism. The questions our old neighbor asked of my father and my father's inability to give a rational answer shocked me to the quick. The angels that guard us, recited in every prayer, had been very real to me. I had lived in strict conformity to the tenets of Jewish Orthodoxy. But I could not forget Mr. Tunick's questions: "What proof have you that there is a God and that he told anything to Moses? And why should I believe that Jews are the only ones that have the truth? And are there not other people just as intelligent as we, and can we prove the Jewish religion is superior to all others?"

After some soul-searching I came to the conclusion that I had no evidence that could effectively answer these questions. I have not since that day ever seen any reason to change that conclusion.

The loss of the religion of my childhood brought no suffering in its train. It seemed to me that the restraints from which I was freed out-balanced the consolations that were lost. Perhaps that is because not all of the consolations were lost. Rational argument could never wholly efface a natural clinging to the joys of Friday night. Much less could it efface the larger spiritual patterns and

---

* From *A Dreamer's Journey,* Chapter 24, copyright, 1949, by *The Free Press.* Permission to reprint was granted by Felix S. Cohen and by the publisher.

values of my childhood religion. Indeed, in my youthful rejection of the Orthodox Jewish observances, I did not feel that I was cutting myself off from religion. I knew that the rejection of ritual is itself deeply rooted in the Hebraic tradition. I could not forget that the Hebrew Prophets, from Amos to Jeremiah, the founders of spiritual monotheism, all made Jahveh despise the ritual with which Israel believed it served Him. Says the God of Amos — and his command is repeated by Micah, Isaiah and Jeremiah:

> I hate, I despise your feast days,
> And will not delight in the day of your
>   solemn assemblies —
> Put thou away from me the noise of thy songs —
> But let justice run down as waters,
> And righteousness as a mighty stream.

If I was a heretic, at least I felt that I was erring in good company. As with ritual, so, I felt, with creed. The essence of religion, it seemed to me, was not in the words uttered with the lips but rather in the faith which shows itself in our moral life. I could not bring myself to think that a just God would condemn the upright and spiritual-minded men I knew in all churches, and outside of all churches, merely because they did not pronounce the right formulas. Beyond any divinity of creed, it seemed to me, there was a God of morality, but even beyond this there was a God of nature. Or to put it in other words, man is a spiritual being in relation not only to his equals, other men, but also in relation to the whole universe. Here again I found myself in company with the Hebrew prophet Micah who strikes at the root of the matter when he says:

> And what doth the Lord require of thee,
> But to do justice and to love mercy,
> And to walk humbly with thy God.

Something more than mercy and justice are required, for one may be just and merciful and still be an intolerable prig. What is needed beyond these in a character that we can revere is humility. This does not mean that we are to bow down before God as we do before a petty tyrant. It means that we need to recognize that we are in a universe which contains a reality which is and always will be beyond all our knowledge and power; with that reality the spiritual faculty seeks communion. It means, too, that we must all be prepared to suffer and be punished for the sins of others; otherwise we are not entitled to the benefits which we all do derive from the virtues of others.

My youthful rejection of the claims of the Jewish religion to absolute truth was subsequently reinforced by philosophical reflections which led me to reject all forms of absolutism, the source of all fanaticism, and all forms of monism — including monotheism. The essence of monotheism is an emphasis upon the harmony of the universe, which seems to me to be most unfortunate in that it tends to dull the sense of resentment against the injustices of the world. I have never been able to reconcile the reality of evil and of the struggle against injustice with the idea of a benevolent and all-powerful deity.

If evil is real, and I am as persuaded of that as of anything else in this world, then God is either the author of evil or else He is defeated by other forces. However comforting the thought of an all-good and all-powerful deity may be in cultivating a wise resignation in the face of evils we cannot surmount, I found myself unable to follow my revered teacher, William James, in considering the comfort that flows from a doctrine any sign of its truth. And making a God in man's image has seemed to me the height of arrogance.

On the other hand I have hesitated to violate ordinary understanding by using the word "God" to refer to an ideal of holiness that enables us to distinguish between the good and evil in men and thus saves us from the idolatrous worship of a humanity that is full of imperfections. Such a conception of God has seemed to me valid, but since I do not generally know what other people have in mind when they ask whether I believe in God, I have generally replied, "That depends upon what you mean by God." This usually brings forth a denunciation of metaphysical quibbling.

There have, of course, been many attempts by rabbis who are not complete strangers to science to formulate a concept of Judaism that may free the Orthodox creed from its incrustations of superstition. But these efforts to rationalize the Jewish faith, and similar attempts to rationalize other historic faiths, have not impressed me. I do not believe that there is any such thing as Judaism as an abstract doctrine — which is what an "ism" is — upon which all Jews can agree. I have heard many definitions of Judaism and they all seem hollow. I know of no religious belief that is common to all Jews, and I know of no belief held by any substantial number of Jews which is not to be found also, in some measure, among other people. Jews are people first, and only Jews incidentally. I have never believed that the Jews, as a people, have to justify their existence. Jews exist because they are human beings, and human beings have a right to exist.

I do not know of any religious doctrine which I share with any large number of my fellow Jews, and certainly there is no political or economic doctrine which unites all Jews. I have always been a Jew because I was born and brought up in a Jewish family. When, in 1899, I was in a position to order my own life, I ceased to observe the traditional Jewish code of ritual practices. This, however, did not carry with it any loss of respect for those who maintained the old observances where such observances represented the expression of an inner conviction. I have always had the highest reverence for those who, like my sainted parents, have a genuine and abiding faith that God listens to their prayers and that His actions are influenced by their petitions and oaths. I have never had any missionary zeal to convert anyone from his own views on religion, or to engage in any polemics with those among whom I was brought up. But I must, in the interest of truth, record my observation that the number of those who outwardly profess Orthodoxy is much greater than of those who really let it influence their lives.

I remember as a boy having a talk with the late Joseph Jacobs. He asked, "Why do your young people on the East Side keep away from the synagogue? Don't they believe in religion?" I replied, "Going to synagogue or not going is a minor matter, Mr. Jacobs. We take religion more seriously than you do." I think that was the truth. True religion must be an expression of the inner soul and cannot be forced on anyone merely because he happens to have been born of a certain ancestry. It seemed to me that in the friction between the older generation and the younger generation which the religious question brought to the fore in the days of my youth, both sides were at fault. The older generation was at fault in not distinguishing between ritual forms and true religious faith. It was lacking in human sympathy with the honest views of the younger generation. It could not learn that the real vitality of a religion does not show itself in the power to resist the advance of new truth but rather in the capacity to adapt itself to whatever new light it can get.

On the other hand there was a certain superficiality in the attitude that many of my generation took towards religion. We used to read accounts of conflict between science and religion in which, we were told, science had gradually conquered. This, however, seemed to me to leave out of consideration the realm where science cannot rule, where neither the telescope nor the microscope can penetrate, the realm of ideal expression. Appropriation or rejection of science thus did not solve the problem of religion. Those who called themselves atheists seemed to be singularly blind, as a rule, to the limitations of our knowledge and to the infinite possibilities beyond us. And those who call themselves materialists appeared to me to be shutting themselves off from philosophy, wisdom, and the life of the spirit, which are certainly not material things. Those of my circle who rejected religion *in toto* seemed to me to be casting away the ideals that had sustained our people through so many generations before we had fashioned guideposts to our own lives that could stand up against the sort of buffeting that the old guideposts had withstood. In this some of us lost sight of the larger view that Thomas Davidson had taught, that we have no right to break away from the past until we have appropriated all its experience and wisdom, and that reverence for the past may go hand in hand with loyalty to the future, "to the Kingdom which doth not yet appear."

The ideal of intellectual integrity compelled me and many others of my generation to reject superstitions that had been bound up with the practices of our Orthodox parents, but it did not prevent us from cherishing the spiritual values which they had found in those practices, and which many others have found in the practices of the other older and younger religions. The struggle between Orthodoxy and active opposition to all religion seemed to me, like so many of the passionate struggles of life, to overlook possibilities and values which a more tolerant and rational outlook could find.

Indeed I marveled then, and have never ceased to marvel, at the fact that on matters where knowledge is readily demonstrable — such as cooking or chemistry — discussions show little of the heated mood of the zealot and fanatic, whereas, in matters on which it is much more difficult to arrive at the truth, such as questions of religion, we are inclined to be very sure of ourselves. Perhaps we try to make up by our vehemence for the lack of demonstrative evidence.

Of course, if you claim to be in possession of a special revelation, then you have a mortgage on the truth of the universe, the other fellow can have nothing true to tell you, and the thing to do is to hold on to your revealed truth with all the ardor that is in you. But then the other fellow is just as certain that he alone has all the truth and there is no use in any argumentation. But if you take your stand on human history and human reason, and recognize, for example, that the claim to the possession of a special revelation of the Jew is, as such, not a bit better than that of the Christian or the Mohammedan, or any of the ten thousand other claims, then, it seemed to me, you must grant that each possesses both truth and error.

Having once made up my mind that the whole truth of the matter did not lie with either side, I saw the religious problem of my own intellectual generation as a problem calling for creative thought rather than simple loyalty. "Before we can appropriate the religion of our ancestors," I wrote in an article on the religious question on the East Side, in June, 1902, "we must build it over again in our own hearts. This holds good not only of religion but of all the products of civilization. Whatever thou hast inherited from thy ancestors, earn in order to possess. Only that which we have worked out ourselves is truly ours."

Twenty years later I was still seeking for a way of uniting naturalism in science with piety towards that which has been revered as noble and sacred in the spiritual history of man. Of all philosophers, it seemed to me that Spinoza had most clearly developed the rational and tolerant attitude to the values of religion for which I had been searching. In my addresses before the American Philosophical Association in 1922 on "The Intellectual Love of God," I undertook to defend the validity of the Spinozistic ideal, "amor Dei intellectualis," as a beacon that may illumine the problems of modern life and thought. Naturalism, for Spinoza, did not import that worldliness which wise men in all generations have recognized as a state of spiritual death. Nor did he conceive of love as a passive emotion. The quest for understanding, Spinoza saw, is an activity, often a breathless activity, that even apart from its practical consequences, is the most divine of human enterprises.

It is true that Spinoza rejects the idea of an anthropomorphic God who will respond to our flattering prayers, reward us for our unsuccessful efforts, and in general compensate us for the harshness of the natural order and the weaknesses of our reason. If, however, religion consists in humility (as a sense of infinite powers beyond our scope), charity or love (as a sense of the mystic potency in our fellow human beings), and spirituality (as a sense of the limitations of all that is merely material, actual or even attainable), then no one was more deeply religious than Spinoza.

And while Spinoza has little regard for the immortality which means the postponement of certain human gratifications to a period beyond our natural life, he does believe in the immortality which we achieve when we live in the eternal present or identify ourselves with those human values that the process of time can never adequately realize or destroy. He thus showed me the path to that serenity which follows a view of life fixed on those things that go on despite all the tragedies and depressions which frighten hysterical people. Above all, Spinoza made clear to me the vision that saves us from the worldliness that drowns out life. We are all like the waves tossed high up by the ocean and breaking on the sands of actuality. If we are to attain true human dignity, we need some sense of our continuity with the past and the future, a consciousness of ourselves not as temporary flies but as waves of a human ocean larger than our own lives and efforts.

Spinoza, like the other great religious teachers and the morally wise men of science, teaches the great lesson of humility — that there are always vast realms beyond our ken or control, and that the great blessing of inner peace is unattainable without a sense of the mystery of creation about us and a wisely cultivated resignation to our mortal but inevitable limitations.

These limitations men surmount only as they learn to subordinate their separate individualities to the interest of families, social or religious groups, nations, races, or that humanity whose life is the whole cosmic drama of which, as thinkers, we are spectators.

In the days of my first youthful revolt against the Jewish observances, I was inclined to regard cultus, prayer and ritual as of little importance in comparison with belief or faith. This was certainly the view that my teacher William James took of the matter. The conclusion he drew from this was that the religious experience of the great mass of people, who follow in the steps of great masters, is of little significance. My own studies of the great historic religions led me, however, to see that ritual, what men do on certain occasions, is a primary fact in human religious experience, and that the beliefs and emotions associated with ritual are more variable than ritual itself, as is shown by the diverse explanations and justifications of the Hebrew Sabbath and the Easter ceremonies.

Indeed the character of the founders of the great religions, as we know it, is largely a product of tradition.

Men cling to sanctified phrases not only because of the insights they contain but even more because, through ritual and repetition, they have become redolent with the wine of human experience. For each of us the symbolism of our childhood offers paths to peace and understanding that can never be wholly replaced by other symbolisms. For me the ancient ceremonies that celebrate the coming and going of life, the wedding ceremony, the *b'rith*, and the funeral service, give an expression to the continuity of the spiritual tradition that is more eloquent than any phrases of my own creation. The ritual may be diluted by English and by modernisms, but the Hebraic God is still a potent symbol of the continuous life of which we individuals are waves. So it is, too, with the celebration of the eternal struggle for freedom, in the family service of the Passover.

Like vivid illustrations in the book of my life are the prayers of my parents, the services at their graves, the memory of an old man chanting funeral songs at the *Jahrzeit* of my dear friend, Dr. Himwich, the unveiling of the monument to the beloved comrade of my life's journeys, and the celebration of the continuity of generations in the Passover services in the home of my parents and in the homes of my children. And though I have never gone back to theologic supernaturalism, I have come to appreciate more than I once did the symbolism in which is celebrated the human need of trusting to the larger vision, according to which calamities come and go but the continuity of life and faith in its better possibilities survive.

7. *Religion in the Making* *

ALFRED NORTH WHITEHEAD *(1861–1947)*

There is no agreement as to the definition of religion in its most general sense, including true and false religion; nor is there any

---

* Reprinted by permission of the publishers from *Religion in the Making*, Lowell Lectures, 1926, The Macmillan Company. The selection is from pages 14–20 and 58–60.

agreement as to the valid religious beliefs, nor even as to what we mean by the truth of religion. It is for this reason that some consideration of religion as an unquestioned factor throughout the long stretch of human history is necessary to secure the relevance of any discussion of its general principles.

There is yet another contrast. What is generally disputed is doubtful, and what is doubtful is relatively unimportant — other things being equal. I am speaking of general truths. We avoid guiding our actions by general principles which are entirely unsettled. If we do not know what number is the product of 69 and 67, we defer any action presupposing the answer, till we have found out. This little arithmetical puzzle can be put aside till it is settled, and it is capable of definite settlement with adequate trouble.

But as between religion and arithmetic, other things are not equal. You *use* arithmetic, but you *are* religious. Arithmetic of course enters into your nature, so far as that nature involves a multiplicity of things. But it is there as a necessary condition, and not as a transforming agency. No one is invariably "justified" by his faith in the multiplication table. But in some sense or other, justification is the basis of all religion. Your character is developed according to your faith. This is the primary religious truth from which no one can escape. Religion is force of belief cleansing the inward parts. For this reason the primary religious virtue is sincerity, a penetrating sincerity.

A religion, on its doctrinal side, can thus be defined as a system of general truths, which have the effect of transforming character when they are sincerely held and vividly apprehended.

In the long run your character and your conduct of life depend upon your intimate convictions. Life is an internal fact for its own sake, before it is an external fact relating itself to others. The conduct of external life is conditioned by environment, but it receives its final quality, on which its worth depends, from the internal life which is the self-realization of existence. Religion is the art and the theory of the internal life of man, so far as it depends on the man himself and on what is permanent in the nature of things.

This doctrine is the direct negation of the theory that religion is primarily a social fact. Social facts are of great importance to religion, because there is no such thing as absolutely independent existence. You cannot abstract society from man; most psychology is herd-psychology. But all collective emotions leave untouched the awful ultimate fact, which is the human being, consciously alone with itself, for its own sake.

Religion is what the individual does with his own solitariness. It runs through three stages, if it evolves to its final satisfaction. It is the transition from God the void to God the enemy, and from God the enemy to God the companion.

Thus religion is solitariness; and if you are never solitary, you are never religious. Collective enthusiasms, revivals, institutions, churches, rituals, bibles, codes of behaviour, are the trappings of religion, its passing forms. They may be useful, or harmful; they may be authoritatively ordained, or merely temporary expedients. But the end of religion is beyond all this.

Accordingly, what should emerge from religion is individual worth of character. But worth is positive or negative, good or bad. Religion is by no means necessarily good. It may be very evil. The fact of evil, interwoven with the texture of the world, shows that in the nature of things there remains effectiveness for degradation. In your religious experience the God with whom you have made terms may be the God of destruction, the God who leaves in his wake the loss of the greater reality.

In considering religion, we should not be obsessed by the idea of its necessary goodness. This is a dangerous delusion. The point to notice is its transcendent importance; and the fact of this importance is abundantly made evident by the appeal to history.

Religion, so far as it receives external expression in human history, exhibits four factors or sides of itself. These factors are ritual, emotion, belief, rationalization. There is definite organized procedure, which is ritual; there are definite types of emotional expression; there are definitely expressed beliefs; and there is the adjustment of these beliefs into a system, internally coherent and coherent with other beliefs.

But all these four factors are not of equal influence throughout all historical epochs. The religious idea emerged gradually into human life, at first barely disengaged from other human interests. The order of the emergence of these factors was in the inverse order of the depth of their religious importance: first ritual, then emotion, then belief, then rationalization.

The dawn of these religious stages is gradual. It consists in an increase of emphasis. Perhaps it is untrue to affirm that the later factors are ever wholly absent. But certainly, when we go far enough back, belief and rationalization are completely negligible, and emotion is merely a secondary result of ritual. Then emotion takes the lead, and the ritual is for the emotion which it generates. Belief then makes its appearance as explanatory of the complex of ritual and emotion, and in this appearance of belief we may discern the germ of rationalization.

It is not until belief and rationalization are well established that solitariness is discernible as constituting the heart of religious importance. The great religious conceptions which haunt the imaginations of civilized mankind are scenes of solitariness: Prometheus chained to his rock, Mahomet brooding in the desert, the meditations of the Buddha, the solitary Man on the Cross. It belongs to the depth of the religious spirit to have felt forsaken even by God. . . .

This point of the origin of rational religion in solitariness is fundamental. Religion is founded on the concurrence of three allied concepts in one moment of self-consciousness, concepts whose separate relationships to fact and whose mutual relations to each other are only to be settled jointly by some direct intuition into the ultimate character of the universe.

These concepts are:

1. That of the value of an individual for itself.

2. That of the value of the diverse individuals of the world for each other.

3. That of the value of the objective world which is a community derivative from the interrelations of its component individuals, and also necessary for the existence of each of these individuals.

The moment of religious consciousness starts from self-valuation, but it broadens into the concept of the world as a realm of adjusted values, mutually intensifying or mutually destructive. The intuition into the actual world gives a particular definite content to the bare notion of a principle determining the grading of values. It also exhibits emotions, purposes, and physical conditions, as subservient factors in the emergence of value.

In its solitariness the spirit asks, What, in the way of value, is the attainment of life? And it can find no such value till it has merged its individual claim with that of the objective universe. Religion is world-loyalty.

8. Science and Religion *

ALBERT EINSTEIN *(1879–)*

It would not be difficult to come to an agreement as to what we understand by science. Science is the century-old endeavor to bring together by means of systematic thought the perceptible phenomena of this world into as thoroughgoing an association as possible. To put it boldly, it is the attempt at the posterior reconstruction of existence by the process of conceptualization. But when asking myself what religion is, I cannot think of an answer so easily. And even after finding an answer which may satisfy me at this particular moment, I still remain convinced that I can never under any circumstances bring together, even to a slight extent, all those who have given this question serious consideration.

At first, then, instead of asking what religion is, I should prefer to ask what characterizes the aspirations of a person who gives me the impression of being religious: a person who is religiously enlightened appears to me to be one who has, to the best of his ability, liberated himself from the fetters of his selfish desires and is preoccupied with thoughts, feelings, and aspirations to which he clings because of their super-personal value. It seems to me that what is important is the force of this super-personal content and the depth of the conviction concerning its overpowering meaningfulness, regardless of whether any attempt is made to unite this content with a Divine Being, for otherwise it would not be possible to count Buddha and Spinoza as religious personalities. Accordingly, a religious person is devout in the sense that he has no doubt of the significance and loftiness of those super-personal objects and goals which neither require nor are capable of rational foundation. They exist with the same necessity and matter-of-factness as he himself. In this sense religion is the age-old endeavor of mankind to become clearly and completely conscious of these values and goals and constantly to strengthen and extend their effects. If one conceives of religion and science according to these definitions then a conflict between them appears impossible. For science can only ascertain what *is*, but not what should be, and outside of its domain value judgments of all

---

* Reprinted by permission of the author and of the Conference on Science, Philosophy and Religion (1941).

kinds remain necessary. Religion, on the other hand, deals only with evaluations of human thought and action; it cannot justifiably speak of facts and relationships between facts. According to this interpretation, the well-known conflicts between religion and science in the past must all be ascribed to a misapprehension of the situation which has been described.

For example, a conflict arises when a religious community insists on the absolute truthfulness of all statements recorded in the Bible. This means an intervention on the part of religion into the sphere of science; this is where the struggle of the Church against the doctrines of Galileo and Darwin belongs. On the other hand, representatives of science have often made an attempt to arrive at fundamental judgments with respect to values and ends on the basis of scientific method, and in this way have set themselves in opposition to religion. These conflicts have all sprung from fatal errors.

Now, even though the realms of religion and science in themselves are clearly marked off from each other, nevertheless there exist between the two, strong reciprocal relationships and dependencies. Though religion may be that which determines the goal, it has, nevertheless, learned from science, in the broadest sense, what means will contribute to the attainment of the goals it has set up. But science can only be created by those who are thoroughly imbued with the aspiration towards truth and understanding. This source of feeling, however, springs from the sphere of religion. To this there also belongs the faith in the possibility that the regulations valid for the world of existence are rational, that is comprehensible to reason. I cannot conceive of a genuine scientist without that profound faith. The situation may be expressed by an image: science without religion is lame, religion without science is blind.

Though I have asserted above, that in truth a legitimate conflict between religion and science cannot exist, I must nevertheless qualify this assertion once again on an essential point, with reference to the actual content of historical religions. This qualification has to do with the concept of God. During the youthful period of mankind's spiritual evolution, human fantasy created gods in man's own image, who, by the operations of their will were supposed to determine, or at any rate to influence, the phenomenal world. Man sought to alter the disposition of these gods in his own favor by means of magic and prayer. The idea of God in the religions taught at present is a sublimation of that old conception of the gods. Its anthropomorphic character is shown, for instance, by the fact that men appeal to the Divine Being in prayers and plead for the fulfillment of their wishes.

Nobody, certainly, will deny that the idea of the existence of an omnipotent, just and omnibeneficent personal God is able to accord men solace, help and guidance; also, by virtue of its simplicity the concept is accessible to the most undeveloped mind. But, on the other hand, there are decisive weaknesses attached to this idea in itself, which have been painfully felt since the beginning of history. That is, if this Being is omnipotent, then every occurrence, including every human action, every human thought, and every human feeling and aspiration is also His work; how is it possible to think of holding men responsible for their deeds and thoughts before such an Almighty Being? In giving out punishment and rewards He would to a certain extent be passing judgment on Himself. How can this be combined with the goodness and righteousness ascribed to Him?

The main source of the present-day conflicts between the spheres of religion and science lies in this concept of a personal God. It is the aim of science to establish general rules which determine the reciprocal connection of objects and events in time and space. For these rules, or laws of nature, absolutely general validity is required — not proven. It is mainly a program, and faith in the possibility of its accomplishment in principle is only founded on partial success. But hardly anyone could be found who would deny these partial successes and ascribe them to human self-deception. The fact that on the basis of such laws we are able to predict the temporal behavior of phenomena in certain domains with great precision and certainty, is deeply embedded in the consciousness of the modern man, even though he may have grasped very little of the contents of those laws. He need only consider that planetary courses within the solar system may be calculated in advance with great exactitude on the basis of a limited number of simple laws. In a similar way, though not with the same precision, it is possible to calculate in advance the mode of operation of an electric motor, a transmission system, or of a wireless apparatus, even when dealing with a novel development.

To be sure, when the number of factors coming into play in a phenomenological complex is too large, scientific method in most cases fails us. One need only think of the weather, in which case prediction even for a few days ahead is impossible. Nevertheless no one doubts that we are confronted with a causal connection whose causal components are in the main known to us. Occurrences in this domain are beyond the reach of exact prediction because of the variety of factors in operation, not because of any lack of order in nature.

We have penetrated far less deeply into the regularities obtaining within the realm of living things, but deeply enough nevertheless to sense at least the rule of fixed necessity. One need only think of the systematic order in heredity, and in the effect of poisons, as for instance alcohol, on the behavior of organic beings. What is still lacking here is a grasp of connections of profound generality, but not a knowledge of order in itself.

The more a man is imbued with the ordered regularity of all events, the firmer becomes his conviction that there is no room left by the side of this ordered regularity for causes of a different nature. For him neither the rule of human nor the rule of divine will exists as an independent cause of natural events. To be sure, the doctrine of a personal God interfering with natural events could never be refuted, in the real sense, by science, for this doctrine can always take refuge in those domains in which scientific knowledge has not yet been able to set foot.

But I am persuaded that such behavior on the part of the representatives of religion would not only be unworthy but also fatal. For a doctrine which is able to maintain itself not in clear light but only in the dark, will of necessity lose its effect on mankind, with incalculable harm to human progress. In their struggle for the ethical good, teachers of religion must have the stature to give up the doctrine of a personal God, that is, give up that source of fear and hope which in the past placed such vast power in the hands of priests. In their labors they will have to avail themselves of those forces which are capable of cultivating the Good, the True, and the Beautiful in humanity itself. This is, to be sure, a more difficult but an incomparably more worthy task.[1] After religious teachers accomplish the refining process indicated, they will surely recognize with joy that true religion has been ennobled and made more profound by scientific knowledge.

If it is one of the goals of religion to liberate mankind as far as

---

[1] This thought is convincingly presented in Herbert Samuel's book, "Belief and Action."

possible from the bondage of egocentric cravings, desires, and fears, scientific reasoning can aid religion in yet another sense. Although it is true that it is the goal of science to discover rules which permit the association and foretelling of facts, this is not its only aim. It also seeks to reduce the connections discovered to the smallest possible number of mutually independent conceptual elements. It is in this striving after the rational unification of the manifold that it encounters its greatest successes, even though it is precisely this attempt which causes it to run the greatest risk of falling a prey to illusions. But whoever has undergone the intense experience of successful advances made in this domain, is moved by profound reverence for the rationality made manifest in existence. By way of the understanding he achieves a far-reaching emancipation from the shackles of personal hopes and desires, and thereby attains that humble attitude of mind towards the grandeur of reason incarnate in existence, which, in its profoundest depths, is inaccessible to man. This attitude, however, appears to me to be religious, in the highest sense of the word. And so it seems to me that science not only purifies the religious impulse of the dross of its anthropomorphism, but also contributes to a religious spiritualization of our understanding of life.

The further the spiritual evolution of mankind advances, the more certain it seems to me that the path to genuine religiosity does not lie through the fear of life, and the fear of death, and blind faith, but through striving after rational knowledge. In this sense I believe that the priest must become a teacher if he wishes to do justice to his lofty educational mission.

9. The Nature and Destiny of Man *

REINHOLD NIEBUHR (1892-   )

The thought of a typical naturalistic philosopher of the twentieth century, John Dewey, advances remarkably little beyond the per-

---

* Reprinted from *The Nature and Destiny of Man* by Reinhold Niebuhr; copyright 1941, 1943 by Charles Scribner's Sons; used by permission of the publishers.

plexities and confusions of the previous centuries. He has the same difficulty in finding a vantage point for reason from which it may operate against the perils of nature and the same blindness toward the new perils of spirit which arise in the "rational" life of man. Dewey is in fact less conscious of the social perils of self-love than either Locke or Hume. In his thought the hope of achieving a vantage point which transcends the corruptions of self-interest takes the form of trusting the "scientific method" and attributing antisocial conduct to the "cultural lag," that is, to the failure of social science to keep abreast with technology. "That coercion and oppression on a large scale exist no honest person can deny," he declares. "But these things are not the product of science and technology but of the perpetuation of old institutions and patterns untouched by the scientific method. The inference to be drawn is clear."[1] The failures of the past and present are due to the fact that the scientific method "has not been tried at any time with use of all the resources which scientific material and the experimental method now put at our disposal."[2] The subordination of intelligence to party passion is attributed to faulty social theories which represent "a kind of political watered-down version of the Hegelian dialectic" and the true liberal must make it clear that this "method has nothing in common with the procedure of organized co-operative inquiry which has won the triumphs of science in the field of physical nature."[3]

Professor Dewey has a touching faith in the possibility of achieving the same results in the field of social relations which intelligence achieved in the mastery of nature. The fact that man constitutionally corrupts his purest visions of disinterested justice in his actual actions seems never to occur to him. Consequently he never wearies in looking for specific causes of interested rather than disinterested action. As an educator, one of his favourite theories is that man's betrayal of his own ideals in action is due to faulty educational techniques which separate "theory and practice, thought and action." He thinks this faulty pedagogy is derived from the "traditional separation of mind and body" in idealistic philosophy.[4]

---

[1] *Liberalism and Social Action*, p. 82. [All quotations from John Dewey's *Liberalism and Social Action* are by permission of G. P. Putnam's Sons.]

[2] *Ibid.*, p. 51.

[3] *Ibid.*, p. 71.

[4] Joseph Ratner, *Philosophy of John Dewey*, p. 381.

In common with his eighteenth-century precursors, he would use the disinterested force of his "freed intelligence" to attack institutional injustices and thus further free intelligence. Despotic institutions represent "relationships fixed in a pre-scientific age" and are the bulwark of anachronistic social attitudes. On the other hand "lag in mental and moral patterns provide the bulwark of the older institutions." [5]

No one expresses modern man's uneasiness about his society and complacency about himself more perfectly than John Dewey. One half of his philosophy is devoted to an emphasis upon what, in Christian theology, is called the creatureliness of man, his involvement in biological and social process. The other half seeks a secure place for disinterested intelligence above the flux of process; and finds it in "organized co-operative inquiry." Not a suspicion dawns upon Professor Dewey that no possible "organized inquiry" can be as transcendent over the historical conflicts of interest as it ought to be to achieve the disinterested intelligence which he attributes to it. Every such "organized inquiry" must have its own particular social locus. No court of law, though supported by age-old traditions of freedom from party conflict, is free of party bias whenever it deals with issues profound enough to touch the very foundation of the society upon which the court is reared. Morever, there can be no "free co-operative inquiry" which will not pretend to have achieved a more complete impartiality than is possible for human instruments of justice. The worst injustices and conflicts of history arise from these very claims of impartiality for biased and partial historical instruments. The solution at which Professor Dewey arrives is therefore an incredibly naive answer to a much more ultimate and perplexing problem than he realizes. It could only have arisen in a period of comparative social stability and security and in a nation in which geographic isolation obscured the conflict of nations, and great wealth mitigated the social conflict within a nation.

Modern naturalism expresses its confidence in the goodness of man either by finding a harmony of nature, conceived in mechanistic or vitalistic terms, to which he can flee from the tensions and conflicts of freedom; or by placing its trust in some principle of order and

---

[5] John Dewey, *ibid.*, p. 76.

harmony in reason in which it really has no right to believe within the limits of its naturalistic presupposition. Idealistic rationalism, on the other hand, has a much more simple approach to its moral optimism. Its confidence in the goodness of man rests upon a sharp distinction between nature and reason, between *nous* and *physis*. The order and inner coherence of reason is regarded as a safe retreat from the chaos of natural impulse; and the power of reason is considered sufficient to master and coerce natural vitality and transmute it into a higher realm of coherence. Such an interpretation of human nature has the advantage of recognizing the total dimension of the human spirit; but it makes the mistake of dividing the human *psyche* too absolutely and of identifying spirit and reason too completely. Its dualism prevents it from understanding the organic relation between nature and reason and the dependence of reason upon nature. Its identification of reason and spirit obscures the fact that human freedom actually transcends the capacities which are usually known as "rational." In other words it repeats the errors of Greek classicism. Consequently it finds a premature security for the freedom of man in the inner coherence of reason and does not see to what degree man may, in his freedom, violate, corrupt and prostitute the canons of reason in his own interest. Its rejection of Christian pessimism rests upon its belief that the rational man is also the good man.

Professor Alfred N. Whitehead, despite the qualified character of his idealism, offers a striking example of this idealistic optimism. He distinguishes between "speculative reason" and "pragmatic reason" and regards the former as the source of virtue and the latter as the root of evil. This distinction is reminiscent of Aristotle's distinction between the active and the passive *nous*. According to Whitehead, the former is the reason "which Plato shares with God," while the latter is the reason which "Ulysses shares with the foxes": "The short-range function of reason characteristic of Ulysses is reason criticizing and emphasizing subordinate purposes of nature which are agents of final causation. This is reason as a pragmatic agent . . . . The other function of reason was connected with the life work of Plato. In this function reason is enthroned above the practical tasks of the world. . . . It seeks with disinterested curiosity an understanding of the world. . . . In this function reason serves only itself. This is speculative reason." Evil arises from the "massive

obscurantism of human nature" and this obscurantism in turn is
defined as "the inertial resistance of practical reason with its millions of years behind it, to interference with its fixed methods arising
from recent habits of speculation." [6]

Thus Whitehead, from the standpoint of a quasi-idealistic theory,
believes the root of evil to lie in the inertia of that very intelligence,
that pragmatic and short-range rational relation to natural impulses
which, in the opinion of Professor Dewey, is man's sole rational
possession. Yet both arrive at a "cultural lag" theory of human
evil and both hope for a society which will ultimately be governed
purely by rational suasion rather than force.[7] Their arrival at this
common goal by contrasting methods is indicative of the power of
moral optimism in modern culture. The rationalistic naturalists
are forced to construct a very shaky and inadequate point of reference from which they can operate against the confusion of natural
impulse. In Professor Dewey's case this is the device of a "free co-
operative inquiry," which is involved in the natural-historical process and yet somehow has a vantage point of pure disinterestedness
above it. The purer rationalist splits the human spirit into a speculative and a pragmatic intelligence; and he assumes that the former
has a vantage point of pure disinterestedness which no type of human
intelligence ever possesses . . . .

The easy conscience of modern culture is practically unanimous,
but not quite. It may be more correct to say that there are practically no exceptions to the easy conscience but there are exceptions
to the general moral optimism. For there are pessimists about
human nature, who are nevertheless of easy conscience, because
they do not hold man himself responsible for the evils in human
nature. Hobbes is a pessimist in regard to the individual; but he
is completely complacent about the moral qualities of the state,
which he introduces to overcome the chaos of individual life. Most
of the other pessimists stand in the romantic tradition. Rousseau's
romanticism is provisionally pessimistic; yet it becomes the very
fountain of optimism in modern educational theory. Nietzsche's

---

[6] *The Function of Reason*, 1929, pp. 23–30. [Quotation by permission of
Princeton University Press.]

[7] Cf. Whitehead, *Adventures of Ideas*, Ch. 5; John Dewey, *Philosophy and
Civilization.*

pessimism is thoroughgoing but even he is able to erect an ultimate optimism upon his conception of the superman, who transmutes the will-to-power into an instrument of social creativity and order. Freud's pessimism is most thoroughgoing, but he finds no conscience to appeal to. His "super-ego" performs the functions of Hobbes's state; but it cannot be given an unconditioned function of discipline, because it is feared that discipline will lead to new disorders in the unconscious life of the individual.

The romantic pessimism which culminates in Freud may be regarded as symbolic of the despair which modern man faces when his optimistic illusions are dispelled; for under the perpetual smile of modernity there is a grimace of disillusion and cynicism.

This undercurrent of romantic pessimism and cynicism does not, however, deflect the main stream of optimism. The fact that modern man has been able to preserve such a good opinion of himself, despite all the obvious refutations of his optimism, particularly in his own history, leads to the conclusion that there is a very stubborn source of resistance in man to the acceptance of the most obvious and irrefutable evidence about his moral qualities. This source of resistance is not primarily modern but generally human. The final sin of man, said Luther truly, is his unwillingness to concede that he is a sinner. The significant contribution of modern culture to this perennial human inclination lies in the number of plausible reasons which it was able to adduce in support of man's good opinion of himself. The fact that many of these reasons stand in contradiction to each other did not shatter modern man's confidence in them; for he could always persuade himself of the truth of at least one of them and it never occurred to him that they might all be false.

Yet they were all false. Whether they found the path from chaos to order to lead from nature to reason or from reason to nature, whether they regarded the harmony of nature or the coherence of mind as the final realm of redemption, they failed to understand the human spirit in its full dimension of freedom. Both the majesty and the tragedy of human life exceed the dimension within which modern culture seeks to comprehend human existence. The human spirit cannot be held within the bounds of either natural necessity or rational prudence. In its yearning toward the infinite lies the source of both human creativity and human sin. In the words of the eminent Catholic philosopher Étienne Gilson: "Epicurus remarked, and not without reason, that with a little bread and water the wise man is the equal of Jupiter himself . . . The fact is, perhaps, that with a little bread and water a man ought to be happy but precisely is not; and if he is not, it is not necessarily because he lacks wisdom, but simply because he is a man, and because all that is deepest in him perpetually gainsays the wisdom offered . . . The owner of a great estate would still add field to field, the rich man would heap up more riches, the husband of a fair wife would have another still fairer, or possibly one less fair would serve, provided only she were fair in some other way . . . This incessant pursuit of an ever fugitive satisfaction springs from troubled depths in human nature . . . The very insatiability of human desire has a positive significance; it means this: that we are attracted by an infinite good." [8]

The fact that man can transcend himself in infinite regression and cannot find the end of life except in God is the mark of his creativity and uniqueness; closely related to this capacity is his inclination to transmute his partial and finite self and his partial and finite values into the infinite good. Therein lies his sin.

Our analysis of modern interpretations of human nature has led to the conviction that the modern mind arrives at contradictory conclusions about the relation of vitality to form in human nature; that the perennial debate between rationalists and romanticists, the one depreciating and the other glorifying the power and the virtue of subrational vitalities, is the historic evidence of this contradiction; that the modern mind fails to find a secure foundation for the individuality which it ostensibly cherishes so highly; and that its estimates of human virtue are too generous and optimistic to accord with the known facts of human history.

In analysing the modern failure in each of these areas of thought we have suggested that the difficulty arises from the lack of a principle of interpretation which can do justice to both the height of human self-transcendence and the organic unity between the spirit of man and his physical life. The modern mind interprets man as either essentially reason, without being able to do justice to his nonrational vitalities, or as essentially vitality without appreciating the

---

[8] *The Spirit of Medieval Philosophy*, pp. 270–272.

extent of his rational freedom. Its metaphysics fails to comprehend the unity of mind and nature, of freedom and necessity, in the actual life of man. In similar fashion it dissipates the sense of individuality, upon which it insists with so much vehemence in the early Renaissance, because it cannot find a foundation in either nature, historical social structure, or universal mind for this individuality. It lacks an anchor or norm for the free individual who transcends both the limitations of nature and the various social concretions of history. Its inability to estimate the evil in man realistically is partly due to the failure of modern culture to see man in his full stature of self-transcendence. The naturalist sees human freedom as little more than the freedom of *homo faber* [8a] and fails to appreciate to what degree the human spirit breaks and remakes the harmonies and unities of nature. The idealist, identifying freedom with reason and failing to appreciate that freedom rises above reason, imagines that the freedom of man is secure, in the mind's impetus toward coherence and synthesis. Neither naturalism nor idealism can understand that man is free enough to violate both the necessities of nature and the logical systems of reason.

All three errors of modern estimates of man, therefore, point to a single and common source of error: Man is not measured in a dimension sufficiently high or deep to do full justice to either his stature or his capacity for both good and evil or to understand the total environment in which such a stature can understand, express and find itself. One might define this total environment most succinctly as one which includes both eternity and time; but the concept of eternity without further definition may be too ambiguous to clarify the point at issue. The eternity which is part of the environment of man is neither the infinity of time nor yet a realm of undifferentiated unity of being. It is the changeless source of man's changing being. As a creature who is involved in flux but who is also conscious of the fact that he is so involved, he cannot be totally involved. A spirit who can set time, nature, the world and being *per se* into juxtaposition to himself and inquire after the meaning of these things, proves that in some sense he stands outside and beyond them.

8a [The man of action].

This ability to stand outside and beyond the world, tempts man to megalomania and persuades him to regard himself as the god around and about whom the universe centres. Yet he is too obviously involved in the flux and finiteness of nature to make such pretensions plausibly. The real situation is that he has an environment of eternity which he cannot know through the mere logical ordering of his experience. The rational faculty by which he orders and interprets his experience (sometimes erroneously regarded as the very eternity in which finiteness rests) is itself a part of the finite world which man must seek to understand. The only principle for the comprehension of the whole (the whole which includes both himself and his world) is therefore inevitably beyond his comprehension. Man is thus in the position of being unable to comprehend himself in his full stature of freedom without a principle of comprehension which is beyond his comprehension.

This is the situation which gives perennial rise to mystic faiths in both east and west, though the east is more addicted to mysticism than the west. The mystic, being conscious of standing somehow beyond the flux of events in the finite world, and fearful lest his finite effort to comprehend this eternal world merely obscure the concept of the eternal with finite perspectives, restricts himself to a purely negative definition of the eternal world. It is everything the finite world is not; or rather it is not anything which the finite world is. He thus arrives at a concept of an undifferentiated eternal unity. With this as his principle of criticism for the finite world, he is forced to regard the finite world as a corruption of, or emanation from the undifferentiated unity of eternity. Since his own particularized existence is a part of this corrupt finite world the pure mystic, who begins by lifting self-consciousness out of the flux of temporal events, must end by negating his own conscious life as part of the temporal world and by seeking absorption into eternity.

The character of Biblical religion must be understood in contrast to this tendency toward self-immolation in mysticism. It is a religion which neither reduces the stature of man to the level of nature, nor yet destroys it in an empty and undifferentiated eternity. Biblical religion is variously defined, in distinction from other religions, as a prophetic or as an apocalyptic religion, or as a religion of revelation. In a religion of revelation, the unveiling of the eternal purpose and will, underlying the flux and evanescence of the world, is expected; and the expectation is fulfilled in personal and social-historical experience.[9]

From the standpoint of an understanding of human nature, the significance of a religion of revelation lies in the fact that both the transcendence of God over, and his intimate relation to, the world are equally emphasized. He is more completely transcendent than the eternity of mystic faith. Mysticism always regards the final depth of human consciousness as in some sense identical with the eternal order, and believes that men may know God if they penetrate deeply enough into the mystery of their own being. But on the other hand the transcendent God of Biblical faith makes Himself known in the finite and historical world. The finite world is not, because of its finiteness, incapable of entertaining comprehensible revelations of the incomprehensible God. The most important characteristic of a religion of revelation is this twofold emphasis upon the transcendence of God and upon His intimate relation to the world. In this divine transcendence the spirit of man finds a home in which it can understand its stature of freedom. But there it also finds the limits of its freedom, the judgment which is spoken against it and, ultimately, the mercy which makes such a judgment sufferable. God's creation of, and relation to, the world on the other hand prove that human finiteness and involvement in flux are essentially good and not evil. A religion of revelation is thus alone able to do justice to both the freedom and the finiteness of man and to understand the character of the evil in him.

The revelation of God to man is always a twofold one, a personal-individual revelation, and a revelation in the context of social-

---

[9] John Oman defines the difference between mystical and apocalyptic religions as follows: "In the former case the eternal is sought as the unchanging by escape from the evanescent; in the latter it is looked for in the evanescent as a revelation of the increasing purpose in its changes." . . . "A mystical religion is, as it should always be understood scientifically, one that seeks the eternal behind the illusion of the evanescent; but in using 'apocalyptic' for any religion which looks for a revealing in the evanescent, the term is extended from its customary use, which is for a religion which expects this in sudden catastrophic form, to one which expects it in any form."—*The Natural and the Supernatural,* pp. 403–409.

historical experience. Without the public and historical revelation the private experience of God would remain poorly defined and subject to caprice. Without the private revelation of God, the public and historical revelation would not gain credence. Since all men have, in some fashion, the experience of a reality beyond themselves, they are able to entertain the more precise revelations of the character and purpose of God as they come to them in the most significant experiences of prophetic history. Private revelation is, in a sense, synonymous with " general" revelation, without the presuppositions of which there could be no "special" revelation. It is no less universal for being private. Private revelation is the testimony in the consciousness of every person that his life touches a reality beyond himself, a reality deeper and higher than the system of nature in which he stands.

St. Paul speaks of this experience of God when he declares that even without a further revelation men are "without excuse" if they do not glorify God as God but become vain in their imagination and make themselves God (Romans 1:20). The experience of God is not so much a separate experience, as an overtone implied in all experience.[10] The soul which reaches the outermost rims of its own consciousness, must also come in contact with God, for He impinges upon that consciousness.

Schleiermacher describes this experience of God as the experience of "unqualified dependence." This is one of its aspects but not its totality. It is one of its aspects because there is, in all human consciousness, at least a dim recognition of the insufficient and dependent character of all finite life, a recognition which implies the consciousness of the reality upon which dependent existence depends. An equally important characteristic of the experience of God is the sense of being seen, commanded, judged and known from beyond ourselves. This experience is described by the Psalmist in the words: "O Lord, thou hast searched me, and known me. Thou

---

10 Professor John Baillie writes very truly: "No matter how far back I go, no matter by what effort of memory I attempt to reach the virgin soil of childish innocence, I cannot get back to an atheistic mentality. As little can I reach a day when I was conscious of myself but not of God as I can reach a day when I was conscious of myself but not of other human beings."—*Our Knowledge of God*, p. 4.

knowest my downsitting and mine uprising . . . and are acquainted with all my ways" (Ps. 139). The Psalmist exults in this relation between God and man and rightly discerns that the greatness and uniqueness of man is as necessary as the greatness of God for such a relationship: "I am fearfully and wonderfully made: marvellous are thy works; and that my soul knoweth right well." If any one should maintain that this sense of the impingement of God upon human life is a delusion by which man glorifies himself, one might call attention to the fact that in the book of Job exactly the same experience is described by one who is not grateful for it but protests against it. The constant demands and judgments of God seem to him to place life under an intolerable strain: "What is man, that thou shouldest magnify him? and that thou shouldest set thine heart upon him? and that thou shouldest visit him every morning, and try him every moment?" He feels that the divine demands are too exacting for human weakness: "let me alone; for my days are vanity," and he looks forward to the day when death will make the visitations of God impossible: "for now shall I sleep in the dust; and thou shalt seek me in the morning, but I shall not be" (Job 7:16-21). This impious protest against the ever-present accusing God is perhaps a more perfect validation of the reality of the experience than any pious words of gratitude for it.

The experience so described is in some sense identical or associated with what is usually called "conscience." The actual nature of conscience is, of course, variously defined in various philosophies. It may be regarded as the social obligations and judgments which all men must face. Or it may be defined as the obligation and judgment under which the rational or intelligible self places the empirical, the sensible or the partial self. The significance of the Biblical interpretation of conscience lies precisely in this, that a universal human experience, the sense of being commanded, placed under obligation and judged is interpreted as a relation between God and man in which it is God who makes demands and judgments upon man. Such an interpretation of a common experience is not possible without the presuppositions of the Biblical faith. But once accepted the assumption proves to be the only basis of a correct analysis of all the factors involved in the experience; for it is a fact that man is judged and yet there is no vantage point in his own life, sufficiently transcendent, from which the judgment can take place. St. Paul describes the three levels of judgment under which men stand, and the relativity of all but the last level in the words: "But to me it is a very small thing that I should be judged of you, or of man's judgment: yea, I judge not mine own self. For I know nothing by myself; yet am I not hereby justified: but he that judgeth me is the Lord" (I Cor. 4:3-4).

It might be argued that the content of a personal experience which can be defined only through the aid of a more historical revelation of the nature of the divine, which enters this experience, while this historical revelation can gain credence only if the personal experience is presupposed, is so involved in a logical circle as to become incredible. But the fact is that all human knowledge is also so involved. All common human experience requires more than the immediate experience to define the character of the object of experience. The reality of the object of experience is not in question, but the exact nature of the reality touched is not clear until it is defined by insights which transcend the immediate perception of the object. If the reality touched is something more than a mere "object" but is itself subject, that is, if its character cannot be fully revealed to us, except as it takes the initiative, the principle of interpretation must be something more than merely the general principles of knowledge which illumine a particular experience. The principle of interpretation must be a "revelation."

Our approach to other human personalities offers an illuminating analogy of the necessity and character of "revelation" in our relation to God. We have various evidence that, when dealing with persons, we are confronting a reality of greater depth than the mere organism of animal life. We have evidence that we are dealing with a "Thou" of such freedom and uniqueness that a mere external observation of its behaviour will not only leave the final essence of that person obscure but will actually falsify it, since such observation would debase what is really free subject into a mere object. This person, this other "Thou" cannot be understood until he speaks to us; until his behaviour is clarified by the "word" which comes out of the ultimate and transcendent unity of his spirit. Only such a word can give us the key by which we understand the complexities of his behaviour. This word spoken from beyond us and to us is both a verification of our belief that we are dealing with a different dimension than animal existence; and also a revelation of the actual and precise character of the person with whom we are dealing.

In the same way, the God whom we meet as "The Other" at the final limit of our own consciousness, is not fully known to us except as specific revelations of His character augment this general experience of being confronted from beyond ourselves.

In Biblical faith these specific revelations are apprehended in the context of a particular history of salvation in which specific historical events become special revelations of the character of God and of His purposes. Without the principle of interpretation furnished by this "special revelation" the general experience or the general revelation involved in conscience becomes falsified, because it is explained merely as man facing the court of social approval or disapproval or as facing his own "best self." In that case, whatever the provisional verdict, the final verdict always is, "I know nothing against myself" and the conclusion drawn from this verdict must be and is, "I am thereby justified." But this conclusion is at variance with the actual facts of the human situation, for there is no level of moral achievement upon which man can have or actually has an easy conscience.

The fact that a culture which identifies God with some level of human consciousness, either rational or super-rational, or with some order of nature, invariably falsifies the human situation and fails to appreciate either the total stature of freedom in man or the complexity of the problem of evil in him, is the most telling negative proof for the Biblical faith. Man does not know himself truly except as he knows himself confronted by God. Only in that confrontation does he become aware of his full stature and freedom and of the evil in him. It is for this reason that Biblical faith is of such importance for the proper understanding of man, and why it is necessary to correct the interpretations of human nature which underestimate his stature, depreciate his physical existence and fail to deal realistically with the evil in human nature, in terms of Biblical faith.

10. Is There Such a Thing as a Teleological Suspension of the Ethical? *

SÖREN KIERKEGAARD *(1813–1855)*

The ethical as such is the universal, it applies to everyone, and the same thing is expressed from another point of view by saying that it applies every instant. It reposes immanently in itself, it has nothing outside itself which is its *telos*,[1] but is itself *telos* for everything outside it, and when this has been incorporated by the ethical it can go no further. Conceived immediately as physical and psychical, the particular individual is the particular which has its *telos* in the universal, and its task is to express itself constantly in it, to abolish its particularity in order to become the universal. As soon as the individual would assert himself in his particularity over against the universal he sins, and only by recognizing this can he again reconcile himself with the universal. Whenever the individual after he has entered the universal feels an impulse to assert himself as the particular, he is in temptation (*Anfechtung*), and he can labor himself out of this only by abandoning himself as the particular in the universal. If this be the highest thing that can be said of man and of his existence, then the ethical has the same character as man's eternal blessedness, which to all eternity and at every instant is his *telos*, since it would be a contradiction to say that this might be abandoned (i.e. teleologically suspended), inasmuch as this is no sooner suspended than it is forfeited. . . .

If this be the case, then Hegel is right when, in dealing with the Good and the Conscience, he characterizes man merely as the particular and regards this character as "a moral form of the evil" which is to be annulled in teleology of the moral, so that the individual who remains in this stage is either sinning or subjected to temptation (*Anfechtung*). On the other hand, he is wrong in talking of faith, wrong in not protesting loudly and clearly against the fact that Abraham enjoys honor and glory as the father of faith, whereas he ought to be prosecuted and convicted of murder.

---

* Reprinted by permission of the Princeton University Press from *Fear and Trembling* by Sören Kierkegaard.
[1] End or fulfillment.

For faith is this paradox, that the particular is higher than the universal — yet in such a way, be it observed, that the movement repeats itself, and that consequently the individual, after having been in the universal, now as the particular isolates himself as higher than the universal. If this be not faith, then Abraham is lost, then faith has never existed in the world — because it has always existed. For if the ethical (i.e. the moral) is the highest thing, and if nothing incommensurable remains in man in any other way but as the evil (i.e. the particular which has to be expressed in the universal), then one needs no other categories than those which the Greeks possessed or which by consistent thinking can be derived from them. This fact Hegel ought not to have concealed, for after all he was acquainted with Greek thought. . . .

Faith is precisely this paradox, that the individual as the particular is higher than the universal, is justified over against it, is not subordinate but superior — yet in such a way, be it observed, that it is the particular individual who, after he has been subordinated as the particular to the universal, now through the universal becomes the individual who as the particular is superior to the universal, *inasmuch as the individual as the particular stands in an absolute relation to the absolute.* This position cannot be mediated, for all mediation comes about precisely by virtue of the universal; it is and remains to all eternity a paradox, inaccessible to thought. And yet faith is this paradox. . . .

That for the particular individual this paradox may easily be mistaken for a temptation (*Anfechtung*) is indeed true, but one ought not for this reason to conceal it. That the whole constitution of many persons may be such that this paradox repels them is indeed true, but one ought not for this reason to make faith something different in order to be able to possess it, but ought rather to admit that one does not possess it, whereas those who possess faith should take care to set up certain criteria so that one might distinguish the paradox from a temptation (*Anfechtung*).

Now the story of Abraham contains such a teleological suspension of the ethical . . . . Abraham's relation to Isaac, ethically speaking, is quite simply expressed by saying that a father shall love his son more dearly than himself. Yet within its own compass the ethical has various gradations. Let us see whether in this story there is to be found any higher expression for the ethical such as would ethically explain his conduct, ethically justify him in suspending the ethical obligation toward his son, without in this search going beyond the teleology of the ethical.

When an undertaking in which a whole nation is concerned is hindered,[2] when such an enterprise is brought to a standstill by the disfavor of heaven, when the angry deity sends a calm which mocks all efforts, when the seer performs his heavy task and proclaims that the deity demands a young maiden as a sacrifice — then will the father heroically make the sacrifice. He will magnanimously conceal his pain, even though he might wish that he were "the lowly man who dares to weep,"[3] not the king who must act royally. And though solitary pain forces its way into his breast and he has only three confidants among the people, yet soon the whole nation will be cognizant of his pain, but also cognizant of his exploit, that for the welfare of the whole he was willing to sacrifice her, his daughter, the lovely young maiden. "O charming bosom! O beautiful cheeks! O bright golden hair!" (v.687). And the daughter will affect him by her tears, and the father will turn his face away, but the hero will raise the knife. — When the report of this reaches the ancestral home, then will the beautiful maidens of Greece blush with enthusiasm, and if the daughter was betrothed, her true love will not be angry but be proud of sharing in the father's deed, because the maiden belonged to him more feelingly than to her father.

When the intrepid judge,[4] who saved Israel in the hour of need, in one breath binds himself and God by the same vow, then heroically the young maiden's jubilation, the beloved daughter's joy, he will turn to sorrow, and with her all Israel will lament her maiden youth; but every free-born man will understand, and every stouthearted woman will admire Jeptha, and every maiden in Israel will wish to act as did his daughter. For what good would it do if Jephtha were victorious by reason of his vow, if he did not keep it? Would not the victory again be taken from the nation?

When a son is forgetful of his duty,[5] when the state entrusts the

---

[2] The Trojan War. When the Greek fleet was unable to set sail from Aulis because of an adverse wind, the seer Calchas announced that King Agamemnon had offended Artemis and that the goddess demanded his daughter, Iphigenia, as a sacrifice of expiation. [Translator's footnote.]

[3] Euripides, *Iphigenia in Aulis*, v. 448. [Translator's footnote.]

[4] Jephtha. Judges 11:30-40.

[5] The son of Brutus, while his father was consul, took part in a conspiracy to restore the king Rome had expelled, and Brutus ordered him to be put to death. [Translator's footnote.]

father with the sword of justice, when the laws require punishment
at the hand of the father, then will the father heroically forget that
the guilty one is his son, he will magnanimously conceal his pain,
but there will not be a single one among the people, not even the son,
who will not admire the father, and whenever the law of Rome is
interpreted, it will be remembered that many interpreted it more
learnedly, but none so gloriously as Brutus.

If, on the other hand, while a favorable wind bore the fleet on
with swelling sails to its goal, Agamemnon had sent that messenger
who fetched Iphigenia in order to be sacrificed; if Jephtha, without
being bound by any vow which decided the fate of the nation, had
said to his daughter, "Bewail now thy virginity for the space of
two months, for I will sacrifice thee"; if Brutus had had a righteous
son and yet would have ordered the lictors to execute him — who
would have understood them? If these three men had replied to the
query why they did it by saying, "It is a trial in which we are
tested," would people have understood them better? . . .

The difference between the tragic hero and Abraham is clearly
evident. The tragic hero still remains within the ethical. He lets
one expression of the ethical find its *telos* in a higher expression of
the ethical; the ethical relation between father and son, or daughter
and father, he reduces to a sentiment which has its dialectic in the
idea of morality. Here there can be no question of a teleological
suspension of the ethical.

With Abraham the situation was different. By his act he over-
stepped the ethical entirely and possessed a higher *telos* outside of
it, in relation to which he suspended the former. For I should very
much like to know how one would bring Abraham's act into relation
with the universal, and whether it is possible to discover any connection whatever between what Abraham did and the universal — except
the fact that he transgressed it. It was not for the sake of saving a
people, not to maintain the idea of the state, that Abraham did this,
and not in order to reconcile angry deities. If there could be a
question of the deity being angry, he was angry only with Abraham,
and Abraham's whole action stands in no relation to the universal;
it is a purely personal undertaking. Therefore, whereas the tragic
hero is great by reason of his moral virtue, Abraham is great by
reason of a personal virtue. In Abraham's life there is no higher
expression for the ethical than this, that the father shall love his son.
Of the ethical in the sense of morality there can be no question in

this instance. Insofar as the universal was present, it was indeed cryptically present in Isaac, hidden as it were in Isaac's loins, and must therefore cry out with Isaac's mouth, "Do it not! Thou art bringing everything to naught."

Why then did Abraham do it? For God's sake, and (in complete identity with this) for his own sake. He did it for God's sake because God required this proof of his faith; for his own sake he did it in order that he might furnish the proof. The unity of these two points of view is perfectly expressed by the word which has always been used to characterize this situation: it is a trial, a temptation (*Fristelse*). A temptation — but what does that mean? What ordinarily tempts a man is that which would keep him from doing his duty, but in this case the temptation is itself the ethical — which would keep him from doing God's will.

Here is evident the necessity of a new category if one would understand Abraham. Such a relationship to the deity paganism did not know. The tragic hero does not enter into any private relationship with the deity, but for him the ethical is the divine, hence the paradox implied in his situation can be mediated in the universal.

Abraham cannot be mediated, and the same thing can be expressed also by saying that he cannot talk. As soon as I talk I express the universal, and if I do not do so, no one can understand me. Therefore if Abraham would express himself in terms of the universal, he must say that his situation is a temptation (*Anfechtung*), for he has no higher expression for that universal which stands above the universal which he transgresses.

Therefore, though Abraham arouses my admiration, he at the same time appalls me. He who denies himself and sacrifices himself for duty gives up the finite in order to grasp the infinite, and that man is secure enough. The tragic hero gives up the certain for the still more certain, and the eye of the beholder rests upon him confidently. But he who gives up the universal in order to grasp something still higher which is not the universal — what is he doing? Is it possible that this can be anything else but a temptation (*Anfechtung*)? And if it be possible, but the individual was mistaken — what can save him? He suffers all the pain of the tragic hero, he brings to naught his joy in the world, he renounces everything — and perhaps at the same instant debars himself from the sublime joy which to him was so precious that he would purchase it at any price. Him the beholder cannot understand nor let his eye rest confidently upon him. . . .

The story of Abraham contains therefore a teleological suspension of the ethical. As the individual he became higher than the universal: this is the paradox which does not permit of mediation. It is just as inexplicable how he got into it as it is inexplicable how he remained in it. If such is not the position of Abraham, then he is not even a tragic hero but a murderer. To want to continue to call him the father of faith, to talk of this to people who do not concern themselves with anything but words, is thoughtless. A man can become a tragic hero by his own powers — but not a knight of faith. When a man enters upon the way, in a certain sense the hard way of the tragic hero, many will be able to give him counsel; to him who follows the narrow way of faith no one can give counsel, him no one can understand. Faith is a miracle, and yet no man is excluded from it; for that in which all human life is unified is passion, and faith is a passion.

What It Is to Become a Christian *

Objectively, becoming or being a Christian is defined as follows:

1. A Christian is one who accepts the doctrine of Christianity; but if it is the *what* of this doctrine which in the last resort decides whether one is a Christian, attention is instantly turned outward, with the intent of learning down to the last detail what then the doctrine of Christianity is, because this 'what' is to decide, not merely what Christianity is, but whether I am a Christian. That same instant begins the erudite, the anxious, the timorous contradictory effort of approximation. Approximation may be protracted indefinitely, and with that the decision whereby one becomes a Christian is relegated to oblivion.

This incongruity has been remedied by the assumption that

---

* Reprinted from the *Concluding Unscientific Postscript* by Sören Kierkegaard by permission from The American-Scandinavian Foundation and the Princeton University Press.

everyone in Christendom is a Christian, that we are all of us what one in a way calls Christians. With this assumption things go better with the objective theories. We are all Christians. The Bible-theory has now to investigate quite objectively what Christianity is (and yet we are in fact Christians and the objective information is assumed to make us Christians, the objective information which we who are Christians shall now for the first time learn to know — for if we are not Christians, the road here taken will never lead us to become such). The Church theory assumes that we are Christians, but now we have to be assured in a purely objective way what Christianity is, in order that we may defend ourselvɩs against the Turk and the Russian and the Roman yoke, and gallantly fight out the battle of Christianity so that we may make our age, as it were, a bridge to the peerless future which already is glimpsed. This is sheer aesthetics. Christianity is an existence-communication, the task is to become a Christian and continue to be one, and the most dangerous of all illusions is to be so sure of being one that one has to defend the whole of Christendom against the Turk — instead of being alert to defend our own faith against the illusion about the Turk.

2. One says, No, not every acceptance of the Christian doctrine makes one a Christian; what it principally depends upon is appro-priation, that one appropriates and holds fast this doctrine quite differently from anything else, that one is ready to live in it and to die in it, to venture one's life for it, etc.

This seems as if it were something. However, the category "quite differently" is a mediocre category, and the whole formula, which makes an attempt to define more subjectively what it is to be a Christian, is neither one thing nor the other; in a way it avoids the difficulty involved in the distraction and deceit of approximation, but it lacks categorical definition. The pathos of approximation which is talked of here is that of immanence; one can just as well say that an enthusiastic lover is so related to his love: he holds fast to it and appropriates it quite differently from anything else, he is ready to live in it and die in it, he will venture everything for it. To this extent there is no difference between a lover and a Christian with respect to inwardness, and one must again recur to the *what*, which is the doctrine — and with that we again come under No. 1.

The pathos of appropriation needs to be so defined that it cannot be confused with any other pathos. The more subjective interpretation is right in insisting that it is appropriation which decides the matter, but it is wrong in its definition of appropriation, which does not distinguish it from every other immediate pathos.

Neither is this distinction made when one defines appropriation as faith, but at once imparts to faith headway and direction toward reaching an understanding, so that faith becomes a provisional function whereby one holds what essentially is to be an object for understanding, a provisional function wherewith poor people and stupid men have to be content, whereas *Privatdocents* and clever heads go further. The mark of being a Christian (i.e. faith) is appropriated, but in such a way that it is not specifically different from other intellectual appropriation where a preliminary assumption serves as a provisional function looking forward to understanding. Faith is not in this case the specific mark of the relationship to Christianity, and again it will be the *what* of faith which decides whether one is a Christian or not. But therewith the thing is again brought back under No. 1.

That is to say, the appropriation by which a Christian is a Christian must be so specific that it cannot be confused with anything else.

3. One defines the thing of becoming and being a Christian, not objectively by the *what* of the doctrine, nor subjectively by appropriation, not by what has gone on in the individual, but by what the individual has undergone: that he was baptized. Though one adjoins to baptism the assumption of a confession of faith, nothing decisive will be gained, but the definition will waver between accentuating the *what* (the path of approximation) and talking indefinitely about acceptance and appropriation, etc., without any specific determination.

If being baptized is to be the definition, attention will instantly turn outward toward the reflection, whether I have really been baptized. Then begins the approximation with respect to a historical fact.

If, on the other hand, one were to say that he did indeed receive the Spirit in baptism and by the witness it bears together with his spirit, he knows that he was baptized — then the inference is inverted, he argues from the witness of the Spirit within him to the fact that he was baptized, not from the fact of being baptized to the possession of the Spirit. But if the inference is to be drawn in this way, baptism is quite rightly not regarded as the mark of the Christian, but inwardness is, and so here in turn there is needed a specific definition of inwardness and appropriation whereby the witness of the Spirit in the individual is distinguished from all other (universally defined) activity of spirit in man.

It is noteworthy moreover that the orthodoxy which especially has made baptism the decisive mark is continually complaining that among the baptized there are so few Christians, that almost all, except for an immortal little band, are spiritless baptized pagans — which seems to indicate that baptism cannot be the decisive factor with respect to becoming a Christian, not even according to the latter view of those who in the first form insist upon it as decisive with respect to becoming a Christian.

Subjectively, what it is to become a Christian is defined thus:

The decision lies in the subject. The appropriation is the paradoxical inwardness which is specifically different from all other inwardness. The thing of being a Christian is not determined by the *what* of Christianity but by the *how* of the Christian. This *how* can only correspond with one thing, the absolute paradox. There is therefore no vague talk to the effect that being a Christian is to accept, and to accept quite differently, to appropriate by faith quite differently (all of them purely rhetorical and fictitious definitions); but *to believe* is specifically different from all other appropriation and inwardness. *Faith is the objective uncertainty along with the repulsion of the absurd held fast in the passion of inwardness, which precisely is inwardness potentiated to the highest degree.* This formula fits only the believer, no one else, not a lover, not an enthusiast, not a thinker, but simply and solely the believer who is related to the absolute paradox.

Faith therefore cannot be any sort of provisional function. He who, from the vantage point of a higher knowledge, would know his faith as a factor resolved in a higher idea has *eo ipso* ceased to believe. Faith *must* not *rest content* with unintelligibility; for precisely the relation to or the repulsion from the unintelligible, the absurd, is the expression for the passion of faith.

This definition of what it is to be a Christian prevents the erudite or anxious deliberation of approximation from enticing the individual into byways, so that be becomes erudite instead of becoming a Christian, and in most cases a smatterer instead of becoming a Christian; for the decision lies in the subject. But inwardness has again found its specific mark whereby it is differentiated from all other inwardness and is not disposed of by the chatty category "quite differently," which fits the case of every passion at the moment of passion.

The psychologist generally regards it as a sure sign that a man is beginning to give up a passion when he wishes to treat the object of it objectively. Passion and reflection are generally exclusive of one another. Becoming objective in this way is always retrogression, for passion is man's perdition, but it is his exaltation as well. In case dialectic and reflection are not used to intensify passion, it is a retrogression to become objective; and even he who is lost through passion has not lost so much as he who lost passion, for the former had the possibility. Thus it is that people in our age have wanted to become objective with relation to Christianity; the passion by which every man is a Christian has become too small a thing for them, and by becoming objective we all of us have the prospect of becoming a *Privatdocent*. . . .

Because people in our age and in the Christendom of our time do not appear to be sufficiently aware of the dialectic of inward appropriation, or of the fact that the "how" of the individual is an expression just as precise and more decisive for what he has than is the "what" to which he appeals — for this very reason there crop up the strangest and (if one is in the humor and has time for it) the most laughable confusions, more comic than even the confusions of paganism, because in them there was not so much at stake, and because the contradictions were not so strident.

An orthodox champion fights in defense of Christianity with the most frightful passion, he protests with the sweat of his brow and with the most concerned demeanor that he accepts Christianity pure and simple, that he will live and die in it — and he forgets that such acceptance is an all too general expression for the relation to Christianity. He does everything in Jesus' name and uses Christ's name on every occasion as a sure sign that he is a Christian and is called to fight in defense of Christendom in our age — and he has no inkling of the little ironical secret that a man, merely by describing the "how" of his inwardness, can show indirectly that he is a Christian without mentioning God's name.[1] A man becomes converted New Year's Eve precisely at six o'clock. With that he is fully prepared. Fantastically decked out wtih the fact of conversion, he now must run out and proclaim Christianity — in a Christian land. Well, of course, even though we are all baptized, every man may well need to become a Christian in another sense. But here is the distinction: there is no lack of information in a Christian land, something else is lacking, and this is a something which the one man cannot directly communicate to the other. And in such fantastic categories would a converted man work for Christianity; and yet he proves (just in proportion as he is the more busy in spreading and spreading) that he himself is not a Christian. For to be a Christian is something so deeply reflected that it does not admit of the aesthetical dialectic which allows one man to be for others something he is not for himself. On the other hand, a scoffer attacks Christianity and at the same time expounds it so reliably that it is a pleasure to read him, and one who is in perplexity about finding it distinctly set forth may almost have recourse to him.

All ironical observations depend upon paying attention to the "how," whereas the gentleman with whom the ironist has the honor to converse is attentive only to the "what." A man protests loudly and solemnly, "This is my opinion." However, he does not confine himself to delivering this formula verbatim, he explains himself further, he ventures to vary the expressions. Yes, for it is not so easy to vary as one thinks it is. More than one student would have got *laudabilis* for style if he had not varied his expressions, and a great multitude of men possess the talent which Socrates so much admired

---

[1] In relation to love (by which I would illustrate again the same thing) it does not hold good in the same sense that a man merely by defining his "how" indicates what or whom it is he loves. All lovers have the "how" of love in common, the particular person must supply the name of his beloved. But with respect to believing (*sensu strictissimo*) it holds good that this "how" is appropriate only to one as its object. If anybody would say, "Yes, but then one can also learn the 'how' of faith by rote and patter"; to this one must reply that it cannot be done, for he who declares it directly contradicts himself, because the content of the assertion must constantly be reduplicated in the form of expression, and the isolation contained in the definition must reduplicate itself in the form. [Author's footnote.]

in Polos: they never say the same thing — about the same. The ironist then is on the watch, he of course is not looking out for what is printed in large letters or for that which by the speaker's diction betrays itself as a formula (our gentleman's "what"), but he is looking out for a little subordinate clause which escapes the gentleman's haughty attention, a little beckoning predicate, etc., and now he beholds with astonishment (glad of the variation — *in variatione voluptas*) that the gentleman *has not* that opinion — not that he is a hypocrite, God forbid! that is too serious a matter for an ironist — but that the good man has concentrated his force in bawling it out instead of possessing it within him. To that extent the gentleman may be right in asserting that he has that opinion which with all his vital force he persuades himself he has, he may do everything for it in the quality of talebearer, he may risk his life for it, in very much troubled times he may carry the thing so far as to lose his life for this opinion — with that, how the deuce can I doubt that the man had this opinion; and yet there may have been living contemporaneously with him an ironist who, even in the hour when the unfortunate gentleman is executed, cannot resist laughing, because he knows by the circumstantial evidence he has gathered that the man had never been clear about the thing himself. Laughable it is, nor is it disheartening that such a thing can occur; for he who with quiet introspection is honest before God and concerned for himself, the Deity saves from being in error, though he be never so simple; him the Deity leads by the suffering of inwardness to the truth. But meddlesomeness and noise are signs of error, signs of an abnormal condition, like wind in the stomach, and this thing of stumbling by chance upon getting executed in a tumultuous turn of affairs is not the sort of suffering which essentially characterizes inwardness.

It is said to have chanced in England that a man was attacked on the highway by a robber who had made himself unrecognizable by wearing a big wig. He falls upon the traveler, seizes him by the throat and shouts, "Your purse!" He gets the purse and keeps it, but the wig he throws away. A poor man comes along the same road, puts it on and arrives at the next town where the traveler had already denounced the crime, he is arrested, is recognized by the traveler, who takes his oath that he is the man. By chance, the robber is present in the court-room, sees the misunderstanding, turns to the judge and says, "It seems to me that the traveler has regard rather to the wig than to the man," and he asks permission to make a trial. He puts on the wig, seizes the traveler by the throat, crying, "Your purse!" — and the traveler recognizes the robber and offers to swear to it — the only trouble is that already he has taken an oath.

So it is, in one way or another, with every man who has a "what" and is not attentive to the "how": he swears, he takes his oath, he runs errands, he ventures life and blood, he is executed — all on account of the wig.

11. What Is Humanistic Religion? *

ERICH FROMM (1900–   )

It would far transcend the scope of this chapter to attempt a review of all types of religion. Even to discuss only those types which are relevant from the psychological standpoint cannot be undertaken here. I shall therefore deal with only one distinction, but one which in my opinion is the most important, and which cuts across nontheistic and theistic religions: that between *authoritarian* and *humanistic* religions.

What is the principle of authoritarian religion? The definition of religion given in the *Oxford Dictionary*, while attempting to define religion as such, is a rather accurate definition of authoritarian religion. It reads: "[Religion is] recognition on the part of man of some higher unseen power as having control of his destiny, and as being entitled to obedience, reverence, and worship."

Here the emphasis is on the recognition that man is controlled by a higher power outside of himself. But this alone does not constitute authoritarian religion. What makes it so is the idea that this power, because of the control it exercises, is *entitled* to "obe-

---

* From *Psychoanalysis and Religion,* by Erich Fromm, Yale University Press, 1950. Reprinted by permission of the publisher.

dience, reverence and worship." I italicize the word "entitled" because it shows that the reason for worship, obedience, and reverence lies not in the moral qualities of the deity, not in love or justice, but in the fact that it has control, that is, has power over man. Furthermore it shows that the higher power has a right to force man to worship him and that lack of reverence and obedience constitutes sin.

The essential element in authoritarian religion and in the authoritarian religious experience is the surrender to a power transcending man. The main virtue of this type of religion is obedience, its cardinal sin is disobedience. Just as the deity is conceived as omnipotent or omniscient, man is conceived as being powerless and insignificant. Only as he can gain grace or help from the deity by complete surrender can he feel strength. Submission to a powerful authority is one of the avenues by which man escapes from his feeling of aloneness and limitation. In the act of surrender he loses his independence and integrity as an individual but he gains the feeling of being protected by an awe-inspiring power of which, as it were, he becomes a part.

In Calvin's theology we find a vivid picture of authoritarian, theistic thinking. "For I do not call it humility," says Calvin, "if you suppose that we have anything left. . . . We cannot think of ourselves as we ought to think without utterly despising everything that may be supposed an excellence in us. This humility is unfeigned submission of a mind overwhelmed with a weighty sense of its own misery and poverty; for such is the uniform description of it in the word of God." [1]

The experience which Calvin describes here, that of despising everything in oneself, of the submission of the mind overwhelmed by its own poverty, is the very essence of all authoritarian religions whether they are couched in secular or in theological language.[2] In authoritarian religion God is a symbol of power and force, He is supreme because He has supreme power, and man in juxtaposition is utterly powerless.

Authoritarian secular religion follows the same principle. Here

---

[1] Johannes Calvin, *Institutes of the Christian Religion* (Presbyterian Board of Christian Education, 1928), p. 681.

[2] See Erich Fromm, *Escape from Freedom* (Farrar & Rinehart, 1941), pp. 141 ff. This attitude toward authority is described there in detail.

the Führer or the beloved "Father of His People" or the State or the Race or the Socialist Fatherland becomes the object of worship; the life of the individual becomes insignificant and man's worth consists in the very denial of his worth and strength. Frequently authoritarian religion postulates an ideal which is so abstract and so distant that it has hardly any connection with the real life of real people. To such ideals as "life after death" or "the future of mankind" the life and happiness of persons living here and now may be sacrificed; the alleged ends justify every means and become symbols in the names of which religious or secular "elites" control the lives of their fellow men.

Humanistic religion, on the contrary, is centered around man and his strength. Man must develop his power of reason in order to understand himself, his relationship to his fellow men and his position in the universe. He must recognize the truth, both with regard to his limitations and his potentialities. He must develop his powers of love for others as well as for himself and experience the solidarity of all living beings. He must have principles and norms to guide him in this aim. Religious experience in this kind of religion is the experience of oneness with the All, based on one's relatedness to the world as it is grasped with thought and with love. Man's aim in humanistic religion is to achieve the greatest strength, not the greatest powerlessness; virtue is self-realization, not obedience. Faith is certainty of conviction based on one's experience of thought and feeling, not assent to propositions on credit of the proposer. The prevailing mood is that of joy, while the prevailing mood in authoritarian religion is that of sorrow and of guilt.

Inasmuch as humanistic religions are theistic, God is a symbol of *man's own powers* which he tries to realize in his life, and is not a symbol of force and domination, having *power over man*.

Illustrations of humanistic religions are early Buddhism, Taoism, the teachings of Isaiah, Jesus, Socrates, Spinoza, certain trends in the Jewish and Christian religions (particularly mysticism), the religion of Reason of the French Revolution. It is evident from these that the distinction between authoritarian and humanistic religion cuts across the distinction between theistic and nontheistic, and between religions in the narrow sense of the word and philosophical systems of religious character. What matters in all such systems is not the thought system as such but the human attitude underlying their doctrines.

One of the best examples of humanistic religions is early Buddhism. The Buddha is a great teacher, he is the "awakened one" who recognizes the truth about human existence. He does not speak in the name of a supernatural power but in the name of reason. He calls upon every man to make use of his own reason and to see the truth which he was only the first to find. Once man takes the first step in seeing the truth, he must apply his efforts to live in such a way that he develops his powers of reason and of love for all human creatures. Only to the degree to which he succeeds in this can he free himself from the bondage of irrational passions. While man must recognize his limitations according to Buddhistic teaching, he must also become aware of the powers in himself. The concept of Nirvana as the state of mind the fully awakened one can achieve is not one of man's helplessness and submission but on the contrary one of the development of the highest powers man possesses. . . .

Zen-Buddhism, a later sect within Buddhism, is expressive of an even more radical anti-authoritarian attitude. Zen proposes that no knowledge is of any value unless it grows out of ourselves; no authority, no teacher can really teach us anything except to arouse doubts in us; words and thought systems are dangerous because they easily turn into authorities whom we worship. Life itself must be grasped and experienced as it flows, and in this lies virtue. . . .

Another illustration of a humanistic religious system is to be found in Spinoza's religious thinking. While his language is that of medieval theology, his concept of God has no trace of authoritarianism. God could not have created the world different from what it is. He cannot change anything; in fact, God is identical with the totality of the universe. Man must see his own limitations and recognize that he is dependent on the totality of forces outside himself over which he has no control. Yet his are the powers of love and of reason. He can develop them and attain an optimum of freedom and of inner strength.

The distinction between authoritarian and humanistic religion not only cuts across various religions, it can exist within the same religion. Our own religious tradition is one of the best illustrations of this point. Since it is of fundamental importance to understand fully the distinction between authoritarian and humanistic religion, I shall illustrate it further from a source with which every reader is more or less familiar, the Old Testament.

The beginning of the Old Testament [3] is written in the spirit of authoritarian religion. The picture of God is that of the absolute ruler of a patriarchal clan, who has created man at his pleasure and can destroy him at will. He has forbidden him to eat from the tree of knowledge of good and evil and has threatened him with death if he transgresses this order. But the serpent, "more clever than any animal," tells Eve, "Ye shall not surely die: For God doth know that in the day ye eat thereof, then your eyes shall be opened, and ye shall be as gods, knowing good and evil." [4] God proves the serpent to be right. When Adam and Eve have transgressed he punishes them by proclaiming enmity between man and nature, between man and the soil and animals, and between men and women. But man is not to die. However, "the man has become as one of us, to know good and evil: and now, lest he put forth his hand, and take also of the tree of life, and eat, and live for ever," [5] God expels Adam and Eve from the garden of Eden and puts an angel with a flaming sword at the east "to keep the way of the tree of life."

The text makes very clear what man's sin is: it is rebellion against God's command; it is disobedience and not any inherent sinfulness in the act of eating from the tree of knowledge. On the contrary, further religious development has made the knowledge of good and evil the cardinal virtue to which man may aspire. The text also makes it plain what God's motive is: it is concern with his own superior role, the jealous fear of man's claim to become his equal.

A decisive turning point in the relationship between God and man is to be seen in the story of the Flood. When God saw "that the wickedness of man was great on the earth . . . it repented the Lord that he had made man and the earth, and it grieved him at his heart. And the Lord said, I will destroy man whom I have created

---

[3] The historical fact that the beginning of the Bible may not be its oldest part does not need to be considered here since we use the text as an illustration of two principles and not to establish a historical sequence.

[4] Genesis 3: 4–5.

[5] *Ibid.* 3:22.

from the face of the earth; both man, and beast, and the creeping thing, and the fowls of the air; for it repenteth me that I have made them." [6]

There is no question here but that God has the right to destroy his own creatures; he has created them and they are his property. The text defines their wickedness as "violence," but the decision to destroy not only man but animals and plants as well shows that we are not dealing here with a sentence commensurate with some specific crime but with God's angry regret over his own action which did not turn out well. "But Noah found grace in the eyes of the Lord," and he, together with his family and a representative of each animal species, is saved from the Flood. Thus far the destruction of man and the salvation of Noah are arbitrary acts of God. He could do as he pleased, as can any powerful tribal chief. But after the Flood the relationship between God and man changes fundamentally. A covenant is concluded between God and man in which God promises that "neither shall all flesh be cut off any more by the waters of a flood; neither shall there any more be a flood to destroy the earth." [7] God obligates himself never to destroy all life on earth, and man is bound to the first and most fundamental command of the Bible, not to kill: "At the hand of every man's brother will I require the life of man." [8] From this point on the relationship between God and man undergoes a profound change. God is no longer an absolute ruler who can act at his pleasure but is bound by a constitution to which both he and man must adhere; he is bound by a principle which he cannot violate, the principle of respect for life. God can punish man if he violates this principle, but man can also challenge God if he is guilty of its violation.

The new relationship between God and man appears clearly in Abraham's plea for Sodom and Gomorrah. When God considers destroying the cities because of their wickedness, Abraham criticizes God for violating his own principles. "That be far from thee to do after this manner, to slay the righteous with the wicked: and that the righteous should be as the wicked, that be far from thee. Shall not the Judge of all the earth do right?" [9]

The difference between the story of the Fall and this argument

---

[6] *Ibid.* 6:5 ff.
[7] *Ibid.* 9:11.
[8] *Ibid.* 9:5.
[9] *Ibid.* 18:25.

is great indeed. There man is forbidden to know good and evil and his position toward God is that of submission — or sinful disobedience. Here man uses his knowledge of good and evil, criticizes God in the name of justice, and God has to yield.

Even this brief analysis of the authoritarian elements in the biblical story shows that at the root of the Judaeo-Christian religion both principles, the authoritarian and the humanistic, are present. In the development of Judaism as well as of Christianity both principles have been preserved and their respective preponderance marks different trends in the two religions.

The following story from the Talmud expresses the unauthoritarian, humanistic side of Judaism as we find it in the first centuries of the Christian era.

A number of other famous rabbinical scholars disagreed with Rabbi Eliezar's views in regard to a point of ritual law. "Rabbi Eliezar said to them: 'If the law is as I think it is then this tree shall let us know.' Whereupon the tree jumped from its place a hundred yards (others say four hundred yards). His colleagues said to him, 'One does not prove anything from a tree.' He said, 'If I am right then this brook shall let us know.' Whereupon the brook ran upstream. His colleagues said to him, 'One does not prove anything from a brook.' He continued and said, 'If the law is as I think then the walls of this house will tell.' Whereupon the walls began to fall. But Rabbi Joshua shouted at the walls and said, 'If scholars argue a point of law, what business have you to fall?' So the walls fell no further out of respect for Rabbi Joshua but out of respect for Rabbi Eliezar did not straighten up. And that is the way they still are. Rabbi Eliezar took up the argument again and said, 'If the law is as I think, they shall tell us from heaven.' Whereupon a voice from heaven said, 'What have you against Rabbi Eliezar, because the law is as he says.' Whereupon Rabbi Joshua got up and said, 'It is written in the Bible: The law is not in heaven. What does this mean? According to Rabbi Jirmijahu it means since the Torah has been given on Mount Sinai we no longer pay attention to voices from heaven because it is written: You make your decision according to the majority opinion.' It then happened that Rabbi Nathan [one of the participants in the discussion] met the Prophet Elijah [who had taken a stroll on earth] and he asked the Prophet, 'What did God himself say when we had this discussion?' The

Prophet answered, 'God smiled and said, My children have won, my children have won.' " [10]

This story is hardly in need of comment. It emphasizes the autonomy of man's reason with which even the supernatural voices from heaven cannot interfere. God smiles, man has done what God wanted him to do, he has become his own master, capable and resolved to make his decisions by himself according to rational, democratic methods. . . .

That early Christianity is humanistic and not authoritarian is evident from the spirit and text of all Jesus' teachings. Jesus' precept that "the kingdom of God is within you" is the simple and clear expression of nonauthoritarian thinking. But only a few hundred years later, after Christianity had ceased to be the religion of the poor and humble peasants, artisans, and slaves (the *Am haarez*) and had become the religion of those ruling the Roman Empire, the authoritarian trend in Christianity became dominant. Even so, the conflict between the authoritarian and humanistic principles in Christianity never ceased. It was the conflict between Augustine and Pelagius, between the Catholic Church and the many "heretic" groups and between various sects within Protestantism. The humanistic, democratic element was never subdued in Christian or in Jewish history, and this element found one of its most potent expressions in the mystic thinking within both religions. The mystics have been deeply imbued with the experience of man's strength, his likeness to God, and with the idea that God needs man as much as man needs God; they have understood the sentence that man is created in the image of God to mean the fundamental identity of God and man. Not fear and submission but love and the assertion of one's own powers are the basis of mystical experience. *God is not a symbol of power over man but of man's own powers.*

Thus far we have dealt with the distinctive features of authoritarian and humanistic religions mainly in descriptive terms. But the psychoanalyst must proceed from the description of attitudes to the analysis of their dynamics, and it is here that he can contribute to our discussion from an area not accessible to other fields of inquiry. The full understanding of an attitude requires an appreciation of those conscious and, in particular, unconscious processes

[10] Talmud, Baba Meziah, 59, b. (My translation.)

occurring in the individual which provide the necessity for and the conditions of its development.

While in humanistic religion God is the image of man's higher self, a symbol of what man potentially is or ought to become, in authoritarian religion God becomes the sole possessor of what was originally man's: of his reason and his love. The more perfect God becomes, the more imperfect becomes man. He *projects* the best he has onto God and thus impoverishes himself. Now God has all love, all wisdom, all justice — and man is deprived of these qualities, he is empty and poor. He had begun with the feeling of smallness, but he now has become completely powerless and without strength; all his powers have been projected onto God. This mechanism of projection is the very same which can be observed in interpersonal relationships of a masochistic, submissive character, where one person is awed by another and attributes his own powers and aspirations to the other person. It is the same mechanism that makes people endow the leaders of even the most inhuman systems with qualities of superwisdom and kindness.[11]

When man has thus projected his own most valuable powers unto God, what of his relationship to his own powers? They have become separated from him and in this process he has become *alienated* from himself. Everything he has is now God's and nothing is left in him. *His only access to himself is through God.* In worshiping God he tries to get in touch with that part of himself which he has lost through projection. After having given God all he has, he begs God to return to him some of what originally was his own. But having lost his own he is completely at God's mercy. He necessarily feels like a "sinner" since he has deprived himself of everything that is good, and it is only through God's mercy or grace that he can regain that which alone makes him human. And in order to persuade God to give him some of his love, he must prove to him how utterly deprived he is of love; in order to persuade God to guide him by his superior wisdom he must prove to him how deprived he is of wisdom when he is left to himself.

But this alienation from his own powers not only makes man feel slavishly dependent on God, it makes him bad too. He becomes a man without faith in his fellow men or in himself, without the ex-

---

[11] Cf. the discussion about symbiotic relationship in *Escape from Freedom,* pp. 158 ff.

perience of his own love, of his own power of reason. As a result the separation between the "holy" and the "secular" occurs. In his worldly activities man acts without love, in that sector of his life which is reserved to religion he feels himself to be a sinner (which he actually is, since to live without love is to live in sin) and tries to recover some of his lost humanity by being in touch with God. Simultaneously, he tries to win forgiveness by emphasizing his own helplessness and worthlessness. Thus the attempt to obtain forgiveness results in the activation of the very attitude from which his sins stem. He is caught in a painful dilemma. The more he praises God, the emptier he becomes. The emptier he becomes, the more sinful he feels. The more sinful he feels, the more he praises his God — and the less able is he to regain himself.

Analysis of religion must not stop at uncovering those psychological processes within man which underly his religious experience; it must proceed to discover the conditions which make for the development of the authoritarian and humanistic character structures, respectively, from which different kinds of religious experience stem. Such a sociopsychological analysis goes far beyond the context of these chapters. However, the principal point can be made briefly. What people think and feel is rooted in their character and their character is molded by the total configuration of their practice of life — more precisely, by the socioeconomic and political structure of their society. In societies ruled by a powerful minority which holds the masses in subjection, the individual will be so imbued with fear, so incapable of feeling strong or independent, that his religious experience will be authoritarian. Whether he worships a punishing, awesome God or a similarly conceived leader makes little difference. On the other hand, where the individual feels free and responsible for his own fate, or among minorities striving for freedom and independence, humanistic religious experience develops. The history of religion gives ample evidence of this correlation between social structure and kinds of religious experience. Early Christianity was a religion of the poor and downtrodden; the history of religious sects fighting against authoritarian political pressure shows the same principle again and again. Judaism, in which a strong anti-authoritarian tradition could grow up because secular authority never had much of a chance to govern and to build up a legend of its wisdom, therefore developed the humanistic aspect of religion to a remarkable degree. Whenever, on the other hand, religion allied itself with secular power, the religion had by necessity to become authoritarian. The real fall of man is his alienation from himself, his submission to power, his turning against himself even though under the guise of his worship of God.

From the spirit of authoritarian religion stem two fallacies of reasoning which have been used again and again as arguments for theistic religion. One argument runs as follows: How can you criticize the emphasis on dependence on a power transcending man; is not man dependent on forces outside himself which he cannot understand, much less control?

Indeed, man is dependent; he remains subject to death, age, illness, and even if he were to control nature and to make it wholly serviceable to him, he and his earth remain tiny specks in the universe. But it is one thing to recognize one's dependence and limitations, and it is something entirely different to indulge in this dependence, to worship the forces on which one depends. To understand realistically and soberly how limited our power is is an essential part of wisdom and of maturity; to worship it is masochistic and self-destructive. The one is humility, the other self-humiliation

We can study the difference between the realistic recognition of our limitations and the indulgence in the experience of submission and powerlessness in the clinical examination of masochistic character traits. We find people who have a tendency to incur sickness accidents, humiliating situations, who belittle and weaken themselves. They believe that they get into such situations against their will and intention, but a study of their unconscious motives shows that actually they are driven by one of the most irrational tendencies to be found in man, namely, by an unconscious desire to be weak and powerless; they tend to shift the center of their life to powers over which they feel no control, thus escaping from freedom and from personal responsibility. We find furthermore that this masochistic tendency is usually accompanied by its very opposite, the tendency to rule and to dominate others, and that the masochistic and the dominating tendencies form the two sides of the authoritarian character structure.[12] Such masochistic tendencies are not always unconscious. We find them overtly in the sexual masochistic perversion where the fulfillment of the wish to be hurt

---

[12] See *Escape from Freedom,* pp. 141 ff.

or humiliated is the condition for sexual excitement and satisfaction. We find it also in the relationship to the leader and the state in all authoritarian secular religions. Here the explicit aim is to give up one's own will and to experience submission under the leader or the state as profoundly rewarding.

Another fallacy of theological thinking is closely related to the one concerning dependence. I mean here the argument that there must be a power or being outside of man because we find that man has an ineradicable longing to relate himself to something beyond himself. Indeed, any sane human being has a need to relate himself to others; a person who has lost that capacity completely is insane. No wonder that man has created figures outside of himself to which he relates himself, which he loves and cherishes because they are not subject to the vacillations and inconsistencies of human objects. That God is a symbol of man's need to love is simple enough to understand. But does it follow from the existence and intensity of this human need that there exists an outer being who corresponds to this need? Obviously that follows as little as our strongest desire to love someone proves that there is a person with whom we are in love. All it proves is our need and perhaps our capacity.

The underlying theme of the preceding chapters is the conviction that the problem of religion is not the problem of God but the problem of man; religious formulations and religious symbols are attempts to give expression to certain kinds of human experience. What matters is the nature of these experiences. The symbol system is only the cue from which we can infer the underlying human reality. Unfortunately the discussion centered around religion since the days of the Enlightenment has been largely concerned with the affirmation or negation of a belief in God rather than with the affirmation or negation of certain human attitudes. "Do you believe in the existence of God?" has been made the crucial question of religionists and the denial of God has been the position chosen by those fighting the church. It is easy to see that many who profess the belief in God are in their human attitude idol worshipers or men without faith, while some of the most ardent "atheists," devoting their lives to the betterment of mankind, to deeds of brotherliness and love, have exhibited faith and a profoundly religious attitude. Centering the religious discussion on the acceptance or denial of the symbol God blocks the understanding of the religious problem as a human problem and prevents the development of that human attitude which can be called religious in a humanistic sense.

Many attempts have been made to retain the symbol God but to give it a meaning different from the one which it has in the monotheistic tradition. One of the outstanding illustrations is Spinoza's theology. Using strictly theological language he gives a definition of God which amounts to saying there is no God in the sense of the Judaeo-Christian tradition. He was still so close to the spiritual atmosphere in which the symbol God seemed indispensable that he was not aware of the fact that he was negating the existence of God in the terms of his new definition.

In the writings of a number of theologians and philosophers in the nineteenth century and at present one can detect similar attempts to retain the word God but to give it a meaning fundamentally different from that which it had for the Prophets of the Bible or for the Christian and Jewish theologians of the Middle Ages. There need be no quarrel with those who retain the symbol God although it is questionable whether it is not a forced attempt to retain a symbol whose significance is essentially historical. However this may be, one thing is certain. The real conflict is not between belief in God and "atheism" but between a humanistic, religious attitude and an attitude which is equivalent to idolatry regardless of how this attitude is expressed — or disguised — in conscious thought.

12. Is Religious Knowledge Possible? *

A. J. AYER (1910–)

This mention of God brings us to the question of the possibility of religious knowledge. We shall see that this possibility has already been ruled out by our treatment of metaphysics. But, as this is a point of considerable interest, we may be permitted to discuss it at some length.

---

* Reprinted by permission of the author and publisher from *Language, Truth and Logic* by A. J. Ayer, Victor Gollancz, Ltd., London, 1936. Recently reissued by Dover Publications, Inc., New York 19, N. Y.

It is now generally admitted, at any rate by philosophers, that
the existence of a being having the attributes which define the god
of any non-animistic religion cannot be demonstratively proved. To
see that this is so, we have only to ask ourselves what are the
premises from which the existence of such a god could be deduced.
If the conclusion that a god exists is to be demonstratively certain,
then these premises must be certain; for, as the conclusion of a
deductive argument is already contained in the premises, any uncertainty there may be about the truth of the premises is necessarily
shared by it. But we know that no empirical proposition can ever
be anything more than probable. It is only *a priori* propositions that
are logically certain. But we cannot deduce the existence of a god
from an *a priori* proposition. For we know that the reason why
a priori propositions are certain is that they are tautologies. And
from a set of tautologies nothing but a further tautology can be
validly deduced. It follows that there is no possibility of demonstrating the existence of a god.

What is not so generally recognised is that there can be no way
of proving that the existence of a god, such as the God of Christianity, is even probable. Yet this also is easily shown. For if the
existence of such a god were probable, then the proposition that he
existed would be an empirical hypothesis. And in that case it
would be possible to deduce from it, and other empirical hypotheses,
certain experimental propositions which were not deducible from
those other hypotheses alone. But in fact this is not possible. It is
sometimes claimed, indeed, that the existence of a certain sort of
regularity in nature constitutes sufficient evidence for the existence
of a god. But if the sentence "God exists" entails no more than
that certain types of phenomena occur in certain sequences, then
to assert the existence of a god will be simply equivalent to asserting
that there is the requisite regularity in nature; and no religious
man would admit that this was all he intended to assert in asserting
the existence of a god. He would say that in talking about God,
he was talking about a transcendent being who might be known
through certain empirical manifestations, but certainly could not be
defined in terms of those manifestations. But in that case the term
"god" is a metaphysical term. And if "god" is a metaphysical term,
then it cannot be even probable that a god exists. For to say that
"God exists" is to make a metaphysical utterance which cannot be
either true or false. And by the same criterion, no sentence which

purports to describe the nature of a transcendent god can possess any literal significance.

It is important not to confuse this view of religious assertions with the view that is adopted by atheists, or agnostics.[1] For it is characteristic of an agnostic to hold that the existence of a god is a possibility in which there is no good reason either to believe or disbelieve; and it is characteristic of an atheist to hold that it is at least probable that no god exists. And our view that all utterances about the nature of God are nonsensical, so far from being identical with, or even lending any support to, either of these familiar contentions, is actually incompatible with them. For if the assertion that there is a god is nonsensical, then the atheist's assertion that there is no god is equally nonsensical, since it is only a significant proposition that can be significantly contradicted. As for the agnostic, although he refrains from saying either that there is or that there is not a god, he does not deny that the question whether a transcendent god exists is a genuine question. He does not deny that the two sentences "There is a transcendent god" and "There is no transcendent god" express propositions one of which is actually true and the other false. All he says is that we have no means of telling which of them is true, and therefore ought not to commit ourselves to either. But we have seen that the sentences in question do not express propositions at all. And this means that agnosticism also is ruled out.

Thus we offer the theist the same comfort as we gave to the moralist. His assertions cannot possibly be valid, but they cannot be invalid either. As he says nothing at all about the world, he cannot justly be accused of saying anything for which he has insufficient grounds. It is only when the theist claims that in asserting the existence of a transcendent god he is expressing a genuine proposition that we are entitled to disagree with him.

It is to be remarked that in cases where deities are identified with natural objects, assertions concerning them may be allowed to be significant. If, for example, a man tells me that the occurrence of thunder is alone both necessary and sufficient to establish the truth of the proposition that Jehovah is angry, I may conclude that, in his usage of words, the sentence "Jehovah is angry" is equivalent to "It is thundering." But in sophisticated religions, though they

---

[1] This point was suggested to me by Professor H. H. Price.

may be to some extent based on men's awe of natural process which they cannot sufficiently understand, the "person" who is supposed to control the empirical world is not himself located in it; he is held to be superior to the empirical world, and so outside it; and he is endowed with super-empirical attributes. But the notion of a person whose essential attributes are non-empirical is not an intelligible notion at all. We may have a word which is used as if it named this "person," but, unless the sentences in which it occurs express propositions which are empirically verifiable, it cannot be said to symbolise anything. And this is the case with regard to the word "god," in the usage in which it is intended to refer to a transcendent object. The mere existence of the noun is enough to foster the illusion that there is a real, or at any rate a possible entity corresponding to it. It is only when we enquire what God's attributes are that we discover that "God," in this usage, is not a genuine name.

It is common to find belief in a transcendent god conjoined with belief in an after-life. But, in the form which it usually takes, the content of this belief is not a genuine hypothesis. To say that men do not ever die, or that the state of death is merely a state of prolonged insensibility, is indeed to express a significant proposition, though all the available evidence goes to show that it is false. But to say that there is something imperceptible inside a man, which is his soul or his real self, and that it goes on living after he is dead, is to make a metaphysical assertion which has no more factual content than the assertion that there is a transcendent god.

It is worth mentioning that, according to the account which we have given of religious assertions, there is no logical ground for antagonism between religion and natural science. As far as the question of truth or falsehood is concerned, there is no opposition between the natural scientists and the theist who believes in a transcendent god. For since the religious utterances of the theist are not genuine propositions at all, they cannot stand in any logical relation to the propositions of science. Such antagonism as there is between religion and science appears to consist in the fact that science takes away one of the motives which make men religious. For it is acknowledged that one of the ultimate sources of religious feeling lies in the inability of men to determine their own destiny; and science tends to destroy the feeling of awe with which men regard an alien world, by making them believe that they can understand and anticipate the course of natural phenomena, and even to some extent control it. The fact that it has recently become fashionable for physicists themselves to be sympathetic towards religion is a point in favour of this hypothesis. For this sympathy towards religion marks the physicists' own lack of confidence in the validity of their hypotheses, which is a reaction on their part from the anti-religious dogmatism of nineteenth-century scientists, and a natural outcome of the crisis through which physics has just passed.

It is not within the scope of this enquiry to enter more deeply into the causes of religious feeling, or to discuss the probability of the continuance of religious belief. We are concerned only to answer those questions which arise out of our discussion of the possibility of religious knowledge. The point which we wish to establish is that there cannot be any transcendent truths of religion. For the sentences which the theist uses to express such "truths" are not literally significant.

An interesting feature of this conclusion is that it accords with what many theists are accustomed to say themselves. For we are often told that the nature of God is a mystery which transcends the human understanding. But to say that something transcends the human understanding is to say that it is unintelligible. And what is unintelligible cannot significantly be described. Again, we are told that God is not an object of reason but an object of faith. This may be nothing more than an admission that the existence of God must be taken on trust, since it cannot be proved. But it may also be an assertion that God is the object of a purely mystical intuition, and cannot therefore be defined in terms which are intelligible to the reason. And I think there are many theists who would assert this. But if one allows that it is impossible to define God in intelligible terms, then one is allowing that it is impossible for a sentence both to be significant and to be about God. If a mystic admits that the object of his vision is something which cannot be described, then he must also admit that he is bound to talk nonsense when he describes it.

For his part, the mystic may protest that his intuition does reveal truths to him, even though he cannot explain to others what these truths are; and that we who do not possess this faculty of intuition can have no ground for denying that it is a cognitive faculty. For we can hardly maintain *a priori* that there are no ways of discovering true propositions except those which we ourselves employ. The answer is that we set no limit to the number of ways in which one may come to formulate a true proposition. We do not in any way deny that a synthetic truth may be discovered by purely intuitive methods as well as by the rational method of induction. But we do say that every synthetic proposition, however it may have been arrived at, must be subject to the test of actual experience. We do not deny *a priori* that the mystic is able to discover truths by his own special methods. We wait to hear what are the propositions which embody his discoveries, in order to see whether they are verified or confuted by our empirical observations. But the mystic, so far from producing propositions which are empirically verified, is unable to produce any intelligible propositions at all. And there-fore we say that his intuition has not revealed to him any facts. It is no use his saying that he has apprehended facts but is unable to express them. For we know that if he really had acquired any in-formation, he would be able to express it. He would be able to indicate in some way or other how the genuineness of his discovery might be empirically determined. The fact that he cannot reveal what he "knows," or even himself devise an empirical test to validate his "knowledge," shows that his state of mystical intuition is not a genuinely cognitive state. So that in describing his vision the mystic does not give us any information about the external world; he merely gives us indirect information about the condition of his own mind.

These considerations dispose of the argument from religious ex-perience, which many philosophers still regard as a valid argument in favour of the experience of a god. They say that it is logically possible for men to be immediately acquainted with God, as they are immediately acquainted with a sense-content, and that there is no reason why one should be prepared to believe a man when he says that he is seeing a yellow patch, and refuse to believe him when he says that he is seeing God. The answer to this is that if the man who asserts that he is seeing God is merely assert-ing that he is experiencing a peculiar kind of sense-content, then we do not for a moment deny that his assertion may be true. But, ordinarily, the man who says that he is seeing God is saying not merely that he is experiencing a religious emotion, but also that there exists a transcendent being who is the object of this emotion; just as the man who says that he sees a yellow patch is ordinarily saying not merely that his visual sense-field contains a yellow sense-content, but also that there exists a yellow object to which the sense-content belongs. And it is not irrational to be prepared to believe a man when he asserts the existence of a yellow object, and to refuse to believe him when he asserts the existence of a transcendent god. For whereas the sentence "There exists here a yellow-coloured material thing" expresses a genuine synthetic proposition which could be empirically verified, the sentence "There exists a transcendent god" has, as we have seen, no literal significance.

We conclude, therefore, that the argument from religious experience is altogether fallacious. The fact that people have religious experiences is interesting from the psychological point of view, but it does not in any way imply that there is such a thing as religious knowledge, any more than our having moral experiences implies that there is such a thing as moral knowledge. The theist, like the moralist may believe that his experiences are cognitive experiences, but, unless he can formulate his "knowledge" in propositions that are empirically verifiable, we may be sure that he is deceiving himself. It follows that those philosophers who fill their books with assertions that they intuitively "know" this or that moral or religious "truth" are merely providing material for the psycho-analyst. For no act of intuition can be said to reveal a truth about any matter of fact unless it issues in verifiable propositions. And all such propositions are to be incorporated in the system of empirical propositions which constitutes science.

13. *Fundamentals of the Christian Religion* *

BLAISE PASCAL *(1623–1662)*

430

The greatness and the wretchedness of man are so evident that the true religion must necessarily teach us both that there is in man some great source of greatness, and a great source of wretchedness. It must then give us a reason for these astonishing contradictions.

---

* From Pascal's *Pensees,* first published in 1670 under the title, *Thoughts of M. Pascal on Religion and on some other subjects.* The translation is by W. F. Trotter and is reprinted by permission of E. P. Dutton & Co., Inc.

In order to make man happy, it must prove to him that there is
a God; that we ought to love Him; that our true happiness is to be
in Him, and our sole evil to be separated from Him; it must recognise that we are full of darkness which hinders us from knowing
and loving Him; and that thus, as our duties compel us to love God,
and our lusts turn us away from Him, we are full of unrighteousness.
It must give us an explanation of our opposition to God and to our
own good. It must teach us the remedies for these infirmities, and
the means of obtaining these remedies. Let us therefore examine
all the religions of the world, and see if there be any other than the
Christian which is sufficient for this purpose.

Shall it be that of the philosophers, who put forward as the chief
good, the good which is in ourselves? Is this the true good? Have
they found the remedy for our ills? Is man's pride cured by placing
him on an equality with God? Have those who have made us equal
to the brutes, or the Mohammedans who have offered us earthly
pleasures as the chief good even in eternity, produced the remedy
for our lusts? What religion, then, will teach us to cure pride and
lust? What religion will in fact teach us our good, our duties, the
weakness which turns us from them, the cause of this weakness,
the remedies which can cure it, and the means of obtaining these
remedies?

All other religions have not been able to do so. Let us see what
the wisdom of God will do.

"Expect neither truth," she says, "nor consolation from men. I
am she who formed you, and who alone can teach you what you are.
But you are now no longer in the state in which I formed you. I
created man holy, innocent, perfect. I filled him with light and
intelligence. I communicated to him my glory and my wonders.
The eye of man saw then the majesty of God. He was not then in
the darkness which blinds him, nor subject to mortality and the
woes which afflict him. But he has not been able to sustain so great
glory without falling into pride. He wanted to make himself his
own centre, and independent of my help. He withdrew himself
from my rule; and, on his making himself equal to me by the
desire of finding his happiness in himself, I abandoned him to himself. And setting in revolt the creatures that were subject to him, I
made them his enemies; so that man is now become like the brutes,
and so estranged from me that there scarce remains to him a dim

vision of his Author. So far has all his knowledge been extinguished or disturbed! The senses, independent of reason, and often the masters of reason, have led him into pursuit of pleasure. All creatures either torment or tempt him, and domineer over him, either subduing him by their strength, or fascinating him by their charms, a tyranny more awful and more imperious.

"Such is the state in which men now are. There remains to them some feeble instinct of the happiness of their former state; and they are plunged in the evils of their blindness and their lust, which have become their second nature.

"From this principle which I disclose to you, you can recognize the cause of those contradictions which have astonished all men, and have divided them into parties holding so different views. Observe, now, all the feelings of greatness and glory which the experience of so many woes cannot stifle, and see if the cause of them must not be in another nature."

For Port-Royal to-morrow (Prosopopœa). — "It is in vain, O men, that you seek within yourselves the remedy for your ills. All your light can only reach the knowledge that not in yourselves will you find truth or good. The philosophers have promised you that, and you have been unable to do it. They neither know what is your true good, nor what is your true state. How could they have given remedies for your ills, when they did not even know them? Your chief maladies are pride, which takes you away from God, and lust, which binds you to earth; and they have done nothing else but cherish one or other of these diseases. If they gave you God as an end, it was only to administer to your pride; they made you think that you are by nature like Him, and conformed to Him. And those who saw the absurdity of this claim put you on another precipice, by making you understand that your nature was like that of the brutes, and led you to seek your good in the lusts which are shared by the animals. This is not the way to cure you of your unrighteousness, which these wise men never knew. I alone can make you understand who you are. . . ."

Adam, Jesus Christ.

If you are united to God, it is by grace, not by nature. If you are humbled, it is by penitence, not by nature.

Thus this double capacity . . .

You are not in the state of your creation.

As these two states are open, it is impossible for you not to recognise them. Follow your own feelings, observe yourselves, and see if you do not find the lively characteristics of these two natures. Could so many contradictions be found in a simple subject?

— Incomprehensible. — Not all that is incomprehensible ceases to exist. Infinite number. An infinite space equal to a finite.

— Incredible that God should unite Himself to us.— This consideration is drawn only from the sight of our vileness. But if you are quite sincere over it, follow it as far as I have done, and recognise that we are indeed so vile that we are incapable in ourselves of knowing if His mercy cannot make us capable of Him. For I would know how this animal, who knows himself to be so weak, has the right to measure the mercy of God, and set limits to it, suggested by his own fancy. He has so little knowledge of what God is, that he does not know what he himself is, and, completely disturbed at the sight of his own state, dares to say that God cannot make him capable of communion with Him.

But I would ask him if God demands anything else from him than the knowledge and love of Him, and why, since his nature is capable of love and knowledge, he believes that God cannot make Himself known and loved by him. Doubtless he knows at least that he exists, and that he loves something. Therefore, if he sees anything in the darkness wherein he is, and if he finds some object of his love among the things on earth, why, if God impart to him some ray of His essence, will he not be capable of knowing and of loving Him in the manner in which it shall please Him to communicate Himself to us? There must then be certainly an intolerable presumption in arguments of this sort, although they seem founded on an apparent humility, which is neither sincere nor reasonable, if it does not make us admit that, not knowing of ourselves what we are, we can only learn it from God.

"I do not mean that you should submit your belief to me without reason, and I do not aspire to overcome you by tyranny. In fact, I do not claim to give you a reason for everything. And to reconcile these contradictions, I intend to make you see clearly, by convincing proofs, those divine signs in me, which may convince you of what I am, and may gain authority for me by wonders and proofs which you cannot reject; so that you may then believe without . . . the things which I teach you, since you will find no other ground for rejecting them, except that you cannot know of yourselves if they are true or not.

"God has willed to redeem men, and to open salvation to those who seek it. But men render themselves so unworthy of it, that it is right that God should refuse to some, because of their obduracy, what He grants to others from a compassion which is not due to them. If He had willed to overcome the obstinacy of the most hardened, He could have done so by revealing Himself so manifestly to them that they could not have doubted of the truth of His essence; as it will appear at the last day, with such thunders and such a convulsion of nature, that the dead will rise again, and the blindest will see Him.

"It is not in this manner that He has willed to appear in His advent of mercy, because, as so many make themselves unworthy of His mercy, He has willed to leave them in the loss of the good which they do not want. It was not then right that He should appear in a manner manifestly divine, and completely capable of convincing all men; but it was also not right that He should come in so hidden a manner that He could not be known by those who should sincerely seek Him. He has willed to make Himself quite recognizable by those; and thus, willing to appear openly to those who seek Him with all their heart, and to be hidden from those who flee from Him with all their heart, He so regulates the knowledge of Himself that He has given signs of Himself, visible to those who seek Him, and not to those who seek Him not. There is enough light for those who only desire to see, and enough obscurity for those who have a contrary disposition."

431

No other religion has recognized that man is the most excellent creature. Some, which have quite recognized the reality of his excellence, have considered as mean and ungrateful the low opinions which men naturally have of themselves; and others, which have thoroughly recognized how real is this vileness, have treated with proud ridicule those feelings of greatness, which are equally natural to man.

"Lift your eyes to God," say the first; "see Him whom you resemble, and who has created you to worship Him. You can make yourselves like unto Him; wisdom will make you equal to Him, if you will follow it." "Raise your heads, free men," says Epictetus. And others say, "Bend your eyes to the earth, wretched worm that you are, and consider the brutes whose companion you are."

What, then, will man become? Will he be equal to God or the brutes? What a frightful difference! What, then, shall we be? Who does not see from all this that man has gone astray, that he has fallen from his place, that he anxiously seeks it, that he cannot find it again? And who shall then direct him to it? The greatest men have failed.

432

Scepticism is true; for, after all, men before Jesus Christ did not know where they were, nor whether they were great or small. And those who have said the one or the other, knew nothing about it, and guessed without reason and by chance. They also erred always in excluding the one or the other. . . .

555

. . . Men blaspheme what they do not know. The Christian religion consists in two points. It is of equal concern to men to know them, and it is equally dangerous to be ignorant of them. And it is equally of God's mercy that He has given indications of both.

And yet they take occasion to conclude that one of these points does not exist, from that which should have caused them to infer the other. The sages who have said there is only one God have been persecuted, the Jews were hated, and still more the Christians. They have seen by the light of nature that if there be a true religion on earth, the course of all things must tend to it as to a centre.

The whole course of things must have for its object the establishment and the greatness of religion. Men must have within them feelings suited to what religion teaches us. And, finally, religion must so be the object and centre to which all things tend, that whoever knows the principles of religion can give an explanation both of the whole nature of man in particular, and of the whole course of the world in general.

And on this ground they take occasion to revile the Christian religion, because they misunderstand it. They imagine that it consists simply in the worship of a God considered as great, powerful, and eternal; which is strictly deism, almost as far removed from the Christian religion as atheism, which is its exact opposite. And thence they conclude that this religion is not true, because they do not see that all things concur to the establishment of this point, that God does not manifest Himself to men with all the evidence which He could show.

But let them conclude what they will against deism, they will conclude nothing against the Christian religion, which properly consists in the mystery of the Redeemer, who, uniting in Himself the two natures, human and divine, has redeemed men from the corruption of sin in order to reconcile them in His divine person to God.

The Christian religion, then, teaches men these two truths; that there is a God whom men can know, and that there is a corruption in their nature which renders them unworthy of Him. It is equally important to men to know both these points; and it is equally dangerous for man to know God without knowing his own wretchedness, and to know his own wretchedness without knowing the Redeemer who can free him from it. The knowledge of only one of these points gives rise either to the pride of philosophers, who have known God, and not their own wretchedness, or to the despair of atheists, who know their own wretchedness, but not the Redeemer.

And, as it is alike necessary to man to know these two points, so is it alike merciful of God to have made us know them. The Christian religion does this; it is in this that it consists.

Let us herein examine the order of the world, and see if all things do not tend to establish these two chief points of this religion: Jesus Christ is the end of all, and the centre to which all tends. Whoever knows Him knows the reason of everything.

Those who fall into error err only through failure to see one of these two things. We can then have an excellent knowledge of God without that of our own wretchedness, and of our own wretchedness without that of God. But we cannot know Jesus Christ without knowing at the same time both God and our own wretchedness.

Therefore I shall not undertake here to prove by natural reasons either the existence of God, or the Trinity, or the immortality of the soul, or anything of that nature; not only because I should not feel myself sufficiently able to find in nature arguments to convince hardened atheists, but also because such knowledge without Jesus

Christ is useless and barren. Though a man should be convinced that numerical proportions are immaterial truths, eternal and dependent on a first truth, in which they subsist, and which is called God, I should not think him far advanced towards his own salvation.

The God of Christians is not a God who is simply the author of mathematical truths, or of the order of the elements; that is the view of heathens and Epicureans. He is not merely a God who exercises His providence over the life and fortunes of men, to bestow on those who worship Him a long and happy life. That was the portion of the Jews. But the God of Abraham, the God of Isaac, the God of Jacob, the God of Christians, is a God of love and of comfort, a God who fills the soul and heart of those whom He possesses, a God who makes them conscious of their inward wretchedness, and His infinite mercy, who unites Himself to their inmost soul, who fills it with humility and joy, with confidence and love, who renders them incapable of any other end than Himself.

All who seek God without Jesus Christ, and who rest in nature, either find no light to satisfy them, or come to form for themselves a means of knowing God and serving Him without a mediator. Thereby they fall either into atheism, or into deism, two things which the Christian religion abhors almost equally.

Without Jesus Christ the world would not exist; for it should needs be either that it would be destroyed or be a hell.

If the world existed to instruct man of God, His divinity would shine through every part in it in an indisputable manner; but as it exists only by Jesus Christ, and for Jesus Christ, and to teach men both their corruption and their redemption, all displays the proofs of these two truths.

All appearance indicates neither a total exclusion nor a manifest presence of divinity, but the presence of a God who hides Himself. Everything bears this character.

. . . Shall he alone who knows his nature know it only to be miserable? Shall he alone who knows it be alone unhappy?

. . . He must not see nothing at all, nor must he see sufficient for him to believe he possesses it; but he must see enough to know that he has lost it. For to know of his loss, he must see and not see; and that is exactly the state in which he naturally is.

. . . Whatever part he takes, I shall not leave him at rest . . .

556

. . . It is then true that everything teaches man his condition, but he must understand this well. For it is not true that all reveals God, and it is not true that all conceals God. But it is at the same time true that He hides Himself from those who tempt Him, and that He reveals Himself to those who seek Him, because men are both unworthy and capable of God; unworthy by their corruption, capable by their original nature.

557

What shall we conclude from all our darkness, but our unworthiness?

558

If there never had been any appearance of God, this eternal deprivation would have been equivocal, and might have as well corresponded with the absence of all divinity, as with the unworthiness of men to know Him; but His occasional, though not continual, appearances remove the ambiguity. If He appeared once, He exists always; and thus we cannot but conclude both that there is a God, and that men are unworthy of Him.

559

We do not understand the glorious state of Adam, nor the nature of his sin, nor the transmission of it to us. These are matters which took place under conditions of a nature altogether different from our own, and which transcend our present understanding.

The knowledge of all this is useless to us as a means of escape from it; and all that we are concerned to know, is that we are miserable, corrupt, separated from God, but ransomed by Jesus Christ, whereof we have wonderful proofs on earth.

So the two proofs of corruption and redemption are drawn from the ungodly, who live in indifference to religion, and from the Jews who are irreconcilable enemies.

560

There are two ways of proving the truths of our religion; one by the power of reason, the other by the authority of him who speaks.

We do not make use of the latter, but of the former. We do not say, "This must be believed, for Scripture, which says it, is divine." But we say that it must be believed for such and such a reason, which are feeble arguments, as reason may be bent to everything.

561

There is nothing on earth that does not show either the wretchedness of man, or the mercy of God; either the weakness of man without God, or the strength of man with God.

562

It will be one of the confusions of the damned to see that they are condemned by their own reason, by which they claimed to condemn the Christian religion.

563

The prophecies, the very miracles and proofs of our religion, are not of such a nature that they can be said to be absolutely convincing. But they are also of such a kind that it cannot be said that it is unreasonable to believe them. Thus there is both evidence and obscurity to enlighten some and confuse others. But the evidence is such that it surpasses, or at least equals, the evidence to the contrary; so that it is not reason which can determine men not to follow it, and thus it can only be lust or malice of heart. And by this means there is sufficient evidence to condemn, and insufficient to convince; so that it appears in those who follow it, that it is grace, and not reason, which makes them follow it; and in those who shun it, that it is lust, not reason, which makes them shun it.

[NOTE: The bibliography for Chapter One appears on page 519.]

Chapter Two

THE EXISTENCE OF GOD

INTRODUCTION

Central to most discussions in the philosophy of religion is the question of the existence of God. What evidence is there that a Deity exists and, if there is evidence, what is the nature and character of such an avowed Being? The answer to this sort of question involves some conception of God. God has been conceived of by most traditional writers on religion as an all-powerful (omnipotent), all-knowing (omniscient), benevolent Being who has created and sustains the universe. Such a God-idea is classified as supernatural in that God is said to be far more than the powers inherent in Nature; not restricted by the natural laws of the universe (*i.e.*, performing supernatural miracles). Because of the historically dominant influence of the supernaturalist traditional conception of God, most of the selections deal with a defense or criticism of supernaturalism.

Many, however, conceive of God as a unifying ideal expressing the highest aspirations and values of men (Ames, Dewey); some as

126

identifiable powers which make for human growth and happiness (Wieman, Kaplan); others as Process which organizes and effects cosmic evolution, directing the emergence of new fields and qualities and which introduces order, harmony and value into the universe, (Whitehead, Boodin, Bergson, Alexander.) In constructing a conception of God, thinkers have often been influenced by intellectual, scientific or emotional considerations. As we have seen in the previous chapter, those opposing the more traditional ideas of God may develop a non-supernatural conception of God of their own, or they may frankly reject the existence of God outright (atheism) or else maintain a deliberate suspension of judgment (agnosticism) on the grounds of insufficient evidence either way.

Traditionalists frequently question the right of those who employ the term "God" in any but the supernaturalist sense. They argue that to apply the term "God" to processes in nature or human ideas is to invite semantic confusion and to hide heresy behind the cloak of traditional terminology.

Traditionalists have also questioned the atheistic position on philosophic grounds. Does the alleged absence of evidence in favor of the existence of God justify the atheistic conclusion that there is no God?

The atheists offer rejoinder by questioning the logic of those who would demonstrate God's existence from the absence of arguments and evidence disproving His existence.

In counterclaim to the agnostic position, traditionalists have asked, can we afford to assume such an attitude on this important issue? Does not agnosticism really take a position in favor of disbelief? For is not absence of belief in God equivalent to disbelief in God? How much evidence and of what kind would be acceptable to tip the scale of belief either way?

Some thinkers have explained the genesis of the God-idea as mere human projection (anthropomorphism), as a substitute father-image (Freud); as a means of dulling the revolutionary spirit of the oppressed (Lenin) or as the sancta of society (Durkheim).

The classic philosophic demonstrations in favor of the existence of God have generally fallen into two categories. Proofs stemming from (1) formal logical considerations (a priori), derived from arguments independent of experiential information and (2) from observational and empirical grounds (a posteriori).

Anselm's argument (ontological proof) illustrates the first method. Let us conceive of a Perfect Being, something greater than which nothing can be thought. Such an idea is that of God. Now if God did not exist, this idea of a Perfect Being would clearly not be of the greatest thing conceivable; for a being which exists is superior to one which does not exist. Therefore for God, the Perfect Being, not to exist, is self-contradictory. God then must be said to exist.

Descartes' formulation of this proof argues the existence of a God on the basis of man's finite ability to conceive of an infinite, Perfect Being. Since the cause of the idea must be at least as great as the idea itself, and since man is far from perfect, the idea of Perfection must have been placed in man's mind by some infinite Being or God who exists.

Similarly, the Thomistic argument (cosmological) argues the logical necessity of assuming some first cause or principle as the only recourse for an intelligible accounting of the origin and movement of things and events. Both Perfection and First Cause are identified as essential characteristics belonging to a transcendent God.

But, can we prove the existence of a being through logic? What do we mean by "existence" as an attribute of God? Is "existence" a predicate like "good" or "powerful"? Is there no alternative other than to assume a first cause? Why should this first cause be called God?

The argument from design (teleological) illustrates the second method. A study of recurrent rhythm of natural events suggests an ordered pattern pointing to some Grand Designer, or Purposeful Intelligence. To some philosophers, the law-abiding character of natural events, and our ability to predict and understand such phenomena seem to imply a planned universe, not to be explained on the basis of chance or coincidence.

On the other hand, is the universe really ordered? How do we account for earthquake, disease, perversion? Has everything which exists a purpose? How do we decide the purpose or purposes of an object? Is everything which carries the mark of design proof of a designing Agent?

On a different level, arguments in favor of the belief in God's existence are offered by pointing to the beneficial effects which are gained from faith in God's power to heal and comfort. The miraculous recovery of many hopelessly ill, the morale and courage gained by faith — do they not testify to God's goodness, power and therefore existence? How else can we explain these recoveries which seem to defy scientific analysis? Such practical arguments (pragmatic) point to the results of security, stability and happiness which faith in God is said to induce in the believers (James). It may be asked whether such arguments prove God's existence or merely cite evidence for the power of belief, regardless of the truth or falsity of the belief held.

Arguments are frequently adduced from testimony of miracles and experiences of Divine revelation by prophets and saints. These arguments are in turn questioned by those who ask whether a miracle at present scientifically inexplicable would be proof of the existence of supernatural powers? How can we be sure that the miracle is caused by God? Does the testimony of the Bible asserting the existence of God, beg the question?

The issue of the existence of God and its proof and counterclaims is an ancient concern which remains very much alive in our contemporary age. Serious attention to these questions remains requisite for either a profound religious faith, or an intelligent rejection of religious beliefs.

H. M. S.

14. How God May Be Known Through Natural Reason *

ST. THOMAS AQUINAS *(1225–1274)*

THE EXISTENCE OF GOD

Because the chief aim of sacred doctrine is to teach the knowledge of God, not only as He is in Himself, but also as He is the beginning of things and their last end, and especially of rational

* Reprinted from the *Summa Theologica* with the kind permission of Benziger Bros., Inc., publishers and copyright owners.

creatures, as is clear from what has been already said, therefore, in our endeavor to expound this science, we shall treat: (1) Of God: (2) Of the rational creatures advance towards God: (3) Of Christ, Who as man, is our way to God.

In treating of God there will be a threefold division:

For we shall consider (1) whatever concerns the Divine Essence. (2) Whatever concerns the distinctions of Persons. (3) Whatever concerns the procession of creatures from Him. Concerning the Divine Essence, we must consider:

(1) Whether God exists? (2) The manner of His existence, or, rather, what is *not* the manner of His existence. (3) Whatever concerns His operations — namely, His knowledge, will, power.

Concerning the first, there are three points of inquiry: — (1) Whether the proposition 'God exists' is self-evident? (2) Whether it is demonstrable? (3) Whether God exists?

First Article:

WHETHER THE EXISTENCE OF GOD IS SELF-EVIDENT?

We proceed thus to the First Article:

Objection 1. It seems that the existence of God is self-evident. Now those things are said to be self-evident to us the knowledge of which is naturally implanted in us, as we can see in regard to first principles. But as Damascene says (*De Fid.* i. 1, 3) *the knowledge of God is naturally implanted in all.* Therefore the existence of God is self-evident.

Obj. 2. Further, those things are said to be self-evident which are known as soon as the terms are known, which the Philosopher (1 *Poster, iii*) says is true of the first principles of demonstration. Thus, when the nature of a whole and of a part is known, it is at once recognized that every whole is greater than its part. But as soon as the signification of the word 'God' is understood, it is at once seen that God exists. For by this word is signified that thing than which nothing greater can be conceived. But that which exists actually and mentally is greater than that which exists only mentally. Therefore, since as soon as the word 'God' is understood it exists mentally, it also follows that it exists actually. Therefore the proposition 'God exists' is self-evident.

Obj. 3. Further, the existence of truth is self-evident. For whoever denies the existence of truth grants that truth does not exist: and, if truth does not exist, then the proposition 'Truth does not exist' is true: and if there is anything true, there must be truth. But God is truth itself: *I am the way, the truth, and the life* (John xiv. 6). Therefore 'God exists' is self-evident.

On the contrary, No one can mentally admit the opposite of what is self-evident; as the Philosopher (Metaph. IV., lect. VI) states concerning the first principles of demonstration. But the opposite of the proposition 'God is' can be mentally admitted: *The fool said in heart, There is no God* (Ps. lii. 1). Therefore, that God exists is not self-evident.

I answer that, A thing can be self-evident in either of two ways; on the one hand, self-evident in itself, though not to us; on the other, self-evident in itself, and to us. A proposition is self-evident because the predicate is included in the essence of the subject, as 'Man is an animal,' for animal is contained in the essence of man. If, therefore, the essence of the predicate and subject be known to all, the proposition will be self-evident to all; as is clear with regard to the first principles of demonstration, the terms of which are common things that no one is ignorant of, such as being and non-being, whole and part, and suchlike. If, however, there are some to whom the essence of the predicate and subject is unknown, the proposition will be self-evident in itself, but not to those who do not know the meaning of the predicate and subject of the proposition. Therefore, it happens, as Boethius says (*Hebdom., the title of which is: 'Whether all that is, is good'*) 'that there are some mental concepts self-evident only to the learned, as that incorporeal substances are not in space.' Therefore I say that this proposition, 'God exists,' of itself is self-evident, for the predicate is the same as the subject; because God is His own existence as will be hereafter shown (Q.III., A.4). Now because we do not know the essence of God, the proposition is not self-evident to us; but needs to be demonstrated by things that are more known to us, though less known in their nature, namely, by effect.

Reply Obj. 1. To know that God exists in a general and confused way is implanted in us by nature, inasmuch as God is man's beatitude. For man naturally desires happiness, and what is naturally desired by man must be naturally known to him. This, however, is not to know absolutely that God exists; just as to know that someone is approaching is not the same as to know that Peter is approaching, even though it is Peter who is approaching; for many there are who imagine that man's perfect good which is happiness, consists in riches, and others in pleasures, and others in something else.

Reply Obj. 2. Perhaps not everyone who hears this word 'God' understands it to signify something than which nothing greater can be thought, seeing that some have believed God to be a body. Yet, granted that everyone understands that by this word 'God' is signified something than which nothing greater can be thought, nevertheless, it does not therefore follow that he understands that what the word signifies exists actually, but only that it exists mentally. Nor can it be argued that it actually exists, unless it be admitted that there actually exists something than which nothing greater can be thought; and this precisely is not admitted by those who hold that God does not exist.

Reply Objection 3. The existence of Truth in general is self-evident, but the existence of a Primal Truth is not self-evident to us.

Second Article:

Whether It Can Be Demonstrated That God Exists?

Objection 3. Further, if the existence of God were demonstrated, this could only be from His effects. But His effects are not proportionate to Him, since He is infinite and His effects are finite; and between the finite and infinite there is no proportion. Therefore, since a cause cannot be demonstrated by an effect not proportionate to it, it seems that the existence of God cannot be demonstrated. . . .

On the contrary, The Apostle says: *The invisible things of Him are clearly seen, being understood by the things that are made* (Rom.i, 20). But this would not be unless the existence of God could be demonstrated through the things that are made; for the first thing we must know of anything is, whether it exists.

I answer that, Demonstration can be made in two ways: One is through the cause, and is called *a priori,*[1] and this is to argue from what is prior absolutely. The other is through the effect, and is called a demonstration, *a posteriori,*[2] this is to argue from what is prior relatively only to us. When an effect is better known to us than its cause, from the effect we proceed to the knowledge of the cause. And from every effect the existence of its proper cause can be demonstrated, so long as its effects are better known to us; because since every effect depends upon its cause, if the effect exists, the cause must pre-exist. Hence the existence of God, in so far as it is not self-evident to us, can be demonstrated from those of His effects which are known to us.

Reply Objection 3. From effects not proportionate to the cause no perfect knowledge of that cause can be obtained. Yet from every effect the existence of the cause can be clearly demonstrated, and so we can demonstrate the existence of God from His effects; though from them we cannot perfectly know God as He is in His essence.

Third Article:

WHETHER GOD EXISTS

We proceed thus to the Third Article: —

Objection 1. It seems that God does not exist: because if one of two contraries be infinite, the other would be altogether destroyed. But the word 'God' means that He is infinite goodness. If, therefore, God existed, there would be no evil discoverable; but there is evil in the world. Therefore God does not exist.

Obj. 2. Further, it is superfluous to suppose that what can be accounted for by a few principles has been produced by many. But

---

[1] [Edit. Ascertained by reason before experience. For example, if "A" is greater than "B" and "B" is greater than "C", then "A" must *a priori* be greater than "C".]

[2] [Edit. Knowledge which is derived as a result of experience. For example, that metal expands when heated is learned *a posteriori.*]

it seems that everything we see in the world can be accounted for by other principles, supposing God did not exist. For all natural things can be reduced to one principle, which is nature; and all voluntary things can be reduced to one principle, which is human reason, or will. Therefore there is no need to suppose God's existence.

On the contrary, It is said in the person of God: *I am Who am* (Exod.iii.14).

I answer that, The existence of God can be proved in five ways.

The first and more manifest way is the argument from motion. It is certain, and evident to our senses, that in the world some things are in motion. Now whatever is in motion is put in motion by another, for nothing can be in motion except it is in potentiality to that towards which it is in motion; whereas a thing moves inasmuch as it is in act. For motion is nothing else than the reduction of something from potentiality to actuality, except by something in a state of actuality. Thus that which is actually hot, as fire, makes wood, which is potentially hot, to be actually hot, and thereby moves and changes it. Now it is not possible that the same thing should be at once in actuality and potentiality in the same respect, but only in different respects. For what is actually hot cannot simultaneously be potentially hot; but it is simultaneously potentially cold. It is therefore impossible that in the same respect and in the same way a thing should be both mover and moved, i.e., that it should move itself. Therefore, whatever is in motion must be put in motion by another. If that by which it is put in motion be itself put in motion by another, and that by another again. But this cannot go on to infinity, because then there would be no first mover, and, consequently, no other mover; seeing that subsequent movers move only inasmuch as they are put in motion by the first mover; as the staff moves only because it is put in motion by the hand. Therefore it is necessary to arrive at a first mover, put in motion by no other; and this everyone understands to be God.

The second way is from the nature of the efficient cause. In the world of sense we find there is an order of efficient causes. There is no case known (neither is it, indeed, possible) in which a thing is found to be the efficient cause of itself; for so it would be prior to itself, which is impossible. Now in efficient causes it is not possible to go on to infinity, because in all efficient causes following in order, the first is the cause of the intermediate cause, and the intermediate is the cause of the ultimate cause, whether the intermediate cause be several, or one only. Now to take away the cause is to take away the effect. Therefore, if there be no first cause among efficient causes, there will be no ultimate, nor any intermediate cause. But if in efficient causes it is possible to go on to infinity, there will be no first efficient cause, neither will there be an ultimate effect, nor any intermediate efficient causes, all of which is plainly false. Therefore it is necessary to admit a first efficient cause, to which everyone gives the name of God.

The third way is taken from possibility and necessity, and runs thus. We find in nature things that are possible to be and not to be, since they are found to be generated, and to corrupt, and consequently, they are possible to be and not to be. But it is impossible for these always to exist, for that which is possible not to be at some time is not. Therefore, if everything is possible not to be, then at one time there could have been nothing in existence. Now if this were true, even now there would be nothing in existence, because that which does not exist only begins to exist by something already existing. Therefore, if at one time nothing was in existence, it would have been impossible for anything to have begun to exist; and thus even now nothing would be in existence — which is absurd. Therefore, not all beings are merely possible, but there must exist something the existence of which is necessary. But every necessary thing either has its necessity caused by another, or not. Now it is impossible to go on to infinity in necessary things which have their necessity caused by another, as has already been proved in regard to efficient causes. Therefore we cannot but postulate the existence of some being having of itself its own necessity, and not receiving it from another, but rather causing in others their necessity. This all men speak of as God.

The fourth way is taken from the gradation to be found in things. Among beings there are some more and some less good, true, noble, and the like. But 'more' and 'less' are predicated of different things, according as they resemble in their different ways something which is the maximum, as a thing is said to be hotter according as it more nearly resembles that which is hottest; so that there is something which is truest, something best, something noblest, and, consequently, something which is uttermost being; for those things that are greatest in truth are greatest in being, as it is written in *Metaph.ii.* Now the maximum in any genus is the cause of all in that genus; as fire, which is the maximum of heat, is the cause of all hot things. Therefore there must also be something which is to all beings the cause of their being, goodness, and every other perfection; and this we call God.

The fifth way is taken from the governance of the world. We see that things which lack intelligence, such as natural bodies, act for an end, and this is evident from their acting always, or nearly always, in the same way, so as to obtain the best result. Hence it is plain that not fortuitously, but designedly, do they achieve their end. Now whatever lacks intelligence cannot move towards an end, unless it be directed by some being endowed with knowledge and intelligence; as the arrow is shot to its mark by the archer. Therefore some intelligent being exists by whom all natural things are directed to their end; and this being we call God.

Reply Obj. 1. As Augustine says (Enchir. XI): *Since God is the highest good, He would not allow any evil to exist in His works, unless His omnipotence and goodness were such as to bring good even out of evil.* This is part of the infinite goodness of God, that He should allow evil to exist, and out of it produce good.

Reply Obj. 2. Since nature works for a determinate end under the direction of a higher agent, whatever is done by nature must needs be traced back to God, as to its first cause. So also whatever is done voluntarily must also be traced back to some higher cause other than human reason or will, since these can change and fail; for all things that are changeable and capable of defect must be traced back to an immovable and self-necessary first principle, as was shown in the body of the *Article.*

15. *God and the Idea of Perfection* *

ST. ANSELM OF CANTERBURY *(1033–1109)*

II

Truly there is a God, although the fool hath said in his heart, "There is no God."

And so, Lord, do thou, who dost give understanding to faith, give

---

* St. Anselm, *Proslogium* (Chapter 2 and 3) and *Appendix* (Chapter 1) (La Salle, Ill.: Open Court Publishing Co., 1939). Reprinted by permission.

me, so far as thou knowest it to be profitable, to understand that thou art as we believe; and that thou art that which we believe. And, indeed, we believe that thou art a being than which nothing greater can be conceived. Or is there no such nature, since the fool hath said in his heart, there is no God? (Psalms xiv. 1). But, at any rate, this very fool, when he hears of this being of which I speak — a being than which nothing greater can be conceived — understands what he hears, and what he understands is in his understanding; although he does not understand it to exist.

For, it is one thing for an object to be in the understanding, and another to understand that the object exists. When a painter first conceives of what he will afterwards perform, he has it in his understanding, but he does not yet understand it to be, because he has not yet performed it. But after he has made the painting, he both has it in his understanding, and he understands that it exists, because he has made it.

Hence, even the fool is convinced that something exists in the understanding, at least, than which nothing greater can be conceived. For, when he hears of this, he understands it. And whatever is understood, exists in the understanding. And assuredly that, than which nothing greater can be conceived, cannot exist in the understanding alone. For, suppose it exists in the understanding alone: then it can be conceived to exist in reality; which is greater.

Therefore, if that, than which nothing greater can be conceived, exists in the understanding alone, the very being, than which nothing greater can be conceived, is one, than which a greater can be conceived. But obviously this is impossible. Hence, there is no doubt that there exists a being, than which nothing greater can be conceived, and it exists both in the understanding and in reality.

III

God cannot be conceived not to exist.—God is that, than which nothing greater can be conceived.—That which can be conceived not to exist is not God.

And it assuredly exists so truly, that it cannot be conceived not to exist. For, it is possible to conceive of a being which cannot be conceived not to exist; and this is greater than one which can be conceived not to exist. Hence, if that, than which nothing greater can be conceived, can be conceived not to exist, it is not that, than which nothing greater can be conceived. But this is an irreconcilable contradiction. There is, then, so truly a being than which nothing greater can be conceived to exist, that it cannot even be conceived not to exist; and this being thou art, O Lord, our God.

So truly, therefore, dost thou exist, O Lord, my God, that thou canst not be conceived not to exist; and rightly. For, if a mind could conceive of a being better than thee, the creature would rise above the Creator; and this is most absurd. And, indeed, whatever else there is, except thee alone, can be conceived not to exist. To thee alone, therefore, it belongs to exist more truly than all other beings, and hence in a higher degree than all others. For, whatever else exists does not exist so truly, and hence in a less degree it belongs to it to exist. Why, then, has the fool said in his heart, there is no God (Psalms xiv 1), since it is so evident, to a rational mind, that thou dost exist in the highest degree of all? Why, except that he is dull and a fool?

IV

How the fool has said in his heart what cannot be conceived.—A thing may be conceived in two ways: (1) when the word signifying it is conceived; (2) when the thing itself is understood. As far as the word goes, God can be conceived not to exist; in reality he cannot.

But how has the fool said in his heart what he could not conceive; or how is it that he could not conceive what he said in his heart? since it is the same to say in the heart, and to conceive.

But, if really, nay, since really, he both conceived, because he said in his heart; and did not say in his heart, because he could not conceive; there is more than one way in which a thing is said in the heart or conceived. For, in one sense, an object is conceived, when the word signifying it is conceived; and in another, when the very entity, which the object is, is understood.

In the former sense, then, God can be conceived not to exist; but in the latter, not at all. For no one who understands what fire and water are can conceive fire to be water, in accordance with the nature of the facts themselves, although this is possible according to the words. So, then, no one who understands what God is can conceive that God does not exist; although he says these words in his heart, either without any or with some foreign, signification. For

God is that than which a greater cannot be conceived. And he who thoroughly understands this, assuredly understands that this being so truly exists, that not even in concept can it be non-existent. Therefore, he who understands that God so exists, cannot conceive that he does not exist.

I thank thee, gracious Lord, I thank thee; because what I formerly believed by thy bounty, I now so understand by thine illumination, that if I were unwilling to believe that thou dost exist, I should not be able not to understand this to be true.

In Behalf of The Fool.

An Answer to the Argument of Anselm in the Proslogium. By Gaunilon, a Monk of Marmoutier.

1. If one doubts or denies the existence of a being of such nature that nothing greater than it can be conceived, he receives this answer:

The existence of this being is proved, in the first place, by the fact that he himself, in his doubt or denial regarding this being, already has it in his understanding; for in hearing it spoken of he understands what is spoken of. It is proved, therefore, by the fact that what he understands must exist not only in his understanding, but in reality also.

And the proof of this is as follows. — It is a greater thing to exist both in the understanding and in reality than to be in the understanding alone. And if this being is in the understanding alone, whatever has even in the past existed in reality will be greater than this being. And so that which was greater than all beings will be less than some being, and will not be greater than all: which is a manifest contradiction.

And hence, that which is greater than all, already proved to be in the understanding, must exist not only in the understanding, but also in reality: for otherwise it will not be greater than all other beings.

2. The fool might make this reply:

This being is said to be in my understanding already, only because I understand what is said. Now could it not with equal justice be said that I have in my understanding all manner of unreal objects, having absolutely no existence in themselves, because I understand these things if one speaks of them, whatever they may be?

Unless indeed it is shown that this being is of such a character that it cannot be held in concept like all unreal objects, or objects whose existence is uncertain: and hence I am not able to conceive of it when I hear of it, or to hold it in concept; but I must understand it and have it in my understanding; because, it seems, I cannot conceive of it in any other way than by understanding it, that is, by comprehending in my knowledge its existence in reality.

But if this is the case, in the first place there will be no distinction between what has precedence in time — namely, the having of an object in the understanding — and what is subsequent in time — namely, the understanding that an object exists; as in the example of the picture, which exists first in the mind of the painter, and afterwards in his work.

Moreover, the following assertion can hardly be accepted: that this being, when it is spoken of and heard of, cannot be conceived not to exist in the way in which even God can be conceived not to exist. For if this is impossible, what was the object of this argument against one who doubts or denies the existence of such a being?

Finally, that this being so exists that it cannot be perceived by an understanding convinced of its own indubitable existence, unless this being is afterwards conceived of — this should be proved to me by an indisputable argument, but not by that which you have advanced: namely, that what I understand, when I hear it, already is in my understanding. For thus in my understanding, as I still think, could be all sorts of things whose existence is uncertain, or which do not exist at all, if some one whose words I should understand mentioned them. And so much the more if I should be deceived, as often happens, and believe in them: though I do not yet believe in the being whose existence you would prove.

3. Hence, your example of the painter who already has in his understanding what he is to paint cannot agree with this argument. For the picture, before it is made, is contained in the artificer's art itself; and any such thing, existing in the art of an artificer, is nothing but a part of his understanding itself. A joiner, St. Augustine says, when he is about to make a box in fact, first has it in his art. The box which is made in fact is not life; but the box which exists in his art is life. For the artificer's soul lives, in which all these things are, before they are produced. Why, then, are these thing

life in the living soul of the artificer, unless because they are nothing else than the knowledge or understanding of the soul itself?

With the exception, however, of those facts which are known to pertain to the mental nature, whatever, on being heard and thought out by the understanding, is perceived to be real, undoubtedly that real object is one thing, and the understanding itself, by which the object is grasped, is another. Hence, even if it were true that there is a being than which a greater is inconceivable: yet to this being, when heard of and understood, the not yet created picture in the mind of the painter is not analogous.

4. Let us notice also the point touched on above, with regard to this being which is greater than all which can be conceived, and which, it is said, can be none other than God himself. I, so far as actual knowledge of the object, either from its specific or general character, is concerned, am as little able to conceive of this being when I hear of it, or to have it in my understanding, as I am to conceive of or understand God himself: whom, indeed, for this very reason I can conceive not to exist. For I do not know that reality itself which God is, nor can I form a conjecture of that reality from some other like reality. For you yourself assert that that reality is such that there can be nothing else like it.

For, suppose that I should hear something said of a man absolutely unknown to me, of whose very existence I was unaware. Through that special or general knowledge by which I know what man is, or what men are, I could conceive of him also, according to the reality itself, which man is. And yet it would be possible, if the person who told me of him deceived me, that the man himself, of whom I conceived, did not exist; since that reality according to which I conceived of him, though a no less indisputable fact, was not that man, but any man.

Hence, I am not able, in the way in which I should have this unreal being in concept or in understanding, to have that being of which you speak in concept or in understanding, when I hear the word *God* or the words, *a being greater than all other beings*. For I can conceive of the man according to a fact that is real and familiar to me: but of God, or a being greater than all others, I could not conceive at all, except merely according to the word. And an object can hardly or never be conceived according to the word alone.

For when it is so conceived, it is not so much the word itself (which is, indeed, a real thing — that is, the sound of the letters and syllables) as the signification of the word, when heard, that is conceived. But it is not conceived as by one who knows what is generally signified by the word; by whom, that is, it is conceived according to a reality and in true conception alone. It is conceived as by a man who does not know the object, and conceives of it only in accordance with the movement of his mind produced by hearing the word, the mind attempting to image for itself the signification of the word that is heard. And it would be surprising if in the reality of fact it could ever attain to this.

Thus, it appears, and in no other way, this being is also in my understanding, when I hear and understand a person who says that there is a being greater than all conceivable beings. So much for the assertion that this supreme nature already is in my understanding.

5. But that this being must exist, not only in the understanding but also in reality, is thus proved to me:

If it did not so exist, whatever exists in reality would be greater than it. And so the being which has been already proved to exist in my understanding, will not be greater than all other beings.

I still answer: if it should be said that a being which cannot be even conceived in terms of any fact, is in the understanding, I do not deny that this being is, accordingly, in my understanding. But since through this fact it can in no wise attain to real existence also, I do not yet concede to it that existence at all, until some certain proof of it shall be given.

For he who says that this being exists, because otherwise the being which is greater than all will not be greater than all, does not attend strictly enough to what he is saying. For I do not yet say, no, I even deny or doubt that this being is greater than any real object. Nor do I concede to it any other existence than this (if it should be called existence) which it has when the mind, according to a word merely heard, tries to form the image of an object absolutely unknown to it.

How, then, is the veritable existence of that being proved to me from the assumption, by hypothesis, that it is greater than all other beings? For I should still deny this, or doubt your demonstration of it, to this extent, that I should not admit that this being is in my understanding and concept even in the way in which many objects whose real existence is uncertain and doubtful, are in my understanding and concept. For it should be proved first that this being itself really exists somewhere; and then, from the fact that it is greater than all, we shall not hesitate to infer that it also subsists in itself.

6. For example: it is said that somewhere in the ocean is an island, which, because of the difficulty, or rather the impossibility, of discovering what does not exist, is called the lost island. And they say that this island has an inestimable wealth of all manner of riches and delicacies in greater abundance than is told of the Islands of the Blest; and that having no owner or inhabitant, it is more excellent than all other countries, which are inhabited by mankind, in the abundance with which it is stored.

Now if some one should tell me that there is such an island, I should easily understand his words, in which there is no difficulty. But suppose that he went on to say, as if by a logical inference: "You can no longer doubt that this island which is more excellent than all lands exists somewhere, since you have no doubt that it is in your understanding. And since it is more excellent not to be in the understanding alone, but to exist both in the understanding and in reality, for this reason it must exist. For if it does not exist, any land which really exists will be more excellent than it; and so the island already understood by you to be more excellent will not be more excellent."

If a man should try to prove to me by such reasoning that this island truly exists, and that its existence should no longer be doubted, either I should believe that he was jesting, or I know not which I ought to regard as the greater fool: myself, supposing that I should allow this proof; or him, if he should suppose that he had established with any certainty the existence of this island. For he ought to show first that the hypothetical excellence of this island exists as a real and indubitable fact, and in no wise as any unreal object, or one whose existence is uncertain, in my understanding.

7. This, in the mean time, is the answer the fool could make to the arguments urged against him. When he is assured in the first place that this being is so great that its non-existence is not even conceivable, and that this in turn is proved on no other ground than the fact that otherwise it will not be greater than all things, the fool may make the same answer, and say:

When did I say that any such being exists in reality, that is, a being greater than all others? — that on this ground it should be proved to me that it also exists in reality to such a degree that it cannot even be conceived not to exist? Whereas in the first place it should be in some way proved that a nature which is higher, that is, greater and better, than all other natures, exists; in order that from this we may then be able to prove all attributes which necessarily the being that is greater and better than all possesses.

Moreover, it is said that the non-existence of this being is inconceivable. It might better be said, perhaps, that its non-existence, or the possibility of its non-existence, is unintelligible. For according to the true meaning of the word, unreal objects are unintelligible. Yet their existence is conceivable in the way in which the fool conceived of the non-existence of God. I am most certainly aware of my own existence; but I know, nevertheless, that my non-existence is possible. As to that supreme being, moreover, which God is, I understand without any doubt both his existence, and the impossibility of his non-existence. Whether, however, so long as I am most positively aware of my existence, I can conceive of my non-existence, I am not sure. But if I can, why can I not conceive of the non-existence of whatever else I know with the same certainty? If, however, I cannot, God will not be the only being of which it can be said, it is impossible to conceive of his non-existence.

ANSELM'S APOLOGETIC.

In Reply to Gaunilon's Answer in Behalf of the Fool.

It was a fool against whom the argument of my Proslogium was directed. Seeing, however, that the author of these objections is by no means a fool, and is a Catholic, speaking in behalf of the fool, I think it sufficient that I answer the Catholic.

I

A general refutation of Gaunilon's argument. It is shown that a being than which a greater cannot be conceived exists in reality.

You say — whosoever you may be, who say that a fool is capable of making these statements — that a being than which a greater cannot be conceived is not in the understanding in any other sense than that in which a being that is altogether inconceivable in terms of reality, is in the understanding. You say that the inference that this being exists in reality, from the fact that it is in the understanding, is no more just than the inference that a lost island most certainly exists, from the fact that when it is described the hearer does not doubt that it is in his understanding.

But I say: if a being than which a greater is inconceivable is not understood or conceived, and is not in the understanding or in concept, certainly either God is not a being than which a greater is inconceivable, or else he is not understood or conceived, and is not in the understanding or in concept. But I call on your faith and conscience to attest that this is most false. Hence, that than which a greater cannot be conceived is truly understood and conceived, and is in the understanding and in concept. Therefore either the grounds on which you try to controvert me are not true, or else the inference which you think to base logically on those grounds is not justified.

But you hold, moreover, that supposing that a being than which a greater cannot be conceived is understood, it does not follow that this being is in the understanding; nor, if it is in the understanding, does it therefore exist in reality.

In answer to this, I maintain positively: if that being can be even conceived to be, it must exist in reality. For that than which a greater is inconceivable cannot be conceived except as without beginning. But whatever can be conceived to exist, and does not exist, can be conceived to exist through a beginning. Hence what can be conceived to exist, but does not exist, is not the being than which a greater cannot be conceived. Therefore, if such a being can be conceived to exist, necesarily it does exist.

Furthermore: if it can be conceived at all, it must exist. For no one who denies or doubts the existence of a being than which a greater is inconceivable, denies or doubts that if it did exist, its non-existence, either in reality or in the understanding, would be impossible. For otherwise it would not be a being than which a greater cannot be conceived. But as to whatever can be conceived, but does not exist — if there were such a being, its non-existence, either in reality or in the understanding, would be possible. Therefore if a being than which a greater is inconceivable can be even conceived, it cannot be non-existent.

But let us suppose that it does not exist, even if it can be conceived. Whatever can be conceived, but does not exist, if it existed, would not be a being than which a greater is inconceivable. If, then, there were a being a greater than which is inconceivable, it would not be a being than which a greater is inconceivable: which is most absurd. Hence, it is false to deny that a being than which a greater cannot be conceived exists, if it can be even conceived; much the more, therefore, if it can be understood or can be in the understanding.

Moreover, I will venture to make this assertion: without doubt, whatever at any place or at any time does not exist — even if it does exist at some place or at some time — can be conceived to exist nowhere and never, as at some place and at some time it does not exist. For what did not exist yesterday, and exists to-day, as it is understood not to have existed yesterday, so it can be apprehended by the intelligence that it never exists. And what is not here, and is elsewhere, can be conceived to be nowhere, just as it is not here. So with regard to an object of which the individual parts do not exist at the same places or times: all its parts and therefore its very whole can be conceived to exist nowhere or never.

For, although time is said to exist always, and the world everywhere, yet time does not as a whole exist always, nor the world as a whole everywhere. And as individual parts of time do not exist when others exist, so they can be conceived never to exist. And so it can be apprehended by the intelligence that individual parts of the world exist nowhere, as they do not exist where other parts exist. Moreover, what is composed of parts can be dissolved in concept, and be non-existent. Therefore, whatever at any place or at any time does not exist as a whole, even if it is existent, can be conceived not to exist.

But that than which a greater cannot be conceived, if it exists, cannot be conceived not to exist. Otherwise, it is not a being than which a greater cannot be conceived: which is inconsistent. By no means, then, does it at any place or at any time fail to exist as a whole: but it exists as a whole everywhere and always.

Do you believe that this being can in some way be conceived or understood, or that the being with regard to which these things are understood can be in concept or in the understanding? For if it cannot, these things cannot be understood with reference to it. But if you say that it is not understood and that it is not in the understanding, because it is not thoroughly understood; you should say that a man who cannot face the direct rays of the sun does not see the light of day, which is none other than the sunlight. Assuredly a being than which a greater cannot be conceived exists, and is in the understanding, at least to this extent — that these statements re- garding it are understood.

16. *Contradictions Involved in the Existence of God* *

LUDWIG FEUERBACH *(1804–1872)*

In the genesis of ideas, the first mode in which reflection on religion, or theology, makes the divine being a distinct being, and places him outside of man, is by making the existence of God the object of a formal proof.

The proofs of the existence of God have been pronounced con- tradictory to the essential nature of religion. They are so, but only in their form as proofs. Religion immediately represents the inner nature of man as an objective, external being. And the proof aims at nothing more than to prove that religion is right. The most per- fect being is that than which no higher can be conceived: God is the highest that man conceives or can conceive. This premiss of the ontological proof — the most interesting proof, because it pro- ceeds from within — expresses the inmost nature of religion. That which is the highest for man, from which he can make no further abstraction, which is the positive limit of his intellect, of his feeling, of his sentiment, that is to him God — *id quo nihil majus cogitari potest.* But this highest being would not be the highest if he did not exist; we could then conceive a higher being who would be superior to him in the fact of existence; the idea of the highest being directly precludes this fiction. Not to exist is a deficiency; to exist is perfection, happiness, bliss. From a being to whom man gives all, offers up all that is precious to him, he cannot withhold the bliss of existence. The contradiction to the religious spirit in the proof of the existence of God lies only in this that the existence is thought of separately, and thence arises the appearance that God

* Ludwig Feuerbach, *The Essence of Christianity,* (Boston: Houghton Mif- flin Co., n. d.). From Chapter XX, pp. 197–203. Reprinted by permission.

is a mere conception, a being existing in idea only, — an appearance, however, which is immediately dissipated; for the very result of the proof is, that to God belongs an existence distinct from an ideal one, an existence apart from man, apart from thought — a real self-existence.

The proof therefore is only thus far discordant with the spirit of religion, that it presents as a formal deduction the implicit enthymeme or immediate conclusion of religion, exhibits in logical relation, and therefore distinguishes, what religion immediately unites; for to religion God is not a matter of abstract thought — he is a present truth and reality. But that every religion in its idea of God makes a latent, unconscious inference, is confessed in its polemic against other religions. "Ye heathens," says the Jew or the Christian, "were able to conceive nothing higher as your deities because ye were sunk in sinful desires. Your God rests on a conclusion, the premisses of which are your sensual impulses, your passions. You thought thus: the most excellent life is to live out one's impulses without restraint; and because this life was the most excellent, the truest, you made it your God. Your God was your carnal nature, your heaven only a free theatre for the passions which, in society and in the conditions of actual life generally, had to suffer restraint." But, naturally, in relation to itself no religion is conscious of such an inference, for the highest of which it is capable is its limit, has the force of necessity, is not a thought, not a conception, but immediate reality.

The proofs of the existence of God have for their aim to make the internal external, to separate it from man.[1] His existence being proved, God is no longer a merely relative, but a noumenal being (*Ding an sich*): he is not only a being for us, a being in our faith, our feeling, our nature, he is a being in himself, a being external to us, — in a word, not merely a belief, a feeling, a thought, but also a real existence apart from belief, feeling, and thought. But such an existence is no other than a sensational existence; i.e., an existence conceived according to the forms of our senses.

---

[1] At the same time, however, their result is to prove the nature of man. The various proofs of the existence of God are nothing else than various highly interesting forms in which the human nature affirms itself. Thus, for example, the physico-theological proof (or proof from design) is the self-affirmation of the calculated activity of the understanding. Every philosophic system is, in this sense, a proof of the existence of God.

The idea of sensational existence is indeed already involved in the characteristic expression "external to us." It is true that a sophistical theology refuses to interpret the word "external" in its proper, natural sense, and substitutes the indefinite expression of independent, separate existence. But if the externality is only figurative, the existence also is figurative. And yet we are here only concerned with existence in the proper sense, and external existence is alone the definite, real, unshrinking expression for separate existence.

Real, sensational existence is that which is not dependent on my own mental spontaneity or activity, but by which I am involuntarily affected, which is when I am not, when I do not think of it or feel it. The existence of God must therefore be in space — in general, a qualitative, sensational existence. But God is not seen, not heard, not perceived by the senses. He does not exist for me, if I do not exist for him; if I do not believe in a God, there is no God for me. If I am not devoutly disposed, if I do not raise myself above the life of the senses, he has no place in my consciousness. Thus he exists only in so far as he is felt, thought, believed in — in addition "for me" is unnecessary. His existence therefore is a real one, yet at the same time not a real one; — a spiritual existence, says the theologian. But spiritual existence is only an existence in thought, in feeling, in belief; so that his existence is a medium between sensational existence and conceptional existence, a medium full of contradiction. Or: he is a sensational existence, to which however all the conditions of sensational existence are wanting; — consequently an existence at once sensational and not sensational, an existence which contradicts the idea of the sensational, or only a vague existence in general, which is fundamentally a sensational one, but which, in order that this may not become evident, is divested of all the predicates of a real, sensational existence. But such an "existence in general" is self-contradictory. To existence belongs full, definite reality.

A necessary consequence of this contradiction is Atheism. The existence of God is essentially an empirical existence, without having its distinctive marks; it is in itself a matter of experience, and yet in reality no object of experience. It calls upon man to seek it in Reality: it impregnates his mind with sensational conceptions and pretensions; hence, when these are not fulfilled — when, on the contrary, he finds experience in contradiction with these concep tions, he is perfectly justified in denying that existence.

Kant is well known to have maintained, in his critique of the proofs of the existence of God, that that existence is not susceptible of proof from reason. He did not merit, on this account, the blame which was cast on him by Hegel. The idea of the existence of God in those proofs is a thoroughly empirical one; but I cannot deduce empirical existence from an a priori idea. The only real ground of blame against Kant is, that in laying down this position he supposed it to be something remarkable, whereas it is self-evident. Reason cannot constitute itself an object of sense. I cannot, in thinking, at the same time represent what I think as a sensible object, external to me. The proof of the existence of God tran- scends the limits of the reason; true, but in the same sense in which sight, hearing, smelling transcend the limits of the reason. It is absurd to reproach reason that it does not satisfy a demand which can only address itself to the senses. Existence, empirical existence is proved to me by the senses alone; and in the question as to the being of God, the existence implied has not the significance of inward reality, of truth, but the significance of a formal, external existence. Hence there is perfect truth in the allegation that the belief that God is, or is not, has no consequence with respect to inward moral dispositions. It is true that the thought: There is a God, is inspiring; but here the "is" means inward reality; here the existence is a movement of inspiration, an act of aspiration. Just in proportion as this existence becomes a prosaic, an empirical truth, the inspiration is extinguished.

Religion, therefore, in so far as it is founded on the existence of God as an empirical truth, is a matter of indifference to the inward disposition. As, necessarily, in the religious cultus, ceremonies, ob- servances, sacraments, apart from the moral spirit or disposition, become in themselves an important fact: so also, at last, belief in the existence of God becomes, apart from the inherent quality, the spiritual import of the idea of God, a chief point in religion. If thou only believest in God — believest that God is, thou art already saved. Whether under this God thou conceivest a really divine being or a monster, a Nero or a Caligula, an image of thy passions, thy revenge, or ambition, it is all one, — the main point is that thou be not an atheist. The history of religion has amply confirmed this

consequence which we here draw from the idea of the divine existence. If the existence of God, taken by itself, had not rooted itself
as a religious truth in minds, there would never have been those
infamous, senseless, horrible ideas of God which stigmatise the
history of religion and theology. The existence of God was a common, external, and yet at the same time a holy thing: — what wonder, then, if on this ground the commonest, rudest, most unholy conceptions and opinions sprang up!

Atheism was supposed, and is even now supposed, to be the
negation of all moral principle, of all moral foundations and bonds:
if God is not, all distinction between good and bad, virtue and vice,
is abolished. Thus the distinction lies only in the existence of God;
the reality of virtue lies not in itself, but out of it. And assuredly
it is not from an attachment to virtue, from a conviction of its
intrinsic worth and importance, that the reality of it is thus bound
up with the existence of God. On the contrary, the belief that God
is the necessary condition of virtue is the belief in the nothingness
of virtue in itself.

It is indeed worthy of remark that the idea of the empirical
existence of God has been perfectly developed in modern times, in
which empiricism and materialism in general have arrived at their
full blow. It is true that even in the original, simple religious
mind, God is an empirical existence to be found in a place, though
above the earth. But here this conception has not so naked, so
prosaic a significance; the imagination identifies again the external
God with the soul of man. The imagination is, in general, the true
place of an existence which is absent, not present to the senses,
though nevertheless sensational in its essence.[2] Only the imagination solves the contradiction in an existence which is at once
sensational and not sensational; only the imagination is the preservative from atheism, — existence affirms itself as a power; with
the essence of sensational existence the imagination associates also

---

[2] "Christ is ascended on high, . . . that is, he not only sits there above, but
he is also here below. And he is gone thither to the very end that he might
be here below, and fill all things, and be in all places, which he could not do
while on earth, for here he could not be seen by all bodily eyes. Therefore he
sits above, where every man can see him, and he has to do with every man."—
Luther (*TH*. xiii. p. 643). That is to say: Christ or God is an object, an existence of the imagination; in the imagination he is limited to no place,—he is
present and objective to every one. God exists in heaven, but is for that
reason omnipresent; for this heaven is the imagination.

the phenomena of sensational existence. Where the existence of God is a living truth, an object on which the imagination exercises itself, there also appearances of God are believed in.[3] Where, on the contrary, the fire of the religious imagination is extinct, where the sensational effects or appearances necessarily connected with an essentially sensational existence cease, there the existence becomes a dead, self-contradictory existence, which falls irrevocably into the negation of atheism.

The belief in the existence of God is the belief in a special existence, separate from the existence of man and Nature. A special existence can only be proved in a special manner. This faith is therefore only then a true and living one when special effects, immediate appearances of God, miracles, are believed in. Where on the other hand, the belief in God is identified with the belief in the world, where the belief in God is no longer a special faith, where the general being of the world takes possession of the whole man, there also vanishes the belief in special effects and appearances of God. Belief in God is wrecked, is stranded on the belief in the world, in natural effects as the only true ones. As here the belief in miracles is no longer anything more than the belief in historical, past miracles, so the existence of God is also only an historical, in itself atheistic conception.

17. Must There Be a First Cause? *

JOHN STUART MILL (1806–1873)

The argument for a First Cause admits of being, and is, presented as a conclusion from the whole of human experience. Every-

---

[3] "Thou has not to complain that thou art less experienced than was Abraham or Isaac. Thou also hast appearances . . . . . Thou hast holy baptism, the supper of the Lord, the bread and wine, which are figures and forms, under and in which the present God speaks to thee, and acts upon thee, in thy ears, eyes, and heart . . . . He appears to thee in baptism, and it is he himself who baptizes thee, and speaks to thee . . . . Everything is full of divine appearances and utterances, if he is on thy side."—Luther (*TH*. ii. p. 466. See also on this subject, *TH*. xix p. 407).

* John Stuart Mill, *Three Essays on Religion* (New York: Henry Holt & Co., 1874). "Theism."

thing that we know (it is argued) had a cause, and owed its existence to that cause. How then can it be but that the world, which is but a name for the aggregate of all that we know, has a cause to which it is indebted for its existence?

The fact of experience however, when correctly expressed, turns out to be, not that everything which we know derives its existence from a cause, but only every event or change. There is in Nature a permanent element, and also a changeable: the changes are always the effects of previous changes; the permanent existences, so far as we know, are not effects at all. It is true we are accustomed to say not only of events, but of objects, that they are produced by causes, as water by the union of hydrogen and oxygen. But by this we only mean that when they begin to exist, their beginning is the effect of a cause. But their beginning to exist is not an object, it is an event. If it be objected that the cause of a thing's beginning to exist may be said with propriety to be the cause of the thing itself, I shall not quarrel with the expression. But that which in an object begins to exist, is that in it which belongs to the changeable element in nature; the outward form and the properties depending on mechanical or chemical combinations of its component parts. There is in every object another and a permanent element, viz., the specific elementary substance or substances of which it consists and their inherent properties. These are not known to us as beginning to exist: within the range of human knowledge they had no beginning, consequently no cause; though they themselves are causes or con-causes of everything that takes place. Experience therefore, affords no evidences, not even analogies, to justify our extending to the apparently immutable, a generalization grounded only on our observation of the changeable.

As a fact of experience, then, causation cannot legitimately be extended to the material universe itself, but only to its changeable phenomena; of these, indeed, causes may be affirmed without any exception. But what causes? The cause of every change is a prior change; and such it cannot but be; for if there were no new antecedent, there would not be a new consequent. If the state of facts which brings the phenomenon into existence, had existed always or for an indefinite duration, the effect also would have existed always or been produced an indefinite time ago. It is thus a necessary part of the fact of causation, within the sphere of our experience that the causes as well as the effects had a beginning in time, and were themselves caused. It would seem therefore that our experience, instead of furnishing an argument for a first cause, is repugnant to it; and that the very essence of causation as it exists within the limits of our knowledge, is incompatible with a First Cause.

But it is necessary to look more closely into the matter, and analyse more closely the nature of the causes of which mankind have experience. For if it should turn out that though all causes have a beginning, there is in all of them a permanent element which had no beginning, this permanent element may with some justice be termed a first or universal cause, inasmuch as though not sufficient of itself to cause anything, it enters as a con-cause into all causation. Now it happens that the last result of physical inquiry, derived from the converging evidences of all branches of physical science, does, if it holds good, land us so far as the material world is concerned, in a result of this sort. Whenever a physical phenomenon is traced to its cause, that cause when analysed is found to be a certain quantum of Force, combined with certain collocations. And the last great generalization of science, the Conservation of Force, teaches us that the variety in the effects depends partly upon the amount of the force, and partly upon the diversity of the collocations. The force itself is essentially one and the same; and there exists of it in nature a fixed quantity, which (if the theory be true) is never increased or diminished. Here then we find, even in the changes of material nature, a permanent element; to all appearance the very one of which we were in quest. This it is apparently to which if to anything we must assign the character of First Cause, the cause of the material universe. For all effects may be traced up to it, while it cannot be traced up, by our experience, to anything beyond: its transformations alone can be so traced, and of them the cause always includes the force itself: the same quantity of force, in some previous form. It would seem then that in the only sense in which experience supports in any shape the doctrine of a First Cause, viz., as the primaeval and universal element in all causes, the First Cause can be no other than Force.

We are, however, by no means at the end of the question. On the contrary, the greatest stress of the argument is exactly at the point which we have now reached. For it is maintained that Mind is the only possible cause of Force; or rather perhaps, that Mind is a Force, and that all other force must be derived from it inasmuch as mind is the only thing which is capable of originating change. This is said to be the lesson of human experience. In the phenomena of inanimate nature the force which works is always a pre-existing force, not originated, but transferred. One physical object moves another by giving out to it the force by which it has first been itself moved. The wind communicates to the waves, or to a windmill, or a ship, part of the motion which has been given to itself by some other agent. In voluntary action alone we see a commencement, an origination of motion; since all other causes appear incapable of this origination experience is in favour of the conclusion that all the motion in existence owed its beginning to this one cause, voluntary agency, if not that of man, then of a more powerful Being.

This argument is a very old one. It is to be found in Plato; not as might have been expected, in the Phaedon, where the arguments are not such as would now be deemed of any weight, but in his latest production, the Leges. And it is still one of the most telling arguments with the more metaphysical class of defenders of Natural Theology.

Now, in the first place, if there be truth in the doctrine of the Conservation of Force, in other words the constancy of the total amount of Force in existence, this doctrine does not change from true to false when it reaches the field of voluntary agency. The will does not, any more than other causes, create Force: granting that it originates motion, it has no means of doing so but by converting into that particular manifestation a portion of Force which already existed in other forms. It is known that the source from which this portion of Force is derived, is chiefly, or entirely, the Force evolved in the processes of chemical composition and decomposition which constitute the body of nutrition: the force so liberated becomes a fund upon which every muscular and even every merely nervous action, as of the brain in thought, is a draft. It is in this sense only that, according to the best lights of science, volition is an originating cause. Volition, therefore, does not answer to the idea of a First Cause; since Force must in every instance be assumed as prior to it; and there is not the slightest colour, derived from experience, for supposing Force itself to have been created by a volition. As far as anything can be concluded from human experience Force has all the attributes of a thing eternal and uncreated.

This, however, does not close the discussion. For though whatever verdict experience can give in the case is against the possibility that Will ever originates Force, yet if we can be assured that neither does Force originate Will, Will must be held to be an agency, if not prior to Force yet coeternal with it: and if it be true that Will can originate, not indeed Force but the transformation of Force from some other of its manifestations into that of mechanical motion, and that there is within human experience no other agency capable of doing so, the argument for a Will as the originator, though not of the universe, yet of the kosmos, or order of the universe, remains unanswered.

But the case thus stated is not conformable to fact. Whatever volition can do in the way of creating motion out of other forms of force, and generally of evolving force from a latent into a visible state, can be done by many other causes. Chemical action, for instance; electricity; heat; the mere presence of a gravitating body; all these causes of mechanical motion on a far larger scale than any volitions which experience presents to us: and in most of the effects thus produced the motion given by one body to another is not, as in the ordinary cases of mechanical action, motion that has first been given to that other by some third body. The phenomenon is not a mere passing on of mechanical motion, but a creation of it out of a force previously latent or manifesting itself in some other form. Volition, therefore, regarded as an agent in the material universe, has no exclusive privilege of origination: all that it can originate is also originated by other transforming agents. If it be said that those other agents must have had the force they give out put into them from elsewhere, I answer, that this is no less true of the force which volition disposes of. We know that this force comes from an external source, the chemical action of the food and air. The force by which the phenomena of the material world are produced, circulates through all physical agencies in a never ending though sometimes intermitting stream. I am, of course, speaking of volition only in its action on the material world. We have nothing to do here with the freedom of the will itself as a mental phenomenon — with the *vexata questio* whether volition is self-determining or determined by causes. To the question now in hand it is only the effects of volition that are relevant, not its origin. The assertion is that physical nature must have been produced by a Will, because nothing but Will is known to us as having the power of originating the production of phenomena. We have seen that, on the contrary, all the power that Will possesses over phenomena is shared, as far as we have the means of judging, by other and much more powerful agents, and that in the only sense in which those agents do not originate, neither does Will originate. No prerogative, therefore, can, on the ground of experience, be assigned to volition above other natural agents, as a producing cause of phenomena. All that can be affirmed by the strongest assertor of the Freedom of the Will, is that volitions are themselves uncaused and are therefore alone fit to be the first or universal Cause. But, even assuming volitions to be uncaused, the properties of matter, so far as experience discloses, are uncaused also, and have the advantage over any particular volition, in being so far as experience can show, eternal. Theism, therefore, in so far as it rests on the necessity of a First Cause, has no support from experience.

To those who, in default of Experience, consider the necessity of a first cause as matter of intuition, I would say that it is needless, in this discussion, to contest their premises; since admitting that there is and must be a First Cause, it has now been shown that several other agencies than Will can lay equal claim to that character. One thing only may be said which requires notice here. Among the facts of the universe to be accounted for, it may be said, is Mind; and it is self-evident that nothing can have produced Mind but Mind.

The special indications that Mind is deemed to give, pointing to intelligent contrivance, belong to a different portion of this inquiry. But if the mere existence of Mind is supposed to require, as a necessary antecedent, another Mind greater and more powerful, the difficulty is not removed by going one step back: the creating mind stands as much in need of another mind to be the source of its existence, as the created mind. Be it remembered that we have no direct knowledge (at least apart from Revelation) of a Mind which is even apparently eternal, as Force, and Matter are: an eternal mind is, as far as the present argument is concerned, a simple hypothesis to account for the minds which we know to exist. Now it is essential to an hypothesis that if admitted it should at least remove the difficulty and account for the facts. But it does not account for Mind to refer one mind to a prior mind for its origin. The problem remains unsolved, the difficulty undiminished, nay, rather increased.

To this it may be objected that the causation of every human mind is matter of fact, since we know that it had a beginning in time. We even know, or have the strongest grounds for believing that the human species itself had a beginning in time. For there is a vast amount of evidence that the state of our planet was once such as to be incompatible with animal life, and that human life is of very much more modern origin than animal life. In any case, therefore, the fact must be faced that there must have been a cause which called the first human mind, nay the very first germ of organic life, into existnce. No such difficulty exists in the supposition of an Eternal Mind. If we did not know that Mind on our earth began to exist, we might suppose it to be uncaused; and we may still suppose this of the mind to which we ascribe its existence.

To take this ground is to return into the field of human experience, and to become subject to its canons, and we are then entitled to ask where is the proof that nothing can have caused a mind except another mind. From what, except from experience, can we know what can produce what — what causes are adequate to what effects? That nothing can consciously produce Mind but Mind, is self-evident, being involved in the meaning of the words; but that there cannot be unconscious production must not be assumed, for it is the very point to be proved. Apart from experience, and arguing on what is called reason, that is on supposed self-evidence, the notion seems to be, that no causes can give rise to products of a more precious or elevated kind than themselves. But this is at variance with the known analogies of Nature. How vastly nobler and more precious, for instance, are the higher vegetables and animals than the soil and manure out of which, and by the properties of which they are raised up! The tendency of all recent speculation is towards the opinion that the development of inferior orders of existence into superior, the substitution of greater elaboration and higher organization for lower, is the general rule of Nature. Whether it is so or not, there are at least in Nature a multitude of facts bearing that character, and this is sufficient for the argument.

Here, then this part of the discussion may stop. The result it leads to is that the First Cause argument is in itself of no value for the establishment of Theism: because no cause is needed for the existence of that which has no beginning; and both Matter and Force (whatever metaphysical theory we may give of the one or the other) have had, so far as our experience can teach us, no beginning — which cannot be said of Mind. The phenomena or changes in the universe have indeed each of them a beginning and a cause, but their cause is always a prior change; nor do the analogies of experience give us any reason to expect, from the mere occurrence of changes, that if we could trace back the series far enough we should arrive at a Primaeval Volition. The world does not, by its mere existence, bear witness to a God: if it gives indications of one, these must be given by the special nature of the phenomena, by what they present that resembles adaptation to an end: of which hereafter. If, in default of evidence from experience, the evidence of intuition is relied upon, it may be answered that if Mind, as Mind, presents intuitive evidence of having been created, the Creative Mind must do the same, and we are no nearer to the First Cause than before. But if there be nothing in the nature of mind which in itself implies a Creator, the minds which have a beginning in time, as all minds have which are known to our experience, must indeed have been caused, but it is not necessary that their cause should have been a prior Intelligence.

18. Does Design in Nature Imply Divine Intelligence? *

DAVID HUME (1711–1776)

Not to lose any time in circumlocutions, said Cleanthes, addressing himself to Demea, much less in replying to the pious declamations of Philo; I shall briefly explain how I conceive this matter. Look round the world: contemplate the whole and every part of it: you will find it to be nothing but one great machine, subdivided into

* David Hume, *Dialogues on Natural Religion*, ed. Prof. Kemp Smith (Edinburgh: Thomas Nelson and Sons, Ltd., 1947). Reprinted by permission.

an infinite number of lesser machines, which again admit of sub-
divisions, to a degree beyond what human sense and faculties can
trace and explain. All these various machines, and even their most
minute parts, are adjusted to each other with an accuracy, which
ravishes into admiration all men, who have ever contemplated them.
The curious adapting of means to ends, throughout all nature, resembles exactly, though it much exceeds, the productions of human
contrivance; of human design, thought, wisdom, and intelligence.
Since therefore the effects resemble each other, we are led to infer,
by all the rules of analogy, that the causes also resemble; and that
the Author of Nature is somewhat similar to the mind of men;
though possessed of much larger faculties, proportioned to the
grandeur of the work, which he has executed. By this argument *a
posteriori*, and by this argument alone, do we prove at once the
existence of a Deity, and his similarity to human mind intelligence.

I shall be so free, Cleanthes, said Demea, as to tell you, that from
the beginning, I could not approve of your conclusion concerning
the similarity of the Deity to men; still less can I approve of the
mediums, by which you endeavor to establish it. What! No demonstration of the being of a God! No abstract arguments! No proofs
a priori! Are these, which have hitherto been so much insisted on by
philosophers, all fallacy, all sophism? Can we reach no farther in
this subject than experience and probability? I will not say, that
this is betraying the cause of a deity: but surely, by this affected
candor, you give advantage to atheists, which they never could
obtain, by the mere dint of argument and reasoning.

What I chiefly scruple in this subject, said Philo, is not so much,
that all religious arguments are by Cleanthes reduced to experience,
as that they appear not to be even the most certain and irrefragable
of that interior kind. That a stone will fall, that fire will burn, that
the earth has solidity, we have observed a thousand times; and
when any new instance of this nature is presented, we draw without
hesitation the accustomed inference. The exact similarity of the
cases gives us a perfect assurance of a similar event; and a stronger
evidence is never desired nor sought after. But wherever you
depart, in the least, from the similarity of the cases, you diminish
proportionably the evidence; and may at last bring it to a very
weak *analogy*, which is confessedly liable to error and uncertainty.
After having experienced the circulation of the blood in human

creatures, we make no doubt that it takes place in Titius and Maevius: but from its circulation in frogs and fishes, it is only a presumption, though a strong one, from analogy, that it takes place in men and other animals. The analogical reasoning is much weaker, when we infer the circulation of the sap in vegetables from our experience, that the blood circulates in animals; and those, who hastily followed that imperfect analogy, are found, by more accurate experiments, to have been mistaken.

If we see a house, Cleanthes, we conclude, with the greatest certainty, that it had an architect or builder; because this is precisely that species of effect, which we have experienced to proceed from that species of cause. But surely you will not affirm, that the universe bears such a resemblance to a house, that we can with the same certainly infer a similar cause, or that the analogy is here entire and perfect. The dissimilitude is so striking, that the utmost you can here pretend to is a guess, a conjecture, a presumption concerning a similar cause; and how that pretension will be received in the world, I leave you to consider.

It would surely be very ill received, replied Cleanthes; and I should be deservedly blamed and detested, did I allow, that the proofs of a Deity amounted to no more than a guess or conjecture. But is the whole adjustment of means to ends in a house and in the universe so slight a resemblance? The economy of final causes? The order, proportion, and arrangement of every part? Steps of a stair are plainly contrived, that human legs may use them in mounting; and this inference is certain and infallible. Human legs are also contrived for walking and mounting; and this inference, I allow, is not altogether so certain, because of the dissimilarity which you remark; but does, therefore, deserve the name only of presumption or conjecture?

Good God! cried Demea, interrupting him, where are we? Zealous defenders of religion allow, that the proofs of a Deity fall short of perfect evidence! And you, Philo, on whose assistance I depended, in proving the adorable mysteriousness of the Divine Nature, do you assent to all these extravagant opinions of Cleanthes? For what other name can I give them? Or why spare my censure, when such principles are advanced, supported by such an authority, before so young a man as Pamphilus?

You seem not to apprehend, replied Philo, that I argue with

Cleanthes in his own way; and by showing him the dangerous con-sequences of his tenets, hope at last to reduce him to our opinion. But what sticks most with you, I observe, is the representation which Cleanthes has made of the argument *a posteriori;* and find-ing, that that argument is like to escape your hold and vanish into air, you think it so disguised, that you can scarcely believe it to be set in its true light. Now, however much I may dissent, in other respects, from the dangerous principles of Cleanthes, I must allow, that he has fairly represented that argument; and I shall endeavor so to state the matter to you, that you will entertain no farther scruples with regard to it.

Were a man to abstract from everything which he knows or has seen, he would be altogether incapable, merely from his own ideas, to determine what kind of scene the universe must be, or to give the preference to one state or situation of things above another. For as nothing which he clearly conceives, could be esteemed im-possible or implying a contradiction, every chimera of his fancy would be upon an equal footing; nor could he assign any just reason, why he adheres to one idea or system, and rejects the others, which are equally possible.

Again; after he opens his eyes, and contemplates the world, as it really is, it would be impossible for him, at first, to assign the cause of any one event; much less, of the whole of things or of the universe. He might set his fancy a rambling; and she might bring him in an infinite variety of reports and misrepresentations. These would all be possible; but being all equally possible, he would never, of himself, give a satisfactory account for his preferring one of them to the rest. Experience alone can point out to him the true cause of any phenomenon.

Now, according to this method of reasoning, Demea, it follows (and is, indeed, tacitly allowed by Cleanthes himself) that order, ar-rangement, or the adjustment of final causes is not, of itself, any proof of design; but only so far as it has been experienced to proceed from that principle. For aught we can know *a priori,* matter may contain the source or spring of order originally, within itself, as well as mind does; and there is no more difficulty in conceiving, that the several elements, from an internal unknown cause, may fall into the most exquisite arrangement, than to conceive that their ideas, in the great universal mind, from a like internal, unknown cause, fall into that arrangement. The equal possibility of both these suppositions is allowed. But by experience we find (according to Cleanthes), that there is a difference between them. Throw several pieces of steel together, without shape or form; they will never arrange themselves so as to compose a watch: stone, and mortar, and wood, without an architect, never erect a house. But the ideas in a human mind, we see, by an unknown, inexplicable economy, arrange themselves so as to form the plan of a watch or house. Experience, therefore, proves, that there is an original principle of order in mind, not in matter. From similar effects we infer similar causes. The adjustment of means to ends is alike in the universe, as in a machine of human contrivance. The causes, therefore, must be resembling.

I was from the beginning scandalized, I must own, with this resemblance, which is asserted, between the Deity and human creatures; and must conceive it to imply such a degradation of the Supreme Being as no sound theist could endure. With your assistance, therefore, Demea, I shall endeavor to defend what you justly called the adorable mysteriousness of the Divine Nature, and shall refute this reasoning of Cleanthes, provided he allows, that I have made a fair representation of it.

When Cleanthes had assented, Philo, after a short pause, proceeded in the following manner.

That all inferences, Cleanthes, concerning fact, are founded on experience, and that all experimental reasonings are founded on the supposition, that similar causes prove similar effects, and similar effects similar causes; I shall not, at present, much dispute with you. But observe, I entreat you, with what extreme caution all just reasoners proceed in the transferring of experiments to similar cases. Unless the cases be exactly similar, they repose no perfect phenomenon. Every alteration of circumstances occasions a doubt concerning the event; and it requires new experiments to prove certainly, that the new circumstances are of no moment or importance. A change in bulk, situation, arrangement, age, disposition of the air, or surrounding bodies; any of these particulars may be attended with the most unexpected consequences: and unless the objects be quite familiar to us, it is the highest temerity to expect with assurance, after any of these changes, an event similar to that which before fell under our observation. The slow and deliberate steps of philosophers, here, if anywhere, are distinguished from the precipitate march of the vulgar, who hurried on by the smallest similitudes, are incapable of all discernment or consideration.

But can you think, Cleanthes, that your usual phlegm and philosophy have been preserved in so wide a step as you have taken, when you compared to the universe, houses, ships, furniture, machines; and from their similarity in some circumstances inferred a similarity in their causes. Thought, design, intelligence, such as we discover in men and other animals, is no more than one of the springs and principles of the universe, as well as heat or cold, attraction or repulsion, and a hundred others, which fall under daily observation. It is an active cause, by which some particular parts of nature, we find, produce alterations on other parts. But can a conclusion, with any propriety, be transferred from parts to the whole? Does not the great disproportion bar all comparison and inference? From observing the growth of a hair, can we learn anything concerning the generation of a man? Would the manner of a leaf's blowing, even though perfectly known, afford us any instruction concerning the vegetation of a tree?

But allowing that we were to take the *operations* of one part of nature upon another for the foundation of our judgment concerning the *origin of the whole* (which can never be admitted), yet why select so minute, so weak, so bounded a principle as the reason and design of animals is found to be upon this planet? What peculiar privilege has this little agitation of the brain which we call *thought*, that we must thus make it the model of the whole universe? Our partiality in our own favor does indeed present it on all occasions; but sound philosophy ought carefully to guard against so natural an illusion.

So far from admitting, continued Philo, that the operations of a part can afford us any just conclusion concerning the origin of the whole, I will not allow any one part to form a rule for another part, if the latter be very remote from the former. Is there any reasonable ground to conclude, that the inhabitants of other planets possess thought, intelligence, reason, or anything similar to these faculties in men? When Nature has so extremely diversified her manner of operation in this small globe; can we imagine, that she incessantly copies herself throughout so immense a universe? And if thought, as we may well suppose, be confined merely to this narrow corner, and has even there so limited a sphere of action; with what propriety can we assign it for the original cause of all things? The narrow views of a peasant, who makes his domestic economy the rule for the government of kingdoms, is in comparison a pardonable sophism.

But were we ever so much assured, that a thought and reason, resembling the human, were to be found throughout the whole universe, and were its activity elsewhere vastly greater and more commanding than it appears in this globe; yet I cannot see, why the operations of a world, constituted, arranged, adjusted, can with any propriety be extended to a world, which is in its embryo state, and is advancing towards that constitution and arrangement. By observation, we know somewhat of the economy, action, and nourishment of a finished animal; but we must transfer with great caution that observation to the growth of a fetus in the womb, and still more, to the formation of an animalcule in the loins of its male parent. Nature, we find, even from our limited experience, possesses an infinite number of springs and principles, which incessantly discover themselves on every change of her position and situation. And what new and unknown principles would actuate her in so new and unknown a situation as that of the formation of a universe, we cannot, without the utmost termerity, pretend to determine.

A very small part of this great system, during a very short time, is very imperfectly discovered to us: and do we thence pronounce decisively concerning the origin of the whole?

Admirable conclusion! Stone, wood, brick, iron, brass, have not, at this time, in this minute globe of earth, an order or arrangement without human art and contrivance: therefore the universe could not originally attain its order and arrangement, without something similar to human art. But is a part of nature a rule for another part very wide of the former? Is it a rule for the whole? Is a very small part a rule for the universe? Is nature in one situation, a certain rule for nature in another situation, vastly different from the former?

And can you blame me, Cleanthes, if I here imitate the prudent reserve of Simonides, who, according to the noted story, being asked by Hiero, *What God was?* desired a day to think of it, and then two days more; and after that manner continually prolonged the term, without ever bringing in his definition or description? Could you even blame me, if I had answered at first *that I did not know*, and was sensible that this subject lay vastly beyond the reach of my faculties? You might cry out sceptic and rallier as much as you pleased: but having found, in so many other subjects, much more familiar, the imperfections and even contradictions of human reason, I never should expect any success from its feeble conjectures, in a subject, so sublime, and so remote from the sphere of our observation. When two species of objects have always been observed to be conjoined together, I can infer, by custom, the existence of one wherever I see the existence of the other: and this I call an argument from experience. But how this argument can have place, where the objects, as in the present case, are single, individual, without parallel, or specific resemblance, may be difficult to explain. And will any man tell me with a serious countenance, that an orderly universe must arise from some thought and art, like the human; because we have experience of it? To ascertain this reasoning, it were requisite, that we have experience of the origin of worlds; and it is not sufficient surely, that we have seen ships and cities arise from human art and contrivance. . . .

Philo was proceeding in this vehement manner, somewhat between jest and earnest, as it appeared to me; when he observed some signs of impatience in Cleanthes, and then immediately stopped short. What I had to suggest, said Cleanthes, is only that you would not abuse terms, or make use of popular expressions to subvert philosophical reasonings. You know, that the vulgar often distinguish reason from experience, even where the question relates only to matter of fact and existence; though it is found, where that reason is properly analyzed, that it is nothing but a species of experience. To prove by experience the origin of the universe from mind is not more contrary to common speech than to prove the motion of the earth from the same principle. And a caviler might raise all the same objections to the Copernican system, which you have urged against my reasonings. Have you other earths, might we say, which you have seen to move? Have. . . .

Yes! cried Philo, interrupting him, we have other earths. Is not the moon another earth, which we see to turn round its center? Is not Venus another earth, where we observe the same phenomenon? Are not the revolutions of the sun also a confirmation, from analogy, of the same theory? All the planets, are they not earths, which revolve about the sun? Are not the satellites moons, which move around Jupiter and Saturn, and along with these primary planets, round the sun? These analogies and resemblances, with others, which I have not mentioned, are the sole proofs of the Copernican system: and to you it belongs to consider whether you have any analogies of the same kind to support your theory.

In reality, Cleanthes, continued he, the modern system of astronomy is now so much received by all inquirers, and has become so essential a part even of our earliest education, that we are not commonly very scrupulous in examining the reasons upon which it is founded. It is now become a matter of mere curiosity to study the first writers on that subject, who had the full force of prejudice to encounter, and were obliged to turn their arguments on every side, in order to render them popular and convincing. But if we peruse Galileo's famous Dialogues concerning the system of the world, we shall find, that that great genius, one of the sublimest that ever existed, first bent all his endeavors to prove, that there was no foundation for the distinction commonly made between elementary and celestial substances. The schools, proceeding from the illusions of sense, had carried this distinction very far; and had established the latter substances to be ingenerable, incorruptible, unalterable, impassable; and has assigned all the opposite qualities to the former. But Galileo, beginning with the moon, proved its similarity in every particular to the earth; its convex figure, its natural darkness when not illuminated, its density, its distinction into solid and liquid, the variations of its phases, the mutual illuminations of the earth and moon, their mutual eclipses, and inequalities of the lunar surface, etc. After many instances of this kind, with regard to all the planets, men plainly saw, that these bodies became proper objects of experience; and that the similarity of their nature enabled us to extend the same arguments and phenomena from one to the other.

In the cautious proceeding of the astronomers, you may read your own condemnation, Cleanthes; or rather may see, that the subject in which you are engaged exceeds all human reason and inquiry. Can you pretend to show any such similarity between the fabric of a house, and the generation of a universe? Have you ever seen nature in any such situation as resembles the first arrangement of the elements? Have worlds ever been formed under your eye? And have you had leisure to observe the whole progress of the phe-

nomenon, from the first appearance of order to its final consummation? If you have, then cite your experience, and deliver your
theory.

How the most absurd argument, replied Cleanthes, in the hands
of a man of ingenuity and invention, may acquire an air of probability! Are you not aware, Philo, that it became necessary for
Copernicus and his first disciples to prove the similarity of the
terrestrial and celestial matter; because several philosophers, blinded
by old systems, and supported by some sensible appearances, had
denied this similarity? But that it is by no means necessary, that
theists should prove the similarity of the works of nature to those of
art; because this similarity is self-evident and undeniable? The
same matter, a like form: what more is requisite to show an analogy
between their causes, and to ascertain the origin of all things from a
divine purpose and intention? Your objections, I must freely tell
you, are no better than the abstruse cavils of those philosophers
who denied motion; and ought to be refuted in the same manner, by
illustrations, examples, and instances, rather than by serious argument and philosophy.

Suppose, therefore, that an articulate voice were heard in the
clouds, much louder and more melodious than any which human art
could ever reach: suppose, that this voice were extended in the same
instant over all nations, and spoke to each nation in its own language
and dialect: suppose, that the words delivered not only contain a
just sense and meaning but convey some instruction altogether
worthy of a benevolent being, superior to mankind: could you
possibly hesitate a moment concerning the cause of this voice?
and must you not instantly ascribe it to some design or purpose?
Yet I cannot see but all the same objections (if they merit that
appellation) which lie against the system of theism, may also be
produced against this inference.

Might you not say, that all conclusions concerning fact were
founded on experience: that when we hear an articulate voice in
the dark, and thence infer a man, it is only the resemblance of the
effects, which leads us to conclude that there is a like resemblance
in the cause: but that this extraordinary voice, by its loudness,
extent, and flexibility to all languages, bears so little analogy to
any human voice, that we have no reason to suppose any analogy
in their causes: and consequently, that a rational, wise, coherent

speech proceeded, you knew not whence, from some accidental whistling of the winds, not from any divine reason or intelligence? You see clearly your own objections in these cavils; and I hope too, you see clearly, that they cannot possibly have more force in the one case than in the other.

But to bring the case still nearer the present one of the universe, I shall make two suppositions, which imply not any absurdity or impossibility. Suppose, that there is a natural, universal, invariable language, common to every individual of human race, and that books are natural productions, which perpetuate themselves in the same manner with animals and vegetables, by descent and propagation. Several expressions of our passions contain a universal language: all brute animals have a natural speech, which, however limited, is very intelligible to their own species. And as there are infinitely fewer parts and less contrivance in the finest composition of eloquence, than in the coarsest organized body, the propagation of an *Illiad* or *Aeneid* is an easier supposition than that of any plant or animal.

Suppose, therefore, that you enter into your library, thus peopled by natural volumes, containing the most refined reason and most exquisite beauty: could you possibly open one of them, and doubt, that its original cause bore the strongest analogy to mind and intelligence? When it reasons and discourses; when it expostulates, argues, and enforces its views and topics; when it applies sometimes to the pure intellect, sometimes to the affections; when it collects, disposes, and adorns every consideration suited to the subject: could you persist in asserting, that all this, at the bottom, had really no meaning, and that the first formation of this volume in the loins of its original parent proceeded not from thought and design? Your obstinacy, I know, reaches not that degree of firmness: even your sceptical play and wantonness would be abashed at so glaring an absurdity.

But if there be any difference, Philo, between this supposed case and the real one of the universe, it is all to the advantage of the latter. The anatomy of an animal affords many stronger instances of design than the perusal of Livy or Tacitus: and any objection which you start in the former case, by carrying me back to so unusual and extraordinary a scene as the first formation of worlds, the same objection has place on the supposition of our vegetating library. Choose, then, your party, Philo, without ambiguity or evasion: assert either that a rational volume is no proof of a rational cause, or admit of a similar cause to all the works of nature.

Let me here observe too, continued Cleanthes, that this religious argument, instead of being weakened by that scepticism, so much affected by you, rather acquires force from it, and becomes more firm and undisputed. To exclude all argument or reasoning of every kind is either affectation or madness. The declared profession of every reasonable sceptic is only to reject abstruse, remote and refined arguments; to adhere to common sense and the plain instincts of nature; and to assent, wherever any reasons strike him with so full a force, that he cannot, without the greatest violence, prevent it. Now the arguments for Natural Religion are plainly of this kind; and nothing but the most perverse, obstinate metaphysics can reject them. Consider, anatomize the eye; survey its structure and contrivance; and tell me, from your own feeling, if the idea of a contriver does not immediately flow in upon you with a force like that of sensation. The most obvious conclusion surely is in favor of design; and it requires time, reflection and study, to summon up those frivolous, though abstruse objections, which can support infidelity. Who can behold the male and female of each species, the correspondence of their parts and instincts, their passions and whole course of life before and after generation, but must be sensible, that the propagation of the species is intended by Nature? Millions and millions of such instances present themselves through every part of the universe; and no language can convey a more intelligible, irresistible meaning, than the curious adjustment of final causes. To what degree, therefore, of blind dogmatism must one have attained, to reject such natural and such convincing arguments?

Some beauties in writing we may meet with, which seem contrary to rules, and which gain the affections, and animate the imagination in opposition to all the precepts of criticism, and to the authority of the established masters of art. And if the argument for theism be, as you pretend, contradictory to the principles of logic; its universal, its irresistible influence proves clearly, that there may be arguments of a like irregular nature. Whatever cavils may be urged; an orderly world, as well as a coherent, articulate speech, will still be received as an incontestable proof of design and intention.

It sometimes happens, I own, that the religious arguments have not their due influence on an ignorant savage and barbarian; not because they are obscure and difficult, but because he never asks himself any question with regard to them. Whence arises the curious structure of an animal? From the copulation of its parents. and these whence? From *their* parents. A few removes set the objects at such a distance, that to him they are lost in darkness and confusion; nor is he actuated by any curiosity to trace them farther. But this is neither dogmatism nor scepticism, but stupidity; a state of mind very different from your sifting, inquisitive disposition, my ingenious friend. You can trace causes from effects: you can compare the most distant and remote objects: and your greatest errors proceed not from barrenness of thought and invention, but from too luxuriant a fertility, which suppresses your natural good sense, by a profusion of unnecessary scruples and objections.

19. *The Moral Argument* *

W. R. SORLEY *(1855–1935)*

The result so far is that the events of the world as a causal system are not inconsistent with the view that this same world is a moral order, that its purpose is a moral purpose. The empirical discrepancies between the two orders, and the obstacles which the world puts in the way of morality, are capable of explanation when we allow that ideals of goodness have not only to be discovered by finite minds, but that for their realisation they need to be freely accepted by individual wills and gradually organised in individual characters. If this principle still leaves many particular difficulties unresolved, it may at least be claimed that it provides the general lines of an explanation of the relation of moral value to experience, and that a larger knowledge of the issues of life than is open to us

---

* W. R. Sorley, *Moral Values and the Idea of God* (New York: Cambridge University Press, 1919). Cited from "The Moral Argument," Chapter 13. Reprinted by permission.

might be expected to show that the particular difficulties also are not incapable of solution.

This means that it is possible to regard God as the author and ruler of the world, as it appears in space and time, and at the same time to hold that the moral values of which we are conscious and the moral ideal which we come to apprehend with increasing clearness express his nature. But the question remains, Are we to regard morality — its values, laws, and ideal —as belonging to a Supreme Mind, that is, to God? It is as an answer to this question that the specific Moral Argument enters. And here I cannot do better than give the argument in the words of Dr. Rashdall:

"An absolute Moral Law or moral ideal cannot exist in material things. And it does not exist in the mind of this or that individual Only if we believe in the existence of a Mind for which the true moral ideal is already in some sense real, a Mind which is the source of whatever is true in our own moral judgments, can we rationally think of the moral ideal as no less real than the world itself. Only so can we believe in an absolute standard of right and wrong, which is as independent of this or that man's actual ideas and actual desires as the facts of material nature. The belief in God, though not (like the belief in a real and an active self) a postulate of there being any such thing as Morality at all, is the logical presupposition of an 'objective' or absolute Morality. A moral ideal can exist no where and nohow but in a mind; an absolute moral ideal can exist only in a Mind from which all Reality is derived.[1] Our moral idea can only claim objective validity in so far as it can rationally be regarded as the revelation of a moral ideal eternally existing in the mind of God." [2]

The argument as thus put may be looked upon as a special and striking extension of the cosmological argument. In its first and most elementary form the cosmological argument seeks a cause for the bare existence of the world and man; to account for them there must be something able to bring them into being: God is the First Cause. Then the order of nature impresses us by its regularity, and we come by degrees to understand the principles of its working and the laws under which the material whole maintains its equilibrium

---

[1] "Or at least a mind by which all Reality is controlled."—Dr. Rashdall's foot note.

[2] H. Rashdall, *The Theory of Good and Evil* (1907) Vol. 11, p. 212.

and the ordered procession of its changes: these laws and this order call for explanation, and we conceive God as the Great Lawgiver. But beyond this material world, we understand relations and principles of a still more general kind; and the intellect of man recognises abstract truths so evident that, once understood, they cannot be questioned, while inferences are drawn from these which only the more expert minds can appreciate and yet which they recognise as eternally valid. To what order do these belong and what was their home when man as yet was unconscious of them? Surely if their validity is eternal they must have had existence somewhere, and we can only suppose them to have existed in the one eternal mind: God is therefore the God of Truth. Further, persons are conscious of values and of an ideal of goodness, which they recognise as having undoubted authority for the direction of their activity; the validity of these values or laws and of this ideal, however, does not depend upon their recognition: it is objective and eternal; and how could this eternal validity stand alone, not embodied in matter and neither seen nor realised by finite minds, unless there were an eternal mind whose thought and will were therein expressed? *God must therefore exist and his nature be goodness.*

The argument in this its latest phase has a new feature which distinguishes it from the preceding phases. The laws or relations of interacting phenomena which we discover in nature are already embodied in the processes of nature. It may be argued that they have their reality therein: that in cognising them we are simply cognising an aspect of the actual world in space and time, and consequently that, if the mere existence of things does not require God to account for it (on the ground urged by Hume that the world, being a singular event, justifies no inference as to its cause), then, equally, we are not justified in seeking a cause for those laws or relations which are, after all, but one aspect of the existing world. It may be urged that the same holds of mathematical relations: that they are merely an abstract of the actual order, when considered solely in its formal aspect. It is more difficult to treat the still more general logical relations in the same fashion; but they too receive verification in reality and in our thought so far as it does not end in confusion. But it is different with ethical values. Their validity could not be verified in external phenomena; they cannot be established by observation of the course of nature. They hold good for persons only: and their peculiarity consists in the fact that their validity is not in any way dependent upon their being manifested in the character or conduct of persons, or even on their being recognised in the thoughts of persons. We acknowledge the good and its objective claim upon us even when we are conscious that our will has not yielded to the claim; and we admit that its validity existed before we recognised it.

This leading characteristic makes the theistic argument founded upon moral values or the moral law both stronger in one respect and weaker in another respect than the corresponding argument from natural law and intelligible relations. It is weaker because it is easier to deny the premiss from which it starts — that is, the objective validity of moral law — than it is to deny the objective validity of natural or mathematical or logical relations. But I am here assuming the objective validity of morality as already established by our previous enquiries: and it is unnecessary to go back upon the question. And, granted this premiss, the argument adds an important point. Other relations and laws (it may be said, and the statement is true of laws of nature at any rate) are embodied in actually existing objects. But the same cannot be said of the moral law or moral ideal. We acknowledge that there are objective values, although men may not recognise them, that the moral law is not abrogated by being ignored, and that our consciousness is striving towards the apprehension of an ideal which no finite mind has clearly grasped, but which is none the less valid although it is not realised and is not even apprehended by us in its truth and fullness. Where then is this ideal? It cannot be valid at one time and not at another. It must be eternal as well as objective. As Dr. Rashdall urges, it is not in material things, and it is not in the mind of this or that individual; but "it can exist nowhere and nohow but in a mind"; it requires therefore the mind of God.

Against this argument, however, it may be contended that it disregards the distinction between validity and existence. Why is it assumed that the moral ideal must exist somehow and somewhere? Validity, it may be said, is a unique concept, as unique as existence, and different from it. And this is true. At the same time it is also true that the validity of the moral ideal, like all validity, is a validity for existents. Without this reference to existence there seems no meaning in asserting validity. At any rate it is clear that it is for existents — namely, for the realm of persons — that the moral ideal is valid. It is also true that the perfect moral ideal does not exist in the volitional, or even in the intellectual, consciousness of these persons: they have not achieved agreement with it in their lives, and even their understanding of it is incomplete. Seeing then that it is not manifested by finite existents, how are we to conceive its validity? Other truths are displayed in the order of the existing world; but it is not so with moral values. And yet the system of moral values has been acknowledged to be an aspect of the real universe to which existing things belong. How are we to conceive its relation to them? A particular instance of goodness can exist only in the character of an individual person or group of persons; an idea of goodness such as we have is found only in minds such as ours. But the ideal of goodness does not exist in finite minds or in their material environment. What then is its status in the system of reality?

The question is answered if we regard the moral order as the order of a Supreme Mind and the ideal of goodness as belonging to this Mind. The difficulty for this view is to show that the Mind which is the home of goodness may also be regarded as the ground of the existing world. That reality as a whole, both in its actual events and in its moral order, can be consistently regarded as the expression of a Supreme Mind has been the argument of the present lecture.

20. Conscience as the Voice of God *

JOHN HENRY NEWMAN (1801–1890)

The feeling of conscience (being, I repeat, a certain keen sensibility, pleasant or painful, — self-approval and hope, or compunction and fear, — attendant on certain of our actions, which in

---

* John Henry Newman, *A Grammar of Assent* (New York: Longmans, Green & Co., Inc., 1930), from Chapter 5, "Belief in One God." Reprinted by permission.

consequence we call right or wrong) is twofold:—it is a moral sense, and a sense of duty; a judgment of the reason and a magisterial dictate. Of course its act is indivisible; still it has these two aspects, distinct from each other, and admitting of a separate consideration. Though I lost my sense of the obligation which I lie under to abstain from acts of dishonesty, I should not in consequence lose my sense that such actions were an outrage offered to my moral nature. Again; though I lost my sense of their moral deformity, I should not therefore lose my sense that they were forbidden to me. Thus conscience has both a critical and a judicial office, and though its promptings, in the breasts of the millions of human beings to whom it is given, are not in all cases correct, that does not necessarily interfere with the force of its testimony and of its sanction: its testimony that there is a right and a wrong, and its sanction to that testimony conveyed in the feelings which attend on right or wrong conduct. Here I have to speak of conscience in the latter point of view, not as supplying us, by means of its various acts, with the elements of morals, which may be developed by the intellect into an ethical code, but simply as the dictate of an authoritative monitor bearing upon the details of conduct as they come before us, and complete in its several acts, one by one.

Let us thus consider conscience then, not as a rule of right conduct, but as a sanction of right conduct. This is its primary and most authoritative aspect; it is the ordinary sense of the word. Half the world would be puzzled to know what was meant by the moral sense; but every one knows what is meant by a good or bad conscience. Conscience is ever forcing on us by threats and by promises that we must follow the right and avoid the wrong; so far it is one and the same in the mind of every one, whatever be its particular errors in particular minds as to the acts which it orders to be done or to be avoided; and in this respect it corresponds to our perception of the beautiful and deformed. As we have naturally a sense of the beautiful and graceful in nature and art, though tastes proverbially differ, so we have a sense of duty and obligation, whether we all associate it with the same particular actions or not. Here, however, Taste and Conscience part company: for the sense of beautifulness, as indeed the Moral Sense, has no special relations to persons, but contemplates objects in themselves; conscience, on the other hand, is concerned with persons primarily, and with actions mainly as viewed in their doors, or rather with self alone and one's own actions, and with others only indirectly and as if in association with self. And further, taste is its own evidence, appealing to nothing beyond its own sense of the beautiful or the ugly, and enjoying the specimens of the beautiful simply for their own sake; but conscience does not repose on itself, but vaguely reaches forward to something beyond self, and dimly discerns a sanction higher than self for its decisions, as evidenced in that keen sense of obligation and responsibility which informs them. And hence it is that we are accustomed to speak of conscience as a voice, — a term which we should never think of applying to the sense of the beautiful; and moreover a voice, or the echo of a voice, imperative and constraining, like no other dictate in the whole of our experience.

And again, in consequence of this prerogative of dictating and commanding, which is of its essence, Conscience has an intimate bearing on our affections and emotions, leading us to reverence and awe, hope and fear, especially fear, a feeling which is foreign for the most part, not only to Taste, but even to the Moral Sense, except in consequence of accidental associations. No fear is felt by any one who recognizes that his conduct has not been beautiful, though he may be mortified at himself, if perhaps he has thereby forfeited some advantage; but, if he has been betrayed into any kind of immorality, he has a lively sense of responsibility and guilt, though the act be no offence against society, — of distress and apprehension, even though it may be of present service to him, — of compunction and regret, though in itself it be most pleasurable, — of confusion of face, though it may have no witnesses. These various perturbations of mind, which are characteristic of a bad conscience, and may be very considerable, —self-reproach, poignant shame, haunting remorse, chill dismay at the prospect of the future, — and their contraries, when the conscience is good, as real though less forcible, self-approval, inward peace, lightness of heart, and the like, — these emotions constitute a generic difference between conscience and our other intellectual senses, — common sense, good sense, sense of expedience, taste, sense of honour, and the like, — as indeed they would also create between conscience and the moral sense, supposing these two were not aspects of one and the same feeling, exercised upon one and the same subject-matter.

So much for the characteristic phenomena, which conscience

presents, nor is it difficult to determine what they imply. I refer once more to our sense of the beautiful. This sense is attended by an intellectual enjoyment, and is free from whatever is of the nature of emotion, except in one case, viz. when it is excited by personal objects; then it is that the tranquil feeling of admiration is exchanged for the excitement of affection and passion. Conscience too, considered as a moral sense, an intellectual sentiment, is a sense of admiration and disgust, of approbation and blame: but it is something more than a moral sense; it is always, what the sense of the beautiful is only in certain cases; it is always emotional. No wonder then that it always implies what that sense only sometimes implies; that it always involves the recognition of a living object, towards which it is directed. Inanimate things cannot stir our affections; these are correlative with persons. If, as is the case, we feel responsibility, are ashamed, are frightened, at transgressing the voice of conscience, this implies that there is One to whom we are responsible, before whom we are ashamed, whose claims upon us we fear. If, on doing wrong, we feel the same tearful, broken-hearted sorrow which overwhelms us on hurting a mother; if, on doing right, we enjoy the same sunny serenity of mind, the same soothing, satisfactory delight which follows on our receiving praise from a father, we certainly have within us the image of some person, to whom our love and veneration look, in whose smile we find our happiness, for whom we yearn, towards whom we direct our pleadings, in whose anger we are troubled and waste away. These feelings in us are such as require for their exciting cause an intelligent being; we are not affectionate towards a stone, nor do we feel shame before a horse or a dog; we have no remorse or compunction on breaking mere human law: yet, so it is, conscience excites all these painful emotions, confusion, foreboding, self-condemnation; and on the other hand it sheds upon us a deep peace, a sense of security, a resignation, and a hope, which there is no sensible, no earthly object to elicit. "The wicked flees, when no one pursueth;" then why does he flee? whence his terror? who is it that he sees in solitude, in darkness, in the hidden chambers of his heart? If the cause of these emotions does not belong to this visible world, the Object to which his perception is directed must be Supernatural and Divine; and thus the phenomena of Conscience, as a dictate, avail to impress the imagination with the picture of a Supreme Governor, a Judge, holy, just, powerful, all-seeing, retributive, and is the creative principle of religion, as the Moral Sense is the principle of ethics.

And let me here refer again to the fact, to which I have already drawn attention, that this instinct of the mind recognizing an external Master in the dictate of conscience, and imaging the thought of Him in the definite impressions which conscience creates, is parallel to that other law of, not only human, but of brute nature, by which the presence of unseen individual beings is discerned under the shifting shapes and colours of the visible world. Is it by sense, or by reason, that brutes understand the real unities, material and spiritual, which are signified by the lights and shadows, the brilliant ever-changing calidoscope, as it may be called, which plays upon their retina? Not by reason, for they have not reason; not by sense, because they are transcending sense; therefore it is an instinct. This faculty on the part of brutes, unless we were used to it, would strike us as a great mystery. It is one peculiarity of animal natures to be susceptible of phenomena through the channels of sense; it is another to have in those sensible phenomena a perception of the individuals to which certain groups of them belong. This perception of individual things is given to brutes in large measures, and that apparently from the moment of their birth. It is by no mere physical instinct, such as that which leads him to his mother for milk, that the new-dropped lamb recognizes each of his fellow lambkins as a whole, consisting of many parts bound up in one, and, before he is an hour old, makes experience of his and their rival individualities. And much more distinctly do the horse and dog recognize even the personality of their masters. How are we to explain this apprehension of things, which are one and individual, in the midst of a world of pluralities and transmutations, whether in the instance of brutes or of children? But until we account for the knowledge which an infant has of his mother or his nurse, what reason have we to take exception at the doctrine, as strange and difficult, that in the dictate of conscience, without previous experiences or analogical reasoning, he is able gradually to perceive the voice, or the echoes of the voice, of a Master, living, personal, and sovereign?

I grant, of course, that we cannot assign a date, ever so early, before which he had learned nothing at all, and formed no mental associations, from the words and conduct of those who have the care of him. But still, if a child of five or six years old, when reason is at length fully awake, has already mastered and appropriated thoughts and beliefs, in consequence of their teaching, in such sort as to be able to handle and apply them familiarly, according to the occasion, as principles of intellectual action, those beliefs at the very least must be singularly congenial to his mind, if not connatural with its initial action. And that such a spontaneous reception of religious truths is common with children, I shall take for granted, till I am convinced that I am wrong in so doing. The child keenly understands that there is a difference between right and wrong; and when he has done what he believes to be wrong, he is conscious that he is offending One to whom he is amenable, whom he does not see, who sees him. His mind reaches forward with a strong presentiment to the thought of a Moral Governor, sovereign over him, mindful, and just. It comes to him like an impulse of nature to entertain it.

It is my wish to take an ordinary child, but one who is safe from influences destructive of his religious instincts. Supposing he has offended his parents, he will all alone and without effort, as if it were the most natural of acts, place himself in the presence of God, and beg of Him to set him right with them. Let us consider how much is contained in this simple act. First, it involves the impression on his mind of an unseen Being with whom he is in immediate relation, and that relation so familiar that he can address Him whenever he himself chooses; next, of One whose goodwill towards him he is assured of, and can take for granted — nay, who loves him better, and is nearer to him, than his parents, further, of One who can hear him, wherever he happens to be, and who can read his thoughts, for his prayer need not be vocal; lastly, of One who can effect a critical change in the state of feeling of others toward him. That is, we shall not be wrong in holding that this child has in his mind the image of an Invisible Being, who exercises a particular providence among us, who is present every where, who is heart-rending, heart-changing, ever-accessible, open to impetration. What a strong and intimate vision of God must he have already attained, if, as I have supposed, an ordinary trouble of mind has the spontaneous effect of leading him for consolation and aid to an Invisible Personal Power!

Moreover, this image brought before his mental vision is the image of One who by implicit threat and promise commands certain things which he, the same child, coincidentally, by the same act of his mind, approves; which receive the adhesion of his moral sense and judgment, as right and good. It is the image of One who is good, inasmuch as enjoining and enforcing what is right and good, and who, in consequence, not only excites in the child hope and fear, — nay (it may be added), gratitude towards Him, as giving a law and maintaining it by reward and punishment, — but kindles in him love towards Him, as giving him a good law, and therefore as being good Himself, for it is the property of goodness to kindle love, or rather the very object of love is goodness; and all those distinct elements of the moral law, which the typical child, whom I am supposing, more or less consciously loves and approves, — truth, purity, justice, kindness, and the like, — are but shapes and aspects of goodness. And having in his degree a sensibility towards them all, for the sake of them all he is moved to love the Lawgiver, who enjoins them upon him. And, as he can contemplate these qualities and their manifestations under the common name of goodness, he is prepared to think of them as indivisible correlative, supplementary of each other in one and the same Personality, so that there is no aspect of goodness which God is not; and that the more, because the notion of a perfection embracing all possible excellences, both moral and intellectual, is especially congenial to the mind, and there are in fact intellectual attributes, as well as moral, included in the child's image of God, as above represented.

Such is the apprehension which even a child may have of his Sovereign, Lawgiver, and Judge; which is possible in the case of children, because, at least, some children possess it, whether others possess it or no; and which, when it is found in children, is found to act promptly and keenly, by reason of the paucity of their ideas. It is an image of the good God, good in Himself, good relatively to the child, with whatever incompleteness; an image before it has been reflected on, and before it is recognized by him as a notion. Though he cannot explain or define the word "God," when told to use it, his acts show that to him it is far more than a word. He listens, indeed, with wonder and interest to fables or tales; he has a dim, shadowy sense of what he hears about persons and matters of this world; but he has that within him which actually vibrates, responds, and gives a deep meaning to the lessons of his first teachers about the will and the providence of God.

How far this initial religious knowledge comes from without, and how much from within, how much is natural, how much implies a special divine aid which is above nature, we have no means of determining, nor is it necessary for my present purpose to determine. I am not engaged in tracing the image of God in the mind of a child or a man to its first origins, but showing that he can become possessed of such an image, over and above all mere notions of God, and in what that image consists. Whether its elements, latent in the mind, would ever be elicited without extrinsic help is very doubtful; but whatever be the actual history of the first formation of the divine image within us, so far is certain, that, by informations external to ourselves, as time goes on, it admits of being strengthened and improved. It is certain too, that whether it grows brighter and stronger, or, on the other hand, is dimmed, distorted, or obliterated, depends on each of us individually, and on his circumstances. It is more than probable that, in the event, from neglect, from the temptations of life, from bad companions, or from the urgency of secular occupations, the light of the soul will fade away and die out. Men transgress their sense of duty, and gradually lose those sentiments of shame and fear, the natural supplements of transgression, which, as I have said, are the witnesses of the Unseen Judge. And, even were it deemed impossible that those who had in their first youth a genuine apprehension of Him, could ever utterly lose it, yet that apprehension may become almost undistinguishable from an inferential acceptance of the great truth, or may dwindle into a mere notion of their intellect. On the contrary, the image of God, if duly cherished, may expand, deepen, and be completed, with the growth, of their powers and in the course of life, under the varied lessons, within and without them, which are brought home to them concerning that same God, One and Personal, by means of education social intercourse, experience, and literature.

To a mind thus carefully formed upon the basis of its natural conscience, the world, both of nature and of man, does but give back a reflection of those truths about the One Living God, which have been familiar to it from childhood. Good and evil meet us daily as we pass through life, and there are those who think it philosophical to act towards the manifestations of each with some sort of impartiality, as if evil had as much right to be there as good, or even a better, as having more striking triumphs and a broader jurisdiction. And because the course of things is determined by fixed laws they consider that those laws preclude the present agency of the Creator in the carrying out of particular issues. It is otherwise with the theology of a religious imagination. It has a living hold on truths which are really to be found in the world, though they are not upon the surface. It is able to pronounce by anticipation, what it takes a long argument to prove — that good is the rule, and evil the exception. It is able to assume that, uniform as are the laws of nature, they are consistent with a particular Providence. It interprets what it sees around it by this previous inward teaching, as the true key of that maze of vast complicated disorder; and thus it gains a more consistent and luminous vision of God from the most unpromising materials. Thus conscience is a connecting principle between the creature and his Creator; and the firmest hold of theological truths is gained by habits of personal religion. When men begin all their works with the thought of God, acting for His sake and to fulfil His will, when they ask His blessing on themselves and their life, pray to Him for the objects they desire, and see Him in the event, whether it be according to their prayers or not, they will find everything that happens tend to confirm them in the truths about Him which live in their imagination, varied and unearthly as those truths may be. Then they are brought into His presence as a Living Person, and are able to hold converse with Him, and that with a directness and simplicity, with a confidence and intimacy, *mutatis mutandis*,[1] which we use towards an earthly superior; so that it is doubtful whether we realize the company of our fellow-men with greater keenness than these favoured minds are able to contemplate and adore the Unseen, Incomprehensible Creator.

21. *The Wager in Favor of God* *

BLAISE PASCAL *(1623–1662)*

We know that there is an infinite, and are ignorant of its nature. As we know it to be false that numbers are finite, it is therefore true that there is an infinity in number. But we do not know what

---

[1] [The required changes being made.]

* Blaise Pascal, *Pensées* (New York: E. P. Dutton & Co., Inc., Everyman's Library Edition, 1948). "Aphorisms," pp. 229–241. Reprinted by permission.

it is. It is false that it is even, it is false that it is odd; for the addition of a unit can make no change in its nature. Yet it is a number, and every number is odd or even (this is certainly true of every finite number). So we may well know that there is a God without knowing what He is. Is there not one substantial truth, seeing there are so many things which are not the truth itself?

We know then the existence and nature of the finite, because we also are finite and have extension. We know the existence of the infinite, and are ignorant of its nature, because it has extension like us, but not limits like us. But we know neither the existence nor the nature of God, because He has neither extension nor limits.

But by faith we know His existence; in glory we shall know His nature. Now, I have already shown that we may well know the existence of a thing, without knowing its nature.

Let us now speak according to natural lights.

If there is a God, He is infinitely incomprehensible, since, having neither parts nor limits, He has no affinity to us. We are then incapable of knowing either what He is or if He is. This being so, who will dare to undertake the decision of the question? Not we, who have no affinity to Him.

Who then will blame Christians for not being able to give a reason for their belief, since they profess a religion for which they cannot give a reason? They declare, in expounding it to the world, that it is a foolishness, *stultiam;* and then you complain that they do not prove it! If they proved it, they would not keep their word; it is in lacking proofs that they are not lacking in sense. "Yes, but although this excuses those who offer it as such, and takes away from them the blame of putting it forward without reason, it does not excuse those who receive it." Let us then examine this point, and say, "God is, or He is not." But to which side shall we incline? Reason can decide nothing here. There is an infinite chaos which separated us. A game is being played at the extremity of this infinite distance where heads or tails will turn up. What will you wager? According to reason, you can do neither the one thing nor the other; according to reason, you can defend neither of the propositions.

Do not then reprove for error those who have made a choice; for you know nothing about it. "No, but I blame them for having made, not this choice, but a choice; for again both he who chooses heads and he who chooses tails are equally at fault, they are both in the wrong. The true course is not to wager at all."

Yes; but you must wager. It is not optional. You are embarked. Which will you choose then? Let us see. Since you must choose, let us see which interests you least. You have two things to lose, the true and the good; and two things to stake, your reason and your will, your knowledge and your happiness; and your nature has two things to shun, error and misery. Your reason is no more shocked in choosing one rather than the other, since you must of necessity choose. This is one point settled. But your happiness? Let us weigh the gain and the loss in wagering that God is. Let us estimate these two chances. If you gain, you gain all; if you lose, you lose nothing. Wager, then, without hesitation that He is. — "That is very fine. Yes, I must wager; but I may perhaps wager too much." — Let us see. Since there is an equal risk of gain and of loss, if you had only to gain two lives, instead of one, you might still wager. But if there were three lives to gain, you would have to play (since you are under the necessity of playing), and you would be imprudent, when you are forced to play, not to chance your life to gain three at a game where there is an equal risk of loss and gain. But there is an eternity of life and happiness. And this being so, if there were an infinity of chances, of which one only would be for you, you would still be right in wagering one to win two, and you would act stupidly, being obliged to play, by refusing to stake one life against three at a game in which out of an infinity of chances there is one for you, if there were an infinity of an infinitely happy life to gain. But there is here an infinity of an infinitely happy life to gain, a chance of gain against a finite number of chances of loss, and what you stake is finite. It is all divided; wherever the infinite is and there is not an infinity of chances of loss against that of gain, there is no time to hesitate, you must give all. And thus, when one is forced to play, he must renounce reason to preserve his life, rather than to risk it for infinite gain, as likely to happen as the loss of nothingness.

For it is no use to say it is uncertain if we will gain, and it is certain that we risk, and that the infinite distance between the *certainty* of what is staked and the *uncertainty* of what will be gained, equals the finite good which is certainly staked against the uncertain infinite. It is not so, as every player stakes a certainty to gain an uncertainty, and yet he stakes a finite certainty to gain a finite uncertainty, without transgressing against reason. There is not an infinite distance between the certainty staked and the uncertainty of the gain; that is untrue. In truth, there is an infinity between the certainty of gain and the certainty of loss. But the uncertainty of the gain is proportioned to the certainty of the stake according to the proportion of the chances of gain and loss. Hence it comes that, if there are as many risks on one side as on the other, the course is to play even; and then the certainty of the stake is equal to the uncertainty of the gain, so far is it from fact that there is an infinite distance between them. And so our proposition is of infinite force, when there is the finite to stake in a game where there are equal risks of gain and loss, and the infinite to gain. This is demonstrable; and if men are capable of any truths, this is one.

"I confess it, I admit it. But, still, is there no means of seeing the faces of the cards?" — Yes, Scripture and the rest, etc. "Yes, but I have my hands tied and my mouth closed; I am forced to wager, and am not free. I am not released, and am so made that I cannot believe. What, then, would you have me do?"

True. But at least learn your inability to believe, since reason brings you to this, and yet you cannot believe. Endeavor then to convince yourself, not by increase of proofs of God, but by the abatement of your passions. You would like to attain faith, and do not know the way; you would like to cure yourself of unbelief, and ask the remedy for it. Learn of those who have been bound like you, and who now stake all their possessions. These are people who know the way which you would follow, and who are cured of an ill of which you would be cured. Follow the way by which they began; by acting as if they believed, taking the holy water, having masses said, etc. Even this will naturally make you believe, and deaden your acuteness. — "But this is what I am afraid of." — And why? What have you to lose?

But to show you that this leads you there, it is this which will lessen the passions, which are your stumbling-blocks.

The end of this discourse. — Now, what harm will befall you in taking this side? You will be faithful, honest, humble, grateful, generous, a sincere friend, truthful. Certainly you will not have those poisonous pleasures, glory and luxury; but will you not have others? I will tell you that you will thereby gain in this life, and that, at each step you take on this road, you will see so great certainty of gain, so much nothingness in what you risk, that you will at last recognise that you have wagered for something certain and infinite, for which you have given nothing.

"Ah! This discourse transports me, charms me," etc.

If this discourse pleases you and seems impressive, know that it is made by a man who has knelt, both before and after it, in prayer to that Being, infinite and without parts, before whom he lays all he has, for you also to lay before Him all you have for your own good and for His glory, that so strength may be given to lowliness.

234

If we must not act save on a certainty, we ought not to act on religion, for it is not certain. But how many things we do on an uncertainty, sea voyages, battles! I say then we must do nothing at all, for nothing is certain, and that there is more certainty in religion than there is as to whether we may see to-morrow; for it is not certain that we may see to-morrow, and it is certainly possible that we may not see it. We cannot say as much about religion. It is not certain that it is; but who will venture to say that it is certainly possible that it is not? Now when we work for to-morrow, and so on an uncertainty, we act reasonably; for we ought to work for an uncertainty according to the doctrine of chance which was demonstrated above.

Saint Augustine has seen that we work for an uncertainty, on sea, in battle, etc. But he has not seen the doctrine of chance which proves that we should do so. Montaigne has seen that we are shocked at a fool, and that habit is all-powerful; but he has not seen the reason of this effect.

All these persons have seen the effects, but they have not seen the causes. They are, in comparison with those who have discovered the causes, as those who have only eyes are in comparison with those who have intellect. For the effects are perceptible by sense, and the causes are visible only to the intellect. And although these effects are seen by the mind, this mind is, in comparison with the mind which sees the causes, as the bodily senses are in comparison with the intellect.

235

Rem viderunt, causam non viderunt.

236

According to the doctrine of chance, you ought to put yourself to the trouble of searching for the truth; for if you die without worshipping the True Cause, you are lost. — "But," say you, "if He had wished me to worship Him, He would have left me signs of His will." — He has done so; but you neglect them. Seek them, therefore; it is well worth it.

237

Chances. — We must live differently in the world, according to these different assumptions: (1) that we could always remain in it; (2) that it is certain that we shall not remain here long, and uncertain if we shall remain here one hour. This last assumption is our condition.

238

What do you then promise me, in addition to certain troubles, but ten years of self-love (for ten years is the chance), to try hard to please without success?

239

Objection. — Those who hope for salvation are so far happy; but they have as a counterpoise the fear of hell.

Reply. — Who has most reason to fear hell: he who is in ignorance whether there is a hell, and who is certain of damnation if there is; or he who certainly believes there is a hell, and hopes to be saved if there is?

240

"I would soon have renounced pleasure," say they, "had I faith." For my part I tell you, "You would soon have faith, if you renounced pleasure." Now, it is for you to begin. If I could, I would give you faith. I cannot do so, nor therefore test the truth of what

you say. But you can well renounce pleasure, and test whether what
I say is true.

241

Order. — I would have far more fear of being mistaken, and of
finding that the Christian religion was true, than of not being mistaken in believing it true.

22. *The Testimony of Mystical Experience* *

RUFUS M. JONES *(1863–1948)*

THE NATURE OF MYSTICAL EXPERIENCE

I shall give one or two impressive present-day experiences, the
first one quoted from James B. Pratt's *Religious Consciousness*
(page 358): "There came an overwhelming sense of a Presence
infinitely pure and true and tender, a Presence that broke through
all preconceived notions and revealed itself to my consciousness
in such beauty and power that after more than twenty-five years
it seems to me the one real thing in my whole life."

The only other experience I shall give is that of my friend, Mar-
garet Prescott Montague, which she described first in the *Atlantic
Monthly* and later in a little book, entitled, *Twenty Minutes of
Reality.* "I only remember," she says, "finding myself in the midst
of wonderful moments, beholding life for the first time in all its
young intoxication of loveliness, in its unspeakable joy, beauty and
importance . . . My inner vision was cleared to the truth so that
I saw the actual loveliness which is always there. . . . Once out of
the gray days of my life I looked into the heart of reality; I witnessed the truth; I have seen life as it really is."

One of the most significant effects of experiences of this sort is
the resulting deepening of life and a marked increase of joy. One
feels as though his specific gravity were suddenly lightened by an
incursion from Beyond the usual margins. The person concerned
goes down to deeper foundations for the structure of life, somewhat

---

* Rufus M. Jones, *The Flowering of Mysticism* (New York: The Macmillan
Co., 1939). From the "Epilogue." Reprinted by permission.

as modern builders have learned to do for the stability of the present-day higher climbing type of steel and concrete structure, or those that may be tested by the force of earthquakes. The opening out of the depth-life of the soul is almost always in evidence in persons who have gained the conviction of direct contact with God. There comes that marked depth of calm and serenity which a touch of eternity brings to life. One is not taken out of the timestream of change and process, but life is undergirded and steadied by a surer foundation which is deep-based in what is felt to be the eternal. So much of life is thin and gasping with rush and hurry that it is an immense asset to have these subbasement resources which bring steadiness and assurance, even in the midst of change and turmoil. There can be a center of inward calm even while the affairs of life are going on in the time-stream.

It is, too, a very great advantage which the mystic has, that what we may call the Over-World — the World of Eternal Spiritual Reality — has become to him as certain and as much a part of the domain which he inhabits as is the world which he sees and touches and which gives him his daily food supplies. In the noble sense of the word "amphibian," he lives in two worlds and finds himself at home in both of them. Francis Thompson's words:

> O world invisible, I view thee;
> O world intangible, I touch thee;
> O world unknowable, I know thee;
> Inapprehensible, I clutch thee.

become as natural and normal expressions of his full life as the act of breathing or the act of swimming is. This Over-World is, of course, an essential feature of Plato's philosophy. It is for him the ground and home of truth and beauty and goodness; it is the realm in which all of our eternal values have their spire-top, and Platonism in all generations has borne faithful testimony to such an Over-World, though sometimes by too great depreciation of *this* world, and sometimes appearing to sunder the two worlds by too wide and unbridgeable a chasm.

It is another great advantage to discover, as the mystic does through his experience, that the human mind is not bound and limited to the world of matter and to the approach of the senses, but that it can be raised by divine assistance to an intimate correspondence with the transcendent and supersensuous realm of reality, and can become a transmission organ of it — of a grace like that in Jesus Christ, a pure love like that in God, who is love, and a communion and fellowship with the Holy Spirit with whom our spirits, however feebly, are akin.

The mystic has found the bridge, the ladder, the scaling-wings, which make both worlds his. Sometimes he seems to break through or reach across, and sometimes he seems aware of a thrust from the Beyond into the now and here. In either case he finds himself no longer theorizing about the world of higher reality; he has found his way into it and partakes of it as his promised land. He is in vital communion with a larger world of Life that surrounds his temporal life. It brings with it the feeling of the essential grandeur of the soul, and it makes the moral purpose of life, which springs from this junction of our life here and the Eternal Over-World the most august thing in the universe. Those great mystical books the Upanishads speak of the infinite personality of man, and the Cambridge Platonists [1] said God is more in the mind of man than anywhere else in the universe.

But here we are confronted with the caveat of the psychologist that these experiences of the mystics are only subjective phenomena, lacking objective reference, and that they, further, are dubious because they are in many cases pathological phenomena and heavily weighted with illusion, hallucination, wishful thinking and auto-suggestion.

I shall deal with the second point first, as it is the easier of the two to dispose of. It is true that there is a serious pathological factor to be faced in the biographies and autobiographies of many of the mystics of history. They often reveal in their lives a longer or shorter period of emotional intensity, with symptoms of hysteria and with tendencies toward mental instability. Mystics are, like most persons of genius, not tightly organized and they are inclined to be influenced by the fringe and marginal consciousness rather than by the focal and attentive center of consciousness. They tend to veer away from the habitual and to have novelty and freshness. This would mean that they might well be more subject to trance and ecstasy and hypnoidal conditions than are normal persons, but it might also mean that they would be more likely when

---

[1] [Edit. A Seventeenth Century school of idealists and Christian Apologists who sought to combat the materialist views of such writers of their time as Thomas Hobbes.]

at their best, to be sensitive to an Over-World of Reality and more likely to be the organs of fresh revelations of it. It is a notable fact that their experiences, and their stabilized faith through what they believe to be their contacts with God, in many cases, in fact usually, result in a unification of personality, in a great increase of dynamic quality — a power to stand the universe — and in a recovery of health and normality. While it must be admitted that this pathological factor, which cannot be ignored, presents an element of liability in the mystic's testimony, there nevertheless seems to me on the whole to be an overwhelming balance of asset in favor of the significance of the mystic's life and message. Hysteria does not unify and construct life as mystical experience indubitably does do.

The fact that the mystic himself puts a heavy stress upon the testimony of immediate consciousness of reality, as contrasted with consciousness of objects mediated through sense contact or impact, seems at the take-off to give some ground for the claim of the critical psychologist that mystical experiences are infected, and "sicklied o'er," with the structural weakness of subjectivity, of a mere private buzzing in the head.

This charge of subjectivity, however, turns out to have much less ground of support than appears from the loudness of its roar. The purely empirical, or phenomenalist psychologist, and it is he who is most apt to make this charge, finds himself admittedly, in his psychological method, shut up to a study of mental phenomena, that is to say, to states of mind which pass before the footlights of consciousness. He has no legitimate way, with his basic theory, of getting out of this "ego-centric predicament" and of establishing the validity of any objects beyond the "spectator mind." He lacks a sound philosophical basis for the objective validity of any kind of experience, even of the world of sense-experience. He needs a much sounder epistemology. If he proposes to treat psychology as confined to the study of "phenomena," i.e., to the study of mental processes, he is himself all the time sloughed in the bottomless bog of subjectivity. He usually fails to take adequate note of what Kant called the transcendental unity of self-consciousness, which is always involved in all perception of objects, and he takes too little note of the interpretative function of this unified and permanently same self in all processes of knowledge.

He furthermore has a far too superficial ground for the validity of our knowledge of ourself, our assurance of the reality of other selves and our experience of the objective aspects of beauty, truth and moral significance. He has not yet adequately studied the depth-life of the inner self or its extrasensory powers. There are in these lives of ours impalpables and intangibles, which determine the issues and destiny of life as surely as bread and other tactual objects do. They cannot be reduced to sense contacts, nor are they purely "subjective" phenomena. They have universal significance. They can be counted on and depended on as certainly as the Himalayas can be.

Finally these experiences of God, these mutual correspondences with the Over-World are felt by the mystic to be as objectively real, as genuinely a subject-object relationship — a self experiencing an Other — as is ever true of any event of life. The conviction of Presence, which attends these experiences, the affirmation of reality, is no whit weaker than is the case when one has an object in his clenched hand. It carries a triumphant sense of certitude. It enables the beholder to stand the universe. It organizes life on the profoundest levels. It wins the assent of the mind and will. It furnishes a dynamic of a unique sort and, again and again, this contact with the unseen in a man's life has been a determining factor in shaping the course of history. It has helped to build the world. In fact, the intuitions of the transcendent, insights of what ought to be and must be, convictions that the Eternal God shuts every door but this one that opens, have been a major factor in the course of human events, and must be taken into account as certainly as Alexander's conquests must be.

23. God and the Subconscious *

WILLIAM JAMES (1842–1910)

The warring gods and formulas of the various religions do indeed

---

* Wm. James, *The Varieties of Religious Experience* (New York: Longmans, Green & Co., 1929). From Chapter entitled "Conclusions." Reprinted by permission.

cancel each other, but there is a certain uniform deliverance in which religions all appear to meet. It consists of two parts: —

1. An uneasiness; and
2. Its solution.

1. The uneasiness, reduced to its simplest terms, is a sense that there is *something wrong about us* as we naturally stand.

2. The solution is a sense that *we are saved from the wrongness* by making proper connection with the higher powers.

In those more developed minds which alone we are studying, the wrongness takes a moral character, and the salvation takes a mystical tinge. I think we shall keep well within the limits of what is common to all such minds if we formulate the essence of their religious experience in terms like these:—

The individual, so far as he suffers from his wrongness and criticises it, is to that extent consciously beyond it, and in at least possible touch with something higher, if anything higher exist. Along with the wrong part there is thus a better part of him, even though it may be but a most helpless germ. With which part he should identify his real being is by no means obvious at this stage; but when stage 2 (the stage of solution or salvation) arrives,[1] the man identifies his real being with the germinal higher part of himself; and does so in the following way. *He becomes conscious that this higher part is conterminous and continuous with a* MORE *of the same quality, which is operative in the universe outside of him, and which he can keep in working touch with, and in a fashion get on board of and save himself when all his lower being has gone to pieces in the wreck.*

It seems to me that all the phenomena are accurately describable in these very simple general terms.[2] They allow for the divided self and the struggle; they involve the change of personal centre and the surrender of the lower self; they express the appearance of exteriority of the helping power and yet account for our sense of

---

[1] Remember that for some men it arrives suddenly, for others gradually, whilst others again practically enjoy it all their life.

[2] The practical difficulties are: 1, to "realize the reality" of one's higher part; 2, to identify one's self with it exclusively; and 3, to identify it with all the rest of ideal being.

union with it; [3] and they fully justify our feelings of security and
joy. There is probably no autobiographic document, among all
those which I have quoted, to which the description will not well
apply. One need only add such specific details as will adapt it to
various theologies and various personal temperaments, and one will
then have the various experiences reconstructed in their individual
forms.

So far, however, as this analysis goes, the experiences are only
psychological phenomena. They possess, it is true, enormous biological worth. Spiritual strength really increases in the subject
when he has them, a new life opens for him, and they seem to him
a place of conflux where the forces of two universes meet; and yet
this may be nothing but his subjective way of feeling things, a mood
of his own fancy, in spite of the effects produced. I now turn to my
second question: What is the objective "truth" of their content? [4]

The part of the content concerning which the question of truth
most pertinently arises is that "MORE of the same quality" with
which our own higher self appears in the experience to come into
harmonious working relation. Is such a "more" merely our own
notion, or does it really exist? If so, in what shape does it exist?
Does it act, as well as exist? And in what form should we conceive
of that "union" with it of which religious geniuses are so convinced?

It is in answering these questions that the various theologies perform their theoretic work, and that their divergencies most come to
light. They all agree that the "more" really exists; though some of
them hold it to exist in the shape of a personal god or gods, while
others are satisfied to conceive it as a stream of ideal tendency
embedded in the eternal structure of the world. They all agree,
moreover, that it acts as well as exists, and that something really is
effected for the better when you throw your life into its hands. It
is when they treat of the experience of "union" with it that their

---

[3] "When mystical activity is at its height, we find consciousness possessed by
the sense of a being at once *excessive* and *identical* with the self: great enough
to be God; interior enough to be *me*. The 'objectivity' of it ought in that
case to be called *excessivity,* rather, or exceedingness." RECEJAC: Essai sur les
fondements de la conscience mystique, 1897, p. 46.

[4] The word "truth" is here taken to mean something additional to bare value
for life, although the natural propensity of man is to believe that whatever
has great value for life is thereby certified as true.

speculative differences appear most clearly. Over this point pantheism and theism, nature and second birth, works and grace and karma, immortality and reincarnation, rationalism and mysticism, carry on inveterate disputes.

At the end of my lecture on Philosophy I held out the notion that an impartial science of religions might sift out from the midst of their discrepancies a common body of doctrine which she might also formulate in terms to which physical science need not object. This, I said, she might adopt as her own reconciling hypothesis, and recommend it for general belief. I also said that in my last lecture I should have to try my own hand at framing such an hypothesis.

The time has now come for this attempt. Who says "hypothesis" renounces the ambition to be coercive in his arguments. The most I can do is, accordingly, to offer something that may fit the facts so easily that your scientific logic will find no plausible pretext for vetoing your impulse to welcome it as true.

The "more" as we called it, and the meaning of our "union" with it, form the nucleus of our inquiry. Into what definite description can these words be translated, and for what definite facts do they stand? It would never do for us to place ourselves offhand at the position of a particular theology, the Christian theology, for example, and proceed immediately to define the "more" as Jehovah, and the "union" as his imputation to us of the righteousness of Christ. That would be unfair to other religions, and, from our present standpoint at least, would be an over-belief.

We must begin by using less particularized terms; and, since one of the duties of the science of religions is to keep religion in connection with the rest of science, we shall do well to seek first of all a way of describing the "more," which psychologists may also recognize as real. The *subconscious self* is nowadays a well-accredited psychological entity; and I believe that in it we have exactly the mediating term required. Apart from all religious considerations, there is actually and literally more life in our total soul than we are at any time aware of. The exploration of the transmarginal field has hardly yet been seriously undertaken, but what Mr. Myers said in 1892 in his essay on the Subliminal Consciousness [5] is as true

[5] Proceedings of the Society for Psychical Research, vol. vii. p. 305. For a full statement of Mr. Myers's views, I may refer to his posthumous work, "Human Personality in the Light of Recent Research," which is already an-

as when it was first written: "Each of us is in reality an abiding psychical entity far more extensive than he knows — an individuality which can never express itself completely through any corporeal manifestation. The Self manifests through the organism; but there is always some part of the Self unmanifested; and always, as it seems, some power of organic expression in abeyance or reserve." Much of the content of this larger background against which our conscious being stands out in relief is insignificant. Imperfect memories, silly jingles, inhibitive timidities, "dissolutive" phenomena of various sorts, as Myers calls them, enters into it for a large part. But in it many of the performances of genius seem also to have their origin; and in our study of conversion, of mystical experiences, and of prayer, we have seen how striking a part invasions from this region play in the religious life.

Let me then propose, as an hypothesis, that whatever it may be on its *farther* side, the "more" with which in religious experience we feel our selves connected is on its *hither* side the subconscious continuation of our conscious life. Starting thus with a recognized psychological fact as our basis, we seem to preserve a contact with "science" which the ordinary theologian lacks. At the same time the theologian's contention that the religious man is moved by an external power is vindicated, for it is one of the peculiarities of invasions from the subconscious region to take on objective appearances, and to suggest to the Subject an external control. In the religious life the control is felt as "higher"; but since on our hypothesis it is primarily the higher faculties of our own hidden mind which are controlling, the sense of union with the power beyond us is a sense of something, not merely apparently, but literally true.

This doorway into the subject seems to me the best one for a science of religions, for it mediates between a number of different points of view. Yet it is only a doorway, and difficulties present

---

ounced by Messrs. Longmans, Green & Co. as being in press. Mr. Myers for the first time proposed as a general psychological problem the exploration of the subliminal region of consciousness throughout its whole extent, and made the first methodical steps in its topography by treating as a natural series a mass of subliminal facts hitherto considered only as curious isolated facts, and subjecting them to a systematized nomenclature. How important this exploration will prove, future work upon the path which Myers has opened can alone show. Compare my paper: "Frederic Myers's Services to Psychology," in the said Proceedings, part xlii., May, 1901.

themselves as soon as we step through it, and ask how far our transmarginal consciousness carries us if we follow it on its remoter side. Here the over-beliefs begin: here mysticism and the conversion-rapture and Vedantism and transcendental idealism bring in their monistic interpretations and tell us that the finite self rejoins the absolute self, for it was always one with God and identical with the soul of the world.[6] Here the prophets of all the different religions come with their visions, voices, raptures, and other openings, supposed by each to authenticate his own peculiar faith.

Those of us who are not personally favored with such specific revelations must stand outside of them altogether and, for the present at least, decide that, since they corroborate incompatible theological doctrines, they neutralize one another and leave no fixed results. If we follow any one of them, or if we follow philosophical theory and embrace monistic pantheism on non-mystical grounds, we do so in the exercise of our individual freedom, and build out our religion in the way most congruous with our personal susceptibilities. Among these susceptibilities intellectual ones play

---

[6] One more expression of this belief, to increase the reader's familiarity with the notion of it:—

"If this room is full of darkness for thousands of years, and you come in and begin to weep and wail, 'Oh, the darkness,' will the darkness vanish? Bring the light in, strike a match, and light comes in a moment. So what good will it do you to think all your lives, 'Oh, I have done evil, I have made many mistakes'? It requires no ghost to tell us that. Bring in the light, and the evil goes in a moment. Strengthen the real nature, build up yourselves, the effulgent, the resplendent, the ever pure, call that up in every one whom you see. I wish that every one of us had come to such a state that even when we see the vilest of human beings we can see the God within, and instead of condemning, say, 'Rise, thou effulgent One, rise thou who art always pure, rise thou birthless and deathless, rise almighty, and manifest your nature.' . . . This is the highest prayer that the Advaita teaches. This is the one prayer: remembering our nature." . . . "Why does man go out to look for a God? . . . It is your own heart beating, and you did not know, you were mistaking it for something external. He, nearest of the near, my own self, the reality of my own life, my body and my soul.—I am Thee and Thou art Me. That is your own nature. Assert it, manifest it. Not to become pure, you are pure already. You are not to be perfect, you are that already. Every good thought which you think or act upon is simply tearing the veil, as it were, and the purity, the Infinity, the God behind, manifests itself—the eternal Subject of everything, the eternal Witness in this universe, your own Self. Knowledge is, as it were, a lower step, a degradation. We are It already; how to know It?" SWAMI VIVEKANANDA: Addresses, No. XII., Practical Vedanta, part iv. pp. 172, 174, London, 1897; and Lectures, The Real and the Apparent Man, p. 24, abridged.

a decisive part. Although the religious question is primarily a question of life, of living or not living in the higher union which opens itself to us as a gift, yet the spiritual excitement in which the gift appears a real one will often fail to be aroused in an individual until certain particular intellectual beliefs or ideas which, as we say, come home to him, are touched.[7] These ideas will thus be essential to that individual's religion; — which is as much as to say that over-beliefs in various directions are absolutely indispensable, and that we should treat them with tenderness and tolerance so long as they are not intolerant themselves. As I have elsewhere written, the most interesting and valuable things about a man are usually his over-beliefs.

Disregarding the over-beliefs, and confining ourselves to what is common and generic, we have in *the fact that the conscious person is continuous with a wider self through which saving experiences come*,[8] a positive content of religious experience which, it seems to me, *is literally and objectively true as far as it goes*. If I now proceed to state my own hypothesis about the farther limits of this extension of our personality, I shall be offering my own over-belief — though I know it will appear a sorry under-belief to some of you — for which I can only bespeak the same indulgence which in a converse case I should accord to yours.

The further limits of our being plunge, it seems to me, into an

---

[7] For instance, here is a case where a person exposed from her birth to Christian ideas had to wait till they came to her clad in spiritistic formulas before the saving experience set in:—

"For myself I can say that spiritualism has saved me. It was revealed to me at a critical moment of my life, and without it I don't know what I should have done. It has taught me to detach myself from worldly things and to place my hope in things to come. Through it I have learned to see in all men, even in those most criminal, even in those from whom I have most suffered, undeveloped brothers to whom I owed assistance, love, and forgiveness. I have learned that I must lose my temper over nothing, despise no one, and pray for all. Most of all I have learned to pray! And although I have still much to learn in this domain, prayer ever brings me more strength, consolation, and comfort. I feel more than ever that I have only made a few steps on the long road of progress; but I look at its length without dismay, for I have confidence that the day will come when all my efforts shall be rewarded. So Spiritualism has a great place in my life, indeed it holds the first place there." Flournoy Collection.

[8] "The influence of the Holy Spirit, exquisitely called the Comforter, is a matter of actual experience, as solid a reality as that of electro-magnetism." W. C. BROWNELL, Scribner's Magazine, vol. xxx, p. 112.

altogether other dimension of existence from the sensible and merely "understandable" world. Name it the mystical region, or the supernatural region, whichever you choose. So far as our ideal impulses originate in this region (and most of them do originate in it, for we find them possessing us in a way for which we cannot articulately account), we belong to it in a more intimate sense than that in which we belong to the visible world, for we belong in the most intimate sense wherever our ideals belong. Yet the unseen region in question is not merely ideal, for it produces effects in this world. When we commune with it, work is actually done upon our finite personality, for we are turned into new men, and consequences in the way of conduct follow in the natural world upon our regenerative change.[9] But that which produces effects within another reality must be termed a reality itself, so I feel as if we had no philosophic excuse for calling the unseen or mystical world unreal.

God is the natural appellation, for us Christians at least, for the supreme reality, so I will call this higher part of the universe by the name of God.[10] We and God have business with each other; and in opening ourselves to his influence our deepest destiny is fulfilled. The universe, at those parts of it which our personal being constitutes, takes a turn genuinely for the worse or for the better

---

[9] That the transaction of opening ourselves, otherwise called prayer, is a perfectly definite one for certain persons, appears abundantly in the preceding lectures. I append another concrete example to reinforce the impression on the reader's mind:—

"Man can learn to transcend these limitations [of finite thought] and draw power and wisdom at will. . . . The divine presence is known through experience. The turning to a higher plane is a distinct act of consciousness. It is not a vague, twilight or semi-conscious experience. It is not an ecstasy; it is not a trance. It is not super-consciousness in the Vedantic sense. It is not due to self-hypnotization. It is a perfectly calm, sane, sound, rational, common-sense shifting of consciousness from the phenomena of sense-perception to the phenomena of seership, from the thought of self to a distinctively higher realm. . . . For example, if the lower self be nervous, anxious, tense, one can in a few moments compel it to be calm. This is not done by a word simply. Again I say, it is not hypnotism. It is by the exercise of power. One feels the spirit of peace as definitely as heat is perceived on a hot summer day. The power can be as surely used as the sun's rays can be focused and made to do work, to set fire to wood." The Higher Law, vol. iv. pp. 4, 6, Boston, August, 1901.

[10] Transcendentalists are fond of the term "Over-soul," but as a rule they use it in an intellectualist sense, as meaning only a medium of communion. "God" is a causal agent as well as a medium of communion, and that is the aspect which I wish to emphasize.

in proportion as each one of us fulfills or evades God's demands. As far as this goes I probably have you with me, for I only translate into schematic language what I may call the instinctive belief of mankind: *God is real since he produces real effects.*

The real effects in question, so far as I have as yet admitted them, are exerted on the personal centres of energy of the various subjects, but the spontaneous faith of most of the subjects is that they embrace a wider sphere than this. Most religious men believe (or "know," if they be mystical) that not only they themselves, but the whole universe of beings to whom the God is present, are secure in his parental hands. There is a sense, a dimension, they are sure, in which we are *all* saved, in spite of the gates of hell and all adverse terrestrial appearances. God's existence is the guarantee of an ideal order that shall be permanently preserved. This world may indeed, as science assures, us, some day burn up or freeze; but if it is part of his order, the old ideals are sure to be brought elsewhere to fruition, so that where God is, tragedy is only provisional and partial and shipwreck and dissolution are not the absolutely final things. Only when this farther step of faith concerning God is taken, and remote objective consequences are predicted, does religion, as it seems to me, get wholly free from the first immediate subjective experience, and bring a *real hypothesis* into play. A good hypothesis in science must have other properties than those of the phenomenon it is immediately invoked to explain, otherwise it is not prolific enough. God, meaning only what enters into the religious man's experience of union, falls short of being an hypothesis of this more useful order. He needs to enter into wider cosmic relations in order to justify the subject's absolute confidence and peace.

That the God with whom, starting from the hither side of our own extra-marginal self, we come at its remoter margin into commerce should be the absolute world-ruler, is of course a very considerable over-belief. Over-belief as it is, though, it is an article of almost every one's religion. Most of us pretend in some way to prop it upon our philosophy, but the philosophy itself is really propped upon this faith. What is this but to say that Religion, in her fullest exercise of function, is not a mere illumination of facts already elsewhere given, not a mere passion, like love, which views things in a rosier light. It is indeed that, as we have seen abundantly. But it is something more, namely, a postulator of new *facts* as well. The world interpreted religiously is not the materialistic world over again, with an altered expression; it must have, over and above the altered expression, *a natural constitution* different at some point from that which a materialistic world would have. It must be such that different events can be expected in it, different conduct must be required.

This thoroughly "pragmatic" view of religion has usually been taken as a matter of course by common men. They have interpolated divine miracles into the field of nature, they have built a heaven out beyond the grave. It is only transcendentalist metaphysicians who think that, without adding any concrete details to Nature, or subtracting any, but by simply calling it the expression of absolute spirit, you make it more divine just as it stands. I believe the pragmatic way of taking religion to be the deeper way. It gives it body as well as soul, it makes it claim, as everything real must claim, some characteristic realm of fact as its very own. What the more characteristically divine facts are, apart from the actual inflow of energy in the faith-state and the prayer-state, I know not. But the over-belief on which I am ready to make my personal venture is that they exist. The whole drift of my education goes to persuade me that the world of our present consciousness is only one out of many worlds of consciousness that exist, and that those other worlds must contain experiences which have a meaning for our life also; and that although in the main their experiences and those of this world keep discrete, yet the two become continuous at certain points, and higher energies filter in. By being faithful in my poor measure to this over-belief, I seem to myself to keep more sane and true. I *can*, of course, put myself into the sectarian scientist's attitude, and imagine vividly that the world of sensations and of scientific laws and objects may be all. But whenever I do this, I hear that inward monitor of which W. K. Clifford once wrote, whispering the word "bosh!" Humbug is humbug, even though it bear the scientific name, and the total expression of human experience, as I view it objectively, invincibly urges me beyond the narrow "scientific" bounds. Assuredly, the real world is of a different temperament — more intricately built than physical science allows. So my objective and my subjective conscience both hold me to the over-belief which I express. Who knows whether the faithfulness of individuals here below to their own poor over-beliefs may not actually help God in turn to be more effectively faithful to his own greater tasks?

24. The Changing Conception of God *

MORDECAI KAPLAN (1882-   )

WHAT BELIEF IN GOD MEANS, FROM THE MODERN POINT OF VIEW

To the modern man, religion can no longer be a matter of entering into relationship with the supernatural. The only kind of religion that can help him live and get the most out of life will be the one which will teach him to identify as divine or holy whatever in human nature or in the world about him enhances human life. Men must no longer look upon God as a reservoir of magic power to be tapped whenever they are aware of their physical limitations. It was natural for primitive man to do so. He sought contact with his god or gods primarily because he felt the need of supplementing his own limited powers with the external forces which he believed were controlled by the gods. He sought their aid for the fertility of his fields, the increase of his cattle, and the conquest of his foes. In time, however— and in the case of the Jewish people early in their history — men began to seek communion with God not so much as the source of power but rather as the source of goodness, and to invoke His aid to acquire control not over the external forces but over those of human nature in the individual and in the mass. With the development of scientific techniques for the utilization of natural forces, and with the revision of our world-outlook in a way that invalidates the distinction between natural and supernatural, it is only as the sum of everything in the world that renders life significant and worthwhile— or holy — that God can be worshiped by man. Godhood can have

---

* Mordecai M. Kaplan, *The Meaning of God in Modern Jewish Religion* (New York: Jewish Reconstructionist Foundation, Inc., 2nd Printing, 1947). Reprinted by permission.

no meaning for us apart from human ideals of truth, goodness, and beauty, interwoven in a pattern of holiness.

To believe in God is to reckon with life's creative forces, tendencies and potentialities as forming an organic unity, and as giving meaning to life by virtue of that unity. Life has meaning for us when it elicits from us the best of which we are capable, and fortifies us against the worst that may befall us. Such meaning reveals itself in our experiences of unity, of creativity, and of worth. In the experience of that unity which enables us to perceive the interaction and interdependence of all phases and elements of being, it is mainly our cognitive powers that come into play; in the experience of creativity which we sense at first hand, whenever we make the slightest contribution to the sum of those forces that give meaning to life, our conative powers come to the fore; and in the experience of worth, in the realization of meaning, in contrast to chaos and meaninglessness, our emotional powers find expression. Thus in the very process of human self-fulfillment, in the very striving after the achievement of salvation, we identify ourselves with God, and God functions in us. This fact should lead to the conclusion that when we believe in God, we believe that reality — the world of inner and outer being, the world of society and of nature — is so constituted as to enable man to achieve salvation. If human beings are frustrated, it is not because there is no God, but because they do not deal with reality as it is actually and potentially constituted.

Our intuition of God is the absolute negation and antithesis of all evaluations of human life which assume that consciousness is a disease, civilization a transient sickness, and all our efforts to lift ourselves above the brute only a vain pretense. It is the triumphant exorcism of Bertrand Russell's dismal credo: "Brief and powerless is man's life. On him and all his race the slow sure doom falls pitiless and dark." It is the affirmation that human life is supremely worth while and significant, and deserves our giving to it the best that is in us, despite, or perhaps because of, the very evil that mars it. This intuition is not merely an intellectual assent. It is the "yea" of our entire personality. "That life is worth living is the most necessary of assumptions," says Santayana, "and were it not assumed, the most impossible of conclusions." The existence of evil, far from silencing that "yea," is the very occasion for articulating it. "The highest type of man," said Felix Adler, "is the one who *in articulo mortis* can bless the universe."

The human mind cannot rest until it finds order in the universe. It is this form-giving trait that is responsible for modern scientific theory. That same need is also operative in formulating a view of the cosmos, which will support the spiritual yearnings of the group and make their faith in the goals and objectives of their group life consistent with the totality of their experience as human beings. Out of this process of thought there arise traditional beliefs as to the origin of the world, man's place in it, his ultimate destiny, the role of one's own particular civilization in the scheme of human history, and all those comprehensive systems of belief that try to bring human experience into a consistent pattern.

But there is one underlying assumption in all these efforts at giving a consistent meaning to life, whether they are expressed in the naïve cosmologies of primitive peoples or in the most sophisticated metaphysical systems of contemporary philosophers, and that is the assumption that life is meaningful. Without faith that the world of nature is a cosmos and not a chaos, that it has intelligible laws which can be unravelled, and that the human reason offers us an instrument capable of unravelling them, no scientific theorizing would be possible. This is another way of saying that science cannot dispense with what Einstein has appropriately named "cosmic religion," the faith that nature is meaningful and hence divine. And just as our inquiry into natural law demands the validation of cosmic religion, so also does our inquiry into moral law and the best way for men to live. It implies the intuition that life inherently yields ethical and spiritual values, that it is holy. The God idea thus expresses itself pragmatically in those fundamental beliefs by which a people tries to work out its life in a consistent pattern and rid itself of those frustrations which result from the distracting confusion of ideals and aims, in a word, beliefs by which it orients itself and the individuals that constitute it to life as a whole.

The purpose of all education and culture is to socialize the individual, to sensitize him to the ills as well as to the goods of life. Yet the more successful we are in accomplishing this purpose, the more unhappiness we lay up for those we educate. "As soon as high consciousness is reached," says A. N. Whitehead, "the enjoyment of existence is entwined with pain, frustration, loss, tragedy." Likewise, the more eager we are to shape human life in accordance with some ideal pattern of justice and cooperation, the more reasons we discover for being dissatisfied with ourselves, with our limitations, and with our environment. If, therefore, culture and social sympathy are not to break our hearts, but to help us retain that sureness of the life-feeling which is our native privilege, they must make room for religious faith which is needed as a tonic to quicken the pulse of our personal existence.

Faith in life's inherent worthwhileness and sanctity is needed to counteract the cynicism that sneers at life and mocks at the very notion of holiness. Against such a cheapening of life's values no social idealism that does not reckon with the cosmos as divine is an adequate remedy. How can a social idealist ask men to deny themselves immediate satisfactions for the sake of future good that they may never see in their lifetime, when he leaves them without any definite conviction that the universe will fulfill the hopes that have inspired their sacrifice, or is even able to fulfill them? If human life does not yield some cosmic meaning, is it not the course of wisdom to pursue a policy of "Eat, drink and make merry, for tomorrow we die"?

Belief in God as here conceived can function in our day exactly as the belief in God has always functioned; it can function as an affirmation that life has value. It implies, as the God idea has always implied, a certain assumption with regard to the nature of reality, the assumption that reality is so constituted as to endorse and guarantee the realization in man of that which is of greatest value to him. If we believe that assumption to be true, for, as has been said, it is an assumption that is not susceptible of proof, we have faith in God. No metaphysical speculation beyond this fundamental assumption that reality assures both the emergence and the realization of human ideals is necessary for the religious life.

God Not Known Unless Sought After

Once this idea is clear in our minds, the next step is to identify those elements in the life about us, in our social heritage and in ourselves, that possess the quality of Godhood. The purpose in setting forth in concrete ethical and rational terms the meaning of God should be twofold: first, to forestall the denial of the divine aspect of reality, and secondly, to counteract the tendency to exaggerate the significance of God-awareness as such, regardless of the irrationality or the immorality of the conduct which accompanies that awareness. *While the immediacy and the dynamic of God-awareness are, no doubt, indispensable to vital religion, their value is dangerously overstressed by those of a romantic or mystic turn of mind.*

Nothing less than the deliberate refusal to be satisfied with the negation of life's inherent worth is likely to keep our minds in a receptive mood for the belief in God. But being in a receptive mood is not enough. We shall not come to experience the reality of God unless we go in search of Him. To be seekers of God, we have to depend more upon our own thinking and less upon tradition. Instead of acquiescing passively in the traditional belief that there is a God, and then deducing from that belief conclusions which are to be applied to human experience and conduct, we must accustom ourselves to find God in the complexities of our experience and behavior. "Seek ye me and live." [1] To seek God, to inquire after Him, to try to discern His reality is religion in action. *The ardent and strenuous search for God in all that we know and feel and do is the true equivalent of the behest, "Thou shalt love the Lord thy God with all thy heart, with all thy soul and with all thy might."* [2] Only by way of participation in human affairs and strivings are we to seek God.

We seek God, whenever we explore truth, goodness and beauty to their uttermost reaches. We must take care, however, not to treat these objects of our striving as independent of one another, for then we are likely to pursue some partial truth, some mistaken goodness, or some illusory beauty. The pursuit of truth, unwedded to an appreciation of goodness and beauty, is likely to issue in the sort of personality that can be absorbed in the scientific investigation of the explosive properties of certain chemicals, wholly indifferent as to whether one's conclusions be made to further war or peace, construction or destruction. The well-meaning fanatics of virtue, who inspired the title of one of Bertrand Russell's essays, "The Evil Good Men Do," are typical of the results of seeking goodness while

---

[1] Amos 5:4.

[2] Deut. 6:5.

underestimating its relationship to truth and beauty. Their intentions are good, but their behavior reminds us that "the road to hell is paved with good intentions." The exclusive pursuit of beauty results in the type of decadent estheticism that fiddles while Rome burns. It issues in an art that is for art's sake rather than for life's sake, and that reaches a *reductio ad absurdum* in forms of artistic expression which communicate no meaning to any except the few artists who happen to subscribe to the same set of artistic dogmas, and to be interested in experimenting with the same techniques.

The penalty for the failure to deal with truth, goodness and beauty as organically related to one another is the failure to reach the conviction of life's true worth. The attainment of that conviction is vouchsafed only to those to whom truth, goodness and beauty are but partial phases of life's meaning. Religion has the one word which seeks to express that meaning in all its depth and mystery. That word is "holiness." It is folly to try to eliminate the concept of holiness from our vocabulary. It is the only accurate term for our deepest and most treasured experiences. The moment any situation evokes from us the awareness that we have to do with something to which no other term than "sacred" is adequate, we are on the point of discovering God. In fact, we already sense His reality.

The part to be played by our religious tradition is to bring to our attention the *sancta* through which the God-awareness has been actualized. But we must take care not to adopt the attitude of the philistine who departmentalizes life into the secular and the holy, and who thereby misses the main significance of holiness, which is compatible only with the wholeness of life. The philistinism which associates sanctity only with certain places and occasions and regards all others as secular is, in effect, a reversion to the primitive magical conception of holiness. Certain sites that, for one reason or another, impressed themselves particularly on the imagination of primitive peoples seemed the special haunts of deity; certain times seemed particularly propitious, others unpropitious for approaching him. Those were then pronounced holy. In our logical thinking we reject such notions as superstition, having been taught by our Prophets to associate the holiness of God with the thought that "the whole earth is filled with His glory." But our emotional reactions often revert to the attitude of primitive religion, and we then associate holiness only with persons, places and events which have been sanctified by traditional rituals. If, however, we relate the ideal of holiness to the worthwhileness and sanctity of life as implicit in the God idea, we invest places, persons and events with sacredness only as they contribute to our awareness of the sanctity of life as a whole, only as they symbolize the holiness that is in all things.

Every effort to articulate our sense of life's worthwhileness in ritual and prayer is a means of realizing the godhood manifested in our personal and social experience. The same appreciation of whatever contributes to our joy in living which is voiced in the traditional prayers of praise and thanksgiving still calls for expression. The same hopeful yearning for unrealized good that is voiced in the traditional prayers of petition needs to be articulated, as one of the means toward its ultimate realization. We may have to revise our liturgy to express with greater truth what we sincerely think and feel when we have God in mind, but we cannot dispense with worship. The departure from the traditional idea of God as a self-existent entity necessarily changes the function of prayer, but by no means destroys it. The institution of worship and the resort to prayer did not have to wait for our day to suffer change in their meaning and functioning. From the time that the conception of God as a kind of magnified human being in form or feeling was banned, prayer could not possibly mean what it did in the earlier periods of Jewish religion, when men naïvely believed that God acted directly in answer to any petition that was addressed to Him. Ever since philosophy invaded the field of Jewish religion, it became difficult to pray in the spirit of those who had never been troubled by philosophic scruples. It is unfortunate that medieval Jewish theologians who took such pains to deprecate the naïve idea of God failed to indicate that prayer must undergo changes in form and meaning to correspond with the more philosophical conception of God that they were urging. But their omission does not alter the fact, first, that any affirmative conception of God must necessarily find expression in prayer, and secondly, that the content of the prayer must correspond with the particular conception of God to which we can whole-heartedly ascribe.

Religious prayer is the utterance of those thoughts that imply either the actual awareness of God, or the desire to attain such awareness. To those who formerly prayed for rain, God was a being who gave or withheld rain as it suited His purpose. There is no room for such prayer in a conception of God in which giving or withholding rain at will does not enter. There will always be need, however, for prayer which voices a yearning for those abilities of mind and body, or for that change of heart and character which would enable us to avail ourselves of such aspects of life as in their totality spell God. By voicing that yearning we take the first step—though only the first step—to its realization. Moreover, there is need for that equivalent of praise of God, which, even more than petition, constituted in the past the principal element of prayer. That equivalent is the affirmation in song, liturgy and symbol of the aspects of life that spell God. Study and work, however, as well as prayer and praise, must express our faith in God, and the whole of life must contribute to *kiddush hashem*, the sanctification of God's name, and to the demonstration of the reality and glory of the divine.

25. An Agnostic's Attitude on the Existence of God *

THOMAS H. HUXLEY (1825–1895)

"The greatest and perhaps the sole use of all philosophy of pure reason is, after all, merely negative, since it serves not as an organon for the enlargement (of knowledge), but as a discipline for its delimitation; and, instead of discovering truth, has only the modest merit of preventing error." (Kant)

When I reached intellectual maturity and began to ask myself whether I was an atheist, a theist, or a pantheist; a materialist or an idealist; a Christian or a freethinker; I found that the more I learned and reflected, the less ready was the answer; until, at last, I came to the conclusion that I had neither art nor part with any of these denominations, except the last. The one thing in which most of these good people were agreed was the one thing in which I differed from them. They were quite sure they had attained a certain "gnosis," — had, more or less successfully, solved the prob-

---

* Thomas H. Huxley, *Science and Christian Tradition* (New York: D. Appleton & Co., 1894). From chapter entitled "Agnosticism." Reprinted by permission.

lem of existence; while I was quite sure I had not, and had a pretty strong conviction that the problem was insoluble. And, with Hume and Kant on my side, I could not think myself presumptuous in holding fast by that opinion. On the contrary, I had, and have, the firmest conviction that I never left the "verace via" — the straight road; and that this road led nowhere else but into the dark depths of a wild and tangled forest. And though I have found leopards and lions in the path; though I have made abundant acquaintance with the hungry wolf, that "with privy paw devours apace and nothing said," as another great poet says of the ravening beast; and though no friendly specter has even yet offered his guidance, I was, and am, minded to go straight on, until I either come out on the other side of the wood, or find there is no other side to it, at least, none attainable by me.

This was my situation when I had the good fortune to find a place among the members of that remarkable confraternity of antagonists, long since deceased, but of green and pious memory, the Metaphysical Society. Every variety of philosophical and theological opinion was represented there, and expressed itself with entire openness; most of my colleagues were -*ists* of one sort or another; and, however kind and friendly they might be, I, the man without a rag of a label to cover himself with, could not fail to have some of the uneasy feelings which must have beset the historical fox when, after leaving the trap in which his tail remained, he presented himself to his normally elongated companions. So I took thought, and invented what I conceived to be the appropriate title of "agnostic." It came into my head as suggestively antithetic to the "gnostic" of Church history, who professed to know so much about the very things of which I was ignorant; and I took the earliest opportunity of parading it at our Society, to show that I, too, had a tail, like the other foxes. To my great satisfaction, the term took; and when the *Spectator* has stood godfather to it, any suspicion in the minds of respectable people, that a knowledge of its parentage might have awakened, was, of course, completely lulled.

That is the history of the origin of the terms "agnostic" and "agnosticism"; and it will be observed that it does not quite agree with the confident assertion of the reverend Principal of King's College, that "the adoption of the term agnostic is only an attempt to shift the issue, and that it involves a mere evasion" in relation to the Church and Christianity.

The last objection (I rejoice, as much as my readers must do, that it is the last) which I have to take to Dr. Wace's deliverance before the Church Congress arises, I am sorry to say, on a question of morality.

"It is, and it ought to be," authoritatively declares this official representative of Christian ethics, "an unpleasant thing for a man to have to say plainly that he does not believe in Jesus Christ."

Whether it is so depends, I imagine, a good deal on whether the man was brought up in a Christian household or not. I do not see why it should be "unpleasant" for a Mohammedan or Buddhist to say so. But that "it ought to be" unpleasant for any man to say anything which he sincerely, and after due deliberation, believes, is, to my mind, a proposition of the most profoundly immoral character.

. . . It ought *not* to be unpleasant to say that which one honestly believes or disbelieves. That it so constantly is painful to do so, is quite enough obstacle to the progress of mankind in that most valuable of all qualities, honesty of word or of deed, without erecting a sad concomitant of human weakness into something to be admired and cherished. The bravest of soldiers often, and very naturally, "feel it unpleasant" to go into action; but a court-martial which did its duty would make short work of the officer who promulgated the doctrine that his men *ought* to feel their duty unpleasant.

I am very well aware, as I suppose most thoughtful people are in these times, that the process of breaking away from old beliefs is extremely unpleasant; and I am much disposed to think that the encouragement, the consolation, and the peace afforded to earnest believers in even the worst forms of Christianity are of great practical advantage to them. What deductions must be made from this gain on the score of the harm done to the citizen by the ascetic other-worldliness of logical Christianity; to the ruler, by the hatred, malice, and all uncharitableness of sectarian bigotry; to the legislator, by the spirit of exclusiveness and domination of those that count themselves pillars of orthodoxy; to the philosopher, by the restraints on the freedom of learning and teaching which every Church exercises, when it is strong enough; to the conscientious soul, by the introspective hunting after sins of the mint and cummin type, the fear of theological error, and the overpowering terror of possible damnation, which have accompanied the Churches like their shadow, I need not now consider; but they are assuredly not small. If agnostics lose heavily on the one side, they gain a good deal on the other. People who talk about the comforts of belief appear to forget its discomforts; they ignore the fact that the Christianity of the Churches is something more than faith in the ideal personality of Jesus, which they create for themselves, *plus* so much as can be carried into practice, without disorganizing civil society, of the maxims of the Sermon on the Mount. Trip in morals or in doctrine (especially in doctrine), without due repentance or retractation, or fail to get properly baptized before you die, and a *plébisite* of the Christians of Europe, if they were true to their creeds, would affirm your everlasting damnation by an immense majority.

Preachers, orthodox and heterodox, din into our ears that the world cannot get on without faith of some sort. There is a sense in which that is as eminently as obviously true; there is another one which, in my judgment, is as eminently as obviously false, and it seems to me that the hortatory, or pulpit, mind is apt to oscillate between the false and the true meanings, without being aware of the fact.

It is quite true that the ground of every one of our actions, and the validity of all our reasonings, rest upon the great act of faith, which leads us to take the experience of the past as a safe guide in our dealings with the present and the future. From the nature of ratiocination it is obvious that the axioms on which it is based can not be demonstrated by ratiocination. It is also a trite observation that, in the business of life, we constantly take the most serious action upon evidence of an utterly insufficient character. But it is surely plain that faith is not necessarily entitled to dispense with ratiocination because ratiocination cannot dispense with faith as a starting-point; and that because we are often obliged, by the pressure of events, to act on very bad evidence, it does not follow that it is proper to act on such evidence when the pressure is absent.

The writer of the epistle to the Hebrews tells us that "faith is the assurance of things hoped for, the proving of things not seen." In the authorized version "substance" stands for "assurance," and "evidence" for "proving." The question of the exact meaning of the two words affords a fine field of discussion for the scholar and the metaphysician. But I fancy we shall be not far from the mark if we take the writer to have had in his mind the profound psychological truth that men constantly feel certain about things for which they strongly hope, but have no evidence, in the legal or logical sense of the word; and he calls this feeling "faith." I may have the most absolute faith that a friend has not committed the crime of which he is accused. In the early days of English history, if my friend could have obtained a few more compurgators of a like robust faith, he would have been acquitted. At the present day, if I tendered myself as a witness on that score, the judge would tell me to stand down, and the youngest barrister would smile at my simplicity. Miserable indeed is the man who has not such faith in some of his fellowmen — only less miserable than the man who allows himself to forget that such faith is not, strictly speaking, evidence; and when his faith is disappointed, as will happen now and again, turns Timon and blames the universe for his own blunders. And so, if a man can find a friend, the hypostasis of all his hopes, the mirror of his ethical ideal, in the Jesus of any, or all, of the Gospels, let him live by faith in that ideal. Who shall or can forbid him? But let him not delude himself with the notion that his faith is evidence of the objective reality of that in which he trusts. Such evidence is to be obtained only by the use of the methods of science, as applied to history and to literature, and it amounts at present to very little.

It appears that Mr. Gladstone some time ago asked Mr. Laing if he could draw up a short summary of the negative creed; a body of negative propositions, which have so far been adopted on the negative side as to be what the Apostles' and other accepted creeds are on the positive; and Mr. Laing at once kindly obliged Mr. Gladstone with the desired articles — eight of them.

If any one had preferred this request to me I should have replied that, if he referred to agnostics, they have no creed; and, by the nature of the case, can not have any. Agnosticism, in fact, is not a creed, but a method, the essence of which lies in the rigorous application of a single principle. That principle is of great antiquity; it is as old as Socrates; as old as the writer who said, "Try all things, hold fast by that which is good"; it is the foundation of the Reformation, which simply illustrated the axiom that every man should be able to give a reason for the faith that is in him; it is the great principle of Descartes; it is the fundamental axiom of modern science. Positively the principle may be expressed: In matters of the intellect follow your reason as far as it will take you without regard to any other consideration. And negatively: In matters of the intellect do not pretend that conclusions are certain which are not demonstrated or demonstrable. That I take to be the agnostic faith, which if a man keep whole and undefiled, he shall not be ashamed to look the universe in the face, whatever the future may have in store for him.

The results of the working out of the agnostic principle will vary according to individual knowledge and capacity, and according to the general condition of science. That which is unproved today may be proved by the help of new discoveries tomorrow. The only negative fixed points will be those negations which flow from the demonstrable limitation of our faculties. And the only obligation accepted is to have the mind always open to conviction. Agnostics who never fail in carrying out their principles are, I am afraid, as rare as other people of whom the same consistency can be truthfully predicted. But, if you were to meet with such a phoenix and to tell him that you had discovered that two and two make five, he would patiently ask you to state your reasons for that conviction, and express his readiness to agree with you if he found them satisfactory. The apostolic injunction to "suffer fools gladly" should be the rule of life of a true agnostic. I am deeply conscious how far I myself fall short of this ideal, but it is my personal conception of what agnostics ought to be.

26. The Criteria of Belief *

WILLIAM KINGDON CLIFFORD (1845–1879)

But because it is not enough to say, "It is wrong to believe on unworthy evidence," without saying also what evidence is worthy,

---

* Wm. Kingdon Clifford, *Lectures and Essays* (London: Macmillan & Co., Ltd., 1879). Vol. II. From chapter entitled "The Ethics of Belief." Reprinted by permission.

we shall now go on to inquire under what circumstances it is lawful
to believe on the testimony of others; and then, further, we shall
inquire more generally when and why we may believe that which
goes beyond our own experience, or even beyond the experience of
mankind.

In what cases, then, let us ask in the first place, is the testimony
of a man unworthy of belief? He may say that which is untrue
either knowingly or unknowingly. In the first case he is lying, and
his moral character is to blame; in the second case he is ignorant
or mistaken, and it is only his knowledge or his judgment which
is in fault. In order that we may have the right to accept his
testimony as ground for believing what he says, we must have
reasonable grounds for trusting his veracity, that he is really trying
to speak the truth so far as he knows it; his knowledge, that he has
had opportunities of knowing the truth about this matter; and his
judgment, that he has made proper use of those opportunities in
coming to the conclusion which he affirms.

However plain and obvious these reasons may be, so that no
man of ordinary intelligence, reflecting upon the matter, could fail
to arrive at them, it is nevertheless true that a great many persons
do habitually disregard them in weighing testimony. Of the two
questions, equally important to the trustworthiness of a witness,
"Is he dishonest?" and "May he be mistaken?" the majority of
mankind are perfectly satisfied if one can, with some show of
probability, be answered in the negative. The excellent moral character of a man is alleged as ground for accepting his statements
about things which he cannot possibly have known. A Mohammedan, for example, will tell us that the character of his Prophet
was so noble and majestic that it commands the reverence even
of those who do not believe in his mission. So admirable was his
moral teaching, so wisely put together the great social machine
which he created, that his precepts have not only been accepted by
a great portion of mankind, but have actually been obeyed. His
institutions have on the one hand rescued the Negro from savagery,
and on the other hand have taught civilisation to the advancing
West; and although the races which held the highest forms of his
faith, and most fully embodied his mind and thought, have all
been conquered and swept away by barbaric tribes, yet the history
of their marvelous attainment remains as an imperishable glory to

Islam. Are we to doubt the word of a man so great and so good? Can we suppose that this magnificent genius, this splendid moral hero, has lied to us about the most solemn and sacred matters? The testimony of Mohammed is clear, that there is but one God, and that he, Mohammed, is his Prophet; that if we believe in him we shall enjoy everlasting felicity, but that if we do not we shall be damned. This testimony rests on the most awful of foundations, the revelation of heaven itself; for was he not visited by the angel Gabriel, as he fasted and prayed in his desert cave, and allowed to enter into the blessed fields of Paradise? Surely God is God and Mohammed is the Prophet of God.

What should we answer to this Mussulman? First no doubt, we should be tempted to take exception against his view of the character of the Prophet and the uniformly beneficial influence of Islam: before we could go with him altogether in these matters it might seem that we should have to forget many terrible things of which we have heard or read. But if we chose to grant him all these assumptions, for the sake of argument, and because it is difficult both for the faithful and for infidels to discuss them fairly and without passion, still we should have something to say which takes away the ground of his belief, and therefore shows that it is wrong to entertain it. Namely this: the character of Mohammed is excellent evidence that he was honest and spoke the truth so far as he knew it; but it is no evidence at all that he knew what the truth was. What means could he have of knowing that the form which appeared to him to be the angel Gabriel was not a hallucination, and that his apparent visit to Paradise was not a dream? Grant that he himself was fully persuaded and honestly believed that he had the guidance of heaven, and was the vehicle of a supernatural revelation, how could he know that this strong conviction was not a mistake? Let us put ourselves in his place; we shall find that the more completely we endeavour to realize what passed through his mind, the more clearly we shall perceive that the Prophet could have had no adequate ground for the belief in his own inspiration. It is most probable that he himself never doubted of the matter, or thought of asking the question; but we are in the position of those to whom the question has been asked, and who are bound to answer it. It is known to medical observers that solitude and want of food are powerful means of producing delusion and of fostering a tendency to mental disease. Let us suppose, then, that I, like Mohammed, go into desert places to fast and pray; what things can happen to me which will give me the right to believe that I am divinely inspired? Suppose that I get information, apparently from a celestial visitor, which upon being tested is found to be correct. I cannot be sure, in the first place, that the celestial visitor is not a figment of my own mind, and that the information did not come to me, unknown at the time to my consciousness, through some subtle channel of sense. But if my visitor were a real visitor, and for a long time gave me information which was found to be trustworthy, this would indeed be good ground for trusting him in the future as to such matters as fall within human powers of verification; but it would not be ground for trusting his testimony as to any other matters. For although his tested character would justify me in believing that he spoke the truth so far as he knew, yet the same question would present itself — what ground is there for supposing that he knows?

Even if my supposed visitor had given me such information, subsequently verified by me, as proved him to have means of knowledge about verifiable matters far exceeding my own; this would not justify me in believing what he said about matters that are not at present capable of verification by man. It would be ground for interesting conjecture, and for the hope that, as the fruit of our patient inquiry, we might by and by attain to such a means of verification as should rightly turn conjecture into belief. For belief belongs to man, and to the guidance of human affairs: no belief is real unless it guide our actions, and those very actions supply a test of its truth.

But, it may be replied, the acceptance of Islam as a system is just that action which is prompted by belief in the mission of the Prophet, and which will serve for a test of its truth. Is it possible to believe that a system which has succeeded so well is really founded upon a delusion? Not only have individual saints found joy and peace in believing, and verified those spiritual experiences which are promised to the faithful, but nations also have been raised from savagery or barbarism to a higher social state. Surely we are at liberty to say that the belief has been acted upon, and that it has been verified.

It requires, however, but little consideration to show that what has really been verified is not at all the supernal character of the Prophet's mission, or the trustworthiness of his authority in matters which we ourselves cannot test, but only his practical wisdom in certain very mundane things. The fact that believers have found joy and peace in believing gives us the right to say that the doctrine is a comfortable doctrine, and pleasant to the soul; but it does not give us the right to say that it is true. And the question which our conscience is always asking about that which we are tempted to believe is not, "Is it comfortable and pleasant?" but, "Is it true?" That the Prophet preached certain doctrines, and predicted that spiritual comfort would be found in them, proves only his sympathy with human nature and his knowledge of it; but it does not prove his superhuman knowledge of theology.

And if we admit for the sake of argument (for it seems that we cannot do more) that the progress made by Moslem nations in certain cases was really due to the system formed and sent forth into the world by Mohammed, we are not at liberty to conclude from this that he was inspired to declare the truth about things which we cannot verify. We are only at liberty to infer the excellence of his moral precepts, or of the means which he devised for so working upon men so as to get them obeyed, or of the social and political machinery which he set up. And it would require a great amount of careful examination into the history of those nations to determine which of these things had the greater share in the result. So that here again it is the Prophet's knowledge of human nature, and his sympathy with it, that are verified; not his divine inspiration or his knowledge of theology.

If there were only one Prophet, indeed, it might well seem a difficult and even an ungracious task to decide upon what points we would trust him, and on what we would doubt his authority; seeing what help and furtherance all men have gained in all ages from those who saw more clearly, who felt more strongly, and who sought the truth with more single heart than their weaker brethren. But there is not only one Prophet; and while the consent of many upon that which, as men, they had real means of knowing and did know, has endured to the end, and been honourably built into the great fabric of human knowledge, the diverse witness of some about that which they did not and could not know remains as a warning to us that to exaggerate the prophetic authority is to misuse it, and to dishonour those who have sought only to help and further us after their power. It is hardly in human nature that a man should quite accurately gauge the limits of his own insight; but it is the duty of those who profit by his work to consider carefully where he may have been carried beyond it. If we must needs embalm his possible errors along with his solid achievements, and use his authority as an excuse for believing what he cannot have known, we make of his goodness an occasion to sin.

To consider only one other such witness: the followers of the Buddha have at least as much right to appeal to individual and social experience in support of the authority of the Eastern saviour. The special mark of his religion, it is said, that in which it has never been surpassed, is the comfort and consolation which it gives to the sick and sorrowful, the tender sympathy with which it soothes and assuages all the natural griefs of men. And surely no triumph of social morality can be greater or nobler than that which has kept nearly half the human race from persecuting in the name of religion. If we are to trust the accounts of his early followers, he believed himself to have come upon earth with a divine and cosmic mission to set rolling the wheel of the law. Being a prince, he divested himself of his kingdom, and of his free will became acquainted with misery, that he might learn how to meet and subdue it. Could such a man speak falsely about solemn things? And as for his knowledge, was he not a man miraculous with powers more than man's? He was born of woman without the help of man; he rose into the air and was transfigured before his kinsmen; at last he went up bodily into heaven from the top of Adam's Peak. Is not his word to be believed in when he testifies of heavenly things?

If there were only he, and no other, with such claims! But there is Mohammed with his testimony; we cannot choose but listen to them both. The Prophet tells us that there is one God, and that we shall live forever in joy or misery, according as we believe in the Prophet or not. The Buddha says that there is no God, and that we shall be annihilated by and by if we are good enough. Both cannot be infallibly inspired; one or other must have been the victim of a delusion, and thought he knew that which he really did not know. Who shall dare to say which? and how can we justify ourselves in believing that the other was not also deluded?

We are led, then, to these judgments following. The goodness and greatness of a man do not justify us in accepting a belief upon the warrant of his authority, unless there are reasonable grounds for supposing that he knew the truth of what he was saying. And there can be no grounds for supposing that a man knows that which we, without ceasing to be men, could not be supposed to verify.

THE LIMITS OF INFERENCE

The question in what cases we may believe that which goes beyond our experience, is a very large and delicate one, extending to the whole range of scientific method, and requiring a considerable increase in the application of it before it can be answered with anything approaching to completeness. But one rule, lying on the threshold of the subject, of extreme simplicity and vast practical importance, may here be touched upon and shortly laid down.

A little reflection will show us that every belief, even the simplest and most fundamental, goes beyond experience when regarded as a guide to our actions. A burnt child dreads the fire, because it believes that the fire will burn it today just as it did yesterday; but this belief goes beyond experience, and assumes that the unknown fire of today is like the known fire of yesterday. Even the belief that the child was burnt yesterday goes beyond present experience, which contains only the memory of a burning, and not the burning itself; it assumes, therefore, that this memory is trustworthy, although we know that a memory may often be mistaken. But if it is to be used as a guide to action, as a hint of what the future is to be, it must assume something about that future, namely, that it will be consistent with the supposition that the burning really took place yesterday; which is going beyond experience. Even the fundamental "I am," which cannot be doubted, is no guide to action until it takes to itself "I shall be," which goes beyond experience. The question is not, therefore, "May we believe what goes beyond experience?" for this is involved in the very nature of belief; but "How far and in what manner may we add to our experience in forming our beliefs?"

And an answer, of utter simplicity and universality, is suggested by the example we have taken; a burnt child dreads the fire. We may go beyond experience by assuming that what we do not know is like what we do know; or in other words, we may add to our experience on the assumption of a uniformity in nature. What this uniformity precisely is, how we grow in the knowledge of it from generation to generation, these are questions which for the present we lay aside, being content to examine two instances which may serve to make plainer the nature of the rule.

From certain observations made with the spectroscope, we infer the existence of hydrogen in the sun. By looking into the spectroscope when the sun is shining on its slit, we see certain definite bright lines: and experiments made upon bodies on the earth have taught us that when these bright lines are seen hydrogen is the source of them. We assume, then, that the unknown bright lines in the sun are like the known bright lines of the laboratory, and that hydrogen in the sun behaves as hydrogen under similar circumstances would behave on the earth.

But are we not trusting our spectroscope too much? Surely, having found it to be trustworthy for terrestrial substances, where its statements can be verified by man, we are justified in accepting its testimony in other like cases; but not when it gives us information about things in the sun, where its testimony cannot be directly verified by man.

Certainly, we want to know a little more before this inference can be justified; and fortunately we do know this. The spectroscope testifies to exactly the same thing in the two cases; namely, that light-vibrations of a certain rate are being sent through it. Its construction is such that if it were wrong about this in one case, it would be wrong in the other. When we come to look into the matter, we find that we have really assumed the matter of the sun to be like the matter of the earth, made up of a certain number of distinct substances; and that each of these, when very hot, has a distinct rate of vibration, by which it may be recognised and singled out from the rest. But this is the kind of assumption which we are justified in using when we add to our experience. It is an assumption of uniformity in nature, and can only be checked by comparison with many similar assumptions which we have to make in other such cases.

But is this a true belief, of the existence of hydrogen in the sun? Can it help in the right guidance of human action?

Certainly not, if it is accepted on unworthy grounds, and without some understanding of the process by which it is got at. But when this process is taken in as the ground of the belief, it becomes a very serious and practical matter. For if there is no hydrogen in the sun, the spectroscope — that is to say, the measurement of rates of vibration — must be an uncertain guide in recognizing different substances; and consequently it ought not to be used in chemical analysis — in assaying, for example — to the great saving of time, trouble, and money. Whereas the acceptance of the spectroscopic method as trustworthy has enriched us not only with new metals, which is a great thing, but with new processes of investigation, which is vastly greater.

For another example, let us consider the way in which we infer the truth of an historical event — say the siege of Syracuse in the Peloponnesian war. Our experience is that manuscripts exist which are said to be and which call themselves manuscripts of the history of Thucydides; that in other manuscripts, stated to be by later historians, he is described as living during the time of the war; and that books, supposed to date from the revival of learning, tell us how these manuscripts had been preserved and were then acquired. We find also that men do not, as a rule, forge books and histories without a special motive; we assume that in this respect men in the past were like men in the present; and we observe that in this case no special motive was present. That is, we add to our experience on the assumption of a uniformity in the characters of men. Because our knowledge of this uniformity is far less complete and exact than our knowledge of that which obtains in physics, inferences of the historical kind are more precarious and less exact than inferences in many other sciences.

But if there is any special reason to suspect the character of the persons who wrote or transmitted certain books, the case becomes altered. If a group of documents give internal evidence that they were produced among people who forged books in the names of others, and who, in describing events, suppressed those things which did not suit them, while they amplified such as did suit them; who not only committed these crimes, but glorified in them as proofs of humility and zeal; then we must say that upon such documents no true historical inference can be founded, but only unsatisfactory conjecture.

We may, then, add to our experience on the assumption of a uniformity in nature; we may fill in our picture of what is and has been, as experience gives it us, in such a way as to make the whole consistent with this uniformity. And practically demonstrative inference — that which gives us a right to believe in the result of it — is a clear showing that in no other way than by the truth of this result can the uniformity of nature be saved.

No evidence, therefore, can justify us in believing the truth of a statement which is contrary to, or outside of, the uniformity of nature. If our experience is such that it cannot be filled up consistently with uniformity, all we have a right to conclude is that there is something wrong somewhere; but the possibility of inference is taken away; we must rest in our experience, and not go beyond it at all. If an event really happened which was not a part of the uniformity of nature, it would have two properties; no evidence could give the right to believe it to any except those whose actual experience it was; and no inference worthy of belief could be founded upon it at all.

Are we then bound to believe that nature is absolutely and universally uniform? Certainly not; we have no right to believe anything of this kind. The rule only tells us that in forming beliefs which go beyond our experience, we may make the assumption that nature is practically uniform so far as we are concerned. Within the range of human action and verification, we may form by help of this assumption, actual beliefs; beyond it, only those hypotheses which serve for the more accurate asking of questions.

To sum up: —

We may believe what goes beyond our experience, only when it is inferred from that experience by the assumption that what we do not know is like what we know.

We may believe the statement of another person, when there is reasonable ground for supposing that he knows the matter of which he speaks, and that he is speaking the truth so far as he knows it.

It is wrong in all cases to believe on insufficient evidence; and where it is presumption to doubt and to investigate, there it is worse than presumption to believe.

[NOTE: The bibliography for Chapter Two ap ears on page 519.]

Chapter Three

GOD AND EVIL

INTRODUCTION

Even proof of God's existence cannot, in itself, assure a reverent and worshipful attitude towards the Supreme Power. For the bare existence of God may be compatible with an evil as well as a good Being, with a Force limited or infinite in wisdom and power, with an entity worthy of devotion or deserving of contempt.

The question of God's attributes thus remains crucial even after the problem of His existence has been resolved affirmatively.

Traditional theology, since the Biblical expression of the problem in the Book of Job, has been concerned with an explanation of the source and existence of evil. How could an all-powerful God allow for war, destruction, and pestilence? Does such evil imply God's limited power or does it mean that God may not be concerned with the good at all?

If, as the Judeo-Christian tradition asserts, God created the world out of nothing (*creatio ex nihilo*), then He alone is responsible for all evil in the world. But if God is all-good, what then is the origin of evil? Does it spring from God's will or from a competing malevolent power?

Theological justification of evil (THEODICY) attempts to obviate

225

such dilemmas. Often this yields fundamental re-interpretations and re-formulations of the God-idea. Some would sacrifice the omnipotence of God so as to preserve His goodness. They insist upon the conception of God as a struggling, finite, totally benevolent Force with whom man must join as partner in a common struggle against evil (McTaggart, Mill, James, Brightman).

Others retain the traditional conception of God as good and omnipotent but dismiss what seems to be evil as unreal, as error and illusion (e.g., Christian Science). Some see in evil a blessing in disguise, a challenge to man which adds spice and adventure to life and stimulates him to overcome obstacles in his personal and social life. In fact, they claim that in conquering evil man attains his deepest satisfactions.

A few have argued that the moral predicates of good and bad are only relative to human values and therefore not embarrassing to the proper conception of God (Spinoza). Others hold that evil must be viewed as privation, the absence of good, and that God cannot be held responsible for that which does not exist except through negation (Maimonides, Augustine).

These are some of the attempts to answer the puzzle of the existence of physical evil. In the next chapter on Free Will we will encounter another perplexing question, namely, how to account for moral evil (i.e., man's voluntary acts which lead to war and injustice).

Can God be considered a good agent and yet allow evil to exist in the hearts of men?

H.M.S.

27. Is There More Evil Than Good in Nature?*

JOHN STUART MILL *(1806–1873)*

Nature

For, how stands the fact? That next to the greatness of these

---

* John Stuart Mill, *Three Essays on Religion* (New York: Henry Holt & Co., 1874). "Nature."

cosmic forces, the quality which most forcibly strikes every one who does not avert his eyes from it, is their perfect and absolute recklessness. They go straight to their end, without regarding what or whom they crush on the road. Optimists, in their attempts to prove that "whatever is, is right," are obliged to maintain, not that Nature ever turns one step from her path to avoid trampling us into destruction, but that it would be very unreasonable in us to expect that she should. Pope's "Shall gravitation cease when you go by?" may be a just rebuke to any one who should be so silly as to expect common human morality from nature. But if the question were between two men, instead of between a man and a natural phenomenon, that triumphant apostrophe would be thought a rare piece of impudence. A man who should persist in hurling stones or firing cannon when another man "goes by," and having killed him should urge a similar plea in exculpation, would very deservedly be found guilty of murder.

In sober truth, nearly all the things which men are hanged or imprisoned for doing to one another, are nature's every day performances. Killing, the most criminal act recognized by human laws, Nature does once to every being that lives; and in a large proportion of cases, after protracted tortures such as only the greatest monsters whom we read of ever purposely inflicted on their living fellow-creatures. If, by an arbitrary reservation, we refuse to account anything murder but what abridges a certain term supposed to be allotted to human life, nature also does this to all but a small percentage of lives, and does it in all the modes, violent or insidious, in which the worst human beings take the lives of one another. Nature impales men, breaks them as if on the wheel, casts them to be devoured by wild beasts, burns them to death, crushes them with stones like the first christian martyr, starves them with hunger, freezes them with cold, poisons them by the quick or slow venom of her exhalations, and has hundreds of other hideous deaths in reserve, such as the ingenious cruelty of a Nabis or a Domitian never surpassed. All this, Nature does with the most supercilious disregard both of mercy and of justice, emptying her shafts upon the best and noblest indifferently with the meanest and worst; upon those who are engaged in the highest and worthiest enterprises, and often as the direct consequence of the noblest acts; and it might almost be imagined as a punishment for them. She mows down those on whose existence hangs the well-being of a whole people, perhaps the prospects of the human race for generations to come, with as little compunction as those whose death is a relief to themselves, or a blessing to those under their noxious influence. Such are Nature's dealings with life. Even when she does not intend to kill, she inflicts the same tortures in apparent wantonness. In the clumsy provision which she has made for that perpetual renewal of animal life, rendered necessary by the prompt termination she puts to it in every individual instance, no human being ever comes into the world but another human being is literally stretched on the rack for hours or days, not unfrequently issuing in death. Next to taking life (equal to it according to a high authority) is taking the means by which we live; and Nature does this too on the largest scale and with the most callous indifference. A single hurricane destroys the hopes of a season; a flight of locusts, or an inundation, desolates a district; a trifling chemical change in an edible root, starves a million of people. The waves of the sea, like banditti seize and appropriate the wealth of the rich and the little all of the poor with the same accompaniments of stripping, wounding, and killing as their human antitypes. Everything in short, which the worst men commit either against life or property is perpetrated on a larger scale by natural agents. Nature has Noyades more fatal than those of Carrier; her explosions of fire damp are as destructive as human artillery; her plague and cholera far surpass the poison cups of the Borgias. Even the love of "order" which is thought to be a following of the ways of Nature, is in fact a contradiction of them. All which people are accustomed to deprecate as "disorder" and its consequences, is precisely a counterpart of Nature's ways. Anarchy and the Reign of Terror are overmatched in injustice, ruin, and death, by a hurricane and a pestilence.

But, it is said, all these things are for wise and good ends. On this I must first remark that whether they are so or not, is altogether beside the point. Supposing it true that contrary to appearances these horrors when perpetrated by Nature, promote good ends, still as no one believes that good ends would be promoted by our following the example, the course of Nature cannot be a proper model for us to imitate. Either it is right that we should kill because nature kills; torture because nature tortures; ruin and devastate because nature does the like; or we ought not to consider at all what nature does, but what is good to do. If there is such a thing as a reductio ad absurdum, this surely amounts to one. If it is a sufficient reason for doing one thing, that nature does it, why not another thing? If not all things, why anything? The physical government of the world being full of the things which when done by men are deemed the greatest enormities, it cannot be religious or moral in us to guide our actions by the analogy of the course of nature. This proposition remain true, whatever occult quality of producing good may reside in those facts of nature which to our perceptions are most noxious, and which no one considers it other than a crime to produce artificially.

But, in reality, no one consistently believes in any such occult quality. The phrases which ascribe perfection to the course of nature can only be considered as the exaggerations of poetic or devotional feeling, not intended to stand the test of a sober examination. No one, either religious or irreligious, believes that the hurtful agencies of nature, considered as a whole, promote good purposes, in any other way than by inciting human rational creatures to rise up and struggle against them. If we believed that those agencies were appointed by a benevolent Providence as the means of accomplishing wise purposes which could not be compassed if they did not exist, then everything done by mankind which tends to chain up these natural agencies or to restrict their mischievous operation, from draining a pestilential marsh down to curing the toothache, or putting up an umbrella, ought to be accounted impious; which assuredly nobody does account them, notwithstanding an undercurrent of sentiment setting in that direction which is occasionally perceptible. On the contrary, the improvements on which the civilized part of mankind most pride themselves, consist in more successfully warding off those natural calamities which if we really believed what most people profess to believe, we should cherish as medicines provided for our earthly state by infinite wisdom. Inasmuch too as each generation greatly surpasses its predecessors in the amount of natural evil which it succeeds in averting, our condition, if the theory were true, ought by this time to have become a terrible manifestation of some tremendous calamity, against which the physical evils we have learnt to overmaster, had previously operated as a preservative. Any one, however, who acted as if he supposed this to be the case, would be more likely, I think to be confined as a lunatic, than reverenced as a saint.

It is undoubtedly a very common fact that good comes out of evil, and when it does occur, it is far too agreeable not to find people eager to dilate on it. But in the first place, it is quite as often true of human crimes, as of natural calamities. The fire of London, which is believed to have had so salutary an effect on the healthiness of the city, would have produced that effect just as much if it had been really the work of the "furor papisticus" so long commemorated on the Monument. The deaths of those whom tyrants or persecutors have made martyrs in any noble cause, have done a service to mankind which would not have been obtained if they had died by accident or disease. Yet whatever incidental and unexpected benefits may result from crimes, they are crimes nevertheless. In the second place, if good frequently comes out of evil, the converse fact, evil coming out of good, is equally common. Every event public or private, which, regretted on its occurrence, was declared providential at a later period on account of some unforeseen good consequence, might be matched by some other event, deemed fortunate at the time, but which proved calamitous or fatal to those whom it appeared to benefit. Such conflicts between the beginning and the end, or between the event and the expectation, are not only as frequent, but as often held up to notice, in the painful cases as in the agreeable; but there is not the same inclination to generalize on them; or at all events they are not regarded by the moderns (though they were by the ancients) as similarly an indication of the divine purposes; men satisfy themselves with moralizing on the imperfect nature of our foresight, the uncertainty of events, and the vanity of human expectations. The simple fact is, human interests are so complicated, and the effects of any incident whatever so multitudinous, that if it touches mankind at all, its influence on them is, in the great majority of cases, both good and bad. If the greater number of personal misfortunes have their good side, hardly any good fortune ever befell any one which did not give either to the same or to some other person, something to regret: and unhappily there are many misfortunes so overwhelming that their favourable side, if it exist, is entirely overshadowed and made insignificant; while the corresponding statement can seldom be made concerning blessings. The effects too of every cause depend so much on the circumstances which accidentally accompany it, that many cases are sure to occur in which even the total result is markedly opposed to the predominant tendency: and thus not only evil has its good and good its evil side, but good often produces an overbalance of evil and evil an overbalance of good. This, however, is by no means the general tendency of either phenomenon. On the contrary, both good and evil naturally tend to fructify, each in its own kind, good producing good, and evil, evil. It is one of Nature's general rules, and part of her habitual injustice, that "to him that hath shall be given, but from him that hath not, shall be taken even that which he hath." The ordinary and predominant tendency of good is towards more good. Health, strength, wealth, knowledge, virtue, are not only good in themselves but facilitate and promote the acquisition of good, both of the same and of other kinds. The person who can learn easily, is he who already knows much: it is the strong and not the sickly person who can do everything which most conduces to health; those who find it is easy to gain money are not the poor but the rich; while health, strength, knowledge, talents, are all means of acquiring riches, and riches are often an indispensable means of acquiring these. Again e converso, whatever may be said of evil turning into good, the general tendency of evil is towards further evil. Bodily illness renders the body more susceptible of disease; it produces incapacity of exertion, sometimes debility of mind, and often the loss of means of subsistence. All severe pain, either bodily or mental, tends to increase the susceptibilities of pain for ever after. Poverty is the parent of a thousand mental and moral evils. What is still worse, to be injured or oppressed, when habitual, lowers the whole tone of the character. One bad action leads to others, both in the agent himself, in the bystanders, and in the sufferers. All bad qualities are strengthened by habit, and all vices and follies tend to spread. Intellectual defects generate moral, and moral, intellectual; and every intellectual or moral defect generates others, and so on without end.

That much applauded class of authors, the writers on natural theology, have, I venture to think, entirely lost their way, and missed the sole line of argument which could have made their speculations acceptable to any one who can perceive when two propositions contradict one another. They have exhausted the resources of sophistry to make it appear that all the suffering in the world exists to prevent greater—that misery exists, for fear lest there should be misery: a thesis which if ever so well maintained, could only avail to explain and justify the works of limited beings, compelled to labour under conditions independent of their own will; but can have no application to a Creator assumed to be omnipotent, who, if he bends to a supposed necessity, himself makes the necessity which he bends to. If the maker of the world *can* all that he will, he wills misery, and there is no escape from the conclusion. The more consistent of those who have deemed themselves qualified to "vindicate the ways of God to man" have endeavoured to avoid the alternative by hardening their hearts, and denying that misery is an evil. The goodness of God, they say, does not consist in willing the happiness of his creatures, but their virtue; and the universe, if not a happy, is a just, universe. But waving the objections to this scheme of ethics, it does not at all get rid of the difficulty. If the Creator of mankind willed that they should all be virtuous, his designs are as completely baffled as if he had willed that they should all be happy: and the order of nature is constructed with even less regard to the requirements of justice than to those of benevolence. If the law of all creation were justice and the Creator omnipotent, then in whatever amount suffering and happiness might be dispensed to the world, each person's share of them would be exactly proportioned to that person's good or evil deeds; no human being would have a worse lot than another, without worse deserts; accident or favouritism would have no part in such a world, but every human life would be the playing out of a drama constructed like a perfect moral tale. No one is able to blind himself to the fact that the world we live in is totally different from this; insomuch that the necessity of redressing the balance has been deemed one of the strongest arguments for another life after death, which amounts to an admission that the order of things in this life is often an example of injustice, not justice. If it be said that God does not take sufficient account of pleasure and pain to make them the reward or punishment of the good or the wicked, but that virtue is itself the greatest good and vice the greatest evil, then these at least ought to be dispensed to all according to what they have done to de-

serve them; instead of which, every kind of moral depravity is en-
tailed upon multitudes by the fatality of their birth; through the fault
of their parents, of society, or of uncontrollable circumstances, certainly through no fault of their own. Not even on the most distorted
and contracted theory of good which ever was framed by religious or
philosophical fanaticism, can the government of Nature be made
to resemble the work of a being at once good and omnipotent.

The only admissible moral theory of Creation is that the Principle
of Good *cannot* at once and altogether subdue the powers of evil,
either physical or moral; could not place mankind in a world free
from the necessity of an incessant struggle with the maleficent
powers, or make them always victorious in that struggle, but could
and did make them capable of carrying on the fight with vigour
and with progressively increasing success. Of all the religious explanations of the order of nature, this alone is neither contradictory
to itself, nor to the facts for which it attempts to account. According
to it, man's duty would consist, not in simply taking care of his
own interests by obeying irresistible power, but in standing forward a not ineffectual auxiliary to a Being of perfect beneficence;
a faith which seems much better adapted for nerving him to exertion than a vague and inconsistent reliance on an Author of Good
who is supposed to be also the author of evil. And I venture to assert
that such has really been, though often unconsciously, the faith of
all who have drawn strength and support of any worthy kind from
trust in a superintending Providence. There is no subject on which
men's practical belief is more incorrectly indicated by the words
they use to express it, than religion. Many have derived a base
confidence from imagining themselves to be favourites of an omnipotent but capricious and despotic Deity. But those who have been
strengthened in goodness by relying on the sympathizing support
of a powerful and good Governor of the world, have, I am satisfied,
never really believed that Governor to be, in the strict sense of the
term, omnipotent. They have always saved his goodness at the
expense of his power. They have believed, perhaps, that he could,
if he willed, remove all the thorns from their individual path, but
not without causing greater harm to some one else, or frustrating
some purpose of greater importance to the general well-being. They

have believed that he could do any one thing, but not any combination of things: that his government, like human government, was a system of adjustments and compromises; that the world is inevitably imperfect, contrary to his intention.[1] And since the exertion of all his power to make it as little imperfect as possible, leaves it no better than it is, they cannot but regard that power, though vastly beyond human estimate, yet as in itself not merely finite, but extremely limited. They are bound, for example, to suppose that the best he could do for his human creatures was to make an immense majority of all who have yet existed, be born (without any fault of their own) Patagonians, or Esquimaux, or something nearly as brutal and degraded, but to give them capacities which by being cultivated for very many centuries in toil and suffering, and after many of the best specimens of the race have sacrificed their lives for the purpose, have at last enabled some chosen portions of the species to grow into something better, capable of being improved in centuries more into something really good, of which hitherto there are only to be found individual instances. It may be possible to believe with Plato that perfect goodness, limited and thwarted in every direction by the intractableness of the material, has done this because it could do no better. But that the same perfectly wise and good Being had absolute power over the material, and made it, by voluntary choice, what it is; to admit this might have been supposed impossible to any one who has the simplest notions of moral good and evil. Nor can any such person, whatever kind of religious phrases he may use, fail to believe, that if Nature and Man are both the works of a Being of perfect goodness, that Being intended Nature as a scheme to be amended, not imitated, by Man.

---

[1] This irresistible conviction comes out in the writing of religious philosophers, in exact proportion to the general clearness of their understanding. It nowhere shines forth so distinctly as in Leibnitz's famous Theodicee, so strangely mistaken for a system of optimism, and, as such, satirized by Voltaire on grounds which do not even touch the author's argument. Leibnitz does not maintain that this world is the best of all imaginable, but only of all possible worlds, which he argues, it cannot but be, inasmuch as God, who is absolute goodness, has chosen it and not another. In every page of the work he tacitly assumes an abstract possibility and impossibility, independent of the divine power; and though his pious feelings make him continue to designate that power by the word Omnipotence, he so explains that term as to make it mean, power extending to all that is within the limits of that abstract possibility.

28. *The Origin of Evil in Nature* *

ST. AUGUSTINE *(353–430)*

But I also as yet, although I held and was firmly persuaded that
Thou our Lord the true God, who madest not only our souls, but
our bodies, and not only our souls and bodies, but all beings, and all
things, wert undefilable and unalterable, and in no degree mutable;
yet understood I not, clearly and without difficulty, the cause of
evil. And yet whatever it were, I perceived it was in such wise to
be sought out, as should not constrain me to believe the immutable
God to be mutable, lest I should become that evil I was seeking out.
I sought it out then, thus far free from anxiety, certain of the untruth
of what these held, from whom I shrunk with my whole heart: for I
saw, that through enquiring the origin of evil, they were filled with
evil, in that they preferred to think that Thy substance did suffer
ill than their own did commit it.

And I strained to perceive what I now heard, that free-will was
the cause of our doing ill, and Thy just judgment of our suffering
ill. But I was not able clearly to discern it. So then endeavouring to
draw my soul's vision out of that deep pit, I was again plunged
therein, and endeavouring often, I was plunged back as often. But
this raised me a little into Thy light, that I knew as well that I had
a will, as that I lived: when then I did will or nill any thing, I was
most sure that no other than myself did will and nill: and I all but
saw that here was the cause of my sin. But what I did against my
will, saw that I suffered rather than did, and I judged not to be
my fault, but my punishment; whereby however, holding Thee to be
just, I speedily confessed myself to be not unjustly punished. But
again I said, Who made me? Did not my God, Who is not only good,
but goodness itself? Whence then came I to will evil and nill good,
so that I am thus justly punished? who set this in me, and ingrafted
into me this plant of bitterness, seeing I was wholly formed by my
most sweet God? If the devil were the author, whence is that same

---

* St. Augustine, *The Confessions of St. Augustine* (New York: E. P. Dutton
& Co., Inc., Everyman's Library Edition, 1909), pp. 113–116, pp. 125–127.
Reprinted by permission.

devil? And if he also by his own perverse will, of a good angel became a devil, whence, again, came in him that evil will whereby he became a devil, seeing the whole nature of angels was made by that most good Creator? By these thoughts I was again sunk down and choked; yet not brought down to that hell of error (where no man confesseth unto Thee), to think rather that Thou dost suffer ill, than that man doth it.

And I sought "whence is evil," and sought in an evil way; and saw not the evil in my very search. I set now before the sight of my spirit the whole creation, whatsoever we can see therein (as sea, earth, air, stars, trees, mortal creatures); yea, and whatever in it we do not see, as the firmament of heaven, all angels moreover, and all the spiritual inhabitants thereof. But these very beings, as though they were bodies, did my fancy dispose in place, and I made one great mass of Thy creation, distinguished as to the kinds of bodies; some, real bodies, some, what myself had feigned for spirits. And this mass I made huge, not as it was (which I could not know), but as I thought convenient, yet every way finite. But Thee, O Lord, I imagined on every part environing and penetrating it, though every way infinite: as if there were a sea, every where, and on every side, through unmeasured space, one only boundless sea, and it contained within it some sponge, huge, but bounded; that sponge must needs, in all its parts, be filled from that unmeasurable sea: so conceived I Thy creation, itself finite, full of Thee, the Infinite; and I said, Behold God, and behold what God hath created; and God is good, yea, most mightily and incomparably better than all these but yet He, the Good, created them good; and see how He environeth and fulfils them. Where is evil then, and whence, and how crept it in hither? What is its root, and what its seed? Or hath it no being? Why then fear we and avoid what is not? Or if we fear it idly, then is that very fear evil, whereby the soul is thus idly goaded and racked. Yea, and so much a greater evil, as we have nothing to fear and yet do fear. Therefore either is that evil which we fear, or else evil is, that we fear. Whence is it then? Seeing God, the Good, hath created all these things good. He indeed, the greater and chiefest Good, hath created these lesser goods; still both Creator and created all are good. Whence is evil? Or, was there some evil matter of which He made, and formed, and ordered it, yet left something in it

which He did not convert into good? Why so then? Had He no
might to turn and change the whole, so that no evil should remain
in it, seeing He is All-mighty? Lastly, why would He make any
thing at all of it, and not rather by the same All-mightiness cause
it not to be at all? Or, could it then be against His will? Or if it
were from eternity, why suffered He it so to be for infinite spaces of
times past, and was pleased so long after to make something out of
it? Or if He were suddenly pleased now to effect somewhat, this
rather should the All-mighty have effected, that this evil matter
should not be, and He alone be, the whole, true, sovereign, and infinite Good. Or if it was not good that He who was good should not
also frame and create something that were good, then, that evil
matter being taken away and brought to nothing, He might form
good matter, whereof to create all things. For He should not be
All-Mighty, if He might not create something good without the aid
of that matter which Himself had not created. These thoughts I
revolved in my miserable heart, overcharged with most gnawing
cares, lest I should die ere I had found the truth; yet was the faith
of Thy Christ, our Lord and Saviour, professed in the Church Catholic, firmly fixed in my heart, in many points, indeed, as yet
unformed, and fluctuating from the rule of doctrine; yet did not my
mind utterly leave it, but rather daily took in more and more of it.

And it was manifested unto me, that those things be good which
yet are corrupted; which neither were they sovereignly good, nor
unless they were good could be corrupted: for if sovereignly good,
they were incorruptible, if not good at all, there were nothing in
them to be corrupted. For corruption injures, but unless it diminished goodness, it could not injure. Either then corruption injures
not, which cannot be; or which is most certain, all which is corrupted
is deprived of good. But if they be deprived of all good, they shall
cease to be. For if they shall be, and can now no longer be corrupted,
they shall be better than before, because they shall abide incor-
ruptibly. And what more monstrous than to affirm things to become
better by losing all their good? Therefore, if they shall be deprived
of all good, they shall no longer be. So long therefore as they are,
they are good: therefore whatsoever is, is good. That evil then which
I sought, whence it is, is not any substance: for were it a substance,
it should be good. For either it should be an incorruptible substance,

and so a chief good: or a corruptible substance; which unless it were good, could not be corrupted. I perceived therefore, and it was manifested to me that Thou madest all things good, nor is there any substance at all, which Thou madest not; and for that Thou madest not all things equal, therefore are all things; because each is good, and altogether very good, because our God made all things very good.

And to Thee is nothing whatsoever evil: yea, not only to Thee, but also to Thy creation as a whole, because there is nothing without, which may break in, and corrupt that order which Thou hast appointed it. But in the parts thereof some things, because unharmonising with other some, are accounted evil: whereas those very things harmonise with others, and are good; and in themselves are good. And all these things which harmonise not together, do yet with the inferior part, which we call Earth, having its own cloudy and windy sky harmonising with it. Far be it then that I should say, "These things should not be": for should I see nought but these, I should indeed long for the better; but still must even for these alone praise Thee; for that Thou art to be praised, do show from the earth, dragons, and all deeps, fire, hail, snow, ice, and stormy wind, which fulfil Thy word; mountains, and all hills, fruitful trees, and all cedars; beasts, and all cattle, creeping things, and flying fowls, kings of the earth, and all people, princes, and all judges of the earth; young men and maidens, old men and young, praise Thy Name. But when, from heaven, these praise Thee, praise Thee, our God, in the heights all Thy angels, all Thy hosts, sun and moon, all the stars and light, the Heaven of heavens, and the waters that be above the heavens, praise Thy Name; I did not now long for things better, because I conceived of all: and with a sounder judgment I apprehended that the things above were better than these below, but altogether better than those above by themselves.

And I perceived and found it nothing strange, that bread which is pleasant to a healthy palate is loathsome to one distempered: and to sore eyes light is offensive, which to the sound is delightful. And Thy righteousness displeaseth the wicked; much more the viper and reptiles, which Thou hast created good, fitting in with the inferior portions of Thy Creation, with which the very wicked also fit in; and that the more, by how much they be unlike Thee; but with the

superior creatures, by how much they become more like to Thee. And
I enquired what inquity was, and found it to be no substance, but
the perversion of the will, turned aside from Thee, O God, the Supreme, towards these lower things, and casting out its bowels, and
puffed up outwardly.

29. Does God Have Purpose? *

BENEDICT SPINOZA *(1632–1677)*

In the foregoing I have explained the nature and properties of
God. I have shown that he necessarily exists, that he is one: that he
is, and acts solely by the necessity of his own nature; that he is the
free cause of all things, and how he is so; that all things are in God,
and so depend on him, that without him they could neither exist nor
be conceived; lastly, that all things are pre-determined by God,
not through his free will or absolute fiat, but from the very nature
of God or infinite power. I have further, where occasion offered,
taken care to remove the prejudices, which might impede the comprehension of my demonstrations. Yet there still remain misconceptions not a few, which might and may prove very grave hindrances
to the understanding of the concatenation of things, as I have explained it above. I have therefore thought it worth while to bring
these misconceptions before the bar of reason.

All such opinions spring from the notion commonly entertained,
that all things in nature act as men themselves act, namely, with
an end in view. It is accepted as certain, that God himself directs
all things to a definite goal (for it is said that God made all things
for man, and man that he might worship him). I will, therefore,
consider this opinion, asking first, why it obtains general credence,
and why all men are naturally so prone to adopt it? Secondly, I
will point out its falsity; and, lastly, I will show how it has given
rise to prejudices about good and bad, right and wrong, praise and

* Benedict Spinoza, *Ethics*, (New York: Tudor Publishing Co., n.d.), Appendix to Part I. Reprinted by permission.

blame, order and confusion, beauty and ugliness, and the like. However, this is not the place to deduce these misconceptions from the nature of the human mind: it will be sufficient here, if I assume as a starting point, what ought to be universally admitted, namely, that all men are born ignorant of the causes of things, that all have the desire to seek for what is useful to them, and that they are conscious of such desire. Herefrom it follows first, that men think themselves free, inasmuch as they are conscious of their volitions and desires, and never even dream, in their ignorance, of the causes which have disposed them to wish and desire. Secondly, that men do all things for an end, namely, for that which is useful to them, and which they seek. Thus it comes to pass that they only look for a knowledge of the final causes of events, and when these are learned, they are content, as having no cause for further doubt. If they cannot learn such causes from external sources, they are compelled to turn to considering themselves, and reflecting what end would have induced them personally to bring about the given event, and thus they necessarily judge other natures by their own. Further, as they find in themselves and outside themselves many means which assist them not a little in their search for what is useful, for instance, eyes for seeing, teeth for chewing, herbs and animals for yielding food, the sun for giving light, the sea for breeding fish, etc., they come to look on the whole of nature as a means for obtaining such conveniences. Now as they are aware, that they found these conveniences and did not make them they think they have cause for believing, that some other being has made them for their use. As they look upon things as means, they cannot believe them to be self-created; but, judging from the means which they are accustomed to prepare for themselves, they are bound to believe in some ruler or rulers of the universe endowed with human freedom, who have arranged and adapted everything for human use. They are bound to estimate the nature of such rulers (having no information on the subject) in accordance with their own nature, and therefore they assert that the gods ordained everything for the use of man, in order to bind man to themselves and obtain from him the highest honors. Hence also it follows, that everyone thought out for himself, according to his abilities, a different way of worshipping God, so that God might love him more than his fellows, and direct the whole course of nature for the satis-

faction of his blind cupidity and insatiable avarice. Thus the prejudice developed into superstition, and took deep root in the human
mind; and for this reason everyone strove most zealously to understand and explain the final causes of things; but in their endeavor to
show that nature does nothing in vain, i.e., nothing which is useless
to man, they only seem to have demonstrated that nature, the gods,
and men are all mad together. Consider, I pray you, the result;
among the many helps of nature they were bound to find some hindrances, such as storms, earthquakes, diseases, etc.: so they declared
that such things happen, because the gods are angry at some wrong
done them by men, or at some fault committed in their worship.
Experience day by day protested and showed by infinite examples,
that good and evil fortunes fall to the lot of pious and impious alike;
still they would not abandon their inveterate prejudice, for it was
more easy for them to class such contradictions among other unknown things of whose use they were ignorant, and thus to retain
their actual and innate condition of ignorance, than to destroy the
whole fabric of their reasoning and start afresh. They therefore laid
down as an axiom, that God's judgments far transcend human understanding. Such a doctrine might well have sufficed to conceal the
truth from the human race for all eternity, if mathematics had not
furnished another standard of verity in considering solely the essence and properties of figures without regard to their final causes.
There are other reasons (which I need not mention here) besides
mathematics, which might have caused men's minds to be directed to
these general prejudices, and have led them to the knowledge of the
truth.

I have now sufficiently explained my first point. There is no need
to show at length, that nature has no particular goal in view, and
that final causes are mere human figments.

Further, this doctrine does away with the perfection of God: for, if
God acts for an object, he necessarily desires something which he
lacks. Certainly, theologians and metaphysicians draw a distinction between the object of want and the object of assimilation; still
they confess that God made all things for sake of himself, not for
the sake of creation. They are unable to point to anything prior to
creation, except God himself, as an object for which God should act,
and are therefore driven to admit (as they clearly must), that God

lacked those things for whose attainment he created means, and further that he desired them.

We must not omit to notice that the followers of this doctrine, anxious to display their talent in assigning final causes, have imported a new method of argument in proof of their theory—namely, a reduction, not to the impossible, but to ignorance; thus showing that they have no other method of exhibiting their doctrine. For example, if a stone falls from a roof on to some one's head and kills him, they will demonstrate by their new method, that the stone fell in order to kill the man; for, if it had not by God's will fallen with that object, how could so many circumstances (and there are often many concurrent circumstances) have all happened together by chance? Perhaps you will answer that the event is due to the facts that the wind was blowing, and the man was walking that way. "But why," they will insist, "was the wind blowing, and why was the man at that very time walking that way?" If you again answer, that the wind had then sprung up because the sea had begun to be agitated the day before, the weather being previously calm, and that the man had been invited by a friend, they will again insist: "But why was the sea agitated, and why was the man invited at that time?" So they will pursue their questions from cause to cause, till at last you take refuge in the will of God—in other words, the sanctuary of ignorance. So, again, when they survey the frame of the human body, they are amazed; and being ignorant of the causes of so great a work of art conclude that it has been fashioned, not mechanically, but by divine and supernatural skill, and has been so put together that one part shall not hurt another.

Hence anyone who seeks for the true causes of miracles, and strives to understand natural phenomena as an intelligent being, and not to gaze at them like a fool, is set down and denounced as an impious heretic by those, whom the masses adore as the interpreters of nature and the gods. Such persons know that, with the removal of ignorance, the wonder which forms their only available means for proving and preserving their authority would vanish also. But I now quit this subject, and pass on to my third point.

After men persuaded themselves, that everything which is created is created for their sake, they were bound to consider as the chief quality in everything that which is most useful to themselves, and to account those things the best of all which have the most beneficial effect on mankind. Further, they were bound to form abstract notions for the explantion of the nature of things, such as GOODNESS, BADNESS, ORDER, CONFUSION, WARMTH, COLD, BEAUTY, DEFORMITY, and so on; and from the belief that they are free agents arose the further notions PRAISE and BLAME, SIN and MERIT.

I will speak of these latter hereafter, when I treat of human nature; the former I will briefly explain here.

Everything which conduces to health and the worship of God they have called GOOD, everything which hinders these objects they have styled BAD; and inasmuch as those who do not understand the nature of things do not verify phenomena in any way, but merely imagine them after a fashion, and mistake their imagination for understanding, such persons firmly believe that there is an ORDER in things, being really ignorant both of things and their own nature. When phenomena are of such a kind, that the impression they make on our senses required little effort of imagination, and can consequently be easily remembered, we say that they are WELL-ORDERED; if the contrary, that they are ILL-ORDERED or CONFUSED. Further, as things which are easily imagined are more pleasing to us, men prefer order to confusion—as though there were any order in nature, except in relation to our imagination—and say that God has created all things in order; thus, without knowing it, attributing imagination to God, unless, indeed, they would have it that God foresaw human imagination, and arranged everything, so that it should be most easily imagined. If this be their theory they would not, perhaps, be daunted by the fact that we find an infinite number of phenomena, far surpassing our imagination, and very many others which confound its weakness. But enough has been said on this subject. The other abstract notions are nothing but modes of imagining, in which the imagination is differently affected, though they are considered by the ignorant as the chief attributes of things, inasmuch as they believe that everything was created for the sake of themselves; and, according as they are affected by it, style it good or bad, healthy or rotten and corrupt. For instance, if the motion whose objects we see communicate to our nerves be conducive to health, the objects causing it are styled BEAUTIFUL; if a contrary motion be excited, they are styled UGLY.

Things which are perceived through our sense of smell are styled fragrant or fetid; if through our taste, sweet or bitter, full-flavored or insipid, if through our touch, hard or soft, rough or smooth, etc.

Whatsoever affects our ears is said to give rise to noise, sound, or harmony. In this last case, there are men lunatic enough to believe that even God himself takes pleasure in harmony; and philosophers are not lacking who have persuaded themselves, that the motion of the heavenly bodies gives rise to harmony—all of which instances sufficiently show that everyone judges of things according to the state of his brain, or rather mistakes for things the forms of his imagination. We need no longer wonder that there have arisen all the controversies we have witnessed and finally scepticism: for, although human bodies in many respects agree, yet in very many others they differ; so that what seems good to one seems bad to to another; what seems well ordered to one seems confused to another; what is pleasing to one displeases another, and so on. I need not further enumerate, because this is not the place to treat the subject at length, and also because the fact is sufficiently well known. It is commonly said: "So many men, so many minds; everyone is wise in his own way; brains differ as completely as palates." All of which proverbs show, that men judge of things according to their mental disposition, and rather imagine than understand; for, if they understood phenomena, they would, as mathematics attest, be convinced, if not attracted, by what I have urged.

We have not perceived, that all the explanations commonly given of nature are mere modes of imagining, and do not indicate the true nature of anything, but only the constitution of the imagination; and, although they have names, as though they were entities, existing externally to the imagination, I call them entities imaginary rather than real; and, therefore, all arguments against us drawn from such abstractions are easily rebutted.

Many argue in this way. If all things follow from a necessity of the absolutely perfect nature of God, why are there so many imperfections in nature? such, for instance, as things corrupt to the point of putridity, loathsome deformity, confusion, evil, sin, etc. But these reasoners are, as I have said, easily confuted, for the perfection of things is to be reckoned only from their own nature and power; things are not more or less perfect, according as they delight or offend human senses, or according as they are serviceable or repugnant to mankind. To those who ask why God did not so create all men, that they should be governed only by reason, I give no answer but this: because matter was not lacking to him for the creation of every degree of perfection from highest to lowest; or, more strictly, because the laws of his nature are so vast, as to suffice for the production of everything conceivable by an infinite intelligence, as I have shown in Prop. xvi.

Such are the misconceptions I have undertaken to note; if there are any more of the same sort, everyone may easily dissipate them for himself with the aid of a little reflection.

30. *Why God Is Not Responsible for Evil* *

MAIMONIDES *(1135–1204)*

As has been proved, the (so-called) evils are evils only in relation to a certain thing, and that which is evil in reference to a certain existing thing, either includes the non-existence of that thing or the non-existence of some of its good conditions. The proposition has therefore been laid down in the most general terms, "All evils are negations." Thus for man death is evil; death is his non-existence. Illness, poverty, and ignorance are evils for man; all these are privations of properties. If you examine all single cases to which this general proposition applies, you will find that there is not one case in which the proposition is wrong, except in the opinion of those who do not make any distinction between negative and positive properties, or between two opposites, or do not know the nature of things,— who, e.g., do not know that health in general denotes a certain equilibrium, and is a relative term. The absence of that relation is illness in general, and death is the absence of life in the case of any animal. The destruction of other things is likewise nothing but the absence of their form.

* Moses Maimonides, *Guide of the Perplexed* (New York: Hebrew Publishing Co., n.d.), from Part III. Reprinted by permission.

After these propositions, it must be admitted as a fact that it cannot be said of God that He directly creates evil, or He has the direct intention to produce evil; this is impossible. His works are all perfectly good. He only produces existence, and all existence is good; whilst evils are of a negative character, and cannot be acted upon. Evil can only be attributed to Him in the way we have mentioned. He creates evil only in so far as He produces the corporeal element such as it actually is; it is always connected with negatives, and on that account the source of all destruction and evil. Those beings that do not possess this corporeal element are not subject to destruction or evil; consequently the true work of God is all good, since it is existence. The book which enlightened the darkness of the world says therefore, "And God saw everything that He had made, and, behold, it was very good" (Gen. i. 31). Even the existence of this corporeal element, low as it in reality is, because it is the source of death and all evils, is likewise good for the permanence of the Universe and the continuation of the order of things, so that one thing departs and the other succeeds. Rabbi Meir therefore explains the words "and behold it was very good" (tobh m'od); that even death was good in accordance with what we have observed in this chapter. Remember what I said in this chapter, consider it, and you will understand all that the prophets and our Sages remarked about the perfect goodness of all the direct works of God. In Bereshith Rabba [1] (chap. i.) the same idea is expressed thus: "No evil comes down from above."

.   .   .   .

All the great evils which men cause to each other because of certain intentions, desires, opinions, or religious principles, are likewise due to non-existence, because they originate in ignorance, which is absence of wisdom. A blind man, for example, who has no guide, stumbles constantly, because he cannot see, and causes injury and harm to himself and others. In the same manner various classes of men, each man in proportion to his ignorance, bring great evils upon themselves and upon other individual members of the species. If men possessed wisdom, which stands in the same relation to the form of man as the sight to the eye, they would not cause any injury

---

[1] [Edit. Midrash, or post-biblical rabbinic exposition of the Book of Genesis.]

to themselves or to others; for the knowledge of truth removes hatred
and quarrels, and prevents mutual injuries. This state of society
is promised to us by the prophet in the words: "And the wolf shall
dwell with the lamb," &c.; "and the cow and the bear shall feed
together," &c.; and "the sucking child shall play on the hole of the
asp." &c. (Isa. xi. 6 seq.) The prophet also points out what will be
the cause of this change; for he says that hatred, quarrel, and fighting
will come to an end, because men will then have a true knowledge
of God. "They shall not hurt nor destroy in all my holy mountain:
for the earth shall be full of the knowledge of the Lord, as waters
that cover the sea" (ibid. ver. 9). Note it.

.   .   .   .

Men frequently think that the evils in the world are more numerous than the good things; many sayings and songs of the nations
dwell on this idea. They say that a good thing is found only excep-
tionally, whilst evil things are numerous and lasting. Not only
common people make this mistake, but even many who believe that
they are wise. Al-Razi wrote a well-known book "On Metaphysics"
(or Theology). Among other mad and foolish things, it contains
also the idea, discovered by him, that there exists more evil than
good. For if the happiness of man and his pleasure in the times of
prosperity be compared with the mishaps that befall him,—such as
grief, acute pain, defects, paralysis of the limbs, fears, anxieties, and
troubles,—it would seem as if the existence of man is a punishment
and a great evil for him. This author commenced to verify his
opinion by counting all the evils one by one; by this means he opposed those who hold the correct view of the benefits bestowed by
God and His evident kindness, viz., that God is perfect goodness, and
that all that comes from Him is absolutely good. The origin of the
error is to be found in the circumstance that this ignorant man, and
his party among the common people, judge the whole universe by
examining one single person. For an ignorant man believes that the
whole universe only exists for him; as if nothing else required any
consideration. If, therefore, anything happens to him contrary to his
expectation, he at once concludes that the whole universe is evil. If,
however, he would take into consideration the whole universe, form
an idea of it, and comprehend what a small portion he is of the Uni-

verse, he will find the truth. For it is clear that persons who have fallen into this wide-spread error as regards the multitude of evils in the world, do not find the evils among the angels, the spheres and stars, the elements, and that which is formed of them, viz., minerals and plants, or in the various species of living beings, but only in some individual instances of mankind. They wonder that a person, who became leprous in consequence of bad food, should be afflicted with so great an illness and suffer such a misfortune; or that he who indulges so much in sensuality as to weaken his sight, should be struck with blindness! and the like. What we have, in truth, to consider is this:—The whole mankind at present in existence, and *a fortiori*,[2] every other species of animals, for an infinitesimal portion of the permanent universe. Comp. "Man is like to vanity" (Ps. cxliv. 4) "How much less man, that is a worm; and the son of man, which is a worm" (Job xxv. 6); "How much less in them who dwell in houses of clay" (ibid. iv. 19) "Behold, the nations are as a drop of the bucket" (Isa. xl. 15). There are many other passages in the books of the prophets expressing the same idea. It is of great advantage that man should know his station, and not erroneously imagine that the whole universe exists only for him. We hold that the universe exists because the Creator wills it so; that mankind is low in rank as compared with the uppermost portion of the universe, viz, with the spheres and the stars; but, as regards the angels, there cannot be any real comparison between man and angels, although man is the highest of all beings on earth; i.e., of all beings formed of the four elements. Man's existence is nevertheless a great boon to him, and his distinction and perfection is a divine gift. The numerous evils to which individual persons are exposed are due to the defects existing in the persons themselves. We complain and seek relief from our own faults; we suffer from the evils which we, by our own free will, inflict on ourselves and ascribe them to God, who is far from being connected with them! Comp. "Is destruction His (work)? No. Ye (who call yourselves) wrongly His sons, you are a perverse and crooked generation" (Deut. xxxii. 5). This is explained by Solomon, who says, "The foolishness of man perverteth his way, and his heart fretteth against the Lord" (Prov. xix. 3).

---

[2] [(Ed. Trans.) "All the more so."]

I explain this theory in the following manner. The evils that befall man are of three kinds:—

(1) The first kind of evil is that which is caused to man by the circumstance that he is subject to genesis and destruction, or that he posesses a body. It is on account of the body that some persons happen to have great deformities or paralysis of some of the organs. This evil may be part of the natural constitution of these persons, or may have developed subsequently in consequence of changes in the elements, e.g., through bad air, or thunderstorms, or landslips. We have already shown that, in accordance with the divine wisdom, genesis can only take place through destruction, and without the destruction of the individual members of the species the species themselves would not exist permanently. Thus the true kindness, and beneficence, and goodness of God is clear. He who thinks that he can have flesh and bones without being subject to any external influence, or any of the accidents of matter, unconsciously wishes to reconcile two opposites, viz., to be at the same time subject and not subject to change. If man were never subject to change there could be no generation; there would be one single being, but no individuals forming a species. Galen, in the third section of his book, "The Use of the Limbs," says correctly that it would be in vain to expect to see living beings formed of the blood of menstruous women and the semen virile, who will not die, will never feel pain, or will move perpetually, or shine like the sun. This dictum of Galen is part of the following more general proposition:—Whatever is formed of any matter receives the most perfect form possible in that species of matter; in each individual case the defects are in accordance with the defects of that individual matter. The best and most perfect being that can be formed of the blood and the semen is the species of man, for as far as man's nature is known, he is living, reasonable, and mortal. It is therefore impossible that man should be free from this species of evil. You will, nevertheless, find that the evils of the above kind which befall man are very few and rare; for you find countries that have not been flooded or burned for thousands of years; there are thousands of men in perfect health, deformed individuals are a strange and exceptional occurrence, or say few in number if you object to the term exceptional,—they are not one-hundredth, not even one-thousandth part of those that are perfectly normal.

(2) The second class of evil comprises such evils as people cause to each other, when, e.g., some of them use their strength against others. These evils are more numerous than those of the first kind; their causes are numerous and known; they likewise originate in ourselves, though the sufferer himself cannot avert them. This kind of evil is nevertheless not widespread in any country of the whole world. It is of rare occurrence that a man plans to kill his neighbour or to rob him of his property by night. Many persons are, however, afflicted with this kind of evil in great wars; but these are not frequent, if the whole inhabited part of the earth is taken into consideration.

(3) The third class of evils comprises those which every one causes to himself by his own action. This is the largest class, and is far more numerous than the second class. It is especially of these evils that all men complain,—only few men are found that do not sin against themselves by this kind of evil. Those that are afflicted with it are therefore justly blamed in the words of the prophet, "This hath been by your means" (Mal. i. 9); the same is expressed in the following passage, "He that doeth it destroyeth his own soul" (Prov. vi. 32). In reference to this kind of evil, Solomon says, "The foolishness of man perverteth his way" (ibid. xix. 3). In the following passage he explains also that this kind of evil is man's own work, "Lo, this only have I found, that God hath made man upright, but they have thought out many inventions" (Eccles. vii. 29), and these inventions bring the evils upon him. The same subject is referred to in Job (v. 6), "For affliction cometh not forth of the dust, neither doth trouble spring out of the ground." These words are immediately followed by the explanation that man himself is the author of this class of evils, "But man is born unto trouble." This class of evils originates in man's vices, such as excessive desire for eating, drinking, and love; indulgence in these things in undue measure, or in improper manner, or partaking of bad food. This course brings diseases and afflictions upon body and soul alike. The sufferings of the body in consequence of these evils are well known; those of the soul are twofold: First, such evils of the soul as are the necessary consequence of changes in the body, in so far as the soul is a force residing in the body; it has therefore been said that the properties of the soul depend on the condition of the body. Secondly, the soul, when accustomed to superfluous things, acquires a strong habit of

desiring things which are neither necessary for the preservation of the individual nor for that of the species. This desire is without a limit, whilst things which are necessary are few in number and restricted within certain limits; but what is superfluous is without end —e.g., you desire to have your vessels of silver, but golden vessels are still better: others have even vessels of sapphire, or perhaps they can be made of emerald or rubies, or any other substance that could be suggested. Those who are ignorant and perverse in their thought are constantly in trouble and pain, because they cannot get as much of superfluous things as a certain other person possesses. They as a rule expose themselves to great dangers, e.g., by sea-voyage, or service of kings, and all this for the purpose of obtaining that which is superfluous and not necessary. When they thus meet with the consequences of the course which they adopt, they complain of the decrees and judgments of God; they begin to blame the time, and wonder at the want of justice in its changes; that it has not enabled them to acquire great riches, with which they could buy large quantities of wine for the purpose of making themselves drunk, and numerous concubines adorned with various kind of ornaments of gold, embroidery, and jewels, for the purpose of driving themselves to voluptuousness beyond their capacities, as if the whole Universe existed exclusively for the purpose of giving pleasure to these low people. The error of the ignorant goes so far as to say that God's power is insufficient, because He has given to this Universe the properties which they imagine cause these great evils, and which do not help all evil-disposed persons to obtain the evils which they seek, and to bring their evil souls to the aim of their desires, though these, as we have shown, are really without limit. The virtuous and wise, however, see and comprehend the wisdom of God displayed in the Universe. Thus David says, "All the paths of the Lord are mercy and truth unto such as keep His covenant and His testimonies" (Ps. xxv. 10). For those who observe the nature of the Universe and the commandments of the Law, and know their purpose, see clearly God's mercy and truth in everything; they seek, therefore, that which the Creator intended to be the aim of man, viz., comprehension. Forced by the claims of the body, they seek also that which is necessary for the preservation of the body, "bread to eat and garment to clothe," and this is very little; but they seek nothing superfluous; with very slight exertion man can obtain it, so long as he is contented with that which is indispensable. All the difficulties and troubles we meet in this respect are due to the desire for superfluous things; when we seek unnecessary things, we have difficulty even in finding that which is indispensable. For the more we desire for that which is superfluous, the more we meet with difficulties; our strength and possessions are spent in unnecessary things, and are wanting when required for that which is necessary. Observe how Nature proves the correctness of this assertion. The more necessary a thing is for living beings, the more easily it is found and the cheaper it is; the less necessary it is, the rarer and dearer it is. E.g., air, water, and food are indispensable to man: air is most necessary, for if man is without air a short time he dies; whilst he can be without water a day or two. Air is also undoubtedly found more easily and cheaper (than water). Water is more necessary than food; for some people can be four or five days without food, provided they have water; water also exists in every country in larger quantities than food, and is also cheaper. The same proportion can be noticed in the different kinds of food; that which is more necessary in a certain place exists there in larger quantities and is cheaper than that which is less necessary. No intelligent person, I think, considers musk, amber, rubies, and emerald as very necessary for man except as medicines; and they as well as other like substances, can be replaced for this purpose by herbs and minerals. This shows the kindness of God to His creatures even to us weak beings. His righteousness and justice as regards all animals are well known; for in the transient world there is among the various kinds of animals no individual being distinguished from the rest of the same species by a peculiar property or an additional limb. On the contrary, all physical, psychical, and vital forces and organs that are possessed by one individual are found also in the other individuals. If any one is somehow different it is by accident in consequence of some exception, and not by a natural property it is also a rare occurrence. There is no difference between individuals of a species in the due course of Nature; the difference originates in the various dispositions of their substances. This is the necessary consequence of the nature of the substance of that species; the nature of the species is not more favourable to one individual than to the other. It is no wrong or injustice that one has many bags o

finest myrrh and garments embroidered with gold, while another
has not those things, which are not necessary for our maintenance;
he who has them has not thereby obtained control over anything that
could be an essential addition to his nature, but has only obtained
something illusory or deceptive. The other, who does not possess
that which is not wanted for his maintenance, does not miss anything
indispensable: "He that gathered much had nothing over, and he
that gathered little had no lack: they gathered every man according
to his eating" (Exod. xvi. 18). This is the rule at all times and in
all places; no notice should be taken of exceptional cases, as we
have explained.

In these two ways you will see the mercy of God toward His creatures, how He has provided that which is required, in proper proportions, and treated all individual beings of the same species with
perfect equality. In accordance with this correct reflection the chief
of the wise men says, "All His ways are judgment" (Deut. xxxii. 4):
David likewise says: "All the paths of the Lord are mercy and
truth" (Ps. xxv. 10); he also says expressly, "The Lord is good to
all; and His tender mercies are over all His works" (ibid. cxlv. 9);
for it is an act of great and perfect goodness that He gave us existence; and the creation of the controlling faculty in animals is a proof
of His mercy towards them, as has been shown by us.

31. *That Evil Is Necessary* *

F. R. TENNANT *(1866–)*

The problem of evil has thus far been discussed with almost exclusive reference to evil of the moral kind. And the solution that
has been presented consists in shewing the tenability of the belief
that in our developing world all things work together, as a whole,
for the highest conceivable good. The possibility of moral evil and

---

* Frederick Robert Tennant, *Philosophical Theology* (Cambridge: The
University Press, 1928), Vol. II. From chapter entitled "The Problem of
Evil." Reprinted by permission.

the actuality of its consequences are inevitable concomitants of the 'best possible' evolutionary world. It is not maintained that everything is good, or that "whatever is, is right," or that partial evil is not evil because it is a condition of universal good. Nor is it implied that every particular evil is directly essential to the emergence of some particular good, or that it has its necessary place, like a dissonance in music, in the harmony of the world-process. When it is asserted that all things work together for good, by 'all things' is not meant each and every single thing, but the sum of things regarded as one whole or complex, the universe as a coherent order.

It is by adhering to this general view that the theist can best face the problem presented by the existence of that form of evil for which human freedom is not necessarily, and generally not at all, responsible: the physical evil, or the pain and suffering occasioned by the course of Nature in sentient beings. Indeed any other position than that which has just been summarised seems obviously inadequate as a basis for the explanation of the forthcomingness of physical ills. In order to reconcile the suffering inflicted by the material world upon mankind and other sentient creatures with the goodness and power of the Creator it is both superfluous and insufficient to seek to shew that in every particular case pain is essential to some special end, or that in each single instance suffering may fulfil some particular providential purpose. To attempt a theodicy on these lines is as hopeless as it would be today to develop a teleological argument from particular instances of adaptedness, after the manner of Paley. But, as there is a wider teleology than Paley's so is there a wider theodicy than that which consists in pleading that human and animal pain are sometimes prophylactic — a warning against danger, or that human suffering is sometimes punitive or purgatorial and thus subservient to benign ends. These assertions are undoubtedly true, and there is no need to belittle their import. But by themselves they will not carry us far towards a theodicy. They but touch the fringe of the problem: or, to change the metaphor, they do not go to the root of the matter. It is useless, again, to minimise the pain of the sentient world, or even to reduce our possibly extravagant and unscientific estimate of its intensity, except for the purpose of arguing that, in spite of pain, animal life is probably happy on the whole: otherwise a single pang of useless or superfluous pain is enough to raise our problem. It involves faulty psychology to assert that pain is the necessary background to pleasure; for a lesser pleasure could seem to yield a sufficient contrast to render the enjoyment of intenser pleasure possible. And if pain be sometimes stimulating, educational, preventative, or remedial, as well as sometimes stunting, crushing, and provocative of moral evil, this fact is only significant for an estimation of the worth-whileness of sentient life. The knife may be necessary to cure the disease, but why the necessity of the disease? The escape from mortal danger may require the painful warning, but why the mortal danger? Or, speaking generally, what are we to make of the remoter evil which renders the nearer evil necessary or salutary? The real problem obviously lies further back than these particular and partial solutions reach. It must be shewn that pain is either a necessary by-product of an order of things requisite for the emergence of the higher goods, or an essential instrument to organic evolution, or both. Short of this, we cannot refute the charge that the world is a clumsy arrangement or an imperfectly adjusted mechanism.

It can be argued, however, that the former of the foregoing alternatives is applicable in the case of human suffering, while the latter of them can be invoked to meet especially the case of animal pain. The suffering of the lower animals is not merely an accidental superfluity emerging out of the evolutionary process, but is essentially instrumental to organic progress. It renders unnecessary a large amount of inheritance of specialised structure and function and so prevents the supression of plasticity; and, as the 'sensitive edge' turned towards danger, or as prophylactic, it is of value for organic progressiveness. Although evil, it is also good for something. Much of human suffering, and many of the outrages of this present life upon our rational prudences and our most sacred affections, on the other hand, seem to be good for nothing, or to be nonessential for the realisation of goodness. If a man already has it in him to meet pain with fortitude and patience, he is not necessarily one whit the better man after actually enduring excruciating tortures; and if an all-powerful being 'appointed' him such tortures, merely in order that his fortitude might pass from potentiality to actuality, such a being would be but a superbrute. However, it can be argued that the forthcomingness of our suffering is inevitably incidental to a moral order in a developing world. It issues ultimately out of what is inappropriately called metaphysical evil, or is a necessary outcome of a determinate cosmos of the particular kind that can sustain rational and moral life. The problem which it raises will therefore be solved if it can be maintained that no suffering such as we experience is superfluous to the cosmos as a coherent system and a moral order, however excessive pain often may be as a means to the accomplishment of specific ends such as are attainable by discipline and chastening.

It cannot be too strongly insisted that a world which is to be a moral order must be a physical order characterised by law or regularity. The routine of Nature may be differently described by the spiritualist, the dualist, etc.; but the diversity of these ultimate explanations of law does not affect the present problem. The theist is only concerned to invoke the fact that law-abidingness, on the scale which science is able to assert its subsistence in Nature as already naturata, is an essential condition of the world being a theatre of moral life. Without such regularity in physical phenomena there could be no probability to guide us: no prediction, no prudence, no accumulation of ordered experience, no pursuit of premeditated ends, no formation of habit, no possibility of character or of culture. Our intellectual faculties could not have developed. And, had they been innate, they would have wasted themselves, as Comte observed, in wild extravagances and sunk rapidly into incurable sloth; while our nobler feelings would have been unable to prevent the ascendancy of the lower instincts, and our active powers would have abandoned themselves to purposeless agitation. All this is obvious; but it has often been ignored in discussion of the problem of physical evil. Nevertheless, Nature's regularity is the key to this problem. Once let it be admitted that, in order to be a theatre for moral life, the world must be largely characterised by uniformity or constancy, and most significant consequences will be seen to follow. It becomes idle to complain, as some writers have done, that the orderliness of the world is too dear at the cost of the suffering and hardship which it entails, and might more or less be dispensed with for the benefit of the sentient and rational beings

which people the world. As Hume admitted, if the "conducting of
the world by general laws" were superseded by particular volitions,
no man could employ his reason in the conduct of his life. And
without rationality, morality is impossible: so, if the moral status
of man be the goal of the evolutionary process, the reign of law is
a sine qua non. It is a condition of the forthcomingness of the
highest good, in spite of the fact that it is not an unmixed good but
a source of suffering. We cannot have the advantages of a determinate order of things without its logically or its causally necessary
disadvantages. Nor can we be evaluating subjects without capacity
to feel. The disadvantages, viz. particular ills, need not be regarded, however, as directly willed by God as ends in themselves
or as particular means, among other equally possible but painless
means, to particular ends. To make use of an ancient distinction,
we may say that God wills them consequently, not antecedently.
That is to say, they are not desired as such, or in themselves, but
are only willed because the moral order, which is willed absolutely
or antecedently by God, cannot be had without them. Now to will a
moral order is to will the best possible world; and it also involves
adoption of what we necessarily, if somewhat anthropomorphically,
must call a determinate world-plan. Such a determinate method of
procedure to realise a definite end in an evolutionary world, however, rules out once and for all any other possible goals and methods.
As Dr. Martineau has put it, the cosmical equation being defined,
only such results as are compatible with the values of its roots
can be worked out, and these must be worked out. All determination is negation. If two consequences follow from a system of propositions, or two physical properties are involved in a configuration
of particles, we cannot have the one without the other, though the
one may be pleasing or beneficial to man and the other may be
painful, or in its immediate effects hurtful. And such a result by
no means implies lack of benevolence or of power on the part of
the Creator, so long as power does not include inconsistency or
indeterminateness. It simply bespeaks the inexorableness of logic,
the compatibility of things, and the self-consistency of the Supreme
Being. That painful events occur in the causal chain is a fact;
but, that there could be a determinate evolutionary world of un-
alloyed comfort, yet adapted by its law-abidingness to the develope-

ment of rationality and morality, is a proposition the burden of proving which must be allotted to the opponent of theism. One can only add that, in so far as experience in this world enables us to judge, such proof seems impossible. To illustrate what is here meant: if water is to have the various properties in virtue of which it plays its beneficial part in the economy of the physical world and the life of mankind, it cannot at the same time lack its obnoxious capacity to drown us. The specific gravity of water is as much a necessary outcome of its ultimate constitution as its freezing-point, or its thirst-quenching and cleansing functions. There cannot be assigned to any substance an arbitrarily selected group of qualities, from which all that ever may prove unfortunate to any sentient organism can be eliminated, especially if one organism's meat is to be another's poison, and yet the world, of which that substance forms a part, be a calculable cosmos. Mere determinateness and fixity of nature involve such and such concatenations of qualities, and rule out others. Thus physical ills follow with the same necessity as physical goods from the determinate 'world-plan' which secures that the world be a suitable stage for intelligent and ethical life.

And if this be so, the disadvantages which accrue from the determinateness and regularity of the physical world cannot be regarded either as absolute or as superfluous evils. They are not absolute evils because they are parts of an order which subserves the highest good in providing opportunity for moral development. And they are not superfluous ills because they are the necessary outcome of that order. They are collateral effects of what, in itself or as a whole, is good because instrumental to the highest good. They are not good, when good is hedonically defined; but they are good for good, when good is otherwise defined, rather than good for nothing.

As in the case of moral evil, so also in the case of physical evil, appeal has sometimes been made from necessary linkages and conditionings to a supposed possibility of their being over-ridden by divine omnipotence. And as it was found absurd to suppose that God could make developing beings at the same time morally free and temptationless, so it involves absurdity to suppose that the world could be a moral order without being a physical cosmos. To save mankind from the painful consequences which flow from a determinate world-order, such as the earthquake and the pestilence, would involve renunciation of a world-order, and therefore of a moral order, and the substitution of a chaos of incalculable miracle. Doubtless some directive agency, or the introduction of new streams of causation into the course of Nature, is conceivable without subversion of such regularity as is requisite for human prudence and without the stultification of our science. But the general suspension of painful events, requisite on the vast scale presupposed in the elimination of physical ills, would abolish order and convert a cosmos into an unintelligible chaos in which anything might succeed upon anything. We should have to "renounce reason" if we would thus be "saved from tears," as Martineau says.

Physical evil, then, must necessarily be. And the goodness of God is vindicated if there be no reason to believe that the world-process involves more misery than Nature's uniformity entails. It is not incumbent on the theist to prove that particular evils are never greater than we judge to be necessary for the production of particular salutary effects: that difficult task confronts only the particular kind of theism which is concerned to dispense with proximate causes and a more or less autonomous world, and regards God as the sole and immediate cause of every natural event, and of every incident in a personal life. According to the theodicy which has here been sketched, it is not necessary to suppose that every specific form of suffering that man undergoes — e.g. the agony of tetanus or of cancer — is antecedently willed by God as a means to some particular end. It can be admitted that excruciating pains are more severe than they need be for evoking virtues such as patience and fortitude, and that to assign them to God's antecedent will would be to attribute devilishness to the Deity. Moreover, the fact that some human beings are born as abortions, as imbecile or insane, seems to be inexplicable on the view that every form of suffering is a particular providence, or an antecedently willed dispensation for educating and spiritually perfecting the person on whom the affliction falls; while to suppose that suffering is inflicted on one person for the spiritual edification of another is again to conceive of God as immoral. But the hardest fact of all for human equanimity, in presence of physical and mental evil, is that the apportionment of suffering among individuals is entirely irreconcilable by us with any divine plan of adjustment of particular afflictions to the particular needs, circumstances, and stages of moral development, of individual sufferers. Even more distressing to human thought than the goading intensity of some kinds of pain is the seemingly chaotic distribution of human ills. If we could trace the utility of particular sufferings with their varying degrees of endurableness, or discern any adaptation of pain to the person's sensibility, moral state, and need of awakening of chastening, then philosophy might be able to agree with the simple-minded piety which assigns a special purpose to every instance of suffering, and finds therein the visitation or appointment of an all-wise and all-good God. But the wind is not tempered to the shorn-lamb; the fieriest trials often overtake those who least need torments to inspire fear, to evoke repentance, or to perfect patience, and also those who, through no fault of their own, lack the mature religious faith and moral experience by which alone they could understand how affliction may be endured for their souls' good. "All things come alike to all: there is one event to the righteous and to the wicked" — to those who may be enabled, and to those who are unable, to profit by severe trial.

Disastrous as these facts are to the extremer forms of the doctrine of divine immanence in Nature, they are compatible with theism such as allows to the created world somewhat of delegated autonomy. According to the wider theodicy which has here been presented, the human afflictions arising from our relations with the physical world are not willed as such by God at all, or for any purpose. They are rather inevitable, if incidental, accompaniments or by-products of the world-order which, as a whole, and by means of its uniformity, is a pre-requisite of the actualisation of the highest good that we can conceive a world as embodying. The world is none the less God's world for its callousness to man; but its autonomy, not the particular incidence of each single ill, is what the religious should attribute to His "appointment."

Further, man himself does not deem his suffering to be an excessive price to pay for the dignity of his ethical status, once he recognises physical evil to be inevitable in a moral world. He is then not compelled to see in his suffering self a mere means either to the perfecting of the race, or to the realisation of a divine purpose, or to the manifestation of the 'glory' of God. And this is an important consideration for any theodicy. For man is an end for himself, whatever else he may be. My ills can only be justified to me if the remoter advantage of there being ills at all be mine: not humanity's or even God's, alone. But in that the remoter advantage is the enjoyment of rational and ethical dignity, the individual man can acquiesce in God's purpose for the world: God's ideal may be his also. It is the assurance that God is fulfilling us individually as well as Himself, and fulfilling us for ourselves as well as for Himself, that makes human life in this bitter-sweet world endurable by the sensitively and delicately minded, the tender-hearted believer. It is because a being of the earth, yet so God-like as man, could not be moulded into the image of God save from within himself, as a person or a free agent, that man can account the payment of the sometimes exorbitant price of the chance of learning love inevitable.

If the doctrine of a future life be a corollary of theism, or an implication of the moral purposiveness and meaning which may reasonably be read into the cosmos, it can be invoked to throw further light on the problem of evil. The balance of felicity and unhappiness in an individual life cannot be struck so long as we confine our thought to experience of the present world alone, if we have reason to believe that the earth is "no goal, but starting-point for man." We may then venture to add to our knowledge the faith that "the sufferings of this present time are not worthy to be compared with the glory that shall be revealed." Pain is indeed none the less pain, nor any kind of evil the less evil, for that it shall be done away, or compensated, or because it is a necessary means or by-product. But its hideousness is somewhat transfigured if, besides being involved in the 'best possible' world, it can be seen to have been "but for a moment" in the time-span of just men made perfect. It is not the reality of evil that is here under consideration, but simply the worth-whileness of this life in which evil has a temporary and necessary place. That should not be estimated by looking only at what may now be seen; but for the idea of compensation hereafter theodicy and theistic religion have no further use. They do not ask us to tolerate the evils of the present world, and to abstain from blaming the Creator for them, because of a compensation stored up for us in another world; they rather insist that in this life, with all its evils, we may already discern the world-purpose of God to be a reign of love.

This life acquires, indeed, a new aspect if death be but translation to another mansion in the Father's house, and exchange of one kind of service for another. And it is a question whether theism, in asserting the world-ground to be a Spirit and the Father of spirits, and in ascribing to the world the role of ministering to rational and moral life, can stop short of adding the doctrine of a future life to its fundamental articles of belief, without stultifying its previously reached interpretation of the world and man. For it would not be a perfectly reasonable world which produced free beings, with Godward aspirations and illimitable ideals, only to cut them off in everlasting death, mocking their hopes and frustrating their purposes. Such spirits, even with their moral status, would after all be pawns, not children of God. Certainly a God who can be worshipped by moral beings must be a respecter of the persons whom He has moulded into His own image. Hence theists generally regard the Supreme Being as a God, not of the dead, but of the living.

32. Do Suffering and Sin Constitute Evidence Against a Providential God? *

JOHN LAIRD *(1887–   )*

On the whole it seems appropriate to begin this discussion of God's common grace by enquiring into the positive evidence in favour of that conception. By doing so we shall supplement a part of the argument in the last lecture. In that lecture we say that if certain things could be shown, for example the propitiousness of physical nature to certain finite spirits, then a theist would be confronted with sundry possible interpretations. We are now asking whether such things can be shown.

---

* John Laird, *Mind and Deity* (New York: Philosophical Library, 1941), from chapter entitled "Providence." Reprinted by permission.

In discussing this worn-out tenacious theme, I shall deal, rather narrowly, with man and his place in the cosmos. This restricted treatment may indeed be parochial, but unless our standards of value have no general significance (in which case the question falls) we are bound to test our general theories in the instance in which the issue seems plainest, and that is with reference to man. For I believe man is the bearer of the highest values with which we have any empirical acquaintance. Again, since the human parish is so very wide, it seems better, because it seems sufficient for present purposes, to limit the discussion to two features of the problem of evil (as it is called) and to discuss, on the one hand, suffering, and on the other hand, sin. There are other "problems" of human evil, such as the "problems" of human transcience, ignorance, ugliness, weakness and poverty of opportunity. Some questions may be begged and some answers stolen when the problem is restricted in the way in which I intend to restrict it now, but its general outlines, I think, should not be appreciably dimmed.

What, then, is the theological "problem" of suffering? What bearing has our suffering upon providential and upon antiprovidential arguments?

There is no problem if the last word on the subject must be simply that suffering occurs, and there is no problem if suffering be not an evil. Again, there is no problem if God be altogether omnipotent and also wholly good, for in that case the existence of any pain whatever (if pain be evil) entails a plain contradiction. Such a God could always bestow the palm without the dust. On the other hand there is a problem for those theists who admit that some at least of the suffering that exists is a genuine evil, and do not renounce every possibility of talking sense about the question by committing themselves to a childish interpretation of "omnipotence."

Philosophers with a Stoical bent have often argued that pain is not an evil. So said Seneca—among other things. According to him [1] the genuine recipients of divine favour were stalwarts like Mucius who kept his hand in the flames, Regulus who preferred Punic torture to un-Roman bad faith, Cato re-opening the self-inflicted wound that had failed to bring him the honourable release of a vanquished patriot. This grim picture would seem to present Seneca with an insoluble "problem of pleasure." For pleasure also exists. According

---

[1] In *De Providentia*.

to Seneca it is the base coin with which the high gods repay base natures, giving unworthy mortals something that they desire but also giving them something that, unlike pain, is an evil.

It is needless, however, to pursue the point. Whether or not pleasure is an unworthy thing, suffering is an evil, for all Seneca's moral rhetoric. It is evil unmitigated unless it is necessary for an ulterior good that swamps or annuls its evil. If, using anthropomorphic language, we were to say that God was indifferent to suffering as such, we should be saying that God was callous. If he applauded the suffering, like the saints in heaven who have sometimes been thought to applaud the sufferings of the damned in hell, he would be cruel.

Accordingly we are usually told in the theodicies that pain is not purposeless, but is a salutary warning in matters of health and is our schoolmaster in matters of moral education. The doctrine is still pretty grim, but it might be true for all that, and it is consistent with the belief in a non-omnipotent providence. The implication, however, would be that no suffering is purposeless, and it is hard to suppose that such is the truth. In the case of animal suffering, for instance (where the moral discipline of the sufferers cannot be a relevant consideration), it is difficult to believe that the suffering of slaughtered animals before humane killing became general was justified in terms of this argument, and also that the diminution of animal suffering after humane killing was generally practised is likewise justified. In the case of human beings the same difficulty would arise in connection with advances in our knowledge and use of anaesthetics. We all know of the arguments that have been raised about the use of anaesthetics in childbirth. More generally, there would be a similar problem regarding the moral effects of a rise in the standard of comfortable living.

Obviously, however, it would be unreasonable to expect that every instance of pain that could be cited conveyed a clearly intelligible benefit either to the sufferer or to some other being, or else had to be adjudged to be an instance of finally unjustifiable evil. "Nothing would be more alarming in reality," von Hugel said, "than to find that religion, when pressed, could give us nothing but just what we want." [2] If the line of argument mentioned above supplied the rudiments of an answer to the question set it

[2] *The Reality of God,* p. 15.

would have done a great deal; for the argument itself has the widest ramifications. If, however, it be assumed, as is not unreasonable, that what appear to be close factual connections should be held to be metaphysically stubborn if not even indissoluble, the above type of argument has strength and soundness. I have spoken of the palm without the dust, but no one seriously supposes that it is possible to win a race without running it, or to run it without a quickened pulse and bursting lungs. That should be clear as a matter of course, and the argument may be persuasively extended in the way that is commonly done. We are told that the conquest of perils and the overcoming of obstacles imply the reality of the perils and of the obstacles. In a psychological way, perhaps indissoluble, it may be said to imply the reality of fears, and doubts, and depression, and actual anguish, if not inevitably, at least generally in the course of nature. In this sense there are joys of earth that would have no place in a sheltered heaven, and some of these, say the explorer's zest or the romantic lover's or even the struggles of an ambitious author, may be sweeter and keener because of the risk and because of the painful struggle. It might further be argued that there would be no risk if there were not, sometimes, an actual disaster.

Such arguments, then, must be accorded a certain weight, but although they are empirical they are also rather high-handed in what they say of empirical fact. We find empirically that some (perhaps much) suffering has a beneficial function, and we are entitled to surmise that frequently, when this beneficial function is not apparent, it may nevertheless occur. On the other hand, it would also be legitimate to surmise that some of the apparent benefits of suffering are illusory; and in any case we should be flying a very speculative kite if we maintained that all suffering must be beneficial because we know that some of it is.

That would have to be said even if we admitted that the very audacity of a hypothesis may be one of its better motives to credence. It may, for instance, be more plausible to explain the hurly-burly of our sensations by supposing that permanent physical objects exist and act than by making suppositions that keep closer to the whirling impermanence of our actual sensory experience. Such ideas outstrip the evidence of our senses (according to many interpretations of that evidence) by a mile; but we are all accustomed to make them. So here. The bolder flights of theistic optimism may seem safer and better credible than a more timid resort to whatever gods there may be. The boldness of these flights, however, should not take the form of suppressing or of denying the anti-providential arguments. Courage of that kind is neither hardheaded nor empirical.

An equally familiar objection to the providential hypothesis is that even if all suffering had some beneficial office, it would still be impossible to defend the amount of suffering that exists. Cancer may give an occasion for fortitude and for a certain melancholy dignity, but, in its case, anodynes are better than dignity and most of the suffering is sheer waste.

In the instance of cancer, this argument may be very forcible, but it relies on a general principle that seems to be exceedingly dubious. How can anyone who told that the existence of some (and of much) suffering is consistent with the government of a benign providence take it upon himself to say how much suffering there ought to be? With what measure does such an one compute the permissible quota of suffering? How, for that matter, does he compute the amount of suffering that exists, how could he determine whether or not this computed quantum of suffering (with or without taking its relation to joy into account) either demanded or was opposed to an explanation in terms of a beneficent providence? It seems to me, as I have suggested in an earlier lecture,[3] that the problem is quite indeterminate, and that, because it is indeterminate, we have no business to speak with confidence either about the need for inferring the existence of a providence on these grounds or about the success of the antiprovidentialists in maintaining the opposite opinion. That, I think, is the decisive feature of this affair.

It is not impressive, I allow, to argue that the pain in the world is of small account. The well-known Epicurean tag that pain is brief if it is severe, and tolerable if it is prolonged, is not very accurate and is not very profound. Agony need not be very brief. If it is brief it may recur. Years of dull misery, seldom alleviated, have often to be borne. Similarly it is difficult to have patience

---

[3] Lecture LX in the First Series.

with the shallow view that there are always compensations for the most shocking events, and that the compensations really do compensate. If that argument were pressed to its extremities, the conclusion would be that it is all one whether cancer is conquered like leprosy and smallpox, whether women are widowed in war or raped in peace, whether torture and flogging persist in a judicial system, whether poison gas is or is not to be used. There is a great deal of pain in the world, and much of it is peculiarly revolting, but I do not see how we are able to conjecture whether there is more of it, or less, than a divine regimen would permit.

In the large, I believe, it is reasonable to hold that there has been and that there is a favourable balance of pleasure over pain on this planet. I think it is true, speaking broadly, that life is sweet and that while there is life there is hope. If the latter statement is true, the former could not easily be false. For hope is glad. If some Miserrimus Doleful tells us that we are the dupes of hope, that, looking back on our lives, we should always say "Never again" if we were candid, that the sight of a healthy little child should always make us sad, thinking of what the poor little mite will have to go through, the answer is clearly that hope is not the less pleasant because it is illusory. The hopefulness of our vitality may not be very creditable to our intelligence, but it is very comforting to the heart.

That, I think, is what we should say on the whole, however true it may be that we are often tempted to think like the Chorus in Murder in the Cathedral:

O, late, late, late!, late is the time, late too late, and rotten the year; Evil the wind, and bitter the sea, and the sky, grey, grey, grey.

So far as I can see, however, this argument is just another illustration of the impossibility of arguing with precision to or against the existence of a benevolent providence from the credit-balance of happiness over suffering. Let it be held that the positive correlation between vitality and hopefulness is something inevitable and in the long run preponderant. It follows that wherever there is life there will be hope, and so that there is some reason for expecting a favourable balance of joy over pain. But life exists. Therefore, by hypothesis, this favourable balance exists whether we are to say of our sorrows, with Seneca, "veniunt non incident," or, contrariwise, "incident non veniunt." [4] The assertion is that a preponderance of happiness is an inevitable characteristic of life as such. That assertion, however, is not evidence that a providence must have contrived the favourable balance that exists in fact, and it is not evidence against that view. The inference to a providential cause of the favourable balance is neither helped nor hindered.

Let us now pass from the problem of physical evil (i.e. of suffering) to the problem of moral evil (i.e. of sin).

The problem of sin is more intricate and more difficult for a theist than the problem of pain, but rather similar arguments are frequently employed in both cases.

Very few theists suggest that sin, if and where it exists, is not an evil. In this respect the Stoics contrasted vice with pain, for they said that depravity and dishonour were genuine evils although mere pain was not. Again, if anyone were disposed to doubt that sin is an evil, he might be reminded that even the illusion of sinfulness is itself an unworthy thing. A hypersensitive conviction of sin is not so good as sinlessness. Apart from that, many sins are plainly most foul. Moreover sin seems often to be a sort of rebellion against the right and the good, and so, in a host of ways, to be thoroughly anomalous in a supposedly moral universe.

Notwithstanding these special features of the problem, however (and notwithstanding many other special features that I shall here neglect) the writers of theodicies are usually disposed to attempt a solution of the problem of moral evil on the same lines as they try to follow in the case of the problem of suffering. Sin is implied, at least indirectly, they say, if high moral character is to be won. There must be a certain liberty to sin (and, therefore, sometimes the actuality of sinning) if moral achievement be genuine. Providence would not be gracious to man if he denied man such opportunities. There must be moral evil if there is to be moral good.

Such an apology for actual sinning seems to be rather weak. In the first place it raises difficulties concerning some of the moral virtues. For example, it seems to involve a theory definitely inconsistent with what we usually believe to be true concerning the

---

4 [(Ed. Trans.) "They are coming; they will not fall by chance. They will fall by chance; they are not coming."]

virtue of purity. Granting that a man may be pure if his heart is cleansed, it is not at all apparent why a garment that is cleansed should be whiter than a garment that has never been stained. Again, even if there ought to be a certain liberty to make mistakes it surely does not follow that there ought to be any liberty to become thoroughly vicious and depraved. Consider, once again, what we commonly hold when a man has been victorious in some terrible moral struggle. We praise his resolution and respect the toughness of his moral fibre, but we do not usually regard him as an ideal man, any more than we think that the conquest of some physical disadvantage is better than physical fitness that had no such disadvantages to overcome. Indeed, I think we might say generally that the struggle with evil tendencies is not a necessary prerequisite of saintliness. That is what Christians have to maintain when they accept the dogma of the Master's sinlessness. They are asserting dogmatically (whether or not the Gospels [5] expressly assert Christ's sinlessness) that the highest moral character does not imply a struggle with vicious tendencies. Passing to lighter instances, I should say that there is a certain plausibility in Plato's suggestion [6] that the best doctors are those who are themselves rather delicate but that there is nothing like a metaphysical necessity about the circumstance.

These comments refer to the peculiar characteristics of many sins and to the heinousness of certain sins rather than to the simple fact of sin's existence. Therefore they lead to the second point in the parallel between misery and wickedness, namely whether, allowing that there may or must be some sinning in a righteously ordered universe, there is any sufficient reason for believing that, in such a universe, there could be as many sins and as revolting sins as there are in this universe. As in the case of suffering it seems to me that the problem put is quite indeterminate and does not admit of an answer. How can we pretend to say how much sin there would be if God's common grace abounds, but does not always

---

[5] John viii. 46 is obviously not decisive. Outside the Gospels, Hebrews iv. 15 is evidence only of the writer's theology, and similarly of Hebrews vii. 26. The same should be said of Paul in 2 Corinthians v. 21, and of John in 1 John iii. 5. It should be noted that Matthew v. 28 forbids us from holding that serious temptation without actual sin is possible.

[6] Rep. 408. d.

bring good out of evil? If we cannot say whether the actual universe favours human morality more than a secular universe would do, how could we say that a providence either should or should not be supposed?

33. The Good in Evil *

JOSIAH ROYCE (1855–1916)

THE RELIGIOUS INSIGHT

So far we have come in joyful contemplation of the Divine Truth. But now is there not a serpent in this Eden also? We have been talking of the infinite goodness; but after all, what shall we still say of that finite "partial evil" of life? We seem to have somehow proved a priori that it must be "universal good." For, as we have said, in the Infinite Life of our ideal there can be no imperfection. This, we have said, is the demonstration that we missed all through our study of the world of the Powers. Since we approached that world from without, and never felt the pulse of its heart's blood, we had nothing but doubt after doubt when we contemplated the evil that seemed to be in it. Our efforts to explain evil seemed hollow and worthless. There might be some deeper truth involved in these efforts; but we knew it not. Well, are we right in declaring that we have altogether overcome our difficulty now? Apparently we are as far as ever from seeing how the partial evil can be the universal good; we only show, from the conception of the infinite itself, that the partial evil must be the universal good. God must see how; and we know this because we know of God. More than this we seem to be unable to suggest.

But will this do? Have we not forgotten one terrible consequence of our doctrine? The partial evil is universal good, is it? There is no evil? All apparent imperfection is an illusion of our partial

---

* Jos. Royce, *The Religious Aspect of Philosophy* (New York: Houghton Mifflin & Co., 1887), from "The Religious Insight." Reprinted by permission

view? So then where is the chance to be in a free way and of our own choice better than we otherwise in truth should be? Is not the arm that is raised to strike down wickedness paralyzed by the very thought that was to give it divine strength? This evil that I fight here in this finite world is a delusion. So then, why fight it? If I do good works, the world is infinitely good and perfect. If I seem to do evil works, the world is in truth no worse. Seeming good is not better than seeming evil, for if it were, then the seeming evil would be a real defect in God, in whose life is everything. If I have never loved aught but God, even so I have never hated aught but God. It is all alike. God does not need just me. Or rather I may say, in so far as he needs me to complete his infinite truth, he already has me from all eternity. I have nothing to do with the business, save to contemplate in dizzy indolence the whirling misty masses of seeming evil, and to say with a sort of amused reverence that they look very ill and opaque to me, but that of course God sees through them clearly enough somehow. The mist is in truth crystalline water, and he has so quick a sense as to look beyond the drops as easily as if they were in the calm unity of a mountain lake. And so, my religion is simply a contemplation of God's wisdom, but otherwise an idle amusement.

So says the man who sees only this superficial view of our doctrine. In so far as, standing once more outside of some evil thing, we say: "That thing yonder looks bad, but God must see it to be good," we do indeed remain indolent, and our religion simply means a sort of stoical indifference to the apparent distinction of good and evil. This is in fact the proper practical attitude of even the most earnest man in the presence of evil that he cannot understand and cannot affect. In such matters we must indeed be content with the passive knowledge. Death and the unavoidable pains of life, the downfall of cherished plans, all the cruelty of fate, we must learn to look at as things to us opaque, but to God, who knows them fully, somehow clear and rational. So regarding them, we must aim to get to the stage of stoical indifference about them. They are to us the accidents of existence. We have no business to murmur about them, since we see that God, experiencing them, somehow must experience them as elements in an absolutely perfect life. For God we regard not as the mysterious power who made

them, and who then may have been limited to the use of imperfect
means, but as the absolute thought that knows them; so that, however inexplicable they must now be to us, they are in themselves
nothing that God vainly wishes to have otherwise, but they are
organically joined with the rest of the glorious whole.

Such is indeed the only present word for us finite minds about
many of the shadows of seeming evil that we have to behold in the
world of the apparently external facts. Such however is not the
last word for us about the only evil that has any immediate moral
significance, namely, the evil that we see, not as an external,
shadowy mist, but as a present fact, experienced in us. Here it is
that the objector just mentioned seems really formidable to us. But
just here it is that we find the answer to him. For in the world of
our own acts we have a wondrous experience. We realize evil, we
fight it, and, at the same time, we realize our fragment of the perfect
divine life in the moment itself of struggling with the evil. And
in this wondrous experience lies the whole solution of the ancient
problem of the existence of moral evil. For instance, I find in myself
a selfish impulse, trying to destroy the moral insight. Now of this
evil impulse I do not say, looking at it objectively: "It is somehow a part of the universal good;" but, in the moment of moral
action I make it, even in the very moment of its sinfulness, a part
of my good consciousness, in overcoming it. The moral insight
condemns the evil that it experiences; and in condemning and conquering this evil it forms and is, together with the evil, the organic
total that constitutes the good will. Only through this inner victory
over the evil that is experienced as a conquered tendency does the
good will have its being. Now since the perfect life of God must
have the absolutely good will, therefore it also must be conscious of
such a victory. Thus the solution of our difficulty begins to appear.
And thus we reap a new religious fruit from our ethical doctrine,
to whose main principles we must once more here refer the reader.

When I experience the victory of the moral insight over the bad
will, I experience in one indivisible moment both the partial evil of
the selfish impulse (which in itself as a separate fact would be
wholly bad) and the universal good of the moral victory, which
has its existence only in the overwhelming of the evil. So, in the
good act, I experience the good as my evil lost in goodness, as a

rebellion against the good conquered in the moment of its birth, as a peace that arises in the midst of this triumphant conflict, as a satisfaction that lives in this restless activity of inner warfare. This child of inner strife is the good, and the only moral good, we know.

What I here have present in me when I do a good act is an element of God's life. I here directly experience how the partial moral evil is universal good; for so it is a relatively universal good in me when, overcoming myself, I choose the universal will. The bad impulse is still in me, but is defeated. In the choice against evil is the very life of goodness, which would be a pale, stupid abstraction otherwise. Even so, to take another view, in the overcoming of our separateness as individuals lies, as we saw in the previous book, our sense of the worth of the universal life. And what we here experience in the single moment of time, and in the narrowness of our finite lives, God must experience, and eternally. In our single good acts we have thus the specimen of the eternal realization of goodness.

But now how simple becomes the answer to that terrible suggestion of a moment since! How simple also the solution of the problem of evil! "If I want to do evil, I cannot," said the objector; "for God the perfect one includes me with the rest, and so cannot in his perfection be hurt by me. Let me do what I will, my act can only seem bad, and cannot be bad. All evil is illusion, hence there is no moral difference in action possible."

"Right indeed," we answer, "but also wrong, because half the truth. The half kills, the whole gives life. Why canst thou not do any absolute evil? Because thy evil intent, which, in its separateness, would be unmixed evil, thy selfish will, thy struggle against the moral insight, this evil will of thine is no lonesome fact in the world, but is an element in the organic life of God. In him thy evil impulse forms part of a total good will, as the evil impulse of the good man forms an element in his realization of goodness. In God thy separateness is destroyed, and with it thy sin as evil. For good will in the infinite is what the good man finds the good will to be in himself, namely, the organic total whose truth is the discovery of the evil. Therefore is God's life perfect, because it includes not only the knowledge of thy finite wicked will, but the insight into its truth as a moment in the real universal will.

If then thou wert good, thou wouldst be good by including the evil impulse in a realization of its evil, and in an acceptance of the higher insight. If thou art evil, then in thyself, as separate being, thou are condemned, and just because thy separate evil is condemned therefore is the total life of God, that includes thee with thy condemnation and with the triumph over thee, good.

This is the ground for the solution of the problem. To go more into detail: Evil is for us of two classes: the external seeming evil, such as death, pain, or weakness of character; and internal evil, namely the bad will itself. Because we know so little, therefore we can never tell whether those externally seen seeming evils are blessings in disguise, or expressions of some wicked diabolical will-power at work about us. Somehow then, we never know exactly how, these seeming great evils must be in God universal good. But with regard to the only evil that we know as an inward experience, and so as a certain reality, namely, the Evil Will, we know both the existence of that and its true relation to universal goodness, because and only because we experience both of them first through the moral insight, and then in the good act. Goodness having its very life in the insight and in its exercise, has as its elements the evil impulse and its correction. The evil will as such may either be conquered in our personal experience, and then we are ourselves good; or it may be conquered not in our thought considered as a separate thought, but in the total thought to which ours is so related, as our single evil and good thoughts are related to the whole of us. The wicked man is no example of God's delight in wickedness, just as the evil impulse that is an element in the good man's goodness, and a very real element too, is no proof that the good man delights in evil. As the evil impulse is to the good man, so is the evil will of the wicked man to the life of God, in which he is an element. And just because the evil will is the only evil that we are sure of, this explanation is enough.

Thus the distinction between good and evil remains as clear as ever. Our difficulty about the matter is removed, not by any barren external theodicy, such as were the forms of guess-work that we criticised in a previous chapter, but by a plain reflection on the moral experience itself. Goodness as a moral experience is for us the overcoming of experienced evil; and in the eternal life of God the realization of goodness must have the same sort of organic relation to evil as it has in us. Goodness is not mere innocence, but realized insight. To the wicked man we say: God is good because in thinking thee he damns thy evil impulse and overwhelms it in a higher thought of which thou art a part. And in so far as thy will is truly evil, thou art in God just as the evil is in the good man; thou are known only to be condemned and overcome. That is thy blessed mission; and this mission of evil such as thine is indeed an eternal one. So that both things are true. The world is wholly good, and thou, such as thou individually art, mayest be damnably evil if so thou desirest.

We do not say then that evil must exist to set the good off by way of external contrast. That view we long since justly rejected. We say only that the evil will is a conquered element in the good will, and is as such necessary to goodness. Our conception of the absolute unity of God's life, and that conception alone, enables us to apply this thought here. No form of dualistic Theism has any chance to apply this, the only satisfactory theodicy. If God were conceived as external to his creatures, as a power that made them beyond himself, the hopeless problems and the unworthy subterfuges of the older theodicies would come back to torment us. As it is, the solution of the problem of evil is given us in the directest and yet in the most unexpected way.

Let us compare this solution with others. Evil, said one thought, before expounded, is an illusion of the partial view, as the shapelessness of the fragment of a statue is no disproof of the real beauty of the whole. We replied in a previous chapter to this notion, by saying that evil seems so positive an element in the world as to make very hard this conception of the partial evil as good universally in the aesthetic sense in which shapelessness of parts may coexist with a total beauty of the statue. For the fragment of the statue is merely an indifferent bit of stone without character. But the evil in the world seems in positive crying opposition to all goodness. Yet now, in the moral experience, we have found a wholly different relation of evil part to good whole. My good act is good just because of the evil that exists in it as conquered element. Without the evil moment actual in it, the total act could be at best innocent, not good. It is good by reason of its structure. That structure includes the evil will, but so includes it that the whole act is good. Even so, as we declare, God's life includes, in the organic total of one conscious eternal instance, all life, and so all goodness and evil. To say that God is nevertheless perfectly good is to say, not that God is innocent, knowing of no evil whatever, and including none; but that he so includes the evil will in the structure of his good will, as the good man, in one indivisible moment, includes his evil will in his good will; and that God is good only because he does so.

Again, to pass to another explanation, it has been said that evil exists in the world as a means to goodness. We objected to this that it puts the evil and the good first in separate beings, in separate acts or moments, and then makes the attainment of the good result dependent on the prior attainment of the separate and independently present evil. Now all that explanation could only explain and justify the acts of a finite Power, which, not yet possessing a given good thing, seeks it through the mediation of some evil. In no wise can this explanation apply to God as infinite. He is no finite Power, nor does he make or get things external to himself. Hence he cannot be said to use means for the attainment of ends. But our explanation does not make evil a means to get the separate end, goodness. We say that the connection is one of organic part with organic whole; that goodness has its life only in the instant of the discovery and inner overcoming of the evil will; and that therefore any life is good in which the evil will is present only as overcome, and so as lost in the good will. We appeal to the moral experience to illustrate how, when we do good, the evil will is present as a real fact in us, which yet does not make us as a whole bad, but just because it is present as an overcome element, is, even for that very reason, necessary to make us good. And we go on to say that even so in God the evil will of all who sin is present, a real fact in the Divine Life, no illusion in so far as one sees that it exists in God and nowhere else, but for that very reason an element, and a necessary element, in the total goodness of the Universal Will, which realized in God, is related to the wills of the sinners as the wills of the good men are related to their evil impulses.

The explanation that evil is needed to contrast with goodness has already been mentioned.

Evil therefore as a supposed real fact, separate from goodness, and a totally independent entity, is and must be an illusion. The objections to this view that we previously urged in Chapter VIII, were all applicable to the world of powers, which we viewed and had to view externally. God's life, viewed internally, as philosophy must view it, is not subject to these criticisms. And the moral experience has taught us how we are to explain the existence of the only partial evil that we clearly know to be even a partial evil, namely, the evil will. The explanation is that the good act has its existence and life in the transcending of experienced present evil. This evil must not be an external evil, beyond the good will, but must be experienced in the same indivisible moment in which it is transcended. That this wondrous union is possible, we simply find as fact in the moral experience. No genuine moral goodness is possible save in the midst of such inner warfare. The absence of the evil impulse leaves naught but innocence or instinct, morally insipid and colorless. Goodness is this organism of struggling elements. Now, as we declare, in the infinite and united thought of God this unity of goodness is eternally present. God's life is this infinite rest, not apart from but in the endless strife, as in substance Heraclitus so well and originally taught.

34. *Why God Must Be Finite* *

JOHN McTAGGART ELLIS McTAGGART *(1866–1925)*

God as Omnipotent

We now come to the relation of omnipotence to goodness. There is evil in the universe. It is not necessary to inquire how great or how small the amount of evil may be. All that is important for the present discussion is that there is some evil, and this is beyond doubt. A single pang of toothache, a single ungenerous thought, in

* John M. E. McTaggart, *Some Dogmas of Religion* (London: Edward Arnold, 1906), "God as Omnipotent." Reprinted by permission.

the midst of a universe otherwise perfectly good, would prove the existence of evil.

The existence of evil is beyond doubt in the sense that no one denies the existence of pain and sin in experience, and that no one denies that pain and sin are, from the point of view of ordinary life, to be considered evil. But it has been asserted that the universe, when looked at rightly, may be completely good. Sometimes the standard is challenged, and it is suggested that pain and sin are really good, though we think them evil. Sometimes our comprehension of the facts is challenged; it is admitted that pain and sin, if they existed, would be bad, but it is maintained that they do not really exist.

The first of these alternatives means complete ethical scepticism. There is no judgement about the good of whose truth we are more certain than the judgement that what is painful or sinful cannot be perfectly good. If we distrust this judgement, we have no reason to put any trust in any judgement of good or evil. In that case we should have no right to call anything or anybody good, and therefore it would be impossible to justify any belief in God, whose definition includes goodness. This objection, therefore, cannot consistently be used, by the believers in an omnipotent God, against the existence of evil.

The second alternative is one which can only be supported by metaphysical arguments of a somewhat abstruse and elaborate nature. To expound and examine these arguments in detail would take us too far from our subject. I will only say briefly that the theory of the unreality of evil now seems to me untenable. Supposing that it could be proved that all that we think evil was in reality good, the fact would still remain that we think it evil. This may be called a delusion or a mistake. But a delusion or mistake is as real as anything else. A savage's erroneous belief that the earth is stationary is just as real a fact as an astronomer's correct belief that it moves. The delusion that evil exists, then is real. But then, to me at least, it seems certain that a delusion or an error which hid from us the goodness of the universe would itself be evil. And so there would be real evil after all. If, again, the existence of the delusion is pronounced to be a delusion, then this second delusion, which would be admitted to be real, must be pronounced evil, since it is now this delusion which deceives us about the true nature of reality, and hides its goodness from us. And so on indefinitely. However many times we pronounce evil unreal, we always leave a reality behind, which in its turn is to be pronounced evil.

An omnipotent God is conceived as creating the universe. In that case it seems a natural inference that he is the cause of all the evil in the universe. But some people, who maintain the existence of a creative omnipotent God, maintain also that the choice of the human will between motives has no cause, and, therefore, is not ultimately caused by the creator. They admit, however, that God could have dispensed with the freedom of the human will, if he had chosen to do so.[1]

We may therefore say that an omnipotent God could have prevented all the evil in the universe if he had willed to do so. It is impossible to deny this, if omnipotence is to have any meaning, for to deny it would be to assert that there was something that God could not do if he willed to do it.

What bearing has this on the question of God's goodness? It is clear that man may act rightly in permitting evil, and even in directly causing it. It is evil that a child should lose his leg, for the loss deprives him of much happiness, and causes him much pain. But the surgeon who performs the operation, and the parent who allows it to be performed, may be perfectly justified. For amputation may be the only alternative to evils much greater than those it produces.

And, again, the production of sin may under certain circumstances be justified. Supposing that it were true — fortunately there is no reason to believe that it is true — that employment as an executioner tended to degrade morally a large proportion of those who were employed, it would by no means follow that men ought not to be induced to act as executioners. The evil results which might follow from having no hangman might far outweigh the evil done to morality by having one.

But the justification in these cases depends entirely on the limited powers of the agents. The father and the surgeon, for example,

---

[1] It seems curious that believers in human free will should often accept the argument for God's existence from the necessity of a first cause. If human volition is not completely determined, the law of causality is not universally valid. And, in that case, what force remains in the argument for a first cause?

are justified because it is only through the evils of amputation that worse evils can be avoided. If they could have avoided those worse evils by some other course that would not have been evil at all, they would not have been justified in deciding on the amputation.

Now the power of an omnipotent God is not limited. He can effect whatever he wills. If he wills to have A without B, he can have A without B, however closely A and B may be connected in the present scheme of the universe. For that scheme also is dependent on his will. It thus appears that his action cannot be justified as the amputation was. It rather resembles that of a father who should first gratuitously break his son's leg, or permit it to be broken, and should then decide for amputation, although a complete cure was possible.

If a man did this we should call him wicked. We do not wait to call a man wicked till he does more evil than good. If a man should, at the risk of his life, save all the crew of a sinking ship but one, and should then, from mere caprice, leave that man to sink, whom he could easily have saved, we should say that he had acted wickedly. Nor is it necessary that a man should do evil for the sake of evil. To desire to attend a concert is not a desire for evil as such, but if I killed a man in order to acquire his ticket I should have acted wickedly.

Now in what way would the conduct of an omnipotent God, who permitted the existence of evil, differ from the conduct of such men, except for the worse? There are palliations of men's guilt, but what palliations could there be for such a God? A man may have lived a long life of virtue before he fell into sin, or again, we may have reason to hope that he will repent and amend. But could we have any reason for hoping that the omnipotent God would repent and amend? It seems difficult to imagine such a reason. Again, a man may be excused to some extent for his sin, if ignorance or folly prevents him from realizing the full meaning of his action. But if an omnipotent God is not omniscient (and it seems most natural to suppose that he is), at any rate he could be so if he chose. Or again, a man may have a genuine repugnance for his sin, and only commit it under extreme temptation. A man who betrays his country under torture is less wicked than if he had betrayed it for money. But an omnipotent God can be forced to nothing, and can therefore not be forced to choose between wickedness and suffering.

Such conduct, then, as we must attribute to an omnipotent God, would be called wicked in men, although the amount of evil for which any man is responsible is insignificant as compared with the sum of all evil, and although men have in most cases excuses which would not apply to an omnipotent God. Yet this being is still called God, by people who admit that goodness is part of the definition of God. Why is God called good, when his action is asserted to be such as would prove a man to be a monster of wickedness? Two lines of defence have been tried. The first is, in substance, that the omnipotent and good God is not really good, the second that he is not really omnipotent.

The form in which the first is put by its supporters is that goodness in God is of a different nature from what it is in man. Thus Mansel says that 'the infliction of physical suffering, the permission of moral evil' and various other things 'are facts which no doubt are reconcilable, we know not how, with the infinite Goodness of God, but which certainly are not to be explained on the supposition that its sole and sufficient type is to be found in the finite goodness of man."[2] And he goes on to say that the difference is not one of degree only, but of kind. Pascal is still more plain-spoken: "What can be more opposed to our wretched rules of justice than the eternal damnation of a child without any will of its own for a sin in which it seems to have had so little share that it was committed six thousand years before the said child came into existence."[3] Nevertheless Pascal continued to call good, and to worship, a God whom he believed to have done this.

But why should the word good be used in two senses absolutely opposed to one another? The senses are not merely different, as they would be if, for example, it was proposed to use the word good to indicate what is generally meant by the word scarlet. For what is called good in God would be called wicked in men, and good and wicked are predicates directly contrary to one another.

Is the alteration to be considered as one of mere caprice? Are the people who say that God is good, while Nero was wicked in the same position as a man who should call Everest a valley, while he called Snowdon a mountain? It seems to me that there is more than this involved, and that the real ground of the alteration is

---

2 *Limits of Religious Thought,* fourth edition, Preface, p. xiii.
3 *Works,* ed. Brunschvicg, ii. p. 348.

that good is a word of praise, and that wicked is a word of blame, and that it is felt to be desirable to praise God rather than to blame him.

But why is it desirable to praise him? Certainly not for the reasons which make us praise Socrates and blame Nero. For the conduct which in God we call good is conduct for some faint and imperfect approximation to which we blame Nero. What other reason is left? I can only see one — that an omnipotent God is, and will remain, infinitely more powerful than Nero ever was.

On this subject Mill has spoken,[4] and it is unnecessary to quote words which form one of the great turning-points in the religious development of the world. Yet when Mill says that rather than worship such a God he would go to hell, it is possible to raise a doubt. To call such a being good, and to worship him, is to lie and to be degraded. But it is not certain that nothing could be a greater evil than to lie and to be degraded. It is not impossible that God's goodness, as explained by Pascal and Mansel, should include the infliction of such tortures, physical and mental, on one who refused to worship him that they would be a greater evil than lying and degradation. Unless it is said that moral degradation is absolutely incommensurable with suffering — and I doubt if this can be maintained — the case does not seem impossible. Nor need the motive of the worshipper be selfish. The goodness of God, like the wickedness of some men, might include the torture of the culprit's friends as well as of himself.

We may doubt, then, whether we should be bound, or justified, in refusing to misapply the predicate good to such an omnipotent being, if the use of the word would diminish our chances of unending torture. But it seems just as likely to increase them. There are, no doubt, men who are prepared to inflict suffering on all who do not flatter them, even when they know that the flattery is empty and undeserved. But, granted that God has some qualities which would be called wicked in men, it does not follow that he has all qualities which would be called wicked in men, and there is no reason to suppose that he has this particular quality. Many men, bad as well as good, are not appeased by such flattery, but rather irritated by it, especially if they know it to be insincere, or to have

---

[4] *Examination of Hamilton,* chap. vii.

been insincere when it began. God may resemble these men rather than the others. Indeed, the probability seems to be that he would do so, since pleasure in such flattery is generally a mark of a weak intellect, and even if God's goodness is like our wickedness, it can scarcely be suggested that his wisdom is like our folly. Or, again, God's goodness may induce him to damn us whatever we do, in which case we shall gain nothing by lying.

When everything is so doubtful there does not seem to be the least prudence in flattery. Nor can we rest our actions on any statement made by God as to the conduct which he will pursue. For, if goodness in God is different from goodness in us, we should have no reason to believe a statement to be true rather than false, even if it were certain that it came from God. Divine goodness may not exclude the desire to destroy our happiness by false statements.

There remains the attempt to save the goodness of an omnipotent God by giving up the reality of his omnipotence, while retaining the name. Various elements in the universe have been taken either as good or as inevitable, and the evil in the universe explained as the necessary consequence of the reality of these elements. Thus, for example, the sin of the universe has been accounted for by the free will of the sinners, and the suffering explained as the necessary consequence, in some way, of the sin. Thus all the evil in the universe, it is asserted, is a necessary consequence of free will, and it is said that free will is so good that God was justified in choosing a universe with all the present evil in it, rather than surrender free will.

Or, again, it is said that it is impossible that there should not be some evil in a universe which was governed according to general laws, and that to be governed according to general laws is so great a perfection in the universe that God did well to choose it with all the evil that it involves.

It seems to me rather difficult to see such supreme value in free will that it would be worth more than the absence of all the present evil of the universe. It might be doubted, even, whether the advantage of unbroken general laws is so great that the evil of the universe would not be cheaply removed at the cost of frequent miracles. But we need not discuss this. For it is quite evident that a God who cannot create a universe in which all men have free will, and which is at the same time free from all evil, is not an omnipotent God, since there is one thing which he cannot do. In the same way, a God who cannot ordain a series of general laws, the uniform working of which would exclude all evil from the universe, is not an omnipotent God.

Or, once more, it is said that a universe without evil would involve in some way the violation of such laws as the law of Contradiction or of Excluded Middle, and that these laws are so fundamental that the existence of evil in the universe is inevitable.

Even if there were any ground for believing that the absence of evil from the universe would violate such laws as these, it is clear that a God who is bound by any laws is not omnipotent, since he cannot alter them. If it is said — as it may very reasonably be said — that these laws are so fundamental that it is unmeaning to speak of a being who is not bound by them, the proper conclusion is not that an omnipotent God is bound by them, but that, if there is a God, he is not omnipotent.

It is necessary to emphasize this point because, remarkable as it may appear, it is not an unusual position to maintain that God is absolutely omnipotent, and, at the same time, to believe that there are certain things he cannot do, and even to be quite certain what those things are.[5] As against such a view as this it seems necessary to emphasize the tolerably obvious fact that, if there is anything which God could not do if he wishes, he is not omnipotent.

It may be said that we are attaching too much importance to a slight inaccuracy of language. If people say that there are certain things which God could not do, then they do not believe him to be omnipotent, and they are simply using the wrong word when they say that they do believe him to be omnipotent.

But then why do they use the word? It seems to me that the confusion of language covers a confusion of thought. Many people are unwilling to accept the idea that God is not omnipotent. It is held to detract from his perfection and to render it difficult to regard him as the creator of the universe.

And there is another point of grave importance. If God is not

----

[5] Cp. for example, Flint's *Theism*. The omnipotence of God is asserted: I.2, III.1, IX.2. In VI.1 and VIII.1 we find statements of some of the things which God cannot do.

omnipotent, the fact that God exists and is good gives us no guarantee that the universe is more good than bad, or even that it is not very bad. If God exists and is good, the universe will of course be as good as he can make it. But, if there are some things that he cannot do, how can we tell that among these impossibilities may not be the impossibility of preventing the world from being more bad than good, or of preventing it from being very bad? If it could be shown that God's power, though limited, was strong enough to prevent this, it could only be by a determination of the precise limits of his power, and, if this could be done at all, it could only be done by an elaborate metaphysical investigation. Such investigations are open to few, and their results are frequently highly controversial. It is not strange that popular theology is unwilling to accept the position that the goodness of the universe can only be proved in such a way.

And thus popular theology has two conflicting impulses. It desires, among other things, to show that the universe is more good than bad — at any rate in the long run. The only means at its disposal for showing this — if it is to remain popular — is its belief in the existence of a God to whose will all evil is repugnant, and who is powerful enough to effect the predominance of good. But if God is to be taken as omnipotent, it is certain that all evil is not repugnant to his will, and if he is to be taken as not omnipotent, it is not certain that he is powerful enough to effect the predominance of good.

The inaccurate use of the word omnipotence hides this dilemma. When popular theology is pressed to reconcile the present existence of evil with the goodness of God, then it pleads that omnipotent does not mean omnipotent, but only very powerful. But when the sceptic has been crushed, and what is wanted is a belief in the future extinction of evil, then omnipotence slides back into its strict meaning, and it is triumphantly asserted that the cause which has an omnipotent God on its side must certainly win. The confusion is unintentional, no doubt, but it is dangerous.

It seems to me that when believers in God save his goodness by saying that he is not really omnipotent, they are taking the best course open to them, since both the personality and the goodness of God present much fewer difficulties if he is not conceived as omnipotent. But then they must accept the consequences of their choice, and realize that the efforts of a non-omnipotent God in favor of good may, for anything they have yet shown, be doomed to almost total defeat. It is not a very cheerful creed, unless it can be supplemented by some other dogmas which can assure us of God's eventual victory. But it is less depressing and less revolting than the belief that the destinies of the universe are at the mercy of a being who, with the resources of omnipotence at his disposal, decided to make a universe no better than this.

In this chapter I have only discussed the view which makes God a being separate from the universe, though all-powerful over it. I have not thought it necessary to consider the view — which has been maintained — according to which the whole of the universe is one omnipotent person, so that God is the sole reality, and we are not his creatures, but parts of himself. This view has not had much influence on religious thought. (Pantheism, indeed, has been and is very powerful, but the prevailing type is that which denies personality to the unity of all things.) And it is so little known, and of so obscure a nature, that I could scarcely have done it justice without expounding the whole philosophical system of each of its principal adherents. It is clear that the arguments given above to prove the inconsistency of omnipotence with personality and goodness would apply to God equally, if this theory of his nature were true. In addition to these there would be the further difficulty that it would require us to regard ourselves as parts of God. The belief that one person could be part of another would, I think, be found very difficult to defend.

35. *A Gradational View of Good and Evil* *

RADOSLAV A. TSANOFF *(1887–   )*

Explain away the evils in the world complacently, and not only does our life lose the tragic note characteristic of deep experience,

---

* Radoslav A. Tsanoff, *Religious Crossroads* (New York: E. P. Dutton & Co., 1942). Extract from the concluding section of Chapter 15, "The Problem of Evil," pp. 332–337. Reprinted by permission.

the felt need of redemption and refuge, but the idea of the Divine loses much of its sublime appeal, which is an appeal by contrast and in crisis. On the other hand, isolate any one part of existence or experience and stigmatize it as evil, and directly the task is imposed on theodicy to clear God of responsibility for this stigma on his perfect creation. Christian thought more than any other has manifested this dual need: not to ignore the gravity of actual evil, yet not to let it shake its ultimate trust.

We may bring together in concise review the more important explanations of evil in religious and philosophical tradition. The pantheistic description of evil as finitude, which we also find in modern absolutism, is unconvincing if it is intended as a theodicy to exonerate Deity; nor does it reach bedrock in its treatment of the problem. Deity is absolutely perfect; among its perfections is its creative or self-manifesting activity; yet all created being, all manifestation is finite and necessarily imperfect. The harmonising of these three propositions taxes the subtlest theodicy. The critical inquirer is more exacting. He asks: Wherein (in what respect and for what reason) is finite existence imperfect, and its imperfections evil? These four-questions-in-one are all on the docket. Pantheistic absolutism is ambiguous in distinguishing and in facing them.

Two accounts of evil, while not ultimate in their probing of its origin, are explicit in their specific description of it. The hedonist, whether optimistic or pessimistic in his final verdict, is specific in identifying good and evil with pleasure and pain. The value of our existence would then depend upon this, whether our experience yields a balance of pleasure or of pain. In theodicy, then, God would have to be vindicated as a provider or as an adjuster of happiness. But such hedonistic audits of human life are scarcely reliable. Can pleasures and pains be calculated, compared, and a balance drawn: by what standard of measure; by each man for himself or by some impartial judge, how chosen; in the actual moment of experience, or in anticipating or in retrospective judgment of it? These questions suggest the perplexities of any comparative measurement of pleasures and pains. But aside from its lack of precision, the more radical defect of hedonistic calculation is its final irrelevance. The fundamental question in valuation is not, whether men are actually happy or unhappy, but whether it is well that they are happy or unhappy in this way or that way. The anguish and revulsion of the prodigal son were the first gleams of hope in his swinish life. On the other hand, what is more revolting than some people's careless enjoyment of their own depravity, like St. Peter's "dog turning to his own vomit again?" So hedonism, whether optimistic or pessimistic, fails through its insufficiency in valuation. The values of our life are too varied and complex to be described simply in terms of pleasure and pain.

Equally subject to criticism as onesided and finally irrelevant is the specific description of good and evil as self-denying benevolence and egoism. This is a widespread idea in religion and in morals. It has fixed itself in language, so that the words "self-denying" and "selfish" are wellnigh synonyms of good and bad. The Gospel directs us to love our neighbor as ourselves; this is the Golden Rule in many religions. Buddhism ascribes all evil to egoism and preaches salvation through extinction of selfishness. So medieval Christian piety declares, as in the *Theologia Germanica*: "Be simply and wholly bereft of Self. . . . Put off thine own will, and there will be no hell." And modern utilitarian ethics emphasizes the benevolent-social intent of hedonism by advocating "the greatest happiness of the greatest number."

Now there is a basic confusion in the reduction of evil and good to egoism and altruism. It is a confusion in the interpretation of the self. The self is not something discrete and substantial that can be 'asserted' or 'denied.' It is an active and continually developing system of purposes and values: purposes and values pursued or achieved, partly sustaining and partly contending with each other. In our every deliberation and decision and act there is an impending reconstitution of self, a personal self-redefinition through choice. Of no action can we say simply that it is selfish or unselfish, for in everything that we say or do some one aspect or direction of our character, some one self, is affirmed, and another or others are denied. What we censure in the "selfish" man is the sort of values which he has chosen and made his own. Contrariwise with our praise of the 'unselfish' — he has not made the egoist's ignoble choice of values.

At the lowest levels of experience, the pursuit of material goods and advantages, men are concerned with values which are not clearly shareable and involve them in conflict. Higher up the scale, we seek goods that are shareable, express and satisfy our social nature. The very highest values of our spiritual life — truth, love, virtue, saintliness — not only can but must be shared to be achieved at all. It is because of this progressive universality of values in the perfection of personality that 'good' confusedly comes to have the connotation of 'unselfish': the isolated-hostile self is here outgrown. Moral downfall does not mean our relapse into selfishness, but a lowering of the values with which we become identified. Throughout the range of our experience we may note this contest between purposes and values, with eventual choice of some and rejection of others. This is Gospel wisdom: the sinner, in saving his life, loses it; the saint, in losing his life for Christ's sake, finds it. Of the abiding values, love is exalted by St. Paul as the greatest. At this summit of spiritual experience we have the utmost self-forgetfulness and absorption in another, and likewise consummate self-affirmation and self-realization. So we may see that the description of evil as self-assertion is ambiguous and misleading.

Good or evil, the value-character of existence, is not to be found in this or in that part of it. Any such division of the world into sheep and goats involves an ultimate dualism, with all its metaphysical and religious perplexities. Good and evil are ever opposed to each other, but theirs is an opposition-in-relation. Value-character is never manifested in isolation but always relatively to certain contexts, and in other contexts and relations is either wholly absent or radically transformed. The abiding or precarious truth of an idea is thus determined by the range of facts that it explains or the evidence that it interprets. What was true in a Ptolemaic setting is error in a Galilean or Newtonian context. Beauty, harmony, justice, all reveal similar relativity. . . . Each level of experience or spiritual development reveals its own standards, progressively exacting. *Noblesse oblige.*

This view of the world of values is gradational. Our career is hierarchical. Our aims and values are not merely different, or indifferently on a par. The difference between them is one that demands a judgment of preference. And this judgment is directional. In the scale of values, it reveals an upward or a downward course of the will. Evil in this view of things is literally degradation, yielding weakly or willfully to lower tastes or standards. Good is the fulfilment of the highest value available for us at whatever level or range of experience we have attained. As level and range are reconstituted at every step, so are the available values, and so likewise the good or evil of whatever choice we make. This basic idea may be illustrated in any field of value-experience, whether individual or social. When the sociologist urges us to develop a historical sense in judging customs and institutions, he is implicitly appealing to this same central idea.

An important point is that the scale of value, unlike the thermometer, has no fixed dividing zero-point, above and below which settled plus and minus values appear. There is no form of family institution forever and at every level of social organization good and alone good, but polygamy at one level yields at another to monogamy, and that in turn has to meet higher and more exacting standards. Mohammed's institution of polygamy was good, in reforming and rising above the existing promiscuity in Arabia; but continued Mohammedan polygamy, in spite of larger and more mature experience, has become a degradation of its family life and an evil. So in art or science, and so in religion. This is a central idea in the Sermon on the Mount, with its spiritualizing of the Mosaic Law and its upward reach to the higher possibilities of man.

In the gradational world of values, then, good or evil are not in the thing or state or position, but *in the direction* manifested. On any scale or ladder the step which we take may be a step up or a step down. So our every act is an ascent or a decline. Your life and mine are as radii in the Circle of Reality. As the Neoplatonists taught us, we may proceed Godward, toward the radiating center, or we may be straying peripherally towards the outer darkness. An act that may be a backsliding for a saint may mark the beginning in the reclamation of a sinner. The important thing is which way the person is turning. Again we should recall the profound words of St. Augustine: "When the will abandons the higher, and turns to what is lower, it becomes evil, not because that is evil to which it turns, but because the turning itself is perverse": *non quia malum est, quo se convertit, sed quia perversa est ipsa conversio.*

Does this mean that good and evil are not radically different, that the difference between them depends on the point of view or the context? This is a confusion. Evil is no more good than sinking is rising. There can be no deeper or more radical difference or opposition than the opposition of direction. The beast is not beastly in his animality; but when man neglects the fulfilment of his human possibilities, to tread the jungle-track of impulse and instinct, then his human degradation is beastliness. Herein is the evil, in the betrayal of the higher choice. Has the tragedy of this moral downfall ever been expressed better than in Hamlet's scene with his mother? How could Queen Gertrude betray her worthy lord to become the adulterous mate of that "mildewed ear" Claudius? —

This was your husband. Look you now what follows.
Here is your husband. . . . Have you eyes?
Would step from this, . . . What judgment to this?

At every level of experience we may recognize the possibility of good and the hazard of evil or degradation. This is a view neither dispiriting or complacent: "Work out your own salvation with fear and trembling." It raises no baffling problems for theodicy. From the least developed being up to God, nature manifests the urge of the higher and the drag of the lower, both natural as expressions of actual operative factors, but not both on a par as expressions of value. And no matter how high our attainment, always the higher prospect is before us with its challenge and with its hazards.

[NOTE: The bibliography for Chapter Three appears on page 520.]

Chapter Four

GOD AND HUMAN FREEDOM

INTRODUCTION

"Think now, who that was innocent ever perished? Or where were the upright cut off? As I have seen, those who plow iniquity and sow trouble reap the same." (Job 4. 7-8) In these words Eliphaz seeks to console Job in his misery and express confidence in the justice and goodness of the Supreme Ruler.

Experience all about us seems to run counter to such comforting advice. The wicked often prosper while the righteous suffer. Further, why did God create man with an "evil inclination" in the first place? Traditionalists often appeal to the greater value of human freedom of the will which, it is said, more than compensates for the evil wrought through human choice. Were God to have created a totally good world in which men lacked the capacity to sin, the world would have been robbed of the essence of morality — freedom. It is thus argued by many traditional theologians that without the ability to choose uncoercedly among alternative actions, man would be reduced to an automaton.

This solution, however, raises as many problems as it attempts to resolve. Why could not an omnipotent and omniscient God create a totally good universe with man yet possessed of free will? If such a condition is deemed somehow logically incompatible, doesn't this imply that God is a finite being, restricted by the bounds of logic? Moreover, if God is truly all-wise, He would surely be capable of rendering absolutely infallible predictions as to man's future actions. With such unqualified Divine prescience, in what sense could it be said that human action is not pre-determined, but free?

Could Eve have refused to yield to temptation and Adam not fallen in sin without belying God's omniscience? (Edwards, Calvin). We are faced with a dilemma. Either man has no free will or God is not all-wise. If the former is the case, what justification is there for punishment or reward; what becomes of sin; and wherein is God's justice in punishing man for evil? If the latter holds, why should man heed God's laws or reverence his wisdom? If God's will is subject to error, is it to be followed out of fear of his power alone?

These questions have led man to still more involved questions. How can the idea of human free will be squared with the scientific attitude which lays such heavy emphasis upon the data for hereditary and environmental determinism? Does ethical responsibility require freedom of choice? Is predictability of an ethical agent's activity evidence of the absence of free will? What do we mean by freedom, determinism and indeterminism? Is the whole problem of the existence of free will within the realm of empirical verification or is it a hopeless pseudo-problem?

H. M. S.

36. God's Foreknowledge Does Not Preclude Man's Free Will *

SAINT AUGUSTINE (353–430)

Augustine: This then definitely moves you, and at this you marvel!—how these two points are not contrary and logically repugnant—The fact that God knows all things future, and the fact that we sin, not by necessity, but by will.

If God knows that a man will sin, you say, it must be that he sins

---

*St. Augustine, *Free Choice of the Will,* trans. by Francis E. Tourscher Philadelphia: The Peter Reilly Co., 1937), from Chapters 3 and 4. Reprinted y permission.

(in fact). The fact then must be. It is not, therefore, the choice of the will, but rather inevitable and fixed necessity that makes it a fact. In this reasoning now you fear that this is established, namely —either it is denied shamelessly that God has foreknowledge of all things; or, if we cannot deny that, then we must acknowledge that man sins, not by reason of will, but by necessity. Or is there any other thing that disurbs you?

Evodius: Nothing else for the present.

A. You think, then, that all things of the universe, of which God has foreknowledge, are done not by will, but by necessity.

E. So do I think, entirely so.

A. Wake up then, and examine yourself a bit, and tell me if you can, what quality of will you are going to have tomorrow:—a will to sin, or a will to do right?

E. I do not know.

A. What now, think you that God, too, does not know?

E. I would not think that by any means.

A. If therefore God knows your will of tomorrow and the wills of all men who are living, or who will live, He foresees future wills: much more surely does He foresee what He will do in reference to just men and in reference to the impious.

E. Assuredly, if I say that God foreknows my works, much more confidently should I say that He foreknows His own works; and that He foresees most surely what He is going to do.

A. Are you then not on your guard, lest it be said to you that God also will do, not by will but by necessity, whatever He is going to do, if all things of which God has foreknowledge are done of necessity, not by will?

E. When I was saying that all things in the universe, which God foreknew to be future, are done of necessity, I was looking at those things only that are done in God's creation, not in Himself. For those things (in God) are everlasting, they are not done (they just are).

A. God, therefore, works nothing in His creation.

E. He has decreed once for all how the order of the universe, which He made, is carried out; and, in the administration of it, there is not anything (done) by a new will.

A. God, then, makes no one happy?

E. He does, surely.

A. Then surely He does so, when that one is made happy.

E. That is true.

A. If, therefore, you will be happy after one year, then after one year He will make you happy.

E. Yes.

A. Therefore He foreknows today what He will do after a year.

E. He always foreknew that. I agree also that He foreknows that, if it is to be so.

A. Tell me now: Are you not his creature, and will your beatitude not be a fact verified in you?

E. Surely, I am his creature, and in me will be the fact that I am happy.

A. Therefore, not by will, but by necessity will beatitude be realized in you, God being the cause of it.

E. God's will is to me necessity.

A. Will you be happy, then, not will it?

E. If I had the power to be happy, straightway I would be happy now, for I will it now; but I am not now happy, because it is not I, but He that makes me happy.

A. Very well does (the force of) truth speak, for you could not perceive otherwise that when we will we do the act of the will. Wherefore nothing is so completely in our power as the will itself. For when we will, immediately, without any interval, the act of the will is realized. Therefore can we say rightly that we grow old, not by reason of our will, but by reason of necessity; or that we die, not by reason of our will, but of necessity, and other things of this like. But who, out of mind, would dare to say: we will, not by means of will?

Wherefore, though God does know our future acts of will, it is not established from that fact, that we will not a thing by means of will. So also, what you said about beatitude—that it is not by yourself that you are made happy, you spoke as if I would deny it: but I say that when in the future you are happy, you will be so, not unwilling but willing to be happy.

Since therefore God foreknows your future happiness, and nothing can be done other than He foreknows, otherwise there would be no foreknowledge: we are not, by consequence, from the logic of this fact, forced to think (what is absolutely absurd and void of truth) that you will be happy, not willing to be happy.

But as the foreknowledge of God does not take away your will to be happy, when (in the future) you shall have begun to be happy, which (will) today is fixed upon the future fact: so too a wrong will (if it is to be in you in the future) is not therefore less your own will, because God has foreknowledge that that will be in the future.

Mark now, I say, how stupidly men say:—"If God foreknows the future act of my will, it must be that I will that which He has foreknown, because nothing can be done, other than He has foreknown."

Astounding unreason! How, then, can other not be done than as God foreknew, if that act of will, which He foreknew, will be no act of will?

I pass over the illogic of like quality, which I mentioned just now, that the same man (objecting) says:—"It must be that I so will." He is endeavoring to do away with will by supposing necessity. For, if it must be that he will, whence can he will, where there is no (choice of) will?

But if he speaks not after this fashion; yet, in another form, says that he has not the act of will in his own power, because it is necessary that he will, then he will be met from that thought, which you expressed, when I asked whether you, in the future, would be happy, not willing to be happy. You answered then that you would be happy now, if the power to be happy were in you. You said that you have the will, but as yet not the power. Then I added that truth has spoken out from you. For we can not deny that we have the power: The fact is that the object which we will is not now within reach. But, if the will itself is wanting in the act of willing, then (so far as wanting) we do not will.

But, if it can not be that while we are willing (in act) we do not will, surely will is present to the willing: and there is not anything else in the power of the will but what the will has present (its own choice to do or not to do). Our will, therefore, would not be will if it were not in our power.

Furthermore, just because it is in our power, it is for us free. For what is not in our power is not for us free; nor can that which we have be non-existent. Thus it follows that we deny not that God has foreknowledge of all our future acts, and it is equally true yet that we will what we will.

For while He has foreknowledge of our will, that of which He has foreknowledge will be, the will therefore (in particular acts) will be because He foreknows that it is the act of the will: and if it is not in our power, then it can not be will in act. Therefore He has foreknowledge also of the power (to choose). By the fact of his foreknowledge power (of choice) is not taken from me—a power which therefore is more certain to be because He whose foreknowledge is not deceived has foreknown that the power will be (in the future mine).

E. Behold, now I deny not that whatsoever God foreknows must be so done; and that He so foreknows our sins, that yet our will remains free, and in our own power to choose.

. . . .

A. What then perturbs you? Or have you perhaps forgotten what our first argument established, or do you not acknowledge that, by no one forcing us, higher or lower or equal (on the same plane of being), but by our own will we do wrong?

E. I dare not deny any of the foregoing: but yet I confess that I do not see how these two are not contradictory—God's foreknowledge of our sins, and our free choice in sinning. For we must acknowledge that God has foreknowledge and that He is just. But I would like to know by what kind of justice He punishes sins which are done necessarily: or how the things which He foresees in the future are not necessarily done: or how, whatsoever is done necessarily in his creation is not be attributed to the Creator.

A. Whence does it appear to you that our free choice is opposed to God's foreknowledge: Is it because it is foreknowledge, or because it is God's foreknowledge?

E. It is because it is God's foreknowledge, chiefly.

A. How then: If you were to have foreknowledge that some one is going to do wrong, would it not follow necessarily that that one does wrong?

E. Surely so that he would sin: for otherwise my foreknowledge would not be foreknowledge, if its objective were nothing certain.

A. It is not therefore (by reason of) God's foreknowledge (properly) that things are done of necessity, which He foreknows, but must foreknowledge; which, if it foreknows not things certain, is not foreknowledge at all.

E. I acknowledge that. But why these questions?

A. Because, unless I am wrong, you would not force one to sin, of whom you had foreknowledge that he will sin; and your foreknowledge itself would not force him, even though the fact of the future sin be beyond all doubt, for otherwise you could not foreknow the future fact. Therefore, just as these two are not contradictory, so that you, by foreknowledge, might know and another might in future act by his own will, so God, forcing no one to sin, yet sees those who will sin by choice of their own will.

Why then not punish in justice what foreknowing He does not force to be done? As you by your memory do not force to be, the things that have passed; so God by his foreknowledge forces not the things to be done that are in the future. And as you remember certain things that you have done; and yet you have not done all that you remember: So God foreknows all things of which He is the author, yet He is not author of all things that He foreknows. But of things, of which He is not the evil author, He is yet the just avenger.

Understand from this, then, by what justice God punishes sins, because He knows the future facts. He does not make them facts (of disorder). If indeed He ought not to inflict punishment upon sinners because He foresees that they will be sinners; then He ought not to reward those who do right, because He foresees quite equally that they will do right.

Moreover let us confess that the fact that nothing is unknown of the future belongs to God's foreknowledge: and that the fact of sin, because it is done by the (created) will, belongs to God's justice; that thus sin is not left unpunished by his judgment, as it is not, by reason of his foreknowledge, forced to be done.

.   .   .   .

Now as to that point which you put third in order: How anything that is done of necessity in God's creature is not to be imputed to the Creator, that rule of piety, which it is fitting for us to recall, will easily admonish that we owe a debt of thanksgiving to our Creator whose generous goodness should be justly praised even if He had made us creatures of some lower plane of being. For though our soul is weakened by sin, it is yet more sublime and more noble than if it were changed into this visible (material) light. And you see how much souls praise God for the eminence of this light—souls, too tied down to the senses of the body.

Wherefore let not the fact that sin-burdened souls are blamed disturb you so as to say in your heart: "It were better if they did not exist."—Comparatively indeed they are an object of vituperation, when our thoughts go back to see what they would be if they had not chosen to sin.

Yet God, the Author of souls, is to be praised most highly in proportion to human power to praise, not only because He ranges them in order justly; but because He so made them that even spoiled by sin they have yet more worth and dignity in every way, than the light of this material creation, for which God is justly praised.

This also I counsel you to avoid—that you say perhaps, not that it were better that they were not made, but that they should have been made other than they are. For whatever occurs to you by right reasoning, know that that is what the Maker of all has done. But it is not right reasoning, but a wrong-minded weakness, when you shall have thought out something that is to be made, than which you would have nothing less excellent; as, having completed the heavens, you were to decide that there is to be no earth—a wrong thought altogether.

Rightly, by reverse, could you find fault, if, leaving out the heavens, you saw the earth made; for then you might say it should have been made as you can by thought know the heavens. When therefore you were to see that to the pattern of which you would bring the earth completed, called not earth, but sky; I think, that, not deprived of a thing more noble, you ought to have no wrong attitude of mind to oppose the making of an inferior earth too. In which earth again, so great is variety in accord with its parts, that nothing that belongs to the outward form of earth occurs to one who thinks, that, in the entire bulk of it, God the Builder of all, did not make.

And indeed, from land most fair and fruitful to land altogether sterile and void, you so come by intermediate steps, that you presume not to find fault in any part, but by comparing with that which is more excellent; and thus, by all the degrees of praise, you ascend to the highest, which yet you would not wish to be alone— (without the lower and intermediate).

How great is the difference, now, between, all the earth and the heavens? For there are placed things humid (clouds) and the nature of the wind currents. Also, out of the four elements, other natures, to us innumerable; but by God they are numbered, and the forms and the shapes of things by Him are varied (made what they are).

In the nature of things (created) therefore there may be something, about which, by your reason, you do not actually think: but what you think by true reason, cannot not be. What is thinkable by ordered normal thought and imagination is not repugnant to nature.—It can exist. Indeed, you can not think out anything better in creation, that has escaped the mind of the Maker of creation. For the human soul, naturally connected with the divine reasons, upon which it depends, when it says: this would be better done than that, if it speaks true, and sees what it says, sees in those reasons, with which it is connected.

It (the rational soul) may believe therefore that God has done, what, by true reason it knows ought to be done; even though it does not see this in things actually existing. Because, even though man could not see the heavens by means of (material) eyes, yet by right reason he could gather that some such thing should have been made. For by thinking man could not see what ought to be done fittingly; but in those (eternal) reasons only, according to which all things are made that are made. But what is not there (in the changeless reasons of things) no one can see by true thinking, just for the reason that it is not true.

On this point men generally go wrong; because, when they have seen things better by means of the mind, they seek them by means of their eyes not in their proper sources. As if (for example) someone grasping by reason (the idea of) perfect rotundity, find fault in the fact that such roundness is not verified in a nut, if he has never seen any round body but fruits of this kind.

So some men indeed, when, by true reason they see that that created nature is more noble, which, while it has free will, yet fixed upon God, has never sinned: seeing then the sins of men, they regret not so that men should cease from their sins, but that men were ever made, saying: Such He ought to make us in quality, that, willing to enjoy always the changeless truth we would never wish to sin. They do not cry out, they are not angry because He forced them to sin: because He made creatures also to whom He gave the choice, if they would, to sin. And such creatures indeed are the Angels who have never sinned, nor will they in future sin.

Wherefore, if you approve the creature that sins not by a most persevering will, it cannot be doubted that you prefer that creature to the one that sins. But just as you, by right reasoning, rank that creature higher, so God the Creator, by ordinance, has placed it higher.

Believe that such a creature is in the heights of heaven: because if the Creator has shown his goodness to create that creature whose future sins He forsees, He would by no means not show that goodness in the making of a creature, that He foreknows will not sin.

That sublime nature (created spirit) has indeed its everlasting beatitude in the constant enjoyment of its Creator, which it merits by an unwavering will of holding to justice. Then that sinful nature too, the spiritual soul of man, having lost happiness in sin, but not forfeited the faculty of recovering happiness, holds its own order, Which nature thus rises higher than that which (perverted) an unchanging will to sin holds (captive to sin).

Between which (angelic nature perverted by sin) and that former persevering in the will of justice, this, the human creature, points a certain middle course, which reaches its height by the humility of repentance. For God did not withhold the bounty of his goodness from that creature, which He foreknew not only would sin, but would persevere in the will of sinning, so as not to give it being.

For as a horse that is astray is better than a stone which is not astray because it has not proper motion and sense to go astray; so is that creature more excellent which sins by free will, than that which sins not because it has not free will.

37. Why Human Will Is Not Free *

JOHN CALVIN (1509–1564)

WHAT GOOD THERE IS IN MAN DUE TO THE GRACE OF GOD

It is necessary, on the other hand, to consider the remedy of

*John Calvin, A Compend of the Institutes of the Christian Religion, ed. H. T. Kerr (Board of Christian Education of the Presbyterian Church in United States of America, 1939), pp. 50–56. Reprinted with the permission of the Westminster Press.

Divine grace, by which the depravity of nature is corrected and healed. . . . God begins the good work in us by exciting in our hearts a love, desire, and ardent pursuit of righteousness; or, to speak more properly, by bending, forming, and directing our hearts towards righteousness; but he completes it, by confirming us to perseverance. . . . If there be in a stone any softness, which, by some application, being made more tender, would be flexible in every direction, then I will not deny the flexibility of the human heart to the obedience of rectitude, provided its imperfections are supplied by the grace of God. . . . If, therefore, when God converts us to the pursuit of rectitude, this change is like the transformation of a stone into flesh, it follows, that whatever belongs to our own will is removed, and what succeeds to it is entirely from God. The will, I say, is removed, not considered as the will; because, in the conversion of man, the properties of our original nature remain entire. I assert also, that it is created anew, not that the will then begins to exist, but that it is then converted from an evil into a good one. . . . Whatever good is in the human will, is the work of pure grace. . . .

But there may be some, who will concede that the will, being, of its own spontaneous inclination, averse to what is good, is converted solely by the power of the Lord; yet in such a manner, that being previously prepared, it has also its own share in the work; that grace, as Augustine teaches, precedes every good work, the will following grace, not leading it, being its companion, not its guide. . . . As it is preceded by grace, I allow you to style it an attendant; but since its reformation is the work of the Lord, it is wrong to attribute to man a voluntary obedience in following the guidance of grace. . . . Nor was it the intention of Augustine, when he called the human will the companion of grace, to assign to it any secondary office next to grace in the good work; but with a view to refute the nefarious dogma broached by Pelagius, who made the prime cause of salvation to consist in human merit, he contends, what was sufficient for his present argum nt, that grace is prior to all merit. . . . The origin of all good clearly appears, from a plain and certain reason, to be from no other than from God alone; for no propensity of the will to any thing good can be found but in the elect. But the cause of election must not be sought in men. Whence we may conclude, that man has not a good will from himself, but that it proceeds from the same decree by which we were elected before the creation of the world. . . .

Concerning perseverance there would have been no doubt that it ought to be esteemed the gratuitous gift of God, had it not been for the prevalence of a pestilent error, that it is dispensed according to the merit of men, in proportion to the gratitude which each person has discovered for the grace bestowed on him. But as that opinion arose from the supposition that it was at our own option to reject or accept the offered grace of God, this notion being exploded, the other falls of course. . . . But here two errors must be avoided; the legitimate use of the grace first bestowed must not be said to be rewarded with subsequent degrees of grace, as though man, by his own industry, rendered the grace of God efficacious; nor must it be accounted a remuneration in such a sense as to cease to be esteemed the free favour of God.

.   .   .   .

The Will of Man Is Not Free

Man is so enslaved by sin, as to be of his own nature incapable of an effort, or even an inspiration, towards that which is good. . . . Augustine somewhere compares the human will to a horse, obedient to the direction of his rider; and God and the devil he compares to riders. "If God rides it, he, like a sober and skilful rider, manages it in graceful manner; stimulates its tardiness; restrains its immoderate celerity; represses its wantonness and wildness; tames its perverseness, and conducts it into the right way. But if the devil has taken possession of it, he, like a foolish and wanton rider, forces it through pathless places, hurries it into ditches, drives it down over precipices, and excites it to obstinacy and ferocity.". . .

Those whom the Lord does not favour with the government of his Spirit, he abandons, in righteous judgment, to the influence of Satan. . . . The blinding of the wicked, and all of those enormities which attend it, are called the works of Satan, the cause of which must nevertheless be sought only in the human will, from which proceeds the root of evil, and in which rests the foundation of the kingdom of Satan, that is, sin. . . . The fathers are sometimes too scrupulous on this subject, and afraid of a simple confession of the truth, lest they should afford an occasion to impiety to speak irreverently and reproachfully of the works of God. Though I highly approve this sobriety, yet I think we are in no danger, if we simply maintain what the Scripture delivers. . . . God is very frequently said to blind and harden the reprobate, and to turn, incline, and influence their hearts. . . .

What liberty man possesses in those actions which in themselves are neither righteous nor wicked, and pertain rather to the corporeal than to the spiritual life . . . has not yet been explicitly stated. Some have admitted him in such things to possess a free choice. . . . But I maintain . . . that God, whenever he designs to prepare the way for his providence, inclines and moves the wills of men even in external things, and that their choice is not so free, but that its liberty is subject to the will of God. That your mind depends more on the influence of God, than on the liberty of your own choice, you must be constrained to conclude, whether you are willing or not, from this daily experience, that in affairs of no perplexity your judgment and understanding frequently fail; that in undertakings not arduous your spirits languish; on the other hand, in things the most obscure, suitable advice is immediately offered; in things great and perilous, your mind proves superior to every difficulty. . . . In the dispute concerning free will, the question is not, whether a man, notwithstanding external impediments, can perform and execute whatever he may have resolved in his mind, but whether in every case his judgment exerts freedom of choice, and his will freedom of inclination.

.   .   .   .

Refutation of Objections Urged in Support of Free Will

They, who endeavour to overthrow (the servitude of the human will) . . . with a false notion of liberty, allege . . . to render it odious, as if it were abhorrent to common sense; and then they attack it with testimonies of Scripture. . . . If sin, say they, be necessary, then it ceases to be sin; if it be voluntary, then it may be avoided. . . . I deny . . . that sin is the less criminal, because it is necessary; I deny also the other consequence, which they infer, that it is avoidable because it is voluntary. For, if any one wish to dispute with God, and to escape His judgment by the pretext of having been incapable of acting otherwise, He is prepared with an answer, which we have elsewhere advanced, that it arises not from creation, but from the corruption of nature, that men, being enslaved by sin, can will nothing but what is evil. . . . The corruption with which we are firmly bound . . . originated in the revolt of the first man from his

Maker. If all men are justly accounted guilty of this rebellion, let them not suppose themselves excused by necessity. . . . The second branch of their argument is erroneous; because it makes an improper transition from what is voluntary to what is free. . . .

They add, that unless both virtues and vices proceed from the free choice of the will, it is not reasonable either that punishments should be inflicted, or that rewards should be conferred on man. . . . In regard to punishments, I reply, that they are justly inflicted on us, from whom the guilt of sin proceeds. For of what importance is it, whether sin be committed with a judgment free or enslaved, so it be committed with the voluntary bias of the passions. . . ? With respect to rewards of righteousness, where is the great absurdity, if we confess that they depend rather on the Divine benignity than on our own merits? . . .

They further allege . . . that if our will has not this ability to choose good or evil, the partakers of the same nature must be either all evil or all good. . . . It is the election of God, which makes this difference between men. We are not afraid to allow, what Paul very strenuously asserts, that all, without exception, are depraved and addicted to wickedness; but with him we add, that the mercy of God does not permit all to remain in depravity. Therefore, since we all naturally labour under the same disease, they alone recover to whom the Lord has been pleased to apply his healing hand. The rest, whom he passes by in righteous judgment, putrefy in their corruption till they are entirely consumed. . . .

They urge further, that exhortations are given in vain, that the use of admonitions is superfluous, and that reproofs are ridiculous, if it be not in the power of the sinner to obey. . . . God does not regulate the precepts of his law by the ability of men, but when he has commanded what is right, freely gives to his elect ability to perform it. . . . We are not alone in this cause, but have the support of Christ and all the Apostles. . . . Does Christ, who declares that without him we can do nothing,[1] on that account the less reprehend and punish those who without him do what is evil? . . . The operations of God on his elect are twofold . . . internally, by his Spirit, externally, by his word. By his Spirit illuminating their minds and forming their hearts to the love and cultivation of righteousness,

---

[1] John xv. 5.

he makes them new creatures. By his word he excites them to desire, seek, and obtain the same renovation. In both he displays the efficacy of his power. . . . When he addresses the same word to the reprobate, though it produces not their correction, yet he makes it effectual for another purpose, that they may be confounded by the testimony of their consciences now, and be rendered more inexcusable at the day of judgment. . . .

Our adversaries are very laborious in collecting testimonies of Scripture; and this with a view, since they cannot refute us with their weight, to overwhelm us with their number. . . . Either, say they, God mocks us, when he commands holiness, piety, obedience, chastity, love, and meekness, and when he forbids impurity, idolatry, unchastity, anger, robbery, pride, and the like; or he requires only such things as we have power to perform. Now, almost all the precepts which they collect, may be distributed into three classes. Some require the first conversion to God; others simply relate to the observation of the law; others enjoin perseverance in the grace of God already received. . . .

Our more subtle adversaries cavil . . . because there is no impediment, they say, that prevents our exerting our own ability, and God assisting our weak efforts. They adduce . . . passages from the Prophets, where the accomplishments of our conversion seems to be divided equally between God and us. "Turn ye unto me, and I will turn unto you." [2] . . . I wish only this single point to be conceded to me, that it is in vain to infer our possession of ability to fulfil the law from God's command to us to obey it; since it is evident, that for the performance of all the Divine precepts, the grace of the Legislator is both necessary for us, and promised to us; and hence it follows, that at least more is required of us than we are capable of performing. . . .

The second description of arguments is nearly allied to the first. They allege the promises, in which God covenants with our will; such as, "Seek good, and not evil, that ye may live." "If ye be willing and obedient, ye shall eat the good of the land; but if ye refuse and rebel, ye shall be devoured with the sword; for the mouth of the Lord hath spoken it." [3] . . . They consider it an absurdity and

---

[2] Zech. i. 3.
[3] Amos v. 14. Isaiah i. 19, 20.

mockery, that the benefits which the Lord offers in the promises are referred to our will, unless it be in our power either to confirm or to frustrate them. . . . I deny that God is cruel or insincere to us, when he invites us to merit his favours, though he knows us to be altogether incapable of doing this. For as the promises are offered equally to the faithful and the impious, they have their use with them both. As by the precepts God disturbs the consciences of the impious, that they may not enjoy too much pleasure in sin without any recollection of his judgments, so in the promises he calls them to attest how unworthy they are of his kindness. For who can deny that it is most equitable and proper for the Lord to bless those who worship him, and severely to punish the despisers of his majesty? God acts, therefore, in a right and orderly manner, when, addressing the impious, who are bound with the fetters of sin, he adds to the promises this condition, that when they shall have departed from their wickedness, they shall then, and not till then, enjoy his favours; even for this sole reason, that they may know that they are deservedly excluded from those benefits which belong to the worshippers of the true God. . . .

The third class of arguments also has a great affinity with the preceding. For they produce passages in which God reproaches an ungrateful people, that it was wholly owing to their own fault that they did not receive blessings of all kinds from his indulgent hand. Of this kind are the following passages: "The Amalekites and the Canaanites are there before you, and yet shall fall by the sword; because ye are turned away from the Lord." [4] "Because I called you, but ye answered not, therefore will I do unto this house as I have done to Shiloh." [5] . . . How, say they, could such reproaches be applicable to those who might immediately reply, It is true that we desired prosperity and dreaded adversity; but our not obeying the Lord, or hearkening to his voice, in order to obtain good and to avoid evil, has been owing to our want of liberty, and subjection to the dominion of sin. It is in vain, therefore, to reproach us with evils, which we had no power to avoid. . . . I ask whether they can exculpate themselves from all guilt. For if they are convicted of any fault, the Lord justly reproaches them with their perverseness,

---

[4] Numb. xiv. 43.
[5] Jer. vii. 13, 14.

as the cause of their not having experienced the advantage of his clemency. Let them answer, then, if they can deny that their own perverse will was the cause of their obstinacy. If they find the source of the evil within themselves, why do they so earnestly inquire after extraneous causes, that they may not appear to have been the authors of their own ruin? . . .

Let us hold this, then, as an undoubted truth, which no opposition can ever shake—that the mind of man is so completely alienated from the righteousness of God, that it conceives, desires, and undertakes every thing that is impious, perverse, base, impure, and flagitious; that his heart is so thoroughly infected by the poison of sin, that it cannot produce any thing but what is corrupt; and that if at any time men do any thing apparently good, yet the mind always remains involved in hypocrisy and fallacious obliquity, and the heart enslaved by its inward perverseness. . . .

38. God's Foreknowledge Disposes Man's Claim to Free Will *

JONATHAN EDWARDS (1703–1758)

Dr. Whitby supposes there is a great difference between God's foreknowledge, and his decrees, with regard to necessity of future events. In his "Discourse on the Five Points," p. 474, etc. he says, "God's prescience has no influence at all on our actions.—Should God, (says he,) by immediate revelation, give me the knowledge of the event of any man's state or actions, would my knowledge of them have any influence upon his actions? Surely none at all—our knowledge doth not affect the things we know, to make them more certain, or more future, than they would be without it. Now, foreknowledge in God is knowledge. As therefore knowledge has no influence on things that are, so neither has foreknowledge on things that shall be. And, consequently, the foreknowledge of any action

---

* Jonathan Edwards, *Inquiry Concerning the Freedom of the Will* (New York: Leavitt & Co., 1851), Vol. II, from Section 12.

that would be otherwise free, cannot alter or diminish that freedom. Whereas God's decree of election is powerful and active, and comprehends the preparation and exhibition of such means as shall unfrustrably produce the end. Hence God's prescience renders no actions necessary." And to this purpose, p. 473, he cites Origen, where he says, "God's prescience is not the cause of things future, but their being future is the cause of God's prescience that they will be:" and Le Blanc, where he says, "This is the truest resolution of this difficulty, that prescience is not the cause that things are future; but their being future is the cause they are foreseen." In like manner, Dr. Clarke, in his "Demonstration of the Being and Attributes of God," pp. 95-99. And the author of the "Freedom of Will in God and the Creature," speaking to the like purpose with Dr. Whitby, represents "Foreknowledge as having no more influence on things known, to make them necessary, than after-knowledge," or to that purpose.

To all which I would say, that what is said about knowledge, its not having influence on the thing known to make it necessary, is nothing to the purpose, nor does it in the least affect the foregoing reasoning. Whether prescience be the thing that *makes* the event necessary or no, it alters not the case. Infallible foreknowledge may *prove* the necessity of the event foreknown, and yet not be the thing which *causes* the necessity. If the foreknowledge be absolute, this *proves* the event known to be necessary, or proves that it is impossible but that the event should be, by some means or other, either by a decree, or some other way, if there be any other way; because, as was said before, it is absurd to say, that a proposition is known to be certainly and infallibly true, which yet may possibly prove not true.

The whole of the seeming force of this evasion lies in this; that, inasmuch as certain foreknowledge does not *cause* an event to be necessary, as a decree does; therefore it does not *prove* it to be necessary, as a decree does. But there is no force in this arguing: for it is built wholly on this supposition, that nothing can *prove*, or *be an evidence* of a thing's being necessary, but that which has a *causal influence to make it so.* But this can never be maintained. If certain foreknowledge of the future existing of an event, be not the thing which first *makes* it impossible that it should fail of existence;

yet it may, and certainly does, *demonstrate* that it is impossible it should fail of it, however that impossibility comes. If foreknowledge be not the cause, but the effect, of this impossibility, it may prove that there is such an impossibility, as much as if it were the cause. It is as strong arguing from the effect to the cause, as from the cause to the effect. It is enough, that an existence, which is infallibly foreknown, cannot fail, whether that impossibility arises from the foreknowledge, or is prior to it. It is as evident, as it is possible anything should be, that it is impossible a thing which is infallibly known to be true, should prove not to be true: therefore there is a necessity that it should be otherwise; whether the knowledge be the cause of this necessity, or the necessity the cause of the knowledge.

All certain knowledge, whether it be foreknowledge or after-knowledge, or concomitant knowledge, proves the thing known now to be necessary, by some means or other; or proves that it is impossible it should not be otherwise than true. I freely allow, that foreknowledge does not prove a thing to be necessary, any more than after-knowledge; but then after-knowledge, which is certain and infallible, proves that it is now become impossible but that the proposition known should be true. Certain after-knowledge proves that it is now, in the time of the knowledge, by some means or other, become impossible but that the proposition which predicates *past* existence on the event, should be true. And so does certain foreknowledge prove, that now, in the time of the knowledge, it is, by some means or other, become impossible but that the proposition which predicates *future* existence on the event, should be true. The necessity of the truth of the propositions, consisting in the present impossibility of the non-existence of the event affirmed, in both cases is the immediate ground of the certainty of the knowledge; there can be no certainty of knowledge without it.

There must be a certainty in things themselves, before they are certainly known, or (which is the same thing) known to be certain. For certainty of knowledge is nothing else but knowing or discerning the certainty there is in the things themselves, which are known. Therefore there must be a certainty in things to be a ground of certainty of knowledge, and to render things capable of being known to be certain. And this is nothing but the necessity of the truth known, or its being impossible but that it should be true; or, in other words, the firm and infallible connection between the subject and predicate of the proposition that contains that truth. All certainty of knowledge consists in the view of the firmness of that connection. (So God's certain foreknowledge of the future existence of any event, is his view of the firm and indissoluble connection of the subject and predicate of the proposition that affirms its future existence. The subject is that possible event; the predicate is its future existing: but if future existence be firmly and indissolubly connected with that event, then the future existence of that event is necessary. If God certainly knows the future existence of an event which is wholly contingent, and may possibly never be, then he sees a firm connection between a subject and predicate that are not firmly connected; which is a contradiction.

I allow what Dr. Whitby says to be true, "That mere knowledge does not affect the thing known, it makes it more certain or more future." But yet, I say, it *supposes* and *proves* the thing to be *already* both *future* and *certain*: i.e. necessarily future. Knowledge of *futurity*, supposes *futurity*; and a *certain knowledge* of futurity, supposes *certain futurity*, antecedent to that certain knowledge. But there is no other certain futurity of a thing, antecedent to certainty of knowledge, than a prior impossibility but that the thing should prove true; or (which is the same thing) the necessity of the event.

I would observe one thing further concerning this matter; it is this: that if it be as those forementioned writers suppose, that God's foreknowledge is not the cause, but the effect, of the existence of the event foreknown; this is so far from showing that this foreknowledge doth not infer the necessity of the existence of that event, that it rather shows the contrary the more plainly. Because it shows the existence of the event to be so settled and firm, that it is as if it had already been; inasmuch as *in effect* it actually exists already; its future existence has already had actual *influence* and *efficiency*, and has *produced an effect*, viz. prescience: the effect exists already; and as the effect supposes, the cause is connected with the cause, and depends entirely upon it, therefore it is as if the future event which is the cause, had existed already. The effect is firm as possible, it having already the possession of existence, and has made sure of it. But the effect cannot be more firm and stable than its cause, ground, and reason. The building cannot be firmer than the foundation.

To illustrate this matter, let us suppose the appearances and images of things in a glass; for instance, a reflecting telescope, to be the real effects of heavenly bodies (at a distance, and out of sight) which they resemble: if it be so, then, as these images in the telescope have had a past actual existence, and it is become utterly impossible now that it should be otherwise than that they have existed; so they, being the true effects of the heavenly bodies they resemble, this proves the existing of those heavenly bodies to be as real, infallible, firm, and necessary, as the existing of these effects; the one being connected with, and wholly depending on, the other. —Now let us suppose future existences some way or other to have influence back, to produce effects beforehand, and cause exact and perfect images of themselves in a glass, a thousand years before they exist, yea, in all preceding ages; but yet that these images are real effects of these future existences, perfectly dependent on, and connected with, their cause; these effects and images having already had actual existence, rendering that matter of their existing perfectly firm and stable, and utterly impossible to be otherwise: this proves in like manner, as in the other instance, that the existence of the things, which are their causes, is also equally sure, firm, and necessary; and that it is alike impossible but that they should be, as if they had been already, as their effects have. And if, instead of images in a glass, we suppose the antecedent effects to be perfect ideas of them in the Divine Mind, which have existed there from all eternity, which are as properly effects, as truly and properly connected with their cause, the case is not altered.

Another thing which has been said by some Arminians, to take off the force of what is urged from God's prescience, against the contingence of the volitions of moral agents, is to this purpose:—"That when we talk of foreknowledge in God, there is no strict propriety in our so speaking; and that although it be true, that there is in God the most perfect knowledge of all events, from eternity to eternity, yet there is no such thing as *before* and *after* in God, but he sees all things by one perfect, unchangeable view, without any succession." To this I answer:

1. It has already been shown, that all certain knowledge proves

the necessity of the truth known; whether it be *before, after,* or *at the same time.* Though it be true, that there is no succession in God's knowledge, and the manner of his knowledge is to us inconceivable, yet thus much we know concerning it, that there is no event, past, present, or to come, that God is ever uncertain of; he never is, never was, and never will be, without infallible knowledge of it. He always sees the existence of it to be certain and infallible. And as he always sees things just as they are in truth, hence there never is in reality anything contingent in such a sense, as that possibility it may happen never to exist. If, strictly speaking, there is no foreknowledge in God, it is because those things which are future to us, are as present to God as if they already had existence; and that is as much as to say, that future events are always in God's view as evident, clear, sure, and necessary, as if they already were. If there never is a time wherein the existence of the event is not present with God, then there never is a time wherein it is not as much impossible for it to fail of existence, as if its existence were present, and were already come to pass.

God's viewing things so perfectly and unchangeably as that there is no succession in his ideas or judgment, does not hinder but that there is properly now, in the mind of God, a certain and perfect knowledge of moral actions of men, which to us are an hundred years hence: yea, the objection supposes this; and therefore it certainly does not hinder but that, by the foregoing arguments, it is now impossible these moral actions should not come to pass.

We know that God knows the future voluntary actions of men in such a sense beforehand, as that he is able particularly to declare, and foretell them, and write them, or cause them to be written down in a book, as he often has done; and that therefore the necessary connection there is between God's knowledge and the event known, does as much prove the event to be necessary beforehand, as if the Divine knowledge were in the same sense before the event, as the prediction or writing is. If the knowledge be infallible, then the expression of it in the written prediction is infallible; that is, there is an infallible connection between that written prediction and the event. And if so, then it is impossible it should ever be otherwise, than that that prediction and the event should agree; and this is the same thing as to say, it impossible but that the event should come to pass; and this is the same as to say, that its coming to pass is necessary. So that it is manifest, that there being no proper succession in God's mind, makes no alteration as to the necessity of the existence of the events which God knows. Yea,

2. This is so far from weakening the proof which has been given of the impossibility of the not coming to pass of future events known, that it establishes that wherein the strength of the foregoing arguments consists, and shows the clearness of the evidence. For,

(1) The very reason why God's knowledge is without succession, is, because it is absolutely perfect, to the highest possible degree of clearness and certainty: all things, whether past, present, or to come, being viewed with equal evidence and fulness; future things being seen with as much clearness as if they were present; the view is always in absolute perfection; and absolute constant perfection admits of no alteration, and so no succession; the actual existence of the thing known, does not at all increase or add to the clearness or certainty of the thing known: God calls the things that are not as though they were; they are all one to him as if they had already existed. But herein consists the strength of the demonstration before given, of the impossibility of the not existing of those things, whose existence God knows; that it is as impossible they should fail of existence, as if they existed already. This objection, instead of weakening this argument, sets it in the clearest and strongest light, for it supposes it to be so indeed, that the existence of future events is in God's view so much as if it already had been, that when they come actually to exist, it makes not the least alteration or variation in his view or knowledge of them.

(2) The objection is founded on the immutability of God's knowledge: for it is the immutability of knowledge that makes his knowledge to be without succession. But this most directly and plainly demonstrates the thing I insist on, viz. that it is utterly impossible the known events should fail of existence. For if that were possible, then it would be possible for there to be a change in God's knowledge and view of things. For if the known event should fail of existence, and not come into being, as God expected, then God would see it, and so would change his mind, and see his former mistake; and thus there would be change and succession in his knowledge. But as God is immutable, and so it is utterly infinitely impossible that

his view should be changed; so it is, for the same reason, just so impossible that the foreknown event should not exist; and therefore the contrary is necessary. Nothing is more impossible than that the immutable God should be changed by the succession of time; who comprehends all things, from eternity to eternity, in one most perfect and unalterable view; so that his whole eternal duration is *vitae interminabilis, tota, simul, et perfecta possessio.*[1]

On the whole I need not fear to say, that there is no geometrical theorem or proposition whatsoever more capable of strict demonstration, than that God's certain prescience of the volitions of moral agents is inconsistent with such a contingence of these events, as is without all necessity; and so is inconsistent with the Arminian notion of liberty.

Corol. 2. Hence the doctrine of the Calvinists, concerning the absolute decrees of God, does not at all infer any more *fatality* in things, than will demonstrably follow from the doctrine of most Arminian divines, who acknowledge God's omniscience and universal prescience. Therefore all objections they make against the doctrine of the Calvinists, as implying Hobbes' doctrine of necessity, or the *stoical* doctrine of *fate*, lie no more against the doctrine of Calvinists than their own doctrine: and therefore it doth not become those divines to raise such an outcry against the Calvinists on this account.

Corol. 3. Hence all arguing, from necessity, against the doctrine of the inability of unregenerate men to perform the conditions of salvation, and the commands of God requiring spiritual duties, and against the Calvinistic doctrine of efficacious grace; I say, all arguings of Arminians (such of them as own God's omniscience) against these things, on this ground, that these doctrines, though they do not suppose men to be under any constraint or coaction, yet suppose them under necessity with respect to their moral actions, and those things which are required of them in order to their acceptance with God; and their arguing against the necessity of men's volitions, taken from the reasonableness of God's commands, promises, and threatenings, and the sincerity of his counsels and invitations; and all objections against any doctrines of the Calvinists, as being inconsistent with human liberty, because they infer necessity; I say, all

---

[1] [(Ed. Trans.) "The complete and at the same time perfect possession of eternal life."]

these arguments and objections must fall to the ground, and be justly esteemed vain and frivolous, as coming from them; being maintained in an inconsistence with themselves, and in like manner levelled against their own doctrine, as against the doctrine of the Calvinists.

39. Does God's Omnipotence Deny Man's Moral Responsibility? *

JOHN McTAGGART ELLIS McTAGGART (1866–1925)

But how about [man's] responsibility towards God? God's judgment—on the hypothesis that there is a God to judge—about the moral state of any man could not be affected by determinism. If the man is bad, he is bad, even if he is so necessarily, and an omniscient being would recognize this badness. But responsibility, as we have seen, involves more than this. A man is not called responsible to his fellow men because they do right to judge him evil, but because they do right to punish him. Now, it is argued by the indeterminists, it could not be right for God to punish men if their actions were inevitably determined by the natures which he had given them, and the circumstances in which he had placed them.

It seems to me that the answer is this. If there is an omnipotent God, we are not responsible to him for our sins either on the determinist view or the indeterminist. If there is a God who is not omnipotent, then we can as well be responsible to him for our sins on the determinist view, as we can on the indeterminist—or, indeed, better, as we shall see later on.

Punishment is painful, and pain is evil. Punishment, again, does not abolish the sin for which it is inflicted—that is in the past, and irrevocable. And sin is evil. Consequently no person can be justified in inflicting punishment if he might have avoided the necessity by preventing the offence, unless the final result of the sin and the punishment should be something better than would have happened

---

* John M. E. McTaggart, *Some Dogmas of Religion* (London: Edward Arnold, 1906). "Free Will." Reprinted by permission.

without either of them.[1] And this case he will not be justified unless
the good result which arises from the sin and the punishment could
not be attained without them. For both the sin and the punishment
are intrinsically evil.

Now on the determinist hypothesis an omnipotent God could have
prevented all sin by creating us with better natures and in more
favourable surroundings. And any good result which might follow
from the sin and the punishment could be obtained by such a God,
in virtue of his omnipotence, without the sin or the punishment.
Thus God would not be justified in punishing sin, though man would
be, because God could attain the desired results without the punishment, while man could not. Hence we should not be responsible for
our sins to God.

But neither should we be responsible to an omnipotent God on
the indeterminist theory. For such a God could have created us
without free will, or without any temptation to misuse it, and then
there would have been no sin. The common answer to this is that
a universe in which we inevitably did good would be lower than one
in which our action, whether for good or for evil, was not completely
determined. Thus God is said to be justified in giving us free will,
and in punishing us when we misuse it.

I cannot see what extraordinary value lies in the incompleteness
of the determination of the will, which should counterbalance all
the sin, and the consequent unhappiness, caused by the misuse of
that will. If God had to choose between making our wills undetermined and making them good, I should have thought he would
have done well to make them good. But we need not decide this point.
For the defence is one which is obviously inconsistent with the idea
of an omnipotent God—if the word omnipotent is taken seriously.
The defence says that God could not secure the benefits—whatever
they are—of undetermined volition without also permitting the evil
of sin. But there is nothing than an omnipotent being cannot do.
Even if the two were logically contradictory, a really omnipotent
being cannot be bound by the law of contradiction. If it seems to
us absurd to suggest that the law of contradiction is dependent on
the will of any person, we must be prepared to say that no person
is really omnipotent.

---

[1] Cp. my *Studies in Hegelian Cosmology*, chap. vi.

Thus, even on the indeterminist hypothesis, we are not responsible for our sins to an omnipotent God. For he could have prevented the sins without introducing any counterbalancing evil into the universe, And, consequently, he would not be justified in checking sin by pain, since pain is intrinsically evil. If God is omnipotent, then, responsibility is impossible on either theory of freedom.

But if there is a God who is not omnipotent, it would be quite possible for the determinist to hold that we are responsible to him for our sins. Such a God might be unable to create a universe without sin, or at any rate unable to do so without producing some greater evil. And he might find it possible, as men do, to check that sin by means of a system of punishments. In that case he would be justified in doing so—provided, of course, that the necessary punishments were not so severe as to be a greater evil than the sin.

And here the determinist is in a better position than the indeterminist. For the indeterminist, as we shall see later on has no right to assert that there is even a probability that the expectation of punishment will alter our volitions. And, without such a probability, no punishment can be justified except vindictive punishment.

It has sometimes been held that the freedom of the human will was the only way in which the goodness of God could be made compatible with the evil in the universe. The evil we perceive in the universe consists—at any rate chiefly, perhaps entirely—of sin and misery. If sin was due to man's free will, and not to God's decree, God, it was said could not be condemned on account of the existence of sin. And the misery could be explained as the justifiable punishment of sin. On the other hand, it was said, if there was no free will, not only would it be impossible to justify the existence of misery, but the sin also must be referred to God as its ultimate cause. And it would become impossible to regard a being as good, to whose nature we must attribute the existence of all the evil of the world.

But as was shown above, if God is omnipotent, it is impossible to account for the evil of the universe in this way. Indeed, if God is omnipotent, it is impossible that he can be good at all. This would not be affected by the freedom of the human will, since the gratuitous permission of evil would be as fatal to the divine goodness as the gratuitous creation of evil. On the other hand, if God is not omnipotent, his goodness would not be impossible upon either theory

as to the human will. For a being of limited power but perfect goodness might well create evil, and not merely allow it, supposing that
the creation of the evil was the only way of avoiding a greater evil
or attaining a greater good.

40. *The Freedom of Man in a Predetermined Universe* *

G. W. LEIBNIZ *(1646–1716)*

OBJECTION III

If it is always impossible not to sin, it is always unjust to punish.
Now it is always impossible not to sin, or rather all sin is necessary.
Therefore it is always unjust to punish.
The minor of this is proved as follows.

First Prosyllogism

Everything predetermined is necessary.
Every event is predetermined.
Therefore every event (and consequently sin also) is necessary.
Again this second minor is proved thus.

Second Prosyllogism

That which is future, that which is foreseen, that which is in-
volved in causes is predetermined.
Every event is of this kind.
Therefore every event is predetermined.

Answer

I admit in a certain sense the conclusion of the second prosyllogism,
which is the minor of the first; but I shall deny the major of the
first prosyllogism, namely that everything predetermined is neces-

---

* G. W. Leibniz, *Theodicy* (London: Routledge & Kegan Paul, Ltd., 1952).
Synopsis of arguments in the *Theodicy*. Reprinted by permission.

sary; taking "necessity," say the necessity to sin, or the impossibility of not sinning, or of not doing some action, in the sense relevant to the argument, that is, as a necessity essential and absolute, which destroys the morality of action and the justice of punishment. If anyone meant a different necessity or impossibility (that is, a necessity only moral or hypothetical, which will be explained presently) it is plain that we would deny him the major stated in the objection. We might content ourselves with this answer, and demand the proof of the proposition denied: but I am well pleased to justify my manner of procedure in the present work, in order to make the matter clear and to throw more light on this whole subject, by explaining the necessity that must be rejected and the determination that must be allowed. The truth is that the necessity contrary to morality, which must be avoided and which would render punishment unjust, is an insuperable necessity, which would render all opposition unavailing, even though one should wish with all one's heart to avoid the necessary action, and though one should make all possible efforts to that end. Now it is plain that this is not applicable to voluntary actions, since one would not do them if one did not so desire. Thus their prevision and predetermination is not absolute, but it presupposes will: if it is certain that one will do them, it is no less certain that one will will to do them. These voluntary actions and their results will not happen whatever one may do and whether one will them or not; but they will happen because one will do, and because one will will to do, that which leads to them. That is involved in prevision and predetermination, and forms the reason thereof. The necessity of such events is called conditional or hypothetical, or again necessity of consequence, because it presupposes the will and the other requisites. But the necessity which destroys morality, and renders punishment unjust and reward unavailing, is found in the things that will be whatever one may do and whatever one may will to do: in a word, it exists in that which is essential. This it is which is called an absolute necessity. Thus it avails nothing with regard to what is necessary absolutely to ordain interdicts or commandments, to propose penalties or prizes, to blame or to praise; it will come to pass no more and no less. In voluntary actions, on the contrary, and in what depends upon them, precepts, armed with power to punish and to reward, very often serve, and are in-

cluded in the order of causes that make action exist. Thus it comes
about that not only pains and efforts but also prayers are effective,
God having had even these prayers in mind before he ordered things,
and having made due allowance for them. That is why the precept
Ora et labora (Pray and work) remains intact. Thus not only those
who (under the empty pretext of the necessity of event) maintain
that one can spare oneself the pains demanded by affairs, but also
those who argue against prayers, fall into that which the ancients
even in their time called "the Lazy Sophism." So the predetermination of events by their causes is precisely what contributes to morality instead of destroying it, and the causes incline the will without
necessitating it. For this reason the determination we are concerned
with is not a necessitation. It is certain (to him who knows all) that
the effect will follow this inclination; but this effect does not follow
thence by a consequence which is necessary, that is, whose contrary
implies contradiction; and it is also by such an inward inclination
that the will is determined, without the presence of necessity. Suppose that one has the greatest possible passion (for example, a great
thirst), you will admit that the soul can find some reason for resisting it, even if it were only that of displaying its power. Thus
though one may never have complete indifference of equipoise, and
there is always a predominance of inclination for the course adopted,
that predominance does not render absolutely necessary the resolution taken.

Objection IV

Whoever can prevent the sin of others and does not so, but rather
contributes to it, although he be fully apprised of it, is accessory
thereto.

God can prevent the sin of intelligent creatures; but he does not
so, and he rather contributes to it by his co-operation and by the
opportunities he causes, although he is fully cognizant of it.

Therefore, etc.

Answer

I deny the major of this syllogism. It may be that one can prevent the sin, but that one ought not to do so, because one could not
do so without committing a sin oneself, or (when God is concerned)

without acting unreasonably. I have given instances of that, and have applied them to God himself. It may be also that one contributes to the evil, and that one even opens the way to it sometimes, in doing things one is bound to do. And when one does one's duty, or (speaking of God) when, after full consideration, one does that which reason demands, one is not responsible for events, even when one foresees them. One does not will these evils; but one is willing to permit them for a greater good, which one cannot in reason help preferring to other considerations. This is a *consequent* will, resulting from acts of *antecedent* will, in which one wills the good. I know that some persons, in speaking of the antecedent and consequent will of God, have meant by the antecedent that which wills that all men be saved, and by the consequent that which wills, in consequence of persistent sin, that there be some damned, damnation being a result of sin. But these are only examples of a more general notion, and one may say with the same reason, that God wills by his antecedent will that men sin not, and that by his consequent or final and decretory will (which is always followed by its effect) he wills to permit that they sin, this permission being a result of superior reasons. One has indeed justification for saying, in general, that the antecedent will of God tends towards the production of good and the prevention of evil, each taken in itself, and as it were detached (*particulariter et secundum quid*:[1] Thom., I, qu. 19, art. 6) according to the measure of the degree of each good or of each evil. Likewise one may say that the consequent, or final and total, divine will tends towards the production of as many goods as can be put together, whose combination thereby becomes determined, and involves also the permission of some evils and the exclusion of some goods, as the best possible plan of the universe demands. Arminius, in his *Antiperkinsus*, explained very well that the will of God can be called consequent not only in relation to the action of the creature considered beforehand in the divine understanding, but also in relation to other anterior acts of divine will. But it is enough to consider the passage cited from Thomas Aquinas, and that from Scotus (I, dist. 46, qu. 11), to see that they make this distinction as I have made it here. Nevertheless if anyone will not suffer this use of the terms, let him put "previous" in place of "antecedent" will, and "final" or "decre-

---

[1] (Ed. Trans.) In particular and according to a certain point of view.

tory" in place of "consequent" will. For I do not wish to wrangle about words.

Objection V

Whoever produces all that is real in a thing is its cause.
God produces all that is real in sin.
Therefore God is the cause of sin.

Answer

I might content myself with denying the major or the minor, because the term "real" admits of interpretations capable of rendering these propositions false. But in order to give a better explanation I will make a distinction. "Real" either signifies that which is positive only, or else it includes also privative beings: in the first case, I deny the major and I admit the minor; in the second case, I do the opposite. I might have confined myself to that; but I was willing to go further, in order to account for this distinction. I have therefore been well pleased to point out that every purely positive or absolute reality is a perfection, and that every imperfection, comes from limitation, that is, from the privative; for to limit is to withhold extension, or the more beyond. Now God is the cause of all perfections, and consequently of all realities, when they are regarded as purely positive. But limitations or privations result from the original imperfection of creatures which restricts their receptivity. It is as with a laden boat, which the river carries along more slowly or less slowly in proportion to the weight that it bears: thus the speed comes from the river, but the retardation which restricts this speed comes from the load. Also I have shown in the present work how the creature, in causing sin, is a deficient cause; how errors and evil inclinations spring from privation; and how privation is efficacious accidentally. And I have justified the opinion of St. Augustine (lib. I, Ad. Simpl., qu. 2) who explains (for example) how God hardens the soul, not in giving it something evil, but because the effect of the good he imprints is restricted by the resistance of the soul, and by the circumstances contributing to this resistance, so that he does not give it all the good that would overcome its evil. "Nec (inquit) ab illo erogatur aliquid quo homo fit deterior, sed tantum quo fit melior non erogatur." [2] But if God had willed to do more here he must needs have produced either fresh natures in his creatures or fresh miracles to change their natures, and this the best plan did not allow. It is just as if the current of the river must needs be more rapid than its slope permits or the boats themselves be less laden, if they had to be impelled at a greater speed. So the limitation or original imperfection of creatures brings it about that even the best plan of the universe cannot admit more good, and cannot be exempted from certain evils, these, however, being only of such a kind as may tend towards a greater good. There are some disorders in the parts which wonderfully enhance the beauty of the whole, just as certain dissonances, appropriately used, render harmony more beautiful. But that depends upon the answer which I have already given to the first objection.

Objection VI

Whoever punishes those who have done as well as it was in their power to do is unjust.

God does so.

Therefore, etc.

Answer

I deny the minor of this argument. And I believe that God always gives sufficient aid and grace to those who have good will, that is to say, who do not reject this grace by a fresh sin. Thus I do not admit the damnation of children dying unbaptized or outside the Church, or the damnation of adult persons who have acted according to the light that God has given them. And I believe that, *if anyone has followed the light he had,* he will undoubtedly receive thereof in greater measure as he has need, even as the late Herr Hulsemann, who was celebrated as a profound theologian at Leipzig, has somewhere observed; and if such a man had failed to receive light during his life, he would receive it at least in the hour of death.

---

[2] [(Ed. Trans.) "Nor (says he) is anything dispensed by him (or from that source) by which a man is made worse, but so much is not dispensed by which a man is made better."]

Objection VII

Whoever gives only to some, and not to all, the means of producing effectively in them good will and final saving faith has not enough goodness.

God does so.

Therefore, etc.

Answer

I deny the major. It is true that God could overcome the greatest resistance of the human heart, and indeed he sometimes does so, whether by an inward grace or by the outward circumstances that can greatly influence souls; but he does not always do so. Whence comes this distinction, someone will say, and wherefore does his goodness appear to be restricted? The truth is that it would not have been in order always to act in an extraordinary way and to derange the connexion of things, as I have observed already in answering the first objection. The reasons for this connexion, whereby the one is placed in more favourable circumstances than the other, are hidden in the depths of God's wisdom; they depend upon the universal harmony. The best plan of the universe, which God could not fail to choose, required this. One concludes thus from the event itself; since God made the universe, it was not possible to do better. Such management, far from being contrary to goodness, has rather been prompted by supreme goodness itself. This objection with its solution might have been inferred from what was said with regard to the first objection; but it seemed advisable to touch upon it separately.

Objection VIII

Whoever cannot fail to choose the best is not free.

God cannot fail to choose the best.

Therefore God is not free.

Answer

I deny the major of this argument. Rather is it true freedom, and the most perfect, to be able to make the best use of one's free will, and always to exercise this power, without being turned aside either by outward force or by inward passions, whereof the one enslaves our bodies and the other our souls. There is nothing less servile and more befitting the highest degree of freedom than to be always led towards the good, and always by one's own inclination, without any constraint and without any displeasure. And to object that God therefore had need of external things is only a sophism. He creates them freely; but when he had set before him an end, that of exercising his goodness, his wisdom determined him to choose the means not appropriate for obtaining this end. To call that a *need* is to take the term in a sense not usual, which clears it of all imperfection, somewhat as one does when speaking of the wrath of God.

Seneca says somewhere, that God commanded only once, but that he obeys always, because he obeys the laws that he willed to ordain for himself: *semel jussit, semper paret*.[3] But he had better have said, that God always commands and that he is always obeyed: for in willing he always follows the tendency of his own nature, and all other things always follow his will. And as this will is always the same one cannot say that he obeys that will only which he formerly had. Nevertheless, although his will is always indefectible and always tends towards the best, the evil or the lesser good which he rejects will still be possible in itself. Otherwise the necessity of good would be geometrical (so to speak) or metaphysical, and altogether absolute; the contingency of things would be destroyed, and there would be no choice. But necessity of this kind, which does not destroy the possibility of the contrary, has the name by analogy only: it becomes effective not through the mere essence of things, but through that which is outside them and above them, that is, through the will of God. This necessity is called moral, because for the wise what is necessary and what is owing are equivalent things; and when it is always followed by its effect, as it indeed is in the perfectly wise, that is, in God, one can say that it is a happy necessity. The more nearly creatures approach this, the closer do they come to perfect felicity. Moreover, necessity of this kind is not the necessity one endeavours to avoid, and which destroys morality, reward and commendation. For that which it brings to pass does not happen whatever one may do and whatever one may will, but

---

[3] [(Ed. Trans.)   "He has commanded once, He always obeys."]

because one desires it. A will to which it is natural to choose well deserves most to be commended; and it carries with it its own reward, which is supreme happiness. And as this constitution of the divine nature gives an entire satisfaction to him who possesses it, it is also the best and the most desirable from the point of view of the creatures who are all dependent upon God. If the will of God had not as its rule the principle of the best, it would tend towards evil, which would be worst of all; or else it would be indifferent somehow to good and to evil, and guided by chance. But a will that would always drift along at random would scarcely be any better for the government of the universe than the fortuitous concourse of corpuscles, without the existence of divinity. And even though God should abandon himself to chance only in some cases, and in a certain way (as he would if he did not always tend entirely towards the best, and if he were capable of preferring a lesser good to a greater good, that is, and evil to a good, since that which prevents a greater good is an evil) he would be no less imperfect than the object of his choice. Then he would not deserve absolute trust; he would act without reason in such a case, and the government of the universe would be like certain games equally divided between reason and luck. This all proves that this objection which is made against the choice of the best perverts the notions of free and necessary, and represents the best to us actually as evil: but that is either malicious or absurd.

41. The Right to Believe in Free Will *

WILLIAM JAMES (1842–1910)

SOME METAPHYSICAL PROBLEMS PRAGMATICALLY CONSIDERED

Let me take up another well-worn controversy, the free-will problem. Most persons who believe in what is called their free-will do so after the rationalistic fashion. It is a principle, a positive faculty

---

* Wm. James, *Pragmatism* (New York: Longman, Green & Co., 1907). "Some Metaphysical Problems." Reprinted by permission.

or virtue added to man, by which his dignity is enigmatically augmented. He ought to believe it for this reason. Determinists, who deny it, who say that individual men originate nothing, but merely transmit to the future the whole push of the past cosmos of which they are so small an expression, diminish man. He is less admirable, stripped of this creative principle. I imagine that more than half of you share our instinctive belief in free-will, and that admiration of it as a principle of dignity has much to do with your fidelity.

But free-will has also been discussed pragmatically, and, strangely enough, the same pragmatic interpretation has been put upon it by both disputants. You know how large a part questions of accountability have played in ethical controversy. To hear some persons, one would suppose that all that ethics aims at is a code of merits and demerits. Thus does the old legal and theological leaven, the interest in crime and sin and punishment abide with us. "Who's to blame? whom can we punish? whom will God punish?"—these preoccupations hang like a bad dream over man's religious history.

So both free-will and determinism have been inveighed against and called absurd, because each, in the eyes of its enemies, has seemed to prevent the "imputability" of good or bad deeds to their authors. Queer antinomy this! Free-will means novelty, the grafting on to the past of something not involved therein. If our acts were predetermined, if we merely transmitted the push of the whole past, the free-willists say, how could we be praised or blamed for anything? We should be "agents" only, not "principals," and where then would be our precious imputability and responsibility?

But where would it be if we had free-will? rejoin the determinists. If a "free" act be a sheer novelty, that comes not from me, the previous me, but ex nihilo, and simply tacks itself on to me, how can I, the previous I, be responsible? How can I have any permanent character that will stand still long enough for praise or blame to be awarded? The chaplet of my days tumbles into a cast of disconnected beads as soon as the thread of inner necessity is drawn out by the preposterous indeterminist doctrine. Messrs. Fullerton and McTaggart have recently laid about them doughtily with this argument.

It may be good ad hominem, but otherwise it is pitiful. For I ask you, quite apart from other reasons, whether any man, woman or child, with a sense for realities, ought not to be ashamed to plead such principles as either dignity or imputability. Instinct and utility between them can safely be trusted to carry on the social business of punishment and praise. If a man does good acts we shall praise him, if he does bad acts we shall punish him—anyhow, and quite apart from theories as to whether the acts result from what was previous in him or are novelties in a strict sense. To make our human ethics revolve about the question of "merit" is a piteous unreality—God alone can know our merits, if we have any. The real ground for supposing free-will is indeed pragmatic, but it has nothing to to with this contemptible right to punish which has made such a noise in past discussions of the subject.

Free-will pragmatically means novelties in the world, the right to expect that in its deepest elements as well as in its surface phenomena, the future may not identically repeat and imitate the past. That imitation en masse is there, who can deny? The general "uniformity of nature" is presupposed by every lesser law. But nature may be only approximately uniform; and persons in whom knowledge of the world's past has bred pessimism (or doubts as to the world's good character, which become certainties if that character be supposed eternally fixed) may naturally welcome free-will as a melioristic doctrine. It holds up improvement as at least possible; whereas determinism assures us that our whole notion of possibility is born of human ignorance, and that necessity and impossibility between them rule the destinies of the world.

Free-will is thus a general cosmological theory of promise, just like the Absolute, God, Spirit, or Design. Taken abstractly, no one of these terms has any inner content, none of them gives us any picture, and no one of them would retain the least pragmatic value in a world whose character was obviously perfect from the start. Elation at mere existence, pure cosmic emotion and delight, would, it seems to me, quench all interest in those speculations, if the world were nothing but a lubberland of happiness already. Our interest in religious metaphysics arises in the fact that our empirical future feels to us unsafe, and needs some higher guarantee. If the past and present were purely good, who could wish that the future might possibly not resemble them? Who could desire free-will? Who would not say, with Huxley, "let me be wound up every day like a watch, to go right fatally, and I ask no better freedom." "Freedom" in a world already perfect could only mean freedom to be worse, and who could be so insane as to wish that? To be necessarily what it is, to be impossibly aught else, would put the last touch of perfection upon optimism's universe. Surely the only possibility that one can rationally claim is the possibility that things may be better. That possibility, I need hardly say, is one that, as the actual world goes, we have ample grounds for desiderating.

Free-will thus has no meaning unless it be a doctrine of relief. As such, it takes its place with other religious doctrines. Between them, they build up the old wastes and repair the former desolations. Our spirit, shut within this courtyard of sense-experience, is always saying to the intellect upon the tower: "Watchman, tell us of the night, if it aught of promise bear," and the intellect gives it then these terms of promise.

Other than this practical significance, the words God, free-will, design, etc., have none. Yet dark tho they be in themselves, or intellectualistically taken, when we bear them into life's thicket with us the darkness there grows light about us. If you stop, in dealing with such words, with their definition, thinking that to be an intellectual finality, where are you? Stupidly staring at a pretentious sham! "Deus est Ens, a se, extra et supra omne genus, necessarium, unum, infinite perfectum, simplex, immutabile, immensum, aeternum, intelligens," [1] etc.,—wherein is such a definition really instructive? It means less than nothing, in its pompous robe of adjectives. Pragmatism alone can read a positive meaning into it, and for that she turns her back upon the intellectualist point of view altogether. "God's in his heaven; all's right with the world!"— That's the real heart of your theology, and for that you need no rationalist definitions.

Why shouldn't all of us, rationalists as well as pragmatists, confess this? Pragmatism, so far from keeping her eyes bent on the immediate practical foreground, as she is accused of doing, dwells just as much upon the world's remotest perspectives.

See then how all these ultimate questions turn, as it were, upon

---

[1] [(Ed. Trans.) God is a Being, from Himself, outside of and above every species, necessary, One, infinitely perfect, indivisible, changeless, boundless eternal; and knowing ..."]

their hinges; and from looking backwards upon principles, upon an erkenntniss theoretische Ich, a God, a Kausalitatsprinzip, a Design, a Free-will, taken in themselves, as something august and exalted above facts,—see, I say, how pragmatism shifts the emphasis and looks forward into facts themselves. The really vital question for us all is, what is this world going to be? What is life eventually to make of itself? The centre of gravity of philosophy must therefore alter its place. The earth of things, long thrown into shadow by the glories of the upper ether, must resume its rights. To shift the emphasis in this way means that philosophic questions will fall to be treated by minds of a less abstractionist type than heretofore, minds more scientific and individualistic in their tone yet not irreligious either. It will be an alteration in "the seat of authority" that reminds one almost of the protestant reformation. And as, to papal minds, protestantism has often seemed a mere mess of anarchy and confusion, such, no doubt, will pragmatism often seem to ultrarationalist minds in philosophy. It will seem so much sheer trash, philosophically. But life wags on, all the same, and compasses its ends, in protestant countries. I venture to think that philosophic protestantism will compass a not dissimilar prosperity.

42. Free Will and the Will of God *

PLOTINUS (204–269)

What do we mean when we assert that something is in our power, when we speak of freedom in ourselves? Moving as we do amid adverse fortunes, compulsions, violent assaults of passion crushing the soul, feeling ourselves mastered by these experiences, going where they lead, we have been brought to doubt whether we dispose of ourselves in any particular.

---

* Plotinus, *The Essence of Plotinus,* (trans. by Stephen Mackenna) by Grace H. Turnbull, copyright 1934 by Grace H. Turnbull. Reprinted by permission of the Oxford University Press. From the chapter, "Free Will and the Will of the One."

This would indicate that we think of our free act as one which we execute of our own choice, in no servitude to chance or necessity or overmastering passion, nothing thwarting the will; the voluntary is conceived as an event amenable to will and occurring or not as our will dictates. Everything will be voluntary that is produced under no compulsion and with knowledge; our free act is what we are masters to perform.[1]

Thus a man might have the power to kill but the act will not be voluntary if in the victim he had failed to recognize his own father. And the knowledge necessary to a voluntary act cannot be limited to certain particulars but must cover the entire field. Why, for example, should killing be involuntary in the failure to recognize a father and not so in the failure to recognize the wickedness of murder? If because the killer ought to have learned, still ignorance of the duty of learning and the cause of that ignorance remain alike involuntary.

We have traced self-disposal to will, will to reasoning and, next, to right reasoning; perhaps to right reasoning we must add knowledge, for however sound opinion and act may be they do not yield true freedom when the adoption of the right course is the result of hazard or of some presentment from the fancy with no knowledge of the foundations of that rightness. We refuse to range under the principle of freedom those whose conduct is directed by fancy which, as we use the word, takes its rise from the humors of the body. Self-disposal belongs to those who, through the activities of Mind live above the states of the body. The spring of freedom is the activity of this Divine Mind; the proposals emanating thence are freedom.

Effort is free once it is towards a fully recognized good; the involuntary is, precisely, motion towards the enforced, away from the Good; servitude lies in being powerless to move towards one's good, being debarred from what is truly one's own good in a menial obedience.

Virtue and Divine Mind are sovereign and must be held the sole foundation of our self-disposal and freedom; both, then, are free. At its discretion virtue sacrifices a man; it may decree the

---

[1] This discussion of what constitutes voluntary and involuntary action derives from Aristotle, *Nicomachean Ethics* III, i-viii; *Eudemian Ethics* II, vi ff.

jettison of life, means, children, country even; it looks to its own aim and not to the safeguarding of anything lower. Thus our freedom of act, our self-disposal, must be referred not to the doing, not to the external thing done, but to the inner activity, to the intellection, to virtue's own vision.

The unembodied is the free; to this our self-disposal is to be referred; herein lies our will which remains free and self-disposing in spite of any orders which it may necessarily utter to meet the external. All that issues from will and is the effect of will is our free action; and in the highest degree all that lies outside the corporeal is purely within the scope of will.

Soul becomes free when, through Divine Mind, it strives unimpeded towards the Good; what it does in that spirit is its free act; Divine Mind is free in its own right. But the Good is the sole object of desire and That whereby the others are self-disposing. Thought insists upon distinguishing between what is subject to others and what is independent, bound under no allegiance, lord of its own act. This state of freedom belongs in the absolute degree to the Eternals in right of that eternity and to other beings in so far as without hindrance they possess or pursue the Good which, standing above them all, must manifestly be the only good which they can reasonably seek.

In us the individual, viewed as body, is far from reality; by Soul, which especially constitutes our being, we participate in reality, are in some degree real; but this is not reality pure. Thus far we are not masters of our being; the reality in us is one thing and we another. Yet we are again in some sense that which is sovereign in us and so even on this level might in spite of all be described as self-disposing. But in That which is wholly what It is — self-existing Reality, without distinction between the total thing and its essence — the being is a unit. There can be no subjection whatever in That to which reality owes its freedom, That in whose nature the conferring of freedom must clearly be vested, preeminently known as the Liberator. Even self-mastery is absent here, not that anything else is master over It, but that where we speak of self-mastery there is a certain duality, act against essence.

Every being in the pursuit of its good seeks to be that good rather than what it is, it judges itself most truly to be when it partakes of its good; in so far as it thus draws on its good its being is its choice. As long as a thing is apart from its good it seeks outside itself; when it holds its good it wills itself; the essence now is not outside of the will, by the good it is in self-possession. If then this Principle is the means of determination to everything else, we see at once that self-possession must belong primally to It, so that through It others in their turn may be self-belonging.

The Good, then, exists; It holds Its existence through choice and will, conditions of Its very being; yet It cannot be a manifold; therefore the will and the essential being must be taken as one identity; the act of the will must be self-determined and the being self-caused; thus reason shows the Supreme to be Its own Author.

The difficulty which the Supreme presents to our mind may be shown thus: We begin by positing space, a place, a chaos; into this existing container, real or fancied, we introduce God and proceed to enquire whence and how He comes to be there projected into the midst of things as though from some height or depth. But the difficulty disappears if we eliminate the spatial figure before we attempt to conceive God; He must not be set in anything either as enthroned in eternal immanence or as having made some entry into things; He is to be conceived as existing alone, with space and all the rest as later than Him. Thus we conceive Him as far as we may, the spaceless; we abolish the notion of any environment; we circumscribe Him within no limit; we attribute no extension to Him: He has no shape, even shape intellectual; He holds no relationship but exists in and for Himself before anything is. He is at the same time lovable and Love itself.[2] God's being and His seeking are identical; once more, then, the Supreme is the self-producing, sovereign of Himself.

Suppose we found such a nature in ourselves, untouched by all that has gathered around us subjecting us to happening and hazard; all that accruement was of the servile and lay exposed to chance. By this new state alone we acquire self-disposal and free act. When

---

[2] Cf. Aristotle, whose Prime Mover imparting motion does so "as a thing that is loved." Metaphysics, XI, vii, e. Cf. also 1st Epistle of St. John IV, 8: "God is love." Also Spenser, An Hymne of Heavenly Love:

"That high eternall powre, which now doth move
In all things, moved in it selfe by love."

we attain to this state and become This alone, what can we say but
that we are more than free, more than self-disposing? Who could
link us to chance, hazard, happening, when we are thus become
veritable Life, entered into That which contains no alloy but is
purely Itself?

Isolate anything else and the being is inadequate; the Supreme
in isolation is still what It was. The First cannot be in the soulless
or in an unreasoning life; such a life is too feeble in being; only
in the measure of approach towards reason is there liberation from
happening; the rational is above chance. Ascending we come upon
the Supreme, not as reason but as reason's better. Thus God is far
removed from all happening; the Root of reason is self-springing.

The Supreme is the Term of all; It is like the principle and
ground of some vast tree of rational life: Itself unchanging, It
gives reasoned being to the growth into which It enters.

The Supreme is everywhere and yet nowhere. He is everywhere
in entirety; He is, at once, that everywhere and everywise; He is
not in the everywhere but is the everywhere as well as the giver
to the rest of things of their being in that everywhere. Holding the
supreme place — rather no holder, but Himself the Supreme — all
lies subject to Him. He is not, therefore, as He happened to be,
but as He acted Himself into being. If then His Act never came to
be but is eternal wakening and a supra-intellection — He is as He
waked Himself to be. This awakening is before being, before Mind,
before rational life, though He is these.

We hold the universe, with its content entire, to be as all would
be if the design of the maker had so willed it, elaborating it with
purpose and prevision by reasoning amounting to a Providence.
All is always so and always so reproduced: therefore the reason-
principles of things must lie always within the producing powers
in a still more perfect form; these Beings of the Divine Realm must
therefore be previous to Providence; all things that exist in the order
of being must lie forever There in their intellectual mode. Before
our universe there exists the Mind of the All, its source and arch-
type. And if the Source is precedent even to this, It must be greater
than Its product, more powerful, having no better or higher. God
Himself, therefore, cannot but be wholly self-poised.

Seeking Him, seek no thing of Him outside; within is to be sought what follows upon Him; Himself do not attempt. He is, Himself, that outer, He the encompassment and measure of all things; or rather, He is within, at the innermost depth; the outer, circling round Him and wholly dependent upon Him, is Divine Mind by contact with Him and in the degree of that contact and dependence; so a light diffused afar from its source, the true light, is but a vestige, though not different in kind from its prior.

Stirred to the Supreme by what has been told, a man must strive to possess It directly; then he too will see. One seeing That as It really is will lay aside all reasoning upon It and simply state It as the Self-Existent; none that has seen would dare to talk of Its happening to be, or indeed be able to utter a word.[3] With all his courage he would stand astounded, unable at any venture to speak of This, with the vision everywhere before the eyes of the soul, unless one deliberately look away, ignoring God, thinking no more upon Him.

When therefore you seek to state or to conceive Him, put all else aside; abstracting all, keep solely to Him; do not look for something to add, rather you have probably not yet sufficiently abstracted from Him in your conception. For even you can take contact with Something about which nothing can be said or grasped, Something which lies away above all and is — It alone — truly free, solely and essentially Itself while all else is self and something other.

43. Does Responsibility Require Indeterminism *

UNIVERSITY OF CALIFORNIA ASSOCIATES

1. The Problem of Free Will

Acts of free will do not exist, since every action is determined and hence constrained. Let us first examine the considerations that

---

[3] Cf. Dante, Paradiso 1: Appendix, pp. 253, 255. Cf. also the testimony of a living mystic: "This vision brings its own proof to the spirit but words cannot declare or explain it."—"A.E.," *The Candle of Vision*, p. 26.

*Adams *et al.*: *Knowledge and Society*, New York, copyright 1938, used by permission of Appleton-Century-Crofts, Inc.

have been supposed to obliterate the distinction between free and constrained actions. It is alleged that what appear to be acts of free will are in reality instances of constrained action. The argument in support of this allegation is as follows: Every event is determined or necessitated by antecedent events. The acts said to be free are no exception. The belief that at the moment of choice I can act in several alternative ways must be an illusion, since at that moment the antecedent events completely determine my conduct. Thus, every voluntary act is constrained to happen by antecedent causes.

It follows at once that there is no distinction between freedom and compulsion. When I think that I am free and that there are alternatives among which I can choose, I am really the victim of an illusion. Since I am powerless to control the causes of my conduct, I am also powerless to control my conduct, for my conduct is determined by its causes, and these causes necessitate the effect. The possibility of controlling my conduct implies that the causes might have been ineffective — that my behavior could have been different, despite the causes that were present. But a cause that does not produce its effect is not really a cause, and hence the doctrine of free will is incompatible with the doctrine that my conduct has causes. Even when my conduct is not constrained by the dictates of a command, it is always constrained by its causes. They compel my compliance with one alternative to the exclusion of all other alternatives just as effectively as the threats that lend force to a command. The *belief* that my conduct is sometimes free from compulsion can be explained by the fact that I often fail to observe the causes which constrain my conduct. But my conduct is never uncaused and therefore never free.

The denial of free will alleged to be inconsistent with certain doctrines of morality, jurisprudence and theology. The denial of free will is said to be inconsistent with certain doctrines of morality, jurisprudence, and theology. Moralists make a distinction between right and wrong action. They tell us that we *ought* to do what is right, and that we *ought not* to do what is wrong. But, whatever we ought to do we must be able to do, and whatever we ought not to do we must be able to abstain from doing. Moralists cannot require us to perform the impossible. When they say that we ought to do a certain thing they imply that we could do it if we wished. Morality thus presupposes the existence of alternatives, all alike capable of realization. Some of these alternatives may be right and others wrong. Whenever we are confronted by such alternatives, moralists urge us to realize the one that is right. Yet, if every one of my actions is determined by antecedent causes, it follows that, in any given situation, I could not have acted in any other way than I did act. If all my actions are performed under the compulsion of a blind necessity, then it cannot be said that I ought to do a thing which, by supposition, it is impossible for me to do. Actions that I *must* perform are unavoidable, and it is therefore futile to exhort me with an *ought*, when I am forced to comply with a *must*.

Jurists hold that I cannot be held responsible for actions that were performed under compulsion, and that I cannot be justly punished for them. Hence, if all voluntary acts are necessitated by antecedent causes, I cannot be held responsible for my actions, since I have no control over their causes. I am not responsible for actions that I could not help, and it would therefore be unjust to punish me for something over which I had no control. We should not condemn a man who commits fraud, arson, or murder, since no man can help doing what he does do. Instead of "punishing" him by sending him to the penitentiary or the electric chair, we should rather attempt to "cure" him by subjecting him to the action of causes which will modify his behavior in the future so that he will never again commit such acts.

Considerations such as these seem to show that the denial of free will jeopardizes the conceptions on which morality and the administration of justice are based. Morality is impossible unless voluntary acts are exceptions to the principle, that *every event is determined by antecedent causes*. In order to insure the possibility of morality, therefore, some philosophers have argued as follows: There is no conclusive evidence in favor either of the truth of the principle or its falsity. For aught we know, it may be false. Let us therefore assume it to be false. If it is, then there are events which are not determined by antecedent causes. Of course, even if there are such events, we have no means of *knowing* that voluntary actions are events of this sort. In the absence of knowledge, we can only *postulate* that voluntary actions are exceptions to the rule of universal causation. But the postulate is justified, because it insures the possibility of morality. Although the freedom of the will is not susceptible of proof, we are justified in assuming free will as a postulate of morality. With this postulate, the validity of the moral "ought" remains unimpaired.

Theology has taken an interest in the problem of free will for two reasons. First, theology shares with morality certain conceptions which become inapplicable to human conduct, or at least lose their force, if the existence of free will is denied. Second, the determination of the attributes of God is dependent on how the problem of free will is decided.

The conceptions which become either inapplicable or nugatory are those of sin, atonement, and repentance. If man has no power to choose between right and wrong the concept of sin ceases to be applicable to his conduct. The characterization of an act as "sinful" implies a moral censure to the effect that the act ought to have been avoided. Similarly, when we exhort a man to atone for his deed we imply that his deed was a manifestation of free will. We cannot ask him to atone for something over which he had no control. Repentance, finally, is a futile gesture, unless freedom is a reality. I feel repentant when I contemplate a deed I wish I had not done — when I am sorry and resolve to do better in the future. This feeling is accompanied by the belief that the deed could have been avoided, had I so desired. But the belief is utterly illusory if freedom is unreal. Not even my future acts will get the benefit of my present mood of repentance unless free will is a reality. If it is not, and if the causes that determined my misdeed are repeated, my misdeed will also be repeated, no matter how repentant I feel now.

The principal problem of theology is to determine the attributes of God. Those that theologians generally regard as essential to the divine nature are "omniscience," "omnipotence," and "goodness." Granting that God is omnipotent, it was in His power either to create man a free agent or not to create him a free agent. Now, some theologians have argued that, if God has created man a free agent, He cannot have complete foreknowledge of his actions, and is therefore not omniscient. The foreknowledge of future events, they have reasoned, presupposes the determination of every event by antecedent events. If man is free, if his actions are not determined by antecedent events, it is impossible to predict the choice he will make between alternative courses of action. To attribute omniscience to God is to assume that man is not a free agent, since every one of his actions must be subject to the compulsion of causes. But if God did not create man a free agent, it follows that God is not good; for God rewards the saint and punishes the sinner. However, rewards and punishments cannot be meted out with justice, as we saw before, unless man is a free agent. If man is not a free agent, the saint's deeds are not to his credit, and the sinner's not to his discredit. The saint simply had the good luck to have his actions determined by propitious causes and does not deserve to be rewarded, since it is God, and not he, who is responsible for the whole causal chain that determines his actions. Likewise, the sinner does not deserve to be punished, since he could not help the misfortune of having had his actions determined by unpropitious causes. God as Creator is responsible for both causal chains, and it is therefore He who deserves to be praised for the deeds of the saint and blamed for those of the sinner. To reward and punish creatures who are not free agents is not consistent with God's goodness. If goodness is a part of the divine nature, it follows that God must have created man a free agent. Hence, God does not possess both the attribute of omniscience and the attribute of goodness. If He possesses the latter, man is a free agent, but in that case He cannot possess the former. If He possesses the former, man is not a free agent, and in that case He cannot possess the latter. We can therefore take our choice: either we can first settle the theological question one way or the other, and thus settle the problem of free will, or else we can first settle the problem of free will one way or the other, and thus settle the theological question.

2. The Confusions that Generate the Problem

The problem of free will is generated through confusing freedom with indetermination and compulsion with determination. In spite of its antiquity, we find today no substantial agreement as to how the problem of free will can be solved. One begins to suspect that a problem, on which so much intellectual effort has been expended without advancing it towards a solution, has not been properly defined. The layman, it was said, regards the freedom of the will, not as a problem, but as a fact to be verified in everyday experience. We encounter difficulties only as we enter into the considerations we have just been examining. Indeed, it is the latter that have given rise to the problem, because they confound the concept of compulsion (or constraint) with the concept of determination (or causation). The traditional formulation of the problem of free will assumes without question that compulsion, constraint, necessitation, determination, and causation are all synonymous. If the problem is to be solved, this assumption must be challenged. Our task, therefore, is to show that compulsion, constraint, and necessitation are not identical in meaning with determination and causation. If we can do this, we shall have shown, at the same time, that the negative of compulsion, constraint, or necessitation — namely, freedom — is not identical in meaning with the negative of determination or causation — namely, indetermination or chance.

We have to inquire into the meanings of two pairs of concepts: freedom and compulsion, determination and indetermination. Once we have established the meanings of these concepts, we can resolve the so-called problem of the freedom of the will into the following questions: (1) Are voluntary actions free or compelled (constrained, necessitated)? (2) Are voluntary actions determined or undetermined? (3) Does responsibility imply freedom? (4) Does responsibility imply indetermination? (5) Do repentance and remorse imply belief in the existence of free will? (6) Do repentance and remorse imply belief in the indetermination of voluntary acts? The problem of free will is generated by substituting the even-numbered for the corresponding odd-numbered questions, and assuming that these questions are of identical import. Thus, for example, the layman has no difficulty in answering the first question. Some of my actions (he will say) are free, and others are necessitated; I am not always free, and I do not always act under constraint. Those of my actions which are not performed under compulsion are called "voluntary." This being the defined meaning of the term "voluntary," it follows that my voluntary actions are free. The layman who believes that voluntary actions are free might also have ideas about their causation. Perhaps he believes that there is no event that happens without a cause. He will therefore believe that human conduct is never a chance phenomenon, but is always determined by antecedent events. Believing that human conduct is sometimes free and also that human conduct is always determined by antecedent causes, he now falls as easy prey to the arguments that generate the problem of free will. He will be told that he cannot assent to both of these propositions, seeing that freedom is incompatible with determination. If he believes in freedom he must believe that his voluntary decisions are not determined by antecedent events. If, however, he believes in the determination of all events without exception, he must believe that even his voluntary decisions, which appear to him to be free, are in reality necessitated. In all likelihood, our layman will be silenced by this argument; but he will also remain unconvinced.

We shall answer the first question as did the layman: human conduct is sometimes free and sometimes subject to compulsion. When my conduct is free it is called voluntary, and voluntary actions are therefore free by definition. To the second question, we shall be unable to give an unqualified answer. But, subject to the qualifications which are explained below, we shall say that human conduct is determined. The third and fifth questions are both answered in the affirmative. The fourth and sixth questions will be answered in the negative. Responsibility implies determination rather than indetermination. Repentance and remorse imply neither a belief in determination nor a belief in indetermination.

3. The Concept of Causal Determination

There is nothing we need add to what has been said about the distinction between freedom and compulsion. I am free when my conduct is under my own control, and I act under constraint when my conduct is controlled by someone else. My conduct is under my own control when it is determined by my own desires, motives, and intentions, and not under my control when it is determined by the desires, motives and intentions of someone else. It is not under my control even when my own desires and intentions are in agreement with those of another person who seeks to control my conduct; for I might have had desires and intentions which did not agree with his, and I should have then been free only had I been able to seek the realization of my own.

All of this is fairly obvious, and it would have been gratuitous to explain the distinction between freedom and constraint, if these terms had not also been used in an entirely different context, where they have given rise to the problem of the freedom of the will and the many puzzling fallacious arguments both for and against it. The concepts of freedom and compulsion, as we have just explained their meaning, are applicable only to the conscious actions of organisms. Thus, compulsion always implies the existence of desires in the consciousness of the organism, or at least the possibility of such desires, which, were it free to act in accordance with them, would result in actions that are incompatible with the actions the organism performs under compulsion. It is the crossing of its own desires by the will of some other organism that is experienced as compulsion. The identification of constraint with determination and of freedom with indetermination would be legitimate, therefore, only if determination connoted everything that is connoted by constraint and if indetermination connoted everything that is connoted by freedom.

4. Laws of Nature and Human Laws

The confusion between determination and compulsion seems to be explained by the fact that we speak of the determination of B by A whenever A and B are connected by a law. The laws of nature, it might be said, hold without exception; they cannot be transgressed. Hence, when A and B are connected by a law, the happening of B is necessitated whenever A has happened. The iron rod cannot avoid expanding when it is being heated, because its failure to do so would involve the violation of one of nature's laws. The law prescribes what the iron must do whenever its temperature is increased.

This sort of argument is undoubtedly encouraged by the view, once widely held and not yet entirely obsolete, that the laws of nature are divine enactments. According to this view, God governs nature as a ruler governs a state, by means of laws. Everything that happens is subject to the control and regulation of His laws. He keeps the planets in their courses by forcing them to follow prescribed orbits, and He compels the iron rod to expand whenever it is subjected to the influence of heat. Human laws are sometimes transgressed. The laws of nature are absolutely binding; they cannot be transgressed.

Human laws are prescriptions; natural laws are descriptions. We have only to state the assumptions of this argument in order to expose the fallacy on which it rests. The argument assumes that human and natural laws have something in common, namely, the fact that they are both prescriptions. Human laws — that is, moral or judicial laws — regulate and control the behavior of human beings; natural laws regulate and control the behavior of nature. Human laws prescribe certain modes of action and prohibit others; natural laws prescribe the manner in which natural processes are to take place. Human laws differ from natural laws solely in the fact that the former are sometimes violated, while the latter are never violated. The argument assumes that human and natural laws are different species of the same genus. It is this assumption that constitutes the fallacy. For human laws are rules of conduct, constraining conduct by the threat of penalties for violation of the rules. They prescribe the things one ought to do and prohibit the things one ought not to do. In short, they are imperatives. But natural laws are not imperatives and they have nothing in common with human laws except the name. To attribute to the former the functions that belong only to the latter is like the fallacy of attributing to the stocks that are sold on stock exchanges the properties of the stocks that grow in gardens. Natural laws do not prescribe the happenings that ought to take place; they describe the happenings that do take place. The law of falling bodies describes how bodies actually fall; it does not prescribe or command how they ought to fall. Similarly, the laws of planetary motion describe how the planets actually move; they do not prescribe orbits to the planets. Again, the laws of economics describe how economic processes actually are connected; they are not rules that prescribe how they ought to be connected.

We are, therefore, victims of a confusion of ideas when we say that the planets are forced or compelled by the laws of planetary motion to follow elliptical orbits, or that the manner in which a body falls is constrained or necessitated by a law. Compulsion, as we have seen, presupposes the existence, or at least the possibility, of desires and intentions, which seek the realization of actions incompatible with the actions performed under compulsion. A planet, not being conscious, could not have the desire to travel on any orbit incompatible with the orbit specified by the laws of planetary motion. Since it has no desires to be crossed, it cannot be forced or compelled to travel on its orbit. But even when the law describes the mechanical behavior of a conscious organism, it exercises no constraint in the proper sense of the word. If I should fall from an airplane and should desire the distance from my starting point to increase as the cube root of the time, my desire would have not the slightest influence on my motion. The distance will increase as the square of the time, whether I desire this to happen or not. Yet it would be incorrect to say that my desires are being crossed, or that my behavior is under constraint, for this implies at least the possibility of resistance or violation. If my resistance were successful, the law of falling bodies would be false. The formula $s = \frac{1}{2}gt^2$ would not describe the behavior of every falling body and would therefore not express a law of nature. If the formula does express a law of nature, then it describes, but does not constrain, even the behavior of a falling man, whatever his desires may be.

Our conclusion remains unaffected in the domain of economic and psychological laws. Although economic laws connect the properties of economic processes, including the activities of human beings, it is not true that they constrain these activities, or that they can be broken by people who do not like them. If, through man's intervention in economic affairs, economic processes are generated that fail to satisfy a given economic "law," we can conclude, not that the "law" has been violated, but only that the alleged law is false. To repeat what was said in Chapter III, we must always reckon with the contingency that what is taken to be a law, according to a scientific hypothesis, may turn out not to be a law after all.

Finally, psychological laws describe the nature of mind; they do not prescribe what the nature of mind ought to be. In particular, the laws of volition are not rules that force me to perform actions which perhaps I should not have performed, had my desires and intentions not been curbed by these laws. They connect my actual wishes and intentions with the circumstances under which they arise, and the nature of my actions with these desires and intentions. I act under compulsion only when I am prevented from realizing the goal I desire or intend. The law that describes the circumstances under which this desire arises does not constrain my action — not even if I should wish to be without this desire. Constraint, to repeat, implies at least the possibility of resistance or of violation.

The difference between a natural and a human law, to sum up, is the difference between a description and a prescription. A description is either true or false; a prescription is neither. A prescription can be obeyed or disobeyed; a description can neither be obeyed nor disobeyed. A prescription is a constraint on action; a description can by its very nature never encounter opposing desires.

5. DETERMINATION VS. INDETERMINATION OF VOLUNTARY ACTS

Now that we have shown that the concepts of determination and indetermination are not identical with the concepts of compulsion and freedom, we return to the questions asked earlier in this chapter. It will be recalled that the problem of free will is generated when questions (2), (4), and (6) are assumed to be identical with questions (1), (3), and (5). We have already dealt with the questions that were concerned with the freedom and compulsion of voluntary actions. There remain the questions that are concerned with their determination and indetermination.

Classification of voluntary acts. Voluntary acts may be divided into those that are motivated and into those that are not. When it is said that every voluntary act is determined by a motive, the term "motive" is used in the sense of "cause." In order to avoid the initial assumption that every voluntary act is determined, we shall not follow this usage. We shall, instead, use the term in the more familiar sense as the "reason" for the sake of which an act is performed. When, for example, I offer an insult to a person I dislike, I may have been motivated by a desire for revenge. If voluntary actions are determined, then motives in the sense specified determine them only partially at best. The mere presence in my consciousness of a desire for revenge is not enough; various external circumstances are also necessary. If the object of my insult had been three thousand miles away, the motive, however strongly I may have been impelled by it, would have been ineffective. The object of my insult must be within hearing distance and I must be aware of his presence, if my desire is to be realized. The factors that determine my action must therefore include at least the sight of the object in addition to the motive.

For our present purposes, it is unnecessary to enter into the question of the existence of hidden motives. The motives that appear in consciousness are often not the real motives from which we act. If the motive from which we are really acting is reprehensible the mind's censor often refuses to allow this motive to enter consciousness. But since a motive is needed to explain the act, consciousness invents a praiseworthy motive suitable as a reasonable explanation of our action and substitutes it for the real motive. Sometimes we become aware of the deception and discover the hidden motives which impel us to action. When this happens we often refrain from the intended act, namely, whenever we are motivated by the desire not to act from reprehensible motives.

There are many voluntary acts that do not proceed from conscious motives. Can it be said, then, that they proceed from hidden or unconscious motives? If so, it is hard to imagine what they might be. When I am told to choose one of the letters of the word "oblique," and I choose the letter "q," my choice is voluntary, but is certainly not explained by any conscious motive. I had no reason to choose the letter "q" in preference to any other letter. And as for hidden motives, what motive would explain why I chose this rather than some other letter? It will not do to say that my action was motivated by the necessity of having to make some choice among the alternatives. That motive fails to explain the uniqueness of the choice that was made. At best, it only explains the fact that I made a choice. Voluntary acts of this sort are, therefore, unmotivated or arbitrary; they have neither genuine nor fictitious motives.

Voluntary acts may be acts of choice or they may not. If a book review has aroused in me a desire to read "Gone With the Wind," this desire is the motive for entering a bookstore and buying a copy. I do not here make a choice from among a number of alternatives, for I am not confronted with the problem whether or not to buy "Gone With the Wind" instead of some other book. My desire is not distracted by the contemplation of other alternatives. When there are other alternatives, however, I have to make a choice. Suppose that I have decided to buy one or another of three different books. I want to read the first for pleasure, the second for instruction, and the third to impress my friends and acquaintances. No matter which alternative I choose, my choice will be motivated: I shall select one of the books when one of the reasons has achieved a greater strength than the others. Thus, I may finally regard it as more important to make an impression on my friends and acquaintances than to increase my knowledge or to seek my pleasure. The victorious reason then becomes the motive of my action and initiates the choice I make. We shall not discuss here the question of how one of these reasons becomes transformed into a motive. The occurrence of this transformation, however, is frequently observed. We often do weigh the different reasons in favor of one or the other of a number of alternative courses of action, until one of the reasons wins. This phenomenon is so common that it has received a name. It is known as the conflict of motives. It would be more accurate to speak of the conflict of reasons or of the conflict of possible motives, since a reason is not a motive until it contributes to the initiation of the action. But this does not take place until the reason becomes strong enough to overcome the opposing reasons.

In accordance with the distinctions we have made, voluntary acts may now be divided into four groups. The first division is between acts of choice and acts that do not involve choice. Each of these groups may in turn be divided into motivated and unmotivated acts. When an act of choice is unmotivated our choice is confined to the alternatives, one of which we intend to realize. When it is motivated our choice is, in general, again confined to these alternatives. We never make a choice among the motives themselves unless such a choice is itself motivated.

With the foregoing considerations in mind we can now turn to questions (2), (4), and (6). Question (2) asks: "Are voluntary actions determined or indetermined?" In accordance with our analysis of the concept of determination this question may be restated as follows: "Are voluntary actions predictable or are they unpredictable?" The predictability of voluntary actions presupposes the existence of laws that connect the properties of voluntary actions with the properties of antecedent events. In order to decide question (2) we must therefore answer the question: "Are there such laws?"

Relative and absolute determination and indetermination. The predictability of an event E is relative to the initial conditions and the laws that connect these initial conditions with the event E. When we know the initial conditions and these laws, we can predict the event. But when there are no laws known to us that connect these initial conditions with events prior to them, we are unable to predict the initial conditions themselves. Hence, when we assert that the initial conditions are also determined, we maintain the existence of these unknown laws. To illustrate: Suppose we observe a rock dislodged by the wind and rolling on a rough stony surface towards the edge of a vertical cliff. From the moment the rock reaches the edge of the cliff we can predict its positions at future moments by means of the law of falling bodies. We may say, therefore, that the falling of the rock is determined. But since there are no laws known to us that connect the position from which the rock starts its rolling motion with the subsequent positions it occupies between this point and the edge of the cliff, we are unable to predict the moment at which it will reach the edge of the cliff. Hence the further assertion that this event is determined is equivalent to saying that these laws exist. Similarly, we are unable to predict the moment at which the rock will be dislodged by the wind, since there are no laws known to us that connect this event with previous states of the rock, the wind pressure, and an indefinite number of other factors. Hence, once more, the assertion that this event is determined is equivalent to saying that these laws exist.

Our assertion that the future positions of the falling rock are predictable, that there are laws that connect these positions with antecedent events, is therefore ambiguous. For the statement lends itself to the following interpretations: (1) There is a law that connects (a) the positions of the falling rock with (b) its initial position at the edge of the cliff; (2) the law required by (1) exists, and there are laws that connect (b) the position of the rock at the edge of the cliff with (c) its initial position at the moment it is dislodged by the wind; (3) the laws required by (1) and (2) exist, and there are laws that connect (c) the position of the rock at the moment it is dislodged by the wind with (d) the previous states of the rock, wind pressure, etc. Interpretation (1) of our statement is consistent with the view that (b), the initial position at the edge of the cliff, is not determined; interpretation (2) with the view that (c), the initial position of the rock when dislodged, is not determined; and interpretation (3) with the view that (d), the collection of previous states, is not determined. Hence if our statement is to be incompatible with the statement of the indeterminist that (b) and therefore (a) is not determined, we must interpret it in accordance with (2);

and if it is to be incompatible with the statement of the indeterminist that (c) and therefore (a) is not determined, we must interpret it in accordance with (3). In general, our statement that (a) can be predicted when event E is known is not incompatible with the statement of the indeterminist that (a) cannot be predicted because event E cannot be predicted. Our statement will be incompatible with that of the indeterminist only if it is equivalent to the statement that *every* event that is connected with (a) by one or more laws is itself connected with antecedent events by laws.

We are now in a position to resolve the ambiguity of the assertion that voluntary actions are determined. When we make the statement that motivated voluntary actions are determined we may intend to maintain one or the other of the following three alternatives:

(i)   There are laws that connect (a) the action with (b) the motive, (c) the character and the dispositions of the person who acts, and (d) the circumstances under which he is acting.

(ii)   The laws required by (i) exist; and there are laws that connect (b) the motive with (c) the character and the dispositions of the person who acts, and (d) the circumstances under which he is acting.

(iii) A. The laws required by (i) exist; and there are laws that connect (b), (c), and (d) with (e) the properties of events preceding (d).

   B. The laws required by (i) and (ii) exist; and there are laws that connect (c) and (d) with (e) the properties of events preceding (d).

When we make the statement that unmotivated voluntary actions are determined we may intend to maintain one or the other of the following two alternatives:

(iv)   There are laws that connect (a) the action with (c) the character and dispositions of the person who acts, and (d) the circumstances under which he is acting.

(v)   The laws required by (iv) exist; and there are laws that connect (c) and (d) with (e) the properties of events preceding (d).

A few explanatory comments will perhaps facilitate the understanding of this exposition of the different ways in which one can understand the proposition that voluntary acts are determined. If we understand this proposition in sense (i) we profess to be able to predict (a) when (b), (c), and (d) are known. We have noted before that a knowledge of (b) alone, the motive of the act, is insufficient for the prediction of voluntary actions. It is also necessary to know (d), that the circumstances exist which make it possible to act on this motive. If the proposition be understood in sense (ii) we profess to be able to predict (b), the motive, when (c) and (d) are known, and hence also (a) by means of the laws whose existence is asserted in (i). It is obvious that we can predict (a) on the knowledge of (c) and (d) alone, if we are able to predict (b). According to (iii. A), we profess to be able to predict (b), (c), and (d), if we know the properties of events preceding (d). If there are laws of the kind required by (iii. A), we should be able to predict, for example, from our knowledge of present or past events, (b) the motive from which I shall act twenty-four hours from now, (c) my character and my dispositions, and (d) the circumstances which will make it possible for me to act on this motive. After these explanations the remaining alternatives should require no further comments.

An indeterminist could accept (i) and still claim that motivated voluntary actions are not determined, on the ground that there are no laws that permit the prediction of (b) the motive of the action. Our statement that motivated voluntary actions are determined must be understood in sense (ii) if it is to conflict with that of the indeterminist. If, however, the indeterminist should accept the predictability of motives, asserted by (ii), we should have to identify our statement with sense (iii), in order to get a statement that is incompatible with that of the indeterminist. There is no danger that the indeterminist would agree also with interpretation (iii). It is therefore unnecessary to interpret our statement as asserting the existence of laws that permit the prediction of (e) in order to get a proposition that is incompatable with that of the indeterminist.

If the indeterminist agrees with the determinist at all, his agreement is confined to (i) and (ii). As far as the statement that motivated voluntary actions are determined is concerned, it is certain that he disagrees with (iii). He may of course also disagree with formulations (i) and (ii), unless he has been impressed by the evidence in favor of the laws required by (i) and (ii). There is little doubt as to the attitude of the indeterminist regarding either formulation of the statement that unmotivated voluntary actions are predictable. Since he denies (iii), he will certainly also reject (v). And in view of the fact that we do not know the laws required by (iv) any more than we know those required by (v), we may take it for granted that he will also reject formulation (iv) of our statement.

The evidence in favor of the determination of voluntary acts. The indeterminist would have difficulty in supporting his disagreement with (i) and (ii). It must be admitted that we do not know the laws required by (i) and (ii), for otherwise we should be able to predict actions and motives with the same degree of reliability with which astronomers are able to predict eclipses. Our knowledge of the laws of volition is much too fragmentary to make predictions such as these possible. But it is nevertheless a fact that we are sometimes able to predict, with a fair degree of accuracy, what a man will do in a given set of circumstances. We feel almost certain that we can do this when we are acquainted with the man's character and dispositions and when we know his motive. Sometimes, indeed, we are even able to predict the motive from which he will act, when we know only his character, his dispositions, and the circumstances under which he is acting. Hence (i) and (ii) have at least some evidence in their favor. More often, to be sure, our predictions are not verified. However, we regard this as showing, not that indetermination is true of motivated voluntary acts, but only that our knowledge of the laws of volition and of human nature is imperfect. Motivated actions, we have found, do exhibit a considerable amount of regularity, and this fact justifies our presumption that the laws required by (i) and (ii) exist. The reason our predictions occasionally fail is not that these laws do not exist, but that we have an inadequate knowledge of them.

The indeterminist is in a somewhat better position to support his disagreement with (iii), (iv), and (v). For he can at least point out that we do not have even a fragmentary knowledge of the required laws. No one can predict the voluntary actions, whether motivated or unmotivated, that I shall perform during the next hour, or even during the next minute. There are no laws known to us that connect present or past events with my future actions. It must therefore be admitted that there is no evidence for either (iii) or (v). With respect to unmotivated actions, we are unable to predict the one that takes place even when we know the nature of the events that immediately precede the action. No one can predict that I will choose the letter "q" when I am engaged in choosing one of the letters of the word "oblique," no matter how much he knows about my character and my dispositions. Hence, there is likewise no evidence to support (iv). But is the lack of evidence a sufficient ground for denying (iii), (iv), and (v)? There was a time when we did not know the laws of planetary motion and were unable to predict the future positions of the planets. We could hardly have regarded our lack of knowledge as evidence that there were no such laws, or that the motions of the planets were chance occurrences. The fact that we had not as yet discovered them was no reason for inferring, either that they would never be discovered or that there were no such laws to discover. To date, we have failed to discover the laws required by (iii), (iv), and (v), but at some future time they may be discovered as were the laws of planetary motion.

We conclude, then, that the statement, voluntary acts are determined, is a presumption. It has some evidence in its favor when it is interpreted in accordance with (i) and (ii). It has no evidence in its favor when it is interpreted in accordance with one or the other of the remaining alternatives. If we believe it to be true when it is interpreted in accordance with those propositions also, it is only because we believe that the law of causality has no exceptions— that every event is connected with antecedent events by one or more laws. Anyway, the lack of evidence for these propositions is no evidence that they are false, as the indeterminist claims they are.

Free and constrained actions are both instances of determination. The presumption that voluntary acts are determined does not imply that voluntary acts, though apparently free, are in reality not free. Acts of free will are distinguished from compulsory actions, as a matter of fact, on the basis of the kinds of causes that determine them. My acts are free when they are determined by my own desires, intentions, and motives; and they are constrained when they are determined by the desires, intentions, and motives of another person. It is not only that freedom, as well as compulsion, is compatible with the assumption of determination, but the distinction between them requires this assumption. For the distinction breaks down unless we assume the determination of voluntary action.

This conclusion is supported by the analogous distinction between "free" and "constrained" motion. The motion of a body is said to be "free" when its motion is completely determined by the initial conditions and the forces acting upon the body. It is said to be "constrained" when its motion is determined not only by the initial conditions and the forces acting upon the body, but also by conditions which are not directly expressible in terms of forces. According to these definitions the motions of a falling body, of a thrown body, of a planet, are free; the motion of a body rolling down an inclined plane, the motion of a train, the motion of an automobile, the motion of a pendulum are all constrained, since they are determined not alone by the forces acting on these bodies, but also by the plane, the rails, the road, or the arc of the pendulum. This is exactly analogous to the distinction between free and constrained action. The initial conditions and the forces that determine the free motion of a body correspond to the desires, intentions, and motives that determine my acts of free will. The conditions that are not directly expressible in terms of forces correspond to the desires, intentions, and motives of a person other than myself. When the motion of a body is determined not only by the former, but also by the latter set of conditions, its motion is constrained. And analogously, when my action is determined not only by my own desires, intentions, and motives, but also by the desires, intentions, and motives of another person, my action is constrained.

The distinction between free and constrained motion is a distinction between two kinds of determining causes. Since this distinction is exactly analogous to the distinction between free and constrained action, it follows that determination is destructive of freedom neither in mechanics nor in ethics, jurisprudence, and theology. The fears of moralists, jurists, and theologians are baseless; the determination of the will is not incompatible with its freedom. The freedom of the will, therefore, need not be timidly assumed as a moral postulate; free will is a psychological fact. If moralists complain that ethics requires the concept of "ought" and that "ought" implies "can," while determination supplies us only with an inexorable "must," we reply that they are confusing determination with compulsion. If jurists object that responsibility requires freedom and that determination is compulsion in disguise, we answer that compulsion is neither identical with determination nor implied by it. If theologians preach that the concepts of sin, repentance, atonement, reward and punishment would be nugatory, if voluntary acts were determined, we retort that there could be no sin, that atonement and repentance would be useless, and that the distribution of rewards and punishments would be a futile gesture, unless voluntary acts were determined.

6. FREEDOM AND RESPONSIBILITY

Responsibility does not imply indetermination. We can now deal rather briefly with questions (4) and (6). Question (4) asks: "Does responsibility imply indetermination?" Responsibility, we have said before, implies freedom; I am not responsible for acts I am forced to perform. Does it also imply indetermination? That the answer must be in the negative is shown by the following considerations. It will be recalled that punishment is justifiable when, and only when, I am responsible for my actions. But if my voluntary actions were not determined, it would be futile to punish me for them. To punish me for the crime of forgery, for example, would be useless unless the punishment tended to deter me from committing acts of forgery in the future. But if voluntary actions are not determined, my future actions are as unpredictable with the punishment as without it. I shall be just as likely to commit the act of forgery in the future, no matter if I am now punished for the commission of such an act, or the act is ignored, or I receive a reward for it. But if punishment accomplishes nothing, it is hard to see what one can mean by its justification. Responsibility therefore implies determination, rather than indetermination.

Repentance and remorse do not imply indetermination. Question (6) asks: "Do repentance and remorse imply belief in the indetermination of voluntary acts?" In accordance with our analysis of the concept of determination, this question may be restated as follows: "When we feel repentant or remorseful, do we believe that there are no laws by means of which the act we repent could have been predicted?" It can be shown very easily that we believe nothing of the sort. Let us first examine our beliefs regarding acts of choice. Before I make a choice among a number of contemplated alternatives, I believe that I can choose any one of them. Both at the time of choice and afterwards, I believe that I could have chosen a different alternative if I had wanted to. Is the earlier belief, at the time of choice, a belief to the effect that there are no laws by means of which my future act can be predicted? Or is it simply the belief that I am free to choose any one of the possible alternatives and that my final choice will not be subject to compulsion? There is no doubt that what I believe in is the freedom and not the indetermination of my choice. Similarly, the later belief, after the choice has been made, is not a belief to the effect that my wanting to choose this rather than that alternative could not have been predicted. It is simply the belief that I was free when I made my choice, that the decision to choose the letter "q" rather than the letter "l" from the word "oblique," for example, was unconstrained, and that any other decision *I had wanted to make* would have been similarly unconstrained.

These conclusions remain unaffected in the special case when motives are present. Before I choose, I believe that I can act on any one of the competing motives. Does this mean anything more than that I believe my choice will be unconstrained? It surely does not mean that I believe my action will not be determined (at least partially) by the victorious motive. Furthermore, at the time of choice and afterwards, I believe that I could have acted on one of the competing motives, and that my action could have been different on that account. This again means no more than that I believe my choice was unconstrained. It is not a belief to the effect either that my choice is not determined by the victorious motive or that the victorious motive is not determined by antecedent events. It is perfectly plain that my choice would have been different had one of the other competing motives been victorious.

Let us turn next to our beliefs regarding voluntary acts that are not acts of choice. Before I act I believe that I can refrain from acting; both at the time of acting and afterwards I believe that I could have refrained from acting, if I had wanted to—these beliefs surely do not claim that I could have wanted to refrain from acting, or that my wanting to act, rather than refrain, was not determined

by antecedent events. The presumption is merely that I was free—
that I was not acting under compulsion.

These conclusions, too, remain unaffected in the special case
when the act is motivated. Before I act, I believe that I can refrain
from acting upon the motive. At the time of acting and afterwards
I believe that I could have done so. These beliefs claim neither
that motives do not determine actions, nor that motives are not
determined by antecedent events. It is obvious that I could have
refrained from acting or that my action would have been different,
if the motive I did act on had been weaker than it was, or if some
other motive had been present. These beliefs do not go so far as
to maintain that this motive could have been weaker than it was,
or that some other motive could have been present. They make only
the modest claim that there was no one who compelled me to act as
I did.

When the beliefs we have about voluntary actions accompany
remorse or repentance they are very intense. We have shown that,
in any event, they do not claim the indetermination of voluntary
action. Since the greater intensity they have in the instance of remorse and repentance does not affect the claim they do make, we
can answer question (6) in the negative.

Solution of the theological problems. It may be of interest to
apply the distinction between determination and compulsion and
that between indetermination and freedom to the solution of the
theological problem we discussed earlier in this chapter. The problem may be stated in the form of four hypothetical propositions.
(1) If God is good, then man is a free agent. (2) If man is a free
agent, then God is not omniscient. (3) If God is omniscient, then
man is not a free agent. (4) If man is not a free agent, then God
is not good. From these four propositions theologians have drawn
the conclusion that God cannot be at once good and omniscient.
This conclusion will not follow if any of these propositions are false.
And since (1) is equivalent to (4) and (2) is equivalent to (3) the
conclusion will be false if either (1) or (2) should turn out to be
false. It is not difficult to show that proposition (1) is true. If
man were not a free agent, God would not be justified in meting out
rewards and punishments for his actions, as He does, and He would
therefore not be good. But proposition (2) is false. The thesis that

God is not omniscient is supposed to be a consequence of the hypothesis that man is a free agent. If this thesis can be established at all it can only be established on the hypothesis of the indetermination of man's voluntary actions. Propositions (2) and (3) depend for their plausibility on the confusion between freedom and indetermination. On the supposition that man's voluntary actions are not determined, God would be unable to predict them if, like mundane scientists, He depended upon a knowledge of laws. If He is not so dependent (and there is no reason to suppose that He is), the indetermination of voluntary actions is no hindrance to his foreknowledge. For it follows from the law of excluded middle that in the instance of every one of my actions I either do *A* or I do *non-A*. If God has access to the truth, He can know which one of these alternatives is true. We conclude therefore, theologians to the contrary, that God's goodness is not incompatible with his omniscience.

Determinism and fatalism. It might be useful, finally, to call attention to the common mistake of identifying determinism—the thesis that every event is connected with antecedent events by one or more laws—with fatalism. Fatalism is a doctrine that is primarily concerned with the destiny of man. The doctrine holds that man's destiny is fixed, decided upon, and recorded in the big ledger of fate. Man's will is no match for the decrees of fate. It is futile to take measures for his welfare, his health, and his safety; for man is powerless to escape his fate. Determinism makes no such ominous statements. If we state the doctrine of fatalism in deterministic terms, it presumably holds that man's voluntary actions are superfluous in determining the circumstances under which his history upon this earth will terminate. Determinism makes no such preposterous claim. Determinism holds instead that all events, not excepting voluntary actions, are connected with preceding as well as with subsequent events by laws. Hence a man's voluntary actions constitute one of the factors in the determination of his future history. In order to predict at the present moment the nature of his eventual demise, it would be necessary to know many more laws than we do know, and it would be necessary to ascertain the state of nature as a whole at this moment. But a complete description of this state would have to include our present resolve to bring this discussion to an end.

44. An Agnostic's Apology *

LESLIE STEPHEN (1832-1904)

Let me say . . . that the whole school which refuses to transcend experience errs from the wickedness of its heart and the consequent dulness of its intellect. Some people seem to think that a plausible and happy suggestion. Let the theologian have his necessary laws of thought, which enable him to evolve truth beyond all need of verification from experience. Where will the process end? The question answers itself. The path has been trodden again and again, till it is as familiar as the first rule of arithmetic. Admit that the mind can reason about the Absolute and the Infinite, and you will get to the position of Spinoza, or to a position substantially equivalent. In fact, the chain of reasoning is substantially too short and simple to be for a moment doubtful. Theology, if logical, leads straight to Pantheism. The Infinite God is everything. All things are bound together as cause and effect. God, the first cause, is the cause of all effects down to the most remote. In one form or other, that is the conclusion to which all theology approximates as it is pushed to its legitimate result.

Here, then, we have an apparent triumph over Agnosticism. But nobody can accept Spinoza without rejecting all the doctrines for which the Gnostics really contend. In the first place, revelation and the God of revelation disappear. The argument according to Spinoza against supernaturalism differs from the argument according to Hume in being more peremptory. Hume only denies that a past miracle can be proved by evidence: Spinoza denies that it could ever have happened. As a fact, miracles and a local revelation were first assailed by Deists more effectually than by sceptics. The old Theology was seen to be unworthy of the God of nature, before it was said that nature could not be regarded through the theological representation. And, in the next place, the orthodox assault upon the value of Pantheism is irresistible. Pantheism can give no ground for morality, for nature is as much the cause of vice as the cause

---

* Sir Leslie Stephen, An Agnostic's Apology (London: Smith, Elder & Co., 1903). Reprinted by permission.

of virtue; it can give no ground for an optimist view of the universe, for nature causes evil as much as it causes good. We no longer doubt, it is true, whether there be a God, for our God means all reality; but every doubt which we entertained about the universe is transferred to the God upon whom the universe is moulded. The attempt to transfer to pure being or to the abstraction Nature the feelings with which we are taught to regard a person of transcendent wisdom and benevolence is, as theologians assert, hopeless. To deny the existence of God is in this sense the same as to deny the existence of no-God. We keep the old word; we have altered the whole of its contents. A Pantheist is, as a rule, one who looks upon the universe through his feelings instead of his reason, and who regards it with love because his habitual frame of mind is amiable. But he has no logical argument as against the Pessimist, who regards it with dread unqualified by love, or the Agnostic, who finds it impossible to regard it with any but a colourless emotion.

The Gnostic, then, gains nothing by admitting the claims of a faculty which at once overturns his conclusions. His second step is invariably to half-retract his first. We are bound by a necessary law of thought, he tells us, to believe in universal causation. Very well, then, let us be Pantheists. No, he says; another necessary law of thought tells us that causation is not universal. We know that the will is free, or, in other words, that the class of phenomena most important to us is not caused. This is the position of the ordinary Deist; and it is of vital importance to him, for otherwise the connection between Deism and morality is, on his own ground, untenable. The ablest and most logical thinkers have declared that the free-will doctrine involves a fallacy, and have unravelled the fallacy to their own satisfaction. Whether right or wrong, they have at least this advantage, that, on their showing, reason is on this point consistent with itself. The advocate of free-will, on the other hand, declares that an insoluble antinomy occurs at the very threshold of his speculations. An uncaused phenomenon is unthinkable; yet consciousness testifies that our actions, so far as they are voluntary, are uncaused. In face of such a contradiction, the only rational state of mind is scepticism. A mind balanced between two necessary and contradictory thoughts must be in a hopeless state of doubt. The Gnostic, therefore, starts by proclaiming that we must all be Agnostics in regard to a matter of primary philosophical importance. If by free-will he means anything else than a denial of causation, his statement is irrelevant.

For, it must be noticed, this is not one of the refined speculative problems which may be neglected in our ordinary reasoning. The ancient puzzles about the one and the many, or the infinite and the finite, may or may not be insoluble. They do not affect our practical knowledge. Familiar difficulties have been raised as to our conceptions of motion: the hare and tortoise problem may be revived by modern metaphysicians; but the mathematician may continue to calculate the movements of the planets and never doubt whether the quicker body will, in fact, overtake the slower. The free-will problem cannot be thus shirked. We all admit that a competent reasoner can foretell the motions of the moon; and we admit it because we know that there is no element of objective chance in the problem. But the determinist asserts, whilst the libertarian denies, that it would be possible for an adequate intelligence to foretell the actions of a man or a race. There is or is not an element of objective chance in the question; and whether there is or is not must be decided by reason and observation, independently of those puzzles about the infinite and the finite, which affect equally the man and the planet. The antideterminist asserts the existence of chance so positively, that he doubts whether God Himself can foretell the future of humanity; or, at least, he is unable to reconcile Divine prescience with his favorite doctrine.

In most practical questions, indeed, the difference is of little importance. The believer in free-will admits that we can make an approximate guess; the determinist admits that our faculty of calculation is limited. But when we turn to the problems with which he Gnostic desires to deal, the problem is of primary importance. Free-will is made responsible for all the moral evil in the world. God made man perfect, but He gave His creature free will. The exercise of that free-will has converted the world into a scene in which the most striking fact, as Newman tells us, is the absence of the Creator. It follows, then, that all this evil, the sight of which leads some of us to Atheism, some to blank despair, and some to Epicurean indifference, and the horror of which is at the root of every vigorous religious creed, results from accident. If even God

could have foretold it, He foretold it in virtue of faculties inconceivable to finite minds; and no man, however exalted his faculties,
could by any possibility have foretold it. Here, then, is Agnosticism
in the highest degree. An inexorable necessity of thought makes it
absolutely impossible for us to say whether this world is the ante-
room to heaven or hell. We do not know, nay, it is intrinsically
impossible for us to know, whether the universe is to be a source
of endless felicity or a ghastly and everlasting torture-house. The
Gnostic invites us to rejoice because the existence of an infinitely
good and wise Creator is a guarantee for our happiness. He adds,
in the same breath, that this good and wise Being has left it to
chance whether His creatures shall all, or in any proportion, go
straight to the devil. He reviles the Calvinist, who dares to think
that God has settled the point by His arbitrary will. Is an arbitrary
decision better or worse than a trusting to chance? We know that
there is a great First Cause; but we add that there are at this moment in the world some twelve hundred million little first causes
which may damn or save themselves as they please.

The free-will hypothesis is the device by which theologians try to
relieve God of the responsibility for the sufferings of His creation.
It is required for another purpose. It enables the Creator to be
also the judge. Man must be partly independent of God, or God
would be at once pulling the wires and punishing the puppets. So
far the argument is unimpeachable; but the device justifies God at
the expense of making the universe a moral chaos. Grant the existence of this arbitrary force called free-will, and we shall be forced
to admit that, if justice is to be found anywhere, it is at least not to
be found in this strange anarchy, where chance and fate are struggling for the mastery.

The fundamental proposition of the anti-determinist, that which
contains the whole pith and substance of his teaching, is this: that
a determined action cannot be meritorious. Desert can only accrue
in respect of actions which are self-caused, or in so far as they are
self-caused; and self-caused is merely a periphrasis for uncaused.
Now no one dares to say that our conduct is entirely self-caused.
The assumption is implied in every act of our lives and every speculation about history that men's actions are determined, exclusively
or to a great extent, by their character and their circumstances.

Only so far as that doctrine is true can human nature be the subject of any reasoning whatever; for reason is but the reflection of external regularity, and vanishes with the admission of chance. Our conduct, then, is the resultant of the two forces, which we may call fate and free-will. Fate is but the name for the will of God. He is responsible for placing us with a certain character in a certain position; He cannot justly punish us for the consequences; we are responsible to Him for the effects of our free-will alone, if free-will exists. That is the very contention of the anti-determinist; let us look for a moment at the consequences.

The ancient difficulty which has perplexed men since the days of Job is this: Why are happiness and misery arbitrarily distributed? Why do the good so often suffer, and the evil so often flourish? The difficulty, says the determinist, arises entirely from applying the conception of justice where it is manifestly out of place. The advocate of free-will refuses this escape, and is perplexed by a further difficulty. Why are virtue and vice arbitrarily distributed? Of all the puzzles of this dark world, or of all forms of the one great puzzle, the most appalling is that which meets us at the corner of every street. Look at the children growing up amidst moral poison; see the brothel and the public-house turning out harlots and drunkards by the thousand; at the brutalised elders preaching cruelty and shamelessness by example; and deny, if you can, that lust and brutality are generated as certainly as scrofula and typhus. Nobody dares to deny it. All philanthropists admit it; and every hope of improvement is based on the assumption that the moral character is determined by its surroundings. What does the theological advocate of free-will say to reconcile such a spectacle with our moral conceptions? Will God damn all these wretches for faults due to causes as much beyond their power as the shape of their limbs or as the orbits of the planets? Or will He make some allowance, and decline to ask for grapes from thistles, and exact purity of life from beings born in corruption, breathing corruption, and trained in corruption? Let us try each alternative.

To Job's difficulty it has been replied that, though virtue is not always rewarded and vice punished, yet virtue *as such* is rewarded, and vice *as such* is punished. If that be true, God, on the free-will hypothesis, must be unjust. Virtue and vice, as the facts irresistibly

prove, are caused by fate or by God's will as well as by free-will—
that is, our own will. To punish a man brought up in a London
slum by the rule applicable to a man brought up at the feet of Christ
is manifestly the height of injustice. Nay, for anything we can tell
— for we know nothing of the circumstances of their birth and education — the effort which Judas Iscariot exerted in restoring the
price of blood may have required a greater force of free-will than
would have saved Peter from denying his Master. Moll Flanders
may put forth more power to keep out of the lowest depths of vice
than a girl brought up in a convent to kill herself by ascetic aus-
terities. If, in short, reward is proportioned to virtue, it cannot be
proportioned to the free-will, which is only one of the factors of
virtue. The apparent injustice may, of course, be remedied by some
unknowable compensation; but for all that appears, it is the height
of injustice to reward equally equal attainments under entirely different conditions. In other words, the theologian has raised a
difficulty from which he can only escape by the help of Agnosticism.
Justice is not to be found in the visible arrangements of the universe.

Let us, then, take the other alternative. Assume that rewards
are proportioned, not to virtue, but to merit. God will judge us by
what we have done for ourselves, not by the tendencies which He
has impressed upon us. The difficulty is disguised, for it is not
diminished, and morality is degraded. A man should be valued,
say all the deepest moralists, by his nature, not by his external acts;
by what he is, not by how he came to be what he is. Virtue is
heaven, and vice is hell. Divine rewards and punishments are not
arbitrarily annexed, but represent the natural state of a being
brought into harmony with the supreme law, or in hopeless conflict
with it. We need a change of nature, not a series of acts uncon-
nected with our nature. Virtue is a reality precisely in so far as it
is a part of nature, not of accident; of our fate, not of our free-
will. The assertion in some shape of these truths has been at the
bottom of all great moral and religious reforms. The attempt to
patch up some compromise between this and the opposite theory
has generated those endless controversies about grace and free-will
on which no Christian Church has ever been able to make up its
mind, and which warn us that we are once more plunging into Agnosticism. In order to make the Creator the judge, you assume that

part of man's actions are his own. Only on that showing can he have merit as against his Maker. Admitting this, and only if we admit this, we get a footing for the debtor and creditor theories of morality — for the doctrine that man runs up a score with Heaven in respect of that part of his conduct which is uncaused. Thus we have a ground for the various theories of merit by which priests have thriven and Churches been corrupted; but it is at the cost of splitting human nature in two, and making happiness depend upon those acts which are not really part of our true selves.

It is not, however, my purpose to show the immorality or the unreasonableness of the doctrine. I shall only remark that it is essentially agnostic. Only in so far as phenomena embody fixed 'laws' can we have any ground for inference in this world, and, *à fortiori*, from this world to the next. If happiness is the natural consequence of virtue, we may plausibly argue that the virtuous will be happy hereafter. If heaven be a bonus arbitrarily bestowed upon the exercise of an inscrutable power, all analogies break down. The merit of an action as between men depends upon the motives. The actions for which God rewards and punishes are the actions or those parts of actions which are independent of motive. Punishment amongst men is regulated by some considerations of its utility to the criminal or his fellows. No conceivable measure of Divine punishment can even be suggested when once we distinguish between divine and natural; and the very essence of the theory is that such a distinction exists. For whatever may be true of the next world, we begin by assuming that new principles are to be called into play hereafter. The new world is summoned into being to redress the balance of tne old. The fate which here too often makes the good miserable and the bad happy, which still more strangely fetters our wills and forces the strong will to goodness, will then be suspended. The motive which persuades us to believe in the good arrangement hereafter is precisely the badness of this. Such a motive to believe cannot itself be a reason for belief. That would be to believe because belief was unreasonable. This world, once more, is a chaos, in which the most conspicuous fact is the absence of the Creator. Nay, it is so chaotic that, according to theologians, infinite rewards and penalties are required to square the account and redress the injustice here accumulated.

What is this, so far as the natural reason is concerned, but the very superlative of agnosticism? The appeal to experience can lead to nothing, for our very object is to contradict experience. We appeal to facts to show that facts are illusory. The appeal to *à priori* is not more hopeful for you begin by showing that reason on these matters is self-contradictory, and you insist that human nature is radically irregular, and there beyond the sphere of reason. If you could succeed in deducing any theory by reason, reason would, on your showing, be at hopeless issue with experience.

There are two questions, in short, about the universe which must be answered to escape from Agnosticism. The great fact which puzzles the mind is the vast amount of evil. It may be answered that evil is an illusion, because God is benevolent; or it may be answered that evil is deserved, because God is just. In one case the doubt is removed by denying the existence of the difficulty, in the other it is made tolerable by satisfying our consciences. We have seen what natural reason can do towards justifying these answers. To escape from Agnosticism we become Pantheists; then the divine reality must be the counterpart of phenomenal nature, and all the difficulties recur. We escape from Pantheism by the illogical device of free-will. Then God is indeed good and wise, but God is no longer omnipotent. By His side we erect a fetish called free-will, which is potent enough to defeat all God's good purposes, and to make His absence from His own universe the most conspicuous fact given by observation; and which, at the same time, is by its own nature intrinsically arbitrary in its action. Your Gnosticism tells us that an almighty benevolence is watching over everything, and bringing good out of all evil. Whence, then, comes the evil? By free-will; that is, by chance! It is an exception, an exception which covers, say, half the phenomena, and includes all that puzzle us. Say boldly at once no explanation can be given, and then proceed to denounce Agnosticism. If, again, we take the moral problem, the Pantheist view shows desert as before God to be a contradiction in terms. We are what He has made us; nay, we are but manifestations of Himself — how can He complain? Escape from the dilemma by making us independent of God, and God, so far as the observed universe can tell us, becomes systematically unjust. He rewards the good and the bad, and gives equal reward to the free agent and the slave of fate. Where are we to turn for a solution?

[NOTE: The bibliography for Chapter Four appears on page 520.]

Chapter Five

CHURCH AND STATE

INTRODUCTION

When two authorities, such as Church and State, both claim dominion over important overlapping areas of man's life, he is confronted by a nice problem of conflicting loyalties.

Some of the outstanding solutions of this problem are offered in the selections of this chapter.

The classical view of the Roman Catholic Church was expressed by St. Augustine (354-430), who held that the Church should be supreme in the political as well as the religious domain, and should have the right to compel obedience to its teachings, for example, by punishing heretics and depriving them of civil rights.

An opposing view of church-state relations was offered by the philosopher Thomas Hobbes (1588-1679) (Selection 45). The problem, as put by Hobbes, is: How can we decide whether to obey God or man, when their commandments are contrary to one another? He solves it neatly by contending that the only law of God that we need worry about is the commandment that we obey our civil sovereigns, for "to resist a civil sovereign is to sin against the laws of God."

Between the positions of St. Augustine, who stood for complete Church dominance, and Hobbes, who advocated complete State dominance, there are many intermediate positions.

Spinoza (1632-1677) (Selection 46) held that since it is the sovereign's duty to maintain the peace, he must have spiritual as well as temporal rights. For if someone else had the power of deciding what is pious or impious, he could veto the acts of the sovereign, and ultimately control him. Spinoza had in mind here only the external rites of religion. Insofar as a man's own beliefs or modes of worship are concerned, he held that the ruler should have no authority. In fact, this is a matter over which he *can* have no authority, since

... no one the whole world over can be forced or legislated into a state of blessedness; the means required for such a consummation are faithful and brotherly admonition, sound education, and above all, free use of the individual judgment. Therefore, as the supreme right of free thinking, even on religion, is in every man's power, and as it is inconceivable that such power could be alienated, it is also in every man's power to wield the supreme right of free judgment in this behalf, and to explain and interpret religion for himself.

Only when questions of public right are involved does the authority of the sovereign take precedence over that of the individual.

John Locke, a contemporary of Spinoza, agreed. He also thought it necessary to distinguish the business of civil government from that of religion, in order to put an end to the controversies that were always arising between the two. It is not the business of the sovereign to tell a man how to get to heaven. "The care of every man's soul," he said, "belongs unto himself." Locke gives several reasons for limiting the sovereign's power. One is that this power consists in outward force, while religion consists in the inward persuasion of the mind. Another reason, and one which had an important influence on such fathers of the Republic as Thomas Jefferson and James Madison, stems from the "variety and contradictions of opinions in religion, wherein the princes of the world are as much divided as in their secular interests." Since one prince would not be more likely to have the exclusive truth in religion than another, while each would think he had, the result would be a desire on the part of each to lead a holy crusade to save men's souls, which would end in war and mutual destruction. Locke's remedy is the principle of mutual toleration of private persons and of churches differing from one another in religion. His views, first presented in his "Essay Concerning Toleration," written in 1667, were revised in 1689, the year of the English Act of Toleration, under the title: *A Letter Concerning Toleration* (Selection 47). It is now recognized that the variety of opposing sects, both in England and in the Colonies, was a potent force in bringing about religious freedom. Voltaire put it with his usual felicity when he said, "If there were one religion in England, its despotism would be terrible; if there were only two, they would destroy each other; but there are thirty, and therefore they live in peace and happiness."

In 1790, while Edmund Burke lectured his countrymen on the necessity of retaining their established church, and of resisting the influence of the revolutionaries in France, across the Atlantic the States were ratifying the Bill of Rights which provided (Amendment I) "that Congress shall make no law respecting an establishment of religion or prohibiting the free exercise thereof. . . ." The selections from Jefferson and Madison, both strongly under the influence of Locke, show how the early battles against an established church, and for religious freedom, were fought and won.

In 1779 Jefferson introduced into the Virginia legislature "An Act for Establishing Religious Freedom" (Selection 48) in which he proclaimed that "no man shall be compelled to frequent or support any religious worship, place or ministry whatsoever, nor shall be enforced, restrained, molested, or burthened in his body or goods, nor shall otherwise suffer on account of his religious opinions or belief; but that all men shall be free to profess, and by argument to maintain, their opinions in matters of religion, and that the same shall in no wise diminish, enlarge, or affect their civil capacities." During the long-drawn-out debate on this Act, there was introduced "A Bill Establishing a Provision for Teachers of the Christian Religion,"* to provide funds for such teachers by an assessment on all citizens. It was in answer to this bill that Madison wrote his famous *Memorial and Remonstrance against Religious Assessments* (Selection 49), in which he gives fifteen reasons for opposing the bill. Religion, he held, was the concern of the individual, but not of the legislature. "Who does not see," he wrote, "that the same authority which can

---

* See p. 408, this volume.

establish Christianity, in exclusion of all other religions, may establish, with the same ease, any particular sect of Christians, in exclusion of all other sects? That the same authority which can force a citizen to contribute three pence only of his property for the support of any one establishment, may force him to conform to any other establishment in all cases whatsoever?" The bill was defeated and Jefferson's Act passed after seven years of controversy.

But today, more than a century and a half later, we are still plagued by dissension, often bitter, on the proper role of the State in matters concerning religion. May a state use tax monies collected from all its citizens to pay for the bus transportation of children to parochial schools? The Supreme Court ruled in the Everson Case (1947) (Selection 52) that the State of New Jersey may do just that. But the decision was hard and close (5-4).

Another perplexing question is whether the various Released Time programs in the public schools, whereby children are given religious training during school hours, are a breach of the First Amendment. We offer in the opinions of Justices Black, Rutledge, Douglas, and Jackson, and in the statement of the Roman Catholic Bishops (1948), many opposing views on these timely subjects.

In the Everson decision (Selection 52), Justice Black, speaking for the Court, said that according to the Constitution, neither the Federal government nor a state government may "pass laws which aid one religion, *aid all religions,* or prefer one religion over another." [1] This view, especially insofar as the italicized portion is concerned, has aroused much debate. Opponents of the view are wont to cite various proclamations by judges that although all religions are equal before the law, nevertheless this is a Christian nation both historically and in its ethical ideals. One of the best known statements is that of Justice David J. Brewer:

"Still again, this is a Christian nation. Not that the people have made it so by any legal enactment, or that there exists an established church, but Christian in the sense that the dominant thought and purpose of the nation accord with the great principles taught by the founder of Christianity." [2]

T. S. Eliot (Selection 50) holds that our society is not a Christian

---

[1] Italics not in original.

[2] Quoted by A. P. Stokes, *Church and State in the United States,* Vol. III, Chap. XXIV, p. 598. See this chapter for a summary and appraisal of the entire controversy. Also Leo Pfeffer, *Church, State, and Freedom,* p. 210–214.

society, but a neutral one; that although our culture is "vestigial of a positive Christianity, it has already advanced [far] towards something else." His tract is an attempt to show the difference between a neutral society ("the society in which we live at present") and a Christian society, which he would like to see. The chief fault of modern society, according to Eliot—and this would be true both of Britain and our own country—is the divorce between religion and politics.

Maritain strikes the same note when he says that the ideals of freedom, equality, and universal brotherhood cannot be attained by political methods and agencies alone, but only when bolstered by a genuine religious fervor, that in fact democracy cannot survive unless the people become infused by the spirit of the Gospels. His *Christianity and Democracy*, from which our selection is drawn (Selection 51) was written during the dark days of the Second World War, in 1942.

For other positions on the relation of church and state the reader is referred to the bibliography on page 521.

D. J. B.

45. How to Reconcile the Obedience Due to Our Civil Sovereign with That Due to God *

THOMAS HOBBES *(1588–1679)*

The most frequent pretext of sedition, and civil war, in Christian commonwealths, hath a long time proceeded from a difficulty, not yet sufficiently resolved, of obeying at once both God and man, then when their commandments are one contrary to the other. It is manifest enough, that when a man receiveth two contrary commands, and knows that one of them is God's, he ought to obey that, and

* An excerpt from the *Leviathan*, first published in 1651.

not the other, though it be the command even of his lawful sovereign, (whether a monarch, or a sovereign assembly), or the command of his father. The difficulty therefore consisteth in this, that men, when they are commanded in the name of God, know not in divers cases, whether the command be from God, or whether he that commandeth do but abuse God's name for some private ends of his own. For as there were in the Church of the Jews, many false prophets, that sought reputation with the people, by feigned dreams and visions; so there have been in all times in the Church of Christ, false teachers, that seek reputation with the people, by fantastical and false doctrines; and by such reputation, (as is the nature of ambition), to govern them for their private benefit.

But this difficulty of obeying both God and the civil sovereign on earth, to those that can distinguish between what is *necessary,* and what is not *necessary for their reception into the kingdom of God,* is of no moment. For if the command of the civil sovereign be such, as that it may be obeyed without the forfeiture of life eternal; not to obey it is unjust; and the precept of the apostle takes place: *Servants obey your masters in all things;* and *Children obey your parents in all things;* and the precept of our Saviour, *The Scribes and Pharisees sit in Moses' chair; all therefore they shall say, that observe and do.* But if the command be such as cannot be obeyed, without being damned to eternal death; then it were madness to obey it, and the council of our Saviour takes place, (*Matth.* x. 28), *Fear not those that kill the body, but cannot kill the soul.* All men therefore that would avoid, both the punishments that are to be in this world inflicted, for disobedience to their earthly sovereign, and those that shall be inflicted in the world to come, for disobedience to God, have need be taught to distinguish well between what is, and what is not necessary to eternal salvation.

All that is NECESSARY *to salvation,* is contained in two virtues, *faith in Christ,* and *obedience to laws.* The latter of these, if it were perfect, were enough to us. But because we are all guilty of disobedience to God's law, not only originally in Adam, but also actually by our own transgressions, there is required at our hands now, not only *obedience* for the rest of our time, but also a *remission of sins* for the time past; which remission is the reward of our faith in Christ. That nothing else is necessarily required to salvation, is manifest from this, that the kingdom of heaven is shut to none but to sinners; that is to say, to the disobedient, or transgressors of the law; nor to them, in case they repent, and believe all the articles of Christian faith necessary to salvation.

The obedience required at our hands by God, that accepteth in all our actions the will for the deed, is a serious endeavour to obey him; and is called also by all such names as signify that endeavour. And therefore obedience is sometimes called by the names of *charity* and *love*, because they imply a will to obey; and our Saviour himself maketh our love to God, and to one another, a fulfilling of the whole law: and sometimes by the name of *righteousness;* for righteousness is but the will to give to every one his own; that is to say, the will to obey the laws: and sometimes by the name of *repentance;* because to repent, implieth a turning away from sin, which is the same with the return of the will to obedience. Whosoever therefore unfeignedly desireth to fulfill the commandments of God, or repenteth him truly of his transgressions, or that loveth God with all his heart, and his neighbour as himself, hath all the obedience necessary to his reception into the kingdom of God. For if God should require perfect innocence, there could no flesh be saved.

But what commandments are those that God hath given us? Are all those laws which were given to the Jews by the hand of Moses, the commandments of God? If they be, why are not Christians taught to obey them? If they be not, what others are so, besides the law of nature? For our Saviour Christ hath not given us new laws, but counsel to observe those we are subject to; that is to say, the laws of nature, and the laws of our several sovereigns: nor did he make any new law to the Jews in his sermon on the Mount, but only expounded the law of Moses, to which they were subject before. The laws of God therefore are none but the laws of nature, whereof the principal is, that we should not violate our faith, that is, a commandment to obey our civil sovereigns, which we constituted over us by mutual pact one with another. And this law of God, that commandeth obedience to the law civil, commandeth by consequence obedience to all the precepts of the Bible; which, as I have proved in the precedent chapter, is there only law, where the civil sovereign hath made it so; and in other places, but counsel; which a man at his own peril may without injustice refuse to obey. . . .

Having thus shown what is necessary to salvation; it is not hard to reconcile our obedience to God, with our obedience to the civil sovereign; who is either Christian, or infidel. If he be a Christian, he alloweth the belief of this article, that *Jesus is the Christ;* and of all the articles that are contained in, or are by evident consequence deduced from it: which is all the faith necessary to salvation. And because he is a sovereign, he requireth obedience to all his own, that is, to all the civil laws; in which also are contained all the laws of nature, that is all the laws of God: for besides the laws of nature, and the laws of the Church, which are part of the civil law, (for the Church that can make laws is the commonwealth), there be no other laws divine. Whosoever therefore obeyeth his Christian sovereign, is not thereby hindered, neither from believing, nor from obeying God. But suppose that a Christian king should from this foundation *Jesus is the Christ,* draw some false consequences, that is to say, make some superstructions of hay or stubble, and command the teaching of the same; yet seeing St. Paul says he shall be saved; much more shall he be saved, that teacheth them by his command; and much more yet, he that teaches not, but only believes his lawful teacher. And in case a subject be forbidden by the civil sovereign to profess some of those his opinions, upon what just ground can he disobey? Christian kings may err in deducing a consequence, but who shall judge? Shall a private man judge, when the question is of his own obedience? Or shall any man judge but he that is appointed thereto by the Church, that is, by the civil sovereign that representeth it? Or if the pope, or an apostle judge, may he not err in deducing of a consequence? Did not one of the two, St. Peter or St. Paul, err in a superstructure, when St. Paul withstood St. Peter to his face? There can therefore be no contradiction between the laws of God, and the laws of a Christian commonwealth.

And when the civil sovereign is an infidel, every one of his own subjects that resisteth him, sinneth against the laws of God, (for such are the laws of nature), and rejecteth the counsel of the apostles, that admonisheth all Christians to obey their princes, and all children and servants to obey their parents and masters in all things. And for their *faith,* it is internal, and invisible; they have the license that Naaman had,[1] and need not put themselves into danger for it. But if they do, they ought to expect their reward in heaven, and not complain of their lawful sovereign; much less make war upon him. For he that is not glad of any just occasion of martyrdom, has not the faith he professeth, but pretends it only, to set some colour upon his own contumacy. But what infidel king is so unreasonable, as knowing he has a subject, that waiteth for the second coming of Christ, after the present world shall be burnt, and intendeth then to obey him, (which is the intent of believing that Jesus is the Christ), and in the mean time thinketh himself bound to obey the laws of that infidel king, (which all Christians are obliged in conscience to do), to put to death or to persecute such a subject?

And thus much shall suffice, concerning the kingdom of God, and policy ecclesiastical. Wherein I pretend not to advance any position of my own, but only to show what are the consequences that seem to me deducible from the principles of Christian politics, (which are the holy Scriptures), in confirmation of the power of civil sovereigns, and the duty of their subjects.

46. Relations Between Church and State *

BENEDICT SPINOZA (1632–1677)

It is shown that the right over matters spiritual lies wholly with the sovereign, and that the outward forms of religion should be in accordance with public peace, if we would obey God aright.

When I said that the possessors of sovereign power have rights over everything, and that all rights are dependent on their decree, I did not merely mean temporal rights, but also spiritual rights; of the latter, no less than the former, they ought to be the interpreters

---

[1] [To obey his sovereign, Naaman is compelled to bow before an idol, and in effect to deny the God of his choice. His action is approved by Elisha, and Hobbes also holds him guiltless. Since belief is a matter of the heart, not of the lips, it is permissible, according to Hobbes, for a subject to obey his sovereign outwardly without really believing what he professes. Since he is acting under compulsion, the belief is, in effect, not really his own, but that of his sovereign. See *Leviathan*, Chapter 42.]

* From *A Theologico-Political Treatise*, Chap. XIX.

and the champions. I wish to draw special attention to this point, and to discuss it fully in this chapter, because many persons deny that the right of deciding religious questions belongs to the sovereign power, and refuse to acknowledge it as the interpreter of Divine right. They accordingly assume full license to accuse and arraign it, nay, even to excommunicate it from the Church, as Ambrosius treated the Emperor Theodosius in old time. However, I will show later on in this chapter that they take this means of dividing the government, and paving the way to their own ascendency. I wish, however, first to point out that religion acquires its force as law solely from the decrees of the sovereign. God has no special kingdom among men except in so far as He reigns through temporal rulers. Moreover, the rites of religion and the outward observances of piety should be in accordance with the public peace and well-being, and should therefore be determined by the sovereign power alone. I speak here only of the outward observances of piety and the external rites of religion, not of piety itself, nor of the inward worship of God, nor the means by which the mind is inwardly led to do homage to God in singleness of heart.

Inward worship of God and piety in itself are within the sphere of everyone's private rights, and cannot be alienated (as I showed at the end of Chapter VII.) What I here mean by the Kingdom of God is, I think, sufficiently clear from what has been said in Chapter XIV. I there showed that a man best fulfils God's law who worships Him, according to His command, through acts of justice and charity; it follows, therefore, that wherever justice and charity have the force of law and ordinance, there is God's kingdom.

I recognize no difference between the cases where God teaches and commands the practice of justice and charity through our natural faculties, and those where He makes special revelations; nor is the form of the revelation of importance so long as such practice is revealed and becomes a sovereign and supreme law to men. If, therefore, I show that justice and charity can only acquire the force of right and law through the rights of rulers, I shall be able readily to arrive at the conclusion (seeing that the rights of rulers are in the possession of the sovereign), that religion can only acquire the force of right by means of those who have the right to command, and that God only rules among men through the instrumentality of earthly potentates. It follows from what has been said, that the practice of justice and charity only acquires the force of law through the rights of the sovereign authority; for we showed in Chapter XVI. that in the state of nature reason has no more rights than desire, but that men living either by the laws of the former or the laws of the latter, possess rights co-extensive with their powers.

For this reason we could not conceive sin to exist in the state of nature, nor imagine God as a judge punishing man's transgressions; but we supposed all things to happen according to the general laws of universal nature, there being no difference between pious and impious, between him that was pure (as Solomon says) and him that was impure, because there was no possibility either of justice or charity.

In order that the true doctrines of reason, that is (as we showed in Chapter IV.), the true Divine doctrines might obtain absolutely the force of law and right, it was necessary that each individual should cede his natural right, and transfer it either to society as a whole, or to a certain body of men, or to one man. Then, and not till then, does it first dawn upon us what is justice and what is injustice, what is equity and what is inequity.

Justice, therefore, and absolutely all the precepts of reason, including love towards one's neighbour, receive the force of laws and ordinances solely through the rights of dominion, that is (as we showed in the same chapter) solely on the decrees of those who possess the right to rule. Inasmuch as the kingdom of God consists entirely in rights applied to justice and charity or to true religion, it follows that (as we asserted) the kingdom of God can only exist among men through the means of the sovereign powers; nor does it make any difference whether religion be apprehended by our natural faculties or by revelation: the argument is sound in both cases, inasmuch as religion is one and the same, and is equally revealed by God, whatever be the manner in which it becomes known to men.

Thus, in order that the religion revealed by the prophets might have the force of law among the Jews, it was necessary that every man of them should yield up his natural right, and that all should, with one accord, agree that they would only obey such commands as God should reveal to them through the prophets. Just as we have shown to take place in a democracy, where men with one consent agree to live according to the dictates of reason. Although the Hebrews furthermore transferred their right to God, they were able to do so rather in theory than in practice, for, as a matter of fact (as we pointed out above) they absolutely retained the right of dominion till they transferred it to Moses, who in his turn became absolute king, so that it was only through him that God reigned over the Hebrews. For this reason (namely, that religion only acquires the force of law by means of the sovereign power) Moses was not able to punish those who, before the covenant, and consequently while still in possession of their rights, violated the Sabbath (Exod. xvi. 27), but was able to do so after the covenant (Numb. xv. 36), because everyone had then yielded up his natural rights, and the ordinance of the Sabbath had received the force of law.

Lastly, for the same reason, after the destruction of the Hebrew dominion, revealed religion ceased to have the force of law; for we cannot doubt that as soon as the Jews transferred their right to the king of Babylon, the kingdom of God and the Divine right forthwith ceased. For the covenant wherewith they promised to obey all the utterances of God was abrogated; God's kingdom, which was based thereupon, also ceased. The Hebrews could no longer abide thereby, inasmuch as their rights no longer belonged to them but to the king of Babylon, whom (as we showed in Chapter XVI.) they were bound to obey in all things. Jeremiah (chap. xxix, verse 7) expressly admonishes them of this fact: "And seek the peace of the city, whither I have caused you to be carried away captives, and pray unto the Lord for it; for in the peace thereof shall ye have peace." Now, they could not seek the peace of the city as having a share in its government, but only as slaves, being, as they were, captives; by obedience in all things, with a view to avoiding seditions, and by observing all the laws of the country, however different from their own. It is thus abundantly evident that religion among the Hebrews only acquired the form of law through the right of the sovereign rule; when that rule was destroyed, it could no longer be received as the law of a particular kingdom, but only as the universal precept of reason. I say of reason, for the universal religion had not yet become known by revelation. We may therefore draw the general conclusion that religion, whether revealed through our natural faculties or through prophets, receives the force of a command solely through the decrees

of the holders of sovereign power; and, further, that God has no
special kingdom among men, except in so far as He reigns through
earthly potentates.

We may now see in a clearer light what was stated in Chapter IV.,
namely, that all the decrees of God involve eternal truth and necessity, so that we cannot conceive God as a prince or legislator giving
laws to mankind. For this reason the Divine precepts, whether revealed through our natural faculties, or through prophets, do not
receive immediately from God the force of a command, but only
from those, or through the mediation of those, who possess the right
of ruling and legislating. It is only through these latter means that
God rules among men, and directs human affairs with justice and
equity.

This conclusion is supported by experience, for we find traces
of Divine justice only in places where just mean bear sway; elsewhere the same lot (to repeat again Solomon's words) befalls the
just and the unjust, the pure and the impure: a state of things which
causes Divine Providence to be doubted by many who think that
God immediately reigns among men, and directs all nature for their
benefit.

As, then, both reason and experience tell us that the Divine right
is entirely dependent on the decrees of secular rulers, it follows that
secular rulers are its proper interpreters. How this is so we shall now
see, for it is time to show that the outward observances of religion,
and all the external practices of piety should be brought into accordance with the public peace and well-being if we would obey God
rightly. When this has been shown we shall easily understand how
the sovereign rulers are the proper interpreters of religion and piety.

It is certain that duties towards one's country are the highest that
man can fulfil; for, if government be taken away, no good thing
can last, all falls into dispute, anger and anarchy reign unchecked
amid universal fear. Consequently there can be no duty towards
our neighbour which would not become an offence if it involved injury to the whole state, nor can there be any offence against our
duty towards our neighbour, or anything but loyalty in what we
do for the sake of preserving the state. For instance: it is in the
abstract my duty when my neighbour quarrels with me and wishes
to take my cloak, to give him my coat also; but if it be thought that

such conduct is hurtful to the maintenance of the state, I ought to bring him to trial, even at the risk of his being condemned to death. For this reason Manlius Torquatus is held up to honour, inasmuch as the public welfare outweighed with him his duty towards his children. This being so, it follows that the public welfare is the sovereign law to which all others, Divine and human, should be made to conform.

Now, it is the function of the sovereign only to decide what is necessary for the public welfare and the safety of the state, and to give orders accordingly; therefore it is also the function of the sovereign only to decide the limits of our duty towards our neighbour—in other words, to determine how we should obey God. We can now clearly understand how the sovereign is the interpreter of religion, and further, that no one can obey God rightly, if the practices of his piety do not conform to the public welfare; or, consequently, if he does not implicitly obey all the commands of the sovereign. For as by God's command we are bound to do our duty to all men without exception, and to do no man an injury, we are also bound not to help one man at another's loss, still less at a loss to the whole state. Now, no private citizen can know what is good for the state, except he learn it through the sovereign power, who alone has the right to transact public business: therefore no one can rightly practise piety or obedience to God, unless he obey the sovereign power's commands in all things. This proposition is confirmed by the facts of experience. For if the sovereign adjudge a man to be worthy of death or an enemy, whether he be a citizen or a foreigner, a private individual or a separate ruler, no subject is allowed to give him assistance. So also though the Jews were bidden to love their fellow-citizens as themselves (Levit. xix. 17, 18), they were nevertheless bound, if a man offended against the law, to point him out to the judge (Levit. v. 1, and Deut. xiii. 8, 9), and, if he should be condemned to death, to slay him (Deut. xvii. 7).

Further, in order that the Hebrews might preserve the liberty they had and might retain absolute sway over the territory they had conquered, it was necessary, as we showed in Chapter XVII., that their religion should be adapted to their particular government, and that they should separate themselves from the rest of the nations: wherefore it was commanded to them, "Love thy neighbour and hate thine enemy" (Matt. v. 43), but after they had lost their dominion and had gone into captivity in Babylon, Jeremiah bid them take thought for the safety of the state into which they had been led captive; and Christ when He saw that they would be spread over the whole world, told them to do their duty by all men without exception; all of which instances show that religion has always been made to conform to the public welfare. Perhaps someone will ask: By what right, then, did the disciples of Christ, being private citizens, preach a new religion? I answer that they did so by the right of the power which they had received from Christ against unclean spirits (see Matt. x. 1). I have already stated in Chapter XVI. that all are bound to obey a tyrant, unless they have received from God through undoubted revelation a promise of aid against him; so let no one take example from the Apostles unless he too has the power of working miracles. The point is brought out more clearly by Christ's command to His disciples, "Fear not those who kill the body" (Matt. x. 28). If this command were imposed on everyone, governments would be founded in vain, and Solomon's words (Prov. xxiv. 21), "My son, fear God and the king," would be impious, which they certainly are not; we must therefore admit that the authority which Christ gave to His disciples was given to them only, and must not be taken as an example for others.

I do not pause to consider the arguments of those who wish to separate secular rights from spiritual rights, placing the former under the control of the sovereign, and the latter under the control of the universal Church; such pretensions are too frivolous to merit refutation. I cannot, however, pass over in silence the fact that such persons are woefully deceived when they seek to support their seditious opinions (I ask pardon for the somewhat harsh epithet) by the example of the Jewish high priest, who, in ancient times, had the right of administering the sacred offices. Did not the high priests receive their right by decrees of Moses (who, as I have shown, retained the sole right to rule), and could they not by the same means be deprived of it? Moses himself chose not only Aaron, but also his son Eleazar, and his grandson Phineas, and bestowed on them the right of administering the office of high priest. This right was retained by the high priests afterwards, but none the less were they delegates of Moses—that is, of the sovereign power. Moses, as we have shown, left no successor to his dominion, but so distributed his prerogatives, that those who came after him seemed, as it were, regents who administer the government when a king is absent but not dead.

In the second commonwealth the high priests held their right absolutely, after they had obtained the rights of principality in addition. Wherefore the rights of the high priesthood always depended on the edict of the sovereign, and the high priests did not possess them till they became sovereigns also. Rights in matters spiritual always remained under the control of the kings absolutely (as I will show at the end of this chapter), except in the single particular that they were not allowed to administer in person the sacred duties in the Temple, inasmuch as they were not of the family of Aaron, and were therefore considered unclean, a reservation which would have no force in a Christian community.

We cannot, therefore, doubt that the daily sacred rites (whose performance does not require a particular genealogy but only a special mode of life, and from which the holders of sovereign power are not excluded as unclean) are under the sole control of the sovereign power; no one, save by the authority or concession of such sovereign, has the right or power of administering them, of choosing others to administer them, of defining or strengthening the foundations of the Church and her doctrines; of judging on questions of morality or acts of piety; of receiving anyone into the Church or excommunicating him therefrom, or, lastly, of providing for the poor.

Those doctrines are proved to be not only true (as we have already pointed out), but also of primary necessity for the preservation of religion and the state. We all know what weight spiritual right and authority carries in the popular mind: how everyone hangs on the lips, as it were, of those who possess it. We may even say that those who wield such authority have the most complete sway over the popular mind.

Whosoever, therefore, wishes to take this right away from the sovereign power, is desirous of dividing the dominion; from such divisions, contentions, and strife will necessarily spring up, as they did of old between the Jewish kings and high priests, and will defy all attempts to allay them. Nay, further, he who strives to deprive the sovereign power of such authority, is aiming (as we have said), at gaining dominion for himself. What is left for the sovereign power to decide on, if this right be denied him? Certainly nothing concerning either war or peace, if he has to ask another man's opinions as to whether what he believes to be beneficial would be pious or impious. Everything would depend on the verdict of him who had the right of deciding and judging what was pious or impious, right or wrong.

When such a right was bestowed on the Pope of Rome absolutely, he gradually acquired complete control over the kings, till at last he himself mounted to the summits of dominion; however much monarchs, and especially the German emperors, strove to curtail his authority, were it only by a hairsbreadth, they effected nothing, but on the contrary by their very endeavours largely increased it. That which no monarch could accomplish with fire and sword, ecclesiastics could bring about with a stroke of the pen; whereby we may easily see the force and power at the command of the Church, and also how necessary it is for sovereigns to reserve such prerogatives for themselves.

If we reflect on what was said in the last chapter we shall see that such reservation conduced not a little to the increase of religion, and piety; for we observed that the prophets themselves, although gifted with Divine efficacy, being merely private citizens, rather irritated than reformed the people by their freedom of warning, reproof, and denunciation, whereas the kings by warnings and punishments easily bent men to their will. Furthermore, the kings themselves, not possessing the right in question absolutely, very often fell away from religion and took with them nearly the whole people. The same thing has often happened from the same cause in Christian states.

Perhaps I shall be asked, "But if the holders of sovereign power choose to be wicked, who will be the rightful champion of piety? Should the sovereigns still be its interpreters?" I meet them with the counter-question, "But if ecclesiastics (who are also human, and private citizens, and who ought to mind only their own affairs), or if others whom it is proposed to entrust with spiritual authority, choose to be wicked, should they still be considered as piety's rightful interpreters?" It is quite certain that when sovereigns wish to follow their own pleasure, whether they have control over spiritual matters or not, the whole state, spiritual and secular, will go to ruin, and it will go much faster if private citizens seditiously assume the championship of the Divine rights.

Thus we see that not only is nothing gained by denying such rights to sovereigns, but on the contrary, great evil ensues. For (as happened with the Jewish kings who did not possess such rights absolutely) rulers are thus driven into wickedness, and the injury and the loss to the state become certain and inevitable, instead of uncertain and possible. Whether we look to the abstract truth, or the security of states, or the increase of piety, we are compelled to maintain that the Divine right, or the right of control over spiritual matters, depends absolutely on the decree of the sovereign, who is its legitimate interpreter and champion. Therefore the true ministers of God's word are those who teach piety to the people in obedience to the authority of the sovereign rulers by whose decree it has been brought into conformity with the public welfare.

There remains for me to point out the cause for the frequent disputes on the subject of these spiritual rights in Christian states; where the Hebrews, so far as I know, never had any doubts about the matter. It seems monstrous that a question so plain and so vitally important should thus have remained undecided, and that the secular rulers could never obtain the prerogative without controversy, nay, nor without great danger of sedition and injury to religion. If no cause for this state of things were forthcoming, I could easily persuade myself that all I have said in this chapter is mere theorizing, or a kind of speculative reasoning which can never be of any practical use. However, when we reflect on the beginnings of Christianity the cause at once becomes manifest. The Christian religion was not taught at first by kings, but by private persons, who, against the wishes of those in power, whose subjects they were, were for a long time accustomed to hold meetings in secret churches, to institute and perform sacred rites, and, on their own authority to settle and decide on their affairs without regard to the state. When, after the lapse of many years, the religion was taken up by the authorities, the ecclesiastics were obliged to teach it to the emperors themselves as they had defined it: wherefore they easily gained recognition as its teachers and interpreters, and the church pastors were looked upon as vicars of God. The ecclesiastics took good care that the Christian kings should not assume their authority, by prohibiting marriage to the chief ministers of religion and to its highest interpreter. They furthermore effected their purpose by multiplying the dogmas of religion to such an extent and so blending them with philosophy that their chief interpreter was bound to be a skilled philosopher and theologian, and to have leisure for a host of idle speculations: conditions which could only be fulfilled by a private individual with much time on his hands.

Among the Hebrews things were very differently arranged: for their Church began at the same time as their dominion, and Moses, their absolute ruler, taught religion to the people, arranged their sacred rites, and chose their spiritual ministers. Thus the royal authority carried very great weight with the people, and the kings kept a firm hold on their spiritual prerogatives.

Although, after the death of Moses, no one held absolute sway, yet the power of deciding both in matters spiritual and matters temporal was in the hands of the secular chief, as I have already pointed out. Further, in order that it might be taught religion and piety, the people was bound to consult the supreme judge no less than the high priest (Deut. xvii. 9, 11). Lastly, though the kings had not as much power as Moses, nearly the whole arrangement and choice of the sacred ministry depended on their decision. Thus David arranged the whole service of the Temple (see 1 Chron. xxviii. 11, 12, &c.) ; from all the Levites he chose twenty-four thousand for the sacred psalms; six thousand of these formed the body from which were chosen the judges and praetors, four thousand were porters, and four thousand to play on instruments (see 1 Chron. xxiii. 4, 5). He further divided them into companies (of whom he chose the chiefs), so that each in rotation, at the allotted time, might perform the sacred rites. The priests he also divided into as many companies; I will not go through the whole catalogue, but refer the reader to 2 Chron. viii. 13, where it is stated, "Then Solomon offered burnt offerings to the Lord . . . . after a certain rate every day, offering according to the commandments of Moses:" and in verse 14, "And he appointed, according to the order of David his father the courses of the priests to their service . . . for so had

David the man of God commanded." Lastly, the historian bears witness in verse 15: "And they departed not from the command- ment of the king unto the priests and Levites concerning any mat- ter, or concerning the treasuries."

From these and other histories of the kings, it is abundantly evi- dent that the whole practice of religion and the sacred ministry depended entirely on the commands of the king.

When I said above that the kings had not the same right as Moses to elect the high priest, to consult God without intermediaries, and to condemn the prophets who prophesied during their reign, I said so simply because the prophets could, in virtue of their mission, choose a new king and give absolution for regicide, not because they could call a king who offended against the law to judgment, or could rightly act against him.

Wherefore if there had been no prophets who, in virtue of a special revelation, could give absolution for regicide, the kings would have possessed absolute rights over all matters both spiritual and temporal. Consequently the rulers of modern times, who have no prophets and would not rightly be bound in any case to receive them (for they are not subject to Jewish law), have absolute possession of the spiritual prerogative, although they are not celibates, and they will always retain it, if they will refuse to allow religious dogmas to be unduly multiplied or confounded with philosophy.

47. A Letter Concerning Toleration

JOHN LOCKE (1632–1704)

But, after all, the principal consideration and which absolutely determines this controversy is this: Although the magistrate's opin- ion in religion be sound, and the way that he appoints be truly evangelical, yet, if I be not thoroughly persuaded thereof in my own mind, there will be no safety for me in following it. No way whatsoever that I shall walk in against the dictates of my conscience will ever bring me to the mansions of the blessed. I may grow rich by an art that I take not delight in, I may be cured of some disease by remedies that I have not faith in; but I cannot be saved by a religion that I distrust and by a worship that I abhor. It is in vain for an unbeliever to take up the outward show of another man's profession. Faith only and inward sincerity are the things that procure acceptance with God. The most likely and most approved remedy can have no effect upon the patient if his stomach reject it as soon as taken; and you will in vain cram a medicine down a sick man's throat which his particular constitution will be sure to turn into poison. In a word, whatsoever may be doubtful in religion, yet this at least is certain that no religion which I believe not to be true can be either true or profitable unto me. In vain, therefore, do princes compel their subjects to come into their church communion, under pretense of saving their souls. If they believe, they will come of their own accord; if they believe not, their coming will nothing avail them. How great soever, in fine, may be the pretense of goodwill and charity, and concern for the salvation of men's souls, men cannot be forced to be saved whether they will or no. And therefore, when all is done, they must be left to their own consciences.

Having thus at length freed men from all dominion over one another in matters of religion, let us now consider what they are to do. All men know and acknowledge that God ought to be publicly worshipped; why otherwise do they compel one another unto the public assemblies? Men, therefore, constituted in this liberty, are to enter into some religious society, that they meet together, not only for mutual edification, but to own to the world that they worship God, and offer unto His Divine Majesty such service as they themselves are not ashamed of, and such as they think not unworthy of Him, nor unacceptable to Him; and finally, that by the purity of doctrine, holiness of life, and decent form of worship, they may draw others unto the love of the true religion, and perform such other things in religion as cannot be done by each private man apart.

These religious societies I call churches; and these, I say, the magistrate ought to tolerate, for the business of these assemblies of the people is nothing but what is lawful for every man in particular to take care of — I mean the salvation of their souls; nor in this case is there any difference between the national church and other separated congregations.

But as in every Church there are two things especially to be considered — the outward form and rites of worship, and the doctrines and articles of faith — these things must be handled each distinctly that so the whole matter of toleration may the more clearly be understood.

Concerning outward worship, I say, in the first place, that the magistrate has no power to enforce by law, either in his own church or much less in another, the use of any rites or ceremonies whatsoever in the worship of God. And this, not only because these churches are free societies, but because whatsoever is practised in the worship of God is only so far justifiable as it is believed by those that practise it to be acceptable unto Him. Whatsoever is not done with that assurance of faith is neither well in itself, nor can it be acceptable to God. To impose such things, therefore, upon any people, contrary to their own judgment, is in effect to command them to offend God, which, considering that the end of all religion is to please Him, and that liberty is essentially necessary to that end, appears to be absurd beyond expression.

But perhaps it may be concluded from hence that I deny unto the magistrate all manner of power about indifferent things, which, if it be not granted, the whole subject matter of lawmaking is taken away. No, I readily grant that indifferent things, and perhaps none but such, are subjected to the legislative power. But it does not therefore follow that the magistrate may ordain whatsoever he pleases concerning anything that is indifferent. The public good is the rule and measure of all lawmaking. If a thing be not useful to the commonwealth, though it be never so indifferent, it may not presently be established by law.

And further, things never so indifferent in their own nature, when they are brought into the church and worship of God, are removed out of the reach of the magistrate's jurisdiction, because in that use they have no connection at all with civil affairs. The only business of the church is the salvation of souls, and it no way concerns the commonwealth, or any member of it, that this or the other ceremony be there made use of. Neither the use nor the omission of any ceremonies in those religious assemblies does either advantage or prejudice the life, liberty, or estate of any man. For example, let it be granted that the washing of an infant with water is in itself an indifferent thing; let it be granted also that the magistrate understand such washing to be profitable to the curing or preventing of any disease the children are subject unto, and esteem the matter weighty enough to be taken care of by a law. In that case he may order it to be done. But will anyone therefore say that a magistrate has the same right to ordain by law that all children shall be baptized by priests in the sacred font in order to the purification of their souls? The extreme difference of these two cases is visible to everyone at first sight. Or let us apply the last case to the child of a Jew, and the thing speaks itself. For what hinders but a Christian magistrate may have subjects that are Jews? Now, if we acknowledge that such an injury may not be done unto a Jew as to compel him, against his own opinion, to practice in his religion a thing that is in its nature indifferent, how can we maintain that anything of this kind may be done to a Christian?

Again, things in their own nature indifferent cannot, by any human authority, be made any part of the worship of God — for this very reason: because they are indifferent. For, since indifferent things are not capable, by any virtue of their own, to propitiate the Deity, no human power or authority can confer on them so much dignity and excellence as to enable them to do it. In the common affairs of life that use of indifferent things which God has not forbidden is free and lawful, and therefore in those things human authority has place. But it is not so in matters of religion. Things indifferent are not otherwise lawful in the worship of God than as they are instituted by God Himself, and as He, by some positive command, has ordained them to be made a part of that worship which He will vouchsafe to accept at the hands of poor sinful men. Nor, when an incensed Deity shall ask us, "Who has required these or suchlike things at your hands?" will it be enough to answer Him that the magistrate commanded them? If civil jurisdiction extend thus far, what might not lawfully be introduced into religion? What hodgepodge of ceremonies, what superstitious inventions, built upon the magistrate's authority, might not (against conscience) be imposed upon the worshippers of God? For the greatest part of these ceremonies and superstitions consists in the religious use of such things as are in their own nature indifferent; nor are they sinful upon any other account than because God is not the author of them. The sprinkling of water, and the use of bread and wine, are both in their own nature and in the ordinary occasions of life altogether indifferent. Will any man therefore say that these things could have been introduced into religion, and made a part of divine worship, if not by divine institution? If any human authority or civil power could have done this, why might it not also enjoin the eating of fish and drinking of ale in the holy banquet as a part of divine worship? Why not the sprinkling of the blood of beasts in churches, and expiations by water or fire, and abundance more of this kind? But these things, how indifferent soever they be in common uses, when they come to be annexed unto divine worship, without divine authority, they are as abominable to God as the sacrifice of a dog. And why is a dog so abominable? What difference is there between a dog and a goat, in respect of the divine nature, equally and infinitely distant from all affinity with matter, unless it be that God required the use of one in His worship, and not of the other? We see, therefore, that indifferent things, how much soever they be under the power of the civil magistrate, yet cannot, upon that pretense, be introduced into religion and imposed upon religious assemblies because, in the worship of God, they wholly cease to be indifferent. He that worships God does it with design to please Him and procure His favor. But that cannot be done by him who, upon the command of another, offers unto God that which he knows will be displeasing to Him, because not commanded by Himself. This is not to please God, or appease His wrath, but willingly and knowingly to provoke Him by a manifest contempt, which is a thing absolutely repugnant to the nature and end of worship.

But it will be here asked: "If nothing belonging to divine worship be left to human discretion, how is it then that churches themselves have the power of ordering anything about the time and place of worship, and the like?" To this I answer that in religious worship we must distinguish between what is part of the worship itself and what is but a circumstance. That is a part of the worship which is believed to be appointed by God and to be well-pleasing to Him, and therefore that is necessary. Circumstances are such things which, though in general they cannot be separated from worship, yet the particular instances or modifications of them are not determined, and therefore they are indifferent. Of this sort are the time and place of worship, habit and posture of him that worships. These are circumstances, and perfectly indifferent, where God has not given any express command about them. For example: amongst the Jews the time and place of their worship, and the habits of those that officiated in it, were not mere circumstances, but a part of the worship itself, in which if anything were defective or different from the institution, they could not hope that it would be accepted by God. But these, to Christians under the liberty of the Gospel, are mere circumstances of worship, which the prudence of every church may bring into such use as shall be judged most subservient to the end of order, decency, and edification. But, even under the Gospel, those who believe the first or the seventh day to be set apart by God, and consecrated still to His worship, to them that portion of time is not a simple circumstance, but a real part of Divine worship, which can neither be changed nor neglected.

In the next place: As the magistrate has no power to impose by his laws the use of any rites and ceremonies in any church, so neither has he any power to forbid the use of such rites and ceremonies as are already received, approved, and practised by any church; because if he did so, he would destroy the church itself; the end of whose institution is only to worship God with freedom after its own manner.

You will say, by this rule, if some congregations should have a mind to sacrifice infants, or (as the primitive Christians were falsely accused) lustfully pollute themselves in promiscuous uncleanliness, or practice any other such heinous enormities, is the magistrate obliged to tolerate them because they are committed in a religious assembly? I answer, No. These things are not lawful in the ordinary course of life, nor in any private house; and therefore neither are they so in the worship of God, or in any religious meeting. But, indeed, if any people congregated upon account of religion should be desirous to sacrifice a calf, I deny that that ought to be prohibited by a law. Meliboeus, whose calf it is, may lawfully kill his calf at home, and burn any part of it that he thinks fit. For no injury is thereby done to anyone, no prejudice to another man's goods. And for the same reason he may kill his calf also in a religious meeting. Whether the doing so be well-pleasing to God or no, it is their part to consider that do it. The part of the magistrate is only to take care that the commonwealth receive no prejudice, and that there be no injury done to any man, either in life or estate. And thus what may be spent on a feast may be spent on a sacrifice. But if peradventure such were the state of things that the interest of the commonwealth required all slaughter of beasts should be forborne for some while, in order to the increasing of the stock of cattle that had been destroyed by some extraordinary murrain, who sees not that the magistrate, in such a case, may forbid all his subjects to kill any calves for any use whatsoever? Only it is to be observed that, in this case, the law is not made about a religious, but a political matter; nor is the sacrifice, but the slaughter of calves, thereby prohibited.

By this we see what difference there is between the church and the commonwealth. Whatsoever is lawful in the commonwealth cannot be prohibited by the magistrate in the church. Whatsoever is permitted unto any of his subjects for their ordinary use neither can nor ought to be forbidden by him to any sect of people for their religious uses. If any man may lawfully take bread or wine, either sitting or kneeling in his own house, the law ought not to abridge him of the same liberty in his religious worship; though in the church the use of bread and wine be very different, and be there applied to the mysteries of faith and rites of divine worship. But those things that are prejudicial to the commonweal of a people in their ordinary use, and are therefore forbidden by laws, those things ought not to be permitted to churches in their sacred rites. Only the magistrate ought always to be very careful that he do not misuse his authority to the oppression of any church, under pretense of public good.

It may be said, what if a Church be idolatrous, is that also to be tolerated by the magistrate? I answer, what power can be given to the magistrate for the suppression of an idolatrous church which may not in time and place be made use of to the ruin of an orthodox one? For it must be remembered that the civil power is the same everywhere, and the religion of every prince is orthodox to himself. If, therefore, such a power be granted unto the civil magistrate in spirituals, as that at Geneva, for example, he may extirpate, by violence and blood, the religion which is there reputed idolatrous;

by the same rule another magistrate, in some neighboring country, may oppress the reformed religion, and, in India, the Christian. The civil power can either change everything in religion, according to the prince's pleasure, or it can change nothing. If it be once permitted to introduce anything into religion, by the means of laws and penalties, there can be no bounds put to it; but it will in the same manner be lawful to alter everything, according to that rule of truth which the magistrate has framed unto himself. No man whatsoever ought therefore to be deprived of his terrestrial enjoyments upon account of his religion. Not even Americans, subjected unto a Christian prince, are to be punished either in body or goods for not embracing our faith and worship. If they are persuaded that they please God in observing the rites of their own country, and that they shall obtain happiness by that means, they are to be left unto God and themselves. Let us trace this matter to the bottom. Thus it is: an inconsiderable and weak number of Christians, destitute of everything, arrive in a pagan country; these foreigners beseech the inhabitants, by the bowels of humanity, that they would succor them with the necessaries of life; those necessaries are given them, habitations are granted, and they all join together and grow up into one body of people. The Christian religion by this means takes root in that country and spreads itself, but does not suddenly grow the strongest. While things are in this condition peace, friendship, faith, and equal justice are preserved amongst them. At length the magistrate becomes a Christian, and by that means their party becomes the most powerful. Then immediately all compacts are to be broken, all civil rights to be violated, that idolatry may be extirpated; and unless these innocent pagans, strict observers of the rules of equity and the law of nature, and no ways offending against the laws of the society, I say, unless they will forsake their ancient religion and embrace a new and strange one, they are to be turned out of the lands and possessions of their forefathers, and perhaps deprived of life itself. Then, at last, it appears what zeal for the church, joined with the desire of dominion, is capable to produce, and how easily the pretense of religion and of the care of souls serves for a cloak to covetousness, rapine, and ambition.

Now whosoever maintains that idolatry is to be rooted out of any place by laws, punishments, fire, and sword, may apply this story to himself. For the reason of the thing is equal, both in America and Europe. And neither pagans there nor any dissenting Christians here can, with any right, be deprived of their worldy goods by the predominating faction of a court-church; nor are any civil rights to be either changed or violated upon account of religion in one place more than another.

But idolatry, say some, is a sin and therefore not to be tolerated. If they said it were therefore to be avoided, the inference were good. But it does not follow that because it is a sin it ought therefore to be punished by the magistrate. For it does not belong unto the magistrate to make use of his sword in punishing everything, indifferently, that he takes to be a sin against God. Covetousness, uncharitableness, idleness, and many other things are sins, by the consent of men, which yet no man ever said were to be punished by the magistrate. The reason is because they are not prejudicial to other men's rights, nor do they break the public peace of societies. Nay, even the sins of lying and perjury are nowhere punishable by laws, unless in certain cases in which the real turpitude of the thing and the offense against God are not considered, but only the injury done unto men's neighbors and to the commonwealth. And what if in another country, to a Mahometan or a pagan prince, the Christian religion seem false and offensive to God; may not the Christians for the same reason, and after the same manner, be extirpated there?

But it may be urged further that, by the law of Moses, idolaters were to be rooted out. True, indeed, by the law of Moses; but that is not obligatory to us Christians. Nobody pretends that everything generally enjoined by the law of Moses ought to be practised by Christians; but there is nothing more frivolous than that common distinction of moral, judicial, and ceremonial law, which men ordinarily make use of. For no positive law whatsoever can oblige any people but those to whom it is given. "Hear, O Israel," sufficiently restrains the obligations of the law of Moses only to that people. And this consideration alone is answer enough unto those that urge the authority of the law of Moses for the inflicting of capital punishment upon idolaters. But, however, I will examine this argument a little more particularly.

The case of idolaters, in respect of the Jewish commonwealth, falls under a double consideration. The first is of those who, being initiated in the Mosaical rites and made citizens of that commonwealth, did afterwards apostatize from the worship of the God of Israel. These were proceeded against as traitors and rebels, guilty of no less than high treason. For the commonwealth of the Jews, different in that from all others, was an absolute theocracy; nor was there, or could there be, any difference between that commonwealth and the church. The laws established there concerning the worship of One Invisible Deity were the civil laws of that people and a part of their political government, in which God Himself was the legislator. Now, if anyone can show me where there is a commonwealth at this time, constituted upon that foundation, I will acknowledge that the ecclesiastical laws do there unavoidably become a part of the civil, and that the subjects of that government both may and ought to be kept in strict conformity with that church by the civil power. But there is absolutely no such thing under the Gospel as a Christian commonwealth. There are, indeed, many cities and kingdoms that have embraced the faith of Christ, but they have retained their ancient form of government, with which the law of Christ hath not at all meddled. He, indeed, hath taught men how, by faith and good works, they may obtain eternal life; but He instituted no commonwealth. He prescribed unto His followers no new and peculiar form of government, nor put He the sword into any magistrate's hand, with commission to make use of it in forcing men to forsake their former religion and receive His.

Secondly, foreigners and such as were strangers to the commonwealth of Israel were not compelled by force to observe the rites of the Mosaical law; but, on the contrary, in the very same place where it is ordered that an Israelite that was an idolater should be put to death [Exod. 22:20, 21], there it is provided that strangers should not be vexed nor oppressed. I confess that the seven nations that possessed the land which was promised to the Israelites were utterly to be cut off, but this was not singly because they were idolaters. For if that had been the reason, why were the Moabites and other nations to be spared? No, the reason is this: God being in a peculiar manner the King of the Jews, He could not suffer the adoration of any other deity (which was properly an act of high treason against Himself) in the land of Canaan, which was His kingdom. For such a manifest revolt could no ways consist with His dominion, which was perfectly political in that country. All idolatry was therefore to be rooted out of the bounds of His kingdom, because it was an acknowledgment of another god, that is to say, another king, against the laws of empire. The inhabitants were also to be driven out, that the entire possession of the land might be given to the Israelites. And for the like reason the Emims and the Horims were driven out of their countries by the children of Esau and Lot, and their lands, upon the same grounds, given by God to the invaders [Deut. 2]. But, though all idolatry was thus rooted out of the land of Canaan, yet every idolater was not brought to execution. The whole family of Rahab, the whole nation of the Gibeonites, articled with Joshua and were allowed by treaty; and there were many captives amongst the Jews who were idolaters, David and Solomon subdued many countries without the confines of the Land of Promise, and carried their conquests as far as Euphrates. Amongst so many captives taken, so many nations reduced under their obedience, we find not one man forced into the Jewish religion and the worship of the true God, and punished for idolatry, though all of them were certainly guilty of it. If anyone indeed, becoming a proselyte, desired to be made a denizen of their commonwealth, he was obliged to submit to their laws, that is, to embrace their religion. But this he did willingly, on his own accord, not by constraint. He did not unwillingly submit, to show his obedience, but he sought and solicited for it as a privilege. And, as soon as he was admitted, he became subject to the laws of the commonwealth by which all idolatry was forbidden within the borders of the land of Canaan. But that law (as I have said) did not reach to any of those regions, however subjected unto the Jews, that were situated without those bounds.

Thus far concerning outward worship. Let us now consider articles of faith.

The articles of religion are some of them practical and some speculative. Now, though both sorts consist in the knowledge of truth, yet these terminate simply in the understanding, those influence the will and manners. Speculative opinions, therefore, and articles of faith (as they are called) which are required only to be believed, cannot be imposed on any church by the law of the land. For it is absurd that things should be enjoined by laws which are not in men's power to perform. And to believe this or that to be true does not depend upon our will. But of this enough has been said already. But (will some say) let men at least profess that they believe. A sweet religion, indeed, that obliges men to dissemble and tell lies, both to God and man, for the salvation of their souls! If the magistrate thinks to save men thus, he seems to understand little of the way of salvation. And if he does it not in order to save them, why is he so solicitious about the articles of faith as to enact them by a law?

Further, the magistrate ought not to forbid the preaching or professing of any speculative opinions in any church, because they have no manner of relation to the civil rights of the subjects. If a Roman Catholic believe that to be really the body of Christ which another man calls bread, he does no injury thereby to his neighbor. If a Jew do not believe the New Testament to be the Word of God, he does not thereby alter anything in men's civil rights. If a heathen doubt of both Testaments, he is not therefore to be punished as a pernicious citizen. The power of the magistrate and the estates of the people may be equally secure whether any man believe these things or no. I readily grant that these opinions are false and absurd. But the business of laws is not to provide for the truth of opinions, but for the safety and security of the commonwealth, and of every particular man's goods and person. And so it ought to be. For the truth certainly would do well enough if she were once left to shift for herself. She seldom has received, and I fear never will receive, much assistance from the power of great men, to whom she is but rarely known and more rarely welcome. She is not taught by laws, nor has she any need of force to procure her entrance into the minds of men. Errors indeed prevail by the assistance of foreign and borrowed succors. But if truth makes not her way into the understanding by her own light, she will be but the weaker for any borrowed force violence can add to her. Thus much for speculative opinions. Let us now proceed to practical ones.

A good life, in which consists not the least part of religion and true piety, concerns also the civil government; and in it lies the safety both of men's souls and of the commonwealth. Moral actions belong therefore to the jurisdiction both of the outward and inward court, both of the civil and domestic governor; I mean both of the magistrate and conscience. Here, therefore, is great danger, lest one

of these jurisdictions intrench upon the other and discord arise between the keeper of the public peace and the overseers of souls. But
if what has been already said concerning the limits of both these
governments be rightly considered, it will easily remove all difficulty
in this matter.

Every man has an immortal soul, capable of eternal happiness or
misery, whose happiness depending upon his believing and doing
those things in this life which are necessary to the obtaining of God's
favor, and are prescribed by God to that end. It follows from thence,
first, that the observance of these things is the highest obligation
that lies upon mankind, and that our utmost care, application, and
diligence ought to be exercised in the search and performance of
them; because there is nothing in this world that is of any consideration in comparison with eternity. Secondly, that seeing one man
does not violate the right of another by his erroneous opinions and
undue manner of worship, nor is his perdition any prejudice to another man's affairs, therefore, the care of each man's salvation belongs only to himself. But I would not have this understood as if I
meant hereby to condemn all charitable admonitions and affectionate
endeavors to reduce men from errors, which are indeed the greatest
duty of a Christian. Anyone may employ as many exhortations and
arguments as he pleases, toward the promoting of another man's
salvation. But all force and compulsion are to be forborne. Nothing
is to be done imperiously. Nobody is obliged in that manner to yield
obedience unto the admonitions or injunctions of another, further
than he himself is persuaded. Every man in that has the supreme
and absolute authority of judging for himself. And the reason is
because nobody else is concerned in it, nor can receive any prejudice
from his conduct therein.

But besides their souls, which are immortal, men have also their
temporal lives here upon earth; the state whereof being frail and
fleeting, and the duration uncertain, they have need of several outward conveniences to the support thereof, which are to be procured
or preserved by pains and industry. For those things that are necessary to the comfortable support of our lives are not the spontaneous
products of nature, nor do offer themselves fit and prepared for our
use. This part therefore draws on another care, and necessarily gives
another employment. But the pravity of mankind being such that

they had rather injuriously prey upon the fruits of other men's labors
than take pains to provide for themselves, the necessity of preserving men in the possession of what honest industry has already acquired, and also of preserving their liberty and strength, whereby
they may acquire what they further want, obliges men to enter into
society with one another, that by mutual assistance and joint force
they may secure unto each other their properties, in the things that
contribute to the comfort and happiness of this life, leaving in the
meanwhile to every man the care of his own eternal happiness, the
attainment whereof can neither be facilitated by another man's
industry, nor can the loss of it turn to another man's prejudice, nor
the hope of it be forced from him by any external violence. But,
forasmuch as men thus entering into societies, grounded upon their
mutual compacts of assistance for the defense of their temporal
goods, may, nevertheless, be deprived of them, either by the rapine
and fraud of their fellow citizens or by the hostile violence of foreigners, the remedy of this evil consists in arms, riches, and multitude of
citizens; the remedy of the other in laws; and the care of all things
relating both to one and the other is committed by the society to
the civil magistrate. This is the original, this is the use, and these are
the bounds of the legislative (which is the supreme) power in every
commonwealth. I mean that provision may be made for the security
of each man's private possessions, for the peace, riches, and public
commodities of the whole people, and, as much as possible, for the
increase of their inward strength against foreign invasions.

48. An Act for Establishing Religious Freedom

THOMAS JEFFERSON (1743–1826)

Well aware that Almighty God hath created the mind free; that
all attempts to influence it by temporal punishments or burdens, or
by civil incapacitations, tend only to beget habits of hypocrisy and
meanness, and are a departure from the plan of the Holy Author of
our religion, who being Lord both of body and mind, yet chose not to

propagate it by coercions on either, as was in his Almighty power
to do; that the impious presumption of legislators and rulers, civil
as well as ecclesiastical, who, being themselves but fallible and unin-
spired men have assumed dominion over the faith of others, setting
up their own opinions and modes of thinking as the only true and
infallible, and as such endeavoring to impose them on others, hath
established and maintained false religions over the greatest part of
the world, and through all time; that to compel a man to furnish
contributions of money for the propagation of opinions which he
disbelieves, is sinful and tyrannical; that even the forcing him to
support this or that teacher of his own religious persuasion, is depriving him of the comfortable liberty of giving his contributions
to the particular pastor whose morals he would make his pattern, and
whose power he feels most persuasive to righteousness, and is with-
drawing from the ministry those temporal rewards, which proceeding
from an approbation of their personal conduct, are an additional
incitement to earnest and unremitting labors for the instruction of
mankind; that our civil rights have no dependence on our religious
opinions, more than our opinions in physics or geometry; that, therefore, the proscribing any citizen as unworthy the public confidence
by laying upon him an incapacity of being called to the offices of
trust and emolument, unless he profess or renounce this or that
religious opinion, is depriving him injuriously of those privileges and
advantages to which in common with his fellow citizens he has
a natural right; that it tends also to corrupt the principles of
that very religion it is meant to encourage, by bribing, with a
monopoly of worldly honors and emoluments, those who will externally profess and conform to it; that though indeed these are
criminal who do not withstand such temptation, yet neither are
those innocent who lay the bait in their way; that to suffer the civil
magistrate to intrude his powers into the field of opinion and to
restrain the profession or propagation of principles, on the supposition of their ill tendency, is a dangerous fallacy, which at once
destroys all religious liberty, because he being of course judge of
that tendency, will make his opinions the rule of judgment, and
approve or condemn the sentiments of others only as they shall
square with or differ from his own; that it is time enough for the
rightful purposes of civil government, for its officers to interfere
when principles break out into overt acts against peace and good

order; and finally, that truth is great and will prevail if left to herself, that she is the proper and sufficient antagonist to error, and has nothing to fear from the conflict, unless by human interposition disarmed of her natural weapons, free argument and debate, errors ceasing to be dangerous when it is permitted freely to contradict them.

Be it therefore enacted by the General Assembly. That no man shall be compelled to frequent or support any religious worship, place or ministry whatsoever, nor shall be enforced, restrained, molested, or burthened in his body or goods, nor shall otherwise suffer on account of his religious opinions or belief; but that all men shall be free to profess, and by argument to maintain, their opinions in matters of religion, and that the same shall in nowise diminish, enlarge, or affect their civil capacities.

And though we well know this Assembly, elected by the people for the ordinary purposes of legislation only, have no power to restrain the acts of succeeding assemblies, constituted with the powers equal to our own, and that therefore to declare this act irrevocable, would be of no effect in law, yet we are free to declare, and do declare, that the rights hereby asserted are of the natural rights of mankind, and that if any act shall be hereafter passed to repeal the present or to narrow its operation, such act will be an infringement of natural right.

49. *Memorial and Remonstrance Against Religious Assessments*

JAMES MADISON (1751–1836)

To the Honorable the General Assembly
of
The Commonwealth of Virginia
A Memorial and Remonstrance

We, the subscribers, citizens of the said Commonwealth, having taken into serious consideration, a Bill printed by order of the last Session of General Assembly, entitled "A Bill establishing a provision for Teachers of the Christian Religion," [1] and conceiving that the same, if finally armed with the sanctions of a law, will be a dangerous abuse of power, are bound as faithful members of a free State, to remonstrate against it, and to declare the reasons by which we are determined. We remonstrate against the said Bill,

1. Because we hold it for a fundamental and undeniable truth, "that Religion or the duty which we owe to our Creator and the Manner of discharging it, can be directed only by reason and conviction, not by force or violence." The Religion then of every man must be left to the conviction and conscience of every man; and it is the right of every man to exercise it as these may dictate. This right is in its nature an unalienable right. It is unalienable; because the opinions of men, depending only on the evidence contemplated by their own minds, cannot follow the dictates of other men: It is unalienable also; because what is here a right towards men, is a duty towards the Creator. It is the duty of every man to render to the Creator such homage, and such only, as he believes to be acceptable to him. This duty is precedent both in order of time and degree of obligation, to the claims of Civil Society. Before any man can be considered as a member of Civil Society, he must be considered as a subject of the Governor of the Universe: And if a member of Civil Society, who enters into any subordinate Association, must always do it with a reservation of his duty to the general authority; much more must every man who becomes a member of any particular Civil Society, do it with a saving of his allegiance to the Universal Sovereign. We maintain, therefore, that in matters of Religion, no man's right is abridged by the institution of Civil Society, and that Religion is wholly exempt from its cognizance. True it is, that no other rule exists, by which any question which may divide a Society, can be ultimately determined, but the will of the majority; but it is also true, that the majority may trespass on the rights of the minority.

2. Because if religion be exempt from the authority of the Society at large, still less can it be subject to that of the Legislative Body. The latter are but the creatures and vicegerents of the former. Their jurisdiction is both derivative and limited: it is limited with regard to the co-ordinate departments, more necessarily is it limited with

---

[1] [The Bill is reprinted as an Appendix to this selection.]

regard to the constituents. The preservation of a free government requires not merely, that the metes and bounds which separate each department of power may be invariably maintained; but more especially, that neither of them be suffered to overleap the great Barrier which defends the rights of the people. The Rulers who are guilty of such an encroachment, exceed the commission from which they derive their authority, and are Tyrants. The People who submit to it are governed by laws made neither by themselves, nor by an authority derived from them, and are slaves.

3. Because, it is proper to take alarm at the first experiment on our liberties. We hold this prudent jealously to be the first duty of citizens, and one of the noblest characteristics of the late Revolution. The freemen of America did not wait till usurped power had strengthened itself by exercise, and entangled the question in precedents. They saw all the consequences in the principle, and they avoided the consequences by denying the principle. We revere this lesson too much, soon to forget it. Who does not see that the same authority which can establish Christianity, in exclusion of all other Religions, may establish with the same ease any particular sect of Christians, in exclusion of all other Sects? That the same authority which can force a citizen to contribute three pence only of his property for the support of any one establishment, may force him to conform to any other establishment in all cases whatsoever?

4. Because, the bill violates that equality which ought to be the basis of every law, and which is more indispensable, in proportion as the validity or expediency of any law is more liable to be impeached. If "all men are by nature equally free and independent," all men are to be considered as entering into Society on equal conditions; as relinquishing no more, and therefore retaining no less, one than another, of their natural rights. Above all are they to be considered as retaining an "equal title to the free exercise of Religion according to the dictates of conscience.' Whilst we assert for ourselves a freedom to embrace, to profess and to observe the Religion which we believe to be of divine origin, we cannot deny an equal freedom to those whose minds have not yet yielded to the evidence which has convinced us. If this freedom be abused, it is an offence against God, not against man: To God, therefore, not to men, must an account of it be rendered. As the Bill violates equality by subjecting

some to peculiar burdens; so it violates the same principle, by granting to others peculiar exemptions. Are the Quakers and Menonists the only sects who think a compulsive support of their religions unnecessary and unwarrantable? Can their piety alone be intrusted with the care of public worship? Ought their Religions to be endowed above all others, with extra-ordinary privileges, by which proselytes may be enticed from all others? We think too favorably of the justice and good sense of these denominations, to believe that they either covet pre-eminencies over their fellow citizens, or that they will be seduced by them, from the common opposition to the measure.

5. Because the bill implies either that the Civil Magistrate is a competent Judge of Religious truth; or that he may employ Religion as an engine of Civil policy. The first is an arrogant pretension falsified by the contradictory opinions of Rulers in all ages, and throughout the world: The second an unhallowed perversion of the means of salvation.

6. Because the establishment proposed by the Bill is not requisite for the support of the Christian Religion. To say that it is, is a contradiction to the Christian Religion itself; for every page of it disavows a dependence on the powers of this world: it is a contradiction to fact; for it is known that this Religion both existed and flourished, not only without the support of human laws, but in spite of every opposition from them; and not only during the period of miraculous aid, but long after it had been left to its own evidence, and the ordinary care of Providence: Nay, it is a contradiction in terms; for a Religion not invented by policy, must have pre-existed and been supported, before it was established by human policy. It is moreover to weaken in those who profess this Religion a pious confidence in its innate excellence, and the patronage of its Author; and to foster in those who still reject it, a suspicion that its friends are too conscious of its fallacies, to trust it to its own merits.

7. Because experience witnesseth that ecclesiastical establishments, instead of maintaining the purity and efficacy of Religion, have had a contrary operation. During almost fifteen centuries, has the legal establishment of Christianity been on trial. What have been its fruits? More or less in all places, pride and indolence in the Clergy; ignorance and servility in the laity; in both, superstition,

bigotry and persecution. Enquire of the Teachers of Christianity for the ages in which it appeared in its greatest lustre; those of every sect, point to the ages prior to its incorporation with Civil policy. Propose a restoration of this primitive state in which its Teachers depended on the voluntary rewards of their flocks; many of them predict its downfall. On which side ought their testimony to have greatest weight, when for or when against their interest?

8. Because the establishment in question is not necessary for the support of Civil Government. If it be urged as necessary for the support of Civil Government only as it is a means of supporting Religion, and it be not necessary for the latter purpose, it cannot be necessary for the former. If Religion be not within the cognizance of Civil Government, how can its legal establishment be said to be necessary to Civil Government: What influence in fact have ecclesiastical establishments had on Civil Society? In some instances they have been seen to erect a spiritual tyranny on the ruins of Civil authority; in many instances they have been seen upholding the thrones of political tyranny; in no instance have they been seen the guardians of the liberties of the people. Rulers who wished to subvert the public liberty, may have found an established clergy convenient auxiliaries. A just government, instituted to secure & perpetuate it, needs them not. Such a government will be best supported by protecting every citizen in the enjoyment of his Religion with the same equal hand which protects his person and his property; by neither invading the equal rights of any Sect, nor suffering any Sect to invade those of another.

9. Because the proposed establishment is a departure from that generous policy, which, offering an asylum to the persecuted and oppressed of every Nation and Religion, promised a lustre to our country, and an accession to the number of its citizens. What a melancholy mark is the Bill of sudden degeneracy? Instead of holding forth an asylum to the persecuted, it is itself a signal of persecution. It degrades from the equal rank of Citizens all those whose opinions in Religion do not bend to those of the Legislative authority. Distant as it may be, in its present form, from the Inquisition it differs from it only in degree. The one is the first step, the other the last in the career of intolerance. The magnanimous sufferer under this cruel scourge in foreign Regions, must view the

Bill as a Beacon on our Coast, warning him to seek some other haven, where liberty and philanthropy in their due extent may offer a more certain repose from his troubles.

10. Because, it will have a like tendency to banish our Citizens. The allurements presented by other situations are every day thinning their number. To superadd a fresh motive to emigration, by revoking the liberty which they now enjoy, would be the same species of folly which has dishonoured and depopulated flourishing kingdoms.

11. Because, it will destroy that moderation and harmony which the forbearance of our laws to intermeddle with Religion, has produced amongst its several sects. Torrents of blood have been spilt in the old world, by vain attempts of the secular arm to extinguish Religious discord, by proscribing all difference in Religious opinions. Time has at length revealed the true remedy. Every relaxation of narrow and rigorous policy, wherever it has been tried, has been found to assuage the disease. The American Theatre has exhibited proofs, that equal and compleat liberty, if it does not wholly eradicate it, sufficiently destroys its malignant influence on the health and prosperity of the State. If with the salutary effects of this system under our own eyes, we begin to contract the bonds of Religious freedom, we know no name that will too severely reproach our folly. At least let warning be taken at the first fruits of the threatened innovation. The very appearance of the Bill has transformed that "Christian forbearance, love and charity," which of late mutually prevailed, into animosities and jealousies, which may not soon be appeased. What mischiefs may not be dreaded should this enemy to the public quiet be armed with the force of a law?

12. Because, the policy of the bill is adverse to the diffusion of the light of Christianity. The first wish of those who enjoy this precious gift, ought to be that it may be imparted to the whole race of mankind. Compare the number of those who have as yet received it with the number still remaining under the dominion of false Religions; and how small is the former! Does the policy of the Bill tend to lessen the disproportion? No; it at once discourages those who are strangers to the light of revelation from coming into the Region of it; and countenances, by example the nations who continue in darkness, in shutting out those who might convey it to

them. Instead of levelling as far as possible, every obstacle to the victorious progress of truth, the Bill with an ignoble and unchristian timidity would circumscribe it, with a wall of defence, against the encroachments of error.

13. Because attempts to enforce by legal sanctions, acts obnoxious to so great a proportion of Citizens, tend to enervate the laws in general, and to slacken the bands of Society. If it be difficult to execute any law which is not generally deemed necessary or salutary, what must be the case where it is deemed invalid and dangerous? and what may be the effect of so striking an example of impotency in the Government, on its general authority.

14. Because a measure of such singular magnitude and delicacy ought not to be imposed, without the clearest evidence that it is called for by a majority of citizens: and no satisfactory method is yet proposed by which the voice of the majority in this case may be determined, or its influence secured. "The people of the respective counties are indeed requested to signify their opinion respecting the adoption of the Bill to the next Session of Assembly." But the representation must be made equal, before the voice either of the Representatives or of the Counties, will be that of the people. Our hope is that neither of the former will, after due consideration, espouse the dangerous principle of the Bill. Should the event disappoint us, it will still leave us in full confidence, that a fair appeal to the latter will reverse the sentence against our liberties.

15. Because, finally, "the equal right of every citizen to the free exercise of his Religion according to the dictates of conscience" is held by the same tenure with all our other rights. If we recur to its origin, it is equally the gift of nature; if we weigh its importance, it cannot be less dear to us; if we consult the Declaration of those rights which pertain to the good people of Virginia, as the "basis and foundation of Government," it is enumerated with equal solemnity, or rather studied emphasis. Either then, we must say, that the will of the Legislature is the only measure of their authority; and that in the plenitude of this authority, they may sweep away all our fundamental rights; or, that they are bound to leave this particular right untouched and sacred: Either we must say, that they may control the freedom of the press, may abolish the trial by jury, may swallow up the Executive and Judiciary Powers of the State; nay

that they may despoil us of our very right of suffrage, and erect themselves into an independent and hereditary assembly: or we must say, that they have no authority to enact into law the Bill under consideration. We the subscribers say, that the General Assembly of this Commonwealth have no such authority: And that no effort may be omitted on our part against so dangerous an usurpation, we oppose to it, this remonstrance; earnestly praying, as we are in duty bound, that the Supreme Lawgiver of the Universe, by illuminating those to whom it is addressed, may on the one hand, turn their councils from every act which would affront his holy prerogative, or violate the trust committed to them: and on the other, guide them into every measure which may be worthy of his blessing, may redound to their own praise, and may establish more firmly the liberties, the prosperity and the Happiness of the Commonwealth.

APPENDIX TO SELECTION 49

*A Bill Establishing a Provision for Teachers of
the Christian Religion* [1]

Whereas the general diffusion of Christian knowledge hath a natural tendency to correct the morals of men, restrain their vices, and preserve the peace of society; which cannot be effected without a competent provision for learned teachers, who may be thereby enabled to devote their time and attention to the duty of instructing such citizens, as from their circumstances and want of education, cannot otherwise attain such knowledge; and it is judged that such provision may be made by the Legislature, without counteracting the liberal principle heretofore adopted and intended to be preserved by abolishing all distinctions of pre-eminence amongst the different societies of communities of Christians;

---

[1] [This bill, which provoked Madison's famous Remonstrance, was introduced into the Virginia Legislature but was never passed. The present version of the bill dates from December 24, 1784.]

Be it therefore enacted by the General Assembly, That for the support of Christian teachers, per centum on the amount, or in the pound on the sum payable for tax on the property within this Commonwealth, is hereby assessed, and shall be paid by every person chargeable with the said tax at the time the same shall become due; and the Sheriffs of the several Counties shall have power to levy and collect the same in the same manner and under the like restrictions and limitations, as are or may be prescribed by the laws for raising the Revenues of this State.

And be it enacted, That for every sum so paid, the Sheriff or Collector shall give a receipt, expressing therein to what society of Christians the person from whom he may receive the same shall direct the money to be paid, keeping a distinct account thereof in his books. The Sheriff of every County shall, on or before the day of   in every year, return to the Court, upon oath, two alphabetical lists of the payments to him made, distinguishing in columns opposite to the names of the persons who shall have paid the same, the society to which the money so paid was by them appropriated; and one column for the names where no appropriation shall be made. One of which lists, after being recorded in a book to be kept for that purpose, shall be filed by the Clerk in his office; the other shall by the Sheriff be fixed up in the Court-house, there to remain for the inspection of all concerned. And the Sheriff, after deducting five per centum for the collection, shall forthwith pay to such person or persons as shall be appointed to receive the same by the Vestry, Elders, or Directors, however denominated of each such society, the sum so stated to be due to that society; or in default thereof, upon the motion of such person or persons to the next or any succeeding Court, execution shall be awarded for the same against the Sheriff and his security, his and their executors or administrators; provided that ten days previous notice be given of such motion. And upon every such execution, the Officer serving the same shall proceed to immediate sale of the estate taken, and shall not accept of security for payment at the end of three months, nor to have the goods forthcoming at the day of sale; for his better direction wherein, the Clerk shall endorse upon every such execution that no security of any kind shall be taken.

And be it further enacted, That the money to be raised by virtue of this Act, shall be by the Vestries, Elders, or Directors of each religious society, appropriated to a provision for a Minister or Teacher of the Gospel of their denomination, or the providing places of divine worship, and to none other use whatsoever; except in the denominations of Quakers and Menonists, who may receive what is collected from their members, and place it in their general fund, to be disposed of in a manner which they shall think best calculated to promote their particular mode of worship.

And be it enacted, That all sums which at the time of payment to the Sheriff or Collector may not be appropriated by the person paying the same, shall be accounted for with the Court in manner as by this Act is directed; and after deducting for his collection, the Sheriff shall pay the amount thereof (upon account certified by the Court to the Auditors of Public Accounts, and by them to the Treasurer) into the public Treasury, to be disposed of under the direction of the General Assembly, for the encouragement of seminaries of learning within the Counties whence such sums shall arise, and to no other use or purpose whatsoever.

THIS ACT shall commence, and be in force, from and after the day of   in the year

A copy from the Engrossed Bill.

JOHN BECKLEY, C. H. D.

50. *The Idea of a Christian Society* *

T. S. ELIOT (1888-   )

In using the term 'Idea' of a Christian Society I do not mean primarily a concept derived from the study of any societies which we may choose to call Christian; I mean something that can only be found in an understanding of the end to which a Christian Society, to deserve the name, must be directed. I do not limit the application of the term to a perfected Christian Society on earth;

* Excerpted from *The Idea of a Christian Society,* copyright, 1940, by T. S. Eliot; Reprinted by permission of Harcourt, Brace and Company, Inc.

and I do not comprehend in it societies merely because some profession of Christian faith, or some vestige of Christian practice, is retained. My concern with contemporary society, accordingly, will not be primarily with specific defects, abuses or injustices but with the question, what—if any—is the 'idea' of the society in which we live? to what end is it arranged?

The Idea of a Christian Society is one which we can accept or reject; but if we are to accept it, we must treat Christianity with a great deal more *intellectual* respect than is our wont; we must treat it as being for the individual a matter primarily of thought and not of feeling. The consequences of such an attitude are too serious to be acceptable to everybody: for when the Christian faith is not only felt, but thought, it has practical results which may be inconvenient. For to see the Christian faith in this way—and to see it in this way is not necessarily to accept it, but only to understand the real issues —is to see that the difference between the Idea of a Neutral Society (which is that of the society in which we live at present) and the Idea of a Pagan Society (such as the upholders of democracy abominate) is, in the long run, of minor importance. I am not at this moment concerned with the means for bringing a Christian Society into existence; I am not even primarily concerned with making it appear desirable; but I am very much concerned with making clear its difference from the kind of society in which we are now living. Now, to understand the society in which he lives, must be to the interest of every conscious thinking person. The current terms in which we describe our society, the contrasts with other societies by which we— of the 'Western Democracies'—eulogise it, only operate to deceive and stupefy us. To speak of ourselves as a Christian Society, in contrast to that of Germany or Russia, is an abuse of terms. We mean only that we have a society in which no one is penalised for the *formal profession of* Christianity; but we conceal from ourselves the unpleasant knowledge of the real values by which we live. We conceal from ourselves, moreover, the similarity of our society to those which we execrate: for we should have to admit, if we recognised the similarity, that the foreigners do better. I suspect that in our loathing of totalitarianism, there is infused a good deal of admiration for its efficiency.

The political philosopher of the present time, even when he is a

Christian himself, is not usually concerned with the possible structure of a Christian state. He is occupied with the possibility of a just State in general, and when he is not an adherent of one or another secular system, is inclined to accept our present system as one to be improved, but not fundamentally altered. Theological writers have more to say that is relevant to my subject. I am not alluding to those writers who endeavour to infuse a vague, and sometimes de-based, Christian spirit into the ordinary conduct of affairs; or to those who endeavour, at moments of emergency, to apply Christian principles to particular political situations. Relevant to my subject are the writings of the Christian sociologists—those writers who criticise our economic system in the light of Christian ethics. Their work consists in proclaiming in general, and demonstrating in particular, the incompatibility of Christian principle and a great deal of our social practice. They appeal to the spirit of justice and humanity with which most of us profess to be inspired; they appeal also to the practical reason, by demonstrating that much in our system is not only iniquitous, but in the long run unworkable and conducive to disaster. Many of the changes which such writers advocate, while deducible from Christian principles, can recommend themselves to any intelligent and disinterested person, and do not require a Christian society to carry them into effect, or Christian belief to render them acceptable: though they are changes which would make it more possible for the individual Christian to live out his Christianity. I am here concerned only secondarily with the changes in economic organisation, and only secondarily with the life of the devout Christian: my primary interest is a change in our social attitude, such a change only as could bring about anything worthy to be called a Christian Society. That such a change would compel changes in our organisation of industry and commerce and financial credit, that it would facilitate, where it now impedes, the life of devotion for those who are capable of it, I feel certain. But my point of departure is different from that of the sociologists and economists; though I depend upon them for enlightenment, and a test of my Christian Society would be that it should bring about such reforms as they propose; and though the kind of 'change of spirit' which can testify for itself by nothing better than a new revivalistic vocabulary, is a danger against which we must be always on guard.

My subject touches also upon that of another class of Christian writer: that of the ecclesiastical controversialists. The subject of Church and State is, again, not my primary concern. It is not, except at moments which lend themselves to newspaper exploitation, a subject in which the general public takes much interest; and at the moments when the public's interest is aroused, the public is never well enough informed to have the right to an opinion. My subject is a preliminary to the problem of Church and State: it involves that problem in its widest terms and in its most general interest. A usual attitude is to take for granted the existing State, and ask: 'What Church?' But before we consider what shall be the relation of Church and State, we should first ask: 'What State?' Is there any sense in which we can speak of a 'Christian State', any sense in which the State can be regarded as Christian? for even if the nature of the State be such, that we cannot speak of it in its Idea as either Christian or non-Christian, yet is it obvious that actual States may vary to such an extent that the relation of the Church to the State may be anything from overt hostility to a more or less harmonious cooperation of different institutions in the same society. What I mean by the Christian State is not any particular political form, but whatever State is suitable to a Christian Society, whatever State a particular Christian Society develops for itself. Many Christians there are, I know, who do not believe that a Church in relation to the State is necessary for a Christian Society; and I shall have to give reasons, in later pages, for believing that it is. The point to be made at this stage is that neither the classical English treatises on Church and State, nor contemporary discussion of the subject, give me the assistance that I need. For the earlier treatises, and indeed all up to the present time, assume the existence of a Christian Society; modern writers sometime assume that what we have is a pagan society: and it is just these assumptions that I wish to question.

Your opinion of what can be done for this country in the future, and incidentally your opinion of what ought to be the relations of Church and State, will depend upon the view you take of the contemporary situation. We can abstract three positive historical points: that at which Christians are a new minority in a society of positive pagan traditions—a position which cannot recur within any future with which we are concerned; the point at which the whole society can be called Christian, whether in one body or in a prior or subsequent stage of division into sects; and finally the point at which practising Christians must be recognised as a minority (whether static or diminishing) in a society which has ceased to be Christian. Have we reached the third point? Different observers will give different reports; but I would remark that there are two points of view for two contexts. The first is that a society has ceased to be Christian when religious practices have been abandoned, when behaviour ceases to be regulated by reference to Christian principle, and when in effect prosperity in this world for the individual or for the group has become the sole conscious aim. The other point of view, which is less readily apprehended, is that a society has not ceased to be Christian until it has become positively something else. It is my contention that we have to-day a culture which is mainly negative, but which, so far as it is positive, is still Christian. I do not think that it can remain negative, because a negative culture has ceased to be efficient in a world where economic as well as spiritual forces are proving the efficiency of cultures which, even when pagan, are positive; and I believe that the choice before us is between the formation of a new Christian culture, and the acceptance of a pagan one. Both involve radical changes; but I believe that the majority of us, if we could be faced immediately with all the changes which will only be accomplished in several generations, would prefer Christianity.

I do not expect everyone to agree that our present organisation and temper of society—which proved, in its way, highly successful during the nineteenth century—is 'negative': many will maintain that British, French and American civilisation still stands integrally for something positive. And there are others who will insist, that if our culture is negative, then a negative culture is the right thing to have. There are two distinct arguments to be employed in rebuttal: one, an argument of principle, that such a culture is undesirable; the other, a judgment of fact, that it must disappear anyway. The defenders of the present order fail to perceive either how far it is vestigial of a positive Christianity, or how far it has already advanced towards something else.

There is one class of persons to which one speaks with difficulty, and another to which one speaks in vain. The second, more numerous and obstinate than may at first appear, because it represents a state of mind into which we are all prone through natural sloth to relapse, consists of those people who cannot believe that things will ever be very different from what they are at the moment. From time to time, under the influence perhaps of some persuasive writer or speaker, they may have an instant of disquiet or hope; but an invincible sluggishness of imagination makes them go on behaving as if nothing would ever change. Those to whom one speaks with difficulty, but not perhaps in vain, are the persons who believe that great changes must come, but are not sure either of what is inevitable, or of what is probable, or of wnat is desirable.

What the Western world has stood for—and by that I mean the terms to which it has attributed sanctity—is 'Liberalism' and 'Democracy'. The two terms are not identical or inseparable. The term 'Liberalism' is the more obviously ambiguous, and is now less in favour; but the term 'Democracy' is at the height of its popularity. When a term has become so universally sanctified as 'democracy' now is, I begin to wonder whether it means anything, in meaning too many things: it has arrived perhaps at the position of a Merovingian Emperor, and wherever it is invoked, one begins to look for the Major of the Palace. Some persons have gone so far as to affirm, as something self-evident, that democracy is the only regime compatible with Christianity; on the other hand, the word is not abandoned by sympathisers with the government of Germany. If anybody ever attacked democracy, I might discover what the word meant. Certainly there is a sense in which Britain and America are more democratic than Germany; but on the other hand, defenders of the totalitarian system can make out a plausible case for maintaining that what we have is not democracy, but financial oligarchy.

Mr. Christopher Dawson considers that 'what the non-dictatorial States stand for to-day is not Liberalism but Democracy', and goes on to foretell the advent in these States of a kind of totalitarian democracy. I agree with his prediction, but if one is considering, not merely the non-dictatorial States, but the societies to which they belong, his statement does less than justice to the extent to which Liberalism still permeates our minds and affects our attitude towards much of life. That Liberalism may be a tendency towards something very different from itself, is a possibility in its nature. For it is something which tends to release energy rather than accumulate it, to relax, rather than to fortify. It is a movement not so much defined by its end, as by its starting point; away from, rather than towards, something definite. Our point of departure is more real to us than our destination; and the destination is likely to present a very different picture when arrived at, from the vaguer image formed in imagination. By destroying traditional social habits of the people, by dissolving their natural collective consciousness into individual constituents, by licensing the opinions of the most foolish, by substituting instruction for education, by encouraging cleverness rather than wisdom, the upstart rather than the qualified, by fostering a notion of *getting on* to which the alternative is a hopeless apathy, Liberalism can prepare the way for that which is its own negation: the artificial, mechanised or brutalised control which is a desperate remedy for its chaos. . . .

With religious Liberalism, however, I am no more specifically concerned than with political Liberalism: I am concerned with a state of mind which, in certain circumstances, can become universal and infect opponents as well as defenders. And I shall have expressed myself very ill if I give the impression that I think of Liberalism as something simply to be rejected and extirpated, as an evil for which there is a simple alternative. It is a necessary negative element; when I have said the worst of it, that worst comes only to this, that a negative element made to serve the purpose of a positive is objectionable. In the sense in which Liberalism is contrasted with Conservatism, both can be equally repellant: if the former can mean chaos, the latter can mean petrifaction. We are always faced both with the question "what must be destroyed?" and with the question "what must be preserved?" and neither Liberalism nor Conservatism, which are not philosophies and may be merely habits, is enough to guide us. . . .

If, then, Liberalism disappears from the philosophy of life of a people, what positive is left? We are left only with the term 'democracy', a term which, for the present generation, still has a Liberal connotation of 'freedom'. But totalitarianism can retain the terms 'freedom' and 'democracy' and give them its own meaning: and its right to them is not so easily disproved as minds inflamed by passion suppose. We are in danger of finding ourselves with nothing to stand for except a *dislike* of everything maintained by Germany and/or Russia: a dislike which, being a compost of newspaper sensations and prejudice, can have two results, at the same time, which appear at first incompatible. It may lead us to reject possible improvements, because we should owe them to the example of one or both of these countries; and it may equally well lead us to be mere imitators *à rebours*, in making us adopt uncritically almost any attitude which a foreign nation rejects. . . .

The more highly industrialised the country, the more easily a materialistic philosophy will flourish in it, and the more deadly that philosophy will be. Britain has been highly industrialised longer than any other country. And the tendency of unlimited industrialism is to create bodies of men and women—of all classes—detached from tradition, alienated from religion, and susceptible to mass suggestion: in other words, a mob. And a mob will be no less a mob if it is well fed, well clothed, well housed, and well disciplined. . . .

My thesis has been, simply, that a liberalised or negative condition of society must either proceed into a gradual decline of which we can see no end, or (whether as a result of catastrophe or not) reform itself into a positive shape which is likely to be effectively secular. We need not assume that this secularism will approximate closely to any system in the past or to any that can now be observed in order to be apprehensive about it: the Anglo-Saxons display a capacity for *diluting* their religion, probably in excess of that of any other race. But unless we are content with the prospect of one or the other of these issues, the only possibility left is that of a positive Christian society. The third will only commend itself to those who agree in their view of the present situation, and who can see that a thoroughgoing secularism would be objectionable, in its consequences, even to those who attach no positive importance to the survival of Christianity for its own sake.

I am not investigating the possible lines of action by which such a Christian society could be brought into being. I shall confine myself to a slight outline of what I conceive to be essential features of this society, bearing in mind that it can neither be mediaeval in form, nor be modelled on the seventeenth century or any previous age. In what sense, if any, can we speak of a 'Christian State'? I would ask to be allowed to use the following working distinctions:

the Christian State, the Christian Community, and the Community of Christians, as elements of the Christian Society.

I conceive then of the Christian State as of the Christian Society under the aspect of legislation, public administration, legal tradition, and form. Observe that at this point I am not approaching the problem of Church and State except with the question: with what kind of State can the Church have a relation? By this I mean a relation of the kind which has hitherto obtained in England; which is neither merely reciprocal tolerance, nor a Concordat. The latter seems to me merely a kind of compromise, of doubtful durability, resting on a dubious division of authority, and often a popular division of loyalty; a compromise which implies perhaps a hope on the part of the rulers of the State that their rule will outlast Christianity, and a faith on the part of the Church that it will survive any particular form of secular organisation. A relation between Church and State such as is, I think, implied in our use of the term, implies that the State is in some sense Christian. It must be clear that I do not mean by a Christian State one in which the rulers are chosen because of their qualifications, still less their eminence, as Christians. A regiment of Saints is apt to be too uncomfortable to last. I do not deny that some advantages may accrue from persons in authority, in a Christian State, being Christians. Even in the present conditions, that sometimes happens; but even if, in the present conditions, *all* persons in positions of the highest authority were devout and orthodox Christians, we should not expect to see very much difference in the conduct of affairs. The Christian and the unbeliever do not, and cannot, behave very differently in the exercise of office; for it is the general ethos of the people they have to govern, not their own piety, that determines the behaviour of politicians. One may even accept F. S. Oliver's affiirmation—following Buelow, following Disraeli — that real statesmen are inspired by nothing else than their instinct for power and their love of country. It is not primarily the Christianity of the statesmen that matters, but their being confined, by the temper and traditions of the people which they rule, to a Christian framework within which to realise their ambitions and advance the prosperity and prestige of their country. They may frequently perform un-Christian acts; they must never attempt to defend their actions on un-Christian principles. . . .

The relation of the Christian State, the Christian Community, and the Community of Christians, may be looked at in connexion with the problem of *belief*. Among the men of state, you would have as a minimum, conscious conformity of behaviour. In the Christian Community that they ruled, the Christian faith would be ingrained, but it requires, as a minimum, only a largely unconscious behaviour; and it is only from the much smaller number of conscious human beings, the Community of Christians, that one would expect a conscious Christian life on its highest social level.

For the great mass of humanity whose attention is occupied mostly by their direct relation to the soil, or the sea, or the machine, and to a small number of persons, pleasures and duties, two conditions are required. The first is that, as their capacity for *thinking* about the objects of faith is small, their Christianity may be almost wholly realised in behaviour: both in their customary and periodic religious observances, and in a traditional code of behaviour towards their neighbours. The second is that, while they should have some perception of how far their lives fall short of Christian ideals, their religious and social life should form for them a natural whole, so that the difficulty of behaving as Christians should not impose an intolerable strain. These two conditions are really the same differently stated; they are far from being realised to-day. . . .

The mass of the population, in a Christian society, should not be exposed to a way of life in which there is too sharp and frequent a conflict between what is easy for them or what their circumstances dictate and what is Christian. The compulsion to live in such a way that Christian behaviour is only possible in a restricted number of situations, is a very powerful force against Christianity; for behaviour is as potent to affect belief, as belief to affect behaviour. . . .

I confine myself therefore to the assertion, which I think few will dispute, that a great deal of the machinery of modern life is merely a sanction for un-Christian aims, that it is not only hostile to the conscious pursuit of the Christian life in the world by the few, but to the maintenance of any Christian society *of* the world. We must abandon the notion that the Christian should be content with freedom of cultus, and with suffering no wordly disabilities on account of his faith. However bigoted the announcement may sound, the Christian can be satisfied with nothing less than a Christian organisation of society—which is not the same thing as a society consisting exclusively of devout Christians. It would be a society in which the natural end of man—virtue and well-being in community —is acknowledged for all, and the supernatural end—beatitude— for those who have the eyes to see it.

I do not wish, however, to abandon my previous point, that a Christian community is one in which there is a unified religious-social code of behaviour. It should not be necessary for the ordinary individual to be wholly conscious of what elements are distinctly religious and Christian, and what are merely social and identified with his religion by no logical implication. I am not requiring that the community should contain more 'good Christians' than one would expect to find under favourable conditions. The religious life of the people would be largely a matter of behaviour and conformity; social customs would take on religious sanctions; there would no doubt be many irrelevant accretions and local emphases and observances—which, if they went too far in eccentricity or superstition, it would be the business of the Church to correct, but which otherwise could make for social tenacity and coherence. The traditional way of life of the community would not be imposed by law, would have no sense of outward constraint, and would not be the result merely of the sum of individual belief and understanding.

The rulers, I have said, will *qua* rulers, accept Christianity not simply as their own faith to guide their actions, but as the system under which they are to govern. The people will accept it as a matter of behaviour and habit. In the abstraction which I have erected, it is obvious that the tendency of the State is toward expediency that may become cynical manipulation, the tendency of the people toward intellectual lethargy and superstition. We need therefore what I have called 'the Community of Christians', by which I mean, not local groups, and not the Church in any one of its senses, unless we call it 'the Church within the Church'. These will be the consciously and thoughtfully practising Christians, especially those of intellectual and spiritual superiority. . . .

If my outline of a Christian society has commanded the assent of the reader, he will agree that such a society can only be realised when the great majority of the sheep belong to one fold. To those who maintain that unity is a matter of indifference, to those who maintain even that a diversity of theological views is a good thing to an indefinite degree, I can make no appeal. But if the desirability of unity be admitted, if the idea of a Christian society be grasped and accepted, then it can only be realised, in England, through the Church of England. This is not the place for discussing the theological position of that Church: if in any points it is wrong, inconsistent, or evasive, these are matters for reform within the Church. And I am not overlooking the possibility and hope of eventual reunion or re-integration, on one side and another; I am only affirming that it is this Church which, by reason of its tradition, its organisation, and its relation in the past to the religious-social life of the people, is the one for our purpose—and that no Christianisation of England can take place without it.

The Church of a Christian society, then, should have some relation to the three elements in a Christian society that I have named. It must have a hierarchical organisation in direct and official relation to the State: in which relation it is always in danger of sinking into a mere department of State. It must have an organisation, such as the parochial system, in direct contact with the smallest units of the community and their individual members. And finally, it must have, in the persons of its more intellectual, scholarly and devout officers, its masters of ascetic theology and its men of wider interests, a relation to the Community of Christians. In matters of dogma, matters of faith and morals, it will speak as the final authority within the nation; in more mixed questions it will speak through individuals. At times, it can and should be in conflict with the State, in rebuking derelictions in policy, or in defending itself against encroachments of the temporal power, or in shielding the community against tyranny and asserting its neglected rights, or in contesting heretical opinion or immoral legislation and administration. At times, the hierarchy of the Church may be under attack from the Community of Christians, or from groups within it: for any organisation is always in danger of corruption and in need of reform from within. . . .

I think that the dangers to which a National Church is exposed, when the Universal Church is no more than a pious ideal, are so obvious that only to mention them is to command assent. Completely identified with a particular people, the National Church may at all times, but especially at moments of excitement, become no more than the voice of that people's prejudice, passion or interest.

But there is another danger, not quite so easily identified. I have maintained that the idea of a Christian society implies, for me, the existence of one Church which shall *aim at* comprehending the whole nation. Unless it has this aim, we relapse into that conflict between citizenship and church-membership, between public and private morality, which to-day makes moral life so difficult for everyone, and which in turn provokes that craving for a simplified, monistic solution of statism or racism which the National Church can only combat if it recognises its position as a part of the Universal Church. But if we allowed ourselves to entertain for Europe (to confine our attention to that continent) the ideal merely of a kind of society of Christian societies, we might tend unconsciously to treat the idea of the Universal Church as only the idea of a supernatural League of Nations. The direct allegiance of the individual would be to his National Church alone, and the Universal Church would remain an abstraction or become a cockpit for conflicting national interests. But the difference between the Universal Church and a perfected League of Nations is this, that the allegiance of the individual to his own Church is secondary to his allegiance to the Universal Church. Unless the National Church is a part of the whole, it has no claim upon me: but a League of Nations which could have a claim upon the devotion of the individual, prior to the claim of his country, is a chimaera which very few persons can even have endeavoured to picture to themselves. I have spoken more than once of the intolerable position of those who try to lead a Christian life in a non-Christian world. But it must be kept in mind that even in a Christian society as well organised as we can conceive possible in this world, the limit would be that our temporal and spiritual life should be harmonised: the temporal and spiritual would never be identified. There would always remain a dual allegiance, to the State and to the Church, to one's countrymen and to one's fellow-Christians everywhere, and the latter would always have the primacy. There would always be a tension; and this tension is essential to the idea of a Christian society, and is a distinguishing mark between a Christian and a pagan society. . . .

To justify Christianity because it provides a foundation of morality, instead of showing the necessity of Christian morality from the truth of Christianity, is a very dangerous inversion; and we may reflect, that a good deal of the attention of totalitarian states has been devoted, with a steadiness of purpose not always found in democracies, to providing their national life with a foundation of morality —the wrong kind perhaps, but a good deal more of it. It is not enthusiasm, but dogma, that differentiates a Christian from a pagan society. . . .

For a long enough time we have believed in nothing but the values arising in a mechanised, commercialised, urbanised way of life: it would be as well for us to face the permanent conditions upon which God allows us to live upon this planet. And without sentimentalising the life of the savage, we might practise the humility to observe, in some of the societies upon which we look down as primitive or backward, the operation of a social-religious-artistic complex which we should emulate upon a higher plane. We have been accustomed to regard 'progress' as always integral; and have yet to learn that it is only by an effort and a discipline, greater than society has yet seen the need of imposing upon itself, that material knowledge and power is gained without loss of spiritual knowledge and power. The struggle to recover the sense of relation to nature and to God, the recognition that even the most primitive feelings should be part of our heritage, seems to me to be the explanation and justification of the life of D. H. Lawrence, and the excuse for his aberrations. But we need not only to learn how to look at the world with the eyes of a Mexican Indian—and I hardly think that Lawrence succeeded—and we certainly cannot afford to stop there. We need to know how to see the world as the Christian Fathers saw it; and the purpose of reascending to origins is that we should be able to return, with greater spiritual knowledge, to our own situation. We need to recover the sense of religious fear, so that it may be overcome by religious hope.

51. Christianity and Democracy *

JACQUES MARITAIN (1882-)

With regard to the relationship between politics and religion—

---

* Reprinted by permission of the publishers from Jacques Maritain, *Christianity and Democracy*, first published 1945 by Geoffrey Bles Ltd.

it is obvious that Christianity and Christian faith cannot be made subservient to democracy as a philosophy of human and political life or to any political form whatsoever. That is a result of the fundamental distinction introduced by Christ between the things that are Caesar's and the things that are God's, a distinction which has been unfolding throughout our history in the midst of accidents of all kinds, and which frees religion from all temporal enslavement by stripping the State of all sacred pretensions; in other words, by giving the State secular standing. No doctrine or opinion of merely human origin, no matter how true it may be, but only things revealed by God, force themselves upon the faith of the Christian soul. One can be a Christian and achieve one's salvation while militating in favour of any political regime whatsoever, always on condition that it does not trespass against natural law and the law of God. One can be a Christian and achieve one's salvation while defending a political philosophy other than the democratic philosophy, just as one was able to be a Christian, in the days of the Roman Empire, while accepting the social regime of slavery, or in the seventeenth century while holding to the political regime of absolute monarchy. But the important thing for the political life of the world and for the solution of this crisis of civilization is by no means to pretend that Christianity is linked to democracy and that Christian faith compels every believer to be a democrat; it is to affirm that democracy is linked to Christianity and that the democratic impulse has arisen in human history as a temporal manifestation of the inspiration of the Gospel. The question does not deal here with Christianity as a religious creed and road to eternal life, but rather with Christianity as leaven in the social and political life of nations and as bearer of the temporal hope of mankind; it does not deal with Christianity as a treasurer of divine truth sustained and propagated by the Church, but with Christianity as historical energy at work in the world. It is not in the heights of theology, it is in the depths of secular conscience and secular existence that Christianity works in this fashion, while sometimes even assuming heretical forms or forms of revolt in which it seems to be denying itself, as though the broken bits of the key to paradise, falling into our destitute lives and combining with the metals of the earth, were more effective in activating the history of this world than the pure essence of the celestial metal. It was not given to believers faithful to Catholic dogma but to rationalists to proclaim in France the rights of man and of the citizen, to Puritans to strike the last blow at slavery in America, to atheistic Communists to abolish in Russia the absolutism of private profit, although this last process would have been less vitiated by the force of error and would have occasioned fewer catastrophes if it had been performed by Christians. Yet the effort to deliver labour and man from the domination of money is an outgrowth of the currents released in the world by the preaching of the Gospel, such as the effort to abolish servitude and the effort to bring about the recognition of the rights of the human person.

Christ sent the sword to the heart of human history. The human race will emerge from the era of great sufferings only when the activity of hidden stimulation, by means of which the Christian spirit moves along and toils at bloody cost in the night of earthly history, will have joined with the activity of illumination, by means of which the Christian spirit restores souls in the truth and life of the kingdom of God. It is not at the end of the present war that this goal will be reached. But the present war reveals to us, as by an apocalyptic sign, the direction in which we must move; and peace, if peace is won, will denote that the creative forces in motion within human history are decidedly set in this direction. . . .

That is why I said above that the democratic impulse burst forth in history as a temporal manifestation of the inspiration of the Gospel. Statesmen know this well, and it is not without reason that in their defence of democracy they are to-day invoking the Sermon on the Mount. In his message of January 4, 1939, which has been said to contain "the outline of that reconstruction in their moral philosophy which the democracies must undertake if they are to survive," [1] President Roosevelt stressed the fact that democracy, respect for the human person, for liberty, and for international good faith find their soundest foundation in religion and furnish religion with its best guarantees. He recently affirmed that "we [the United Nations] shall seek . . . the establishment of an international order in which the spirit of Christ shall rule the hearts of men and nations." [2]

In an important speech delivered on May 8, 1942, Henry A. Wal-

---

[1] Walter Lippmann, New York Herald Tribune, Jan. 7, 1939.

[2] Letter to the American Bishops, Catholic News, Jan. 17, 1942.

lace, the Vice-President of the United States, declared in turn: "The Idea of freedom . . . is derived from the Bible with its extraordinary emphasis on the dignity of the individual. Democracy is the only true political expression of Christianity." [3] Toward the close of his life, Chateaubriand had expressed the same thought. And in his book, *The Two Sources of Morality and Religion,* Henri Bergson also stated that because in the republican slogan "the essential thing is fraternity," we must state that "democracy is evangelical in essence." To the misfortune and confusion of ideas of the modern world, Rousseau and Kant dressed democratic thought up in their sentimental and philosophical formulas. We know, however, "how much Kant owed to his pietism, and Rousseau to an interplay of Protestantism and Catholicism." [4] The sources of the democratic ideal must be sought many centuries before Kant and Rousseau.

Not only does the democratic state of mind proceed from the inspiration of the Gospel, but it cannot exist without it. To keep faith in the forward march of humanity despite all the temptations to despair of man that are furnished by history, and particularly contemporary history; to have faith in the dignity of the person and in common humanity, in human rights and in justice—that is, in essentially spiritual values; to have, not in formulas but in reality, the sense of and respect for the dignity of the people, which is a spiritual dignity and is revealed to whoever knows how to love it; to sustain and revive the sense of equality without sinking into a levelling equalitarianism; to respect authority, knowing that its wielders are only men, like those they rule, and derive their trust from the consent or the will of the people whose vicars or representatives they are; to believe in the sanctity of law and in the efficacious virtue—efficacious at long range—of political justice in face of the scandalous triumphs of falsehood and violence; to have faith in liberty and in fraternity, an heroical inspiration and an heroical belief are needed which fortify and vivify reason, and which none other than Jesus of Nazareth brought forth in the world.

Let us also consider the immense burden of animality, of egoism, and of latent barbarism that men bear within themselves and which

---

[3] *The Price of Free World Victory,* speech delivered May 8, 1942 before the Free World Association.

[4] Henri Bergson, *The Two Sources of Morality and Religion,* p. 243, English edition.

keeps social life still terribly far from achieving its truest and most elevated aims. Let us realize this fact that the part of instinct and irrational forces is even greater in communal existence than in individual existence, and that at the moment when the people enter into history by claiming their political and social majority, large portions of humanity remain in a state of immaturity or suffer from morbid complexes accumulated in the course of time, and are still no more than the rough draft or the preparation of that fruit of civilization which we call a people. Let us understand that in order to enjoy its privileges as an adult in political life without running the risk of failure a people must be able to act naturally; then we will understand that the era has still not passed when for democracy itself force—righteous force—apart from its normal role in the policing of societies, must also play a subsidiary role of protecting against the return of the instinct of domination, exploitation or anarchic egoism. And above all we will understand that, with a view to curtailing as much as possible and eliminating by degrees these subsidiary functions of force, more than ever democracy needs the evangelical ferment in order to be realized and in order to endure. The lasting advent of the democratic state of mind and of the democratic philosophy of life requires the energies of the Gospel to penetrate secular existence, taming the irrational to reason and becoming embodied in the vital dynamism of the tendencies and instincts of nature, in order to fashion and stabilize in the depths of the sub-conscious those reflexes, habits and virtues without which the intellect which leads action fluctuates with the wind and wasting egoism prevails in man. It was Joseph de Maistre who said: "Wherever a religion other than the Christian religion holds sway, there slavery is sanctioned, and wherever the Christian religion weakens, the nation becomes, in exact proportion, less capable of general liberty. . . . Government alone cannot govern, it needs either slavery which reduces the number of active wills in the State, or divine force, which by a kind of spiritual grafting, destroys the natural harshness of these wills, and enables them to work together without harm to one another." [5]

It is not enough for a population or a section of the population to have Christian faith and be docile to the ministers of religion in order to be in a position properly to judge political matters. If this

---

[5] *Le Pape*, Book III, Chapter 2.

population has no political experience, no taste for seeing clearly for itself nor a tradition of initiative and critical judgment, its position with respect to politics grows more complicated, for nothing is easier for political counterfeiters than to exploit good principles for purposes of deception, and nothing is more disastrous than good principles badly applied. And, moreover, nothing is easier for human weakness than to merge religion with prejudices of race, family or class, collective hatreds, passions of a clan and political phantoms which compensate for the rigours of individual discipline in a pious but insufficiently purified soul. Politics deal with matters and interests of the world and they depend upon passions natural to man and upon reason. But the point I wish to make here is that without goodness, love and charity, all that is best in us—even divine faith, but passions and reason much more so—turns in our hands to an unhappy use. The point is that right political experience cannot develop in people unless passions and reason are oriented by a solid basis of collective virtues, by faith and honour and thirst for justice. The point is that without the evangelical instinct and the spiritual potential of a living Christianity, political judgment and political experience are ill protected against the illusions of selfishness and fear; without courage, compassion for mankind, and the spirit of sacrifice the ever-thwarted advance toward an historical ideal of generosity and fraternity is not conceivable.

As Bergson has shown in his profound analyses, it is the urge of a love infinitely stronger than the philanthropy commended by philosophers which caused human devotion to surmount the closed borders of the natural social groups—family group and national group—and extended it to the entire human race, because this love is the life in us of the very love which has created being and because it truly makes of each human being our neighbor. Without breaking the links of flesh and blood, of self-interest, tradition and pride which are needed by the body politic, and without destroying the rigorous laws of existence and conservation of this body politic, such a love extended to all men transcends and at the same time transforms from within the very life of the group, and tends to integrate all humanity into a community of nations and peoples in which men will be reconciled. For the kingdom of God is not miserly, the communion which is its supernatural privilege is not jealously guarded; it wants to spread and refract this communion outside its own limits, in the imperfect shapes and in the universe of conflicts, malice and bitter toil which make up the temporal realm. That is the deepest principle of the democratic ideal, which is the secular name for the ideal of Christendom. That is why, Bergson writes, "democracy is evangelical in essence and . . . its motive power is love." [6]

Yet in the same way it also appears that the democratic ideal runs against the grain of nature, whose law is not evangelical love. ". . . They were false democracies, those cities of antiquity, based on slavery, relieved by this fundamental iniquity of the biggest and most excruciating problems." [7] Democracy is a paradox and a challenge hurled at nature, at that thankless and wounded human nature whose original aspirations and reserves of grandeur it evokes. In the democratic ideal, and "in the democratic frame of mind" we must see, Bergson writes, "a great effort running against the grain of nature"—which does not mean an effort contrary to nature, but an effort to straighten nature, an effort linked to the developments of reason and justice and which must take place in history under the influence of the Christian leaven; an effort that requires that nature and the temporal order be elevated by the action of this leaven within their own realm, in the realm of civilization's movement. If the development of machinery and the great conquests which we have seen in the realm of matter and techniques demand "an increment of soul" in order to become true instruments of liberation, it is also by means of this increment of soul that democracy will be realized. Its progress is bound up with the spiritualization of secular existence.

52. *The Everson Case* *

JUSTICE HUGO BLACK *(1886–   )*

FOR THE COURT

The "establishment of religion" clause of the First Amendment

---

[6] Henri Bergson, op. cit. p. 243.

[7] ibid.

* [The Supreme Court of the United States, 1947, 330 U. S. 1. Only a brief excerpt from Justice Black's *Opinion* is reprinted.]

means at least this: Neither a state nor the Federal Government can set up a church. Neither can pass laws which aid one religion, aid all religions, or prefer one religion over another. Neither can force nor influence a person to go to or to remain away from church against his will or force him to profess a belief or disbelief in any religion. No person can be punished for entertaining or professing religious beliefs or disbeliefs, for church attendance or non-attendance. No tax in any amount, large or small, can be levied to support any religious activities or institutions, whatever they may be called, or whatever form they may adopt to teach or practice religion. Neither a state nor the Federal Government can, openly or secretly, participate in the affairs of any religious organization or groups and vice versa. In the words of Jefferson, the clause against establishment of religion by law was intended to erect a wall of separation between church and state."[1]

JUSTICE WILEY B. RUTLEDGE *(1894–1949)*

DISSENTING OPINION

Congress shall make no law respecting an establishment of religion, or prohibiting the free exercise thereof . . . . U. S. Const., Amend. I.

Well aware that Almighty God hath created the mind free; . . . . that to compel a man to furnish contributions of money for the propagation of opinions which he disbelieves, is sinful and tyrannical; . . . .

WE, THE GENERAL ASSEMBLY, DO ENACT, That no man shall be compelled to frequent or support any religious worship, place, or ministry whatsoever, nor shall be enforced, restrained, molested, or burthened in his body or goods, nor shall otherwise suffer, on account of his religious opinions or belief . . . .

I cannot believe that the great author of those words,[1a] or the men who made them law, could have joined in this decision. Neither so

---

[1] [This phrase was first used by Jefferson in a talk to the Danbury Baptists Association. He said: "Believing with you that religion is a matter which lies solely between man and his God, that he owes account to none other for his faith or his worship, that the legislative powers of government reach actions only, and not opinions, I contemplate with sovereign reverence that act of the whole American people which declared that their legislature should make no law respecting an establishment of religion, or prohibiting the free exercise thereof, thus building a wall of separation between church and state."]

[1a] [See Selection 48.]

high nor impregnable today as yesterday is the wall raised between church and state by Virginia's great statute of religious freedom and the First Amendment, now made applicable to all the states by the Fourteenth. New Jersey's statute sustained is the first, if indeed it is not the second breach to be made by this Court's action. That a third, and a fourth, and still others will be attempted, we may be sure. For just as *Cochran v. Board of Education,* 281 U.S. 370, has opened the way by oblique ruling for this decision, so will the two make wider the breach for a third. Thus with time the most solid freedom gives way steadily before continuing corrosive decision.

This case forces us to determine squarely for the first time what was "an establishment of religion" in the First Amendment's conception; and by that measure to decide whether New Jersey's action violates its command. The facts may be stated shortly, to give setting and color to the constitutional problem.

By statute New Jersey has authorized local boards of education to provide for the transportation of children "to and from school other than a public school" except one operated for profit wholly or in part, over established public school routes, or by other means when the child lives "remote from any school." The school board of Ewing Township has provided by resolution for "the transportation of pupils of Ewing to the Trenton and Pennington High Schools and Catholic Schools by way of public carrier. . . ."

Named parents have paid the cost of public conveyance of their children from their homes in Ewing to three public high schools and four parochial schools outside the district. Semiannually the Board has reimbursed the parents from public school funds raised by general taxation. Religion is taught as part of the curriculum in each of the four private schools, as appears affirmatively by the testimony of the superintendent of parochial schools in the Diocese of Trenton.

The Court of Errors and Appeals of New Jersey, reversing the Supreme Court's decision, 132 N.J.L.98, 39 A. 2d 75, has held the Ewing board's action not in contravention of the state constitution or statutes or of the Federal Constitution. 133 N.J.L.350, 44 A. 2d 333. We have to consider only whether this ruling accords with the prohibition of the First Amendment implied in the due process clause of the Fourteenth.

Not simply an established church, but any law respecting an

establishment of religion is forbidden. The Amendment was broadly but not loosely phrased. It is the compact and exact summation of its author's views formed during his long struggle for religious freedom. In Madison's own words characterizing Jefferson's Bill for Establishing Religious Freedom, the guaranty he put in our national charter, like the bill he piloted through the Virginia Assembly, was "a Model of technical precision, and perspicuous brevity." Madison could not have confused "church" and "religion," or "an established church" and "an establishment of religion."

The Amendment's purpose was not to strike merely at the official establishment of a single sect, creed or religion, outlawing only a formal relation such as had prevailed in England and some of the colonies. Necessarily it was to uproot all such relationships. But the object was broader than separating church and state in this narrow sense. It was to create a complete and permanent separation of the spheres of religious activity and civil authority by comprehensively forbidding every form of public aid or support for religion. In proof the Amendment's wording and history unites with this Court's consistent utterances whenever attention has been fixed directly upon the question.

"Religion" appears only once in the Amendment. But the word governs two prohibitions and governs them alike. It does not have two meanings, one narrow to forbid "an establishment" and another, much broader, for securing "the free exercise thereof." "Thereof" brings down "religion" with its entire and exact content, no more and no less, from the first into the second guaranty, so that Congress and now the states are as broadly restricted concerning the one as they are regarding the other.

No one would claim today that the Amendment is constricted, in "prohibiting the free exercise" of religion, to securing the free exercise of some formal or creedal observance, of one sect or of many. It secures all forms of religious expression, creedal, sectarian or non-sectarian, wherever and however taking place, except conduct which trenches upon the like freedoms of others or clearly and presently endangers the community's good order and security. For the protective purposes of this phase of the basic freedom, street preaching, oral or by distribution of literature, has been given "the same high estate under the First Amendment as . . . worship in the churches and preaching from the pulpits." And on this basis parents have been held entitled to send their children to private, religious schools, *Pierce v. Society of Sisters*, 268 U. S. 510. Accordingly, daily religious education commingled with secular is "religion" within the guaranty's comprehensive scope. So are religious training and teaching in whatever form. The word connotes the broadest content, determined not by the form or formality of the teaching or where it occurs, but by its essential nature regardless of those details.

"Religion" has the same broad significance in the twin prohibition concerning "an establishment." The Amendment was not duplicitous. "Religion" and "establishment" were not used in any formal or technical sense. The prohibition broadly forbids state support, financial or other, of religion in any guise, form or degree. It outlaws all use of public funds for religious purposes. . . .

Compulsory attendance upon religious exercises went out early in the process of separating church and state, together with forced observance of religious forms and ceremonies. Test oaths and religious qualification for office followed later. These things none devoted to our great tradition of religious liberty would think of bringing back. Hence today, apart from efforts to inject religious training or exercises and sectarian issues into the public schools, the only serious surviving threat to maintaining that complete and permanent separation of religion and civil power which the First Amendment commands is through use of the taxing power to support religion, religious establishments, or establishments having a religious foundation whatever their form or special religious function.

Does New Jersey's action furnish support for religion by use of the taxing power? Certainly it does, if the test remains undiluted as Jefferson and Madison made it, that money taken by taxation from one is not to be used or given to support another's religious training or belief, or indeed one's own. Today as then the furnishing of "contributions of money for the propagation of opinions which he disbelieves" is the forbidden exaction; and the prohibition is absolute for whatever measure brings that consequence and whatever amount may be sought or given to that end.

The funds used here were raised by taxation. The Court does not dispute, nor could it, that their use does in fact give aid and encouragement to religious instruction. It only concludes that this aid is not "support" in law. But Madison and Jefferson were concerned with aid and support in fact, not as a legal conclusion "entangled in precedents." Remonstrance, Par. 3.[2] Here parents pay money to send their children to parochial schools and funds raised by taxation are used to reimburse them. This not only helps the children to get to school and the parents to send them. It aids them in a substantial way to get the very thing which they are sent to the particular school to secure, namely, religious training and teaching.

Believers of all faiths, and others who do not express their feeling toward ultimate issues of existence in any creedal form, pay the New Jersey tax. When the money so raised is used to pay for transportation to religious schools, the Catholic taxpayer to the extent of his proportionate share pays for the transportation of Lutheran, Jewish and otherwise religiously affiliated children to receive their non-Catholic religious instruction. Their parents likewise pay proportionately for the transportation of Catholic children to receive Catholic instruction. Each thus contributes to "the propagation of opinions which he disbelieves" in so far as their religions differ, as do others who accept no creed without regard to those differences. Each thus pays taxes also to support the teaching of his own religion, an exaction equally forbidden since it denies "the comfortable liberty" of giving one's contribution to the particular agency of instruction he approves.

New Jersey's action therefore exactly fits the type of exaction and the kind of evil at which Madison and Jefferson struck. Under the test they framed it cannot be said that the cost of transportation is no part of the cost of education or of the religious instruction given. That it is a substantial and a necessary element is shown most plainly by the continuing and increasing demand for the state to assume it. Nor is there pretense that it relates only to the secular instruction given in religious schools or that any attempt is or could be made toward allocating proportional shares as between the secular and the religious instruction. It is precisely because the instruction is religious and relates to a particular faith, whether one or another, that parents send their children to religious schools under the *Pierce* doctrine.[3] And the very purpose of the state's contribution is to de-

---

[2] [See Selection 49].

[3] [In the *Pierce* case, the Supreme Court invalidated an Oregon law outlawing parochial schools. This, in effect, authorized parents to send their children to such schools, if they so desired, instead of to public schools.]

fray the cost of conveying the pupil to the place where he will receive not simply secular, but also and primarily religious, teaching and guidance.

Indeed the view is sincerely avowed by many of various faiths, that the basic purpose of all education is or should be religious, that the secular cannot be and should not be separated from the religious phase and emphasis. Hence, the inadequacy of public or secular education and the necessity for sending the child to a school where religion is taught. But whatever may be the philosophy or its justification, there is undeniably an admixture of religious with secular teaching in all such institutions. That is the very reason for their being. Certainly for purposes of constitutionality we cannot contradict the whole basis of the ethical and educational convictions of people who believe in religious schooling.

Yet this very admixture is what was disestablished when the First Amendment forbade "an establishment of religion." Commingling the religious with the secular teaching does not divest the whole of its religious permeation and emphasis or make them of minor part, if proportion were material. Indeed, on any other view, the constitutional prohibition always could be brought to naught by adding a modicum of the secular.

An appropriation from the public treasury to pay the cost of transportation to Sunday school, to weekday special classes at the church or parish house, or to the meetings of various young people's religious societies, such as the Y. M. C. A., the Y. W. C. A., the Y. M. H. A., and the Epworth League, could not withstand the constitutional attack. This would be true, whether or not secular activities were mixed with the religious. If such an appropriation could not stand, then it is hard to see how one becomes valid for the same thing upon the more extended scale of daily instruction. Surely constitutionality does not turn on where or how often the mixed teaching occurs.

Finally, transportation, where it is needed, is as essential to education as any other element. Its cost is as much a part of the total expense, except at times in amount, as the cost of textbooks, of school lunches, of athletic equipment, of writing and other materials; indeed of all other items composing the total burden. Now as always the core of the educational process is the teacher-pupil relationship. Without this the richest equipment and facilities would go for naught.

See *Judd v. Board of Education*, 278 N. Y., 200, 212, 15 N. E. 2d 576, 582. But the proverbial Mark Hopkins conception [4] no longer suffices for the country's requirements. Without buildings, without equipment, without library, textbooks and other materials, and without transportation to bring teacher and pupil together in such an effective teaching environment, there can be not even the skeleton of what our times require. Hardly can it be maintained that transportation is the least essential of these items, or that it does not in fact aid, encourage, sustain and support, just as they do, the very process which is its purpose to accomplish. No less essential is it, or the payment of its cost, than the very teaching in the classroom or payment of the teacher's sustenance. Many types of equipment, now considered essential, better could be done without.

For me, therefore, the feat is impossible to select so indispensable an item from the composite of total costs, and characterize it as not aiding, contributing to, promoting or sustaining the propagation of beliefs which it is the very end of all to bring about. Unless this can be maintained, and the Court does not maintain it, the aid thus given is outlawed. Payment of transportation is no more, nor is it any the less essential to education, whether religious or secular, than payment for tuitions, for teachers' salaries, for buildings, equipment and necessary materials. Nor is it any the less directly related, in a school giving religious instruction, to the primary religious objective all those essential items of cost are intended to achieve. No rational line can be drawn between payment for such larger, but not more necessary, items and payment for transportation. The only line that can be drawn is one between more dollars and less. Certainly in this realm such a line can be no valid constitutional measure. *Murdock v. Pennsylvania*, 319 U. S. 105; *Thomas v. Collins*, 323 U. S. 516. Now, as in Madison's time, not the amount but the principle of assessment is wrong.

But we are told that the New Jersey statute is valid in its present application because the appropriation is for a public, not a private purpose, namely, the promotion of education, and the majority accept this idea in the conclusion that all we have here is "public welfare legislation." If that is true and the Amendment's force can be thus destroyed, what has been said becomes all the more per-

---

4 [Mark Hopkins (1802–1887), former president of Williams College, defined a university as a log with a teacher at one end and a student at the other.]

tinent. For then there could be no possible objection to more extensive support of religious education by New Jersey.

If the fact alone be determinative that religious schools are engaged in education, thus promoting the general and individual welfare, together with the legislature's decision that the payment of public moneys for their aid makes their work a public function, then I can see no possible basis, except one of dubious legislative policy, for the state's refusal to make full appropriation for support of private, religious schools, just as is done for public instruction. There could not be, on that basis, valid constitutional objection.[*]

Of course paying the cost of transportation promotes the general cause of education and the welfare of the individual. So does paying all other items of educational expense. And obviously, as the majority say, it is much too late to urge that legislation designed to facilitate the opportunities of children to secure a secular education serves no public purpose. Our nation-wide system of public education rests on the contrary view, as do all grants in aid of education, public or private, which is not religious in character.

These things are beside the real question. They have no possible materiality except to obscure the all-pervading, inescapable issue. Cf. *Cochran v. Board of Education*, supra. Stripped of its religious phase, the case presents no substantial federal question. *Ibid.* The public function argument, by casting the issue in terms of promoting the general cause of education and the welfare of the individual, ignores the religious factor and its essential connection with the transportation, thereby leaving out the only vital element in the case. So of course do the "public welfare" and "social legislation" ideas, for they come to the same thing.

We have here then one substantial issue, not two. To say that

---

[*] If it is part of the state's function to supply to religious schools or their patrons the smaller items of educational expense, because the legislature may say they perform a public function, it is hard to see why the larger ones also may not be paid. Indeed, it would seem even more proper and necessary for the state to do this. For if one class of expenditures is justified on the ground that it supports the general cause of education or benefits the individual, or can be made to do so by legislative declaration, so even more certainly would be the other. To sustain payment for transportation to school, for text-books, for other essential materials, or perhaps for school lunches, and not for what makes all these things effective for their intended end, would be to make a public function of the smaller items and their cumulative effect, but to make wholly private in character the larger things without which the smaller could have no meaning or use.

New Jersey's appropriation and her use of the power of taxation for raising the funds appropriated are not for public purposes but are for private ends, is to say that they are for the support of religion and religious teaching. Conversely, to say that they are for public purposes is to say that they are not for religious ones.

This is precisely for the reason that education which includes religious training and teaching, and its support, have been made matters of private right and function, not public, by the very terms of the First Amendment. That is the effect not only in its guaranty of religion's free exercise, but also in the prohibition of establishments. It was on this basis of the private character of the function of religious education that this Court held parents entitled to send their children to private, religious schools. *Pierce v. Society of Sisters, supra.* Now it declares in effect that the appropriation of public funds to defray part of the cost of attending those schools is for a public purpose. If so, I do not understand why the state cannot go farther or why this case approaches the verge of its power.

In truth this view contradicts the whole purpose and effect of the First Amendment as heretofore conceived. The "public function"—"public welfare"—"social legislation" argument seeks, in Madison's words, to "employ Religion (that is, here, religious education) as an engine of Civil policy." Remonstrance, Par. 5. It is of one piece with the Assessment Bill's preamble, although with the vital difference that it wholly ignores what that preamble explicitly states.

Our constitutional policy is exactly the opposite. It does not deny the value or the necessity for religious training, teaching or observance. Rather it secures their free exercise. But to that end it does deny that the state can undertake or sustain them in any form or degree. For this reason the sphere of religious activity, as distinguished from the secular intellectual liberties, has been given the twofold protection and, as the state cannot forbid, neither can it perform or aid in performing the religious function. The dual prohibition makes that function altogether private. It cannot be made a public one by legislative act. This was the very heart of Madison's Remonstrance, as it is of the Amendment itself.

It is not because religious teaching does not promote the public or the individual's welfare, but because neither is furthered when the state promotes religious education, that the Constitution forbids it to do so. Both legislatures and courts are bound by that distinction. In failure to observe it lies the fallacy of the "public function" —"social legislation" argument, a fallacy facilitated by easy transference of the argument's basing from due process unrelated to any religious aspect to the First Amendment.

By no declaration that a gift of public money to religious uses will promote the general or individual welfare, or the cause of education generally, can legislative bodies overcome the Amendment's bar. Nor may the courts sustain their attempts to do so by finding such consequences for appropriations which in fact give aid to or promote religious uses. Cf. *Norris v. Alabama*, 294 U. S. 587, 590; *Hooven & Allison Co. v. Evatt*, 324 U. S. 652, 659; *Akins v. Texas*, 325 U. S. 398, 402. Legislatures are free to make, and courts to sustain, appropriations only when it can be found that in fact they do not aid, promote, encourage or sustain religious teaching or observances, be the amount large or small. No such finding has been or could be made in this case. The Amendment has removed this form of promoting the public welfare from legislative and judicial competence to make a public function. It is exclusively a private affair.

The reasons underlying the Amendment's policy have not vanished with time or diminished in force. Now as when it was adopted the price of religious freedom is double. It is that the church and religion shall live both within and upon that freedom. There cannot be freedom of religion, safeguarded by the state, and intervention by the church or its agencies in the state's domain or dependency on its largess. Madison's Remonstrance, Par. 6,8. The great condition of religious liberty is that it be maintained free from sustenance, as also from other interferences, by the state. For when it comes to rest upon that secular foundation it vanishes with the resting. *Id.*, Par. 7, 8. Public money devoted to payments of religious costs, educational or other, brings the quest for more. It brings too the struggle of sect against sect for the larger share or for any. Here one by numbers alone will benefit most, there another. That is precisely the history of societies which have had an established religion and dissident groups. *Id.*, Par. 8, 11. It is the very thing Jefferson and Madison experienced and sought to guard against, whether in its blunt or in its more screened forms. *Ibid.* The end of such strife cannot be other than to destroy the cherished liberty. The dominating group will achieve the dominant benefit; or all will embroil the state in their dissensions. *Id.*, Par. 11.

Exactly such conflicts have centered of late around providing transportation to religious schools from public funds. The issue and the dissension work typically in Madison's phrase, to "destroy that moderation and harmony which the forbearance of our laws to intermeddle with Religion, has produced amongst its several sects." *Id.*, Par. 11. This occurs, as he well knew, over measures at the very threshold of departure from the principle. *Id.* Par. 3, 9, 11.

In these conflicts wherever success has been obtained it has been upon the contention that by providing the transportation, the general cause of education, the general welfare, and the welfare of the individual will be forwarded; hence that the matter lies within the realm of public function, for legislative determination. State courts have divided upon the issue, some taking the view that only the individual, others that the institution receives the benefit. A few have recognized that this dichotomy is false, that both in fact are aided.

The majority here does not accept in terms any of those views. But neither does it deny that the individual or the school, or indeed both, are benefited directly and substantially. To do so would cut the ground from under the public function—social legislation thesis. On the contrary, the opinion concedes that the children are aided by being helped to get to the religious schooling. By converse necessary implication as well as by the absence of express denial, it must be taken to concede also that the school is helped to reach the child with its religious teaching. The religious enterprise is common to both, as is the interest in having transportation for its religious purposes provided.

Notwithstanding the recognition that this two-way aid is given and the absence of any denial that religious teaching is thus furthered, the Court concludes that the aid so given is not "support" of religion. It is rather only support of education as such, without reference to its religious content, and thus becomes public welfare legislation. To this elision of the religious element from the case is added gloss in two respects, one that the aid extended partakes of the nature of a safety measure, the other that failure to provide it would make the state unneutral in religious matters, discriminating against or hampering such children concerning public benefits all others receive.

As will be noted, the one gloss is contradicted by the facts of record and the other is of whole cloth with the "public function" argument's excision of the religious factor. But most important is that this approach, if valid, supplies a ready method for nullifying the Amendment's guaranty, not only for this case and others involving small grants in aid for religious education, but equally for larger ones. The only thing needed will be for the Court again to transplant the "public welfare—public function" view from its proper nonreligious due process bearing to First Amendment application, holding that religious education is not "supported" though it may be aided by the appropriation, and that the cause of education generally is furthered by helping the pupil to secure that type of training.

This is not therefore just a little case over bus fares. In paraphrase of Madison, distant as it may be in its present form from a complete establishment of religion, it differs from it only in degree; and is the first step in that direction. *Id.*, Par. 9. Today as in his time "the same authority which can force a citizen to contribute three pence only . . . for the support of any one (religious) establishment, may force him" to pay more; or "to conform to any other establishment in all cases whatsoever." And now, as then, "either . . . we must say, that the will of the Legislature is the only measure of their authority; and that in the plenitude of this authority, they may sweep away all our fundamental rights; or, that they are bound to leave this particular right untouched and sacred." Remonstrance, Par. 15.

The realm of religious training and belief remains, as the Amendment made it, the kingdom of the individual man and his God. It should be kept inviolately private, not "entangled . . . in precedents" or confounded with what legislatures legitimately may take over into the public domain.

No one conscious of religious values can be unsympathetic toward the burden which our constitutional separation puts on parents who desire religious instruction mixed with secular for their children. They pay taxes for others' children's education, at the same time the added cost of instruction for their own. Nor can one happily see benefits denied to children which others receive, because in conscience they or their parents for them desire a different kind of training others do not demand.

But if those feelings should prevail, there would be an end to our historic constitutional policy and command. No more unjust or discriminatory in fact is it to deny attendants at religious schools the cost of their transportation than it is to deny them tuitions, sustenance for their teachers, or any other educational expense which others receive at public cost. Hardship in fact there is which none can blink. But, for assuring to those who undergo it the greater, the most comprehensive freedom, it is one written by design and firm intent into our basic law.

Of course discrimination in the legal sense does not exist. The child attending the religious school has the same right as any other to attend the public school. But he foregoes exercising it because the same guaranty which assures this freedom forbids the public school or any agency of the state to give or aid him in securing the religious instruction he seeks.

Were he to accept the common school, he would be the first to protest the teaching there of any creed or faith not his own. And it is precisely for the reason that their atmosphere is wholly secular that children are not sent to public schools under the *Pierce* doctrine. But that is a constitutional necessity, because we have staked the very existence of our country on the faith that complete separation between the state and religion is best for the state and best for religion. *Remonstrance*, Par. 8, 12.

That policy necessarily entails hardship upon persons who forego the right to educational advantages the state can supply in order to secure others it is precluded from giving. Indeed this may hamper the parent and the child forced by conscience to that choice. But it does not make the state unneutral to withhold what the Constitution forbids it to give. On the contrary it is only by observing the prohibition rigidly that the state can maintain its neutrality and avoid partisanship in the dissensions inevitable when sect opposes sect over demands for public moneys to further religious education, teaching or training in any form or degree, directly or indirectly. Like St. Paul's freedom, religious liberty with a great price must be bought. And for those who exercise it most fully, by insisting upon religious education for their children mixed with secular, by the terms of our Constitution the price is greater than for others.

The problem then cannot be cast in terms of legal discrimination or its absence. This would be true, even though the state in giving aid should treat all religious instruction alike. Thus, if the present statute and its application were shown to apply equally to all religious schools of whatever faith, yet in the light of our tradition it could not stand. For then the adherent of one creed still would pay for the support of another, the childless taxpayer with others more fortunate. Then too there would seem to be no bar to making appropriations for transportation and other expenses of children attending public or other secular schools, after hours in separate places and classes for their exclusively religious instruction. The person who embraces no creed also would be forced to pay for teaching what he does not believe. Again, it was the furnishing of "contributions of money for the propagation of opinions which he disbelieves" that the fathers outlawed. That consequence and effect are not removed by multiplying to all-inclusiveness the sects for which support is exacted. The Constitution requires, not comprehensive identification of state with religion, but complete separation. . . .

Two great drives are constantly in motion to abridge, in the name of education, the complete division of religion and civil authority which our forefathers made. One is to introduce religious education and observances into the public schools. The other, to obtain public funds for the aid and support of various private religious schools. See Johnson, *The Legal Status of Church-State Relationships in the United States* (1934) ; Thayer, *Religion in Public Education* (1947) ; Note (1941) 50 Yale L.J. 917. In my opinion both avenues were closed by the Constitution. Neither should be opened by this Court. The matter is not one of quantity, to be measured by the amount of money expended. Now as in Madison's day it is one of principle, to keep separate the separate spheres as the First Amendment drew them; to prevent the first experiment upon our liberties; and to keep the question from becoming entangled in corrosive precedents. We should not be less strict to keep strong and untarnished the one side of the shield of religious freedom than we have been of the other.

53. A Catholic View on Church and State *

FRANCIS CARDINAL SPELLMAN (1889–) AND OTHERS

The inroads of secularism in civil life are a challenge to the Christian citizen—and indeed to every citizen with definite religious convictions. The essential connection between religion and good citizenship is deep in our American tradition. Those who took the lead in establishing our independence and framing our Constitution were firm and explicit in the conviction that religion and morality are the strong supports of national well-being, that national morality cannot long prevail in the absence of religious principle, and that impartial encouragement of religious influence on its citizens is a proper and practical function of good government.

This American tradition clearly envisioned the school as the meeting place of these helpful interacting influences. The third article of the Northwest Ordinance passed by Congress in 1787, reenacted in 1790, and included in the Constitutions of many states, enjoins: "Religion, morality and knowledge being necessary to good citizenship and the happiness of mankind, schools and the means of education shall forever be encouraged." This is our authentic American tradition on the philosophy of education for citizenship.

In the field of law our history reveals the same fundamental connection between religion and citizenship. It is through law that government exercises control over its citizens for the common good and establishes a balance between their rights and duties. The American concept of government and law started with the recognition that man's inalienable rights—which it is the function of government to protect—derive from God, his Creator. It thus bases human law, which deals with man's rights and their correlative duties in society, on foundations that are definitely religious, on principles that emerge from the definite view of man as a creature of God.

This view of man anchors human law to the natural law, which is the moral law of God made clear to us through the judgments of human reason and the dictates of conscience. The natural law, as an outstanding modern legal commentator has written, "is binding

---

* An official statement of the Roman Catholic Bishops of the United States, as reported in *The New York Times,* Nov. 21, 1948, reprinted by permission of *The New York Times.*

over all the globe, in all countries and at all times; no human laws are of any validity if contrary to this," Thus human law is essentially an ordinance of reason, not merely a dictate of will on the part of the state. In our authentic American tradition this is the accepted philosophy of law.

On this basically religious tradition concerning the preparation of the citizen through education and the direction of the citizen through law, secularism has in the past century exercised a corrosive influence. It has banned religion from tax-supported education and is now bent on destroying all cooperation between government and organized religion in the training of our future citizens. It has undermined the religious foundations of law in the mind of many men in the legal profession and has predisposed them to accept the legalistic tyranny of the omnipotent state. It has cleverly exploited, to the detriment of religion and good citizenship, the delicate problem of cooperation between Church and State in a country of divided religious allegiance.

That concrete problem, delicate as it is, can, without sacrifice of principle, be solved in a practical way when good-will and a spirit of fairness prevail. Authoritative Catholic teaching on the relations between Church and State, as set forth in Papal Encyclicals and in the treatises of recognized writers on ecclesiastical law, not only states clearly what these relations should normally be under ideal conditions, but also indicates to what extent the Catholic Church can adapt herself to the particular conditions that may obtain in different countries.

Examining, in the full perspective of that teaching, the position which those who founded our nation and framed its basic law took on the problem of Church-State relations in our own country, we find that the First Amendment to our Constitution solved that problem in a way that was typically American in its practical recognition of existing conditions and its evident desire to be fair to all citizens of whatever religious faith.

To one who knows something of history and law, the meaning of the First Amendment is clear enough from its own words: "Congress shall make no laws [sic] respecting an establishment of religion or forbidding [sic] the free exercise thereof." The meaning is even clearer in the records of the Congress that enacted it. Then, and throughout English and Colonial history, an "establishment of religion" meant the setting up by law of an official Church which would receive from the government favors not equally accorded to others in the cooperation between government and religion — which was simply taken for granted in our country at that time and has, in many ways, continued to this day. Under the First Amendment, the Federal Government could not extend this type of preferential treatment to one religion as against another, nor could it compel or forbid any state to do so.

If this practical policy be described by the loose metaphor "a wall of separation between Church and State," that term must be understood in a definite and typically American sense. It would be an utter distortion of American history and law to make that practical policy involve the indifference to religion and the exclusion of cooperation between religion and government implied in the term "separation of Church and State" as it has become the shibboleth of doctrinaire secularism.

Within the past two years secularism has scored unprecedented victories in its opposition to governmental encouragement of religious and moral training, even where no preferential treatment of one religion over another is involved. In two recent cases,[1] the Supreme Court of the United States has adopted an entirely novel and ominously extensive interpretation of the "establishment of religion" clause of the First Amendment. This interpretation would bar any cooperation between government and organized religion which would aid religion, even where no discrimination between religious bodies is in question.

This reading of the First Amendment, as a group of non-Catholic religious leaders recently noted, will endanger "forms of cooperation between Church and State which have been taken for granted by the American people," and "greatly accelerate the trend toward the secularization of our culture."

Reluctant as we are to criticize our supreme judicial tribunal, we cannot but observe that when the members of that tribunal write long and varying opinions in handing down a decision, they must expect that intelligent citizens of a democracy will study and appraise these opinions. The Journal of the American Bar Association,

---

[1] [The Everson Case, 330 U. S. 1 (1947) and The McCollum Case 333 U. S. 203 (1948)].

in a critical analysis of one of the cases in question, pertinently remarks: "The traditionally religious sanctions of our law, life and government are challenged by a judicial propensity which deserves the careful thought and study of lawyers and people."

Lawyers trained in the American tradition of law will be amazed to find that in the McCollum case the majority opinions pay scant attention to logic, history, or accepted norms of legal interpretation.

Logic would demand that what is less clear be defined by what is more clear. In the present instance we find just the reverse. The carefully chiselled phrases of the First Amendment are defined by the misleading metaphor "the wall of separation between Church and State."[1] This metaphor of Jefferson specifies nothing except that there shall be no "established Church," no state religion. All the rest of its content depends on the letter of the law that sets it up and can in the concrete imply anything from the impartial cooperation between government and free religious bodies (as in Holland and traditionally in our own country) all the way down to persecution of religion (as in France at the turn of the century). As was pointedly remarked in a dissenting opinion: "A rule of law cannot be drawn from a metaphor."

A glance at the history of Jefferson's own life and work would have served as a warning against the broad and devastating application of his "wall of separation" metaphor that we find in this case. The expression first appears in a letter written by Jefferson in 1802 and, significantly enough, in a context that makes it refer to the "free exercise of religion" clause rather than to the "establishment of religion" clause of the First Amendment.

Twenty years later Jefferson clearly showed in action that his concept of "separation of church and state" was far different from the concept of those who now appeal to his metaphor as a norm of interpretation. As the rector of the State University of Virginia, Jefferson proposed a system of cooperation between the various religious groups and the university which goes far beyond anything under consideration in the case at hand. And Mr. Madison, who had proposed the First Amendment and who led in carrying it through to enactment by Congress, was one of the visitors of the University of Virginia who approved Jefferson's plan.

Even one who is not a lawyer would expect to find in the opinion

---

1 [See Footnote 1, p. 430.]

of the Court some discussion of what was in the mind of the members of Congress when they framed and adopted the First Amendment. For it would seem that the intent of the legislator should be of capital importance in interpreting any law when a doubt is raised as to the objective meaning of the words in which it is framed. In regard to the "establishment of religion" clause, there is no doubt of the intent of the legislator. It is clear in the record of the Congress that framed it and of the State Legislatures that ratified it. To them it meant no official Church for the country as a whole, no preferment of one religion over another by the Federal Government — and at the same time no interference by the Federal Government in the Church-State relations of the individual states.

The opinion of the Court advances no reason for disregarding the mind of the legislator. But that reason is discernible in a concurring opinion adhered to by four of the nine judges. There we see clearly the determining influence of secularist theories of public education — and possibly of law. One cannot but remark that if this secularist influence is to prevail in our Government and its institutions, such a result should, in candor and logic and law, be achieved by legislation adopted after full popular discussion and not by the judicial procedure of an ideological interpretation of our Constitution.

We, therefore, hope and pray that the novel interpretation of the First Amendment recently adopted by the Supreme Court will in due process be revised. To that end we shall peacefully, patiently and perseveringly work.

We feel with deep conviction that for the sake of both good citizenship and religion there should be a reaffirmation of our original American tradition of free cooperation between government and religious bodies — cooperation involving no special privilege to any group and no restriction on the religious liberty of any citizen.

We solemnly disclaim any intent or desire to alter this prudent and fair American policy of government in dealing with the delicate problems that have their source in the divided religious allegiance of our citizens.

We call upon our Catholic people to seek in their faith an inspiration and a guide in making an informed contribution to good citizenship. We urge members of the legal profession in particular to develop and apply their special competence in this field. We stand ready to cooperate in fairness and charity with all who believe in God and are devoted to freedom under God to avert the impending danger of a judicial "establishment of secularism" that would ban God from public life. For secularism is threatening the religious foundations of our national life and preparing the way for the advent of the omnipotent state.

54. The New York Released Time Case *

JUSTICE WILLIAM O. DOUGLAS (1898–   )

FOR THE COURT

There is much talk of the separation of Church and State in the history of the Bill of Rights and in the decisions clustering around the First Amendment. See *Everson* v. *Board of Education*, 330 U. S. 1; *McCollum* v. *Board of Education, supra.* There cannot be the slightest doubt that the First Amendment reflects the philosophy that Church and State should be separated. And so far as interference with the "free exercise" of religion and an "establishment" of religion are concerned, the separation must be complete and unequivocal. The First Amendment within the scope of its coverage permits no exception; the prohibition is absolute. The First Amendment, however, does not say that in every and all respects there shall be a separation of Church and State. Rather, it studiously defines the manner, the specific ways, in which there shall be no concert or union or dependency one on the other. That is the common sense of the matter. Otherwise the state and religion would be aliens to each other — hostile, suspicious, and even unfriendly. Churches could not be required to pay even property taxes. Municipalities would not be permitted to render police or fire protection to religious groups. Policemen who helped parishioners into their places of worship would violate the Constitution. Prayers in

---

* 343 U S. 306 (1952). [By a vote of 6–3 the Court upheld the constitutionality of New York's Released Time program. Justice Douglas wrote the Court's opinion, while Justices Black, Jackson, and Frankfurter each wrote dissenting opinions.]

our legislative halls; the appeals to the Almighty in the messages of the Chief Executive; the proclamations making Thanksgiving Day a holiday; "so help me God" in our courtroom oaths — these and all other references to the Almighty that run through our laws, our public rituals, our ceremonies would be flouting the First Amendment. A fastidious atheist or agnostic could even object to the supplication with which the Court opens each session: "God save the United States and this Honorable Court."

We would have to press the concept of separation of Church and State to these extremes to condemn the present law on constitutional grounds. The nullification of this law would have wide and profound effects. A Catholic student applies to his teacher for permission to leave the school during hours on a Holy Day of Obligation to attend a mass. A Jewish student asks his teacher for permission to be excused for Yom Kippur. A Protestant wants the afternoon off for a family baptismal ceremony. In each case the teacher requires parental consent in writing. In each case the teacher, in order to make sure the student is not a truant, goes further and requires a report from the priest, the rabbi, or the minister. The teacher in other words cooperates in a religious program to the extent of making it possible for her students to participate in it. Whether she does it occasionally for a few students, regularly for one, or pursuant to a systematized program designed to further the religious needs of all the students does not alter the character of the act.

We are a religious people whose institutions presuppose a Supreme Being. We guarantee the freedom to worship as one chooses. We make room for as wide a variety of beliefs and creeds as the spiritual needs of man deem necessary. We sponsor an attitude on the part of government that shows no partiality to any one group and that lets each flourish according to the zeal of its adherents and the appeal of its dogma. When the state encourages religious instruction or cooperates with religious authorities by adjusting the schedule of public events to sectarian needs, it follows the best of our traditions. For it then respects the religious nature of our people and accommodates the public service to their spiritual needs. To hold that it may not would be to find in the Constitution a requirement that the government show a callous indifference to religious groups. That would be preferring those who believe in no religion over those who do believe. Government may not finance

religious groups nor undertake religious instruction nor blend secular and sectarian education nor use secular institutions to force one
or some religion on any person. But we find no constitutional requirement which makes it necessary for government to be hostile
to religion and to throw its weight against efforts to widen the
effective scope of religious influence. The government must be
neutral when it comes to competition between sects. It may not
thrust any sect on any person. It may not make a religious observance compulsory. It may not coerce anyone to attend church,
to observe a religious holiday, or to take religious instruction. But
it can close its doors or suspend its operations as to those who want
to repair to their religious sanctuary for worship or instruction. No
more than that is undertaken here.

This program may be unwise and improvident from an educational or a community viewpoint. That appeal is made to us on a
theory, previously advanced, that each case must be decided on the
basis of "our own prepossessions." See *McCollum* v. *Board of Education, supra,* p. 238. Our individual preferences, however, are not
the constitutional standard. The constitutional standard is the separation of Church and State. The problem, like many problems in
constitutional law, is one of degree. See *McCollum* v. *Board of
Education, supra,* p. 231.

In the *McCollum* case the classrooms were used for religious instruction and the force of the public school was to promote that
instruction. Here, as we have said, the public schools do no more
than accommodate their schedules to a program of outside religious
instruction. We follow the *McCollum* case.[1] But we cannot expand
it to cover the present released time program unless separation of

---

[1] Three of us—THE CHIEF JUSTICE, MR. JUSTICE DOUGLAS and MR. JUSTICE
BURTON—who join this opinion agreed that the "released time" program
involved in the *McCollum* case was unconstitutional. It was our view at the
time that the present type of "released time" program was not prejudged by
the *McCollum* case, a conclusion emphasized by the reservation of the question in the separate opinion by MR. JUSTICE FRANKFURTER in which MR. JUS-
TICE BURTON joined. See 333 U. S. at 225 where it was said, "Of course, 'released
time' as a generalized conception, undefined by differentiating particularities,
is not an issue for Constitutional adjudication. Local programs differ from
each other in many and crucial respects. . . . It is only when challenge is made
to the share that the public schools have in the execution of a particular 'released time' program that close judicial scrutiny is demanded of the exact
relation between the religious instruction and the public educational system
in the specific situation before the Court."

Church and State means that public institutions can make no adjustments of their schedules to accommodate the religious needs of the people. We cannot read into the Bill of Rights such a philosophy of hostility to religion.

JUSTICE HUGO BLACK *(1886–)*

An Excerpt From His Dissenting Opinion

Here the sole question is whether New York can use its compulsory education laws to help religious sects get attendants presumably too unenthusiastic to go unless moved to do so by the pressure of this state machinery. That this is the plan, purpose, design and consequence of the New York program cannot be denied. The state thus makes religious sects beneficiaries of its power to compel children to attend secular schools. Any use of such coercive power by the state to help or hinder some religious sects or to prefer all religious sects over nonbelievers or vice versa is just what I think the First Amendment forbids. In considering whether a state has entered this forbidden field the question is not whether it has entered too far but whether it has entered at all. New York is manipulating its compulsory education laws to help religious sects get pupils. This is not separation but combination of Church and State.

The Court's validation of the New York system rests in part on its statement that Americans are "a religious people whose institutions presuppose a Supreme Being." This was at least as true when the First Amendment was adopted; and it was just as true when eight justices of this Court invalidated the released time system in *McCollum* on the premise that a state can no more "aid all religions" than it can aid one.[2] It was precisely because Eighteenth

---

[2] A state policy of aiding "all religions" necessarily requires a governmental decision as to what constitutes "a religion." Thus is created a governmental power to hinder certain religious beliefs by denying their character as such. See, *e. g.*, the regulations of the New York Commissioner of Education providing that, "The courses in religious observance and education must be maintained and operated by or under the control of a *duly constituted* religious body or of *duly constituted* religious bodies." (Emphasis added.) This provides precisely the kind of censorship which we have said the Constitution forbids. *Cantwell* v. *Connecticut,* 310 U. S. 296, 305.

Century Americans were a religious people divided into many fighting sects that we were given the constitutional mandate to keep church and state completely separate. Colonial history had already shown that, here as elsewhere zealous sectarians entrusted with governmental power to further their causes, would sometimes torture, maim and kill those they branded "heretics," "atheists" or "agnostics."[3] The First Amendment was therefore to insure that no one powerful sect or combination of sects could use political or governmental power to punish dissenters whom they could not convert to their faith. Now as then, it is only by wholly isolating the state from the religious sphere and compelling it to be completely neutral, that the freedom of each and every denomination and of all nonbelievers can be maintained. It is this neutrality the Court abandons today when it treats New York's coercive system as a program which *merely* "encourages religious instruction or cooperates with religious authorities." The abandonment is all the more dangerous to liberty because of the Court's legal exaltation of the orthodox and its derogation of unbelievers.

Under our system of religious freedom, people have gone to their religious sanctuaries not because they feared the law but because they loved their God. The choice of all has been as free as the choice of those who answered the call to worship moved only by the music of the old Sunday morning church bells. The spiritual mind of man has thus been free to believe, disbelieve, or doubt, without repression, great or small, by the heavy hand of government. Statutes authorizing such repression have been stricken. Before today, our judicial opinions have refrained from drawing invidious distinctions between those who believe in no religion and those who do believe. The First Amendment has lost much if the religious follower and the atheist are no longer to be judicially regarded as entitled to equal justice under law.

State help to religion injects political and party prejudices into a holy field. It too often substitutes force for prayer, hate for love, and persecution for persuasion. Government should not be allowed, under cover of the soft euphemism of "co-operation," to steal into the sacred area of religious choice.

---

[3] Wertenbaker, *The Puritan Oligarchy*, 213–214.

JUSTICE ROBERT H. JACKSON *(1892–)*

DISSENTING OPINION

This released time program is founded upon a use of the State's power of coercion, which, for me, determines its unconstitutionality. Stripped to its essentials, the plan has two stages, first, that the State compel each student to yield a large part of his time for public secular education and, second, that some of it be "released" to him on condition that he devote it to sectarian religious purposes.

No one suggests that the Constitution would permit the State directly to require this "released" time to be spent "under the control of a duly constituted religious body." This program accomplishes that forbidden result by indirection. If public education were taking so much of the pupils' time as to injure the public or the student's welfare by encroaching upon their religious opportunity, simply shortening everyone's school day would facilitate voluntary and optional attendance at Church classes. But that suggestion is rejected upon the ground that if they are made free many students will not go to the Church. Hence, they must be deprived of freedom for this period, with Church attendance put to them as one of the two permissible ways of using it.

The greater effectiveness of this system over voluntary attendance after school hours is due to the truant officer who, if the youngster fails to go to the Church schoool, dogs him back to the public schoolroom. Here schooling is more or less suspended during the "released time" so the nonreligious attendants will not forge ahead of the churchgoing absentees. But it serves as a temporary jail for a pupil who will not go to Church. It takes more subtlety of mind than I possess to deny that this is governmental constraint in support of religion. It is as unconstitutional, in my view, when exerted by indirection as when exercised forthrightly.

As one whose children, as a matter of free choice, have been sent to privately supported Church schools, I may challenge the Court's suggestion that opposition to this plan can only be antireligious, atheistic, or agnostic. My evangelistic brethren confuse an objection to compulsion with an objection to religion. It is possible to hold a faith with enough confidence to believe that what should be rendered to God does not need to be decided and collected by Caesar.

The day that this country ceases to be free for irreligion it will cease to be free for religion—except for the sect that can win political power. The same epithetical jurisprudence used by the Court today to beat down those who oppose pressuring children into some religion can devise as good epithets tomorrow against those who object to pressuring them into a favored religion. And, after all, if we concede to the State power and wisdom to single out "duly constituted religious" bodies as exclusive alternative for compulsory secular instruction, it would be logical to also uphold the power and wisdom to choose the true faith among those "duly constituted." We start down a rough road when we begin to mix compulsory public education with compulsory godliness.

A number of Justices just short of a majority of the majority that promulgates today's passionate dialectics joined in answering them in *Illinois ex rel. McCollum* v. *Board of Education*, 333 U. S. 203. The distinction attempted between that case and this is trivial, almost to the point of cynicism, magnifying its nonessential details and disparaging compulsion which was the underlying reason for invalidity. A reading of the Court's opinion in that case along with its opinion in this case will show such difference of overtones and undertones as to make clear that the *McCollum* case has passed like a storm in a teacup. The wall which the Court was professing to erect between Church and State has become even more warped and twisted than I expected. Today's judgment will be more interesting to students of psychology and of the judicial processes than to students of constitutional law.

[NOTE: The bibliography for Chapter Five appears on page 521.]

Chapter Six

IMMORTALITY

INTRODUCTION

The view that man, or some part of him—the soul—continues in some sense to exist after death, is found in ancient and in contemporary writings, in non-literate and in civilized cultures, in the east and in the west. But it is not always interpreted in the same way.

Some take it quite literally, basing their belief on alleged contacts with spirits of the deceased.[1] Others accept the view but with much less assurance. They do not base it on sense experience; and they admit that they are unable to prove that it is correct. But it is a pleasant theory which no sceptic has ever disproved. It could be true. So why not accept it? Going one step further, there are those who ardently desire immortality, perhaps in order to conquer their dread of death or of extinction, and have become believers because their belief fulfills their wish. Still others agree that the proofs and disproofs of immortality are equally invalid. Claiming no knowledge of a future life, they feel that as long as there is a possibility of immortality for believers, it would be prudent to live as if the soul were eternal. A more religious variation of the "as if" phi-

---

[1] See, for example, Malinowski, "Baloma, the Spirits of the Dead in the Trobriand Islands" reprinted in *Magic, Science and Religion*, The Free Press, 1948. Also Oliver Lodge, *Why I Believe in Personal Immortality*.

losophy is the view of Unamuno—more religious because it is based on moral considerations rather than on concern for one's own survival. As he puts it, "Act so that in your own judgment and in the judgment of others you may merit eternity, act so that you may become irreplaceable, act so that you may not merit death." Or, as he expresses it in another version, "act as if you were to die tomorrow, but to die in order to survive and be eternalized."

Plato devotes a good part of the *Phaedo* to the proofs of immortality which Socrates, in his last hours, offers to his companions. But Socrates nowhere says that he was himself convinced by these proofs. When Crito says: "How shall we bury you?", Socrates replies, "Though I have spoken many words in the endeavour to show that when I have drunk the poison, I shall leave you and go to the joys of the blessed, these words of mine, with which I was comforting you and myself have had, as I perceive, no effect upon Crito." Words of comfort—that's what they were, at least in part. And this is how many "believers" regard immortality—as a comforting thought. It may not be possible to prove that man has an immortal soul, but neither can it be disproved. So why not believe, if that way lies serenity, rather than torment yourself with thoughts of annihilation? [2] Critics of this view say that if one attains serenity by accepting the doctrine of survival in spite of the absence of positive supporting evidence, he is living in a fool's paradise. A defender of James has replied that one who remains wretched because he rejects, in spite of the absence of contrary evidence, a possibly true belief in survival, is, of his own free will, living in a fool's hell. [3] And he continues: "I submit that the fool's paradise is anyway better than the fool's hell."

Nevertheless, there have been some, like Spinoza, who have managed to avoid the unhappy choice between a fool's paradise and a fool's hell. "A free man," wrote Spinoza, "thinks of nothing less than of death, and his wisdom is a meditation not of death but of life."

But how many are there who can attain this blessed state of freedom? And how many have turned for comfort to the belief in

---

[2] See Selection 3, this volume, William James, *The Will to Believe*.

[3] C. J. Ducasse, *A Philosophical Scrutiny of Religion*, Chapter 9. New York: The Ronald Press, 1953.

immortality? Forty years ago Prof. Leuba determined to find the answers to these questions. He sent questionnaires to many historians, scientists, psychologists, sociologists, and philosophers, asking them about their own beliefs in God and immortality.[4] His statistics revealed that less than half of those questioned believed in a personal God, that there were more believers in immortality than in God, and that among the more distinguished, unbelief is very much more prevalent than among the less distinguished. The answers also showed that the belief in immortality "rested on no scientifically established fact or convincing argument, but upon the usefulness rightly or wrongly ascribed to [the belief]." Perhaps the most remarkable outcome of Leuba's investigation was his inability to secure any statistics from philosophers. Unlike their colleagues, they returned blank questionnaires in large numbers, because they were uncertain how such key terms as "God" and "immortality" were being used. Expressing a desire to cooperate, they nevertheless felt that because of the many different interpretations of immortality, "yes" or "no" answers to such questions as: "Do you believe in personal immortality for all men?" would have little or no value.

Some of the important conceptions of immortality which have been advanced by philosophers are presented and analyzed in the selections of this chapter.

D. J. B.

55. Did Jesus Believe in Immortality? *

LEO TOLSTOY (1828–1910)

According to the doctrine of the Hebrews man is man, exactly as he is — in other words, he is mortal. Life is in him only as life perpetuated from one generation to another, in a race. According

---

[4] James H. Leuba, *The Belief in God and Immortality*, 2nd edition, The Open Court Publishing Company, Chicago, 1921.

* An excerpt from "My Religion" by Leo Tolstoy.

to the doctrine of the Hebrews only one nation possesses in itself the possibility of life.

When God said, "Ye shall live, and not die," he addressed these words to the people. The life that God breathed into man is mortal for each separate human being; this life is perpetuated from generation to generation, if men fulfil the covenant with God, that is, obey the conditions imposed by God. After having propounded the Law, and having told them that this Law was to be found not in heaven, but in their own hearts, Moses said to the people:—

"See, I have set before you this day life and good, and death and evil; in that I command you this day to love the Eternal, to walk in his ways, and to keep his commandments, that you may live. . . . I call heaven and earth to witness against you this day, that I have set before you life and death, the blessing and the curse: therefore choose life, that you may live, you and your seed: to love the Eternal, to obey his voice, and to cleave unto him: for from him is your life, and the length of your days." [2]

The principal difference between our conception of human life and that possessed by the Jews is, that while we believe that our mortal life, transmitted from generation to generation, is not the true life, but a fallen life, a life temporarily depraved, — the Jews, on the contrary, believed this life to be the true and supreme good, given to man on condition that he will obey the will of God. From our point of view, the transmission of the fallen life from generation to generation is the transmission of a curse; from the Jewish point of view, it is the supreme good to which man can attain, on condition that he accomplish the will of God.

On this Hebraic conception of life Christ founded His doctrine of the true or eternal life, which He contrasted with the personal and mortal life. Christ said to the Jews:—

"Search the Scriptures; for in them you think you have eternal life." [3]

The young man asked Christ what he must do to have eternal life. Christ said in reply:—

"If thou wilt enter into life, keep the commandments." He did

---

[2] Deut. xxx. 15–19.
[3] John v. 39.

not say "eternal life," but simply "life." [4] To the same question propounded by the scribe, the answer was, *"This do, and thou shalt live";* [5] here also, He says "live" simply, and does not add "forever." From these two instances, we know what Christ meant by eternal life; whenever He made use of the phrase in speaking to the Jews, He employed it in exactly the same sense in which it was expressed in their own law,—the accomplishment of the will of God is the eternal life.

In contrast with a temporary, isolated and personal life, Christ taught of the eternal life which in Deuteronomy God promised to Israel, — with this difference, that while according to the notion of the Jews the eternal life was to be perpetuated solely by them, the chosen people, and that whoever wished to possess this life must follow the exceptional laws given by God to Israel, according to Christ's teaching the eternal life is perpetuated in the son of man, and that to obtain it we must practise Christ's commands, which express the will of God for all humanity.

As opposed to the personal life, Christ taught us, not of a life beyond the grave, but of a universal life united with the life of humanity, past, present, and to come, the life of the son of man.

According to the teaching of the Hebrews, the personal life could be saved from death only by accomplishing the will of God as propounded in the Mosaic law. On this condition only the life of the Hebrews would not perish, but would pass from generation to generation of the chosen people of God.

According to Christ's teaching, the personal life is saved from death likewise by the accomplishment of the will of God as propounded in Christ's command. Only on this condition, according to Christ's teaching, the personal life does not perish, but becomes eternal and immutable in the son of man. The difference is, that while the worship of God as established by Moses was worship of one people's God, Christ's worship of the Father is the worship of the God of all men. The perpetuity of life in the posterity of a people is doubtful, because the people itself may disappear, and perpetuity depends upon a posterity in the flesh. Perpetuity of life, according to Christ's teaching, is indubitable, because life, accord-

[4] Matt. xix. 17.
[5] Luke x. 28.

ing to His teachings, is transferred to the son of man who lives in harmony with the will of the Father.

But let us grant that Christ's words concerning the last judgment and the consummation of the age, and other words reported in the Gospel of John, are a promise of a life beyond the grave for the souls of mortal men, — it is none the less true that His teachings in regard to the light of life and the kingdom of God have the same meaning for us that they had for His hearers eighteen centuries ago; that is, that the only real life is the life of the son of man according to the Father's will.

It is easier to admit this than to admit that the doctrine of the true life, according to the Father's will, contains the conception of immortality and a life beyond the grave.

Perhaps it is fairer to presuppose that man, after this terrestrial life passed in the satisfaction of personal desires, will enter upon the possession of an eternal personal life in paradise, with all imaginable enjoyments; perhaps this is fairer, but to believe that this is so, to endeavor to persuade ourselves that for our good actions we shall be recompensed with eternal felicity, and for our bad actions punished with eternal torments, — to believe this, does not aid us in understanding Christ's teaching, but, on the contrary, deprives Christ's teaching of its chief foundation.

All Christ's teaching goes to persuade His disciples who recognize the illusoriness of the personal life to renounce it, and merge it in the life of all humanity, in the life of the son of man. Now the doctrine of the immortality of the individual soul does not impel us to renounce the personal life; on the contrary, it affirms the continuance of individuality forever.

According to the notion of the Jews, the Chinese, the Hindus, and all men who do not believe in the dogma of the fall and the redemption, life is life as it is. A man is united with a woman, engenders children, cares for them, grows old, and dies. His children grow up, and his life continues, it passes on from one generation to another without interruption, like everything else in the world, — stones, metals, earth, plants, animals, stars. Life is life, and we must make the best of it.

To live for self alone is not reasonable. And so men, from their earliest existence, have sought for some reason for living aside from the gratification of their own desires; they live for their children, for their families, for their nation, for humanity, for all that does not die with the personal life.

On the other hand, according to the doctrine of our Churches, human life, the supreme good that is known to us, is but a very small portion of another life of which we are deprived for a season. Our life, according to this conception, is not the life that God intended or was obliged to give us. Our life is degenerate and fallen, a mere fragment, a mockery of life, compared with the real life which we think God ought to give us. The principal object of our life, according to this theory, is not to try to live this mortal life conformably to the will of the Giver of Life; or to render it eternal in the generations of men, as the Hebrews believed; or to identify ourselves with the will of the Father, as Christ taught; no, it is to believe that after this unreal life the true life will begin.

Christ did not speak of the imaginary life that God ought to give us, and that God for some unexplained reason did not give us. The theory of the fall of Adam, of eternal life in paradise, of an immortal soul breathed by God into Adam, was unknown to Christ; He never spoke of it, never by one word made the slightest allusion to its existence.

Christ spoke of life as it is, as it always will be; we speak of an imaginary life which has never existed. How, then, can we understand Christ's teaching?

Christ did not anticipate such a singular change of view in His disciples. He supposed that all men understood that the destruction of the personal life is inevitable, and He revealed to them an imperishable life. He offers true peace to those that suffer; but to those that believe that they are certain to possess more than Christ gives, His doctrine cannot give anything. I am going to exhort a man to toil, assuring him that in return for it he will receive food and clothing; and suddenly this man is persuaded that he is already a millionaire. Evidently he will pay no attention to my exhortations. So it is with regard to Christ's teachings. Why should I toil for bread when I can be rich without labor? Why should I trouble myself to live this life according to the will of God, when without doing so I am sure of a personal life for all eternity?

Every notion of a personal life not based on the renunciation of self, the service of humanity, of the son of man, is a phantom which vanishes at the first application of reason. I cannot doubt that my personal life will perish, but the life of the world according to the will of the Father will not perish, and that only identification with it gives me the possibility of salvation. It is not much in comparison with the sublime belief in the future life! It is not much, but it is sure.

I am lost in a snowstorm. Some one assures me— and it seems to him so—that he sees a light in the distance, that it is in the village, but it only seems so to him and to me because we want to have it so; we strive to reach this light, but we never can find it. Another plows through the snow; he seeks and finds the road, and he cries to us, "Go not that way, the lights you see are false, you will wander to destruction; here is the hard road, I feel it beneath my feet; it will bring us home." It is very little. When we had faith in those lights that gleamed in our deluded eyes, there seemed to be somewhere yonder a village, a warm izba, deliverance, rest; and now in exchange for it we have nothing but the solid road. But if we continue to travel toward the imaginary lights we shall perish; if we follow the road, we shall surely escape.

What, then, ought I to do, if I alone understood Christ's teaching, and I alone had trust in it among a people who neither understand it nor obey it?

What was I to do—to live like the rest of the world, or to live according to Christ's teaching? I understood Christ's teaching as expressed in His commands, and I saw that the practice of these commands would bring happiness to me and to all men in the world. I understood that the fulfilment of these commands is the will of that first cause from which my life sprang.

More than this, I saw that whatever I did I should die like a brute after a senseless life if I did not fulfil the will of the Father, and that the only chance of salvation lay in the fulfilment of His will.

Doing as all men do, I unquestionably act contrary to the welfare of all men, I unquestionably act contrary to the will of the Giver of Life, I unquestionably forfeit the sole possibility of bettering my desperate condition. Doing as Christ commands me, I continue the work common to all men who had lived before me; I contribute to the welfare of all men now living and of those who will live after me; I obey the command of the Giver of Life; I do the only thing that can save me.

56. The Christian Hope of Immortality *

A. E. TAYLOR (1869–1945)

Suppose, then, that we make a beginning by asking ourselves the question whether, as intelligent men, we can believe at all in a life which is not destroyed by the dissolution of the body. Are there insuperable difficulties in the way of any such belief, and if there are not, are there any positive reasons, weak or strong, for believing? May we believe at all, and if we may, is there any reason why we should? I think we may at least say at once that there are clearly no sufficient reasons for simply refusing to entertain the belief. The alleged proofs of its absurdity amount only to this, that we know (or at least believe with full conviction) that we all have to die, and that when a man has once died we have no evidence that he is anything any longer. For all that we can tell he may simply have ceased to be. Now this "argument" is clearly worthless, and should really be left to "free thinkers" who are only half-wits. All that it really proves is something which Christianity would never dream of denying, namely, that at death a man's existence as an animate and intelligent person ceases to be certifiable for the surviving observers (at least unless we are willing to admit the reality of the comparatively rare and always disputable cases of "apparitions of the deceased"). Our friend who has died will no longer be seen and heard among us, even his inanimate body, which for a time we can still observe, will sooner or later fall to pieces and, in the main, be resolved into imperceptible constituents. The living man, then, by dying has ceased to be what he was before, an object accessible to our perception. But this is no proof whatever that he has simply

* Reprinted by permission of the publisher from A. E. Taylor, *The Christian Hope of Immortality,* Chapter 2, published in 1947 by The Macmillan Company.

ceased to be. The mere fact that something has become imperceptible is no proof that it has become non-existent. And the fact that the deceased person is no longer a recognizable object for us is no proof that he is not still a very real object indeed for intelligences (if there are such intelligences, and we have no right to assume that there are not), who are not cramped by the narrow limits set by our organs of sensibility to the range of our perceptions. We are never safe in declaring that anything which our senses cannot detect must be nothing at all.

And in the case of a conscious self or a person there is a further consideration to be taken into account. The very word "existence" as applied to a *person* has a double sense. It may mean existence as one *object* among others perceptible by *other* persons as part of their "environment". But it may also mean existence as a *subject* aware of itself, and it is not at all self-evident or demonstrable that these two senses, or modalities, of existence *must* always go together. We are not entitled to say, for example, that a person or self cannot be aware of itself without also being aware of objects which are not itself; there are even certain experiences which would suggest that this assertion would be false. We do sometimes seem to be aware of our own being, and of well-being or the contrary, without being aware of anything else. And equally it is by no means clear that I might not be fully aware of my own being, though no one else in the universe was aware of my presence as part of his "environment". These are at least logical possibilities, and since they are logical possibilities, we should be careful to remember that, though we may all have seen others die, none of us has had the experience of dying in his own person. We know what kind of change occurs "objectively" in our environment when another dies; we do not know what the experienced change is to the *subject* who dies, and never shall know this until we die ourselves. (Even then we shall not know if to die is really to become nothing at all.) We have, then, no right to argue that the person who ceases to be capable of detection as an object going to make up our perceptible environment has ceased to be a *subject* with a continued experience of his own. For all that the ascertainable facts can tell us, he may literally simply have entered on "another life".

But though this might be a sufficient rejoinder to mere confident dogmatism about the impossibility of life beyond death, it is not sufficient ground for entertaining any serious hopes. If we are to believe in anything it is not enough that the thing in question should not be a logical impossibility; we must have adequate positive grounds for our belief. We are thus led to ask where, if anywhere, such positive grounds for belief in life eternal and indestructible may be found. If we set aside for the present grounds directly borrowed from the experience of the religious life itself, we may say, I think, that warrant for the belief has commonly been sought along one or more of three lines: the appeal to certain alleged observable facts which are taken to prove the case, the appeal to a metaphysical theory of the nature of personality, or rational selfhood, the appeal to the character and requirements of the moral law. Some preliminary remarks may be made about each of these lines of argument.

As to the appeal (which covers the whole of the case for "survival" put forward by "spiritualists") to certain alleged facts of an unusual kind which, it is said, may be made matter of actual exact observation under experimental conditions, it is certainly wise to keep an open mind in dealing with such supposed facts. It is certain, and is freely admitted by those who make most of the "evidence" of this kind, that in many cases the supposedly "supernormal facts" are only taken to be so because they have been observed and reported by persons who have had insufficient training in rigidly accurate observation and description of the observed, and again that, for reasons too patent to require stating, there is a constant tendency to fraud on the part of reputed possessors of "supernormal" powers of perception; the temptations to cheat are so strong and so subtle that the "percipient" himself may often be quite uncertain whether he has cheated or not. These are certainly reasons for treating all evidence of this kind with great circumspection, and perhaps for rejecting the great bulk of it, but they do not necessarily prove the whole of it to be worthless. Most of the "supernormal" or abnormal occurrences appealed to may be really only perfectly normal events ill-observed or ill-described; many of them may be produced by conscious or unconscious trickery; it does not follow that there are no genuine disturbing and perplexing facts, inexplicable by the simple assumptions of the complacent materialistic science of the nineteenth century; the "high-and-mighty" attitude of too many "scientific men", who simply decline to examine the alleged facts at all, is not really creditable to their intelligence.

What does make this appeal to "spiritualistic phenomena" of little or no value for our purpose is that, even if we admitted the alleged "evidence" in bulk, it is at once ambiguous and, for us, irrelevant. It is ambiguous, since at the most all that it proves is that the exceptional experiences on which it relies admit of no explanation by currently recognized scientific laws. This, even if completely made out, does not in the least show that the rival "spiritist" explanation is sound; the true explanation might be different from both. Even if it could be sufficiently demonstrated that some of the "phenomena" must be deliberately produced by agents other than embodied human beings, it would not follow that these agents are departed men and women. As F. H. Bradley put it, the strongest conviction that can be produced in this fashion takes the form "if that was not my late brother's spirit, it must have been the devil," and the second alternative is always possibly the right one. If we grant the existence of normally invisible selves who can, from time to time, intervene in the course of affairs around us, we have no right to say that all these agents must be deceased human beings; we cannot simply refuse to face the possibility that they are malevolent or mischievous non-human agents who contrive a masquerade of this kind for our delusion.

In any case the alleged evidence is irrelevant to the Christian hope of the "better" life. It would be something to have apparent proof that the men who were wise and virtuous while they were among us are wiser and more virtuous now that they have left our company. But what we really find is very different. Utterances which profess to come from beings who were once great poets or philosophers are doggerel or twaddle; the preachments of the, "spirits" of men who were great moralists are sentimental puerilities. The life which would be disclosed by such revelations, if we took them seriously, would not be a life nearer to God, the fountain of wisdom and goodness; it would rather be one of intellectual and moral idiocy. I do not think it too much to say of the most harmless of these "messages from beyond the tomb" that, if they are what they claim to be, we can only hope that the unseen world, like the seen, has its homes for the feeble-minded, and that it is with their inmates that our occultists are in communication.

More promising is the line of thought represented by Plato and so many of the great philosophers since Plato's day who have tried to prove by considerations of metaphysics that a self, or at any rate a rational self, a *person*, is, in its intrinsic nature indestructible, and being also in its intrinsic nature rational, can only be exposed to the dangers of intellectual and moral unreason temporarily and incidentally while the connection with a gross and corruptible body is maintained. This is the thought which at bottom inspires all the repeated attempts of philosophers to demonstrate the "natural immortality of the human soul." One would never wish to speak without becoming respect of reasonings which have satisfied the minds of such men as Plato, St. Thomas Aquinas, and Leibniz. Yet it can hardly be doubted that the verdict of impartial reflection on all these arguments must be that while they are impressive, and in various degrees suggestive, they are all inconclusive.

For example, in reply to the particular argument which had the most extended and long continued vogue of them all, down to the time of Kant, the argument from the alleged absolute *simplicity* of the rational soul to its indissolubility and so to its indestructibility, it might manifestly be replied that it is by no means obvious that a personality is something absolutely simple; it may rather have a complexity of very high order; and even if its simplicity be granted, the reasoning, it might be said, points in the wrong direction; it is the complex, not the simple, which is most capable of adequate self-adjustment to great and varied changes in "environment"; the simpler the soul is conceived to be, the more likely is it to be at the mercy of variations in its surroundings. To the reasoning which finally commended itself to Plato, that "souls" are original creators of "motion", not requiring, like other things, to be set moving from without, and therefore, since they depend only upon themselves for their motion, can never cease to "move", and so to be alive, it might be answered, with at least an appearance of plausibility, that, to raise no further difficulties, it is at least certain that in the world of our daily experience the "motions" of the soul recurrently sink to the level of the all but complete unconsciousness of dreamless sleep or deep swoon; what then is to exclude the possibility that at death they sink permanently to a level of deeper unconsciousness still, and in that case, what kind of eternal life worth wasting a thought upon does the argument promise us? At most it can, by itself, do no more than suggest the bare possibility that death too is a profounder sleep from which there may be a waking, but suggestion is something very different from assurance. Or we may take the argument which is developed with such power at the end of the Platonic *Republic*, that nothing can be directly destroyed except by a "malady" or "evil" which is specific to its own nature (as, for example, a man must die of some derangement which is specifically a derangement of the animal organism, and poisonous food or air can only kill him indirectly by first inducing such a specific malady of his own nature). Now the one specific malady of the soul is "injustice" or wickedness; but we can easily see from experience that wickedness has, of itself, no tendency to destroy the self; the very wicked man in society is, in fact, often unusually mentally alert and alive. Since the one thing which is an intrinsic malady of the soul thus has no tendency to put an end to its existence, we may conclude that this existence is unending. Clearly the probative force of this reasoning depends on the assumption made all through that the "cause of a thing's dissolution" must always be looked for without and not within, and this assumption may at least be doubted until cogent justification has been offered for it.

There remains the practically widely influential moral argument for the life to come. Of this, too, a wise man would never speak without due respect. It is often misrepresented as though it was no more than a childish insistence that we shall get a certain thing merely because we very much wish to get it; we should very much like to go on living indefinitely, *ergo* we shall do so; we should all like a good time for ourselves and those of whom we approve, and to give a bad time to those whom we dislike or disapprove, and therefore, as we know that we cannot count on the fulfilment of these wishes in this life, there must be a world to come where they will be fulfilled. Hopes entertained with no better reason than this would certainly be perilous enough, but the real force of the moral argument cannot be judged by the caricatures of it put forward by the more unintelligent among unbelievers, nor yet by the very unsatisfactory statements of it sometimes advanced by the more unintelligent among believers.

The real point of the argument can be better seen from a consideration of two characteristic utterances of two outstanding figures of the eighteenth century, Voltaire and Kant. In his well-known poem *On the Lisbon Earthquake* Voltaire is facing the moral problem suggested by the calamity: "Is there any sign in the order of nature that the source of that order is either intelligent or morally righteous?" His answer is that the course of the world's history appears to have no intelligible meaning at all, to say nothing of any moral significance — *if* what we see of life is all that there is to see (a conclusion in which he might have claimed to be treading in the steps of St. Paul). But we do not know that it is all, and so the last faltering word of the poem is that we are not wholly bereft of *hope*. In Kant's *Critique of Practical Reason* the wavering hope of Voltaire's poem has become a sturdy *faith*. Kant's thought is that the unqualified and absolute reverence for the moral law which is the inner spring of all genuinely moral action does not permit the man of integrity to doubt that the law which has this claim on the absolute reverence of every rational being is the supreme law of the universe, no matter what the appearances to the contrary. But the moral law itself unconditionally demands from every one of us a complete and utter conformity to itself, an inward holiness, which no man achieves in his life on earth; it also imperatively demands that in the end a man shall be happy — that is, his will shall take real effect — only in proportion as it deserves to do so by its conformity to moral law. If we absolutely reverence the moral law, then, we must believe that there is an endless future before us in which we can make unending advance to complete holiness of will, and that the course of nature is under the sovereignty of a moral and all-wise reader of hearts who will so shape it that the deserved "happiness", which the good man cannot directly seek after without degrading duty into a means to an ulterior end, shall come to him unsought in the degree to which he deserves it, and because he deserves it.

The question is thus not one about what we should *like* to have; probably most of us would by no means like to have a "happiness" sternly proportioned to the single-mindedness of our devotion to duty for its own sake. For which of us is thus devoted to duty as he knows he ought to be? The thought is rather that if the scheme of things is a reasonable scheme at all, and not a nightmare, it must realize a purpose, and that purpose must be one of which, *if* we could have it set before us, as we cannot while we are still actors in the temporal drama, intelligence and conscience would approve. It is no proof that the scheme of things is irrational to say that I, with my circumscribed range of vision, do not see its justification, but to doubt that it *has* such a justification would be denying its rationality, the very presupposition on which science itself, no less than morality, is founded. And the denial cannot be escaped if the life we see is all the life there is.

Thus stated, the moral argument deserves all respect. It states no more than the demand every intelligent and virtuous person is entitled to make of the universe, if it is to approve itself to his reason and conscience. But if we treat it, as Kant proposed to do, as the one and only ground of hopes about our destiny, it discloses an obvious weakness. It tells us, indeed, what the universe must be if reason and conscience can approve of it, what the universe is, if it is true that moral law is supreme throughout it. But how do we know that the moral law is thus supreme? No one is clearer than Kant himself on the point that there can be no question of demonstration. We reverence the moral law unreservedly not because we can *prove* that it is entitled to this reverence, but because we should be already vicious at heart if we did not. After all, then, it may be said this reverence for the moral law may be no more than an illegitimate deification of rules and prohibitions of our own devising. They may be as important as the moralist pleases for our parochial affairs on this planet, but with what shadow of right do we convert them into a legislation for the whole universe? If we have not the right to do this, has Kant any ground left for his faith? A universe of which the measure is given by what we see in this life would be unsatisfactory to reason and conscience. *Soit*; but what if the real universe *is* unsatisfactory, the product, as Hume put it, of an author who is childish or senile? Or, it may be, the work of no "author" at all? Clearly if we are to meet these objections, we cannot trust to the "moral argument" alone. It will have at least to be integrated with "metaphysical" considerations of what is implied in the very existence of an historical world, and perhaps also with considerations of a directly religious order. Otherwise we shall be attempting the impossible task of extracting information about that which is solely from premises which deal with what ought to be.

57. Thoughts on the Death of Socrates *

PLATO *(B.C. 427–347)*

Apology

Let no man fear death or fear anything but disgrace. Some one will say: And are you not ashamed, Socrates, of a course of life which is likely to bring you to an untimely end? To him I may fairly answer: There you are mistaken: a man who is good for anything ought not to calculate the chance of living or dying; he ought only to consider whether in doing anything he is doing right or wrong — acting the part of a good man or of a bad. Whereas, upon your view, the heroes who fell at Troy were not good for much, and the son of Thetis above all, who altogether despised danger in comparison with disgrace; and when he was so eager to slay Hector, his goddess mother said to him, that if he avenged his companion Patroclus, and slew Hector, he would die himself — "Fate," she said, in these or the like words, "waits for you next after Hector"; he, receiving this warning, utterly despised danger and death, and instead of fearing them, feared rather to live in dishonour, and not to avenge his friend. "Let me die forthwith," he replies, "and be avenged of my enemy, rather than abide here by the beaked ships, a laughing-stock and a burden of the earth." Had Achilles any thought of death and danger? For wherever a man's place is, whether the place which he has chosen or that in which he has been placed by a commander, there he ought to re-

---

* From *The Dialogues of Plato*, translated by Benjamin Jowett, London: The Clarendon Press, 1892. Excerpts are from the *Apology* and *Phaedo*.

main in the hour of danger; he should not think of death or of anything but of disgrace. And this, O men of Athens, is a true saying. **Socrates, who has often faced death in battle, will not make any condition in order to save his own life; for he does not know whether death is a good or an evil.** Strange, indeed, would be my conduct, O men of Athens, if I, who, when I was ordered by the generals whom you chose to command me at Potidaea and Amphipolis and Delium, remained where they placed me, like any other man, facing death—if now, when, as I conceive and imagine, God orders me to fulfil the philosopher's mission of searching into myself and other men, I were to desert my post through fear of death, or any other fear; that would indeed be strange, and I might justly be arraigned in court for denying the existence of the gods, if I disobeyed the oracle because I was afraid of death, fancying that I was wise when I was not wise. For the fear of death is indeed the pretence of wisdom, and not real wisdom, being a pretence of knowing the unknown; and no one knows whether death, which men in their fear apprehend to be the greatest evil, may not be the greatest good. Is not this ignorance of a disgraceful sort, the ignorance which is the conceit that a man knows what he does not know? And in this respect only I believe myself to differ from men in general, and may perhaps claim to be wiser than they are: — that whereas I know but little of the world below, I do not suppose that I know: but I do know that injustice and disobedience to a better, whether God or man, is evil and dishonourable, and I will never fear or avoid a possible good rather than a certain evil.

He must always be a preacher of philosophy. And therefore if you let me go now, and are not convinced by Anytus, who said that since I had been prosecuted I must be put to death; (or if not that I ought never to have been prosecuted at all); and that if I escape now, your sons will all be utterly ruined by listening to my words — if you say to me, Socrates, this time we will not mind Anytus, and you shall be let off, but upon one condition, that you are not to enquire and speculate in this way any more, and that if you are caught doing so again you shall die; — if this was the condition on which you let me go, I should reply: Men of Athens, I honour and love you; but I shall obey God rather than you, and while I have life and strength I shall never cease from the practice and teaching of philosophy, exhorting any one whom I meet and saying to him after my manner: You, my friend, — a citizen of the great and mighty and wise city of Athens, — are you not ashamed of heaping up the greatest amount of money and honour ʳnd reputation, and caring so little about wisdom and truth and the greatest improvement of the soul, which you never regard or heed at all? And if the person with whom I am arguing, says: Yes, but I do care; then I do not leave him or let him go at once; but I proceed to interrogate and examine and cross-examine him, and if I think that he has no virtue in him, but only says that he has, I reproach him with undervaluing the greater, and overvaluing the less. And I shall repeat the same words to every one whom I meet, young and old, citizen and alien, but especially to the citizens, inasmuch as they are my brethren.

"Necessity is laid upon me: 'I must obey God rather than man.'" For know that this is the command of God; and I believe that no greater good has ever happened in the States than my service to the God. For I do nothing but go about persuading you all, old and young alike, not to take thought for your persons or your properties, but first and chiefly to care about the greatest improvement of the soul. I tell you that virtue is not given by money, but that from virtue comes money and every other good of man, public as well as private. This is my teaching, and if this is the doctrine which corrupts the youth, I am a mischievous person. But if any one says that this is not my teaching, he is speaking an untruth. Wherefore, O men of Athens, I say to you, do as Anytus bids or not as Anytus bids, and either acquit me or not; but whichever you do, understand that I shall never alter my ways, not even if I have to die many times.

He had shown that he would sooner die than commit injustice at the trial of the generals and under the tyranny of the Thirty. I can give you convincing evidence of what I say, not words only, but what you value far more — actions. Let me relate to you a passage of my own life which will prove to you that I should never have yielded to injustice from any fear of death and that "as I should have refused to yield" I must have died at once. I will tell you a tale of the courts, not very interesting perhaps, but never-

theless true. The only office of State which I ever held, O men of
Athens, was that of senator: the tribe Antiochis, which is my tribe,
had the presidency at the trial of the generals who had not taken
up the bodies of the slain after the battle of Arginusae; and you
proposed to try them in a body, contrary to law, as you all thought
afterwards; but at the time I was the only one of the Prytanes who
was opposed to the illegality, and I gave my vote against you; and
when the orators threatened to impeach and arrest me, and you
called and shouted, I made up my mind that I would run the risk,
having law and justice with me, rather than take part in your
injustice because I feared imprisonment and death. This happened
in the days of the democracy. But when the oligarchy of the Thirty
was in power, they sent for me and four others into the rotunda,
and bade us bring Leon the Salaminian from Salamis, as they
wanted to put him to death. This was a specimen of the sort of
commands which they were always giving with the view of implicating as many as possible in their crimes; and then I showed,
not in word only but in deed, that, if I may be allowed to use such
an expression, I cared not a straw for death, and that my great and
only care was lest I should do an unrighteous or unholy thing. For
the strong arm of that oppressive power did not frighten me into
doing wrong; and when we came out of the rotunda the other four
went to Salamis and fetched Leon, but I went quietly home. For
which I might have lost my life, had not the power of the Thirty
shortly afterwards come to an end. And many will witness to my
words.

They will be accused of killing a wise man. Not much time will
be gained, O Athenians, in return for the evil name which you will
get from the detractors of the city, who will say that you killed
Socrates, a wise man; for they will call me wise, even although I
am not wise; when they want to reproach you. If you had waited
a little while, your desire would have been fulfilled in the course
of nature.

Why could they not wait a few years? For I am far advanced
in years, as you may perceive, and not far from death. I am speaking now not to all of you, but only to those who have condemned
me to death. And I have another thing to say to them: You think
that I was convicted because I had no words of the sort which would

have procured my acquittal — I mean, if I had thought fit to leave
nothing undone or unsaid. Not so; the deficiency which led to my
conviction was not of words — certainly not. But I had not the
boldness or impudence or inclination to address you as you would
have liked me to do, weeping and wailing and lamenting, and saying and doing many things which you have been accustomed to
hear from others, and which, as I maintain, are unworthy of me.
I thought at the time that I ought not to do anything common or
mean when in danger: nor do I now repent of the style of my defence; I would rather die having spoken after my manner, than
speak in your manner and live. For neither in war nor yet at law
ought I or any man use every way of escaping death. Often in
battle there can be no doubt that if a man will throw away his arms,
and fall on his knees before his pursuers, he may escape death; and
in other dangers there are other ways of escaping death, if a man
is willing to say and do anything. The difficulty, my friends, is not
to avoid death, but to avoid unrighteousness; for that runs faster
than death. I am old and move slowly, and the slower runner has
overtaken me, and my accusers are keen and quick, and the faster
runner, who is unrighteousness, has overtaken them. And now I
depart hence condemned by you to suffer the penalty of death, —
they too go their ways condemned by the truth to suffer the penalty
of villainy and wrong; and I must abide by my award — let them
abide by theirs. I suppose that these things may be regarded as
fated, — and I think that they are well.

Death either a good or nothing. Let us reflect in another way,
and we shall see that there is great reason to hope that death is a
good; for one of two things — either death is a state of nothingness
and utter unconsciousness, or, as men say, there is a change and
migration of the soul from this world to another.

A profound sleep. Now, if you suppose that there is no consciousness, but a sleep like the sleep of him who is undisturbed even by
dreams, death will be an unspeakable gain. For if a person were
to select the night in which his sleep was undisturbed even by
dreams, and were to compare with this the other days and nights
of his life, and then were to tell us how many days and nights he
had passed in the course of his life better and more pleasantly than
this one, I think that any man, I will not say a private man, but
even the great king will not find many such days or nights, when

compared with the others. Now, if death be of such a nature, I say that to die is gain; for eternity is then only a single night. But if death is the journey to another place, and there, as men say, all the dead abide, what good, O my friends and judges, can be greater than this? If, indeed, when the pilgrim arrives in the world below, he is delivered from the professors of justice in this world, and finds the true judges who are said to give judgment there, Minos and Rhadamanthus and Aeacus and Triptolemus, and other sons of God who were righteous in their own life, that pilgrimage will be worth making.

How blessed to have a just judgment passed on us; to converse with Homer and Hesiod; to see the heroes of Troy, and to continue the search after knowledge in another world! What would not a man give if he might converse with Orpheus and Musaeus and Hesiod and Homer? Nay, if this be true, let me die again and again. I myself, too, shall have a wonderful interest in there meeting and conversing with Palamedes, and Ajax the son of Telamon, and any other ancient hero who has suffered death through an unjust judgment; and there will be no small pleasure, as I think, in comparing my own sufferings with theirs. Above all, I shall then be able to continue my search into true and false knowledge; as in this world, so also in the next; and I shall find out who is wise, and who pretends to be wise, and is not. What would not a man give, O judges, to be able to examine the leader of the great Trojan expedition; or Odysseus or Sisyphus, or numberless others, men and women too! What infinite delight would there be in conversing with them and asking them questions! In another world they do not put a man to death for asking questions: assuredly not. For besides being happier than we are, they will be immortal, if what is said is true.

Wherefore, O judges, be of good cheer about death, and know of a certainty, that no evil can happen to a good man, either in life or after death. He and his are not neglected by the gods; nor has my own approaching end happened by mere chance. But I see clearly that the time had arrived when it was better for me to die and be released from trouble; wherefore the oracle gave no sign. For which reason, also, I am not angry with my condemners, or with my accusers; they have done me no harm, although they did not mean to do me any good; and for this I may gently blame them.

Do to my sons as I have done to you. Still, I have a favour to ask of them. When my sons are grown up, I would ask you, O my friends, to punish them; and I would have you trouble them, as I have troubled you, if they seem to care about riches, or anything, more than about virtue; or if they pretend to be something when they are really nothing, — then reprove them, as I have reproved you, for not caring about that for which they ought to care, and thinking that they are something when they are really nothing. And if you do this, both I and my sons will have received justice at your hands.

The hour of departure has arrived, and we go our ways — I to die, and you to live. Which is better God only knows.

Phaedo

We may now say, not life makes alive, but the soul makes alive; and the soul has a life-giving power which does not admit of death and is therefore immortal. Tell me, then, what is that of which the inherence will render the body alive?

The soul, he replied.

And is this always the case?

Yes, he said, of course.

Then whatever the soul possesses, to that she comes bearing life?

Yes, certainly.

And is there any opposite to life?

There is, he said.

And what is that?

Death.

Then the soul, as has been acknowledged, will never receive the opposite of what she brings.

Impossible, replied Cebes.

And now, he said, what did we just now call that principle which repels the even?

The odd.

And that principle which repels the musical or the just?

The unmusical, he said, and the unjust.

And what do we call that principle which does not admit of death?

The immortal, he said.

And does the soul admit of death?

No.

Then the soul is immortal?

Yes, he said.

And may we say that this has been proven?

Yes, abundantly proven, Socrates, he replied.

Supposing that the odd were imperishable, must not three be imperishable?

Of course.

And if that which is cold were imperishable, when the warm principle came attacking the snow, must not the snow have retired whole and unmelted — for it could never have perished, nor could it have remained and admitted the heat?

True, he said.

Again, if the uncooling or warm principle were imperishable, the fire when assailed by cold would not have perished or have been extinguished, but would have gone away unaffected?

Certainly, he said.

And the same may be said of the immortal: if the immortal is also imperishable, the soul when attacked by death cannot perish; for the preceding argument shows that the soul will not admit of death, or ever be dead, any more than three or the odd number will admit of the even, or fire, or the heat in the fire, of the cold. Yet a person may say: "But although the odd will not become even at the approach of the even, why may not the odd perish and the even take the place of the odd?" Now to him who makes this objection, we cannot answer that the odd principle is imperishable; for this has not been acknowledged, but if this had been acknowledged, there would have been no difficulty in contending that at the approach of the even the odd principle and the number three took their departure; and the same argument would have held good of fire and hate and any other thing.

Very true.

The immortal is imperishable, and therefore the soul is imperishable. And the same may be said of the immortal: if the immortal is also imperishable, then the soul will be imperishable as well as immortal; but if not, some other proof of her imperishableness will have to be given.

No other proof is needed, he said; for if the immortal, being eternal, is liable to perish, then nothing is imperishable.

Yes, replied Socrates, and yet all men will agree that God, and the essential form of life, and the immortal in general, will never perish.

Yes, all men, he said — that is true; and what is more, gods, if I am not mistaken, as well as men.

Seeing then that the immortal is indestructible, must not the soul, if she is immortal, be also imperishable?

Most certainly.

Then when death attacks a man, the mortal portion of him may be supposed to die, but the immortal retires at the approach of death and is preserved safe and sound?

True.

At death the soul retires into another world. Then, Cebes, beyond question, the soul is immortal and imperishable, and our souls will truly exist in another world!

I am convinced, Socrates, said Cebes, and have nothing more to object; but if my friend Simmias, or any one else, has any further objection to make, he had better speak out, and not keep silence, since I do not know to what other season he can defer the discussion, if there is anything which he wants to say or to have said.

But I have nothing more to say, replied Simmias; nor can I see any reason for doubt after what has been said. But I still feel and cannot help feeling uncertain in my own mind, when I think of the greatness of the subject and the feebleness of man.

Yes, Simmias, replied Socrates, that is well said: and I may add that first principles, even if they appear certain, should be carefully considered; and when they are satisfactorily ascertained, then, with a sort of hesitating confidence in human reason, you may, I think, follow the course of the argument; and if that be plain and clear, there will be no need for any further enquiry.

Very true.

"Wherefore, seeing all these things, what manner of persons ought we to be?" But then, O my friends, he said, if the soul is really immortal, what care should be taken of her, not only in respect of the portion of time which is called life, but of eternity! And the danger of neglecting her from this point of view does indeed appear to be awful. If death had only been the end of all, the wicked would have had a good bargain in dying, for they would have been happily quit not only of their body, but of their own evil together with their souls. But now, inasmuch as the soul is manifestly immortal, there is no release or salvation from evil except the attainment of the highest virtue and wisdom. For the soul when on her progress to the world below takes nothing with her but nurture and education; and these are said greatly to benefit or greatly to injure the departed, at the very beginning of his journey thither.

The attendant genius of each brings him after death to the judgment. For after death, as they say, the genius of each individual, to whom he belonged in life, leads him to a certain place in which the dead are gathered together, whence after judgment has been given they pass into the world below, following the guide, who is appointed to conduct them from this world to the other: and when they have there received their due and remained their time, another guide brings them back again after many revolutions of ages. Now this way to the other world is not, as Aeschylus says in the Telephus, a single and straight path — if that were so no guide would be needed, for no one could miss it; but there are many partings of the road, and windings, as I infer from the rites and sacrifices which are offered to the gods below in places where three ways meet on earth.

The different destinies of pure and impure souls. The wise and orderly soul follows in the straight path and is conscious of her surroundings; but the soul which desires the body, and which, as I was relating before, has long been fluttering about the lifeless frame and the world of sight, is after many struggles and many sufferings hardly and with violence carried away by her attendant genius; and when she arrives at the place where the other souls are gathered, if she be impure and have done impure deeds, whether foul murders or other crimes which are the brothers of these, and the works of brothers in crime — from that soul every one flees and turns away; no one will be her companion, no one her guide, but alone she wanders in extremity of evil until certain times are fulfilled, and when they are fulfilled, she is borne irresistibly to her own fitting habitation; as every pure and just soul which has passed through life in the company and under the guidance of the gods has also her own proper home.

When he had done speaking, Crito said: And have you any commands for us, Socrates — anything to say about your children, or any other matter in which we can serve you?

Nothing particular, Crito, he replied: only, as I have always told you, take care of yourselves; that is a service which you may be ever rendering to me and mine and to all of us, whether you promise to do so or not. But if you have no thought for yourselves, and care not to walk according to the rule which I have prescribed for you, not now for the first time, however much you may profess or promise at the moment, it will be of no avail.

We will do our best, said Crito: And in what way shall we bury you?

In any way that you like; but you must get hold of me, and take care that I do not run away from you. Then he turned to us, and added with a smile: — I cannot make Crito believe that I am the same Socrates who has been talking and conducting the argument; he fancies that I am the other Socrates whom he will soon see, a dead body—and he asks, How shall he bury me?

The dead body which remains is not the true Socrates. And though I have spoken many words in the endeavor to show that when I have drunk the poison I shall leave you and go to the joys of the blessed, — these words of mine, with which I was comforting you and myself, have had, as I perceive, no effect upon Crito. And therefore I want you to be surety for me to him now, as at the trial he was surety to the judges for me: but let the promise be of another sort; for he was surety for me to the judges that I would remain, and you must be my surety to him that I shall not remain, but go away and depart; and then he will suffer less at my death, and not be grieved when he sees my body being burned or buried. I would not have him sorrow at my hard lot, or say at the burial, Thus we lay out Socrates, or, Thus we follow him to the grave or bury him; for false words are not only evil in themselves, but they inflict the soul with evil. Be of good cheer then, my dear Crito, and say that you are burying my body only, and do with that whatever is usual, and what you think best.

When he had spoken these words, he arose and went into a chamber to bathe; Crito followed him and told us to wait. So we remained behind, talking and thinking of the subject of discourse, and also of the greatness of our sorrow; he was like a father of whom we were being bereaved, and we were about to pass the rest of our lives as orphans.

He takes leave of his family. When he had taken the bath his children were brought to him (he had two young sons and an elder one); and the women of his family also came, and he talked to them and gave them a few directions in the presence of Crito; then he dismissed them and returned to us.

Now the hour of sunset was near, for a good deal of time had passed while he was within. When he came out, he sat down with us again after his bath, but not much was said.

The humanity of the jailer. Soon the jailer, who was the servant of the Eleven, entered and stood by him, saying: — To you, Socrates, whom I know to be the noblest and gentlest and best of all who ever came to this place, I will not impute the angry feeling of other men, who rage and swear at me, when, in obedience to the authorities, I bid them drink the poison — indeed, I am sure that you will not be angry with me; for others, as you are aware, and not I, are to blame. And so fare you well, and try to bear lightly what must needs be — you know my errand. Then bursting into tears he turned away and went out.

Socrates looked at him and said: I return your good wishes, and will do as you bid. Then turning to us, he said, How charming the man is: since I have been in prison he has always been coming to see me, and at times he would talk to me, and was as good to me as could be, and now see how generously he sorrows on my account. We must do as he says, Crito; and therefore let the cup be brought, if the poison is prepared: if not, let the attendant prepare some.

Crito would detain Socrates a little while. Yet, said Crito, the sun is still upon the hill-tops, and I know that many a one has taken the draught late, and after the announcement has been made to him, he has eaten and drunk, and enjoyed the society of his beloved: do not hurry — there is time enough.

Socrates thinks that there is nothing to be gained by delay. Socrates said: Yes, Crito, and they of whom you speak are right in so acting, for they think that they will be gainers by the delay; but I am right in not following their example, for I do not think that I should gain anything by drinking the poison a little later; I should only be ridiculous in my own eyes for sparing and saving a life which is already forfeit. Please then to do as I say, and not to refuse me.

The poison is brought. Crito made a sign to the servant, who was standing by; and he went out, and having been absent for some time, returned with the jailer carrying the cup of poison. Socrates said: You, my good friend, who are experienced in these matters, shall give me directions how I am to proceed. The man answered: You have only to walk about until your legs are heavy, and then to lie down, and the poison will act.

He drinks the poison. At the same time he handed the cup to Socrates, who in the easiest and gentlest manner, without the least fear or change of colour or feature, looking at the man with all his eyes, Echecrates, as his manner was, took the cup and said: What do you say about making a libation out of this cup to any god? May I, or not? The man answered: We only prepare, Socrates, just so much as we deem enough. I understand, he said: but I may and must ask the gods to prosper my journey from this to the other world — even so — and so be it according to my prayer. Then raising the cup to his lips, quite readily and cheerfully he drank off the poison.

The company of friends are unable to control themselves. And hitherto most of us had been able to control our sorrow; but now when we saw him drinking, and saw too that he had finished the draught, we could no longer forbear, and in spite of myself my own tears were flowing fast; so that I covered my face and wept, not for him, but at the thought of my own calamity in having to part from such a friend. Nor was I the first; for Crito, when he found himself unable to restrain his tears, had got up, and I followed; and at that moment, Apollodorus, who had been weeping all the time, broke out in a loud and passionate cry which made cowards of us all.

Says Socrates, "A man should die in peace." Socrates alone retained his calmness: What is this strange outcry? he said. I sent away the women mainly in order that they might not misbehave in this way, for I have been told that a man should die in peace. Be quiet then, and have patience. When we heard his words we were ashamed, and refrained our tears; and he walked about until, as he said, his legs began to fail, and then he lay on his back, according to directions, and the man who gave him the poison now and then looked at his feet and legs; and after a while he pressed his foot hard, and asked him if he could feel; and he said, No; and then his leg, and so upwards and upwards, and showed us that he was cold and stiff. And he felt them himself, and said: When the poison reaches the heart, that will be the end.

The debt to Asclepius. He was beginning to grow cold about the groin, when he uncovered his face, for he had covered himself up, and said—they were his last words—he said: Crito, I owe a cock to Asclepius; will you remember to pay the debt? The debt shall be paid, said Crito; is there anything else? There was no answer to this question; but in a minute or two a movement was heard, and the attendants uncovered him; his eyes were set, and Crito closed his eyes and mouth.

Such was the end, Echecrates, of our friend; concerning whom I may truly say, that of all men of his time whom I have known, he was the wisest and justest and best.

58. *Eternal Life* *

A. SETH PRINGLE-PATTISON *(1856–1931)*

In the theory of Karma, reincarnation is not put forward as the goal of desire. So much at least will be evident from the discussion in the preceding lecture. Christian writers are accustomed to speak of "the hope of immortality," and theologians frequently use the phrase "a blessed immortality"; but, for the millions who really believe in it, reincarnation is not a "hope," it is rather, one might say, a "doom" to which they must submit. It is explicitly part of the wheel of becoming; and the endlessness of the process, instead of being an attraction ("On and always on," as Tennyson says), operates on the imagination like a nightmare. The sustaining hope is that, after the lapse of ages, release from the wheel may be

---

* From *The Idea of Immortality,* The Gifford Lectures, 1922, Lecture VII, reprinted by permission of the publisher, The Clarendon Press.

attained, that is to say, the cessation of finite or separate being, either by absorption into Brahma or, as it would seem in Buddhism, by actual extinction. It is obvious, therefore, that if we mean by immortality simply an endless continuance of our individual existence, opinions may differ as to the desirability of such a gift or endowment.

Twenty years ago the American Branch of the Society for Psychical Research issued a *questionnaire* on "Human Sentiment with regard to a Future Life," and the first two questions were:

(1) Would you prefer to live after death or not?

(2) If you would prefer to live after death, do you desire a future life whatever the conditions might be, or, if that is not so, what would have to be its character to make the prospect seem tolerable?

The replies received were not very instructive and perhaps not sufficiently representative,[1] but Plutarch has left us his answers to the precise terms of these two questions, and he professes to speak for the vast majority of mankind. "The hope of eternity and the yearning for life," he writes, "is the oldest, as it is the greatest, of human desires." "I might almost say that all men and women would readily submit themselves to the teeth of Cerberus, and to the punishment of carrying water in a sieve, if only they might remain in existence and escape the doom of annihilation."[2] Milton has put the same sentiment in the mouth of one of the rebel angels contemplating the alternative of annihilation in an access of the divine wrath.[3] But the nearest modern parallel to Plutarch's passage is perhaps to be found in Heine's lines shortly before his death; and the force of the feeling that they represent will be best realized if we remember that they were written from the "mattress-grave" in Paris, where he had lingered for so many years:

> O Gott, wie hasslich bitter ist das Sterben!
> O Gott, wie suss und traulich lasst sich's leben
> In diesem traulich sussen Erdennest! [4]

---

[1] That is, on the whole, Dr. Schiller's opinion of the statistical results which he published in the *Proceedings of the Society for Psychical Research*, vol. xviii (1903).

[2] *Non posse suaviter vivi secundum Epicurum*, 1104.

[3] *Paradise Lost*, ii. 146-51.

[4] ["Oh God! how terribly bitter it is to die!
Oh God! how sweet and cozy it is to live
In this cozy and sweet earthly nest."]

The words recall Claudio's passionate recoil from the thought of impending death in *Measure for Measure:*

> This sensible warm motion to become
> A kneaded clod.

But Claudio's ignoble dread, like Hamlet's hesitation, is due not to the idea of extinction, but to "what we fear of death," "what dreams may come."

> The weariest and most loathèd worldly life
> That age, ache, penury, and imprisonment
> Can lay on nature, is a paradise
> To what we fear of death.

Heine was not troubled by such fears: it was just the blankness of death that wrung the words from him. "How our soul struggles against the thought of the cessation of our personality, of eternal annihilation! The *horror vacui* which we ascribe to nature is really inborn in the human heart." So had he written some years earlier in the well-known postscript to his *Romanzero.* Yet the attitude which these two writers so vehemently express is certainly not universal. We have just seen how widely divergent is the voice of Eastern philosophy and Eastern religion. As it has been neatly put, the width of the divergence between East and West may be estimated from the fact that "the destiny which in one hemisphere has been propounded as the final reward of virtue is regarded in the other as the extreme penalty of obstinate wickedness."[5] Where the theory of annihilation has found favour in Christian circles, its acceptance has usually been due to a recoil from the thought of the eternal duration of future punishment. But the profound weariness and sense of oppression, which the thought of the endlessness of future existence is capable of engendering, is not confined to the East. In the West, too, it is found prompting the hope —

> That even the weariest river
> Winds somewhere safe to sea.[6]

Eternal rest is the deepest longing of many an over-driven body and tortured soul.

> Sleep after toil, port after stormy seas,
> Ease after war, death after life, does greatly please.[7]

---

[5] Article on "Annihilation" by Rev. G. C. Joyce in Hasting's *Encyclopaedia of Religion and Ethics.*

[6] Swinburne, "Garden of Proserpine."

[7] *Faerie Queen*, Bk. I. ix. 40.

Buddha avowedly links his doctrine to the thought of the suffer‐
ing or sorrow which accompanies all finite existence, and Brahman‐
ism emphasizes the emptiness, the illusory character of the finite.
But it is not merely the pessimism of Eastern thought that underlies
its view here. Perhaps we should not be wrong in saying that the
East is naturally more speculative than the West, and therefore
thinks out and realizes more fully the implications of a metaphysical
idea like that of endlessness. The Western temperament, with its
active bias, is content for the most part to take the doctrine of
immortality pragmatically, as equivalent to the belief that death
does not end all, without developing its further consequences. Only,
perhaps, in connexion with the doctrine of eternal punishment has
there been any vivid attempt to realize and to apply these conse‐
quences. The unendingness of the penal fire was a theme on which
preachers loved to dilate as embodying a horror greater even than
the cruelty of the tortures depicted.

Questi non hanno speranza di morte

is one of Dante's most terrible lines. Yet it does not require the
experience of the damned to produce this sense of intolerableness. It
is sufficient to concentrate our thoughts, or we might better say our
imagination, on mere endlessness or pure succession. A personal
immortality, so conceived, instead of being felt as a state of blessed‐
ness, oppresses us like a burden too heavy to be borne. "Is it *never*
to end?" (I quote one homely utterance.) "The thought appalls. I,
little I, to live a million years — and another million — and another!
My tiny light to burn for ever."[8] We did not require, in short, to
wait for Hegel to tell us that the endless progress in time or in space
is the false infinite. The feeling is instinctive. It is the aimlessness
of the process which afflicts the mind; for it is a progress which leads
nowhere, which has no goal, seeing that, after ages of forward move‐
ment, you are precisely as distant from the imagined end as when
you started.

But this impression is produced, it will be said, only because we
allow ourselves to be gorgonized by the idea of empty time and the
endless succession of its moments, apart from the experiences which
fill them. As each moment of time, looked at thus abstractly, is
exactly like every other, progress inevitably appears as a change
which is no change. But if we think of the content of our experi‐

---

[8] Quoted by Dr. S. H. Mellone, *The Immortal Hope*, p. 6.

ences, it is argued, the afflicting illusion will disappear. In thinking of an immortal life we may, and ought to, think of it, not as the simple continuance of a being in existence at the same level of all his powers and attainments, but as a progress or advance in a real sense, a continuous growth towards the stature of a perfect humanity. The idea of growth, it is urged, liberates us from the oppressiveness of an unchanging identity. With ever new insights opened to us, and ever new conquests achieved, there can be no question of existence palling upon the taste. In the nature of things, the process can have no end; but, absorbed in each stage as it opens before us, we need not be distracted by the empty thought of the series of future stages still to be traversed. The future, in such a case, would not break upon us until it was present. It is clear, I think, that we are here on the road to a more satisfactory theory, but the improvement lies rather in the stress laid on the quality of the experiences than on the idea of growth as such. Kant's argument for the immortality of the soul based on the conception of the moral life as an infinite process of approximation to perfect virtue, might, I suppose, be taken as a typical application, from the ethical side, of the idea of growth. But such a process is still perilously like the *progressus in indefinitum;* it has, indeed, often been attacked on that ground. The infinite distance of the goal — nay, its explicit unreachableness — is the thought which inspires the argument; and hence the spectre of the future is inevitably conjured up with all the tension of the time-process. Unless we can rise to some experience satisfying in itself, we are not likely to reach a tenable theory of immortality. And, if we are to realize such an experience, we must pass beyond morality to religion, in which the life of finite struggle and endeavour is somehow transcended — where we escape, therefore, from the implications of the time-process, of which the moral life, in the strictest sense of the word, is the typical expression.

Accordingly we find both theologians and philosophers insisting on the idea of an "eternal life," not as something in the future, a continuance of existence after our earthly life is ended, but as an experience, a state of being, to be enjoyed here and now. So, for example, in Schleiermacher's famous declaration: "The goal and the character of the religious life is not the immortality desired and believed in by many. . . . It is not the immortality that is outside of time, behind it or rather after it, and which still is in time. It is the immortality which we can have now in this temporal life. In the midst of finitude to be one with the Infinite, and in every moment to be eternal, that is the immortality of religion."[9] The idea is very commonly put forward, as it is in this passage of Schleiermacher's, in opposition to banal and selfishly personal conceptions of a future life, which have nothing religious about them; and hence such statements are often interpreted as implying that the enjoyment of the eternal life described is limited to the opportunities afforded by the present life. They are taken as definitely negating the idea of personal immortality in any ordinary sense of the term. This negative attitude is, no doubt, adopted by many: they put forward the possibility of realizing eternal life here and now *in place of* the further life which we ordinarily mean by immortality. Schleiermacher himself, at least during the earlier part of his career, seems to have held such a view. There is recounted in Dr. Martineau's *Study of Religion* the touching story of his ineffectual efforts to console a young widow whose husband, according to Schleiermacher's teaching, had "melted away into the great All." But eternity and immortality are by no means necessarily exclusive terms: on the contrary, our experience here and now may carry in it "the power of an endless life," and be in truth the only earnest or guarantee of such a life.

It is a commonplace of philosophical criticism that the term "eternal," when strictly and properly used, does not mean endless continuance *in* time, but a quality of experience which transcends time altogether. Thus in Spinoza, where the contrast is specially emphasized, eternity means rational necessity. We know things "under a certain form of eternity" when we see them not as isolated contingent events, but as necessary parts of a single system, each integral to the whole. It is of the nature of reason *(de natura rationis)* so to regard things, and the perception of this timeless necessity is a very real experience. Mr. Bertrand Russell has told our own generation afresh, in this connexion, that "mathematics [is] . . . capable of a stern perfection such as only the greatest art can show. The true spirit of delight, the exaltation, the sense of being more than man, which is the touchstone of the highest excellence, is to be found in mathematics as surely as in poetry." (*Philosophical Essays*, p. 73.) For Spinoza the necessity of reason is not divorced, as with

---

[9] The closing sentences of the second of his *Reden über die Religion.*

Mr. Russell, from actual existence. It is Spinoza's vision of the universe as in all its parts a system of divine necessity which creates in him "the intellectual love of God," that supreme emotion which expels lower or merely selfish desires, because it is itself joy and peace, the perfect satisfaction of the mind (*vera mentis acquiescentia*). "All our happiness or unhappiness," he tells us, "depends solely on the quality of the object on which our love is fixed. . . . But love towards an object eternal and infinite feeds the mind with a joy that is pure with no tinge of sadness." (*De Intellectus Emendatione*, sections 9 and 10.) Such is the life of "thoughts immortal and divine" of which we found Plato and Aristotle also speaking as opening up to the thinker a present immortality.[10] For Spinoza this "eternal life" is realized in the intellectual vision of truth and harmony; and, as he twice over reminds us in the *Short Treatise*, Truth — the ultimate or all-embracing Truth — is God Himself. This is the "intuition" (*scientia intuitiva*) in which knowledge culminates.

But Art, or, to put it more widely, the perception of Beauty, also yields us experiences under a similar "form of eternity."

> A thing of beauty is a joy for ever:
> Its loveliness increases; it will never
> Pass into nothingness.

Art, it has been said, is the wide world's memory of things. Think only of some of the great stories which have delighted generation after generation, the tale of Troy, the wanderings of Odysseus, the history of Don Quixote. Think of the figures of drama, every turn of whose fate is graven upon our mind and heart, "forms more real than living man," who trod the boards centuries before our coming, and on whom the curtain will rise as many ages after we have gone. Or take the forms bequeathed to us by the sculptor's art, or some melody of immortal loveliness. Perhaps this sense of bodiless immortality is most vividly realized by the ordinary person in the case of a musical work, as the sounds fill the air and the instruments give its harmonies and sequences once more a brief existence for the bodily ear.

In Art, as Schopenhauer loved to insist,[11] the objects we contemplate have the eternity and universality of the Platonic Ideas. They

---

[10] [See, for example, Plato's *Phaedrus*, *Phaedo*, *Laws*, and Aristotle's *Ethics*.]

[11] *The World as Will and Idea*, Bk. III. English translation vol. i, pp. 219–346.

are lifted out of the stream of becoming which constitutes individual existence; and in contemplating them we are emancipated from the tyranny of the Will, that is to say, of selfish desire. In aesthetic perception our knowledge is pure and disinterested; our objectivity is complete. "The subject and the object mutually fill and penetrate each other completely." Science, based on the principle of causality, is constantly investigating the relations of its object to other things, and is involved, thereby, in an endless quest. "Art is everywhere at its goal, for it plucks the object of its contemplation out of the world's course, and has it isolated before it. And this particular thing, which in that stream was a small perishing part, becomes to art the representative of the whole, an equivalent of the endless multitude in space and time. The course of time stops; relations vanish for it; only the essential, the Idea, is its object." Our individuality has fallen from us: "we are only that *one* eye of the world which looks out from all knowing creatures, but only in man can become perfectly free from the service of the will." "Then all at once the peace which we were always seeking, but which fled from us on the former path of the desires, comes to us of its own accord and it is well with us: we keep a Sabbath from the penal slavery of the will; the wheel of Ixion stands still." [12] Many, accordingly, have celebrated Art in this strain, as the only refuge of the spirit from the miseries and weariness of the actual world,

> The weariness, the fever, and the fret,
> Here where men sit and hear each other groan.

To such natures — to Keats, from whom I have quoted, to Goethe and Schiller at certain points in their career — Art thus becomes a religion, or at least is made to do duty for one.[13] Such moments, however, of selfless contemplation and aesthetic enjoyment cannot be more than intermittent, Schopenhauer confesses, and therefore Art cannot achieve that perfect and final deliverance which we seek from the misery of existence. For that we must go, he teaches, to religion, to a religion like Buddhism, which inculcates the resolute extermination of the will to live.

---

[12] Schopenhauer speaks mainly of beauty as perceived through the medium of art, but he does not fail to point out that "a single free glance into nature" may have the same emancipating effect: this is the secret of nature's wonderful restorative and calming power.

[13] Cf. Schiller, *Das Ideal und das Leben*.

It is in religion, after all, that the term "eternal life" is most familiar to us. It occurs constantly in the New Testament as the designation of a frame of mind or spiritual attitude which is intended to be realized here and now. The meaning of the phrase in early Christian usage can hardly be fully understood, however, without a glance at the Jewish apocalyptic beliefs, so prominent in men's minds at the time, with which it was at first closely associated, but with which it comes to be in a sense contrasted. We have seen in a previous Lecture how slow was the growth of an effective doctrine of a future life among the Hebrews. When it did arise, it was associated with the national hope of a Messianic kingdom. "The day of Jahveh," originally conceived simply as a judgment on the enemies of Israel executed by the national god, and the inauguration of a new period of material prosperity under his protection, had been transformed by the prohpets into the idea of a day of judgment upon Israel itself for the nation's sins; and with the rise of a true monotheism (from the seventh century onwards) this judgment was extended to include all the nations of the earth. The result of the prophesied judgment was to be the establishment of the righteous and penitent remnant of Israel under a prince of the house of David, or a dynasty of such warrior kings and righteous rulers. Other nations — the Gentiles — were either to be destroyed, according to the bitter nationalism of some of the prophets, or, according to the larger-hearted, brought into this divinely established kingdom by conversion. The kingdom was to be set up on this present earth and would last for ever, and the righteous dead of Israel were to be raised from Sheol to participate in its blessedness.[14]

This was the first form of the apocalyptic idea, but in course of time — about the close of the second century B.C. — it came to be realized that the earth (whether as we know it or as transformed into "a new heaven and a new earth") was unfit to be the scene of such an eternal kingdom: the Kingdom of God could be realized

---

[14] So in Isaiah xxvi. 19, a passage considered by the critics to date from the late Persian period: "Thy dead shall arise, the inhabitants of the dust shall awake and sing for joy; for a dew of lights is thy dew, and the earth shall produce the shades." So again, more definitely, in Daniel xii. 2. Formerly it had been believed that the Messianic kingdom would be shared only by the living. Cf. Professor H. R. Mackintosh, *Immortality and the Future*, p. 34. I have adopted Professor Mackintosh's rendering of the passage from Isaiah.

only in a spiritual world to come. The idea of a Messianic reign of the saints upon earth was not abandoned, but it was conceived as temporary in duration (sometimes as lasting a thousand years), and as a prelude to the final judgment which inaugurates the eternal kingdom of God. The important point, however, remains the same, namely, the sharp distinction drawn between "the present age," in which the powers of wickedness hold sway, and "the coming age," when the divine kingdom will be realized. The appearance of the Messiah, now conceived as a supernatural being — "the Son of man" or "the Son of God" — is the event which is to mark the advent, or at least the near approach, of the new age. Such were the convictions of the religious part of the Jewish nation in the time of Jesus, and this eschatology meets us everywhere in the New Testament. The sense of the imminence of the coming of the Kingdom is universal. "The Kingdom of Heaven is at hand" was the text of John the Baptist's preaching, and the phrase was appropriated and applied by Jesus in his own way. The first idea which the words roused in the minds of his hearers was the thought of this future dispensation, to be ushered in catastrophically by the appearance of the Messiah on the clouds of heaven to judge the world.[15] Jesus himself appears to have shared the general belief that this event would take place within the life-time of those whom he was addressing: "There be some standing here which shall not taste of death, till they see the Son of man coming in his Kingdom." (Matt. xvi. 28.) "This generation shall not pass, till all these things be fulfilled." (Matt. xxiv. 34.) When he sent out the Twelve on their preaching mission, he is represented as saying that, before their return, the expected event would have taken place: "Verily I say unto you, Ye shall not have gone over the cities of Israel, till the Son of man be come." (Matt. x. 23.) We need not wonder, therefore, if, in spite of the rest of their Master's teaching about the spiritual nature of the Kingdom, the disciples continued to give his sayings about it this future reference, and had to be rebuked for the thoroughly mundane hopes of reward and distinction which they linked with its establishment.

Yet, from the beginning of his teaching, Jesus made the inheri-

---

[15] Or, in the case of those who recognized in Jesus the Messiah or the Christ already come, the *second* coming of the Messiah, in power.

tance of this kingdom dependent on purely spiritual conditions. He taught not simply, like John the Baptist or the prophets before him, that the kingdom of heaven was at hand, but that it was already a present fact — "in their midst" or "within them"; and, in so doing, he stepped out of the ranks of the Hebrew prophets and came forward as the bearer of a new message from God to man. And the gospel he proclaimed was not a promise of future reward for certain beliefs about himself, but, as every genuinely religious message must be, a gospel of deliverance, a message of present salvation: "Come unto me, all ye that labour and are heavy laden, and *I will give you rest.* Take my yoke upon you and learn of me; for I am meek and lowly in heart: and *ye shall find rest unto your souls.*" (Matt. xi. 28-9.) It is an insight which changes the face of the world and "makes all things new." Above all it is an insight into what salvation really means. Not a password enabling a man to escape dire penalties in the future or admitting him to great rewards, but a change of the inner man, the adoption of a new attitude towards life and its happenings. The changed attitude is not to be understood as the condition of salvation, in the sense that salvation is something different from the spiritual state and externally added to it. As St. Paul says, "To be spiritually minded *is* life and peace." (Rom. viii. 6.) This, then, is the salvation of the soul, the only salvation that matters, as the Platonic Socrates had already so impressively insisted: and when Jesus says "A man's *life* consisteth not in the abundance of the things which he possesseth" (Luke xii. 15), or "What shall it profit a man if he shall gain the whole world and lose his own *soul?*" (Mark viii. 36), the words "life" and "soul" are clearly used in the Platonic sense and not in an eschatological reference. Hence we have the antithesis of "life" and "death," so recurrent in the New Testament, both terms being used to signify a present spiritual state. The message of the Gospel is continually referred to as a message of "life," and the change it effects is described as a passage from "death unto life." The antithesis is equated by St. Paul with his own favourite contrast between the flesh and the spirit. "To be carnally minded is death; but to be spiritually minded is life and peace." "The law of the spirit of life in Christ Jesus hath made me free from the law of sin and death . . . The body is dead because of sin, but the spirit is life because of

righteousness." (Rom. viii. 1-10.) He also inweaves with his statement that other sense of "death," contained in the most characteristic teaching of Jesus, that "whosoever will save his life shall lose
it: and whosoever will lose his life for my sake shall find it." (Matt.
xvi. 25.) This is, in his own emphatic phrase, the very "word of the
cross" (I Cor. i. 18), life through death. We must die to self—to
selfish desires and egoistic cravings—before we can find our true
self in that wider life which is at once the love of the brethren and
the love of God.[16] In this sense, St. Paul protests, he dies daily: only
by dying with Christ, "crucifying the flesh with the passions and the
lusts thereof" (Gal. v. 24, Revised Version), can we share with him
the higher life to which he showed the way. As sharing that life,
"walking in Him," "complete in Him," St. Paul describes believers
as already "risen with Christ." Thus the death and resurrection of
Jesus, which he accepted (we know) as historical facts, and his own
resurrection, to which he undoubtedly looked forward as a future
event, became for the Apostle, as a religious thinker, a description
of the eternal nature of the spiritual life, symbols of an experience
daily realized. It is in this sense that Christ is said to have brought
life and immortality to light through the gospel (2 Tim. i. 10).
"This gift to men" (I purposely quote a strictly orthodox commentator) "is not the inculcation of the truth of an endless existence, nor any dogma of the soul's deathless perpetuity, but the
revelation of a higher life." [17]

Life, in the mystical sense indicated, often more specifically
"eternal life," is the very burden of the Fourth Gospel and the
Johannine Epistles.[18] "I am come," says the Johannine Christ, "that
they might have life, and that they might have it more abundantly."
(John x. 10.) "He that eateth my flesh and drinketh my blood hath
eternal life." (John vi. 54.) This spiritual sense both of life and of
resurrection forms the kernel of the Lazarus story, where it expressly emphasized against the literalism of Martha. "Martha saith
unto him, I know that he shall rise again in the resurrection at the
last day. Jesus said unto her, I am the resurrection and the life: he
that believeth in me, though he were dead, yet shall he live: and

---

[16] Cf. I John iii. 14–17.

[17] S. D. F. Salmond, *Christian Doctrine of Immortality*, p. 393.

[18] The expression "eternal life" occurs "some seventeen times in the Gospel
and six times in the Epistles." Salmond, *op. cit.,* p. 489.

whosoever liveth and believeth in me shall never die." (John xi.
24-6.) So again: "The hour cometh *and now is*, when the dead shall
hear the voice of the Son of God, and they that hear shall live."
(John v. 25.) This is the same spiritual sense of life and resurrection as an accomplished fact that we have in St. Paul. The dead
here are the spiritually dead who are to be quickened or made alive.
"This is life eternal, that they should know thee, the only true God,
and Jesus Christ whom thou hast sent." (John xvii. 3.) Similarly in
the Epistles: "God hath given to us eternal life, and this life is in
his Son. He that hath the Son hath life." (I John v. 11-12.) "We
know that we have passed from death unto life, because we love the
brethren. He that loveth not his brother abideth in death." (I John
iii. 14.) "He that loveth not, knoweth not God; for God is love. . . .
If we love one another, God abideth in us, and his love is perfected
in us." (I John iv. 8-12.) "This is the true God, and eternal life."
(I John v. 20.)

The emphatic present tense throughout these passages is evidence
sufficient of the writer's meaning. Eternal life is not a state of existence to follow upon physical death, but an all-satisfying present
experience of the love of God in Christ. It is, as the theologians say,
"participation in the being of the spiritual Christ." The fruit of
such an experience (to quote St. Paul's list) is "love, joy, peace."
(Gal. v. 22.) "My peace I give unto you," says the Johannine
Christ. (John xiv. 27.) "These things have I spoken unto you, that
your joy might be full." (John xv. 11.) "And ye shall know the
truth, and the truth shall make you free." (John viii. 32.) This is
the eternal life in the midst of time which is claimed by the saints
as an immediate experience, one which time can neither increase nor
diminish, one to which considerations of time are, in fact, indifferent,
because we are at rest in the present.

Needless to say, such experience is not the exclusive property of
any single faith. Much controversy has raged, for example, round
the meaning of the Buddhist Nirvana. The term is ordinarily translated nothingness or annihilation. At his death, we are told, the
perfected saint becomes extinct, like the flame of an expiring fire.
That appears to be the natural result of the insight he has gained into
the root of all evil and the way of deliverance; and the term is so
applied by Buddhists themselves. Yet the Buddha himself, when

urged by his disciples, expressly declined to answer yea or nay to the question whether the man who has won deliverance will exist or not after death—on the ground that "this is a matter which does not make for things needful to salvation, nor for that which concerns a holy life." [19] What he had taught, he said, was only the cause of suffering and the path which leads to its cessation. The primary reference of the word, is, therefore, not to any future event —to what may happen after death—but to the insight on which that ultimate deliverance may be supposed to follow—to the extinction of all the fires of desire and the perfect peace resulting therefrom. Nirvana, in its original intention, is that immediate emancipation from all the passions and cares of life which renunciation brings with it, a state of mind to be attained here and now, the peace which the world can neither give nor take away, and which is the supreme and only blessedness. "There is no spot, O King, East, South, West, or North, above, below or beyond, where Nirvana is situate, and yet Nirvana is, and he who orders his life aright . . . may realize it, whether he lives in Greece, in China, in Alexandria or Kosala." [20] Apart from the fundamental pessimism of Buddhism, the words of Jesus and those of the Buddha often strikingly resemble one another in their recurring emphasis on rest and peace. And the language of Buddhist hymns is not so different from that of Christian devotion. Take, for instance, these short examples rendered by Mrs. Rhys Davids (pp. 177, 185.):—

> Nirvana have I realized, and gazed
> Into the mirror of the Holy Law.
> I, even I, am healed of my hurt.
> Low is my burden laid, my task is done,
> My heart is wholly set at liberty.

> . . . .

> Nor is there any bliss greater than peace.
> These things to know, e'en as they really are,
> This is Nirvana, crown of happiness.

Religion is thus, as Hegel has finely said, [21] "the realm where all the riddles of the world are solved, all the contradictions of probing thought are unveiled, and all pangs of feeling cease, the region of

---

[19] Mrs. Rhys Davids, *Buddhism*, p. 179.
[20] *Ibid.* p. 232.
[21] *Werke*, xi, pp. 3–4 (in the opening paragraph of the *Philosophy of Religion*).

eternal truth, of eternal rest. The whole complexity of human relations, activities, enjoyments, everything that man values and es-
teems, wherein he seeks his happiness, his glory, his pride—all find
their final centre in religion, in the thought, the consciousness, the
feeling of God. . . . God is known in religion. Religion just means
being occupied with this object. In this occupation the spirit casts
off all its finitude; in it it finds its satisfaction and perfect freedom.
All nations accordingly have looked upon this religious consciousness as their true dignity, as the Sunday of their lives; every care
and anxiety, this 'bank and shoal of time' itself, vanishes in this
aether, in the immediate feeling of devotion or of hope."

It is, then, on the possibility of such experiences as we have been
considering that any valid theory of immortality must be based.
Their reality is beyond dispute, whether reached in the apprehension
of Truth, through Beauty, or through Goodness. By whatever gate
a man may enter, the eternal foundations of the world are there
discovered to him, and he knows that in his hold on these realities
lies all that is worth striving for, all that is of value in his life. The
being of these realities and his own relation to them "stand sure"
beyond the risks of time and change, even the change which we call
death. He who has tasted eternal life is not wont to be troubled in
heart about the question of his personal survival; for such survival
would mean nothing to him, if he were separated from the object in
which he has found his true life. His immortality lies for him in
his union with the eternal object on which his affections are set, and
he seeks no other assurance.

59. If You Were To Die Tomorrow *

MIGUEL DE UNAMUNO (1864–1936)

Man is said to be a reasoning animal. I do not know why he has
not been defined as an affective or feeling animal. Perhaps that

---

* Reprinted by permission of Macmillan & Co. Ltd. from *The Tragic Sense
of Life,* 1926, by Miguel de Unamuno.

which differentiates him from other animals is feeling rather than reason. More often I have seen a cat reason than laugh or weep. Perhaps it laughs or weeps inwardly—but then perhaps, also inwardly, the crab resolves equations of the second degree.

And thus, in a philosopher, what must needs most concern us is the man.

Take Kant, the man Immanuel Kant, who was born and lived at Königsberg, in the latter part of the eighteenth century and the beginning of the nineteenth. In the philosophy of this man Kant, a man of heart and head—that is to say, a man—there is a significant somersault, as Kierkegaard, another man—and what a man!—would have said, the somersault from the *Critique of Pure Reason* to the *Critique of Practical Reason*. He reconstructs in the latter what he destroyed in the former, in spite of what those may say who do not see the man himself. After having examined and pulverized with his analysis the traditional proofs of the existence of God, of the Aristotelian God, who is the God corresponding to the abstract God, the unmoved prime Mover, he reconstructs God anew; but the God of the conscience, the Author of the moral order—the Lutheran God, in short. This transition of Kant exists already in embryo in the Lutheran notion of faith.

Kant reconstructed with the heart that which with the head he had overthrown. And we know, from the testimony of those who knew him and from his testimony in his letters and private declarations, that the man Kant, the more or less selfish old bachelor who professed Philosophy at Königsberg at the end of the century of the Encyclopedia and the goddess of Reason, was a man much preoccupied with the problem—I mean with the only real vital problem, the problem that strikes at the very root of our being, the problem of our individual and personal destiny, of the immortality of the soul. The man Kant was not resigned to die utterly. And because he was not resigned to die utterly he made that leap, that immortal somersault, from the one Critique to the other.

Whosoever reads the *Critique of Practical Reason* carefully and without blinkers will see that, in strict fact, the existence of God is therein deduced from the immortality of the soul, and not the immortality of the soul from the existence of God. The categorical imperative leads us to a moral postulate which necessitates in its turn, in the teleological or rather eschatological order, the immortality of the soul, and in order to sustain this immortality God is introduced. All the rest is the jugglery of the professional of philosophy.

The man Kant felt that morality was the basis of eschatology, but the professor of philosophy inverted the terms.

Another professor, the professor and man William James, has somewhere said that for the generality of men God is the provider of immortality. Yes, for the generality of men, including the man Kant, the man James, and the man who writes these lines which you, reader, are reading.

Talking to a peasant one day, I proposed to him the hypothesis that there might indeed be a God who governs heaven and earth, a Consciousness of the Universe, but that for all that the soul of every man may not be immortal in the traditional and concrete sense. He replied: "Then wherefore God?" So answered, in the secret tribunal of their consciousness, the man Kant and the man James. Only in their capacities as professors they were compelled to justify rationally an attitude in itself so little rational. Which does not mean, of course, that the attitude is absurd.

.   .   .   .

The problem is tragic and eternal, and the more we seek to escape from it, the more it thrusts itself upon us. Four-and-twenty centuries ago, in his dialogue on the immortality of the soul, the serene Plato—but was he serene?—spoke of the uncertainty of our dream of being immortal and of the *risk* that the dream might be vain, and from his own soul there escaped this profound cry—Glorious is the risk! Glorious is the risk that we are able to run of our souls never dying—a sentence that was the germ of Pascal's famous argument of the wager.

Faced with this risk, I am presented with arguments designed to eliminate it, arguments demonstrating the absurdity of the belief in the immortality of the soul; but these arguments fail to make any impression upon me, for they are reasons and nothing more than reasons, and it is not with reasons that the heart is appeased. I do not want to die—no; I neither want to die nor do I want to want to die; I want to live for ever and ever and ever. I want this "I" to live

—this poor "I" that I am and that I feel myself to be here and now, and therefore the problem of the duration of my soul, of my own soul, tortures me.

I am the centre of my universe, the centre of the universe, and in my supreme anguish I cry with Michelet, "Mon moi, ils m'arrachent mon moi!" What is a man profited if he shall gain the whole world and lose his own soul? (Matt. xvi. 26). Egoism, you say? There is nothing more universal than the individual, for what is the property of each is the property of all. Each man is worth more than the whole of humanity, nor will it do to sacrifice each to all save in so far as all sacrifice themselves to each. That which we call egoism is the principle of psychic gravity, the necessary postulate. "Love thy neighbour as thyself," we are told, the presupposition being that each man loves himself; and it is not said "love thyself." And, nevertheless, we do not know how to love ourselves.

Put aside the persistence of your own self and ponder what they tell you. Sacrifice yourself to your children! And sacrifice yourself to them because they are yours, part and prolongation of yourself, and they in their turn will sacrifice themselves to their children, and these children to theirs, and so it will go on without end, a sterile sacrifice by which nobody profits. I came into the world to create my self, and what is to become of all our selves? Live for the True, the Good, the Beautiful! We shall see presently the supreme vanity and the supreme insincerity of this hypocritical attitude.

"That art thou!" they tell me with the Upanishads. And I answer: Yes, I am that, if that is I and all is mine, and mine the totality of things. As mine I love the All, and I love my neighbour because he lives in me and is part of my consciousness, because he is like me, because he is mine.

Oh, to prolong this blissful moment, to sleep, to eternalize oneself in it! Here and now, in this discreet and diffused light, in this lake of quietude, the storm of the heart appeased and stilled the echoes of the world! Insatiable desire now sleeps and does not even dream; use and wont, blessed use and wont, are the rule of my eternity; my disillusions have died with my memories, and with my hopes my fears.

And they come seeking to deceive us with a deceit of deceits, telling us that nothing is lost, that everything is transformed, shifts and changes, that not the least particle of matter is annihilated, not the least impulse of energy is lost, and there are some who pretend to console us with this! Futile consolation! It is not my matter or my energy that is the cause of my disquiet, for they are not mine if I myself am not mine—that is, if I am not eternal. No, my longing is not to be submerged in the vast All, in an infinite and eternal Matter or Energy, or in God; not to be possessed by God, but to possess Him, to become myself God, yet without ceasing to be I myself, who am now speaking to you. Tricks of monism avail us nothing; we crave the substance and not the shadow of immortality.

Materialism, you say? Materialism? Without doubt; but either our spirit is likewise some kind of matter or it is nothing. I dread the idea of having to tear myself away from my flesh; I dread still more the idea of having to tear myself away from everything sensible and material, from all substance. Yes, perhaps this merits the name of materialism; and if I grapple myself to God with all my powers and all my senses, it is that He may carry me in His arms beyond death, looking into these eyes of mine with the light of His heaven when the light of earth is dimming in them for ever. Self-illusion? Talk not to me of illusion—let me live!

They also call this pride—"stinking pride" Leopardi called it—and they ask us who are we, vile earthworms, to pretend to immortality; in virtue of what? wherefore? by what right? "In virtue of what?" you ask; and I reply, In virtue of what do we now live? "Wherefore?"—and wherefore do we now exist? "By what right?" —and by what right are we? To exist is just as gratuitous as to go on existing for ever. Do not let us talk of merit or of right or of the wherefore of our longing, which is an end in itself, or we shall lose our reason in a vortex of absurdities. I do not claim any right or merit; it is only a necessity; I need it in order to live.

And you, who are you? you ask me; and I reply with Obermann, "For the universe, nothing; for myself, everything!" Pride? Is it pride to want to be immortal? Unhappy men that we are! 'Tis a tragic fate, without a doubt, to have to base the affirmation of immortality upon the insecure and slippery foundation of the desire for immortality; but to condemn this desire on the ground that we believe it to have been proved to be unattainable, without undertaking the proof, is merely supine. I am dreaming . . .? Let me dream, if this dream is my life. Do not awaken me from it. I believe in the immortal origin of this yearning for immortality, which is the very substance of my soul. But do I really believe in it. . .? And wherefore do you want to be immortal? you ask me, wherefore? Frankly, I do not understand the question, for it is to ask the reason of the reason, the end of the end, the principle of the principle.

.   .   .   .

But it is in our endeavour to represent to ourselves what the life of the soul after death really means that uncertainty finds its surest foundation. This it is that most shakes our vital desire and most intensifies the dissolvent efficacy of reason. For even if by a mighty effort of faith we overcome that reason which tells and teaches us that the soul is only a function of the physical organism, it yet remains for our imagination to conceive an image of the immortal and eternal life of the soul. This conception involves us in contradictions and absurdities, and it may be that we shall arrive with Kierkegaard at the conclusion that if the mortality of the soul is terrible, not less terrible is its immortality.

But when we have overcome the impediment of reason, when we have achieved the faith, however painful and involved in uncertainty it may be, that our personal consciousness shall continue after death, what difficulty, what impediment, lies in the way of our imagining to ourselves this persistence of self in harmony with our desire? Yes, we can imagine it as an eternal rejuvenescence, as an eternal growth of ourselves, and as a journeying towards God, towards the Universal Consciousness, without ever an arrival, we can imagine it as. . . . But who shall put fetters upon the imagination, once it has broken the chain of the rational?

.   .   .   .

Once again I must repeat that the longing for the immortality of the soul, for the permanence, in some form or another, of our personal and individual consciousness, is as much of the essence of religion as is the longing that there may be a God. The one does not exist apart from the other, the reason being that fundamentally they are one and the same thing. But as soon as we attempt to give a concrete and rational form to this longing for immortality and permanence, to define it to ourselves, we encounter even more difficulties than we encountered in our attempt to rationalize God.

The universal consent of mankind has again been invoked as a means of justifying this immortal longing for immortality to our own feeble reason. *Permanere animos arbitratur consensu nationum omnium*, said Cicero, echoing the opinion of the ancients (*Tuscul. quaest.*, xvi., 36). But this same recorder of his own feelings confessed that, although when he read the arguments in favour of the immortality of the soul in the *Phaedo* of Plato he was compelled to assent to them, as soon as he put the book aside and began to revolve the problem in his own mind, all his previous assent melted away, *assentio omnis illa illabitur* (*Cap.* xi. 25). And what happened to Cicero happens to us all, and it happened likewise to Swedenborg, the most daring visionary of the other world. Swedenborg admitted that he who discourses of life after death, putting aside all erudite notions concerning the soul and its mode of union with the body, believes that after death he shall live in a glorious joy and vision, as a man among angels; but when he begins to reflect upon the doctrine of the union of the soul with the body, or upon the hypothetical opinion concerning the soul, doubts arise in him as to whether the soul is thus or otherwise, and when these doubts arise, his former idea is dissipated (*De coelo et inferno*, § 183). Nevertheless, as Cournot says, "it is the destiny that awaits me, *me* or my *person*, that moves, perturbs and consoles me, that makes me capable of abnegation and sacrifice, whatever be the origin, the nature or the essence of this inexplicable bond of union, in the absence of which the philosophers are pleased to determine that my person must disappear" (*Traité*, etc., § 297).

.   .   .   .

And the supreme commandment that arises out of love towards God, and the foundation of all morality, is this: Yield yourself up entirely, give your spirit to the end that you may save it, that you may eternalize it. Such is the sacrifice of life.

The individual *qua* individual, the wretched captive of the instinct of preservation and of the senses, cares only about preserving himself, and all his concern is that others should not force their way into his sphere, should not interrupt his idleness; and in return for their abstention or for the sake of example he refrains from forcing himself upon them, from interrupting their idleness, from disturbing them, from taking possession of them. "Do not do unto others what you would not have them do unto you," he translate thus: I do not interfere with others—let them not interfere with me. And he shrinks and pines and perishes in this spiritual avarice and this repellent ethic of anarchic individualism: each one for himself. And as each one is not himself, he can hardly live for himself.

But as soon as the individual feels himself in society, he feels himself in God, and kindled by the instinct of perpetuation he glows with love towards God, and with a dominating charity he seeks to perpetuate himself in others, to perennialize his spirit, to eternalize it, to unnail God, and his sole desire is to seal his spirit upon other spirits and to receive their impress in return. He has shaken off the yoke of his spiritual sloth and avarice.

.   .   .   .

What is our heart's truth, anti-rational though it be? The immortality of the human soul, the truth of the persistence of our consciousness without any termination whatsoever, the truth of the human finality of the Universe. And what is its moral proof? We may formulate it thus: Act so that in your own judgment and in the judgment of others you may merit eternity, act so that you may become irreplaceable, act so that you may not merit death. Or perhaps thus: Act as if you were to die to-morrow, but to die in order to survive and be eternalized. The end of morality is to give personal, human finality to the Universe; to discover the finality that belongs to it—if indeed it has any finality—and to discover it by acting.

More than a century ago, 1804, in Letter XC of that series that constitutes the immense monody of his *Obermann*, Sénancour wrote the words which I have put at the head of this chapter—and of all the spiritual descendants of the patriarchal Rousseau, Sénancour was the most profound and the most intense; of all the men of heart and feeling that France has produced, not excluding Pascal, he was the most tragic. "Man is perishable. That may be; but let us perish resisting, and if it is nothingness that awaits us, do not let us so act that it shall be a just fate." Change this sentence from its negative to the positive form—"And if it is nothingness that awaits us, let us so act that it shall be an unjust fate"—and you get the firmest basis of action for the man who cannot or will not be a dogmatist.

60. *Ideal Immortality* *

GEORGE SANTAYANA *(1863–1952)*

The length of life a subject for natural science. At no point are the two ingredients of religion, superstition and moral truth, more often confused than in the doctrine of immortality, yet in none are they more clearly distinguishable. Ideal immortality is a principle revealed to insight; it is seen by observing the eternal quality of ideas and validities, and the affinity to them native to reason or the cognitive energy of mind. A future life, on the contrary, is a matter for faith or presumption; it is a prophetic hypothesis regarding occult existences. This latter question is scientific and empirical, and should be treated as such. A man is, forensically speaking, the same man after the nightly break in his consciousness. After many changes in his body and after long oblivion, parcels of his youth may be revived and may come to figure again among the factors in his action. Similarly, if evidence to that effect were available, we might establish the resurrection of a given soul in new bodies or its activity in remote places and times. Evidence of this sort has in fact always been offered copiously by rumour and superstition. The operation of departed spirits, like that of the gods, has been recognised in many a dream, or message, or opportune succour. The Dioscuri and Saint James the Apostle have appeared—preferably on white horses—in sundry battles. Spirits duly invoked have repeated forgotten gossip and revealed the places where crimes had been committed or treasure buried. More often, perhaps, ghosts have walked the night without

---

* Excerpts from Chapters XIII and XIV of *Reason in Religion*. Copyright 1905 by Charles Scribner's Sons, 1933 by George Santayana; used by permission of the publishers.

any ostensible or useful purpose, apparently in obedience to some ghastly compulsion that crept over them in death, as if a hesitating sickle had left them still hanging to life by one attenuated fibre. The mass of this evidence, ancient and modern, traditional and statistical, is beneath consideration; the palpitating mood in which it is gathered and received, even when ostensibly scientific, is such that gullibility and fiction play a very large part in the report; for it is not to be assumed that a man, because he speaks in the first person and addresses a learned society, has lost the primordial faculty of lying.

. . . .

Possible forms of survival. Many a man dies too soon and some are born in the wrong age or station. Could these persons drink at the fountain of youth at least once more they might do themselves fuller justice and cut a better figure at last in the universe. Most people think they have stuff in them for greater things than time suffers them to perform. To imagine a second career is a pleasing antidote for ill-fortune; the poor soul wants another chance. But how should a future life be constituted if it is to satisfy this demand, and how long need it last? It would evidently have to go on in an environment closely analogous to earth; I could not, for instance, write in another world the epics which the necessity of earning my living may have stifled here, did that other world contain no time, no heroic struggles, or no metrical language. Nor is it clear that my epics, to be perfect, would need to be quite endless. If what is foiled in me is really poetic genius and not simply a tendency toward perpetual motion, it would not help me if in heaven, in lieu of my dreamt-of epics, I were allowed to beget several robust children. In a word, if hereafter I am to be the same man improved I must find myself in the same world corrected. Were I transformed into a cherub or transported into a timeless ecstasy, it is hard to see in what sense I should continue to exist. Those results might be interesting in themselves and might enrich the universe; they would not prolong my life nor retrieve my disasters.

For this reason a future life is after all best represented by those frankly material ideals which most Christians—being Platonists—are wont to despise. It would be genuine happiness for a Jew to rise again in the flesh and live for ever in Ezekiel's New Jerusalem, with its ceremonial glories and civic order. It would be truly agreeable for any man to sit in well-watered gardens with Mohammed, clad in green silks, drinking delicious sherbets, and transfixed by the gazelle-like glance of some young girl, all innocence and fire. Amid such scenes a man might remain himself and might fulfil hopes that he had actually cherished on earth. He might also find his friends again, which in somewhat generous minds is perhaps the thought that chiefly sustains interest in a posthumous existence. But to recognise his friends a man must find them in their bodies, with their familiar habits, voices, and interests; for it is surely an insult to affection to say that he could find them in an eternal formula expressing their idiosyncrasy. When, however, it is clearly seen that another life, to supplement this one, must closely resemble it, does not the magic of immortality altogether vanish? Is such a reduplication of earthly society at all credible? And the prospect of awakening again among houses and trees, among children and dotards, among wars and rumours of wars, still fettered to one personality and one accidental past, still uncertain of the future, is not this prospect wearisome and deeply repulsive? Having passed through these things once and bequeathed them to posterity, is it not time for each soul to rest? The universe doubtless contains all sorts of experiences, better and worse than the human; but it is idle to attribute to a particular man a life divorced from his circumstances and from his body.

Even vicarious immortality intrinsically impossible. Not only is man's original effort aimed at living for ever in his own person, but, even if he could renounce that desire, the dream of being represented perpetually by posterity is no less doomed. Reproduction, like nutrition, is a device not ultimately successful. If extinction does not defeat it, evolution will. Doubtless the fertility of whatever substance may have produced us will not be exhausted in this single effort; a potentiality that has once proved efficacious and been actualised in life, though it should sleep, will in time revive again. In some form and after no matter what intervals, nature may be expected always to possess consciousness. But beyond this planet and apart from the human race, experience is too little imaginable to be interesting. No definite plan or ideal of ours can find its realisation except in ourselves. Accordingly, a vicarious physical immortality always remains an unsatisfactory issue; what is thus to be preserved is but a counterfeit of our being, and even that counterfeit is confronted by omens of a total extinction more or less remote. A note of failure and melancholy must always dominate in the struggle against natural death.

This defeat is not really problematical, or to be eluded by reviving ill-digested hopes resting entirely on ignorance, an ignorance which these hopes will wish to make eternal. We need not wait for our total death to experience dying; we need not borrow from observation of others' demise a prophecy of our own extinction. Every moment celebrates obsequies over the virtues of its predecessor; and the possession of memory, by which we somehow survive in representation, is the most unmistakable proof that we are perishing in reality. In endowing us with memory, nature has revealed to us a truth utterly unimaginable to the unflective creation, the truth of mortality. Everything moves in the midst of death, because it indeed *moves;* but it falls into the pit unawares and by its own action unmakes and disestablishes itself, until a wonderful visionary faculty is added, so that a ghost remains of what has perished to reveal that lapse and at the same time in a certain sense to neutralise it.

Intellectual victory over change. The more we reflect, the more we live in memory and idea, the more convinced and penetrated we shall be by the experience of death; yet, without our knowing it, perhaps, this very conviction and experience will have raised us, in a way, above mortality. That was a heroic and divine oracle which, in informing us of our decay, made us partners of the gods' eternity, and by giving us knowledge poured into us, to that extent, the serenity and balm of truth. As it is memory that enables us to feel that we are dying and to know that everything actual is in flux, so it is memory that opens to us an ideal immortality, unacceptable and meaningless to the old Adam, but genuine in its own way and undeniably true. It is an immortality in representation—a representation which envisages things in their truth as they have in their own day possessed themselves in reality. It is no subterfuge or superstitious effrontery, called to disguise or throw off the lessons of experience; on the contrary, it is experience itself, reflection itself, and knowledge of mortality. Memory does not reprieve or postpone the changes which it registers, nor does it itself possess a permanent duration; it is, if possible, less stable and more mobile than primary sensation. It is, in point of existence, only an internal and complex kind of sensibility. But in intent and by its significance it plunges to the depths of time; it looks still on the departed and bears witness to the truth that, though absent from this part of experience, and incapable of returning to life, they nevertheless existed once in their own right, were as living and actual as experience is to-day, and still help to make up, in company with all past, present, and future mortals, the filling and value of the world.

As the pathos and heroism of life consists in accepting as an opportunity the fate that makes our own death, partial or total, serviceable to others, so the glory of life consists in accepting the knowledge of natural death as an opportunity to live in the spirit. The sacrifice, the self-surrender, remains real; for, though the compensation is real, too, and at moments, perhaps, apparently overwhelming, it is always incomplete and leaves beneath an incurable sorrow. Yet life can never contradict its basis or reach satisfactions essentially excluded by its own conditions. Progress lies in moving forward from the given situation, and satisfying as well as may be the interests that exist. And if some initial demand has proved hopeless, there is the greater reason for cultivating other sources of satisfaction, possibly more abundant and lasting. Now, reflection is a vital function; memory and imagination have to the full the rhythm and force of life.

The glory of it. But these faculties, in envisaging the past or the ideal, envisage the eternal, and the man in whose mind they predominate is to that extent detached in his affections from the world of flux, from himself, and from his personal destiny. This detachment will not make him infinitely long-lived, nor absolutely happy, but it may render him intelligent and just, and may open to him all intellectual pleasures and all human sympathies.

There is accordingly an escape from death open to man; one not found by circumventing nature, but by making use of her own expedients in circumventing her imperfections. Memory, nay, perception itself, is a first stage in this escape, which coincides with the acquisition and possession of reason. When the meaning of successive perceptions is recovered with the last of them, when a survey is made of objects whose constitutive sensations first arose independently, this synthetic moment contains an object raised above time on a pedestal of reflection, a thought indefeasibly true in its ideal deliverance, though of course fleeting in its psychic existence. Existence is essentially temporal and life foredoomed to be mortal, since its basis is a process and an opposition; it floats in the stream of time, never to return, never to be recovered or repossessed. But ever since substance became at some sensitive point intelligent and reflective, ever since time made room and pause for memory, for history, for the consciousness of time, a god, as it were, became incarnate in mortality and some vision of truth, some self-forgetful satisfaction, became a heritage that moment could transmit to moment and man to man. This heritage is humanity itself, the presence of immortal reason in creatures that perish. Apprehension, which makes man so like a god, makes him in one respect immortal; it quickens his numbered moments with a vision of what never dies, the truth of those moments and their inalienable values.

Reason makes man's divinity. To participate in this vision is to participate at once in humanity and in divinity, since all other bonds are material and perishable, but the bond between two thoughts that have grasped the same truth, of two instants that have caught the same beauty, is a spiritual and imperishable bond. It is imperishable simply because it is ideal and resident merely in import and intent. The two thoughts, the two instants, remain existentially different; were they not two they could not come from different quarters to unite in one meaning and to behold one object in distinct and conspiring acts of apprehension. Being independent in existence, they can be united by the identity of their burden, by the common worship, so to speak, of the same god. Were this ideal goal itself an existence, it would be incapable of uniting anything; for the same gulf which separated the two original minds would open between them and their common object. But being, as it is, purely ideal, it can become the meeting-ground of intelligences and render their union ideally eternal. Among the physical instruments of thought there may be rivalry and impact—the two thinkers may compete and clash—but this is because each seeks his own physical survival and does not love the truth stripped of its accidental associations and provincial accent. Doctors disagree in so far as they are not truly doctors, but, as Plato would say, seek, like sophists and wage-earners, to circumvent and defeat one another. The conflict is physical and can extend to the subject-matter only in so far as this is tainted by individual prejudice and not wholly lifted from the sensuous to the intellectual plane. In the ether there are no winds of doctrine. The intellect, being the organ and source of the divine, is divine and single; if there were many sorts of intellect, many principles of perspective, they would fix and create incomparable and irrelevant worlds. Reason is one in that it gravitates toward an object, called truth, which could not have the function it has, of being a focus for mental activities, if it were not one in reference to the operations which converge upon it.

This unity in truth, as in reason, is of course functional only, not physical or existential. The beats of thought and the thinkers are innumerable; indefinite, too, the variations to which their endowment and habits may be subjected. But the condition of spiritual communion or ideal relevance in these intelligences is their possession of a method and grammar essentially identical. Language, for example, is significant in proportion to the constancy in meaning which words and locutions preserve in a speaker's mind at various times, or in the minds of various persons. This constancy is never absolute. Therefore language is never wholly significant, never exhaustively intelligible. There is always mud in the well, if we have drawn up enough water. Yet in peaceful rivers, though they flow, there is an appreciable degree of translucency. So, from moment to moment, and from man to man, there is an appreciable element of unanimity, of constancy and congruity of intent. On this abstract and perfectly identical function science rests together with every rational formation.

And his immortality. The same function is the seat of human immortality. Reason lifts a larger or smaller element in each man to the plane of ideality according as reason more or less thoroughly leavens and permeates the lump. No man is wholly immortal, as no philosophy is wholly true and no language wholly intelligible; but only in so far as intelligible is a language a language rather than a noise, only in so far as true is a philosophy more than a vent for cerebral humours, and only in so far as a man is rational and immortal is he a man and not a sensorium.

It is hard to convince people that they have such a gift as intelligence. If they perceive its animal basis they cannot conceive its ideal affinities or understand what is meant by calling it divine; if they perceive its ideality and see the immortal essences that swim into its ken, they hotly deny that it is an animal faculty, and invent ultramundane places and bodiless persons in which it is to reside; as if those celestial substances could be, in respect to thought, any less material than matter or, in respect to vision and life, any less instrumental than bodily organs. It never occurs to them that if nature has added intelligence to animal life it is because they belong together. Intelligence is a natural emanation of vitality. If eternity could exist otherwise than as a vision in time, eternity would have no meaning for men in the world, while the world, men, and time would have no vocation or status in eternity. The travail of existence would be without excuse, without issue or consummation, while the conceptions of truth and of perfection would be without application to experience, pure dreams about things preternatural and unreal, vacantly conceived, and illogically supposed to have something to do with living issues. But truth and perfection, for the very reason that they are not problematic existences but inherent ideals, cannot be banished from discourse. Experience may lose any of its data; it cannot lose, while it endures, the terms with which it operates in becoming experience. Now, truth is relevant to every opinion which looks to truth for its standard, and perfection is envisaged in every cry for relief, in every effort at betterment. Opinions, volitions, and passionate refusals fill human life. So that when the existence of truth is denied, truth is given the only status which it ever required —it is conceived.

It is the locus of all truths. Nor can any better defense be found for the denial that nature and her life have a status in eternity. This statement may not be understood, but if grasped at all it will not be questioned. By having a status in eternity is not meant being parts of an eternal existence, petrified or congealed into something real but motionless. What is meant is only that whatever exists in time, when bathed in the light of reflection, acquires an indelible character and discloses irreversible relations; every fact, in being recognised, takes its place in the universe of discourse, in that ideal sphere of truth which is the common and unchanging standard for all assertions. Language, science, art, religion, and all ambitious dreams are compacted of ideas. Life is as much a mosaic of notions as the firmament is of stars; and these ideal and transpersonal objects, bridging time, fixing standards, establishing values, constituting the natural rewards of all living, are the very furniture of eternity, the goals and playthings of that reason which is an instinct in the heart as vital and spontaneous as any other. Or rather, perhaps, reason is a supervening instinct by which all other instincts are interpreted, just as the *sensus communis* or transcendental unity of psychology is a faculty by which all perceptions are brought face to face and compared. So that immortality is not a privilege reserved for a part only of experience, but rather a relation pervading every part in varying measure. We may, in leaving the subject, mark the degrees and phases of this idealisation.

Epicurean immortality, through the truth of existence. Animal sensation is related to eternity only by the truth that it has taken place. The fact, fleeting as it is, is registered in ideal history, and no inventory of the world's riches, no true confession of its crimes, would ever be complete that ignored that incident. This indefeasible character in experience makes a first sort of ideal immortality, one on which those rational philosophers like to dwell who have not speculation enough to feel quite certain of any other. It was a consolation to the Epicurean to remember that, however brief and uncertain might be his tenure of delight, the past was safe and the present sure. "He lives happy," says Horace, "and master over himself, who can say daily, I have lived. To-morrow let Jove cover the sky with black clouds or flood it with sunshine; he shall not thereby render vain what lies behind, he shall not delete and make never to have existed what once the hour has brought in its flight." Such self-concentration and hugging of the facts has no power to improve them; it gives to pleasure and pain an impartial eternity, and rather tends to intrench in sensuous and selfish satisfactions a mind that has lost faith in reason and that deliberately ignores the difference in scope and dignity which exists among various pursuits. Yet the reflection is staunch and in its way heroic; it meets a vague and feeble aspiration, that looks to the infinite, with a just rebuke; it points to real satisfactions, experienced successes, and asks us to be content with the fulfilment of our own wills. If you have seen the world, if you have played your game and won it, what more would you ask for? If you have tasted the sweets of existence, you should be satisfied; if the experience has been bitter, you should be glad that it comes to an end.

Of course, as we have seen, there is a primary demand in man which death and mutation contradict flatly, so that no summons to cease can ever be obeyed with complete willingness. Even the suicide trembles and the ascetic feels the stings of the flesh. It is the part of philosophy, however, to pass over those natural repugnances and overlay them with as much countervailing rationality as can find lodgment in a particular mind. The Epicurean, having abandoned politics and religion and being afraid of any far-reaching ambition, applied philosophy honestly enough to what remained. Simple and healthy pleasures are the reward of simple and healthy pursuits; to chafe against them because they are limited is to import a foreign and disruptive element into the case; a healthy hunger has its limit, and its satisfaction reaches a natural term. Philosophy, far from alienating us from those values, should teach us to see their perfection and to maintain them in our ideal. In other words, the happy filling of a single hour is so much gained for the universe at large, and to find joy and sufficiency in the flying moment is perhaps the only means open to us for increasing the glory of eternity.

Logical immortality, through objects of thought. Moving events, while remaining enshrined in this fashion in their permanent setting, may contain other and less external relations to the immutable. They may represent it. If the pleasures of sense are not cancelled when they cease, but continue to satisfy reason in that they once satisfied natural desires, much more will the pleasures of reflection retain their worth, when we consider that what they aspired to and reached was no momentary physical equilibrium but a permanent truth. As Archimedes, measuring the hypothenuse, was lost to events, being engaged in an event of much greater transcendence, so art and science interrupt the sense for change by engrossing attention in its issues and its laws. Old age often turns pious to look away from ruins to some world where youth endures and where what ought to have been is not overtaken by decay before it has quite come to maturity. Lost in such abstract contemplations, the mind is weaned from mortal concerns. It forgets for a few moments a world in which it has so little more to do and so much, perhaps, still to suffer. As a sensation of pure light would not be distinguishable from light itself, so a contemplation of things not implicating time in their structure becomes, so far as its own deliverance goes, a timeless existence. Unconsciousness of temporal conditions and of the very flight of time makes the thinker sink for a moment into identity with timeless objects. And so immortality, in a second ideal sense, touches the mind.

Ethical immortality, through types of excellence. The transitive phases of consciousness, however, have themselves a reference to eternal things. They yield a generous enthusiasm and love of good which is richer in consolation than either Epicurean self-concentration or mathematical ecstasy. Events are more interesting than the terms we abstract from them, and the forward movement of the will is something more intimately real than is the catalogue of our past experiences. Now the forward movement of the will is an avenue to the eternal. What would you have? What is the goal of your endeavour? It must be some success, the establishment of some order, the expression of some experience. These points once reached, we are not left merely with the satisfaction of abstract success or the consciousness of ideal immortality. Being natural goals, these ideals are related to natural functions. Their attainment does not exhaust but merely liberates, in this instance, the function concerned, and so marks the perpetual point of reference common to that function in all its fluctuations. Every attainment of perfection in an art—as for instance in government—makes a return to perfection easier for posterity, since there remains an enlightening example, together with faculties predisposed by discipline to recover their ancient virtue. The better a man evokes and realises the ideal the more he leads the life that all others, in proportion to their worth, will seek to live after him, and the more he helps them to live in that nobler fashion. His presence in the society of immortals thus becomes, so to speak, more pervasive. He not only vanquishes time by his own rationality, living now in the eternal, but he continually lives again in all rational beings.

Since the ideal has this perpetual pertinence to mortal struggles, he who lives in the ideal and leaves it expressed in society or in art enjoys a double immortality. The eternal has absorbed him while he lived, and when he is dead his influence brings others to the same absorption, making them, through that ideal identity with the best in him, reincarnations and perennial seats of all in him which he could rationally hope to rescue from destruction. He can say, without any subterfuge or desire to delude himself, that he shall not wholly die; for he will have a better notion than the vulgar of what constitutes his being. By becoming the spectator and confessor of his own death and of universal mutation, he will have identified himself with what is spiritual in all spirits and masterful in all apprehension; and so conceiving himself, he may truly feel and know that he is eternal.

[NOTE: The bibliography for Chapter Six appears on page 521.]

BIBLIOGRAPHY

CHAPTER 1: WHAT IS RELIGION?

Bergson, Henri, *The Two Sources of Morality and Religion*, New York: Henry Holt and Co., 1935.

Ducasse, C. J., *A Philosophical Scrutiny of Religion*. New York: The Ronald Press, 1953.

Durkheim, Emile, *The Elementary Forms of Religious Life*. London: George Allen and Unwin, Ltd., 1915.

Frazer, J. G., *The Golden Bough*. (12 vols.) London: Macmillan, 1920-1923.

Freud, Sigmund, *The Future of an Illusion*. New York: Horace Liveright Co., 1928.

Hegel, Georg W., *Lectures on the Philosophy of Religion*. London: K. Paul, Trench, Trübner & Co., Ltd., 1895.

James, William, *The Varieties of Religious Experience*. New York: Longmans, Green and Co., 1902.

Kant, Immanuel, *Religion Within the Limits of Reason Alone*. Chicago: The Open Court Publishing Co., 1934. (Germany 1793).

Leuba, James H., *A Psychological Study of Religion*. New York: The Macmillan Co., 1912.

Lowie, Robert H., *Primitive Religion*. New York: Boni and Liveright, 1924.

Malinowski, Bronislaw, *Magic, Science, and Religion*. Boston: Beacon Press, 1948.

Noss, John B., *Man's Religions*. New York: The Macmillan Co., 1949.

Plato, *Euthyphro*. New York: The Liberal Arts Press, 1948.

CHAPTER 2: THE EXISTENCE OF GOD

Alexander, Samuel, *Space, Time and Deity*, Vol. II, London: Macmillan Co., 1927.

Ames, Edward Scribner, *Religion*, New York: Henry Holt & Co., 1929.

Berkeley, George, *Three Dialogues between Hylas and Philonous*, LaSalle Ill: The Open Court Publishing Co., 1947, pp. 91–100 from the Third Dialogue.

Boodin, G. Elof, *God and Creation*, New York: Macmillan Co., 1934.

Catholic Encyclopedia, Article entitled "Revelation," New York: Appleton Co., 1907–14.

Descartes, R., *Meditations*, New York: Liberal Arts Press, 1951, pp. 36–47 from Part III.

Dewey, John, *A Common Faith*, New Haven: Yale University Press, 1934.

Gilson, Etienne, *God and Philosophy*, London: Oxford University Press, 1941.

Hocking, Wm. Ernest, *The Meaning of God in Human Experience*, New Haven: Yale University Press, 1934.

Lewis, C. S., *Miracles*, London: The Centenary Press, 1947, Chapter VIII, "On Probability."

Wieman, N., MacIntosh, and Otto, *Is There a God?* Chicago: Willet & Clark Co., 1932.

Wisdom, John, *"Gods,"* Proceedings of the Aristotelian Society, 1944. (Reprinted in Wisdom, John, *Philosophy and Psychoanalysis*, Oxford: Basil Blackwell, 1953.)

Chapter 3: God and Evil

Bible, Book of Job.

Buber, Martin, *Images of Good and Evil*, London: Routledge and Paul, 1952.

De Burgh, W. G., *From Morality to Religion*, Bedford-Row, England: MacDonald and Evans, 1938, pp. 222–230.

Joad, Cyril E., *God and Evil*, New York: Harper & Bros., 1943.

Laird, John, *Mind and Deity*, New York: Philosophy Library, 1941.

Niebuhr, Reinhold, *Moral Man and Immoral Society*, New York: Charles Scribners Sons, 1932.

Plato, *Euthyphro*, New York: Random House, 1948.

Rashdall, Hastings, *The Theory of Good and Evil*, Vol. II, Second Edition, London: Oxford University Press, 1924.

Russell, Bertrand, *Mysticism and Logic*, "A Free Man's Worship," New York: Longmans, Green & Co., 1918.

Spinoza, Benedict, *Ethics*, New York: Tudor Publishing Co., N. D., Part IV, "Of Human Bondage."

Tennant, Frederick Robert, *Philosophical Theory*, Vol. II, Cambridge: The University Press, 1928, 1930.

Tsanoff, Radoslav, *The Nature of Evil*, New York: Macmillan Co., 1931.

Chapter 4: God and Human Freedom

Barnes, Ernest Wm., *Scientific Theory and Religion*, Cambridge: The University Press, 1935.

Bennett, W., *Religion and Free Will*, Oxford: The Clarendon Press, 1913.

Berdayev, N., *Freedom and the Spirit of Man*, New York: Charles Scribners Sons, 1935, Chapter 5, "Redemption and Evil."

Bergson, Henri, *Time and Free Will*, New York: Macmillan Co., 1921.

d'Arcy, C. F., *God and Freedom in Human Experience*, London: Edward Arnold, 1915, Chapters 5 and 6.

Feigl and Sellars, *Readings in Philosophical Analysis*, "The Freedom of the Will," New York: Appleton, Century, Crofts, 1951, p. 594.

Leibniz, G. W., "Theodicy," in *Selected Writings in Philosophy*, New York: Appleton-Century, 1939.

Palmer, George Herbert, *The Problem of Freedom*, New York: Houghton-Mifflin, 1911.

Von Hildebrand, D., *Christian Ethics*, New York: David McKay Co., 1953.

CHAPTER 5: CHURCH AND STATE

Augustine, Saint, *The City of God*, Modern Library, New York: Random House, 1950.

Barth, Karl, *The Church and the Political Problem of Our Day.* New York: C. Scribner's Sons, 1939.

Blau, Joseph, *Cornerstones of Religious Freedom in America.* Boston: The Beacon Press, 1949.

Calvin, John, *God and Political Duty.* New York: The Liberal Arts Press, 1950.

Hobbes, Thomas, *Leviathan.* Oxford: Clarendon Press, 1909.

Leo XIII, Pope, "Encyclical on the Constitution of States." *The Great Encyclical Letters of Pope Leo XIII.* New York, Cincinnati: Benziger Bros., 1903.

Maritain, Jacques, *Christianity and Democracy.* London: Geoffrey Bles, 1945.

Milton, John, *Areopagitica.* New York: The Macmillan Co., 1927.

Pfeffer, Leo, *Church, State, and Freedom.* Boston: The Beacon Press, 1953.

Stokes, Anson Phelps, *Church and State in the United States.* (3 vols.) New York: Harper & Bros., 1950.

Williams, Roger, *The Bloudy Tenent of Persecution for Cause of Conscience.* Exerpted in Blau, Joseph, *Cornerstones of Religious Freedom in America.* Boston: The Beacon Press, 1949.

CHAPTER 6: IMMORTALITY

Dickinson, G. Lowes, *Is Immortality Desirable?* Boston and New York: Houghton Mifflin Co., 1909.

Ducasse, C. J., *Nature, Mind and Death*. LaSalle, Illinois: Open Court Publishing Co., 1951.

Finkelstein, Louis, "The Beginnings of the Jewish Doctrine of Immortality." From *Freedom and Reason*, edited by Salo W. Baron, Ernest Nagel, and Koppel S. Pinson. New York: The Free Press, 1951.

Frazer, J. G., *The Belief in Immortality*. London: Macmillan and Company, Ltd., 1913.

Holmes, John Haynes, *Is Death the End?* New York: Putnam's, 1915.

Hume, David, *Of the Immortality of the Soul*, Volume 4 of *The Philosophical Works of David Hume*. London: Longmans, 1882.

James, William, *Human Immortality*. Boston: Houghton, Mifflin & Co., 1898.

Kant, Immanuel, *Critique of Practical Reason*. Translated by T. K. Abbott as Kant's *Theory of Ethics*. Longmans, Green & Co., Sixth Edition, pages 218–220, 1909.

Lamont, Corliss, *The Illusion of Immortality*. New York: G. P. Putnam's Sons, 1935.

Leuba, James H., *The Belief in God and Immortality*. Chicago: The Open Court Publishing Company, 1921.

Lodge, Sir Oliver, *Why I Believe in Personal Immortality*. Cassell and Co. Ltd., 1939.

McTaggart, J. M. E., *Some Dogmas of Religion*. London: Edward Arnold, 1906.

Mill, John Stuart, "The Utility of Religion," and "Theism" (Part III) in *Three Essays on Religion*. New York: Longmans, Green & Co., 1923.

Plotinus, *The Essence of Plotinus*. Pages 140–145. Based on the translation of Stephen Mackenna. New York: Oxford University Press, 1934.

INDEX

INDEX